IBPS & SBI

Preliminary & Mains Examination

BANK CLERK

Dhruva Dhankher

Published by :

Invincible Publication

Published by:

Invincible Publication Pvt Ltd
201A, SAS Tower, Sector 38, Gurugram, Haryana – 122003
Phone: +91-124-4034247, +91 9599066061
Website : www.invinciblepublishers.com

Sales Office : - 4760-61/23, Basement, Pratap Street, Ansari Road,
Daryaganj, New Delhi - 110002
Phone: +91-11-40198405
Email: invinciblepublishers@gmail.com

ISBN : 978-93-5886-021-4
Book Name : IBPS & SBI Bank Clerk

First Edition: September 2023

Printed at: Goyal Offset Works Pvt. Ltd.

Table of Content

IBPS/SBI Clerk Exam

Like every year, the recruitment process for IBPS/SBI Clerk is being conducted. Before preparing for the exam, it is important to know about its pattern and procedure. In this era of tough competition, only that candidate can succeed, who has prepared properly for the exam. Accurate preparation is possible only when you analyze the past exams properly. Exam pattern enables candidates to grasp the significance of each topic and the allotted time for solving related questions. Come, let's know about them.

As part of this examination, candidates are required to successfully clear two main stages of selection- Prelims and Mains.

Prelims Exam Scheme

S No.	Name of Tests	No. of Questions	MaximumMarks	Time allotted for each test
1	English Language	30	30	20 minutes
2	Numerical Ability	35	35	20 minutes
3	Reasoning Ability	35	35	20 minutes
	Total	100	100	60 Minutes (1 Hour)

Mains Exam Scheme

S No.	Name of Tests	No. of Questions	Maximum Marks	Time allotted for each test
1	General/ Financial Awareness	50	50	35 minutes
2	General English	40	40	35 minutes
3	Reasoning Ability & Computer Aptitude	50	60	45 minutes
4	Quantitative Aptitude	50	50	45 minutes
	Total	190	200	160 minutes

Candidates have to work very hard to score better marks in the exam. They need to focus on determining the new topics from the beginning and the most important thing is they should have the utmost excitement and attention in learning the challenging topics.

Make a timetable for yourself, and start preparing for the exam without any distractions. As the subjects are fewer, applicants need to more attentive in learning the process. For getting a better rank in this exam, you need to be more attentive to the preparation. Accuracy is one of the most important ones of the learning process. So do practice well.

Since there is negative marking for wrong answers to the questions, mark the questions only after being sure of the answer. Practice is essential to solve as many questions as possible in the stipulated time. 20 sets are given for your practice which includes 10 practice sets (5 sets each for prelims and mains) and 10 previous years solved question papers (5 solve papers each for prelims and mains).

I hope this book will prove to be very useful.

IBPS Clerk Prelims

Practice Set – 1

English Language

***Directions (1-10)**: In the following passage there are blanks, each of which has been numbered. These numbers are printed below the passage and against each, five words are suggested, one of which fits the blank appropriately. Find out the appropriate word in each case.*

President Barack Obama's recent statement of his Afghanistan policy has again **(1)** the intractable situation the United States has **(2)** since it led the invasion of the country in 2001. In his State of the Union address to the Congress on January 28, Mr. Obama said the mission there would be **(3)** by the end of the year, and that thereafter the U.S. and its allies would **(4)** a "unified Afghanistan", as it took responsibility for itself. With the agreement of the Afghan government, a "small force" could **(5)** to train and **(6)** Afghan forces and carry out counterterrorism operations against any AI – Qaeda **(7)**. Washington has **(8)** 60,000 of its troops from Afghanistan since Mr. Obama took office in 2009, but 36,500 remain, with 19,000 from other countries in the NATO – ISAF coalition. Western plans are for a residual force of 8,000 to 12,000, two – thirds of them American, but sections of the U.S. military have **(9)** a U.S. strength of 10,000 with 5,000 from the rest of the coalition. Mr. Obama is discussing the **(10)** with senior officers.

1.
(1) Revealed (2) Communicated
(3) Imparted (4) Unveiled
(5) told

2.
(1) resisted (2) evaded
(3) flouted (4) given
(5) faced

3.
(1) managed (2) attended
(3) completed (4) initiated
(5) attained

4.
(1) respect (2) subdue
(3) suffer (4) support
(5) neglect

5.
(1) pause (2) depart
(3) honour (4) remain
(5) prevail

6.
(1) sustain (2) face
(3) serve (4) reinforce
(5) assist

7.
(1) opinions (2) facts
(3) scraps (4) vestiges
(5) remnants

8.
(1) advanced (2) diverted
(3) withdrawn (4) switched
(5) detached

9.
(1) Mentioned (2) Sanctioned
(3) Intimated (4) Suggested
(5) pointed

10.
(1) options (2) preferences
(3) privileges (4) grants
(5) reflections

***Directions (11-20)**: Read the passage given below and answer the following questions*

Firms are said to be in perfect competition when the following conditions occur: (1) many firms produce identical products; (2) many buyers are available to buy the product, and many sellers are available to sell the product; (3) sellers and buyers have all relevant information to make rational decisions about the product being bought and sold; and (4) firms can enter and leave the market without any restrictions—in other words, there is free entry and exit into and out of the market.

A perfectly competitive firm is known as a price taker, because the pressure of competing firms forces them to accept the **prevailing** equilibrium price in the market. If a firm in a perfectly competitive market raises the price of its product by so much as a penny, it will lose all of its sales to competitors. When a wheat grower, wants to know what the going price of wheat is, he or she has to go to the computer or listen to the radio to check. The market price is determined solely by supply and demand in the entire market and not the individual farmer. Also, a perfectly competitive firm must be a very small player in the overall market, so that it can increase or decrease output without noticeably affecting the overall quantity supplied and price in the market.

A perfectly competitive market is a **hypothetical** extreme; however, producers in a number of industries do face many competitor firms selling highly similar goods, in which case they must often act as price takers. Agricultural markets are often used as an example. The same crops grown by different farmers are largely interchangeable. According to the United States Department of Agriculture monthly reports, in 2015, U.S. corn farmers received an average price of $6.00 per bushel and wheat farmers received an average price of $6.00 per bushel. A corn farmer who attempted to sell at $7.00 per bushel, or a wheat grower who attempted to sell for $8.00 per bushel, would not have found any buyers. A perfectly competitive firm will not sell below the equilibrium price either. Why should they when they can sell all they want at the higher price?

11. According to the passage, why is a perfectly competitive **firm** a price taker?

(1) A perfectly competitive firm is a price taker as it cannot afford to sell its products below the market price

(2) A perfectly competitive firm is a price taker as prices are determined by the buyers and not sellers of goods

(3) A perfectly competitive firm produces products that are identical to the products produced by its competitors

(4) A perfectly competitive firm cannot charge above the market price as it will lose all its customers

(5) None of the above

12. According to the author, who determines the price of wheat?

(1) The Government
(2) Market Supply and Demand
(3) Individual Farmers
(5) None of the above
(4) Wheat Buyers

13. The rules of perfect competition would definitely not apply to which of the following **firms**?

(I) A wheat farmer

(II) A firm that produces standardized nuts and bolts

(III) A utilities company that has monopoly over electricity supply to an area

(IV) A firm that has an exclusive patent over its products

(1) I and II only
(2) I, II and III only
(3) II, III and IV only
(4) I, III and IV only
(5) III and IV only

14. Why is agriculture a good example of perfect competition?

(1) There is very little distinction between same crops produced by different farmers

(2) It is a highly regulated market where prices are determined by the market
(3) There is a large amount of fluctuation in demand and supply from one season to another
(4) Data about farming is easily available from the US Dept of Agriculture
(5) None of the above

15. Why, according to the author, must a perfectly competitive firm be a small player in the overall market?
(1) The firm should not have higher bargaining power due to its significant size
(2) The firm should not have higher profit margins than its competitors due to economies of scale
(3) The increase or decrease in output of the firm should not alter the supply available in the market and hence indirectly affect the market price
(4) A large player may affect the flow of information in the overall market thereby distorting the market price
(5) None of the above

16. Which of the following can be inferred from the information given in the passage?
(I) A perfectly competitive market does not exist in real life
(II) A firm in a perfectly competitive market cannot sell its products below market price due to regulations
(III) Agriculture is the only sector in which there is perfect competition

(1) I only	(2) II only
(3) I and II only	(4) III only
(5) II and III only	

17. From the passage, it can be inferred that the author is a

(1) Wheat Farmer	(2) Economist
(3) Agricultural Scientist	(4) Manufacturer
(5) Book Critic	

18. What is the purpose of the passage?
(1) To encourage perfect competition in all fields
(2) To explain how an individual producer is a price taker in a perfectly competitive market
(3) To explain why perfect competition is hurting our farmers
(4) To explain supply and demand economics to the reader
(5) None of the above

19. Choose the word that is synonymous with the word "Prevailing" as used in the passage.

(1) Deterministic	(2) Conquering
(3) Current	(4) Popular
(5) Redundant	

20. Choose the word that is synonymous with the word "Hypothetical" as used in the passage.

(1) Theoretical	(2) Incidental
(3) Exploitative	(4) Superlative
(5) Abstract	

***Directions (21-25)**: Which of the phrases (1), (2), (3) and (4) given below each statement should replace the phrase printed in bold in the sentence to make it grammatically correct? If the sentence is correct as it is given and 'No correction is required', mark (5) as the answer.*

21. Soon after the Tsunami had killed thousands of people along the coasts of southern India, parliament passes a bill that proposed to set up an institutional mechanism to respond promptly to natural disasters.

(1) passed a bill that proposed
(2) passes a bill with purpose
(3) pass a bill proposing
(4) passed a bill which propose
(5) No correction required

22. Denial of wages forced scientists and teachers at the agriculture universities throughout the country to go on strike, crippling crucial research that could help the state of agriculture in the country.

(1) from going on strike
(2) which went on strike
(3) on going for a strike
(4) for going to strike
(5) No correction required

23. In an attempt to boost their profits many edible oil producing companies have been engaging themselves in propaganda against commonly used oils and promoting exotic and expensive varieties of oils as healthier options.

(1) as most healthiest options
(2) as less healthy option
(3) as a healthier option
(4) as much healthiest option
(5) No correction required

24. Thanks to numerous government initiatives, rural masses which was earlier unaware of the luxuries of urban ways of living are now connected to the same lifestyle.

(1) who was earlier unaware
(2) which were earlier aware
(3) who were earlier conversant
(4) who were earlier unaware
(5) No correction required

25. Over the last few months, while most industries are busy in restructuring operations, cutting costs and firing, the Indian pharmaceutical and healthcare industry was adding manpower and giving salary hikes.

(1) as many industries are
(2) while most industries were
(3) while many industries is
(4) where many industries were
(5) No correction required

***Directions (26-30)**: Which of the phrases 1, 2, 3 and 4 given below each sentence should replace the word/ phrase printed in bold in the sentence to make it grammatically correct? If the sentence is correct as it is given and no correction is required, mark 5 as the answer.*

26. US Secretary of State made it clear that time running out for diplomacy over Iran's nuclear programme and said that talks aimed at preventing Tehran from acquiring a nuclear weapon would resume in April.

(1) runs out
(2) was running out
(3) ran out
(4) run
(5) No correction required

27. While the war of the generals rage on, somewhere in small town India, Wonderful things are happeing, quetly and minus fanfare.

(1) rage (2) raging
(3) rages on (4) raged on
(5) No correcton required

28. According to WWF, the small island nation of Samoa was the first in switch off its lights for Earth Hour

(1) first ot switch of (2) the first to switch off
(3) the first of switch off (4) first in switch of
(5) No correction required

29. The campaign is significant because not just the youths are directly appealing to the world but because thier efforts challenge the chimera of normalcy in the area.

(1) not just because (2) just not because
(3) not just (4) because just
(5) No Correction required

30. The doctor's association has threatened to go on indefinite strike support of their teachers.

(1) on supporting to (2) to supporting
(3) for support (4) in support of
(5) No correction required

Numerical Ability

31. The LCM of two numbers a and b is 20. Find the number of unordered pairs (a, b)?

(1) 8 (2) 9
(3) 7 (4) 10
(5) None of the above

32. The largest number that divides 43, 91 and 183 and leaves the same remainder in each case is

(1) 16 (2) 8
(3) 9 (4) 13
(5) 4

33. In a temple, the first bell rings at intervals of 2 seconds, the second bell rings at intervals of 4 seconds and so on till the fifth bell, which rings at intervals of 10 seconds. How many times do all the bells ring together in a half-an-hour period?

(1) 60 (2) 45
(3) 120 (4) 15
(5) 30

34. What is the smallest number which when multiplied by 10 is exactly divisible by 12, 18, 24 and 32?

(1) 288 (2) 144
(3) 1440 (4) 552
(5) None of the above

35. The ratio of two numbers is 5:6. The product of the HCF and LCM of the two numbers is 120. What is the HCF of the two numbers?

(1) 2 (2) 4
(3) 6 (4) 8
(5) 1

36. The sum of two numbers is 65 and the HCF of the two numbers is 5. If the LCM of the two numbers is 180, what is the sum of the reciprocals of the two numbers?

(1) 11/13 (2) 11/625
(3) 13/625 (4) 11/180
(5) 13/180

37. What is the greatest number which divides

1070 and 1265 and leaves remainders 3 and 4 respectively?

(1) 91 (2) 93
(3) 95 (4) 97
(5) 101

38. What is the LCM of 1/3, 1/4 and 1/5?

(1) 1 (2) 2
(3) 1/2 (4) 1/6
(5) None of the above

39. 1254 ÷ 254 × 55 = 5?

(1) 7 (2) 9
(3) 11 (4) 13
(5) none of the above

40. $\frac{1}{7} of 2\frac{5}{8} \div \frac{3}{4} + \frac{1}{3} + \frac{1}{6}$

(1) 1 (2) 0
(3) 1/7 (4) 2
(5) None of the above

***Directions (41-45)**: Find the wrong number in given series sequence.*

41. 1, 4, 15, 64 325, 1955

(1) 15 (2) 64
(3) 325 (4) 1955
(5) None of these

42. 6, 12, 21, 33, 49, 66

(1) 21 (2) 33
(3) 49 (4) 66
(5) None of these

43. 6, 11.5, 19, 28.5, 41

(1) 6 (2) 11.5
(3) 41 (4) 28.5
(5) None of these

44. 5, 26, 82, 214, 401, 702

(1) 26 (2) 82
(3) 214 (4) 401
(5) None of these

45. 5, 20, 73, 274, 1049

(1) 20 (2) 73
(3) 274 (4) 1049
(5) None of these

***Directions (46-50)**: Study the following bar graph carefully and answer the questions given below.*

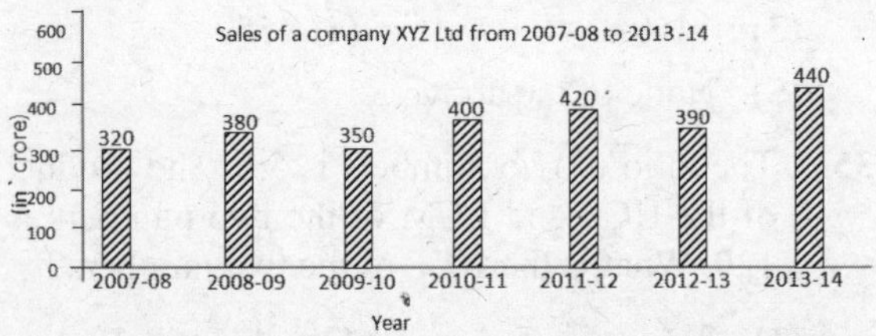

46. What were the average sales of the company per year from 2010-11 to 2013-14?

(1) 402.5 crore (2) 412.5 crore
(3) 422.5 crore 8. (4) 432.5 crore
(5) None of these

47. What is the increase in the sales of the company from 2007-08 to 2013–14?

(1) 60 crore (2) 80 crore
(3) 100 crore (4) 120 crore
(5) None of these

48. What is the ratio of the sales of the company in 2008-09 to the sales of the company in 2011–12?

(1) 19: 21 (2) 21: 23
(3) 23: 25 (4) 25: 27
(5) None of these

49. What was the percentage increase in the sales of the company from 2009–10 to 2011 to 12?

(1) 10% (2) 15%
(3) 20% (4) 25%
(5) None of these

50. In which of the given years was the increase/ decrease in the sales compared to respective previous year the least?

(1) 2010–11 (2) 2011 -12
(3) 2012–13 (4) 2013–14

(5) None of these

51. A sum becomes 10/9 times itself in 1 yr. Find the rate of simple interest.

(1) 11 1/2 % (2) 11 1/9%
(3) 12 1/2% (4) 121/9%
(5) None of these

52. Ananya and Anjali started a business by investing money in the ratio 3:4 respectively. After some months Aditi joined the business by investing half the amount as Ananya. What percentage of the total profit will Aditi earn?

(1) 10% (2) 15%
(3) 20% (4) 25%
(5) Cannot be determined

53. If I walk at 4 km/h, I miss the bus by 10 min. If I walk at 5 km/h, I reach 5 min before the arrival of the bus. How far I walk to reach the bus stand?

(1) 5 km (2) 5.5 km
(3) 6 km (4) 7.5 km
(5) None of these

54. The speed of a boat in still water is 15 km/h and the rate of current is 3 km/h. The distance travelled down steam in 12 minutes is:

(1) 3.3 km (2) 2.9 km
(3) 2.4 km (4) 3.6 km
(5) None of these

55. 6 men finish one-fourth work in 2 days. The number of additional men required for finishing the same work in 2 days is?

(1) 18 men (2) 24 men
(3) 28 men (4) 14 men
(5) None of these

56. A tank is filled in 5 hours by three pipes A, B and C. The pipe C is twice as fast as B and B is twice as fast as A. How much time will pipe A alone take to fill the tank?

(1) 22 hrs
(2) 27 hrs
(3) 35 hrs
(4) cannot be determined
(5) None of these

57. A dishonest milkman plans to adulterate milk by adding water. If water is freely available, how many liters of water should he add to 5 liters of milk, so that, by selling the milk at cost price, he makes a profit of 20%?

(1) 2 liters (2) 1 liter
(3) 3 liters (4) 5 liters
(5) None of the above

58. Rita's present age is four times her daughter's present age and two-thirds of her mother's present age. The total of the present ages of all of them is 154 years. What is the difference between Rita's and her mohter's present age?

(1) 28 years
(2) 34 years
(3) 32 years
(4) Cannot be determined
(5) None of these

59. If SP = Rs. 84, % gain = 20%, then CP =?

(1) Rs. 60 (2) Rs. 65
(3) Rs. 70 (4) RS. 75
(5) None of these

60. On combining two groups of students having 30 and 40 average marks respectively in an exam, the resultant group has an average score of 34. Find the ratio of the number of students in the first group to the number of students in the second group.

(1) 2 : 1 (2) 3 : 2
(3) 3 : 1 (4) 4 : 3
(5) None of these

61. The edge of an ice cube is 14 cm. The volume of the largest cylindrical ice cube that can be formed out of it is

(1) 2200 cu. cm (2) 2000 cu. Cm
(3) 2156 cu. cm (4) 2400 cu. Cm
(5) None of these

62. A rope makes 125 rounds of a cylinder with base radius 15 cm. How many times can it go round a cylinder with base radius 25 cm?

(1) 100 (2) 75
(3) 80 (4) 65
(5) None of these

63. If 6 boys and 6 girls have to sit in a round circular music chair. So, that there is a girl between every 2 boys. Find the number of ways they can sit?

(1) $6! \times 5!$ (2) $6! \times 4!$
(3) $6! \times 3!$ (4) $6! \times 2!$

(5) None of these

64. The LCM of two numbers is 360, and their HCF is 15. If one of the numbers is 45, what is the value of the remainder when the other number is divided by 7?

(1) 1 (2) 2
(3) 3 (4) 4
(5) 0

***Directions (65)**: Study the following table carefully to answer the questions.*

Rate of interest (pcpa) offered by five companies on deposits under different schemes

Company → Scheme ↓	A	B	C	D	E
I	8.5	9.0	8.0	8.5	9.0
II	9.5	8.5	9.0	9.0	8.5
III	8.0	8.0	7.5	8.5	8.5
IV	10.0	9.5	10.5	9.5	10.0

65. Mr. Lal invested Rs. 30000 in company A under Scheme II, which offers simple interest and Rs. 48000 in Company D under Scheme II, which offers compound interest. What will be the total amount of interest earned by Mr Lal in two years?

(1) Rs. 14728.80
(2) Rs. 17428.50
(3) Rs. 14827.70
(4) Rs. 16728.20
(5) None of these

Reasoning Ability

66. Which of the following expressions will be true if the expression $R > O = A > S < T$ as definitely true?

(1) $O > T$ (2) $S < R$
(3) $T > A$ (4) $S = O$
(5) $T < R$

67. Which of the following symbols should replace the question mark (?) in the given expression in order to make the expression '$P > A$' as well as '$T \leq L$' definitely true?

$P > L\ ?\ A \geq N = T$

(1) $\leq$ (2) $>$
(3) $<$ (4) $\geq$ (or) $=$
(5) either $\leq$ or $<$

68. Which of the following symbols should be placed in the blank spaces respectively (in the same order from left to right) in order to complete the given such a manner that makes the expressions '$B > N$' as well as '$D \leq L$' definitely true?

B ___ L ___ O ___ N ___ D

(1) =, =, ≥, >= (2) , ≥, =, >
(3) >, <, =, ≤ (4) >,=, =,≥
(5) >, =, ≥, >

69. Which of the following letters should be placed in the blank spaces respectively (in the same order from left to right) in order to complete the given expression in such a manner that makes the expression '$A < P$' definitely false?

$\_\_ < \_\_ < \_\_ > \_\_$

(1) L, N, P, A
(2) L, A, P, N

(3) A, L, P, N (4) N, A, P, L
(5) P, N, A, L

70. Which of the following symbols should be placed in the blank spaces respectively (in the same order from left to right) in order to complete the given expression in such a manner that makes the expressions 'F > N' and 'U > D' definitely false?

F_O_U_N_D

(1) <, <, >, = (2) <, =, =, >
(3) <, =, =, < (4) ≥, =, =, ≥
(5) >, >, =, <

***Directions (71-75)**: Study the following information carefully and answer the questions given below.*

B, D, M, K, P, Q, W and H are sitting around a circle facing at the centre. M is to the immediate right of B who is 4th to the right of K. P is 2nd to the left of B and is 4th to the right of W.Q is 2nd to the right of D who is 2nd to the right of H.

71. Who is third to the right of B?
(1) W (2) M
(3) K (4) H
(5) None of these

72. Which of the following represents the immediate neighbours of D?
(1) PQ (2) KH
(3) PH (4) KQ
(5) PK

73. Who is third to the right of W?
(1) P (2) D
(3) K (4) R
(5) Data inadequate

74. Who is second to the left of P?
(1) D
(2) H
(3) K
(4) Data inadequate
(5) None of these

75. Who is to the immediate left of B?
(1) Q
(2) P
(3) W
(4) Data inadequate
(5) None of these

***Directions (76-80)**: Study the following information carefully and answer the given questions:*

Eight friends L, M, N, O, P, Q, R and S are sitting around a square table in such a way that four of them sit at four corners of the square while four sit in the middle of each of the four sides. The ones who sit at the four 4 corners face outside while those who sit in the middle of the sides face the centre.

- Only one person sits between L and Q. L sits at middle of one of the series.
- O sits third to the right of Q.
- Both R and S are immediate neighbours of L.
- M sits second to left of N.
- N is neither an immediate neighbour of Q nor S.

76. Four of the following five are alike in a certain way and so form a group. Which is the one that does not belong to that group?
(1) L (2) R
(3) S (4) O
(5) P

77. Who sits third to the left of Q?
(1) M (2) S
(3) R (4) N
(5) P

78. How many people sit between M and S when counted from the right hand side of S?
(1) One (2) Three
(3) None
(4) Two

(5) Four

79. Which of the following is true regarding P?

(1) P sits exactly between M and N.
(2) O sits second to right of P.
(3) None of the given options is true.
(4) L sits immediate right of P.
(5) Q is an immediate neighbour of P.

80. What is the position of P with respect to S?

(1) Fourth to the left
(2) Second to the right
(3) Second to the left
(4) Third to the right
(5) Third to the left

***Directions (81-85)**: Study the following information to answer the given questions.*

Ten people are sitting in two parallel rows having five people each, in such a way that there is an equal distance between adjacent person. In row 1-V, W, X, Y and Z are seated (but not necessarily in the same order) and all of them are facing North. In row 2-F, G, H, I and J are seated (but not necessarily in the same order) and all of the are facing South. Therefore, in the given seating arrangement, each member seated in a row faces another member of the other row.

- Y sits third to the left of W. The one who faces Y sits second to the right of F.
- Only one person sits between F and I.
- H and J are immediate neighbours of each other. J does not sit at any of the extreme ends of the line.
- The one faces G sits to the immediate right of Z.
- X is not an immediate neighbour of Z.

81. Who amongst the following faces H?

(1) Y (2) V
(3) Z (4) W
(5) X

82. Who amongst the following sits to the immediate left of the person who sits exactly in the middle of row-2?

(1) J (2) H
(3) I (4) G
(5) F

83. Four of the following five are alike in a certain way based on the given seating arrangement and thus form a group. Which is the one that does not belong to that group?

(1) H (2) I
(3) W (4) Y
(5) X

84. Who amongst the following sits third to the right of the person who faces X?

(1) G (2) F
(3) J (4) I
(5) H

85. Which of the following is true regarding V?

(1) None of the given options is true.
(2) An immediate neighbour of V faces F.
(3) X is an immediate neighbour of V.
(4) W sits to immediate right of V.
(5) V faces I.

***Directions (86-87)**: Observe the arrangement below and answer the questions that follow:*

T H U 0 $ & G # 3 M 1 % A 5 W 7 < @ 9 Q P 8

86. Of the five options below, only one of them is different from the pattern of the other four. Select that option.

(1) 3A1 (2) H&0
(3) @8Q (4) AW<
(5) G13

87. Select the element that's sixth to the left of the seventh element from the right.

(1) 1 (2) M
(3) % (4) 3
(5) None of the above

***Directions (88)**: Study the following arrangement carefully and answer the question given below:*

B 2 M E J % R 5 @ N D I P 4 © T 3 9 F U I $ 6 H J A 7 * G Q #

88. Four of the following five are alike in a certain way based on their positions in the above arrangement and so form a group. Which is the one that does not belong to that group?

(1) 5NI **(2)** 9U$
(3) HA* **(4)** 7G#
(5) DPT

89. What should come next in the following letter series based on English alphabet?

CEA IKG OQM ?

(1) STW **(2)** WUS
(3) SWU **(4)** UWS
(5) None of these

90. What should come next in the following letter series based on English alphabet?

BDB HJH NPN ?

(1) STS **(2)** WUW
(3) UWU **(4)** TVT
(5) None of these

***Directions (88)**: Study the following arrangement carefully and answer the question given below:*

In a family of 8 people, G is the mother of B. H has two daughters–G and D. F is H's only granddaughter. E is D's father. C is the brother of B. B is A's son.

91. How many children does D have?

(1) 0 **(2)** 1
(3) 2 **(4)** Either 0 or 1
(5) Either 1 or 2

92. How is D related to C?

(1) Uncle **(2)** Aunt
(3) Brother **(4)** Sister
(5) Can't be determined

93. A person rode his bicycle Northwards, then turned left and rode one km and again turned left and rode 2km. He found himself exactly one km West of his starting point. How far did he ride Northwards initially?

(1) 1 km **(2)** 2km
(3) 3km **(4)** 4km
(5) 5km

94. Anup starts from point A and travels towards north for 8 km and then he turns to his left and travels for 15 km to reach point B. What is the distance between A and B and the direction to which Anup is finally facing?

(1) 17 km, West. **(2)** 23 km, East.
(3) 19 km, West. **(4)** 21 km, East.
(5) None of these

***Directions (95-99)**: Study the following arrangement carefully and answer the question given below:*

(I) P, Q, R, S, T, and U are six members of a group which three are males and three are females.
(II) There are two engineers, two lawyers, one teacher and one doctor in the group.
(III) Q, T, P, and R are two married couples and no person in the group has the same profession.
(IV) T, a teacher with blue dress married a male Lawyer with brown dress.
(V) Colour of the dresses of both the husbands and that of both the wives is the same.
(VI) Two persons have blue dress, two have brown and the remaining one each has black and green.
(VII) P is a male engineer and whose sister S is also an engineer.

(VIII) Q is a doctor.

95. Which of the following group of female members?

(1) QSU (2) QSR
(3) QST (4) QTU
(5) None of these

96. Who is wife of P?

(1) R (2) T
(3) S (4) Q
(5) None of these

97. What is the colour of U's dress?

(1) Black
(2) Green
(3) Black or Green
(4) Data inadequate
(5) None of these

98. Which of the following is a pair of married ladies?

(1) QT
(2) PR
(3) TS
(4) Data inadequate
(5) None of these

99. What is the profession of R?

(1) Teacher
(2) Lawyer
(3) Engineer
(4) Doctor
(5) Cannot be determined

100. In certain code language "WINDOW" is written as "SJJEKX". Then what is the code for the word "SIMPLE"?

(1) "OJHIQF" (2) "OJIHQF"
(3) "TENLMA" (4) "OJIQHF"
(5) None of these.

Answers With Explanations

1. **(1)** The rest of the options are inappropriate in the context of the given sentence.

2. **(5)** The rest of the options are inappropriate in the context of the given sentence.

3. **(3)** The rest of the options are inappropriate in the context of the given sentence.

4. **(4)** The rest of the options are inappropriate in the context of the given sentence.

5. **(4)** The rest of the options are contextually inappropriate.

6. **(5)**

7. **(5)**

8. **(3)** The rest of the options are inappropriate in the context of the given sentence.

9. **(4)**

10. **(1)** The rest of the options are incorrect in the context of the given sentence.

11. **(4)**

12. **(2)** The price of wheat is not decided by individual farmers and is decided solely by the supply and demand in the market.

13. **(5)**

14. **(1)**

15. **(3)**

16. **(1)**

17. **(2)**

18. **(2)**

19. **(3)** Current is synonymous with prevailing as used in the passage.

20. **(1)** Hypothetical, as used in the passage, means theoretical.

21. **(1)** The sentence is in the simple past tense. So, the correct option is (1).

22. **(5)** The sentence is grammatically correct.

23. **(5)**

24. **(4)** Masses is plural, so 'was' should be replaced by 'were' and 'which' should also be replaced by 'who'.

25. **(2)** The sentence is in past tense. So, 'were' should be used in place of 'are'.

26. **(2)** 'Was' is missing in the sentence.

27. **(3)** War is singular. So, it should be 'rages on'.

28. **(2)**

29. **(1)**

30. **(4)**

31. **(1)** The pairs are (1,20), (2,20), (4,20) , (5,20), (10,20), (20,20), (4,5), (4,10). Hence, the number of unordered pairs is 8.

32. **(5)** The required number = HCF of (91–43), (183–91) and (183–43)

= HCF of (48, 92, 140) = 4

33. **(4)** The LCM of 2, 4, 6, 8 and 10 is 120. Hence, the bells ring together once every 120 seconds or 2 minutes. So, they ring together 15 times in a half-an-hour period.

34. **(2)** The LCM of the numbers is 288.

So, multiples of 288 are divisible by all the numbers.

LCM of 288 and 10 = 1440.

Hence, the required number = 144

35. **(1)** Let the two numbers be 5h and 6h where h is the HCF of the numbers.

Product of the numbers = Product of LCM and HCF.

$30h^2 = 120$

h = 2

So, the HCF of the two numbers is 2

36. **(5)** Let the numbers be ha and hb.

HCF of the numbers = h

LCM of the numbers = hab.

Sum of reciprocals = (a+b)/hab h(a+b) = 65

h = 5

(a+b) = 13

hab = LCM = 180

So, sum of reciprocals = 13/180

37. **(4)** The required number = HCF of (1070–3, 1265–4)

= HCF of (1067, 1261) 1067 = 11×97 and 1261 = 13×97

Hence, HCF = 97

38. **(1)** LCM of fractions = LCM of numerators/ HCF of denominators

HCF of (3, 4, 5) = 1

Hence, LCM of the three fractions = 1/1 = 1

39. **(2)** 1254 ÷ 254 × 55 = 5?

$125^4 = 5^{12}$ *and* $25^4 = 5^8$

40. **(1)**

41. **(4)** 4 = 1×2+2

15 = 4×3+3

64 = 15×4+4

325 = 64×5+5

1956 = 325×6+6

42. **(3)** 2×2+2 = 6

3×3+3 = 12

4×4 + 5= 21

5×5 +8 = 33

6×6 + 12 = 48

43. **(3)** 1.5×2 + 3 = 6

2.5×3 + 4 = 11.5

3.5×4 + 5 = 19

4.5×5 + 6 = 28.5

5.5×6 + 7 = 40

44. **(3)** 1×2+3=5

4×5+6 = 26

8×9+10 = 82

13×14+15 = 212

19×20 + 21 =401

26×27 +28 = 702

45. **(3)** 12 + 4= 5

$2^2 + 16 = 20$

$3^2 + 64 = 73$

$4^2 + 256 = 272$

$5^2 + 1024 = 1049$

46. **(2)**

47. **(4)**

48. **(1)**

49. **(3)**

50. **(2)**

51. **(2)** Let the sum be Rs. X.

Amount = Rs. 10x/9

T= 1 year

SI = Rs. (10x/9)-x = Rs. x/9

R = [(100×SI)/(P×T)]

= (100×x/9×1/x)%

= (100/9)%

= 11 1/9%

52. **(5)**

53. **(1)** Let the required distance be d km/h

Then, d/4-d/5=15min =1/4 h

d 1/20=1/4

d = 5km

54. **(4)** Speed downstream = (15 + 3) kmph = 18 kmph. Distance traveled = (18×12/60)km = 3.6 km.

55. **(1)**

Time taken by 6 men to finish the whole work = 8 days

Let the number of men required be x.

8×6 = 2 x

x = (8 x 6)/2 = 24

The required men = 24-6 men = 18 men

56. **(3)** Suppose pipe A alone takes x hours to fill the tank.

Then, pipes B and C will take x/2 and x/4 hours respectively to fill the tank. 1/x+2/x+4/x=1/5

7/ =1/5

x = 5hrs

57. **(2)** Let the milkman mix 'x' liters of water in 5 liters of milk and the CP of milk be Rs M per liter

CP of 5 liters of milk = 5M

CP of (5+x) liters of the mixture = 5M

SP of (5+x) liters of milk = (5+x)M

Profit = (5+x)M–5M)/5M

= 20/100 = 1/5

5Mx = 5M

x = 1

Hence, the milkman should mix 1 liter of water in every 5 liters of milk to make a profit of 20% by selling the mixture at the CP of milk

58. **(1)** Let Rita's age be x.

Mother's age = 3x/2

Daughter's age = x/4

x + 3x/2 + x/4 = 154

11x/4 = 154

x = 56

Hence, difference of ages = x/2 = 28 years

59. **(3)**

CP = (100×SP)/((100+gain%))

=(100×84)/120

= Rs. 70

60. **(2)**

Required ratio = (40-34)/(34-30)

= 6/4 = 3/2

61. **(3)**

Volume = π x r² x h

= 22 x 7 x 7 x 14 = 2156

62. **(2)**

63. **(1)** Circular permutation = n! (n–1)!

Hence Number of ways = 6! (6–1)! = 6! × 5!

64. **(1)** Let the second number be x.

LCM x HCF = Product of the two numbers

360 × 15 = x × 45

x = 120

65. **(1)**

(30000×9.5×2)/100 + (48000× 109/100× 109/100- 48000)

= 5700 + (57028.8–48000)

= 5700 + 9028.8 = Rs. 14728.80

66. **(2)** From expression R > O = A > S < T, the two conclusions are made R > O> S < T

R > A> S < T

Hence from the above expression S < R is definitely true.

67. **(4)** The given expression is P > L ? A N = T In order to satisfy the condition that 'P > A' as well as 'T ≤ L' we should replace '?' with '' (or) = symbol i.e. P > L ≥ A ≥ N = T satisfies

both the condition.

P > L = A ≥ N = T satisfies both the condition.

68. **(4)** In order to satisfy the condition i.e. 'B > N' as well as 'D≤L' for the given expression, the expression should be written as B > L = O = N ≥ D From this expression, it is clear that B > N and D <= L

69. **(5)**

70. **(3)**

For questions (71-75):

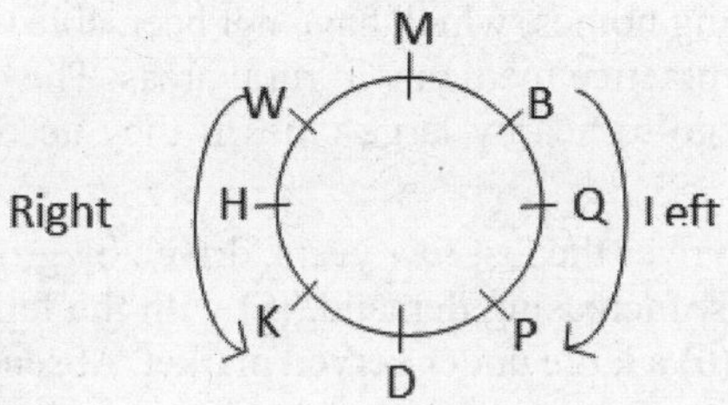

71. **(4)**

72. **(5)**

73. **(2)**

74. **(3)**

75. **(1)**

For questions (76-80):

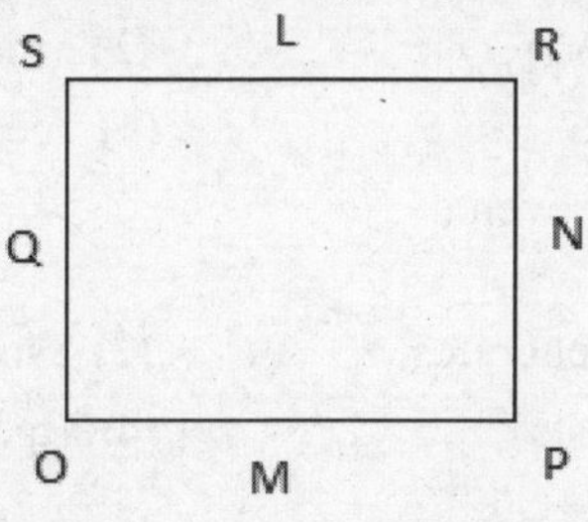

76. **(1)**

77. **(3)**

78. **(5)**

79. **(5)**

80. **(1)**

For questions (81-85):

81. **81.** (1)

82. **(4)**

83. **(3)**

84. **(3)**

85. **(2)**

86. **(4)** The options have an element, the element four positions to it's right and then the element two positions to it's right.

87. **(2)** The element required is 13th from the right.

88. **(5)**

89. **(4)**

90. **(4)**

For questions (91-92):

91. **(4)**

92. **(2)**

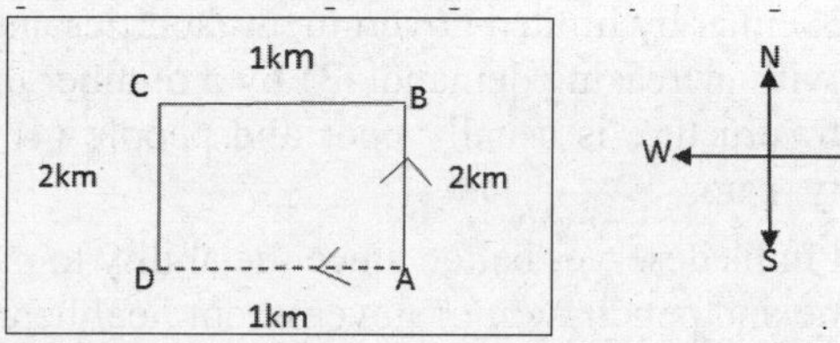

93. **(2)**

94. **(1)**

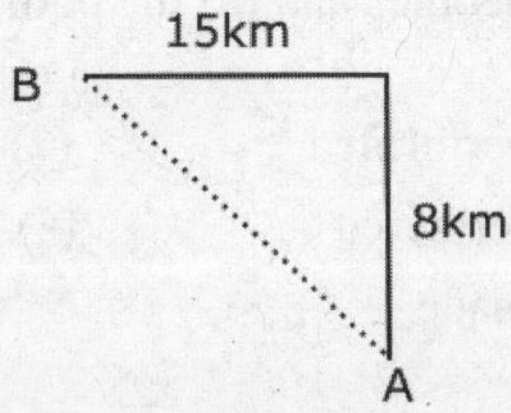

For questions (95-99):

RT and PQ are married couples as T married to a lawyer and Q is a doctor and P is a male engineer.

Q: Doctor, female, blue dress

P: Engineer, Male, brown dress

T: Teacher, female, blue dress

R: Lawyer, Male, brown dress

S: Engineer, female, black/green dress

U: Lawyer, male, black/green dress

95. **(3)**

96. **(4)**

97. **(3)**

98. **(1)**

99. **(2)**

100. **(4)** Based on -4, +1, -4, +1, -4, +1

IBPS Clerk Prelims

Practice Set – 2

English Language

***Directions (1-10)**: In the following passage there are blanks, each of which has been numbered. These numbers are printed below the passage and against each, five words/phrases are suggested, one of which fits the blank appropriately. Find out the appropriate word/phrase in each case.*

Rural healthcare in India is **(1)** by a huge gap between supply and demand. Currently, rural healthcare needs are **(2)** either by limited government facilities and private nursing homes, which have not been able to keep pace with increasing demand, **(3)** by a number of quacks who practice medicine in rural areas. The quality of infrastructure is usually poor and people **(4)** up having to go to nearby large cities if they need high-quality care.

Rural India deserves better, since the ability to pay has gone up over the last few years, driven by growth in income and penetration of government healthcare programmes. Increasing demand, **(5)** with the failure of existing infrastructure to scale, has resulted in rural healthcare **(6)** a large under-served market. Absence of a viable business model **(7)** conversion of the huge rural expenditure on health into an economic activity that generates incomes and **(8)** the poor. It is this **(9)** that entrepreneurs are looking to **(10)**.

1.
(1) performed (2) displayed
(3) furthered (4) characterized
(5) made

2.
(1) stopped (2) met
(3) elevated (4) discussed
(5) set

3.
(1) also (2) nor
(3) but (4) or
(5) and

4.
(1) end (2) give
(3) fed (4) start
(5) set

5.
(1) couple (3) mentioning
(2) combined (4) engaged
(5) resulting

6.
(1) become (2) happening
(3) being (4) exists
(5) is

7.
(1) to (2) makes
(3) so (4) ceasing
(5) prevents

8.
(1) generates (2) supplies
(3) lists (4) turns
(5) serves

9.
(1) gap (2) truth
(3) progress (4) catastrophes
(5) divides

10.
(1) fills (2) access
(3) plug (4) form
(5) distance

***Directions (11-15)**: Which of the phrases (1), (2), (3) and (4) given below each sentence should replace the word/phrase printed in bold in the sentence to make it grammatically correct? If the sentence is correct as it is given and 'No correction is required', mark (5) as the answer.*

11. A freezing morning accompanied by a dense cover of fog set the toning for the coming weekend.

(1) keeping tone
(2) started the toning
(3) kept the tone
(4) set the tone
(5) No correction required

12. The jail is in the news again **with the finding** of a pistol and some bullets?

(1) to finding
(2) with find
(3) finding
(4) on found
(5) No correction required

13. The space-crunched city throws up several stories of struggle that schools **have had putup with** to win playgrounds for their students?

(1) have had to put up to
(2) had put up on
(3) have had to put up with
(4) had to put up to
(5) No correction required

14. **Emotions rang high** as both families were taken to the police station last night?

(1) Emotions went higher
(2) Emotion became high
(3) Emotionally high
(4) Emotions ran high
(5) No Correction required

15. Work at all the court complexes was paralysed as lawyers **went on a day-long strike** as a mark of protest?

(1) for a one day strike
(2) for a strike
(3) on a day's long strike
(4) on a day-long striking
(5) No correction required

***Directions (16-20)**: Rearrange the following five sentences (A), (B), (C), (D) and (E) in the proper sequence to form a meaningful paragraph; then answer the questions given below them.*

(A) The policy makers in most of the developing economies recognise this importance and have been implementing a host of programmes and measures to achieve rural developments objectives.

(B) While some of these countries have achieved impressive results from those programmes and measures, others have failed to make a significant dent in the problem of persistent rural underdevelopment.

(C) The socio-economic disparities between rural and urban areas are widening and creating tremendous pressure on the social and economic fabric of many such developing economics

(D) These factors, among many others, tend to highlight the importance of rural development.

(E) Although millions of rural people have escaped poverty as a result of rural development in many Asian Countries, a large majority of rural people continue to suffer from persistent poverty.

16. Which of the following should be the **THIRD** sentence after rearrangement?

(1) A
(2) B
(3) C
(4) D
(5) E

17. Which of the following should be the **LAST (FIFTH)** sentence after rearrangement?
(1) A (2) B
(3) C (4) D
(5) E

18. Which of the following should be the **FOURTH** sentence after rearrangement?
(1) C (2) B
(3) A (4) D
(5) E

19. Which of the following should be the **FIRST** sentence after rearrangement?
(1) A (2) B
(3) C (4) D
(5) E

20. Which of the following should **SECOND** sentence after rearrangement?
(1) D (2) E
(3) C (4) B
(5) A

***Directions (21-25)**: Each question below has two blanks, each blank indicating that something has been omitted. Choose the set of words for each blank which best fits the meaning of the sentence as a whole.*

21. Forest department officials said that when the elephants were made to —- from their trucks, they went straight to the spot where they had been —- during the camp.
(1) jump, killed (2) alight, tied
(3) enter, hurt (4) step, played
(5) exit, enjoyed

22. Excise officials seized pouches of whisky —- a bus travelling —- Maharashtra.
(1) from, to (2) in, for
(3) for, towards (4) inside, on
(5) through, till

23. Organisations —— for the victims —- the inhuman and unjust attitude of the gov- ernment.
(1) fighting, applauded (2) lobbying, supported
(3) working, condemned (4) stand, opposed
(5) trying, spoke

24. A collision between two buses —- six people dead, —- the driver of one of the buses.
(1) made, also (2) left, including
(3) caused, combined (4) resulted, except
(5) got, surpassing

25. The court —- revenue authorities and PCB officials to —- teams and visit pharma units
(1) directed, form (2) announced, arrange
(3) commanded, display (4) ruled, make
(5) told, carve

***Directions (26-30): Read** each sentence to find out whether there is any grammatical error or idiomatic error in it. The error, if any, will be in one part of the sentence. The number of that part is the answer. If there is 'No error', the answer is 5. (Ignore errors of punctuation, if any)*

26. (1) The transit system's underground/ (2) tunnels and stations will/ (3) be constructed/ (4) next heritage structures./ (5) No error

27. (1) Residents have been planting/ (2) the ornamental trees outside/ (3) their homes and in lawns to/ (4) add beauty and give their place a grand look./ (5) No error

28. (1) A diamond jeweller's peon/ (2) tipped off a gang/ (3) about the gold (4) in his employer's vault./ (5) No error

29. (1) He said that the performance of the Indian team/ (2) was satisfactory at the international meet/ (3) and that they learnt a lot from/ (4) watching top seeded players through action at the grand slam/ (5)No error

30. (1) Watching the Exponential /(2) talent of world tennis/ (3) Was the best things/ (4) to happen to him./ (5) No error

Numerical Ability

31. The retail price of a water geyser is Rs. 1265. If the manufacturer gains 10%, the wholesale dealer gains 15% and the retailer gains 25%, then the cost of the product is:

(1) Rs. 800 (2) Rs. 900
(3) Rs. 700 (4) Rs. 600
(5) None of these

32. A pipe can fill a cistern in 6 hrs. Due to a leak in its bottom, it is filled in 7 hrs. When the cistern is full, in how much time will it be emptied by the leak?

(1) 42 hrs (2) 40 hrs
(3) 43 hrs (4) 45 hrs
(5) None of these

33. Ram travels a certain distance at 3 km/h and reaches 15 minutes late. If he travels at 4 km/h, he reaches 15 minutes earlier. The distance he has to travel is:

(1) 4.5 km (2) 6 km
(3) 7.2 km (4) 12 km
(5) None of these

34. In a mixture of 45 litres, the ratio of milk and water is 3 : 2. How much water must be added to make the ratio 9 : 11?

(1) 10 litres (2) 15 litres
(3) 17 litres (4) 20 litres
(5) None of these

35. A person can row with the stream at 8 Km per hour and against the stream at 6 Km an hour. The speed of the current is:

(1) 1 Km/h (2) 2 Km/h
(3) 4 Km/h (4) 5Km/h
(5) None of these

36. A father's age is three times the sum of the ages of his two children, but 20 years hence his age will be equal to the sum of their ages. Then, the father's age is:

(1) 30 years (2) 40 years
(3) 35 years (4) 45 years
(5) None of these

37. A sum was put at simple interest at a certain rate for 3 years. Had it been put at 1% higher rate, it would have fetched Rs. 5100 more. The sum is:

(1) Rs. 170000 (2) Rs. 150000
(3) Rs. 125000 (4) Rs. 120000
(5) None of these

38. From among 36 teachers in a school, one principal and one vice-principal are to be appointed. In how many ways can this be done?

(1) 1260 (2) 1250
(3) 1240 (4) 1800
(5) None of these

39. A card is drawn at random from a well-shuffled pack of 52 cards. What is the probability of getting a two of hearts or a two diamonds?

(1) 1/26 (2) 2/17
(3) 1/13 (4) 4/13
(5) None of these

40. A sum is invested for 3 years at compound interest at 5%, 10% and 20% respectively. In three years, if the sum amounts to Rs. 16,632, then find the sum.

(1) Rs. 11000 (2) Rs. 12000 (3) Rs. 13000 (4) Rs. 14000

(5) None of these

***Directions (41-45): Table** shows the mobile phones sold on different days by different sellers. Read the table carefully and answer the questions.*

Mobiles Phones Sellers \ Days→	Monday	Tuesday	Wednesday	Thursday	Friday	Saturday	Sunday
P	40	45	48	28	50	24	20
Q	90	92	27	12	16	98	26
R	80	36	30	13	28	62	47
S	60	46	12	64	52	34	76
T	48	18	58	69	70	10	15

41. Find the difference of mobile phones sold by P and R together on Monday to the mobile phones sold by S and T on Wednesday?

(1) 60 (2) 50
(3) 80 (4) 20
(5) None of these

42. Find the ratio of mobile phone sold by Q on Tuesday and Saturday together to the mobile phone sold by R on Thursday and Sunday together?

(1) 7 : 19 (2) 19 : 5
(3) 19 : 6 (4) 2 : 5
(5) None of these

43. Mobile phones sold by P and S together on Wednesday is what percent of mobile phone sold by T on Sunday?

(1) 400% (2) 200%
(3) 100% (4) 50%
(5) None of these

44. What is the average of mobile phone sold by Q on Wednesday, T on Sunday and S on Monday ?

(1) 24 (2) 36
(3) 30 (4) 28
(5) None of these

45. The mobiles sold by P on Thursday are of two types i.e. Windows phone and Android phone in ratio 3 : 4. Find the number of Windows phones sold by P on Thursday?

(1) 14 (2) 24
(3) 16 (4) 12
(5) None of these

***Directions (46-55):** What should come in place of question mark (?) in following simplification problems?*

46. 45% of 600+? % of 480 = 390

(1) 20 (2) 25
(3) 30 (4) 40
(5) None of these

47. 65% of 240+ ? % of 150 = 210

(1) 45 (2) 46
(3) 32 (4) 36
(5) None of these

48. $4\frac{2}{3}+7\frac{1}{6}-5\frac{2}{9}=?$

(1) $6\frac{2}{3}$ (2) $6\frac{2}{9}$
(3) $6\frac{11}{18}$ (4) $6\frac{7}{18}$
(5) None of these

49. $\frac{2}{3}$ *of* $1\frac{2}{3}$ *of* 75% *of* 540 = ?

(1) 378 (2) 756

(3) 252 (4) 332
(5) None of these

50. 555.05 + 55.50 + 5.55 + 5 + 0.55 = ?
(1) 621.65 (2) 655.75
(3) 634.85 (4) 647.35
(5) None of these

51. 1425 + 8560 + 1680 ÷ 200 = ?
(1) 58.325 (2) 9973.4
(3) 56.425 (4) 9939.4
(5) None of these

52. ? % of 800 = 293 – 22% of 750
(1) 14 (2) 18
(3) 12 (4) 16
(5) 20

53. 25.6% of 250 + √? = 119
(1) 4225 (2) 3025
(3) 2025 (4) 5625
(5) None of these

54. $4\frac{5}{6}-5\frac{5}{9}=?-2\frac{1}{3}+\frac{11}{18}$
(1) $\frac{3}{4}$ (2) $2\frac{1}{18}$
(3) $1\frac{7}{9}$ (4) $1\frac{11}{18}$
(5) None of these

55. [30% of {(80% of 850) ÷ 34}] = ?
(1) 5 (2) 4
(3) 6 (4) 8
(5) 9

56. The sides of a triangle are in the ratio of 1/2 :1/3 : 1/4. If the perimeter is 52 cm, then the length of the smallest side is:
(1) 9 cm (2) 10 cm
(3) 11 cm (4) 12 cm
(5) None of these

57. If A's salary is 25% higher than B's salary, then how much per cent is B's salary lower than A's?
(1) 15% (2) 20%
(3) 25% (4) 33.33%
(5) None of these

58. Ravi sells an article at a gain of 121 %. 2 If he had sold it at Rs. 22.50 more, he would have gained 25% The cost price of the article is:
(1) Rs. 162 (2) Rs. 140
(3) Rs. 196 (4) Rs. 180
(5) None of these

59. A certain job was assigned to a group of men to do it in 20 days. But 12 men did not turn up for the job and the remaining men did the job in 32 days. The original number of men in the group was:
(1) 32 (2) 34
(3) 36 (5) None of these
(4) 40

60. A vessel contains liquid P and Q in the ratio 5 : 3. If 16 litres of the mixture are removed and the same quantity of liquid Q is added, the ratio become 3 : 5. What quantity does the vessel hold?
(1) 35 litres (2) 45 litres
(3) 40 litres (4) 50 litres
(5) None of these

***Directions (61-65): What** should come in place of question mark (?) in following simplification problems?*

61. 50% of 250 + √? = 165
(1) 1700 (2) 1600
(3) 1800 (4) 2000
(5) None of these

62. 140% of 56 + 56% of 140 = ?
(1) 78.4 (2) 158.6
(3) 156.6 (4) 87.4
(5) None of these

63. $1\frac{1}{4}+1\frac{5}{9}\times1\frac{5}{8}\div6\frac{1}{2}=?$
(1) 17 (2) 27
(3) 42 (4) 18
(5) None of these

64. 999.09 + 99.90 + 9.99 + 9 + 0.99 =?

(1) 1118.97 (2) 1128.97
(3) 1218.97 (4) 1139.97
(5) None of these

65. 20% of [{(220% of 40) – 10}]% of 500 = ?

(1) 58 (2) 68
(3) 98 (4) 78
(5) None of these

Reasoning Ability

***Directions (66-70)**: In each of the question, relationships between some elements are shown in the statements(s). These statements are followed by conclusions numbered I and II. Read the statements and give the answer.*

(1) If only conclusion I follows.
(2) If only conclusion II follows.
(3) If either conclusion I or II follows.
(4) If neither conclusion I nor II follows.
(5) If both conclusions I and II follow.

66. **Statements:** $A < B > N = M, B \leq V, M > R$
Conclusions: I. $B > R$ **II.** $V > A$

67. **Statements:** $D < E > F = G > H = I \leq J$
Conclusions: I. $F > I$ **II.** $J \geq E$

68. **Statements:** $M < N < O > P, N < E$
Conclusions: I. $E < M$ **II.** $E > O$

69. **Statements:** $C \geq D < E = F \geq G, C < W$
Conclusions: I. $E = G$ **II.** $G < E$

70. **Statements:** $R < T < S < P > Q, R > X$
Conclusions: I. $S < Q$ **II.** $X < S$

***Direction (71-75): Study** the following information carefully and answer the question given below-*

Eight people viz. G, H, I, J, K, L, M and N lives in a Building on different floors from top to bottom (such as ground floor numbered as 1 and top is numbered as 8) but not necessarily in the same order.

There is a gap of three floors between J and L and both of them lives on odd number of floor. N lives just above H, who lives on even numbered floor. I lives on floor number 6.Only one person lives between L and M. J lives above I. Three persons live between K and H.

71. Who among the following lives on ground floor?

(1) N (2) J
(3) K (4) M
(5) None of these

72. Who among the following lives immediately below L?

(1) K (2) I
(3) G (4) H
(5) None of these

73. How many persons live between I and H?

(1) One (2) Three
(3) Five (4) Two
(5) None of these

74. Who among the following lives on Top floor?

(1) N (2) J
(3) K (4) M
(5) None of these

75. Which of the following combination is false?

(1) J-7 (2) L-3
(3) G-2 (4) H-4
(5) N-1

76. In a row of children facing North, Rajan is twelfth from the right end and is fifth to the right of Satyarthiwho is tenth from the left end. How many total numbers of children are there in the row?

(1) 29
(2) 28

(3) 26 (4) 27

(5) None of these

77. Raj leaves his home and goes straight 20 meters, then turns right and goes 10 meters. He turns left and goes 30 meters and finally turns right and starts walking. If he is now moving in the north direction, then in which direction did he start his walking?

(1) East (2) West

(3) North (4) South

(5) None of these

***Directions (78-82)**: In each of the questions given below, a group of digits/letter is given followed by four combinations of symbols numbered (a), (b), (c) and (d). You have to find out which of the four combinations correctly represents the group of digits/letters based on the symbol codes and the conditions given below. If none of the four combinations represents the group of digits correctly, give (e) i.e. 'None of these' as the answer.*

Condition for coding the group elements:

Digit	Z	L	F	1	I	5	7	A	E	B	2	X	6	W
Symbol	@	!	$	^	µ	Δ	Å	&	>	≠	<	®	£	∞

(I) If the first letter is Vowel and the last digit is divisible by 2, then both are to be coded as +.

(II) If the first as well as the last digit is odd, then both are to be coded by the code of the first digit.

(III) If the first letter is consonant and the last digit is odd number, then the code of first and last elements are to be interchanged.

78. X6ZF1

(1) ^®$@£∞ (2) ^@$∞<!

(3) ^®£@$∞ (4) ∞®@>!<

(5) None of these

79. FE1XI6

(1) ∞^@<!£ (2) $<^^£@

(3) $>^®µ£ (4) $<^@^£

(5) None of these

80. 5L2IA1

(1) Δ!<µ&Δ (2) Δ!&^<µ

(3) Δ!<µ^& (4) µ&Δ!<^

(5) None of these

81. E2ZA6

(1) &>!^@ (2) @<@&!

(3) @&<@& (4) +<@&+

(5) None of these

82. IZ2W2

(1) @≠^$& (2) +@<∞+

(3) <∞µ@≠ (4) @≠>!^

(5) None of these

***Directions (83-87)**: **Read** the following information carefully and answer the questions given below.*

A, B, C, D, E, F, G and H are eight members standing in a row (not necessarily in the same order) facing north. C and B have as many members between them as G and C have between them. D, who is 4th from the extreme left end, is 2nd to the left of E. G is 3rd place away from one of the extreme end. Neither B nor C sits any extreme end. F sits immediate right of A.

83. How many persons sit between G and B?

(1) One (2) Three

(3) Two (4) Four

(5) None of these

84. Who among the following persons sits at extreme ends?

(1) A, G (2) B, C

(3) F, H (4) H, A

(5) None of these

85. Who sits second to the right of E?

(1) B (2) H
(3) G (4) C
(5) None of these

86. Who sits third to the left of G?

(1) A (2) None
(3) F (4) E
(5) B

87. Who sits immediate left of C?

(1) A (2) H
(3) C (4) D
(5) None of these

88. Find the odd one out?

(1) ACB (2) DFE
(3) GIH (4) JLK
(5) MNO

***Directions (89-93): Study** the following number sequence and answer the questions following it.*

9 3 2 4 5 7 9 5 8 1 5 0 6 4 2 9 8 2 6 3 5 9 8 2 1 5 4 3 2 1

89. How many odd numbers are there in the numeric series which are immediately preceded by a number, which is a whole square?

(1) One (2) Two
(3) Three (4) More than three
(5) None of these

90. If all the odd numbers are dropped from the series, which number will be eighth to the left of eleventh number from the left end?

(1) 2 (2) 8
(3) 6 (4) 4
(5) None of these

91. If 1 is subtracted from all odd numbers and 2 is subtracted from all even numbers in the given number series, then which number will be sixteenth from the right end?

(1) 0 (2) 2
(3) 3 (4) 8
(5) 6

92. If the position of the 1st and the 16th numbers, the 2nd and the 17th numbers, and so on up to the 15th and the 30th numbers, are interchanged, which number will be 7th to the right of 19th number from the right end?

(1) 5 (2) 9
(3) 8 (4) 4
(5) None of these

93. How many total even numbers which is immediately preceded by a 'whole cube' or 'immediately preceded by a whole square' in the above sequence?

(1) Four (2) Five
(3) Three (4) Six
(5) None of these

***Directions (94–98)**: In each question below are given some statements followed by two conclusions numbered I and II. You have to take the given statements to be true even if they seem to be at variance with commonly known facts. Read all the conclusions and then decide which of the given conclusions logically follows/follow from the given statements, disregarding commonly known facts. Give answer*

(1) If only conclusion I follows.
(2) If only conclusion II follows.
(3) If either conclusion I or II follows.
(4) If neither conclusion I nor II follows.
(5) If both conclusions I and II follow.

94. Statements: All shirts are skirts. No skirt is top. All tops are kurta.
Conclusions: I. All shirts are kurta.
II. Some kurta are skirts.

95. **Statements:** Some chocolate are chips. Some chips are jelly. All jelly are whoppers.
Conclusions: I. Some jelly are chips.
II. All chocolate being whoppers is a possibility

96. **Statements:** Some frooti are Maaza. No Maaza is slice. All slice are fanta.
Conclusions: I. Some frooti are definitely not slice.
II. Some fanta are definitely not Maaza.

97. **Statements:** All carbon are oxygen.
All Nitrogen are carbon. Some oxygen are Sulphur.
Conclusions I. All Nitrogen being Sulphur is a possibility.
II. All Nitrogen are not oxygen.

98. **Statements:** All September are October.
No October is November. No November is December.
Conclusions: I. Some September are not November.
II. No October is December.

***Directions (99-100): Following** questions are based on the five words given below, Study the following words and answer the following questions.*

NOW SAD WAF RAT CAT

(The new words formed after performing the mentioned operations may not necessarily be a meaningful English word.)

99. If the given words are arranged in the order as they appear in a dictionary from left to right, which of the following will be the fourth from the left end?
(1) WAF **(2)** NOW
(3) SAD **(4)** CAT
(5) RAT

100. How many letters are there in the English alphabetical series between the second letter of the word which is second from the right end and the third letter of the word which is second from the left end?
(1) Two **(2)** Three
(3) Four **(4)** Five
(5) None of these

Answers with Explanations

1. (4)
2. (2)
3. (4)
4. (1)
5. (2)
6. (3)
7. (5)
8. (5)
9. (1)
10. (3)
11. (4)
12. (5)
13. (4)
14. (4)
15. (5)
16. (4)
17. (2)
18. (3)
19. (5)
20. (3)
21. (2)
22. (1)
23. (3)
24. (2)
25. (1)
26. (4)
27. (2)
28. (5)
29. (4)
30. (3)

31. **(1)** CP = (100/110) × (100/115) × (100/125) × 1265
= Rs. 800

32. **(1)** In one hour, 1/6 of the cistern can be filled
In one hour, only 1/7 of the cistern can be

filled due to leak in its bottom.

∴ In one hour 1/6 – 1/7 = 1/42 of the cistern is empty

∴ The whole cistern will be emptied in 42 hrs

33. **(2)**

34. **(2)**

35. **(1)** Let the speed of the current be x km/h and speed of the person in still water be y km/h.

∴ $y + x = 8$

$y - x = 6$ ∴ $y = 7, x = 1$

∴ Speed of the current = 1 km/h.

36. **(1)** Let the father's age be x years and age of his children be a and b years

$(a + b) = x/3$

And $(a + b) + 20 + 20 = x + 20$

$x/3 + 20 = x$

$x = 30$ years

37. **(1)**

38. **(1)** One principal can be appointed in 36 days

One vice-principal appointed in remaining 35 ways

∴ Total no. of ways = 36 × 35 = 1260.

39. **(2)**

40. **(2)**

41. **(2)** Required diff. = (40 + 80) – (12 + 58)

= 120 – 70 = 50

42. **(3)** Required ratio =(92+98)/(13+47) = 19 ⇒ 6

43. **(1)** Required % = [(48+12)/15]×100 = 400%

44. **(5)** Average = (27+15+60)/3 = 34

45. **(4)** Windows phones sold by P on Thursday

= 3/7 × 28 =12

46. **(2)** 45% of 600 + ?% of 480

270 + 4.8 ×? = 390

? = 25

47. **(3)**

48. **(4)**

49. **(1)**

50. **(1)** ? = 555.05 + 55.50 + 5.55 + 5 + 0.55

= 621.65

51. **(5)** ? = 1425 + 8560 + 1680 ÷ 200

= 1425 + 8560 + 8.4

= 9993.4

52. **(4)**

53. **(2)** 250 × 25.6% + √? = 119

64 + √? = 119

√? = 119 – 64 = 55

54. **(5)**

55. **(3)**

56. **(4)** Sides of a triangle are in ratio 1/2 : 1/3 : 1/4 i.e. 6 : 4: 3

Let the sides be 6x, 4x and 3x, respectively.

∴ 13x = 52 ∴ x = 4

∴ Sides of the triangle are 24 cm, 16 cm and 12 cm, respectively.

57. **(2)**

58. **(4)** 12.5% = Rs 22.50

CP = Rs 180

59. **(1)** Suppose x = original number of men in the group

∴ (x- 12) men did the job in 32 days

∴ 20x = 32(x – 12)

i.e., x = 32

60. **(3)**

61. **(2)** 50% of 250 + √? = 165

125 + √? = 165

√? = 40

∴ ? = (40)2 = 1600

62. **(5)** 140% of 56 + 56% of 140 = ?

= 78.4 + 78.4 = 156.8

63. **(5)**

64. **(1)** 999.09 + 99.90 + 9.99 + 9 + 0.99 = 1118.97

65. **(4)**

66. **(5)** I. B > R (True) II. V > A (True)

67. **(1)** I. F > I (True) II. J ≥ E (False)

68. **(4)** I. E < M (False) II. E>O (False)

69. **(3)** I. E =G (False) II. G< E (False)

70. **(2)** I. S < Q (False) II. X < S (True)

For questions (71-75):

Floors	Persons
8	K
7	J
6	I
5	N
4	H
3	L
2	G
1	M

71. (4)
72. (3)
73. (1)
74. (3)
75. (5)
76. (3) Sathyarthi's position from left end = 10th Sathyarthi's position from right end
= 17thTotal number of children in the row
= 10 + 17 – 1 = 26
77. (2) Raj started walking towards west.
78. (3) By using condition (iii) the code of WX-6ZF1 will be ^®£@$∞.
79. (3) The code of FE1XI6 will be $>^®µ£.
80. (a) By using condition (ii) the code of 5L2IA1 will be Δ!<µ&Δ.
81. (4) By using condition (i) the code of E2ZA6 will be +<@&+.
82. (2) By using condition (i) the code of IZ2W2 will be +@<∞+.

For questions (83-87):

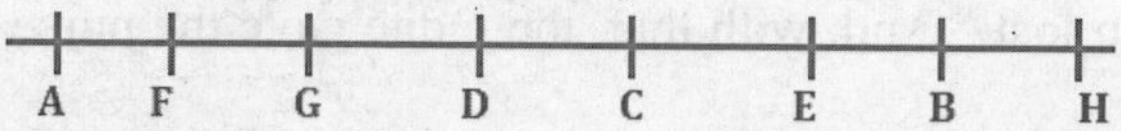

83. (2)
84. (4)
85. (2)
86. (2)
87. (5)
88. (4)

1 3 2 ACB   4 6 5 DFE   7 9 8 GIH   10 12 11 JLK   13 14 15 MNO

So, the odd one out will be MNO.

89. (4) More than three
90. (2)
91. (1)
92. (4)
93. (2)
94. (4)

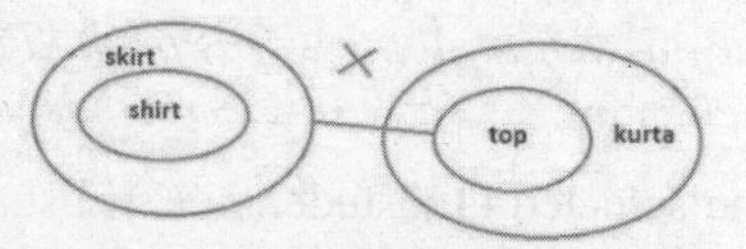

95. (5)

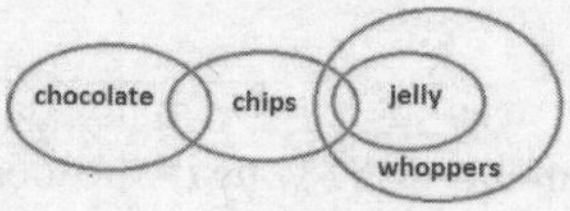

96. (5)

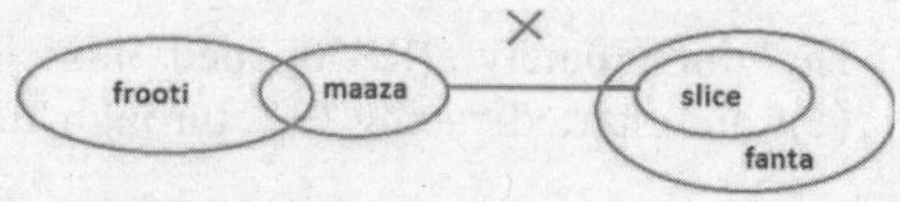

97. (1)

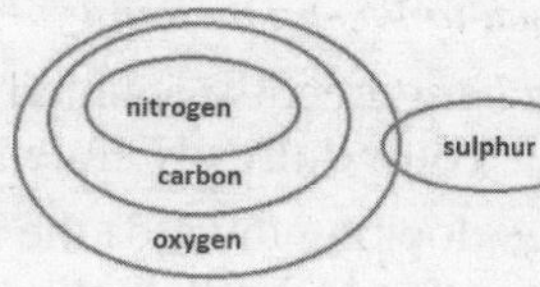

98. (1)

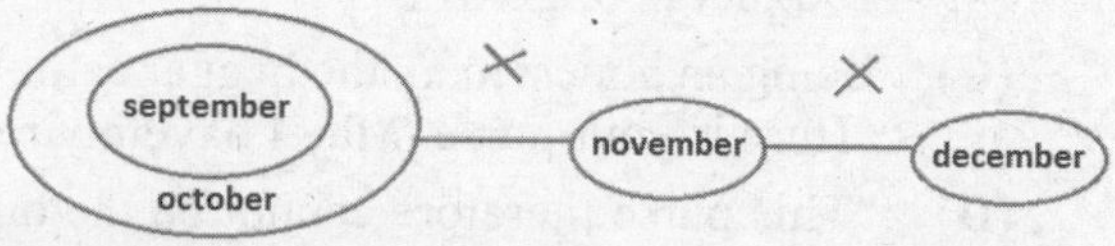

99. (3)
100. (1)

IBPS Clerk Prelims

Practice Set – 3

English Language

***Directions (1-5):** In each question below, four words printed in bold type are given. These are numbered* **(l)**, **(2)**, **(3)** *and* **(4)**. *One of these words printed in bold may either be wrongly spelt or inappropriate in the context of the sentence. Find out the word that is inappropriate or wrongly spelt, if any. The number of that word is your answer. If all the words printed in bold are correctly spelt and appropriate in the context of the sentence then mark* **(5)** *i.e. "All Correct' as your answer.*

1. All the selected (1)/ students' (2)/ list would be displayed (3)/ on the countar. (4)/ all Correct (5)

2. The ship (1)/ was at sea for many days and finally (2)/ anchored (3)/ near the cost-line. (4)/ All Correct (5)

3. He immediately (l)/ opened his journal (2)/ and started racing (3)/ through the first paragraph. (4)/ All Correct (5)

4. For lunch, Payal choosed (1)/ to eat a large bowl (2)/ of salad and a big glass (3)/ of fruit Juice. (4)/ All Correct (5)

5. What had once been only a whimsical (1)/ idea has developed (2)/ a strong fan following (3)/ because of develop (4)/ believers. All Correct (5)

***Directions (6-10):** Rearrange the following six sentences/group of sentences (A), (B), (C), (D), (E) and (F} in the proper sequence to form a meaningful paragraph: then answer the questions given below them.*

(A) The merchant greedily counted his gold and said, "The purse I dropped had 200 pieces of gold in it. You've already stolen more than the reward! Go away or I will tell the police."

(B) The judge, looking towards the merchant said, "You stated that the purse you lost contained 200 pieces of gold. Well, that's a considerable cost. But, the purse this beggar found had only 100 pieces of gold".

(C) Being an honest man, the beggar came forward and handed the purse to the merchant saying, "Here is your purse. May I have my reward not'

(D) "This purse therefore cannot be the one you lost." And. with that, the judge gave the purse and all the gold to the beggar.

(E) A beggar found a leather purse that someone had dropped in the marketplace. On opening it, he discovered that it contained 100 pieces of gold. Then he heard a merchant shout, "A reward! A reward to the one who finds my leather purse".

(F) "I am an honest man," said the beggar defiantly. "Let us take this matter to the court. The Judge patiently listened to both sides of the story.

6. Which of the following should be the **FIRST** sentence after the rearrangement?

(1) E **(2)** B
(3) D **(4)** C
(5) F

7. Which of the following should be the **FOURTH** sentence after the rearrangement?

(1) D **(2)** F
(3) B **(4)** E
(5) C

8. Which of the following should be the **FIFTH** sentence after the rearrangements

(1) E **(2)** D
(3) B **(4)** C

(5) F

9. Which of the following should be the SIXTH (LAST) sentence after the rearrangement?

(1) A (2) D
(3) F (4) E
(5) C

10. Which of the following should be the **SECOND** sentence after the rearrangement?

(1) A (2) D
(3) F (4) B
(5) C

***Directions (11-20):** Read the following passage carefully and answer the questions given below it. Certain words have been printed in bold to help you locate them while answering some of the questions.*

Govind's father was a rich land- lord, who was loved and respected by all his tenants. When he died, he left large tracts of land to Govind. But Govind did not **spend** a single day looking after his land. He had a funny idea, that there existed a magic potion which, if it was poured on any object would turn it into gold. He spent all his time trying to learn more about this potion. People took advantage of him and cheated him. His wife grew anxious. Given the amount of money Govind was spending, she was sure that they would soon be paupers.

One day, a widely respected sage who had been to the Himalayas came to their town. Govind asked him about the potion. To his surprise the sage answered, "I have learnt how to brew such a potion. But it is a difficult process." "Tell me!" insisted Govind, hardly able to believe his luck. "You have to collect the dew which settles on the leaves of a banana tree every morning during winter. There is a condition though. The tree should be planted and watered regularly with your own hands. Store the collected dew in an earthen vessel and when you have five litres, bring it to me. I will recite a sacred mantra to trans- form the dew into the potion. A drop of the potion will be sufficient to change any object into gold."

Govind was worried. "Winter is only for a few months in the year. It will take me years to collect the dew." "You can plant as many trees as you want," replied the sage. Govind went home and after talking to his wife, began clearing the large fields which has been lying vacant for years. He planted rows of banana saplings. He tended them with great care. His wife helped him too. She would take the banana crop to market and get a good price. Over the years the plantation grew and finally after six years Govind had five litres of dew. He went to the sage who smiled, uttered a mantra and sprinkled a few drops of dew on a copper vessel. To Govind's dismay, nothing happened. "You have cheated me!" he shouted at the sage.

The sage however smiled. Govind's wife then came forward with a box. The sage opened it and revealed stacks of gold coins inside. Turning to Govind he said, "You worked hard on your land and created a plantation. Your wife sold the produce in the market. It was your hard work which created this wealth, not magic. If I had told you this earlier, you would not have listened. " Govind understood the wisdom behind the sage's words and worked even harder from that day on.

11. Why did Govind's father give him large plots of land?

(1) It was his way of instilling a sense of responsibility in his son
(2) Govind was his only son and sole heir
(3) To provide Govind with sufficient funds to pursue his interest of discovering a magic potion
(4) He wanted Govind to continue to look after the tenants
(5) None of these

12. Which of the following can be said about the sage?

(1) He was cunning and plotted with Govind's wife to cheat him
(2) He had no magical powers as such and used to swindle people
(3) He was a good judge of people
(4) He did not deserve his good reputation
(5) He was dishonest because he had cheated Govind out of his gold

13. Why was Govind's wife worried?

(1) Govind had no knowledge of farming

and could not cultivate the land he had inherited from his father

(2) Govind had not friends because he was obsessed with finding a potion which would turn anything into gold

(3) Govind only interested in studying under different sages and neglected his family duties

(4) Since Govind had devoted all his time and wealth to finding a magic potion they would soon be poor

(5) Govind's experiments to find a magic potion were dangerous

14. Why did Govind's wife help him in the fields?

(A) To support her husband in his endeavour to find a magic potion

(B) The sage had advised her to help her husband succeed.

(C) He needed someone to help him collect the dew.

(1) None
(2) Only (A)
(3) Both (A) and (B)
(4) All (A), (B) and (C)
(5) None of these

15. Why did Govind decide to cultivate a banana crop?

(1) The soil of his land was suitable only for cultivating bananas
(2) It was the most highly priced commodity in the region
(3) It could be grown at any time of the year including winter
(4) His wife pressurised him to do so
(5) The ingredient for the magic potion could only be obtained from a banana tree

16. What made Govind angry with the sage?

(1) The sage had conspired with Govind's wife against him
(2) He had forgotten the magic spell and all Govind's hard work was in vain
(3) He had lost a good deal of money in cultivating bananas
(4) The sage had made a fool of him in front of other villagers
(5) None of these

17. Which of the following is **TRUE** in the context of the passage?

(A) Govind was easily fooled by people

(B) Govind was preserving by nature

(C) The sage had never actually been to the Himalayas

(1) Only (A)
(2) Both (A) and (B)
(3) Only (C)
(4) Both (A) and (C)
(5) None of these

Directions (18-19): *Choose the word which is most similar in meaning to the word printed in bold as used in the passage.*

18. SPEND

(1) pay
(2) bought
(3) devote
(4) settle
(5) empty

19. LYING

(1) sleeping (2) dishonest (3) relaxing (4) remaining (5) untruthful

Directions: *Choose the word which is most opposite in meaning to the word printed in bold as used in the passage.*

20. DISMAY

(1) joy (2) interest (3) desire (4) humour (5) luck

Directions (21-30): *Read each sentence to find out whether there is any grammatical error in it. The error if any will be in one part of the sentence, the number of that part will be the answer. If there is No error, the answer is (5) i.e. 'no error'. (Ignore the errors of punctuation, if any.)*

21. As he walked over cafeteria (1)/ he noticed that his stride (2)/ was just a little more bouncier than (3)/ when he had first walked into the school. (4)/ No error (5)

22. The shepherd counted (1)/ his sheep and found (2)/ that one of (3)/ them is missing. (4)/ No error (5)

23. The teacher were (1)/ impressed by her performance (2)/ and asked her to (3)/ participate in the competition. (4)/ No error (5)

24. At last he had (1)/ come home again but (2)/ was very sad because (3)/ he is missing his pet sorely. (4)/ No error (5)

25. You might not have (1)/ heard about the ice-cube collectors before (2)/ but are really not (3)/ strongest as they sound. (4)/ No error (5)

26. The explanation was not (1)/ an total failure because people (2)/ came to realise that the club could work (3)/ if people cared enough about it. (4)/ No error (5)

27. Each morning they (1)/ emptied they trays (2)/ into large garbage cans (3)/ which were placed in the street. (4)/ No error (5)

28. The story was (1)/ about how an (2)/ intelligent man had saving (3)/ himself from being robbed. (4)/ No error (5)

29. The painter was (1)/ ask to paint (2)/ picture of the king (3)/ sitting on his throne. (4)/ No error (5)

30. Most of the people which (1)/ have been victims (2)/ of extreme violence (3)/ are too frightened to report it to the police. (4)/ No error (5)

Numerical Ability

31. The upstream speed of a boat is 18 km/hr which is 500% more than the speed of stream. Find how much distance boat will cover in 3 hours while travelling in downstream.

(1) 66 km (2) 63 km
(3) 72 km (4) 75 km
(5) 78 km

32. If $A^2 - B^2 = 252$ and $A + B = 42$ then find the value of 'B'?

(1) 18 (2) 16
(3) 14 (4) 20
(5) 22

33. A alone can do a work in 40 days. The ratio of time taken by A and B to do the same work is 5 : 3. Then, find in how many days both will complete the work together?

(1) 18 days (2) 12 days
(3) 20 days (4) 15 days
(5) 10 days

34. A train having speed of 72 km/hr crosses a pole in 18 sec and a platform in 33 sec. Find the length of platform?

(1) 320 m (2) 300 m
(3) 330 m (4) 360 m

(5) 350 m

35. The circumference of a circle is 66 cm. Find the approximate area of square if the radius of circle is two times of the side of a square.

(1) 18 cm² (2) 32 cm²
(3) 25 cm² (4) 36 cm²
(5) 28 cm²

***Directions (36-40):** What approximate value should come in place of question mark (?) in the following questions?*

36. $\sqrt{1443.98} \div 18.98 + 328.1 = ? \times 22.01$

(1) 10 (2) 12
(3) 18 (4) 15
(5) 22

37. 29.98% of 880.001 = ? + 110.9

(1) 144 (2) 153
(3) 158 (4) 160
(5) 163

38. $(?)^2 + 255.93 = 49.932\%$ of 800.112

(1) 12 (2) 8
(3) 15 (4) 18
(5) 6

39. $3\sqrt{1728.01} + ? = 256.01$

(1) 230 (2) 235
(3) 238 (4) 241
(5) 244

40. 74.91% of ? = $(17.932)^2$

(1) 420 (2) 425
(3) 408 (4) 432
(5) 444

***Directions (41-45):**-Find the wrong number in the given number series questions.*

41. 100, 118, 136, 149, 160, 167, 172

(1) 172 (2) 160
(3) 100 (4) 118
(5) 136

42. 1.5, 2.5, 6, 24, 100, 505, 3036

(1) 1.5 (2) 6
(3) 100 (4) 3036
(5) 2.5

43. 160, 80, 80, 120, 240, 600, 900

(1) 240 (2) 120
(3) 160 (4) 900
(5) 600

44. 5040, 2520, 840, 210, 42, 8, 1

(1) 8 (2) 5040
(3) 840 (4) 1
(5) 42

45. 15, 17, 26, 151, 200, 929, 1050

(1) 17 (2) 1050
(3) 15 (4) 929
(5) 26

***Directions (46-50):** There are total five departments in a company. There are total 90 employees in Finance department which is 25% of total employees in the company. 2/9 of the total employees of the company are working in HR department. Employees working in Sales department is 25% more than that in HR department. Ratio between employees working in Security and Housing department is 4 : 5.*

46. Find number of employees working in HR department is what percent more than number of employees working in Security department?

(1) 250% (2) 200%
(3) 150% (4) 100%
(5) 50%

47. Find the average number of employees working in Sales, Finance and Housing department?

(1) 60 (2) 70
(3) 80 (4) 90
(5) 100

48. Number of employees in Housing department is how much more than number of employees in Security department?

(1) 10 (2) 20
(3) 30 (4) 40
(5) 50

49. In Security department, 40% are female employees then find total male employees working in Security department?

(1) 16 (2) 40
(3) 32 (4) 8
(5) 24

50. Ratio between total number of male and female employees in HR department is 2 : 3. Find total number of female employees working in HR department?

(1) 32 (2) 48
(3) 64 (4) 40
(5) 56

Directions (51-60): What value should come in place of question mark (?) in the following questions?

51. $?^2 = 4^2 + 8^2 - 31$

(1) 6 (2) 7
(3) 8 (4) 9
(5) 10

52. $13 \times 6 + ? \times 4 = 18 \times 7$

(1) 6 (2) 8
(3) 10 (4) 12
(5) 14

53. 40% of ? = 25% of 320 + 75% of 160

(1) 500 (2) 400
(3) 300 (4) 200
(5) 100

54. $112 + 62 = ? + 37$

(1) 130 (2) 110
(3) 120 (4) 140
(5) 150

55. $(360/?) = 12 \times 6 - 33$

(1) 9 (2) 5
(3) 6 (4) 7
(5) 8

56. $\sqrt{225} + \sqrt{441} = ?2$

(1) 3 (2) 4
(3) 5 (4) 6
(5) 8

57. $16 \times 8 - ? = 26$

(1) 64 (2) 32
(3) 128 (4) 192
(5) 96

58. $16 \times 54 \div 36 + 6 = ?$

(1) 144/7 (2) 30
(3) 20 (4) 24
(5) 16

59. $? = \sqrt{6 \times 3 \times 5 + 50\% \text{ of } 620}$

(1) 14 (2) 16
(3) 18 (4) 10
(5) 20

60. $6^2 = \dfrac{18 \times 8 - ? \times 2}{3}$

(1) 36 (2) 27
(3) 18 (4) 9
(5) 54

Directions (61-65):–Table given below shows marks obtained by four students in four different subjects in an exam. Study the data carefully and answer the following questions

Subjects Students	English	Hindi	Science	Maths
Paul	65	60	80	65
Aditya	75	75	60	75
Neeraj	85	55	95	85

Sandy	60	60	65	60

61. Marks scored by Sandy in English and Maths together is what percent of the Marks scored by Aditya and Neeraj in English together?
(1) 25% (2) 50%
(3) 75% (4) 100%
(5) 125%

62. Find the ratio of total marks scored by all four students together in Hindi to total marks scored by all four students together in Science?
(1) 5 : 6 (2) 57 : 50
(3) 1 : 1 (4) 20 : 19
(5) 6 : 5

63. Total marks scored by Paul are how much more/less than total marks scored by Neeraj?
(1) 70 (2) 60
(3) 40 (4) 50
(5) 80

64. Find the average of the marks scored by Aditya in English, Hindi and Science together?
(1) 65 (2) 85
(3) 80 (4) 75
(5) 70

65. If maximum marks for each subject are 100 then find what percentage of total marks is obtained by Sandy?
(1) 64.25% (2) 61.25%
(3) 67.25% (4) 70.25%
(5) 73.25%

Reasoning Ability

Directions (66-70): *Read the following information carefully and answer the questions given below.*

Six persons J, P, Q, R, V, Z are sitting in a row. Some of them are facing north while some of them are facing south. J sits second from one of the extreme end of the row. P sits third to the right of J. R is not an immediate neighbor of P and Z. Both the immediate neighbors of V faces opposite direction. Both the Immediate neighbors of Z faces same direction. V sits second to the left of P. Q sits to the right of R. R faces north. Q faces same direction as Z.

66. Four of the following five are alike in a certain way, and so form a group. Which of the following does not belong to the group?
(1) R, V (2) V, P
(3) J, P (4) V, Q
(5) J, R

67. What is the position of Q with respect to Z?
(1) Second to the left (2) Third to the right
(3) Third to the left (4) Fifth to the right
(5) Second to the right

68. Who amongst the following sits exactly between Z and J?
(1) R (2) P
(3) Q (4) Both V and Q
(5) V

69. How many persons in the given arrangement are facing North?
(1) More than four (2) Four
(3) One (4) Three
(5) Two

70. Who is sitting 4th to the right of Q?
(1) R (2) Z
(3) P (4) J
(5) None of these

Directions (71-73): *Some statements are given followed by two conclusions. You have to consider the statements to be true even if they seem to be at variance from commonly known facts. You have to decide which of the following conclusions follow from the given statements:*

71. **Statements:** No symbol is letter.

All expression are letter. Some symbols are word.

Conclusions: I. No word is letter.

II. Some symbols being expression is possibility.

(1) Only I follows
(2) Only II follows
(3) Either I or II follows
(4) Neither I nor II follows
(5) Both I and II follow

72. **Statements:** Some logic are answers.

All keys are answers.

Conclusions: I. All keys are logic.

II. No keys are logic.

(1) Only I follows
(2) Only II follows
(3) Either I or II follows
(4) Neither I nor II follows
(5) Both I and II follow

73. **Statement:** All numbers are digits.

Some numbers are points. Some points are marks.

Conclusions: I. Some points are digits.

All marks being numbers is a possibility.

(1) Only I follows
(2) Only II follows
(3) Either I or II follows
(4) Neither I nor II follows
(5) Both I and II follow

Directions (74-78): *Read the following information carefully and answer the questions given below.*

Seven boxes M, N, O, P, Q, R, S are arranged one above another. Only two boxes are placed above box P. Only one box is placed between box S and P. As many as boxes are placed between box S and Q as between box Q and M. Three boxes are placed between box N and O. N is placed above O.

74. How many total numbers of boxes are placed in between box S and Q?

(1) Two
(2) One
(3) Three
(4) More than three
(5) None

75. Which of the following is true regarding Box N?

(1) Three boxes are placed between box Q and N
(2) Box N is placed below Q
(3) Box N is placed at top
(4) Only one box is placed above box N
(5) No box is placed between box N and R

76. Which box is placed at top?

(1) S
(2) N
(3) Q
(4) R

(5) M

77. Which box is placed immediately above box Q?

(1) M (2) P

(3) S (4) N

(5) R

78. How many boxes are placed in between R and M?

(1) Two (2) One

(3) Three (4) More than three

(5) None

Directions (79-83): *Answer these questions based on the following information.*

In a certain code:

"arrange things in order" is coded as –**"po gb ik mn"**

"order for new things" is coded as –**"po gb fc bv"**

"new places to order" is coded as –**"gb cq bv ra"**

"places in unknown country" is coded as – **" de ra lf ik"**

79. What will be the code for "order"?

(1) Gb (2) Fc

(3) Cq (4) Ik

(5) can't be determined

80. What may be the code for "things to vanish"?

(1) po cq hx (2) po vm ik

(3) cq fc ik (4) either (1) or (2)

(5) None of these

81. What will be the code for "arrange"?

(1) Gb (2) Mn

(3) Cq (4) Ik

(5) can't be determined

82. What may be the code for "in country"?

(1) lf ik (2) de ik

(3) po gb (4) either (1) or (2)

(5) None of these

83. "bv" is the code for?

(1) things (2) new

(3) arrange (4) places

(5) None of these

Directions (84-88): *Read the following information carefully and answer the questions given below.*

Six persons A, C, Q, R, T, Y were born in six different months January, April, May, August, September, December of a year. Three persons were born in between A and Y. A was born before Y. No one was born in between C and A. Two persons were born in between C and R. T was born before Q.

84. Who among the following was born in May?

(1) C (3) Q

(2) A (4) T

(5) Y

85. How many persons were born between A and Q?

(1) One (2) Three

(3) Four (4) Two

(5) None of these

86. How many persons born were before R?

(1) One (2) Three

(3) Four

(4) Two

(5) None of these

87. Who among the following is the oldest?

(1) C (2) A

(3) Q (4) T

(5) Y

88. Which of the following is not true regarding Y?

(1) Four persons born between C and Y

(2) R was born before Y

(3) Q is born immediately after Y

(4) Only Q was born between Y and R

(5) No one was born after Y

89. A family consists of five members A, P, R, T, H. P is wife of A. R is the daughter of A. R has only one brother T. H is daughter-in-law of P. How is H related to R?

(1) Mother (2) sister-in-law
(3) daughter (4) daughter-in-law
(5) None of these

90. If the digits of the number "46752983" are arranged in increasing order form left to right within the number, then how many digits will remain on the same position after the applied operation?

(1) Two (2) One
(3) Three (4) Four
(5) None of these

91. How many meaningful words can be made by using letters 'A', 'E', 'L' and 'T', keeping L as the first letter of the word?

(1) One (2) Two
(3) Three (4) Four
(5) None of these

Directions (92-96): *Read the following information carefully and answer the questions given below.*

Point E is 15m east of point B. Point G is 20m north of point E. Point K is 10m east of point G. Point M is 30m south of point K. Point P is 20m west of point M. Point L is 10m north of point P.

92. If Point V is 10m east of point S and Point S is 10m north of point L, then what will be the distance between point E and V?

(1) 10m (2) 15m
(3) 20m (4) 5m
(5) 25m

93. What is the total distance between point B and L?

(1) 10 m (2) 15 m
(3) 20 m (4) 5 m
(5) 30 m

94. If Point Z is 10m north of point M, then point what is the distance between point E and Z?

(1) 10 m (2) 15 m
(3) 20 m (4) 25 m
(5) 30 m

95. Point K is in which direction from point P?

(1) South (2) South-east
(3) North (4) North-east
(5) North-west

96. Four of the following five are alike in a certain way, and so form a group. Which of the following does not belong to the group?

(1) P, L (2) P, M
(3) G, E (4) L, E
(5) G, B

Directions (97-100): *These questions are based on the following arrangement. Study it carefully and answer the questions below it.*

1 3 5 3 4 5 9 2 8 7 2 3 6 5 2 7 3 8 1 2 1 8 4 9 8 1 2 4 7 3 5 2 4 8 9 8 2 4

97. Which element is exactly midway between the seventh element from the left end and sixteenth from the right end?

(1) 8 (2) 2
(3) 5 (4) 6
(5) 7

98. How many perfect squares are there to the right of the fourteenth element from the right end?

(1) Two (2) One
(3) Three (4) Four
(5) more than four

99. How many perfect cubes are there in the above arrangement, each of which is immediately preceded by an odd number and immediately followed by an even number?

(1) None (2) Three
(3) Two (4) One
(5) More than three

100. How many such odd digits are there in the given arrangement, each of which is immediately followed and preceded by an

odd number?

(1) None (2) One (3) Two (4) Three

(5) More than three

Answers with Explanations

1. (4)
2. (4)
3. (3)
4. (1)
5. (4)
6. (1)
7. (2)
8. (3)
9. (2)
10. (5)
11. (2)
12. (3)
13. (4)
14. (5)
15. (5)
16. (2)
17. (1)
18. (3)
19. (4)
20. (1)
21. (3)
22. (4)
23. (1)
24. (4)
25. (4)
26. (2)
27. (5)
28. (3)
29. (2)
30. (1)

31. (3) Let the speed of stream be x km/h

Speed of upstream = x ×600/100 = 18

x = 3km/h

Speed of boat in still water = 18 + 3 = 21 km/h

Distance covered in 3 hours in downstream = (21 + 3) × 3 = 72 km

32. (1) (A + B)(A – B) = 252

42 × (A– B) = 252 [A + B = 42 given]

(A– B) = 6 …(i)

And A + B = 42 …(ii)

Solving equation (i) and (ii),

B = 18

33. (4) Let the time taken by A and B be 5 x days and 3 x days respectively.

5 x = 40 days

x = 8 days

B's time = 3 × 8 = 24 days

Time taken by both together to complete the work = 15 days

34. (2) Speed of train = 72 km/h = 20 m/s

Length of train = 18 × 20 = 360 m

Length of (train + platform)

= 20 × 33 = 660 m

∴ Length of platform = 660 m – 360 m = 300 m

35. (5) 2πr = 66 cm

2 × 22/7 × r = 66 cm

r =21/2 cm

Side of a square = 21/4 cm

∴ Area of square = (side)^2 = (21/4)2 ≈ 28 cm^2

36. (4) √1444 ÷ 19 + 328 = ? × 22

2 + 328 = ? × 22

⇒ ? = 15

37. (2) 30% of 880 = ? + 111

? = 264 – 111 = 153

38. (1) (?)2 + 256 = 400

(?)2 = 144

? = 12

39. (5) 12 + ? = 256

⇒ ? = 244

40. (4)

100 [119] 136 149 160 167 172

+19 +17 +13 +11 +7 +5

41. (4)

1.5 2.5 [7] 24 100 505 3036

×1+1 ×2+2 ×3+3 ×4+4 ×5+5 ×6+6

42. (2)

160 80 80 120 240 600 [1800]

×0.5 ×1 ×1.5 ×2 ×2.5 ×3

43. (4)

5040 2520 840 210 42 [7] 1

÷2 ÷3 ÷4 ÷5 ÷6 ÷7

44. (1)

45. (3)

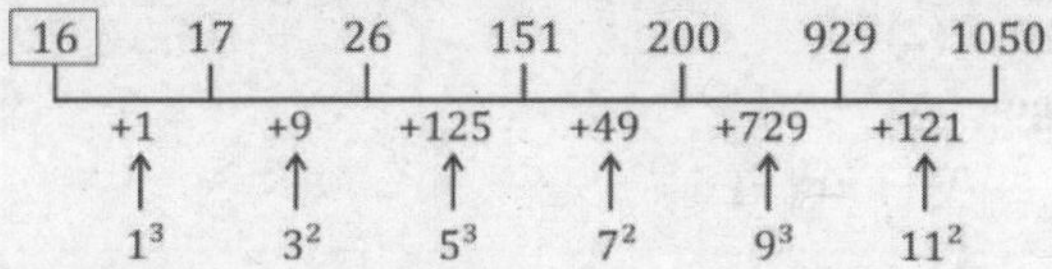

For questions (46-50):

Sales	Finance	HR	Security	Housing	Total
100	90	80	40	50	360

46. **(4)**

47. **(3)**

48. **(1)**

49. **(5)**

50. **(2)**

51. **(2)** ?2 = 42 + 82 − 31

?2 = 16 + 64 − 31 = 80 − 31 = 49

? = 7

52. **(4)** 13 × 6 +? × 4 = 18 × 7

78 +? × 4 = 126

? = 12

53. **(1)** 40% of ? = 25% of 320 + 75% of 160

2/5 × ? = 80 + 120

? = 200 ×5/2 = 500

54. **(3)** 112 + 62 =? +37

121 + 36 − 37 =?

? = 120

55. **(5)**

56. **(4)**

57. **(1)** 16 × 8−? = 26

128 − 64 =? ⇒ ? = 64

58. **(2)** 16 × 54 ÷ 36 + 6 =?

? = 24 + 6 = 30

59. **(5)**

60. **(3)**

61. **(3)**

62. **(1)**

63. **(4)** Total marks scored by Paul

= 65 + 60 + 80 + 65 = 270

Total marks scored by Neeraj

= 85 + 55 + 95 + 85 = 320

Required difference = 320 − 270 = 50

64. **(5)**

65. **(2)**

For questions (66-70):

66. **(4)**

67. **(1)**

68. **(5)**

69. **(2)**

70. **(4)**

71. **(4)**

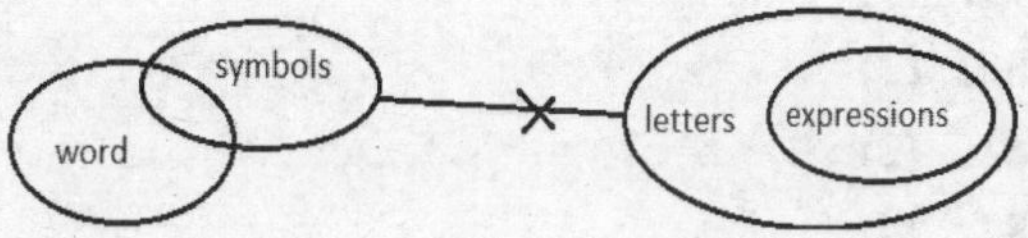

72. **(4)**

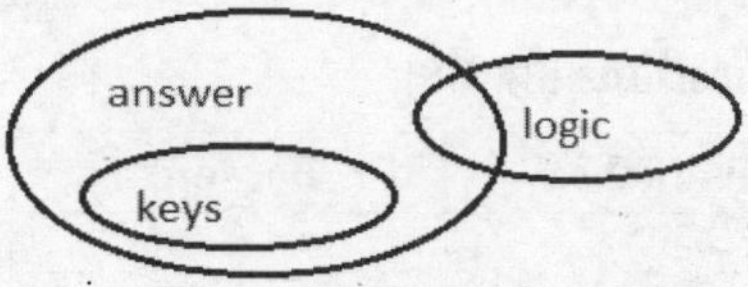

73. **(5)**

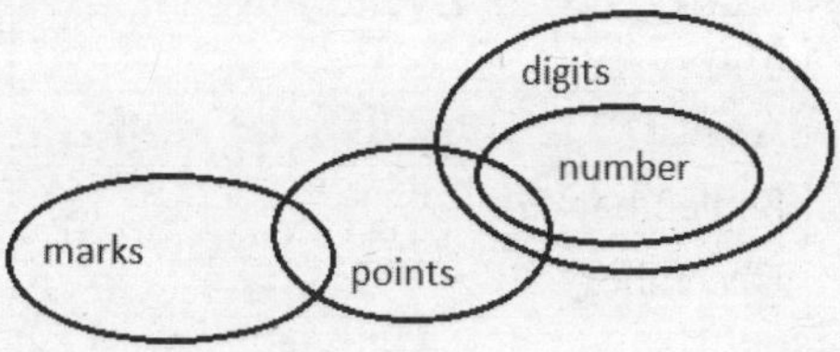

For questions (74-78):

Boxes
S
N
P
Q
R
O
M

74. **(1)**

75. **(4)**

76. **(1)**

77. **(2)**

78. **(2)**

For questions (79-83):

Word	Code
Places	ra
Order	gb
New	bv
To	cq
Things	po
For	fc
In	ik
Arrange	mn
Unknown/country	de/lf

79. (1)
80. (1)
81. (2)
82. (4)
83. (2)

For questions (84-88):

Months	Persons
January	C
April	A
May	T
August	R
September	Q
December	Y

84. (4)
85. (4)
86. (2)
87. (1)
88. (2)
89. (3)

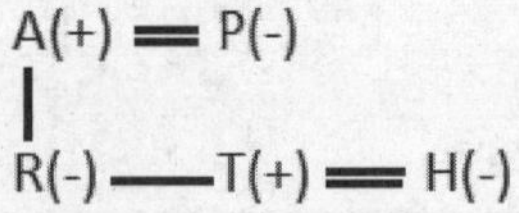

90. (1)

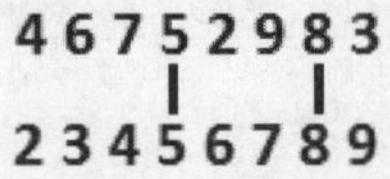

91. (2) LATE, LEAT

For questions (92-96):

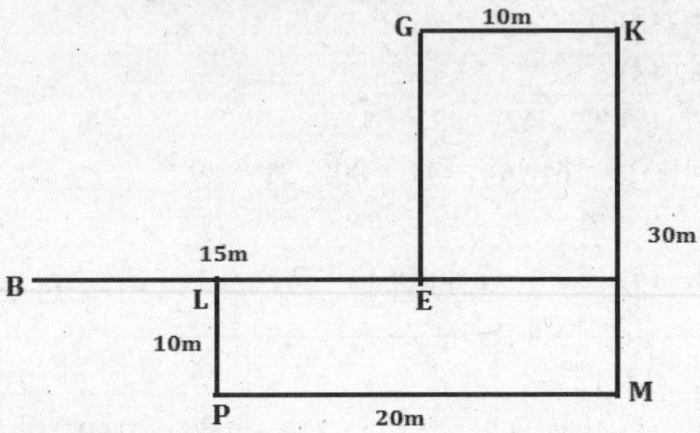

92. (1)
93. (4)
94. (1)
95. (4)
96. (5)
97. (2)
98. (5)
99. (3)
100. (4)

IBPS Clerk Prelims

Practice Set – 4

English Language

Directions (1-10): *Read the passage carefully and answer the questions given below it. Certain words/ phrases have been given in bold to help you locate them while answering some of the questions.*

Once upon a time, there lived a washerman in a village. He had a donkey by the name of Udhata. He used to carry loads of clothes to the river bank and back home everyday.

The donkey was not satisfied with the food that was given to him by his master to eat. So he wandered into the nearby fields stealthily and ate the crops growing there. Once, the donkey, while wandering around, happened to meet a fox. Soon, both of them became friends and began to wander together in search of delicious food. One night, the donkey and the fox were eating water-melons in a field. The water- melons were so tasty, that the donkey ate in a large quantity. Having eaten to his appetite, the donkey became so happy that he was compelled by an intense desire to sing. He told the fox that he was in such a good mood that he had to express his happiness in a melodious tone. 'Don't be a fool. If you sing, the people sleeping in and around this field will wake up and beat us black and blue with sticks,' said the fox worriedly.

`You are a dull fellow', the donkey said hearing the words of fox. 'Singing makes one happy and healthy. No matter what comes. I'll definitely sing a song." The fox became worried to see the donkey adamant to sing a song in the midst of the field, while the owner was still sleeping only a little distance away. Seeing his adamance, he said to the donkey, 'Friend, wait a minute before you start first, let me jump over to the other side of the fence for my safety.' Saying so the fox jumped over to the other side of the fence without losing a moment. The donkey began in his so-called melodious tone. Hearing, suddenly, a donkey braying in the field, the owner woke up from his sleep. He picked up his stick lying by his side and ran towards the donkey who was still braying happily. The owner of the field looked around and saw the loss caused by the donkey. He became very angry and beat him so ruthlessly that the donkey was physically incapacitated temporarily. He, somehow, managed to drag himself out of the field with great difficulty.

The fox looked at the donkey and said in a sympathetic tone, T m sorry to see you in this pitiable condition. I had already warned you, but you didn't listen to my advice.' The donkey too realised his folly and hung his head in shame.

1. Why did donkey want to sing?

(1) Donkey was so happy that he was compelled by an intense desire to sing.

(2) He wanted to wake up the people sleeping around.

(3) Fox told the donkey to sing a song.

(4) He wanted to prove that he was a good singer.

(5) None of the above

2. What was donkey's reaction when fox suggested him not to sing a song?

(1) Donkey agreed with fox and did not sing a song.

(2) Donkey chose to dance instead of singing a song.

(3) Donkey became angry and did not talk to fox after that.

(4) Donkey didn't pay attention to fox's words and sang a song.

(5) None of the above

3. What happened when donkey sang a song?

(1) The fox clapped for the donkey.

(2) The villagers praised donkey and gave him a gift.

(3) The fox started dancing.

(4) The owner woke up and beat the don-

key ruthlessly.

(5) None of the above

4. How did donkey came to know the fox?

(1) Both were childhood friends.

(2) Donkey happened to meet the fox in the field while wandering around in the search of delicious food.

(3) They used to work together for the washerman from the starting.

(4) Fox once saved donkey's life.

(5) None of the above

5. Which of the following statement is false according to the passage?

(1) The donkey realised his mistake in the end.

(2) The donkey was not satisfied with the food given to him by his master.

(3) Donkey didn't want to sing but he was compelled to do that.

(4) The owner of the field woke LIP after hearing to the donkey's voice.

(5) None of the above

***Directions (6-8):** Choose the word/group of words which is most similar in meaning to the word/group of words as used in the passage.*

6. **STEALTHILY**

(1) Superstitiously

(2) Secretly

(3) Honestly

(4) Openly

(5) Overtly

7. **COMPELLED**

(1) Discouraged

(2) Delayed

(3) Suspended

(4) Forced

(5) Demanded

8. **ADAMANCE**

(1) Easy going

(2) Yielding

(3) Flexible

(4) Mischievous

(5) Rigid

***Directions (9-10) :** Choose the word/group of words which is most opposite in meaning of the word/group of words as used in the passage*

9. **FOLLY**

(1) Stupidity

(2) Madness

(3) Advanceness

(4) Sageness

(5) Sharpness

10. **PITIABLE**

(1) Miserable

(2) Misfortunate

(3) Pathetic

(4) Honourable

(5) Commendable

***Directions (11-15):** Rearrange the following six sentences A, B, C, D, E and Fin the proper sequence to form a meaningful paragraph and then answer the questions given below.*

(A) Anything that you touch will turn into gold. The king was delighted with his good fortune.

(B) Even though he was very rich, he always craved for more and more.

(C) Everything he touched turned into gold. He turned trees, grass, tables, chairs, flowers, and vases into gold.

(D) One day, he called his court magician and commanded, find me a spell that can get me more treasures than I already have.

(E) King Midas was a very greedy king.

(F) The magician said, Your Majesty, I can give you a power that no one else in this world has.

11. Which of the following should be the **FIRST** sentence after rearrangement?

(1) F (2) E
(3) B (4) A
(5) C

12. Which of the following should be the **SECOND** sentence after rearrangement?

(1) A (2) B
(3) C (4) E
(5) D

13. Which of the following should be the **THIRD** sentence after rearrangement?

(1) E (2) F
(3) D (4) C
(5) B

14. Which of the following should be the **FOURTH** sentence after rearrangement?

(1) A (2) B
(3) F (4) E
(5) C

15. Which of the following should be the LAST (SIXTH) sentence after rearrangement?

(1) C (2) A
(3) B (4) D
(5) F

Directions (16-20) : *Read each sentence to find out whether there is any grammatical or idiomatic error in it. The error, if any, will be in one part of the sentence. The number of that part is the answer. If there is 'No error', the answer is (5). (Ignore errors of punctuation, if any.)*

16. Harsh Vardhan said he was looking for*ard/(1) to serve his roots, as he had spend/(2) the first 15 years of his life/(3) in the streets of old Delhi.(4) No error (5)

17. A family office has to/(1) execute all tasks related to/(2) manage the wealth of/(3) the upper-rich family. (4) No error (5)

18. Service providers in the financial industry, specially private banks/(1) and wealth management firms, are increasingly/(2) forced to standardise /(3) products to optimise profit.(4) No error (5)`

19. Social or impact funds are private equity-like funds/(1) that pool money from investors/(2) and put it to work in a portfolio of ventures /(3) that meet the funds objective.(4) No error (5)

20. While residential land purchases/(1) have benefitted many investors/(2) buying land can be risky/(3) especially for a NRI.(4) No error(5)

Directions (21-25) : *In each question below, four words printed in bold type are given. These are indicated as (1), (2),(3) and (4). One of these words printed in bold may either be wrongly spelt or inappropriate in the context of the sentence. Find out the word that is inappropriate or wrongly spelt, if any. The number of that word is your answer. If all the words printed in bold are correctly spelt and appropriate in the context of the sentence then mark (5) i.e. All correct', as your answer.*

21. All the competitors/(1) completed /(2) the race/(3) with just one excepsion./(4) All correct (5)

22. Poor posture/(1) can lead/(2) to muscular/(3) problems/(4) in later life. All correct (5)

23. The pump/(1) shut off/(2) as a result/(3) of a mechanikal/(4) failure. All correct (5)

24. The Principal/(1) gave a very pompous/(2) speach/(3) about 'The portals of learning'./(4)All correct (5)

25. Copeing/(1) with her mother's long illness/(2) was a heavy load/(3) to bear./(4) All correct (5)

Directions (26-30) : *In the following passage, some of the words have been left out. Each of which is indicated by a number. Find the suitable word from the options given against each number and fill up the blanks with appropriate words to make the paragraph meaningfully complete.*

A camel and a jackal were-friends. One day, the jackal ...(26)... his friend to a big sugarcane farm. It was on the opposite side of a river. After a ...(27)... meal, the jackal began to howl loudly. The frightened camel pleaded ...(28)... the jackal not to do so. The Jackal said, "Friend, I have this habit after every meal. I cannot help it." Soon the farmers arrived and gave a sound thrashing to the camel.

When the camel crossed the river, the jackal joined him on his back. In the midstream, the camel took a deliberate dip ...(29)... the water. When the jackal cried out in terror, the camel said casually "I have the habit of rolling in the water after every meal." The poor jackal was . ..(30)...

26.
(1) Brought (2) bought
(3) took (4) taken
(5) invites

27.
(1) daily (2) desirous
(3) delicacy (4) dinner
(5) sumptuous

28.
(1) to (2) for
(3) on (4) with
(5) before

29.
(1) onto (2) in
(3) within (4) down
(5) on

30.
(1) sank (2) sinking
(3) drowning (4) drowned
(5) wetting

Reasoning Ability

Directions (31-34): *In each of the question, relationships between some elements are shown in the statements. These statements are followed by conclusions numbered I and II. Read the statements and give the answer.*

(1) If only conclusion I follows.
(2) If only conclusion II follows.
(3) If either conclusion I or II follows.
(4) If neither conclusion I nor II follows.
(5) If both conclusions I and II follow.

31. Statements: $P < R \leq M = L > O \leq V > Y$
Conclusions: I. $L > P$ **II.** $O > R$

32. Statements: $A \geq B > D = F < E \leq C$
Conclusions: I. $B > E$ **II.** $D < C$

33. Statements: $A = E \geq D \geq C < F \leq B$
Conclusions: I. $C < A$ **II.** $A = C$

34. Statements: $F \geq N = O > P \leq K > T$
Conclusions: I. $K < F$ **II.** $N < K$

Directions (35-39): *Study the following information carefully and answer the question given below-*

Seven people viz. A, B, C, D, E, F and G lives in a building on seven different floors such as ground floor is numbered 1, the floor just above is numbered 2 and so on till top floor numbered as seven but not necessarily in the same order.

There are less than three floors above A. Only one person lives between C and A. G lives immediately below D. D lives on an even number floor. B lives immediately above A. F lives above E. F does not lives on the 5th floor. F does not lives on an even number floor.

35. Four of the following five belongs to a group find the one that does not belongs to that group?

(1) CD (2) EC
(3) FB (4) AB
(5) GC

36. Who among the following lives on the top floor?

(1) E (2) B
(3) F (4) D
(5) None of these

37. Number of person lives above F is same as the number of persons below?

(1) B (2) D
(3) C (4) G
(5) None of these

38. How many floors are there above the floor on which G lives?

(1) One (2) Two
(3) Three (4) More than Four
(5) Four

39. Who lives immediately below A?

(1) D (2) E
(3) F (4) C
(5) None of these

Directions (40-44): *Study the following sequence and answer the given questions.*

A @ 3 % 4 E N M $ 8 & 6 L D S ♠ 9 8 6 Q Y Z 1 7 % R O G ♦ 2 I B 2 U &

40. Which of the following element is twelfth to the left of the twentieth element from the left end of the given arrangement?

(1) 6 (2) &
(3) M (4) $
(5) None of these

41. If all the symbols are dropped from the series, which element will be fourth to the right of the one which is twelfth from the right end?

(1) 9 (2) O
(3) R (4) 7
(5) None of these

42. How many such numbers are there in the given series which are immediately preceded by a symbol and followed by a letter?

(1) None (2) One
(3) Two (4) Three
(5) Four

43. Four of the following five are alike in a certain way and forms a group find the one that does not belongs to that group?

(1) 3E% (2) R♦2
(3) M&$ (4) D9S
(5) Y7Z

44. What should come in place of question mark (?) in the following series based on the above arrangement?

34% N$M 6DL 8Q6 = ?

(1) %OR (2) 7Z%
(3) O%R (4) R%O
(5) R%7

Directions (45-49): *Study the following information carefully and answer the question given below-*

Seven people viz. P, Q, R, S, T, U and V are sitting around a circular table having equal distance between them. All of them are facing inside.

P sits immediate right of Q. Only one person sits between P and S (either from left or right). U sits third to the right of S. T is an immediate neighbor of U. R sits second to the left of V.

45. If all the persons are arranged according to the alphabetical order in anticlockwise direction starting from P, then how many persons position will remain unchanged (except P)?

(1) Three (2) One
(3) Two (4) None
(5) None of these

46. How many persons sits between Q and U, if counted from the left of Q?

(1) One (2) Two
(3) Three (4) None
(5) None of these

47. Who sits second to the right of T?

(1) P (2) Q
(3) R (4) S
(5) None of these

48. Four of the following five belongs to a group find the one that does not belongs to that group?

(1) VQ (2) PV
(3) RT (4) SU
(5) TQ

49. Who among the following sits second to the left of the one who sits 4th to the right of V?

(1) U (2) T
(3) R (4) S
(5) None of these

Directions (50-52): *In each of the questions below are given some statements followed by two conclusions. You have to take the given statements to be true even if they seem to be at variance with commonly known facts. Read all the conclusions and then decide which of the given conclusions logically follows from the given statements, disregarding commonly known facts. Give answer*

50. **Statements:** Only a few lamps are bottles. No bottle is ship.

Conclusions I. Some ships are definitely not lamps.

II. All lamps can never be ships.

(1) Both I and II follow
(2) Either I or II follows
(3) Only II follows.
(4) Only I follow.
(5) Neither I nor II follows

51. **Statements:** All bamboos are sticks. No bamboos is a fish.

Conclusions: I. Some sticks are fish.

II. No sticks are fish.

(1) Both I and II follow
(2) Either I or II follows
(3) Only II follows.
(4) Only I follows.
(5) Neither I nor II follows

52. **Statements:** Only a few wells are mats. All pillows are mats.

Conclusions: I. At least some pillows are wells.

II. All wells can never be pillow.

(1) Both I and II follow
(2) Either I or II follows
(3) Only II follows.
(4) Only I follow.
(5) Neither I nor II follows

Directions (53-57): *Study the following information carefully and answer the question given below-*

There are ten persons are sitting in two parallel row such that five persons are sitting in each row. A, B, C, D and E are sitting in row 1 and faces north and M, N, O, P and R are sitting in row 2 and faces south such that persons sitting in row 1 faces the persons sitting row 2.

B sits immediate right of A. Neither A nor B sits at the extreme ends. Two person sits between P and N. B faces the one who sits on the immediate left of P. M sits on the immediate right of R. C sits at the end of the row. D sits on the left of E. D does not face R.

53. Four of the following five belongs to a group find the one that does not belongs to that group?

(1) O (2) C
(3) D (4) P
(5) N

54. Who among the following sits second to the left of the one who faces B?

(1) R (2) N
(3) O (4) M

(5) None of these

55. How many persons sits on the left of N?

(1) One (2) Two
(3) No one (4) Three
(5) None of these

56. How many persons sits between D and C?

(1) One (2) Two
(3) Three (4) No One
(5) Can't be determined

57. Who among the following faces A?

(1) M (2) N
(3) O (4) R
(5) None of these

58. IF 'He will Say' is coded as '1 3 9' and 'Say To Him' is coded as '3 5 2' and 'He May Do' is coded as '8 7 9' then what will be the code of 'will'?

(1) 3 (2) 1
(3) 9 (4) 8
(5) Can't be determined

59. How many pairs of letters are there in the word "MINUTE" each of which have as many letters between them in the word as they have between them in the English alphabetical series?

(1) Three (2) One
(3) Two (4) More than three
(5) None

***Directions (60-63):** Study the following information carefully and answer the question given below-*

There are six persons i.e. A, B, C, D, E and F who all are of different weight. No two persons have same weight. Only two persons are lighter than A. B is heavier than A but lighter than C and D. F is heavier than E but lighter than D. D is not the heaviest. The weight of 2nd heaviest person is 115 kg and the weight of lightest is 56 kg.

60. How many persons are heavier than F?

(1) One (2) Two
(3) Three (4) Four
(5) None of these

61. If the sum of weight of E and A is 131 and the sum of weight of D and B is 213, then what is the sum of weight of A and B?

(1) 172 (2) 173
(3) 174 (4) 175
(5) None of these

62. Which among the following person is the 2nd heaviest?

(1) A (2) B
(3) C (4) D
(5) None of these

63. Which of the following statement is true?

(A) Only two persons are heavier than B.
(B) Sum of weight of D and E is 171 Kg.
(C) Weight of E is 58 Kg.

(1) Only II (2) Both I and II
(3) Both III and II (4) All are True
(5) Only III

***Directions (64-65):** Study the following information carefully and answer the question given below-*

Uncertain number of persons are sitting in a linear row facing north. B sits fifth to the left of E. Two persons sits between B and D. D sits second position from one of the extreme end. Five persons sits between S and E. S is not an immediate neighbor of B. As many as persons sits between E and S as between S and C. As many as persons sits between D and B as between B and F. C sits third position from the extreme end.

64. How many persons are sitting in the row?

(1) 21 (2) 23
(3) 24 (4) 26
(5) Can't be determined

65. If G sits 2nd to the right of S, then what is the position of G from right end?

(1) 7 (2) 9
(3) 8 (4) 6
(5) None of these

Numerical Ability

66. 1, 2, 5, 16, 65, 328, 1957

(1) 5 (2) 328
(3) 16 (4) 1957
(5) 65

67. 4, 11, 25, 46, 74, 129, 151

(1) 129 (2) 11
(3) 151 (4) 4
(5) 46

68. 84, 96, 83, 95, 80, 94, 81

(1) 95 (2) 81
(3) 83 (4) 80
(5) 84

69. 3, 5, 8, 17, 33, 58, 94

(1) 8 (2) 94
(3) 58 (4) 3
(5) 5

70. A boat covers 36 km in upstream in 2 hours and 66 km in downstream in 3 hours. Find the speed of boat in still water?

(1) 21km/h (2) 19 km/h
(3) 20.5 km/h (4) 20 km/h
(5) 19.5 km/h

71. Two inlet taps A and B can fill a tank in 36 minutes and 60 minutes respectively. Find the time taken by both the taps together to fill 1/6th of the tank?

(1) 3 minutes (2) 15/4 minutes
(3) 7/2 minutes (4) 10/3 minutes
(5) None of these

72. If circumference of first circle is 132 cm and circumference of second circle is 110 cm then find the difference between areas of both the circle?

(1) 423.5 cm^2 (2) 412.5 cm^2
(3) 420 cm^2 (4) 422.4 cm^2
(5) 419.8 cm^2

73. In 64 liter of pure milk, 20 liter of water is mixed and then half of the mixture is taken out. When x liter of water is added again then ratio of water to that of the milk becomes 1:2. Find value of x?

(1) 10 liter (2) 8 liter
(3) 12 liter (4) 6 liter
(5) 9 liter

74. Total cost of x pens and (x-2) pencils is Rs 424. If one pencil and one pen costs Rs 4 and Rs 20 respectively then find x?

(1) 16 (2) 18
(3) 15 (4) 20
(5) 21

75. A is 6 years younger than B and ratio of present age of B to C is 12:5. If ratio of present age of A to C is 2:1 then find present age of B?

(1) 20 years (2) 30 years
(3) 24 years (4) 18 years
(5) None of these

***Directions (51-55):** Given bar graph shows the data of two types of school buses X and Y for three schools A, B and C. Study the chart carefully and answer the following questions.*

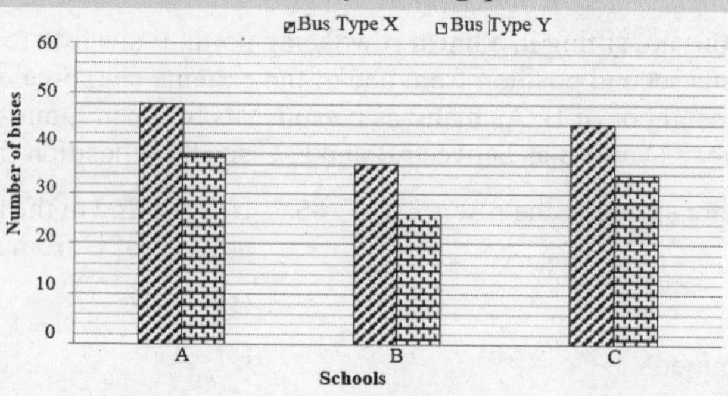

76. What is the average number of X type buses from school B and school C together?

(1) 40 (2) 70
(3) 30 (4) 59
(5) 54

77. X type buses from school A are how much more than that of X type buses from school B?

(1) 55.29% (2) 25%
(3) 5.29% (4) 45.80%
(5) 33.33%

78. What is the average number of all the buses from school B?

(1) 43 (2) 39
(3) 31 (4) 54
(5) 59

79. What is the difference of average number of all buses from school A and average number of all buses from school C?

(1) 16 (2) 4
(3) 8 (4) 24
(5) 12

80. Which school has maximum number of buses?

(1) School B
(2) School C
(3) School A & School C
(4) School A & School B
(5) School A

***Directions (81-85):** Given below are two equations in each question, which you have to solve and give answer*

(1) if $x > y$
(2) if $x \geq y$
(3) if $y > x$
(4) if $y \geq x$
(5) if $x = y$ or no relation can be established

81. I. $2x^2 - 5x + 2 = 0$ II. $2y^2 - 9y + 2 = 0$

82. I. $3x^2 + 7x + 4 = 0$ II. $y^2 + 9y + 20 = 0$

83. I. $x^2 - 7x + 10 = 0$ II. $y^2 - 14y + 45 = 0$

84. I. $x^2 - 3x = 4$ II. $y^2 + 6y + 8 = 0$

85. I. $x^2 - 3x = 10$ II. $y^2 + 7y + 10 = 0$

***Directions (86-90):** Following are the details of three shopkeepers and numbers of items sold by them on three different days*

Shopkeepers	Monday	Tuesday	Wednesday
A	160	240	210
B	200	180	320
C	150	330	280

86. Find the ratio of items sold by A and B on Monday to items sold by B and C on Wednesday?

(1) 5 : 3 (2) 3 : 5
(3) 3 : 4 (4) 4 : 7
(5) 5 : 8

87. Find the average number of items sold by all 3 shopkeepers on Wednesday?

(1) 280 (2) 290
(3) 270 (4) 250
(5) 260

88. Items sold by A and B together on Tuesday is what percentage of items sold by B and C on Wednesday?

(1) 70% (2) 75%
(3) 60% (4) 65%
(5) 80%

89. Find the difference of number of items sold by B on Monday and Tuesday together and items sold by A on Tuesday and Wednesday?

(1) 80 (2) 60
(3) 50 (4) 70
(5) 100

90. Find the ratio of items sold by B on all 3 days together to the items sold by C on all 3 days?

(1) 35 : 38 (2) 38 : 35
(3) 30 : 34 (4) 30 : 38
(5) 35 : 41

91. Marked price of an article is Rs 250 more than cost price of that article and it is sold at a discount of 15% on marked price. Find the cost price of the article if the profit percent earned is 27.5%?

(1) Rs 600 (2) Rs 550
(3) Rs 500 (4) Rs 750
(5) Rs 900

92. In year 2016, ratio of boys to girls in a school is 36:19. And in year 2017, number of boys is increased by 1440 and number of girls is increased by 15%. If in 2017, there were total increase in the number of students is 1725 then find the increased number of boys in the school.

(1) 7240 (2) 5440
(3) 6040 (4) 4440
(5) 5040

93. If ratio of salary of A to that of B is 1:3 and each spends 15% of his salary on house rent. Find the house rent paid by A if remaining amount with A and B together is Rs 42500.

(1) Rs 1800 (2) Rs 1845
(3) Rs 1785 (4) Rs 1760
(5) Rs 1875

94. A started a business by investing Rs. 50,000. After 6 months B joined him by investing Rs. 75,000. After another 6 months C joined with Rs. 1,25,000. What is the ratio of profit shared after 2 years among A, B and C?

(1) 4 : 5 : 6 (2) 8 : 9 : 10
(3) 8 : 9 : 12 (4) 4 : 5 : 8
(5) None of these

95. At what rate will a sum of Rs. 1000 amounts to Rs. 1102.50 in 2 years at compound interest?

(1) 6.5% (2) 6%
(3) 5% (4) 5.5%
(5) None of these

Directions (96-100): What should come in place of question mark (?) in the following questions?

96. $?^2 = 40\%$ of 5/11 of 352

(1) 12 (2) 16
(3) 6 (4) 4
(5) 8

97. $?2 = (\sqrt{144}+\sqrt{676}) \div 4$

(1) 6 (2) 16
(3) 8 (4) 2
(5) 4

98. $\left(\frac{?-0.5}{0.2}\right)=\frac{120}{2}$

(1) 30 (2) 12.5
(3) 25 (4) 17.5
(5) 22.5

99. $60\%\ 0\ ? - \sqrt{324} = 222$

(1) 600 (2) 250
(3) 200 (4) 400
(5) 350

100. $\frac{2^2 \times 3^2}{(90 \div ?)} = \sqrt{64}$

(1) 15 (2) 12
(3) 10 (4) 11
(5) 16

Answers with Explanation

1. (1)
2. (4)
3. (4)
4. (2)
5. (3)
6. (2)
7. (4)
8. (5)
9. (3)
10. (5)
11. (2)
12. (2)
13. (3)
14. (3)
15. (1)
16. (2)
17. (3)
18. (5)
19. (1)
20. (4)
21. (4)
22. (5)
23. (4)
24. (3)
25. (1)
26. (3)
27. (5)
28. (4)
29. (2)
30. (4)

For questions (31-34):

31. (1)
32. (2)
33. (3)
34. (4)

For questions (35-39):

Floors	Person
7	F
6	B
5	A
4	E
3	C
2	D
1	G

35. (5)
36. (3)
37. (4)
38. (4)
39. (2)
40. (3)
41. (3)
42. (4)
43. (2)
44. (1)

For questions (45-49):

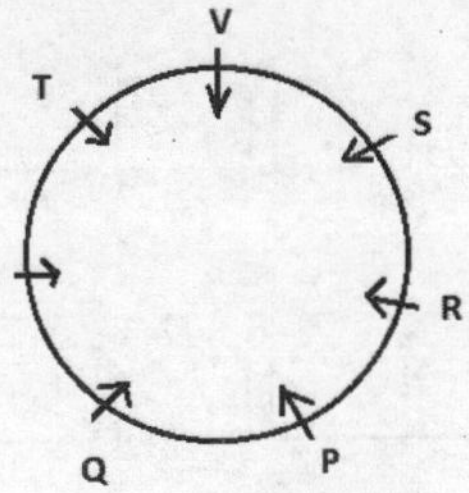

45. (3)
46. (4)
47. (2)
48. (5)
49. (1)
50. (3)

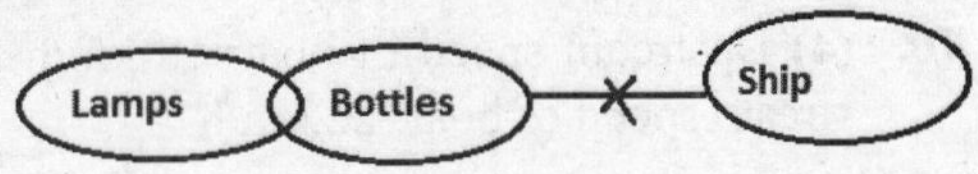

51. (b)

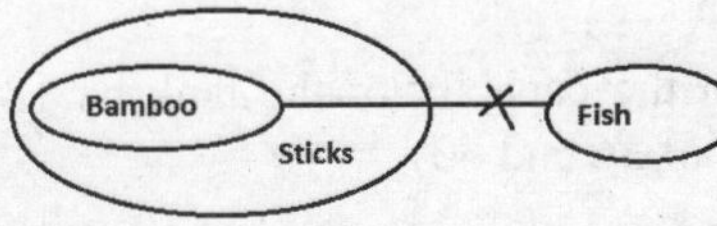

52. (3)

For questions (53-57):

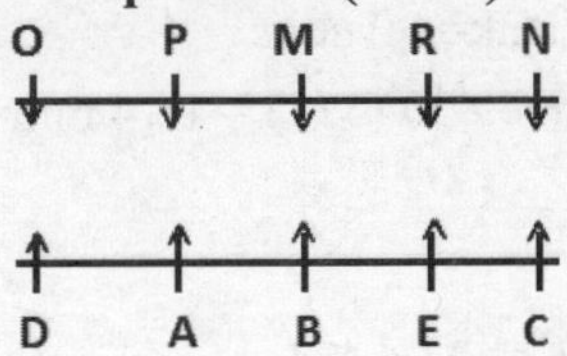

53. (4)
54. (2)
55. (3)
56. (3)
57. (5)
58. (2)
59. (3)

For questions (60-63):

C > D (115kg) > B > A > F > E (56kg)

60. (4)
61. (2)
62. (4)
63. (2)

For questions (64-65):

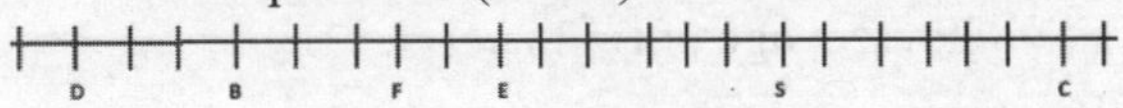

64. (3)
65. (1)

66. (2) $1 \times 1 + 1 = 2$

$2 \times 2 + 1 = 5$

$5 \times 3 + 1 = 16$

$16 \times 4 + 1 = 65$

$65 \times 5 + 1 = 326$

$6 + 1 = 1957$

67. (1)

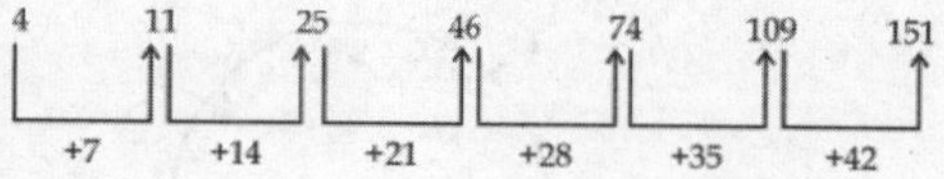

68. (4)

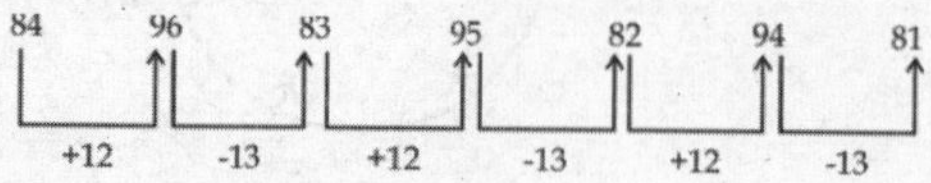

69. (5)

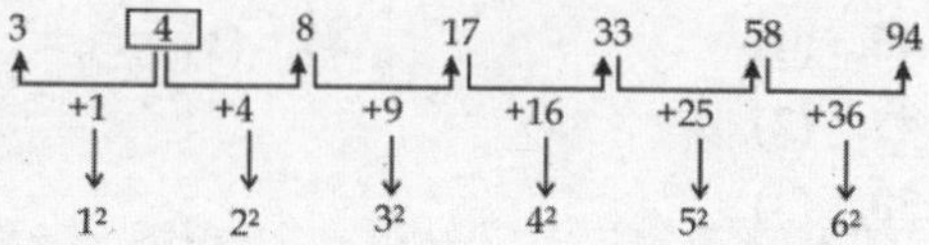

70. (4) Upstream speed of boat=18 km/h Down-stream speed of boat=22 km/h

Speed of boat in still water= (18+22)/2 = 20 km/h

71. (2) Let the capacity of the tank be 180 units (LCM of 36 and 60)

Efficiency of tap A=5 units/ minute

Efficiency of tap B=3 units/minute

1/6th of the tank= 30 units

Required time= 30/(5+3) = 15/4 minutes

72. (1)

73. (5)

74. (2) $20x + 4 \times (x - 2) = 424$

$24x = 432$

$x = 18$

75. (5) Let present age of B and C be 12x years and 5x years respectively.

Present age of A=$10x$ years

According to the question,

$12x - 10x = 6$

$x = 3$

Present age of B=36 years

76. (1)

77. (5)

78. (3)

79. (2)

80. (5) Total buses from school A = 48 + 38 = 86

Total buses from school B = 36 + 26 = 62

Total buses from school C = 44 + 34 = 78

Hence, School A has maximum number of buses.

81. (5)

82. (1)

83. (4)

84. (1) I. $x^2 - 3x - 4 = 0$

$x^2 - 4x + x - 4 = 0$

$(x - 4)(x + 1) = 0$

$x = 4, -1$

II. $y^2 + 6y + 8 = 0$

$y^2 + 2y + 4y + 8 = 0$

$(y + 2)(y + 4) = 0$

$y = -2, -4$

$x > y$

85. (2) I. $x^2 - 3x = 10$

$x^2 - 5x + 2x - 10 = 0$

$(x - 5)(x + 2) = 0$

$x = -2, 5$

II. $y^2 + 7y + 10 = 0$

$y^2 + 5y + 2y + 10 = 0$

$(y + 5)(y + 2) = 0$

$y = -2, -5$

$x \geq y$

86. (2)

87. (3)

88. (1)

89. (4) Items sold by B on Monday and Tuesday = 200 + 180 = 380

Items sold by A on Tuesday and Wednesday = 240 + 210 – 450

∴ Required difference = 450 – 380 =70

90. (1)

91. (3)

92. (5) Let the number of students in the exam be 55x

Then number of boys= 36x Number of girls=19x

According to the question,

$55x + 1725 = (36x + 1440) + 19x \times 1.15$

$x = 100$

Increased number of boys=3600+1440=5040

93. (5) Let the salary of A and B be Rs 100x and Rs 300x respectively

According to the question,

$85x + 255x = 42500 \Rightarrow x = 125$

House rent paid by A=Rs 1875

94. (2)

95. (3)

96. (5)

97. (5)

98. (2) (? −0.5) = 60 × 0.2

? = 12 + 0.5 = 12.5

99. (4)

100. (3)

IBPS Clerk Prelims

Practice Set – 5

English Language

***Directions (1-8):** Read the following passage carefully and answer the questions given below them.*

With regard to employment, the term feminisation can be used to denote presence of women in a particular sector or industry where there is a disproportionate concentration of women; for instance, in the service industry, agriculture, or the garment industry. The Government of India in the Economic Survey (2017-2018) stated that the agricultural sector in India is undergoing feminisation. In the face of shrinking employment opportunities in agriculture, men diversified into the rural non-farm sector, and male out- migration emerged as a major livelihood strategy. Since women did not feature predominantly in either of these trends, most rural women are still engaged in agriculture, mostly as labourers and cultivators (with a disproportionate number of agricultural labourers being Dalit women).

One reason for the feminisation of agricultural labour is that capital prefers to employ women. Women are more willing to accept low-paid irregular work, are easy to hire and fire, are thought to be docile and hardworking, and certain jobs are typified as women's work. All these factors combined with gendered division of work are an important explanation for feminisation. Together, they keep production costs in check and enable capital accumulation. Against the backdrop of rural distress and agrarian crisis, rural men sought employment outside agriculture. Inside villages, they took to non-farm work as casual labourers in construction, brick kilns, mills, or worked as drivers, carpenters, teachers, and so on. An important point to note here is that such jobs, while more readily available and better remunerated than agricultural labour, are socially perceived as 'male work'. Many of these jobs are better paid, more esteemed, and involve arduous physical labour.

The participation of women in the rural, non-farm economy is few and far between, and depends on local socio-cultural value systems. In this context, women often remain in the villages, and therefore in agricultural work. At best, they are supplementary income earners; the concept of a 'breadwinner' is strongly associated with men. Social norms and a gendered division of labour. In line with patriarchal social roles, women are responsible for reproduction and care activities. With male out-migration, women have additionally taken on the role of providing for their households on a daily basis, since are irregular. This means that they now have to take care of their own farming and also work as agricultural wage labourers.

Within agriculture, there exists a gendered division of labour. Women undertake work such as weeding, threshing, and paddy transplantation—tasks that might not require physical strength. Patriarchy is so deeply rooted that even though women might do male tasks like ploughing and spade work in their own fields, they might not as wage labourers. A woman doing a 'man's job' would most likely invite ridicule.

1. As per Economic Survey (2017-18) what is/are the main reason(s) that agriculture in India is undergoing feminisation?

I. The challenges of agricultural employment in India.

II. Men ventured out to non-farm sectors and out- migrating for better prospects and stable livelihood.

III. Women want to earn for themselves and build a career out of it.

(1) Only (I)
(2) Only (II)
(3) Only (I) and (III)
(4) Only (I) and (II)
(5) All (I), (II) and (III)

2. According to the passage, how do the local socio- cultural norms make rural women far less pliable than their male counterparts?

I. Since the "breadwinner" tag is only associated with the male population, women's income is considered as supplementary thus they mostly confine to villages and engage in agricultural activities.

II. The deeply rooted gender division society perceives women as a caregiver. With males out-migrating, women have taken the responsibility of aiding the family through their agricultural wages.

III. Even in farming, women only take those jobs that are not considered as "man's job" just to avoid getting ridiculed.

(1) Only (I)
(2) Only (II)
(3) Only (III)
(4) Only (I) and (III)
(5) All (I), (II) and (III)

3. Why capitalists prefer to employ women?

I. The conventional wisdom states that women are more likely to accept low paid irregular jobs and also, they are easy to hire and fire.

II. women are prejudiced to be docile and hardworking, and certain jobs are typified as women's work.

III. After nurturing the family, women want to earn extra income and capitalists use this in their favour.

(1) Only (I)
(2) Only (II)
(3) Only (III)
(4) Only (I) and (II)
(5) All (I), (II) and (III)

4. After going through the passage characterised author's tone.

(1) condescending
(2) cynical
(3) laudatory
(4) satirical
(5) acerbic

5. Which of the following words can fit grammatically and contextually into the blank given in the passage?

(1) remittances
(2) supplementary
(3) invoice
(4) evasions
(5) consideration

6. Which of the following words can REPLACE the word "**arduous**" given in the passage?

(1) fragile
(2) onerous
(3) effortless
(4) exciting
(5) None of these

7. Which of the following words can REPLACE the word "**ridicule**" given in the passage?

(1) applause
(2) derision
(3) praise
(4) approval

(5) None of these

8. Which of the following words is the OPPOSITE of "**shrinking**" as per passage?

(1) wither
(2) shrivel
(3) expanding
(4) condense
(5) None of these

Directions (9-13): *In the following paragraph few words are missing and for each of this word five options are given. Choose the correct option for the respective blank, which is grammatically and contextually accurate.*

Water ____(9) ____is the lack of freshwater resources to satisfy water demand. It is ____(10) ____by partial or no satisfaction of expressed demand, economic competition for water quantity or quality, disputes between users, irreversible groundwater____ (11) ____, and negative effects on the environment. It affects every continent and was categorised in 2019 by the World Economic Forum as one of the largest global risks with respect to its ____ (12) ____ impact over the next decade.

One-third of the global population (2 billion people) live under situations of severe water scarcity at least one month of the year. Half a billion people in the world ____ (13) ____by severe water scarcity all year round. Half of the world's largest cities have been facing water scarcity.

9.

(1) drainage
(2) clog
(3) scarcity
(4) abundance
(5) surplus

10.

(1) manifested
(2) attested
(3) hidden
(4) certify
(5) transparent

11.

(1) augmentation
(2) depletion
(3) expenditure
(4) dwindle
(5) impoverishment

12.

(1) latent
(2) thinkable
(3) potential
(4) probability
(5) reality

13.

(1) Affected
(2) effected
(3) aftermath
(4) pompous
(5) grandiose

Directions (14-17): *Each question consists three sentences which may or may not have errors. Mark the correct sentence(s) as your answer. If there is no correct sentence then mark (e) that is "All sentences are incorrect".*

14.

I. Before the exam she felt surely of excelling, but when the exam started, she realized that it is not going to be so easy.

II. I know that eventually he will succumb to me and confess that he has committed a crime

III. In his valedictory speech he said nothing worth listening to.

(1) Only (I)
(2) Only (II)
(3) Only (III)
(4) Only (I) and (II)
(5) All sentences are incorrect

15.

I. Just before the match I asked him whom he thought was going to win.

II. My nephew, who is in Bangalore, is eager to travel to Delhi in this winter.

III. One of my uncles is seriously ill and is in the intensive care unit.

(1) Only (I)
(2) Only (II)
(3) Only (III)
(4) Only (II) and (III)
(5) All sentences are incorrect

16.

I. The man was dressed simply but his eyes were beaming with knowledge.

II. when he used to walk along the road, a wild dog started chasing him.

III. A pair of trouser have been bought by me.

(1) Only (I)
(2) Only (II)
(3) Only (III)
(4) Only (I) and (III)
(5) All sentences are incorrect

17.

I. The business tycoon returned back to the corridors of Indian cricket by bagging the franchise of the IPL.

II. Things will go the same as they were, unless you yourself look into it.

III. The thirsty dogs drank up all the water.

(1) Only (I)
(2) Only (II)
(3) Only (III)
(4) Only (I) and (III)
(5) All sentences are incorrect

Directions (18-25): *In each sentence some portion is in bold, which may or may not need improvement. Choose the correct replacement for that portion that makes the sentence grammatically and contextually correct. If the sentence is correct as it is, then mark "No improvement required".*

18. Prime Minister Narendra Modi expressed his gratitude to doctors, nurses and all **whom worked at** crossing the milestone of 100 crore covid doses.

(1) those who worked on
(2) those whom worked at
(3) those who worked upon
(4) whom working on
(5) No improvement required

19. The leader repeatedly said that his mission was **not by merely to achieve** hundred percent literacy.

(1) to more achieving
(2) merely to achieve
(3) for merely to achieve
(4) in order to achieve
(5) No improvement required

20. Stating that the lockdown had opened up new vistas such as conduct of online classes, the Madras High Court **impressed upon the need to continue** the virtual mode of education for the benefit of those in need of it.

(1) impressed by the need to continue
(2) impresses with the need to continue
(3) impressed along with need of continuing
(4) impresses from the need for continue
(5) No Improvement Required

21. **No sooner I saw** him than I ran away.

(1) As soon as I see
(2) No sooner did I see
(3) No sooner had I seen him
(4) No sooner had I seen him
(5) No improvement

22. Rohan met with an accident and immediately **admitted to the hospital.**
(1) admitted to hospital
(2) admitted to a hospital
(3) admitted into a hospital
(4) has admitted to a hospital
(5) No improvement required

23. Our journey to Manali was **far from being comfortable**, as the road was bumpy.
(1) far from comfortability
(2) far not comfortable
(3) far not comforting
(4) far and not being comfortable
(5) No improvement required

24. I **have been ringing the doorbell** five times but no one answered.
(1) Had been ringing the doorbell
(2) have rung the doorbell
(3) ringing the doorbell
(4) has rung the doorbell
(5) No improvement required

25. There **has been a sharp decline of** the profit of the company this year.
(1) have been a sharp decline of
(2) has a sharp decline in
(3) has been a sharp decline in
(4) have been a sharp decline
(5) No correction required

Directions (26-30): *In each question four words are given in bold, in which one of them might be misspelt or grammatically incorrect. Choose the incorrect word as your answer. If all the words are correct, mark (s) i.e. No correction required.*

26. What makes plastic so (A) **convenient** in our day-to- day lives it's (B) **cheap** also makes it (C) **ubiquoitous**, resulting in one of our planet's greatest environmental (D) **challenges**.
(1) A
(2) B
(3) C
(4) D
(5) No correction required

27. The country argues that deep and (A) **significent** cuts to fossil fuel use can (B) **affect** the development (C) **trajectory** of its and other (D) **developing** countries.
(1) A
(2) B
(3) C
(4) D
(5) No correction required

28. James was told to (A) **forfeit** all contact with (B) **convicted** felons if he did not want to (C) **violate** the terms of his (D) **payrole**.
(1) A
(2) B
(3) C
(4) D
(5) No correction required

29. While social media has mobilised help in a way our (A) **infrastructure** was unable to, and many could find the aid they needed in (B) critical times, what was once an escape from reality is now an (C) overwelming source of information and (D) distressing news.
(1) A
(2) B
(3) C
(4) D
(5) No correction required

30. Considering, however, the numbers of venomous and (A) **innocuous** snakes that occur in most (B) **tropical** countries, it might be supposed that (C) **mimicry** in this order of

reptiles would be of commoner(D) **occurence** than appears to be the case.

(1) A (2) B (3) C (4) D

(5) No correction required

Numerical Ability

Directions (31-35): *Line graph given below shows number of passengers travelling in five (A, B, C, D & E) different compartment of a trains. Read the data carefully and answer the questions.*

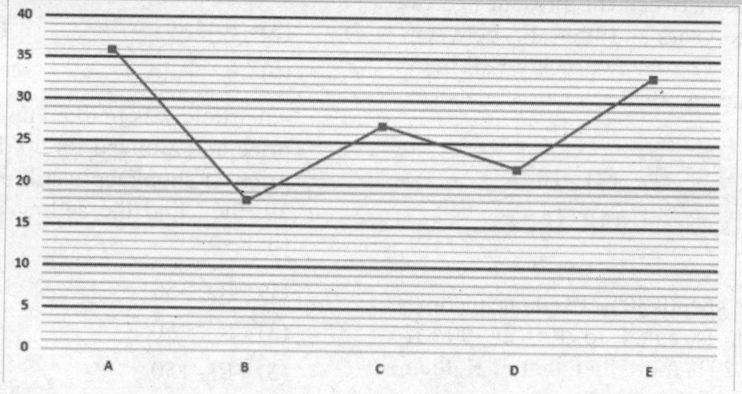

31. Total passengers in E are what percent less than total passengers in A?

(1) 6 ¼ % (2) 8 ⅓%

(3) 6 ⅓% (4) 6 ⅔%

(5) 5%

32. Find average number of passengers in A, C & E?

(1) 32 (2) 30

(3) 36 (4) 33

(5) 27

33. Find the ratio of total passenger in B to that of in D?

(1) 7 : 9 (2) 9 : 10

(3) 11 : 9 (4) 9 : 13

(5) 9 : 11

34. Total passenger in C and E together are what percent more than total passenger in A?

(1) 33 ⅓% (2) 66 ⅔%

(3) 66 ⅓% (4) 50%

(5) 60%

35. Find total number of passengers traveling in B, C & D together?

(1) 69 (2) 65

(3) 67 (4) 63

(5) 71

Directions (36-40): *What will come in the place of question (?) mark in following questions?*

36. 12, 12, 24, 72, ?, 1440

(1) 256 (2) 288

(3) 284 (4) 296

(5) 316

37. 16, 17.8, 21.4, 28.6, 43, ?

(1) 69.8 (2) 72.8

(3) 73.8 (4) 70.8

(5) 71.8

38. 12, 7, 8, 13, ?, 68.5

(1) 28 (2) 27

(3) 26 (4) 27.5

(5) 26.5

39. 72, 79, 65, 93, ?, 149

(1) 36 (2) 31

(3) 33 (4) 37

(5) 35

40. 8, 9, 19, 58, 233, ?

(1) 1164 (2) 1166

(3) 1156 (4) 1152

(5) 1158

41. If the difference between the present age of P and Q is three years and the ratio between the age of P and Q after two years will be 5 : 4, then find the age of P after two years (in years)?

(1) 15 (2) 13

(3) 18 (4) 16

(5) 14

42. A and B both spend 30% of their income together which is equal to Rs. 26400. If income of A is 20% more than that of B, then find the income of B (in Rs.)?

(1) 52000 (2) 48000

(3) 40000 (4) 36000

(5) 30000

43. If a man invests equal sum at the same rate of interest on simple interest for T and T+4 years and the respective ratio of interest gets by man is 1:2 respectively, then find 'T'?

(1) 6 (2) 2

(3) 5 (4) 3

(5) 4

44. 12 women can complete a work in 64 day, then find how many women will be required to complete 2/3 rd of the same work in 16 days?

(1) 28 (2) 24

(3) 36 (4) 32

(5) 48

45. A train running at the speed of 72 kmph crosses a pole in 30 seconds. Find the time taken by the same train to cross the pole with the speed of 54 kmph (in sec)?

(1) 42 (2) 48

(3) 54 (4) 45

(5) 40

46. The upstream speed and downstream speed of a boat is 10 kmph and 14 kmph respectively and boat travelled for T hours & 6 hours in upstream and downstream respectively. If the distance travelled in downstream is 44 km more than upstream, then find the value of 'T'

(1) 4 (2) 3

(3) 6 (4) 5

(5) 8

47. An article was marked up by 50% above cost price and allowed Rs 50 discount on marked price. If shopkeeper still made a profit of Rs. 50, then find the selling price of the article (in Rs.)?

(1) Rs. 350 (2) Rs. 300

(3) Rs. 250 (4) Rs. 200

(5) Rs. 150

48. A & B invested Rs. X and Rs. (X + 800) for same period of time in a business. If A gets Rs. 3200 as profit share out of total profit of Rs. 6800, then find 'X'?

(1) 7800 (2) 6000

(3) 8400 (4) 7200

(5) 6400

49. A vessel contains mixture of milk and water in the ration of 3 : 1 respectively. If 20 liters mixture taken out from the vessel and now the difference between milk and water in the remaining mixture is 70 liters, then find initial mixture in vessel (in liters)?

(1) 240 (2) 160

(3) 120 (4) 80

(5) 180

50. Perimeter of a rectangle is 2 cm more than circumference of a circle and area of circle is 616 cm^2. If breath of rectangle is equal to radius of circle, then find length of rectangle (in cm)?

(1) 35 (2) 33

(3) 31 (4) 21

(5) 27

***Directions (51-55):** Table given below shows number of orders received by three (P, Q & R) companies of their three (A, B & C) items. Read the data carefully and answer the questions.*

Companies	A	B	C
P	80	60	50
Q	40	70	90
R	80	100	30

51. Total orders of item A & B received by R is how much more than total orders of item B & C received by Q?

(1) 50 (2) 10
(3) 40 (4) 20
(5) 30

52. Find total orders (all three items) received by R is what percent more than that of total orders (all three items) received by Q?

(1) 5% (2) 12.5%
(3) 10% (4) 15%
(5) 20%

53. Find ratio of total orders of item A & B received by P to total orders of item B & C received by Q?

(1) 7 : 9 (2) 8 : 7
(3) 4 : 7 (4) 5 : 6
(5) 7 : 8

54. Find average number of orders of item B received by Q & R is what percent of total orders of item A received by P?

(1) 104 ¼ % (2) 106 ¼ %
(3) 108 ¼ % (4) 102 ¼ %
(5) 110 ¼ %

55. Find total orders of item A, B & C received by P?

(1) 210 (2) 220
(3) 190 (4) 180
(5) 200

***Directions (56-65):** What should come in place of question mark (?) in following questions?*

56. (48% of 625) ÷ 0.75 = ?

(1) 800 (2) None of these
(3) 40 (4) 4000
(5) 400

57. $\frac{(4)^3+(18)^2}{7^2+121-73}=?$

(1) 1 (2) 2
(3) 4 (4) 5
(5) 3

58. $(4)^2\times 2=\frac{(16)^2}{\sqrt[4]{16}}$

(1) 2 (2) 3
(3) 4 (4) 1
(5) None of these

59. $4\times(?+120)=(8)^3$

(1) 6 (2) 12
(3) 8 (4) 4
(5) 16

60. ? + 432 – 205 = 550

(1) 384 (2) 244
(3) 224 (4) 276
(5) 324

61. $12\times 8+(?)^2=(14)^2$

(1) 10 (2) 12
(3) 8 (4) 6
(5) 9

62. 40% of 400 + ? % of 300 = 250

(1) 40 (2) 36
(3) 25 (4) 30
(5) 20

63. $\sqrt{441} \div 7 = ? - 180$

(1) 185 (2) 183

(3) 187 (4) 184

(5) 182

64. $\sqrt{576} - \sqrt{144} + \sqrt{729} = 36 + ?$

(1) 1 (2) 4

(3) 5 (4) 2

(5) 3

65. $119 + 41 + 9 = ?^2$

(1) 10 (2) 13

(3) 17 (4) 8

(5) 16

Reasoning Ability

Directions (66-70): *Study the following information carefully and answer the questions given below:*

Eight persons i.e. D, Q, G, H, K, S, E and W are sitting around a square table in such a way that four persons sit at the corner side of the table and other four persons sit in the middle side of the table. The persons who sit at the corner side are facing away from the center and the persons who sit in the middle side are facing towards the center. D sits at the corner side of the table. One person sits between D and G. Q sits third to the right of G. Three persons sit between Q and E. W sits second to the right of E. W is not an immediate neighbour of D. H sits second to the right of K.

66. Who among the following sits second to the right of S?

(1) Q (2) E

(3) D (4) W

(5) None of these

67. How many persons sit between D and W when counted from the right of D?

(1) Three (2) Four

(3) One (4) Two

(5) None of these

68. Who among the following sits second to the left of G?

(1) (a) D (2) (b) K

(3) (c) H (4) (d) S

(5) None of these

69. Who among the following are the immediate neighbours to each other?

(1) K, E (2) Q, D

(3) G, H (4) W, S

(5) None of these

70. Four of the following five are alike in a certain way and hence form a group. Find the one who does not belong to that group?

(1) E (2) D

(3) G (4) (d) K

(5) H

Directions (71-74): *Study the following sequence of numbers and alphabets and answer the given questions-*

P 4 S A W 5 8 F 9 1 R E 7 2 O 3 7 5 1 B 6 K G N

71. How many numbers are there which are immediately preceded by a vowel?

(1) One (2) None

(3) Two (4) (d) Three

(5) None of these

72. If all the numbers are removed from the given series, then which among the following element is seventh from the right end?

(1) E (2) O

(3) F (4) R

(5) None of these

73. If all the consonants are removed from the given series, then which among the following element is ninth from the left end?

(1) 2 (2) O

(3) 3 (4) 7

(5) None of these

74. Which among the following element is fifth to

the left of twelfth element from the left end?

(1) F (2) 8

(3) 9 (4) 1

(5) None of these

Directions (75-77): Study the following information carefully and answer the questions given below:

Five persons A, B, C, D and E have different heights. Less than two persons are shorter than D. As many persons are taller than D as shorter than C. A is taller than B but shorter than E. B is not the shortest person. The height of third tallest person is 86 cm.

75. If the height of shortest person is 68 cm, then what may be the height of B?

(1) 69 cm

(2) 81 cm

(3) 78 cm

(4) All the given heights

(5) None of these

76. How many persons are taller than C?

(1) None (2) One

(3) Two (4) Three

(5) None of these

77. Who among the following is just shorter than E?

(1) None (3) A

(2) C (4) D

(5) None of these

Directions (78-81): In each of the questions below are given some statements followed by some conclusions. You have to take the given statements to be true even if they seem to be at variance with commonly known facts. Read all the conclusions and then decide which of the given conclusions logically follows from the given statements disregarding commonly known facts.

78. Statements: All Greens are Yellows. No Yellows are Black.

Conclusions: I. No Greens are Black.

II. Some Greens are Black.

(1) If only conclusion I follows.

(2) If only conclusion II follows.

(3) If either conclusion I or II follows.

(4) If neither conclusion I nor II follows.

(5) If both conclusions I and II follow.

79. Statements: All Chairs are Sofas. Only a few Sofas are Beds. No Beds are Curtains.

Conclusions: I. Some Sofas are not Beds.

II. Some Sofas are not Curtains.

(1) If only conclusion I follows.

(2) If only conclusion II follows.

(3) If either conclusion I or II follows.

(4) If neither conclusion I nor II follows.

(5) If both conclusions I and II follow.

80. Statements: Only a few Coffee are Tea. **All** Tea is Drinks. **Only** a few Drinks are Cold drinks.

Conclusions: I. Some Tea is not Cold drinks.

II. No Coffee are Drinks.

(1) If only conclusion I follows.

(2) If only conclusion II follows.

(3) If either conclusion I or II follows.

(4) If neither conclusion I nor II follows.

(5) If both conclusions I and II follow.

81. Statements: All Flowers are Trees. Only a few **Trees** are Gardens. No Gardens are Lawns.

Conclusions: I. All Lawns can never be Trees

II. Some Flowers can be Gardens

(1) If only conclusion I follows.

(2) If only conclusion II follows.

(3) If either conclusion I or II follows.

(4) If neither conclusion I nor II follows.

(5) If both conclusions I and II follow.

Directions (82-86): Study the following information carefully and answer the questions given below:

Seven persons A, B, C, D, E, F and G are sitting in row and all are facing towards north but not necessarily in the same order. B sits second from one of the extreme ends. Three persons sit between D and B. Two persons sit between D and A. C sits to the immediate left of A. F sits to left of C but is not an immediate neighbour of C. More than two persons sit between F and E.

82. How many persons sit to the left of F?
(1) Two (2) None
(3) One (4) Three
(5) None of these

83. Who among the following sits third to the right of G?
(1) E (2) C
(3) B (4) F
(5) None of these

84. Who among the following persons sit at the extreme ends?
(1) F, A (2) A, E
(3) G, E (4) F, E
(5) None of these

85. How many persons sit between D and E?
(1) Two (2) Four
(3) Three (4) One
(5) None of these

86. Who among the following sits to the immediate left of E?
(1) G (2) A
(3) B (4) D
(5) None of these

Directions (87-88): Study the following information carefully and answer the questions given below:

Point D is 10m north of point P. Point Y is 14m east of point D. Point Q is 8m north of point Y. Point S is 20m west of point Q. Point H is 8m south of point S.

87. What is the shortest distance between point H and point D?
(1) 8m (2) 6m
(3) 4m (4) 10m
(5) None of these

88. In which direction is point P with respect to point Q?
(1) South east (2) North west
(3) South west (4) North east
(5) None of these

Directions (89-92): Study the following information carefully and answer the questions given below:

There are certain number of persons sitting in a row facing towards north direction. A sits fifth to the right of B. Two persons sit between C and B. D sits fourth to the left of C. Four persons sit to the left of D. The number of persons sit between D and B is same as the number of persons sit between B and F. F sits at fourth position from one of the extreme ends.

89. How many persons sit between B and D?
(1) None (2) Six
(3) Five (4) Four
(5) None of these

90. How many persons sit in the row?
(1) Twenty (2) Twenty-one
(3) Twenty-two (4) Nineteen
(5) None of these

91. Who among the following sits second to the right of A?
(1) None (2) C
(3) D (4) F
(5) None of these

92. How many persons sit to the right of B?
(1) Nine (2) Ten
(3) Eight (4) Eleven
(5) None of these

93. How many such pairs of letters are there in

the meaningful word 'MATCHES' each of which has as many letters between them in the word as in the English alphabet (From both backward and forward)?

(1) Two (2) One
(3) More than three (4) Three
(5) None of these

Directions (94-98): *Study the following sequence carefully and answer the given questions.*

COT IVY PEA FOX MRU

94. If we add 'L' after first letter in every word, then how many meaningful words will be formed?

(1) None (2) Three
(3) Two (4) One
(5) None of these

95. If third letter of each word is replaced by its succeeding letter according to English alphabetical order, then in how many words vowels will appear more than once?

(1) Two (2) One
(3) None (4) Three
(5) None of these

96. If all the words are arranged according to English alphabetical order from left to right, then which word will appear fourth from the left end?

(1) MRU (2) FOX
(3) PEA (4) IVY
(5) None of these

97. If all the letters are arranged according to English alphabetical order within each word, then in how many words vowel will appear at second position?

(1) One (2) None
(3) Two (4) Three
(5) None of these

98. How many letters are there in English alphabetical series between the first letter of the second word from the left end and third letter of the third word from the right end?

(1) Five (2) Six
(3) Seven (4) Four
(5) None of these

99. If in the number '35982476', 1 is added to each even digit and 2 is subtracted from each odd digit, then which digits will not appear twice in the number thus obtained?

(1) Only 1 (2) Only 9
(3) Both '1' and '9' (4) Only 5
(5) None of these

Directions (100): *Study the following information carefully and answer the questions given below:*

Six people P, Q, R, S, T and U have events on different dates 7th and 12th of different months i.e. January, February and March. D has event on even numbered date in the month having 31 days. The number of persons have event before D is same as the number of persons have event after A. One person has event between A and C. F has event before C. B has event just before E.

100. How many persons have event before B?

(1) Two (2) None
(3) Three (4) One
(5) None of these

Answers with Explanations

1. (4)
2. (5)
3. (4)
4. (5)
5. (1)
6. (2)
7. (2)
8. (3) "Expanding" means "to enlarge" which is opposite of the word "shrinking".
9. (3)
10. (1)
11. (b) The sentence is clearly referring ground-water reduction thus the correct answer is "depletion" which means "reduction".
12. (3) "Potential" is the correct word as it means "possible".
13. (1) "Affected" is the correct word as it means "to influence or have an impact on something".
14. (2)
15. (4)
16. (1)
17. (3)
18. (1) The correct answer is "those who worked on".
19. (2) "Merely to achieve" is the correct form.
20. (5)
21. (2) The sentence that starts with "no sooner" follows inversion rules. So, the correct form is "no sooner did I see".
22. (1) "Admitted to hospital" is the correct answer.
23. (5)
24. (2) The given sentence is in present perfect tense and its correct structure is "S+ has/have+ v3".
25. (3)
26. (3) The correct spelling is "ubiquitous".
27. (1) The correct spelling is "significant".
28. (4) The correct spelling is "parole".
29. (3) The correct spelling is "overwhelming".
30. (4) The correct word is "occurrence".
31. (2)
32. (1)
33. (5) Required ratio = 18 : 22 = 9 : 11
34. (2)
35. (3) Required number of passengers = 18 + 27 + 22 = 67
36. (2) $12 \times 1 = 12$

    $12 \times 2 = 24$

    $24 \times 3 = 72$

    $? = 72 \times 4 = 288$

    $288 \times 5 = 1440$
37. (5) $16 + 1.8 = 17.8$

    $17.8 + 3.6 = 21.4$

    $21.4 + 7.2 = 28.6$

    $28.6 + 14.4 = 43$

    $? = 43 + 28.8 = 71.8$
38. (2) $12 \times 0.5 + 1 = 7$

    $7 \times 1 + 1 = 8$

    $8 \times 1.5 + 1 = 13$

    $? = 13 \times 2 + 1 = 27$

    $27 \times 2.5 + 1 = 68.5$
39. (4) $72 + 7 = 79$

    $79 - 14 = 65$

    $65 + 28 = 93$

    $? = 93 - 56 = 37$

    $37 + 112 = 149$
40. (2) $8 \times 1 + 1 = 9$

    $9 \times 2 + 1 = 19$

    $19 \times 3 + 1 = 58$

    $58 \times 4 + 1 = 233$

    $233 \times 5 + 1 = 1166$
41. (1)
42. (3)
43. (5)
44. (4)
45. (5)
46. (1) $14 \times 6 - 10 \times T = 44$

    $10T = 40 \Rightarrow T = 4$

47. (3)
48. (5)
49. (2)
50. (3)
51. (4) Required difference = (80 + 100) – (70 + 90) = 20
52. (1) Total orders (all three items) received by R
    = (80 + 100 + 30) = 210
    Total orders (all three items) received by Q
    = (40 + 70 + 90) = 200
    Required percentage = 5%
53. (5) Total orders of item A & B received by P
    = 80 + 60 = 140
    Total orders of item B & C received by Q
    = 70 + 90 = 160
    Required ratio = 140 : 160 = 7 : 8
54. (2)
55. (3) Required sum = 80 + 60 + 50 = 190
56. (5)
57. (3)
58. (2)
59. (3)
60. (5) ? + 432 – 206 = 550
    ? = 550 – 226
    ? = 324
61. (1) $(?)^2 = 196 - 96$
    $?^2 = 100 \Rightarrow ? = 10$
62. (4)
63. (2)
64. (5) 24 – 12 + 27 = 36 + ?
    ? = 13
65. (2) $119 + 41 + 9 = ?^2$
    ? = 13

For questions (66-70):

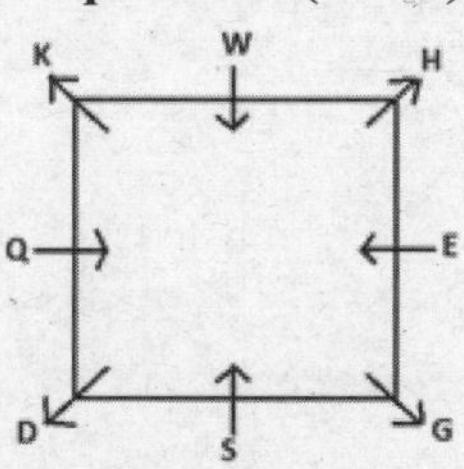

66. (2)
67. (4)
68. (3)
69. (2)
70. (1)
71. (3)
72. (4)
73. (1)
74. (2)

For questions (75-77):

C > E > A (86) > B > D

75. (4)
76. (1)
77. (3)
78. (1)

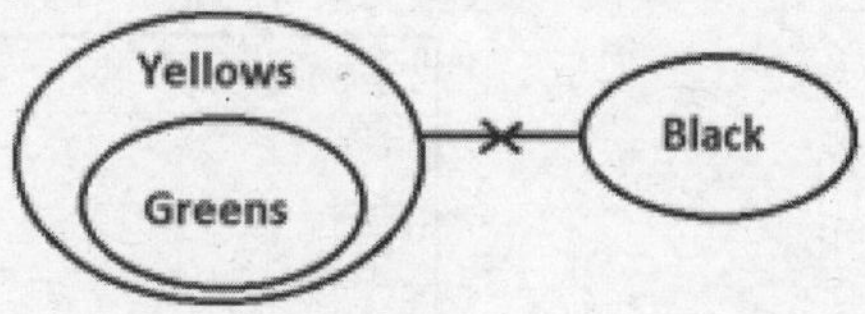

79. (5)

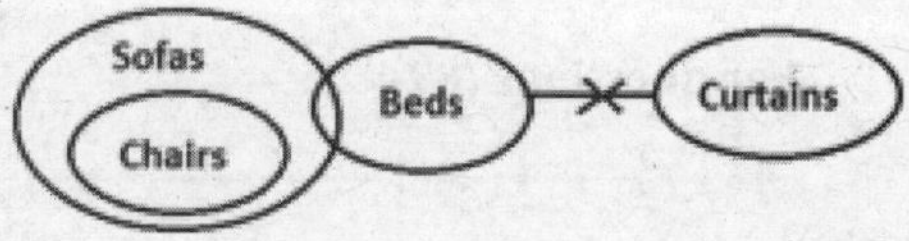

80. (4)

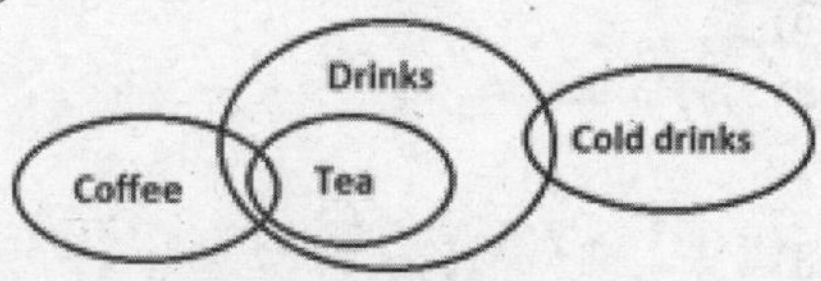

81. (2)

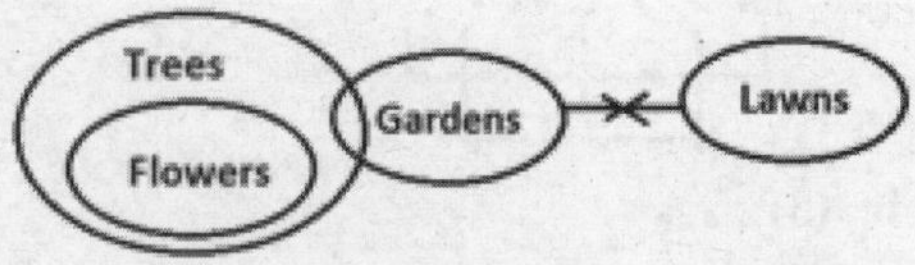

For questions (82-86):

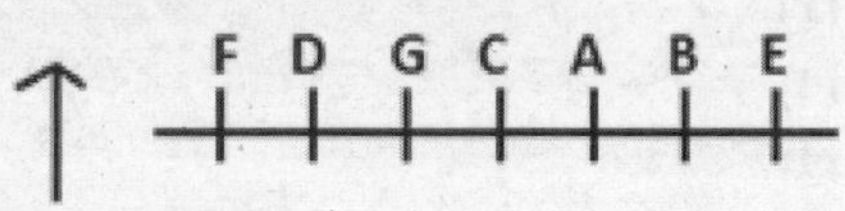

82. (2)
83. (3)
84. (4)

85. (2)

86. (3)

87. (2)

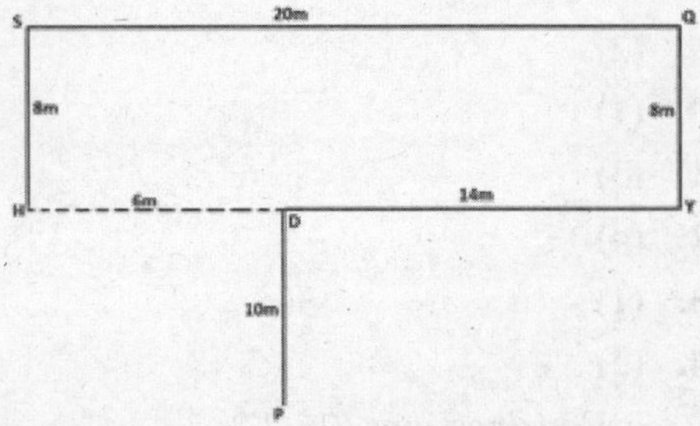

88. (3)

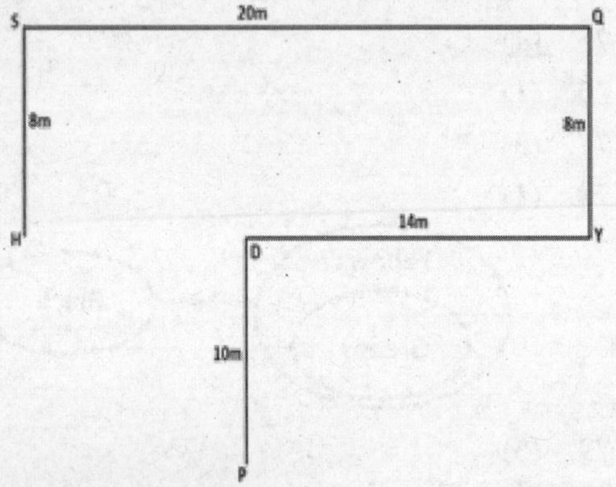

For questions (89-92):

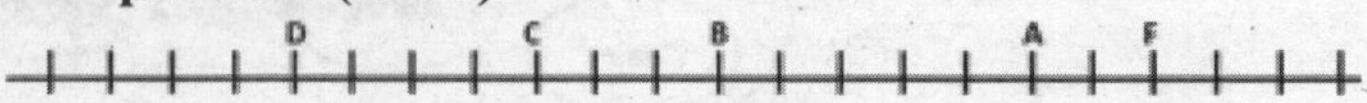

89. (2)

90. (3)

91. (4)

92. (2)

93. (3)

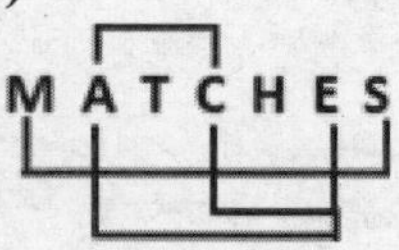

94. (3)

95. (2)

96. (1)

97. (4)

98. (3)

99. **(3):** 3 5 9 8 2 4 7 6

1 3 7 9 3 5 5 7

For question (100):

Months	7th	12th
January	A	F
February	C	B
March	E	D

100. (3)

IBPS Clerk Mains

Practice Set – 6

General English

Directions (1-5): *Read the following sentences to find out whether there is any grammatical error in them. The error, if any, will be in one part of the sentence. Mark the part with the error as your answer. If there is no error, mark 'No error' as your answer.* (*Ignore the error of punctuation, if any*)

1. Such manufacturing plant will/generated employment for/over 1000 skilled professional/over the next five years.

(1) Such manufacturing plant will

(2) generated employment for

(3) over 1000 skilled professionals

(4) over the next five years

(5) No Error

2. On account of the falling it/its revenue and profitability/the company has received/a lower credit rating this year.

(1) On account of the falling in

(2) its revenue and profitability

(3) the company has received

(4) a lower credit rating this year

(5) No error

3. The panel appointed by/the government has recommended/the removal of these ambiguity/in the draft of the taxation law.

(1) The panel appointed by

(2) the government has recommended

(3) the removal of these ambiguity

(4) in the draft of the taxation law

(5) No Error

4. With the Reserve Bank of Indian handling out/licenses for new banks as well as/new types of banks such as Payment banks/Public Sector Bank will face many challenges.

(1) With the Reserve Bank of India handling out

(2) licenses for new banks as well as

(3) new types of banks such as Payment banks,

(4) Public sector Banks will face many challenges .

(5) No error

5. When the Emperor heard of/the saga's wit and intelligence/he sent to a messenger to/invite him to the court.

(1) When the Emperor heard of

(2) the saga's wit and intelligence

(3) he sent to a messenger to

(4) invite him to the court

(5) No error

Directions (6-15): *Read the following passage carefully and answers the given questions. Certain words/phrases have been I bold to help you locate them while answering some of the questions.*

Once an old lady lost her eyesight and became blind. She called a doctor and agreed to pay him a very big amount if he cured her. But she has a condition that she would not give a single penny, if she was not **cured.** The doctor came to her house daily for treatment. Day after day he started stealing the lady's house. In order to do this, he **delayed** curing the lady. He finally cured the lady after he had removed all the furniture and valuable articles from the lady. But the lady refused to pay the fees and said that she was not fully cured.

The doctor **registered** a case against her. On being asked by judge in the court as to why she was not paying the fee, the sharp lady told the court that her eye sight had not fully restored as she could not see, her furniture and other articles in the house. The judge was very clever. He **gathered** what was going on and punished the doctor.

6. Which of the following can be said about the doctor?

A. He spent the rest of his life in prison.

B. He was outwitted by the old lady.

C. He believed he could get away with his deception.

(1) Only A (2) A and B

(3) Only C (4) B and C

(5) A, B, and C

7. Which of the following is true according to the story?

(1) The lady was still partially blind, hence refused to pay the doctor.

(2) The judge in the court was not intelligent.

(3) The doctor's in fact was not successful.

(4) The lady had taken advantage of the doctor's naiveté.

(5) All the given statements are true.

8. Choose the word which is most **opposite** in meaning to the word **'Registered'** given in **bold** as used in the passage.

(1) Lodged (2) Withdrew

(3) Dislocated (4) Uncalculated

(5) Dismembered

9. Choose the word which is most **similar** in meaning to the word **'Gathered'** given in **bold** as used in passage.

(1) Collected (2) Accumulated

(3) Rounded (4) Amassed

(5) Understood

10. Which of the following can be the most appropriate title for the story?

(1) The Skilled Doctor

(2) The Blind One Who Saw All

(3) The Rich Lady's House

(4) The Court of Mercy and Justice

(5) The Iron Lady

11. Which of the following can be said about old lady?

A. She was dumb. B. She fought for justice.

C. She was a cheat.

(1) Only A (2) Only B

(3) A and C (4) Only C

(5) A, B, and C

12. Choose the word which is most **similar** in meaning to the word **'Cured'** given in **bold** as used in passage.

(1) Healed (2) Rested

(3) Stationed (4) Lifted

(5) Sighted

13. Which one of the following aspects of the doctor's personality comes across very strongly in the story?

(1) He was arrogant. (2) He was empathetic

(3) He was rich (4) He was a cheat.

(5) He was gullible

14. Why did the lady not complain when her furniture was being stolen?

(1) She had no use for it

(2) She had no idea that it was happening even after she was cured.

(3) She always wanted to pay the doctor in kind and not cash.

(4) She intended to sell it anyway and thought the doctor was doing her a favour.

(5) Other than those given as options.

15. Choose the word which is most **opposite** in meaning to the word **'Delayed'** given in **bold** as used in passage.

(1) Slowed (2) Patented

(3) Protected (4) Absolved

(5) Expedited

Directions (16-20): *Pick out the most effective word from the given words to fill in the blank to make the sentence meaningful complete.*

16. The gentleman came to know that the villager was in .... of money.

(1) dire (2) desire

(3) demand (4) wise

(5) need

17. Two crows .... each other to see who could fly the highest.

(1) thought (2) challenged

(3) argued (4) kill

(5) wants

18. .... All the other man in Alaska, Sheena's father did not have a steady job.

(1) Well (2) Like
(3) From (4) So
(5) Similar

19. Kevin was eagerly .... for the summer holidays to begin.
(1) counted (2) waiting
(3) longed (4) thinking
(5) around

20. Suddenly there was a flash of lightening .... By thunderstorm.
(1) followed (2) knowing
(3) crossing (4) spilt
(5) taking

Directions (21-25): *Rearrange the given six sentences A, B, C, D, E and F in a proper sequence so as to form a meaningful paragraph and then answer the given questions.*

A. Immediately the crowd dispersed leaving Joja to deal with his donkey as he thought fit.
B. Many people gathered around them and started asking why he was beating the poor animal.
C. In anger and desperation Joja began to belabor it with a stick.
D. Joja was on his way to the market with a basketful of vegetables, loaded on his donkey when suddenly halfway there the donkey stopped and even after trying hard, did not budge.
E. "I can see you come from a large and bud-mouthed family," he said to his donkey with sarcasm.
F. Joja gave his donkey an admiring look and said, 'Had I known you had so many relatives to defend you I would never have hit you.

21. Which of the following should be the Sixth (Last) sentence after rearrangement?
(1) E (2) D
(3) A (4) B
(5) F

22. Which of the following should be the Second sentence after rearrangement?
(1) A (2) B
(3) F (4) D
(5) C

23. Which of the following should be the fourth sentence after rearrangement?
(1) A (2) B
(3) C (4) F
(5) D

24. Which of the following should be the first sentence after rearrangement?
(1) A (2) C
(3) B (4) F
(5) D

25. Which of the following should be the fifth sentence after rearrangement?
(1) E (2) D
(3) A (4) F
(5) C

Directions (26-30): *In each question below, a sentence with four words printed in bold type is given. These are numbered as* (*a*), (*b*) *and* (*c*) *and* (*d*). *One of these four words printed in bold may be either wrongly spelt or inappropriate in the context of the sentence. Find out the word which is wrongly spelt or inappropriate, if any. The letter of that word is your answer. If all the words printed in bold are correctly spelt and also appropriate in the text of the sentence, mark* (*e*) *i.e., 'All correct' as your answer.*

26. **Out** of the two **mules** that Roma had, one **fall** in the **well.**
(1) Out (2) Mules
(3) Fall (4) Well
(5) All correct

27. Snow white is **under threat** from her **evil** September who wants to be the **fairest** in the village.
(1) under (2) threat
(3) evil (4) fairest
(5) All correct

28. Nobody **realizes** that over two billion people **across** the **globe** now speak this **language.**
(1) realizes (2) across

(3) globe (4) language

(5) All correct

29. **Tried** of seeing the land he loves **cluttered** with trash, Thurman the turtle **decided** to take **action.**

(1) Tried (2) Cluttered

(3) Decided (4) Action

(5) All Correct

30. During his **chase** to catch a rabbit, he **sprang** into a small bush from where he came out not with the rabbit but with a huge **throne** in his **palm.**

(1) Chase (2) Sprang

(3) Thorne (4) Palm

(5) All correct

Directions (31-40): *In the given passage there are blanks, each of which has been numbered. Against each, five words are suggested, one of which fits the blank appropriately. Find out the appropriate word in each case.*

Two baby coyotes once lost their way while travelling through a forest. Tired and frightened, they walked on and on ....31......... One of them sat down and burst into tears. The other tried to ....32.........him and said a small prayer. 'Dear God, please help us find our way ....33......... home.' The God took pity and created dark clouds in the sky. "Yippee!" ....34......... the coyote who believed his prayer had been answered. The other began to cry ....35......... The rain began to fall .... and the entire forest was soon.........36......... The coyotes were swept away by the.........37......... of the water. 'This is so much fun. We'll soon be home!' shouted ....38......... joyfully. The other kept his eyes tightly shut and began to curse as they were tossed ....39......... by the swirling waters. As the waters swept past, the coyote, whose eyes were open in ....40......... looking at the world, suddenly jumped towards something. He had seen his mother who grabbed him and led him to safety. The other coyote kept his eyes shut and was swept to sea.

31. (1) that (2) till

(3) upto (4) sudden

(5) instead

32. (1) hut (2) push

(3) comfort (4) teach

(5) plead

33. (1) back (2) to

(3) from (4) early

(5) go

34. (1) happy (2) whispered

(3) feels (4) cried

(5) shouting

35. (1) tears (2) much

(3) lot (4) fervent

(5) harder

36. (1) inundate (2) flourishing

(3) clearly (4) flooded

(5) dry

37. (1) space (2) area

(3) force (4) puddle

(5) part

38. (1) him (2) one

(3) them (4) each

(5) both

39. (1) about (2) almost

(3) into (4) above

(5) softly

40. (1) death (2) wonder

(3) doubt (4) miracle

(5) shock

Reasoning Ability & Computer Aptitude

Directions (41-45): *Study the information carefully and answer the following questions:*

Eight friends P, Q, R, S, T, V, W and Y are sitting around a square table in such a way that four of them sit at four corners of the square while four sit in the middle of each of the four sides. The ones who sit at the four corners faces the centre while those who sit in the middle of the sides face outside. S sits third to the right of P. P faces the centre. Y is not an immediate neighbor of P or S. T sits third to the right of R. R does not sit in the middle of any of the sides and also R is not an immediate neighbor of Y. Only one person sits between P and V. Q is not an immediate neighbor of V.

41. If all the persons are made to sit in alphabetical order in clockwise direction, starting from P, the positions of how many (excluding P) will remain unchanged as compared to their original seating positions?
(1) None (2) One
(3) Two (4) Three
(5) Four

42. Which of the following is true regarding Y?
(1) T is not immediate neighbor of Y
(2) Y sits in the middle of one of the sides
(3) R sits second to left of Y
(4) P and V are immediate neighbors of Y
(5) None is true

43. Who amongst the following sits fourth to the left of V?
(1) Y (2) R
(3) T (4) Q
(5) W

44. What is the position of Q with respect to R?
(1) Immediately to the left
(2) Second to the left
(3) Third to the left
(4) Third to the right
(5) Immediately to the right

45. Four of the following five are alike in a certain way and so form a group. Which is the one that does not belong to the group?
(1) T (2) W
(3) V (4) S
(5) Q

Directions (46-50): *Study the information carefully and answer the following questions:*

A building has eight floors from 1 to 8 in such a way that ground floor is numbered 1, the above floor is numbered 2 and so on. The top most floor is numbered 8. Eight persons G, P, M, R, Q, A, D and C are staying each on one of these floors. A is staying on floor 6. There is a gap of three persons between G and R. C is staying on the topmost floor. Neither P nor M is staying on the floor 5. Q is staying middle of P and M. R is staying on the floor 1. M is not an immediate neighbor of G.

46. Who is staying on the floor no. 7?
(1) A (2) P
(3) D (4) R
(5) M

47. How many persons are staying between D and P?
(1) Three (2) Four
(3) Two (4) One
(5) None of these

48. Who is staying on the second floor?
(1) Q (2) M
(3) P (4) A
(5) Q or M

49. If all persons are arranged in alphabetical order such as A occupies floor 1 then who will occupy floor 5?
(1) G (2) Q
(3) R (4) M
(5) P

50. Immediate neighbors of the person who is staying in floor 3?
(1) R and P (2) A and P
(3) G and M (4) P and M
(5) D and G

Directions (51-55): *Study the following information to answer the questions.*

Twelve people are sitting in two parallel rows containing 6 people each, in such a way that there is an equal distance between adjacent persons. In row-1 P, Q, R, S, T, and U are seated and all of them are facing south. In row-2 A, B, C, D, E and F are seated and all facing North. Therefore in the given seating arrangement each member seated in a row faces another member of the outer row.

S sits third to right of Q, either S or Q sits an extreme end of line. The one who faces Q sits second to right of E. Two people sits between B and F. Neither B nor F sits at an extreme end of the line. The immediate end of line. The immediate neighbour of B faces the person who sits third to left of P, R and T are immediate neighbours of the each other. C sits second to the left of A. T does not face the immediate neighbour of D.

51. Who amongst the following sits at the extreme ends of the rows?
(1) S, D (2) Q, A
(3) U, F (4) Q, E
(5) P, D

52. Who amongst the following faces S?
(1) A (2) B
(3) C (4) D
(5) F

53. How many persons are seated between U and R?
(1) One (2) Two
(3) Three (4) Four
(5) None

54. Which of the following is true regarding T?
(1) F faces T
(2) U is an immediate neighbour of T
(3) F faces the one who is second to right of T
(4) T sits at one of the extreme ends of the line
(5) Q sits second to the right of T.

55. Four of the following five are alike in a certain way based on the given arrangement and so form a group which is the one that does not being not being to that group?
(1) A-T (2) B-T
(3) F-P (4) C-U
(5) E-Q

Directions (56-60): *Study the following arrangement carefully and answer the questions given below:*

1 R Z T 4 A 9 $ D F 1 U # B # 8 H I © X M H 3 2 P $ 5 N P 6 D

56. How many such consonants are there in the above arrangement, each of which is immediately preceded by a consonant and immediately followed by a number?
(1) None (2) One
(3) Two (4) Three
(5) More than three

57. How many such numbers are there in the above arrangement, each of which is immediately preceded by a letter but not immediately followed by a symbol?
(1) None (2) One
(3) Two (4) Three
(5) More than three

58. How many such vowels are there in the above arrangement, each of which is immediately followed by a symbol?
(1) None (2) One
(3) Two (4) Three
(5) More than three

59. Four of the following five are alike in a certain way based on their positions in the above arrangement and so form a group. Which is the one that does not belong to that group?
(1) RTA (2) 9DF
(3) ##H (4) 5PD
(5) IXH

60. Which of the following is the fourth to the left of the twelfth from the left end?
(1) % (2) $
(3) 2 (4) H
(5) None of these

Directions (61-65): *In these questions, relationship between different elements is shown in the statements. These statements are followed by two conclusions.*

Mark answer
(1) If only conclusion I follows.
(2) If only conclusion II follows.
(3) If either conclusion I or II follows.
(4) If neither conclusion I nor II follows.
(5) If both conclusions I and II follow.

61. **Statements:** $X > P > Q \geq R, X = Y, X \leq Z$
Conclusions: I. $Y > R$ II. $R > Z$

62. **Statements:** $P \geq Q, S \leq T, X = Y, X > Z$
Conclusions: I. $S = Q$ II. $X > Q$

63. **Statements:** $S \leq T, T > R, T = W$
Conclusions: I. $R < S$ II. $S < W$

64. Statements: $X = Y \leq Z > W$

Conclusions: I. $Z = X$ II. $Z > X$

65. Statements: $S > R$, $Y = X \leq Z$, $S < Y$

Conclusions: I. $Y > R$ II. $R > Z$

Directions (66-70): *In each question below are given three statements followed by four conclusions numbered I, II, III and IV. You have to take the given statements to be true even if they seem to be at variance with commonly known facts. Read all the conclusions and then decide which of the given conclusions logically follows from the given statements, disregarding commonly known facts.*

66. Statements:

(*a*) Only copies are books.
(*b*) No copies are pens.
(*c*) Only dusters are pens.

Conclusions:

I. All books are copies.
II. All pens are dusters.
III. All dusters are pens.
IV. No books are pens.

(1) All follow
(2) Only III and IV follow
(3) Only I and II follow
(4) Only I, II and IV follow
(5) None of these

67. Statements:

(*a*) Only cars are motorcycles.
(*b*) No motorcycles are bikes.
(*c*) Some bikes are scooters.

Conclusions:

I. Some bikes are cars.
II. No bikes are cars.
III. Some scooters are not motorcycles.
IV. No bikes are motorcycles.

(1) Only III and IV follow
(2) Either I or II, III and IV follow
(3) Only either I or II follows
(4) Only II, III and IV follow
(5) None of these

68. Statements:

(*a*) All pens are pencils.
(*b*) No pencil are clips.
(*c*) No pencils are dusters.

Conclusions:

I. Some dusters are not pens.
II. Some pens are not clips.
III. All pencils are pens.
IV. Some pens are pencils.

(1) Only I, II and IV follow
(2) Only IV follows
(3) All follow
(4) None follows
(5) None of these

69. Statements:

(*a*) All erasers are pens.
(*b*) All erasers are dusters.
(*c*) Some erasers are sharpeners.

Conclusions:

I. Some pens are not sharpeners.
II. Some duster are not sharpeners.
III. No dusters are pens.
IV. All pens are dusters.

(1) None follows
(2) Only I, II and III follow
(3) Only I, II and IV follow
(4) Only I and II follow
(5) None of these

70. Statements:

(*a*) Some horses are dogs.
(*b*) All dogs are cats.
(*c*) No cats are rats.

Conclusions:

I. Some horses are not cats.
II. Some dogs are rats.
III. No horses are rats.
IV. Some rats are not horses.

(1) None follows
(2) All follow
(3) Only I and II follow
(4) Only II and III follow
(5) None of these

Directions (71-75): *Study the following information to answer the given questions.*

In a certain code language

'firefighters are armymen' is written as 'tee meekee',

'courageous people are armymen' is written as 'kee loo nee tee',

'courageous being enthusiastic' is written as 'loo pee jee',

'people are enthusiastic' is written as 'kee nee pee' and

'positive people are unpleasant' is written 'nee kee dee see'.

71. What is the code for 'being'?

(1) Loo (2) Jee
(3) Kee (4) Pee
(5) None of these

72. Which of the following may be the possible code for 'unpleasant firefighters are positive'?

(1) dee see tee mee (2) dee see kee mee
(3) see tee mee kee (4) dee see jee lee
(5) None of these

73. What does 'pee' stand for?

(1) Courageous (2) Positive
(3) Armymen (4) enthusiastic
(5) None of these

74. Which of the following is represented by the code 'see jee tee pee dee kee loo'?

(1) unpleasant armymen enthusiastic being are positive firefighters
(2) unpleasant armymen enthusiastic courageous positive are being
(3) unpleasant armymen being enthusiastic are positive people
(4) unpleasant armymen being enthusiastic people
(5) None of these

75. Which of the following is the code for 'firefighters armymen belong to positive people'?

(1) tee kee cee que loo dee
(2) mee cee loo dee kee see
(3) mee tee cee loo dee kee
(4) mee tee kee cee que dee
(5) Can't be determined

Directions (76-80): *In each of the questions given below, one question and below it two statements I and II are given. You have to determine whether the data given in the statements is sufficient to answer the question or not.*

Answer (1) if the data given in statement I is sufficient to answer the question whereas data given only in statement II is not sufficient to answer the question.

Answer (2) if the data given only in statement II is sufficient to answer the question whereas data given only in statement I is not sufficient to answer the question.

Answer (3) if the data given either only in statement I or only in statement II is sufficient to answer the question.

Answer (4) if the combined data given in statement I and statement II are not sufficient to answer the question.

Answer (5) if the combined data given in statement I and statement II are necessary to answer the question.

76. In which month of the year did the construction of the building begin?

I. The construction engineer correctly remembers that the construction began before September but after May and that particular month did not have 31 days.
II. The builder correctly remembers that the construction began after February but before October and the fact that, that particular month did not have 31 days.

77. Each of A, B, C, D and E are of different heights. Who is the third tallest among these?

I. E is only shorter than B.
II. C is only taller than A.

78. How many sisters does K have?

I. M is sister of K.
II. Mother of K has three children.

79. In a row of thirty students facing north, what is the position of R from left end?

I. There are twelve students between R and Q.

II. T is tenth from right and there are sixteen students between T and R.

80. How is 'go' written in a code language?

I. In that code language 'go over there' is written as 'pa da na'

II. In that code language 'go and sit' is written as 'sa ka pa'.

81. Windows 7 is an example of a(n)

(1) application software
(2) browser
(3) Operating system
(4) Shareware
(5) None of these

82. A(n) .... program provides access to Web resources.

(1) Web (2) ISP
(3) Browser (4) URL
(5) None of these

83. Which of the following is not a logic gate?

(1) AND (2) NOR
(3) NAND (4) NAT
(5) None of these

84. A modem could be attached to which port?

(1) Parallel port
(2) ASYNA port
(3) Keyboard connector
(4) Video port
(5) None of these

85. The binary system uses powers of

(1) 2 (2) 10
(3) 8 (4) 16
(5) None of these

86. Expand RDBMS.

(1) Relative Database Management System
(2) Rational Database Minimize System
(3) Relational Database Management System
(4) Relational Database Maximize System
(5) None of these

87. .... is a set of instructions.

(1) Hardware (2) Code
(3) Language (4) Program
(5) All of these

88. Which memory is nonvolatile and may be written only once?

(1) RAM (2) EE-ROM
(3) RAM (4) PROM
(5) None of these

89. Main storage is also called

(1) accumulator (2) control unit
(3) register unit (4) memory
(5) None of these

90. In which language is a source program written?

(1) English (2) Symbolic
(3) High-level (4) Machine
(5) None of these

Quantitative Aptitude

Directions (91-92): *Which number comes in the place of the question mark* (?)?

91. 1, 27, 125, 343, ?

(1) 512 (2) 1000
(3) 729 (4) 216
(5) 1024

92. 5, 25, 61, 113, ?

(1) 144 (2) 181
(3) 165 (4) 200
(5) 245

93. A and B can complete a piece of work in 80 and 120 days respectively. They together start the work but A left after 20 days. After another 12 days C joined B and now they complete the work in 28 more days. In how many days C can complete the work, working alone?

(1) 100 days (2) 112 days
(3) 120 days (4) 126 days
(5) None of these

94. 33.33% of 150 + 66.66% of 180 = ?% of 1700

(1) 30 (2) 25

(3) 20 (4) 10
(5) 15

95. The area of a square is the same as that of a circle. What is the ratio of the side of the square to the radius of the circle?
(1) $1 : \pi$ (2) $1 : \sqrt{\neq}$
(3) $\sqrt{\neq} : 1$ (4) $\pi^2 : 1$
(5) None of the above

96. 5.88% of 85 + 5% of 200 = ?
(1) 13 (2) 15
(3) 16 (4) 17
(5) 18

97. Present age of a father is 3 times the present age of his son. 4 years later father's age is 13 more than 2 times of his son's age. What is present age of father?
(1) 54 (2) 53
(3) 51 (4) 63
(5) 52

98. A person bought an article on 40% discount and sold it at 50% more than the marked price. What profit did he get?
(1) 250% (2) 150%
(3) 350% (4) 200%
(5) None of these

99. 25% of 400 + 33.33% of 30 = ?
(1) 110 (2) 120
(3) 130 (4) 140
(5) 150

100. Which number comes in the place of the question mark (?)
11, 44, 99, 176, ?
(1) 274 (2) 266
(3) 275 (4) 265
(5) 300

101. Find SI if P = Rs. 1000, R = 20% per annum and duration is 4 years
(1) Rs. 400 (2) Rs. 600
(3) Rs. 800 (4) Rs. 850
(5) None of these

102. In a right angled triangle, two sides are of the same length. Which of the options is one of the angles of that triangle?
(1) 30 (2) 45
(3) 60 (4) 75
(5) None of the above

103. 7.69% of 130 + 6.66% of 150 = ?
(1) 20 (2) 21
(3) 22 (4) 23
(5) 24

104. The price of a book is first increased by 10% and then decreased by 5%, then the net change in the price will be
(1) 4.2% increase (2) 4.5% increase
(3) 4.2% decrease (4) 4.5% decrease
(5) None of these

105. 11.11% of 90 + 8.33% of 120 = ?
(1) 20 (2) 30
(3) 40 (4) 50
(5) 60

106. 20% of 200 + 7.14% of 140 = ?
(1) 30 (2) 40
(3) 50 (4) 60
(5) 70

107. A boat's speed with the current is 15 kmph and the boat's speed against the current is 5 kmph. What is the speed of the current?
(1) 15 kmph (2) 10 kmph
(3) 5 kmph (4) 20 kmph
(5) None of the above

108. An express train travelled at an average speed of 75 km/h stopping for 5 min every 125 km. How long did it take to reach its destination 375 km from the starting point?
(1) 6 h 30 min (2) 4 h 45 min
(3) 3 h 15 min (4) 5 h 10 min
(5) None of these

109. 16.66% of 600 + 9.09% of 110 = ?
(1) 110 (2) 120
(3) 130 (4) 140
(5) 150

110. Ramesh is thrice as old as Kishore and Nirmal is half the age of Ramesh. If the sum of their ages is 99, then what is the age of Nirmal?
(1) 18 (2) 27
(3) 20 (4) 35
(5) None of these

111. 3.44% of 290 + 20% of 580 = ?% of 630

(1) 60 (2) 50
(3) 40 (4) 30
(5) 20

112. What is the number of words formed from the letters of the word 'JOKE' So that the vowels and consonants alternate?

(1) 4 (2) 8
(3) 12 (4) 18
(5) None of these

Directions (113-117): *Study the following bar-graph and pie-chart carefully to answer the questions given below.*

Number of participants in an event from six different regions.

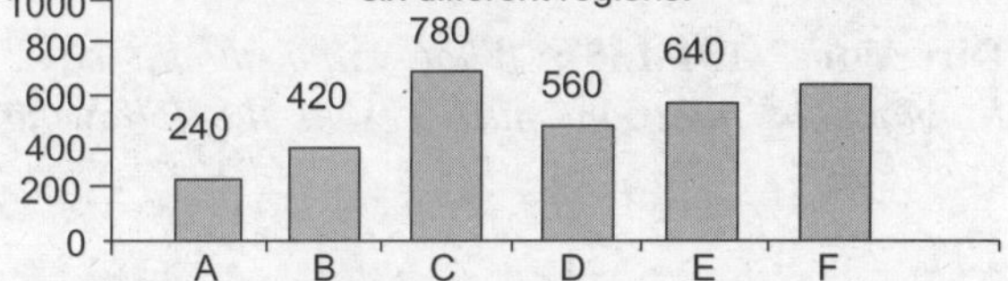

Number of males who participated different regions.

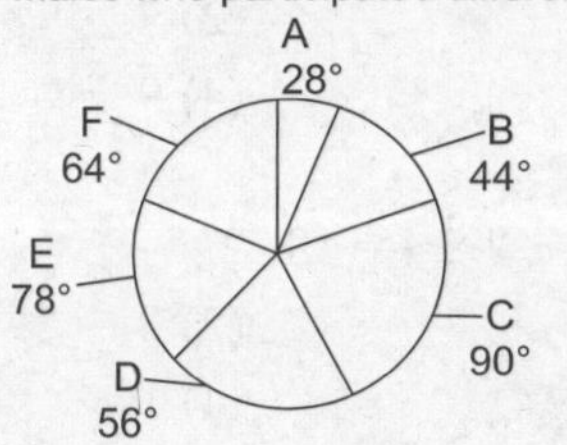

Total number of males who participated = 2,160

113. How many more males have participated from E than from B?

(1) 186 (2) 204
(3) 224 (4) 236
(5) None of these

114. How many females have participated from A and C together?

(1) 236 (2) 252
(3) 274 (4) 312
(5) None of these

115. From which region, maximum number of females participated?

(1) B (2) C
(3) D (4) E
(5) None of these

116. From how many regions, is the number of females participated less than 60% of the respective male participants?

(1) 1 (2) 2
(3) 3 (4) 4
(5) None of these

117. What is the ratio of the percentage of females among the persons who participated from B to the percentage from B to the percentage of females who participated from B to the percentage of females among the persons who participated from D?

(1) 3 : 4 (2) 6 : 7
(3) 13 : 14 (4) 15 : 19
(5) None of these

118. 3 pipes when opened for 3 hours can fill 3 buckets. How many buckets can 2 pipes open for 2 hours approximately fill?

(1) 2/3 buckets (2) 2 buckets
(3) 1 bucket (4) 4/3 buckets
(5) None of the above.

119. What is the LCM of the following fractions? 2/3, 4/7, 1/4

(1) 1 (2) 2
(3) 4 (4) 7
(5) 8

120. Gopi started a business and invested Rs. 48000 at the start of it. Raghav joined him after 2 months and invested Rs. 42000. Two years after Gopi started the business, there was a profit of Rs. 41520. What is Raghav's share of the profit?

(1) Rs. 18480 (2) Rs. 23040
(3) Rs. 14840 (4) Rs. 15600
(5) Rs. 19600

121. 12.5% of 64 + 11.11% of 90 = ?

(1) 18 (2) 19
(3) 20 (4) 22
(5) 24

122. 5.26% of 95 + 5.88% of 170 = ?

(1) 16 (2) 15
(3) 14 (4) 13
(5) 17

123. Which number comes in the place of the question mark (?)?

2, 6, 12, 20, 30, ?

(1) 50 (2) 44

(3) 45 (4) 42

(5) 55

124. Which number comes in the place of the question mark (?)?

16, 25, 36, 49, 64, ?

(1) 121 (2) 100

(3) 81 (4) 144

(5) 196

125. A person borrowed Rs. 2000 at 5% per annum simple interest and immediately lent it at 6% per annum simple interest. At the end of 21/2 yr he collected the amount and settled his loan. What was his profit?

(1) Rs. 45 (2) Rs. 40

(3) Rs. 50 (4) Rs. 56

(5) None of these

Directions (126-130): *There are total five departments in a company. There are total 90 employees in Finance department which is 25% of total employees in the company. 2/9 of the total employees of the company are working in HR department. Employees working in Sales department is 25% more than that in HR department. Ratio between employees working in Security and Housing department is 4 : 5.*

126. Find number of employees working in HR department is what percent more than number of employees working in Security department?

(1) 250% (2) 200%

(3) 150% (4) 100%

(5) 50%

127. Find the average number of employees working in Sales, Finance and Housing department?

(1) 60 (2) 70

(3) 80 (4) 90

(5) 100

128. Number of employees in Housing department is how much more than number of employees in Security department?

(1) 10 (2) 20

(3) 30 (4) 40

(5) 50

129. In Security department, 40% are female employees then find total male employees working in Security department?

(1) 16 (2) 40

(3) 32 (4) 8

(5) 24

130. Ratio between total number of male and female employees in HR department is 2 : 3. Find total number of female employees working in HR department?

(1) 32 (2) 48

(3) 64 (4) 40

(5) 56

Directions (131-135): *What value should come in place of question mark* **(?)** *in the following questions?*

131. $?^2 = 4^2 + 8^2 - 31$

(1) 6 (2) 7

(3) 8 (4) 9

(5) 10

132. $13 \times 6 + ? \times 4 = 18 \times 7$

(1) 6 (2) 8

(3) 10 (4) 12

(5) 14

133. 40% of ? = 25% of 320 + 75% of 160

(1) 500 (2) 400

(3) 300 (4) 200

(5) 100

134. $11^2 + 6^2 = ? + 37$

(1) 130 (2) 110

(3) 120 (4) 140

(5) 150

135. $(360/?) = 12 \times 6 - 3^3$

(1) 9 (2) 5

(3) 6 (4) 7

(5) 8

Directions (136-140): *Table given below shows marks obtained by four students in four different subjects in an exam. Study the data carefully and answer the following questions.*

Subjects / Students	English	Hindi	Science	Maths
Paul	65	60	80	65
Aditya	75	75	60	75
Neeraj	85	55	95	85
Sandy	60	60	65	60

136. Marks scored by Sandy in English and Maths together is what percent of the Marks scored by Aditya and Neeraj in English together?
(1) 25% (2) 50%
(3) 75% (4) 100%
(5) 125%

137. Find the ratio of total marks scored by all four students together in Hindi to total marks scored by all four students together in Science?
(1) 5 : 6 (2) 57 : 50
(3) 1 : 1 (4) 20 : 19
(5) 6 : 5

138. Total marks scored by Paul are how much more/less than total marks scored by Neeraj?
(1) 70 (2) 60
(3) 40 (4) 50
(5) 80

139. Find the average of the marks scored by Aditya in English, Hindi and Science together?
(1) 65 (2) 85
(3) 80 (4) 75
(5) 70

140. If maximum marks for each subject are 100 then find what percentage of total marks is obtained by Sandy?
(1) 64.25% (2) 61.25%
(3) 67.25% (4) 70.25%
(5) 73.25%

General Awareness

141. In which country did the ISSF Junior World Championships 2023 take place?
(1) Russia (2) China
(3) South Korea (4) Japan
(5) India

142. Where does JRD Tata Sports Complex Stadium?
(1) Lucknow (2) Ranchi
(3) Kolkata (4) Patna
(5) Jamshedpur

143. Where is the headquarters of the Intergovernmental Panel on Climate Change (IPCC) located?
(1) New Delhi (2) France
(3) Geneva (4) New York
(5) London

144. What is the total allocation received by PM-JAY under the Union Budget 2023?
(1) Rs. 7200 crores (2) Rs. 4200 crores
(3) Rs. 5600 crores (4) Rs. 2700 crores
(5) Rs. 7020 crores

145. An .... is used by startups to bypass the rigorous and regulated capital-raising process required by venture capitalists or banks.
(1) Ending Coin Offering
(2) Initial Coin Offering
(3) Banking Coin Offering
(4) External Coin Offering
(5) Economy Coin Offering

146. The .... is where overnight (one day) loans can be availed by banks to meet liquidity.
(1) Call Money (2) Notice Money
(3) Short Money (4) Half Money
(5) Soft Money

147. Name the organisation, which regulates microfinance given by NBFC?
(1) RBI (2) SEBI
(3) NABARD (4) SIDBI
(5) IRDAI

148. What is the name of the newly inaugurated International Exhibition-cum-Convention Centre in Delhi?

(1) Pragati Maidan (2) Bharat Mandapam
(3) Bharat Puram (4) Atal Complex
(5) None of these

149. CAGR is the mean annual growth rate of an investment over a specified period of time longer than one year. CAGR stands for-
(1) Compound Annual General Rate
(2) Compound Annual Growth Rate
(3) Compound Annual Growth Ratio
(4) Cancel Annual Growth Rate
(5) Compound Assembly Growth Rate

150. Dr Virendra Kumar is the member of Lok Sabha. His Constituency is
(1) Darbhanga, Bihar
(2) Allahabad, UttarPradesh
(3) Tikamgarh, MadhyaPradesh
(4) Haridwar, Uttarakhand
(5) Jaipur, Rajasthan

151. Rashtriya Chemicals and Fertilizers Limited (RCF) is one of the most revered public sector undertakings in India. Where is the head office of Rashtriya Chemicals and Fertilizers Limited?
(1) Pune (2) New Delhi
(3) Mumbai (4) Chennai
(5) Kolkata

152. An ELSS is a diversified equity mutual fund which has a majority of the corpus invested in equities. What is the meaning of "L" in ELSS?
(1) Least (2) Limited
(3) Lose (4) Level
(5) Linked

153. Credit card facility has not given by which institution?
(1) Payment Banks
(2) Nationalised Banks
(3) Public Sector Banks
(4) Regional Rural Banks
(5) Foreign Banks

154. Which Indian city recently joined the World Cities Culture Forum (WCCF)?
(1) Bengaluru (2) Bhopal
(3) Imphal (4) Patna
(5) Agra

155. National Institute of Securities Markets (NISM) is a public trust, established by
(1) NABARD (2) SEBI
(3) RBI (4) SIDBI
(5) IRDAI

156. .... is an accounting term that refers to the process of allocating the cost of an intangible asset or reduction in amount of loan over a period of time.
(1) Liability (2) Inflation
(3) Depreciation (4) NPA
(5) Amortization

157. The government stated that post the abolition of the FIPB, ministries will have to decide on FDI proposals within .... of the application and any rejection will need concurrence of the DIPP.
(1) 30 days (2) 70 days
(3) 40 days (4) 60 days
(5) 50 days

158. CRISIL pioneered the first corporate sector rating in 1988. It is what type of a company?
(1) Lender (2) Geographical
(3) Analytical (4) Insurance
(5) None of the given options is true

159. Multilateral Investment Guarantee Agency (MIGA) is an international financial institution which offers political risk insurance and credit enhancement guarantees. Where is the head office of MIGA?
(1) Vienna (2) Washington DC
(3) Paris (4) London
(5) New York

160. Private sector lender HDFC Bank Ltd has been declared a domestic-systemically important bank (D-SIB), the Reserve Bank of India (RBI). On what basis D-SIB tag is given to banks?
(1) Banks with assets that exceed 2% of GDP will be considered part of this class of lenders
(2) Banks with assets that exceed 5% of GDP

will be considered part of this class of lenders

(3) Banks with assets that exceed 15% of GDP will be considered part of this class of lenders

(4) Banks with assets that exceed 7% of GDP will be considered part of this class of lenders

(5) Banks with assets that exceed 10% of GDP will be considered part of this class of lenders

161. The MPC of India is a committee of the Reserve Bank of India that is responsible for fixing the benchmark interest rate in India. What is the meaning of "P" in MPC?

(1) Policy (2) Production
(3) Purchase (4) Product
(5) Primary

162. Paris Agreement (PACC) is related to-

(1) Global Warming (2) Climate Change
(3) Pollution (4) Fuel Consumption
(5) Carbon Copy

163. Loan disbursed under MUDRA yojna is insured by-

(1) SEBI (2) Banking Lokpal
(3) CGTMSE (4) RBI
(5) DICGC

164. According to SBI Research economists, when is India projected to become the third-largest economy in the world?

(1) FY 27 (2) FY 26
(3) FY 25 (4) FY 28
(5) None of these

165. .... is a specific division of banking related to the creation of capital for other companies, governments and other entities.

(1) Narrow Banking
(2) Current Banking
(3) Universal Banking
(4) Retail Banking
(5) Investment banking

166. In which of the following state, the Achanakmar Wildlife Sanctuary situated?

(1) Rajasthan (2) Kerala
(3) West Bengal (4) Chhattisgarh
(5) Odisha

167. A .... is a bank certificate issued in more than one country for shares in a foreign company.

(1) Gross national product (GNP)
(2) Global Depositary Receipt (GDR)
(3) Gross domestic product (GDP)
(4) Society for Worldwide Interbank Financial Telecommunication (SWIFT)
(5) Eurobond

168. .... is a secure messaging standard developed to serve as a platform for intra-bank and inter-bank applications.

(1) Structured Financial Messaging System (SFMS)
(2) Centralized Funds Management Systems (CFMS)
(3) Society for Worldwide Interbank Financial Telecommunication (SWIFT)
(4) Institute for Development & Research in Banking Technology (IDRBT)
(5) Electronic Funds Transfer (EFT)

169. Which international alliance was recently launched by India to conserve major big cat species on Earth?

(1) International Big Cat Alliance (IBCA)
(2) International Cheetah Alliance (ICA)
(3) International Panther Protection Alliance (IPPA)
(4) World Jaguar Consortium (WJC)
(5) None of these

170. A .... is the risk of default on a debt that may arise from a borrower failing to make required payments.

(1) current risk (2) export risk
(3) operational risk (4) market risk
(5) credit risk

171. The .... risk is the risk that an investment's value will change due to a change in the absolute level of interest rates, in the spread between two rates, in the shape of the yield curve.

(1) current risk (2) interest risk

(3) operational risk (4) market risk
(5) credit risk

172. Surya Pratap Shukla is present governor of which state?
(1) Arunachal Pradesh
(2) Maharashtra
(3) Uttar Pradesh
(4) Himachal Pradesh
(5) Jharkhand

173. Balphakram National Park is home to wide species of plants and animals and is located in the midst of the Garo Hills in-
(1) Meghalaya
(2) Mizoram
(3) Arunachal Pradesh
(4) Manipur
(5) Tripura

174. Vienna is the capital and largest city of
(1) Canada (2) Australia
(3) Yemen (4) Russia
(5) Austria

175. How long will the ACROSS scheme be implemented for in the next finance cycle?
(1) 5 (2) 3
(3) 8 (4) 7
(5) 10

176. LAF is a monetary policy tool which allows banks to borrow money through repurchase agreements or repos. What is the meaning of "L" in LAF?
(1) Lose (2) Lesson
(3) Lease (4) Labour
(5) Liquidity

177. FATF is an inter-governmental body established in 1989 by the Ministers of its Member jurisdictions. What is the meaning of "A" in FATF?
(1) Agriculture (2) Assets
(3) Association (4) Action
(5) Assembly

178. The Ukai Dam is the largest reservoir in which state?
(1) Rajasthan (2) Maharashtra
(3) Gujarat (4) Punjab
(5) Kerala

179. Who is a leading Indian economist and Vice Chairman of NITI Aayog?
(1) Narendra Modi (2) Suman Bery
(3) Bibek Debroy (4) Dr Rajeev Kumar
(5) V K Saraswat

180. How many women members were nominated to the panel of Vice-Chairpersons in Rajya Sabha for the first time?
(1) 1 (2) 2
(3) 3 (4) 4
(5) 5

181. Dhirubhai Ambani Solar Park is a 40-megawatt (MW AC) photovoltaic power station in-
(1) Rajasthan (2) Gujarat
(3) Maharashtra (4) Kerala
(5) West Bengal

182. "Hand-in-Hand" is the annual exercise between-
(1) Japan and Russia
(2) India and China
(3) USA and Sri Lanka
(4) France and India
(5) India and Japan

183. Who has been appointed as the new Chief Justice of Bombay High Court?
(1) Justice Ragini Singh
(2) Justice Madan Dhingra
(3) Justice D K Upadhyay
(4) Justice M K Sinha
(5) None of these

184. Sanjeev Stalin is related to which game?
(1) Cricket (2) Football
(3) Tennis (4) Archery
(5) Wrestling

185. NACH is a centralised system, launched with an aim to consolidate multiple ECS systems running across the country and provides a framework for the harmonization of standard & practices and removes local barriers/inhibitors. What is the meaning of "H" in

NACH?

(1) House (2) Home
(3) Handle (4) Host
(5) Honest

186. Which among the following Indian States has became first Indian state to call online attention adjournment motions and proposals?

(1) Kerala (2) Maharashtra
(3) Gujarat (4) Rajasthan
(5) Haryana

187. Bharatiya Reserve bank Note Mudran press located in Salboni, West Bengal and another one in-

(1) Hoshangabad (2) Mysore
(3) Nashik (4) Mumbai
(5) Noida

188. .... of a bank is the ratio of deposits in current and saving accounts to total deposits.

(1) RASA ratio (2) FARA ratio
(3) SADA ratio (4) NASA ratio
(5) CASA ratio

189. What percentage of stake did Mahindra & Mahindra acquire in RBL Bank?

(1) 3.53% (2) 5.2%
(3) 9.3% (4) 16%
(5) 6.7%

190. Who was Lekh Tandon?

(1) Indian filmmaker and actor
(2) Indian Writer and Dancer
(3) Indian Composer and Doctor
(4) Indian Producer and Musician
(5) None of the given options is true

Answers With Explanations

1. (2) 'Will or Shall' are followed by first form of verb. So 'generated' should be replaced by 'generate'.
2. (1)
3. (3) 'these ambiguity' is incorrect. It should be 'these ambiguities'.
4. (2)
5. (3)
6. (4)
7. (3)
8. (2)
9. (5)
10. (2)
11. (2)
12. (1) Cured means to recover from illness.
13. (4)
14. (5)
15. (5) Delayed means 'was late'. Its opposite is 'expedited'.
16. (5)
17. (2)
18. (2)
19. (2)
20. (1)
21. (3)
22. (5)
23. (4)
24. (5)
25. (1)
26. (3) The sentence is in the past tense. So 'fall' should be replaced by 'fell'.
27. (4)
28. (3)
29. (1)
30. (3) The word thorn is spelt incorrectly.
31. (2)
32. (3) One was weeping comfort is the appropriate word.
33. (a) back is the correct option.
34. (4) Sentences are in past tense.
35. (5)
36. (4)
37. (3)
38. (2)
39. (1)
40. (2)

For questions (41-45):

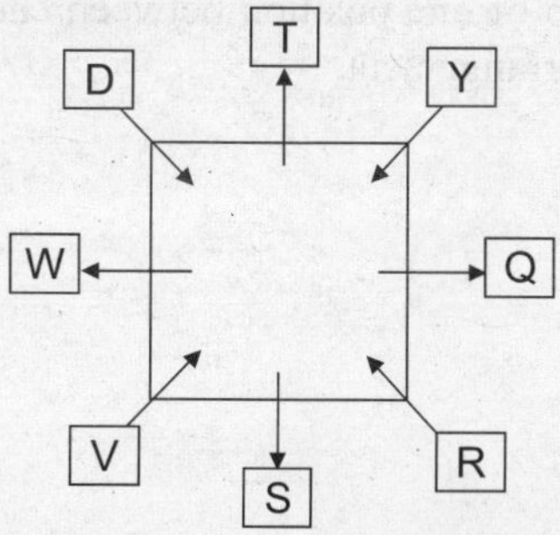

41. (1)
42. (3)
43. (1)
44. (5)
45. (3)

For questions (46-50):

Floor No.	Person
8	C
7	D
6	A
5	G
4	P
3	Q
2	M
1	R

46. (3)
47. (3)
48. (2)
49. (4)
50. (4)

For questions (51-55):

P	U	S	T	R	Q
C	F	A	E	B	D

51. (5)
52. (1)
53. (2)
54. (3)
55. (5)
56. (5) There are 4 such combinations – ZT4, DF1, MH3, NP6.
57. (5) There are 4 such combinations – T4A, F1U, H32, P6D
58. (3) There are 2 such combinations – U#, I©.
59. (2) Except 9DF, every other combination has a gap of one position between each letter in the arrangement.
60. (2)
61. (1)
62. (4)
63. (4)
64. (3)
65. (1)
66. (4)

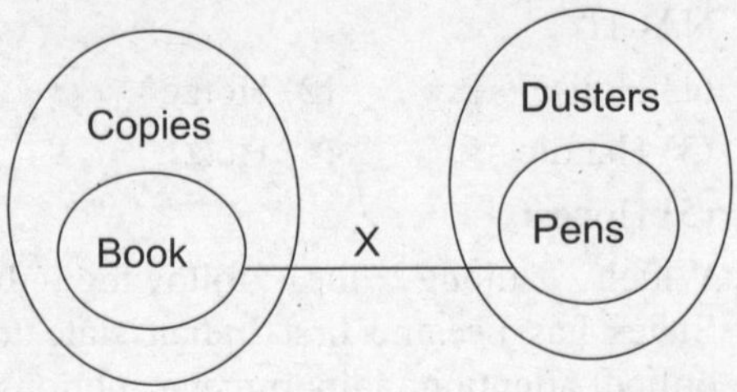

67. (2)

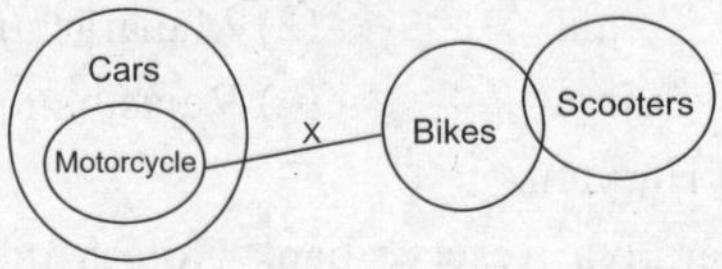

68. (1)

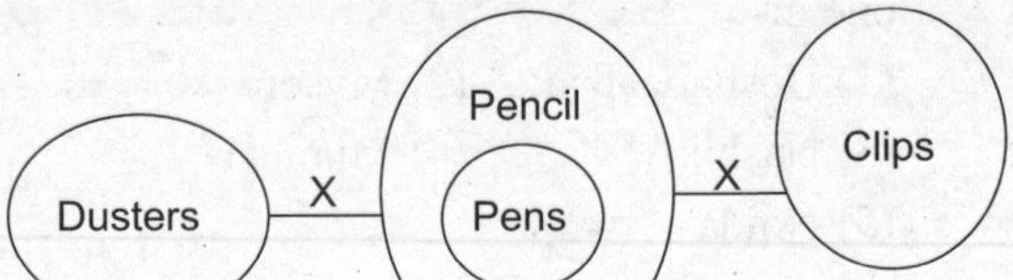

69. (1)

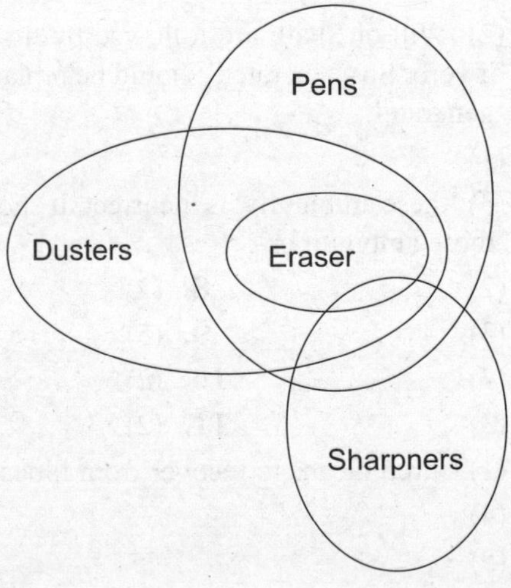

70. (1)

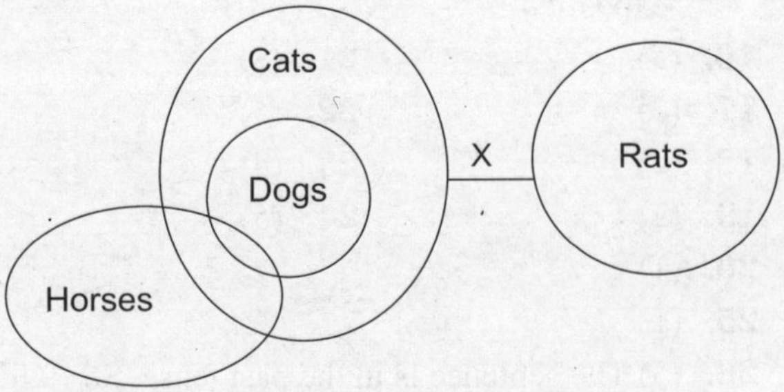

For questions (71-75):

Are	kee
Armymen	tee
Firefighters	mee
Enthusiastic	pee
People	nee
Courageous	loo
Being	jee
positive/unpleasant	dee/see

71. (2)
72. (2)
73. (4)
74. (2)
75. (5)

For questions (76-80):

76. (1) Only I is sufficient.
77. (5) D is third tallest among these.
78. (4) It cannot be determined from both the statements that how many sisters K have.
79. (2)
80. (5) Code for go is 'pa'.
81. (3)
82. (3)
83. (4)
84. (1)
85. (1)
86. (3)
87. (3)
88. (4)
89. (4)
90. (3)
91. (3) $1^3 = 1$
$3^3 = 27$
$5^3 = 125$
$7^3 = 343$
$9^3 = 729$
92. (2) $1^2 + 2^2 = 5$
$3^2 + 4^2 = 25$
$5^2 + 6^2 = 61$
$7^2 + 8^2 = 113$
$9^2 + 10^2 = 181$
93. (2) A did the work for 20 days.
B did the work for $(20 + 12 + 38) = 60$ days
C did the work for 28 days.
Let C alone can complete the work in x days.
Fraction of work did by A + Fraction of work did by B + Fraction of work did by C = 1
$20/80 + 60/120 + 28/x = 1$
$x = 28 \times 4 = 112$ days
C alone can complete the work in 112 days
94. (4)
95. (3)
96. (2)
97. (3) Let the present age of son be x.
Hence father's age will be $3x$.
4 years later, $(x + 4) \times 2 + 13 = 3x + 4$
$x = 17$ and $3x = 51$
98. (2) Let the marked price be Rs. 100.
Then CP = 100 – 40 = Rs. 60
SP = 100 + 50 = Rs. 150
Profit = 150 – 60 = 90
Profit% = 90/60 × 100 =150%
99. (1)
100. (3) $1 \times 11 = 11$
$2 \times 22 = 44$
$3 \times 33 = 99$
$4 \times 44 = 176$
$5 \times 55 = 275$
101. (3) S.I = PRT/100
= (1000 × 20 × 4)/100
= Rs. 800
102. (2) If two sides of the right angled triangle are equal, it is a right angled isosceles triangle. So, the angles of the triangle are 45°, 45° and 90°.
103. (1)
104. (2) Let the original price be Rs. 100.
New final price = 95% of (110% of Rs. 100)
= Rs. 95/100 × 110/100 × 100 = Rs. 104.5
∴ Increase in price = 4.5%
105. (1)
106. (3)
107. (3) Let the speed of the boat be 'x' and the speed of the river be 'y'.
So, $x - y = 5$ and $x + y = 15$
From both equations,
$2x = 20$

$x = 10$

Hence $y = 5$ kmph

Speed of the current = 5 kmph

108. (4) Time taken to cover 375 km

= (375/75)h = 5 h

Number of stoppages = 375/125 – 1 = 2

Total time to stoppages = (5 × 2) min = 10 min

Hence, total time taken = 5 h 10 min

109. (1)

110. (2) Let the age of Kishore be x.

Given that Ramesh is thrice as old as Kishore.

So, the age of Ramesh = $3x$

Also, Kishore is half the age of Ramesh.

So, age of Kishore = $3x/2 = 1.5x$

The sum of their ages = $99 = x + 3x + 1.5x$

Hence, $x = 99/5.5 = 18$

So, the age of Nirmal = $1.5x = 27$

111. (5)

112. (2) Word name: 'JOKE' Vowels: O, E Consonants: J, K

∴ Possible arrangement beginning with consonant: JOKE, KOJE, JEKO, KEJO = 4

Numbers beginning with vowel: OJEK, OKEJ, EJOK, EKOJ = 4 Numbers

Required number = 4 + 4 = 8 numbers

113. (2) Required number of males

= (78° – 44°)/(360°) × 2160

= 34/360 × 2160

= 34 × 6 = 204

114. (4) Total number of females participated from A and C together = 72 + 240 = 312

115. (5)

116. (4)

117. (3)

118. (4)

119. (3) LCM of fractions = LCM of the numerators/ HCF of the denominators.

LCM of 2, 4 and 1 is 4

HCF of 3, 7 and 4 is 1

Hence, the LCM of the given fractions is 4/1 = 4

120. (1)

121. (1)

122. (2)

123. (4) 2 + 4 = 6

6 + 6 = 12

12 + 8 = 20

20 + 10 = 30

30 + 12 = 2

124. (3) $4^2 = 16$

$5^2 = 25$

$6^2 = 36$

$7^2 = 49$

$8^2 = 64$

$9^2 = 81$

125. (3) SI = Rs. (2000 × 5/2 × 5 × 1/100)= Rs. 250

For lent money,

SI = Rs. (2000 × 5/2 × 6 × 1/100) = Rs. 300

His profit = Rs. (300 – 250) = Rs. 50

For questions (126-130):

Sales	Finance	HR	Security	Housing	Total
100	90	80	40	50	360

126. (4)

127. (3)

128. (1)

129. (5)

130. (2)

131. (2) $?^2 = 4^2 + 8^2 - 31$

$?^2 = 16 + 64 - 31 = 80 - 31 = 49$

$? = 7$

132. (4) 13 × 6 + ? × 4 = 18 × 7

78 + ? × 4 = 126

? = 12

133. (1) 40% ? = 25% of 320 + 75% of 160

2/5 × ? = 80 + 120

? = 200 ×5/2 = 500

134. (3) $11^2 + 6^2 = ? + 37$

121 + 36 – 37 = ?

? = 120

135. (5)

136. (3)

137. (1)

138. (4) Total marks scored by Paul

= 65 + 60 + 80 + 65 = 270

Total marks scored by Neeraj

= 85 + 55 + 95 + 85 = 320

Required difference = 320 – 270 = 50

139. (5)
140. (2)
141. (3)
142. (5)
143. (3)
144. (1)
145. (2)

146. (1) The call money market (CMM) the market where overnight (one day) loans can be availed by banks to meet liquidity.

147. (1) NBFC & MFI in India are regulated by the Reserve Bank of India (RBI) within the framework of the RBI Act, 1934.

148. (2) The Prime Minister of India, Narendra Modi, inaugurated the International Exhibition-cum-Convention Centre (IECC) named 'Bharat Mandapam' at the revamped Pragati Maidan complex in Delhi.

149. (2) Compound Annual Growth Rate - CAGR.

150. (3) Dr Virendra Kumar's Constituency is in Tikamgarh, Madhya Pradesh.

151. (3) Rashtriya Chemicals and Fertilizers Limited (RCF) is a Mini Ratna company. Its headquarter located in Mumbai.

152. (5) Equity Linked Savings Scheme – ELSS.

153. (1) Credit card facility has not given by Payment Banks.

154. (1) Bengaluru, the capital of Karnataka, became the first Indian city to join the World Cities Culture Forum (WCCF).

155. (2) National Institute of Securities Markets (NISM) established by the Securities and Exchange Board of India (SEBI).

156. (5)

157. (4)

158. (3) CRISIL is a analytical company providing ratings, research, and risk and policy advisory services.

159. (2) The Head Office of MIGA is in Washington DC, USA.

160. (1)

161. (1) Monetary Policy Committee – MPC

162. (2)

163. (3) Credit Guarantee Fund Trust for Micro and Small Enterprises – CGTMSE.

164. (4) SBI Research economists stated that India will become the third-largest economy by FY28, two years earlier than previously projected.

165. (5)

166. (4) It is an Indian sanctuary in Mungeli district, Chhattisgarh State.

167. (2) Global Depository Receipt – GDR

168. (1) Structured Financial Messaging System – SFMS

169. (1)
170. (5)
171. (2)
172. (4)

173. (1) Balphakram National Park is home to wide species of plants and animals and is located in the midst of the Garo Hills in Meghalaya.

174. (5)

175. (1) The ACROSS scheme is approved for continuation in the next finance cycle of five years, *i.e.*, from 2021 to 2026.

176. (5) Liquidity Adjustment Facility – LAF

177. (4) Financial Action Task Force – FATF

178. (3) The Ukai Dam, constructed across the Tapti River, is the largest reservoir in Gujarat.

179. (2)

180. (4) Four women members were nominated to the panel of Vice-Chairpersons in Rajya Sabha, constituting 50% of the total members.

181. (1)
182. (2)
183. (3)
184. (2)

185. (1) National Automated Clearing House – NACH

186. (4)

187. (2)

188. (5)

189. (1)

190. (1)

IBPS Clerk Mains

Practice Set – 7

General English

Directions (1-8): *Read the following passage carefully and answer the questions given below it.*

One of the major concerns of many European physicians today is the alarming increase in the incidence of suicides across the Continent. Recent studies indicate that more Europeans take their own lives than they die on the highways. While the traditionally high suicide rates in Austria, Hungary, Switzerland and Scandinavia have remained relatively stable, the low rates in Latin and Catholic countries have begun to grow dramatically in the last 20 years. Among some age groups in Ireland, the increase is to the order of 100 percent. In many parts of Europe, suicide has long been common among older people. In parts of Hungary, which holds Europe's record for suicides with a rate of 41 a year per one lakh people, the rate among the elderly is 300. In France it is 114, while the overall rate is 20.8. By comparison the overall suicide rate in the United States is 12.3. In Japan, it is 17.3.

The greatest concern of European specialists is the increasing number of young people who take their own lives. Since 1960s the suicide rate among young French men between the ages of 15 and 29 has tripled. A third of Danish men who die between the ages of 25 and 34 kill themselves.

Experts see the transformation of European society as the key to the recent increases in European suicides. The modernization of the workforce, the increasing social and geographical mobility and the consequent breakdown of old family structures and support networks all play a role. In a comparative study of suicide in 20 European countries over two decades, it was found that factors such as divorce, unemployment, the number of working women in a society, the number of children and the prevalence of religion, combined with the presence of violent crimes and alcohol abuse, are useful in predicting the rise and fall of suicide rates. As European Southern tier becomes more prosperous, families are becoming smaller, relationship less stable and suicides are increasing. In Eastern Europe, where change is coming even faster, suicide rates are expected to flare up for a rather long period of time.

As traditional family support systems have weakened in the U. S., Canada and Britain, State and community services have worked to fill the gap with counseling and hotlines. But there has been a setback to this very recently. More and more people are beginning to consider the way they die as an equally personal choice. This has been fuelled by a whole new range of "how-to-do-it" books hitting the market, a few of them even topping the best-seller list. The authors usually justify their works as human aids for the aged and infirm. Suicide is portrayed essentially as self-inflicted euthanasia, itself a hotly debated issue. As a consequence of this, an increasing number of people in Europe are now directly confronting their own mortality.

1. What, according to the passage, has exactly been the greatest concern of European specialists?

(1) Increase in the number of young people committing suicide

(2) Increase in the number of Danish men killing themselves

(3) Increase in the number of older people committing suicide

(4) Increase in the number of French people killing themselves

(5) None of these

2. Which of the following has not been mentioned in the passage as a reason for the gradual escalation in European suicide rate?

(1) The breakdown of traditional family structures

(2) The migration of people from one place to another

(3) The growing unemployment problem

(4) The mobility of people on the social scale

(5) None of these

3. According to the passage, the finding of the comparative study of suicide in 20 countries was that

(1) divorce and unemployment led to violent crimes and alcoholic abuse.

(2) suicide rate could be predicted on the basis of certain socio-cultural factors.

(3) violent crimes and alcohol abuse are the main reasons for suicides.

(4) the prevalence of religion was combined with the presence of violent crimes and alcohol abuse.

(5) suicide rates may rise or fall and are difficult to predict.

4. What has been mentioned in the passage as regards the suicide rate in Switzerland?

(1) The increase in the suicide rate in Switzerland has been higher than that of other European countries.

(2) There has not been any appreciable change in the suicide rate in Switzerland over the few years.

(3) Switzerland's suicide rate has been the same as that of other countries like Austria, Hungary and Scandinavia.

(4) There has been a steady increase in the suicide rate in Switzerland over the past 20 years.

(5) Switzerland's suicide rate has been traditionally stable, but has been growing over the last 20 years.

5. Which of the following statements is TRUE in the context of the passage?

(1) Some places in Hungary have a yearly suicide rate of 300 elderly people per one lakh people.

(2) The overall suicide rate in Ireland has increased by 700 percent in the last 20 years.

(3) The suicide rate in Latin and Catholic countries has remained low over the last 20 years.

(4) In France, 114 individuals per one lakh people commit suicide every year.

(5) In Japan, the suicide rate of elderly people is 17.3 a year per one lakh people.

6. The activities of State and community services are yielding less results in recent times on account of the

(1) growing resistance to counselling and hotlines by the people

(2) increase in the number of the aged and the terminally ill resorting to euthanasia

(3) weakening of traditional family support systems

(4) ever-increasing number of people committee suicide out of frustration

(5) increase in the number of people exerting their personal choice in deciding the way they die

7. Which of the following statements is NOT TRUE in the context of the passage?

(1) Lesser number of Europeans are today dying of highway accidents than killing themselves.

(2) One-third of men between the ages of 25 and 34 who kill themselves are Danish.

(3) The overall suicide rate in America is 12.3 a year per one lakh people.

(4) An overall suicide rate of 41 a year per one lakh people has been found in parts of Hungary.

(5) During the 1960s the suicide rate of 15-29 year old French men was only one-third of what it is today.

8. What has been mentioned in the passage regarding Europe's Southern part?

(1) Suicide rates are remaining stable there.

(2) Unemployment is comparatively more there.

(3) The living standards of the people are improving there.

(4) There are smaller families there.

(5) Economic transformation is relatively faster there.

Directions (9-15): *Read the following passage carefully and answer the questions given below it.*

From 'apparel to aerospace', 'steel to

software', the pace of technological innovation is quickening. No longer can companies afford to miss generation of technology and expect to remain competitive. Adding to the pressure, innovations are increasingly crossing industry boundaries; a new fiber developed by the textile industry has potential for building materials and medical equipment. Some companies are adept at using a diversity of technologies to create new products that transform markets. But many others are floundering because they rely on a technology strategy that no longer works in such a fast changing environment. The difference between success and failure is not how much a company spends on research and development (R&D), but how it approaches it.

There are two possible approaches. Either a company can invest in R&D that replaces an older generation of technology the 'break through' approach-or its focus on combining existing technologies into hybrid technologies– the 'technologies fusion' approach. It blends incremental technical improvements from several previously separate field of technology to create products that revolutionise markets.

In a world where the old maxim 'one technology one industry' no longer applies, a singular breakthrough strategy is inadequate; companies need to include both the breakthrough and fusion approaches in their technology strategy. Relying on breakthroughs alone fails because it focuses the R&D efforts to narrowly, ignoring the possibilities of combining technologies. Yet many western companies still rely almost exclusively– on the breakthrough approach. The reasons are complex: a distrust of outside innovations and not-invented here engineering and arrogance and aversion to sharing research results.

9. Which of the following is false according to the passage?

(1) Technological innovation is taking place at a fast pace

(2) All technological innovations have applicability in other industries

(3) Companies failing to adopt new technology may fail.

(4) Companies which adopt technologies of other industries have an advantage

(5) Technology becomes obsolete in a fast changing environment.

10. Which of the following would correctly reflect the position regarding the two approaches to technology adoption?

(1) Both the approaches are to be used at the same time

(2) 'Breakthrough' approach is only to be used

(3) 'Technology fusion' approach is only to be used

(4) 'Breakthrough approach' is preferable for many companies

(5) None of these

11. Which of the following has the same meaning as the word 'generation' as it has been used in-the passage?

(1) Family (2) Class

(3) Offspring (4) Phase

(5) Level

12. Which of the following features of technology has been highlighted most prominently by the author of the passage?

(1) Its improper utilization by some companies

(2) The speed at which innovations are happening

(3) The expenses involved in developing technology

(4) The two approaches to adopting technology

(5) None of these

13. What does the author want to highlight by using the example 'apparel to aerospace' and 'steel to software'?

(1) Many industries are trying to improve technology

(2) His knowledge about the various industries

(3) The wide spread of technological innovations

(4) The speed of the technological innovation

(5) None of these

14. What, according to the author, is adding to the pressure on the companies?

(1) Applicability of technologies of other industries to them
(2) Increasing speed of technological innovations
(3) Work load on their R & D departments
(4) Finding funds for increased R & D activities
(5) Demand from customers for improved products

15. What is the immediate effect, according to the passage, if a company does not innovate?
(1) It closes down.
(2) It ceases to be competitive in the market.
(3) The prices of its products go up.
(4) Its R & D departments close down.
(5) It adds pressure on itself.

Directions (16-20): *Pick out the word opposite or nearly so in the meaning of the given words.*

16. EXTRAVAGANT
(1) Developing (2) Wonderful
(3) Disappearing (4) Economical
(5) Real

17. VIVID
(1) Peculiar (2) Uncanny
(3) Evocative (4) Stifle
(5) Ceases

18. DESULTORY
(1) Isolated (2) Manifest
(3) Pertinent (4) Customization
(5) Frequent

19. ERUDITE
(1) Aversion (2) Sleazy
(3) Sagacious (4) Loquacious
(5) Disheveled

20. DEBONAIR
(1) Awkward (2) Windy
(3) Balmy (4) Sportive
(5) Stormy

Directions (21-23): *In each of the questions given below a sentence is given with a blank which is followed by five options that provide us with the possible alternatives for the blank. The blank must be filled by one of the idioms or phrases given in the options.*

21. We missed our flight to Paris because the connecting flight was late and to they made us pay for a new ticket as if it was our fault!
(1) break a leg
(2) hit the books
(3) add insult to injury
(4) cut the corners
(5) scratch someone's back

22. I can't believe that was our test. I think it was easier than some of our homework! It was a ....
(1) whole new ball game
(2) new lease of life
(3) dime's worth
(4) bit of fluff
(5) piece of cake

23. His birthday was supposed to be a surprise! I can't believe you .... Now he knows!
(1) let the cat out of bag
(2) keep your cool
(3) keep a straight face
(4) fate worse than death
(5) face like thunder

Directions (24-25): *In the question given below few sentences are given which are grammatically correct and meaningful. Connect them by the word given above the statements in the best possible way without changing the intended meaning. Choose your answer accordingly from the options to form a correct, coherent sentence.*

24. BECAUSE
A. The federal department has twice rejected LePage's requests for centralization
B. LePage has been in a tug of war with the regional boards for control of the federal money for several years.
C. Lepage didn't work in collaboration with federal department as required.
D. The organization claims that LePage has broken federal law by refusing to release the funds within 30 days of them having become available in August.

(1) Only B-D (2) Only D-A
(3) Both C-B and D-A
(4) Only A-C
(5) None of these

25. BY THE TIME

A. The storm crawls up the East Coast Wednesday and Thursday.

B. It's expected to gust with strong 30 to 50 mph winds.

C. That's a signal that the storm is going to get more intense, quickly.

D. Once the storm reaches New England, it may bring dangerous, power line-snapping blizzard conditions and coastal flooding.

(1) Only A-B (2) Only B-C
(3) Only D-C (4) Only D-B
(5) Only C-A

Directions (26-28): *Five statements are given below, labelled a, b, c, d and e. Among these, four statements are in logical order and form a coherent paragraph. From the given options, choose the option that does not fit into the theme of the paragraph.*

26. (1) Digital radio works by turning sound into digital signals for transmission and then decoding them at the other end using digital radio receivers;

(2) The result is close-to-CD-quality sound output.

(3) Digital radio is to normal radio what digital television is to your standard analog TV.

(4) It's the most significant upgrade to happen since the introduction of FM in Australia in the 1970s and the leap in quality is comparable to FM versus AM.

(5) Although DAB has the potential to provide better sound quality than FM, governments may end up filling the DAB bandwidth with as many channels as possible which may divide the bit-rate (the rate of data transfer) among these broadcasts. As a result, if the DAB bandwidth is choked, it may suffer a drop in quality.

27. (1) India has developed complex election expenditure, political party funding, and reporting and disclosure laws.

(2) Competitive political parties and election campaigns are central to the health of democracies.

(3) Parties and campaigns require significant resources to be effective.

(4) Current state funding measures include provision of free time on public broadcasters for national parties in general elections and for registered state parties in state legislature elections.

(5) However, these laws may have perverse impacts on the electoral system: they tend to drive campaign expenditure underground and foster a reliance on unaccounted funds or "black money."

28. (1) Many analysts feel that these are opening gambits to create uncertainty as bargaining ploy with the adversary.

(2) Minor incidents had been taking place since long.

(3) When man-made disaster looms, sane voices come together to ward it off.

(4) However, with the coming of Mr. Donald Trump to the White House matters have taken a more serious turn, to the extent that things could get out of hand and even lead to war should the two powers not negotiate and come to a solution acceptable to both sides.

(5) Such a disaster is clearly looming in the South China Sea, brought on by the two leading powers of the world, China and the USA; the former by militarising the islands, the latter by objecting to it.

Directions (29-30): *In each of the following questions, various sentences are given and you have to choose the one which has some or any grammatical error in it. In the questions where option (e) all are correct is given and all the sentences are grammatically correct choose option (5) as the correct choice.*

29. (1) The potassium found in potatoes is said to reduce cholesterol level, blood pressure and controls heart problems.

(2) The calcium and magnesium content in potatoes can help ease rheumatism.
(3) Health experts and nutritionists say that turnip juice has more Vitamin C than orange juice.
(4) To watch even a single plant grow from seedling to small and big with more leaves each day and find them flowering and giving fruits can give you happiness untold.
(5) All are correct.

30. (1) Everyone who desires to participate in the good to be obtained must share in the act.
(2) As we have seen above, all must participate that none may be in a position to reproach the rest.
(3) While Dean had no desire to participate in the new and perilous sport of ice climbing, he didn't share Cynthia total perplexity at why a sane human being would even consider subjecting himself or herself to such uncomfortable danger.
(4) They were dressed like the others, and seemed to participate in the general joy.
(5) He being the best student in the class, Gopal was chosen to participate in the competition.

Directions (31-35): *In the following passage there are blanks, each of which has been numbered. These numbers are printed below the passage and against each, five words are suggested, one of which fits the blank appropriately. Find out the appropriate word that fits the blank.*

In these days of economic liberalization, globalization, etc. materialistic values have assumed **(31)** importance. Money, physical comforts and luxuries are the most sought after aspects. There has been **(32)** competition. Such competition **(33)** stress. The stress leads to **(34)** of health of the people. Indian culture has **(35)** its striking uniqueness, as against the Western culture.

31. (1) Usual (2) Little
(3) Tangible (4) Least
(5) greater

32. (1) Critical (2) Unhealthy
(3) Unequalled (4) No
(5) absolute

33. (1) Releases (2) Deserves
(3) Generates (4) Demonstrates
(5) suppresses

34. (1) Neglect (2) Illness
(3) Generation (4) Deterioration
(5) encroachment

35. (1) maintained (2) illustrated
(3) marginalized (4) bestowed
(5) forsaken

Directions (36-40): *In the following passage there are blanks, each of which has been numbered and one word has been suggested alongside the blank. These numbers are printed below the passage and against each, five options are given. Find out the appropriate word which fits the blank appropriately. If the word written alongside the blank fits the passage, choose option '5' (No correction required) as the correct choice.*

Significantly, in remarking **(36)** who a whistle-blower is, the law goes beyond government officials who boost **(37)** corruption they come across in the course of their work. It includes any other person or non-governmental organisation. The importance of such radical **(38)** expansion is underlined by the fact that in the last few years, more than 65 people have been killed for exposing corruption in the government on the basis of instruction **(39)** they obtained under the Right to Information (RTI) Act. The RTI law has guaranteed **(40)** the common man to have access to information from public authorities — which only government officials were earlier privy to — making every citizen a potential whistle-blower.

36. (1) Characterize (2) Assigning
(3) Defining (4) Illustrating
(5) No correction required

37. (1) Unfolds (2) Proves
(3) Inform (4) Expose
(5) No correction required

38. (1) progressive (2) intermittent
(3) shifting (4) mobile
(5) No correction required

39. (1) advice (2) information
(3) knowledge (4) experience

(5) No correction required

40. (1) Revoked (2) Licensed (3) Enabled (4) Empowered
(5) No correction required

Reasoning Ability & Computer Aptitude

Directions (41-45): *Study the given information carefully to answer the given questions.*

A, B, C, D, E, F and G are seven different mobile phones which has different storage spaces, *i.e* 256 mb, 500 mb, 1 gb, 2 gb, 8 gb, 16 gb and 32 gb but not necessarily in the same order.

The mobile phone which has 256 mb storage space is immediately above A. There are only two mobile phones between D and the mobile phones which have of 256 mb storage space. The mobile phones which has 1 gb storage space is above D but not immediately above D. Only three mobile phones are between C and the mobile phones which have 1 gb storage space. The mobile phones which has 32 gb storage space is immediately above C. The mobile phones which is of 2 gb storage space is immediately above the mobile phones G. Only one mobile phone is there between mobile phone B and mobile phone E. Mobile phone B is above E. Neither mobile phone B nor mobile phone A is of 8 gb storage space. Mobile phone A has not 500 mb storage space. There is only one mobile phone between mobile phone E and G. Mobile phones G is not of 16 gb or 8 gb storage space. Neither mobile phone D nor G is of 500 mb storage space. Mobile phone G is not below mobile phone A.

41. How many mobile phones are there between mobile phone D and mobile phone G?
(1) One (2) Two
(3) Three (4) Four
(5) None

42. What is the storage space of mobile phone F?
(1) 32 gb (2) 256 mb
(3) 1 gb (4) 2 gb
(5) Can't be determined

43. Find the pair of storage space and mobile phone which is not correctly matched.
(1) B-2 gb (2) F-1 gb
(3) A-16 gb (4) G-256 mb
(5) None of these

44. Which of the following conditions is correct regarding 8 gb storage space with respect to E?
(1) There is one mobile phone between E and 8 gb storage space mobile phones.
(2) E is immediately above 8 gb storage space mobile phone.
(3) 8 gb storage space is related to the mobile phone immediately above E.
(4) All the above are true
(5) None of the above is true

45. Which of the following storage spaces belongs to 'A'?
(1) 256 mb (2) 2 gb
(3) 8 gb (4) 500 mb
(5) None of these.

Directions (46-48): *In each of the question below are given three statements followed by three conclusions numbered I, II and III. You have to take the given statements to be true even if they seem to be at variance with commonly known facts. Read all the conclusions and then decide which of the given conclusions logically follow(s) from the given statements, disregarding commonly known facts:*

46. Statements: Some Gujrat are karnal. Some karnal are haryana. Some haryana are delhi.
Conclusions:
I. Atleast some delhi are Gujrat.
II. There is a possibility that all delhi are karnal.
III. No delhi is karnal.
(1) None follows
(2) I and II follow
(3) Only II follows
(4) Only either II or III follows
(5) Only I and either II or III follow

47. Statements: All doc are pdf. Some pdf are ppt. All ppt are xls.
Conclusions:
I. At least some xls are pdf.
II. Some pdf are doc.

III. All xls are doc is a possibility.

(1) I and II follow (2) I and III follow
(3) II and III follow (4) All follow
(5) None of the above

48. Statements: All windows are microsoft. All ios are Microsoft. All microsoft are android.

Conclusions:

I. All windows are android is a possibility.
II. All ios is android.
III. At least some android are microsoft.

(1) I and II follow (2) I and III follow
(3) II and III follow (4) All follow
(5) None of the above

Directions (49-53): *Study the following information carefully to answer the given questions.*

W, X, Y, Z, M, N and O going to three different malls GIP, DLF and SRS with at least two of them in any of these malls. Each of them has a favourite colour–Green, Blue, Red, White, Black, Violet and Purple. X going to DLF mall with M.

M's favourite colour is Purple. Those who went to GIP mall do not like Green and White colour. The one who likes Blue colour is going only with O in SRS mall. The one who's favourite Colour is Black does not go in the same mall with either M or O. W does not go in DLF mall. W likes Violet colour. Z and N going in the same mall. N does not like Red colour. The one who's favourite colour is White does not go in DLF mall.

49. W, Z and N are going in which mall?
(1) Cannot be determined
(2) GIP
(3) DLF
(4) SRS
(5) None of these

50. What is the favourite colour of M?
(1) Violet (2) White
(3) Purple (4) Black
(5) None of these

51. Which of the following combinations is true?
(1) W–SRS–Blue (2) O–GIP–Black
(3) N–SRS–White (4) Z–GIP–Red
(5) None of these

52. Y goes in which mall?
(1) GIP (2) DLF
(3) SRS (4) Cannot be determined
(5) None of these

53. Whose favourite colour is White?
(1) X (2) W
(3) O (4) Z
(5) None of these

Directions (54-58): *Following questions are based on the five three-digit given below.*

519 328 746 495 837

54. If half of the second highest number is subtracted from the third highest number, what will be the value?
(1) 156 (2) 146
(3) 213 (4) 314
(5) None of these

55. If the positions of the first and the third digits in each of the numbers are interchanged, which of the following will be the second digit of the lowest number?
(1) 1 (2) 2
(3) 4 (4) 9
(5) 3

56. If in each number the third digit becomes the first digit, the first digit becomes the second digit and the second digit becomes the third digit, which of the following will be the second digit of the lowest number?
(1) 1 (2) 2
(3) 4 (4) 9
(5) 3

57. Which of the following represents the difference between the first and the second digits of the second highest number?
(1) 4 (2) 1
(3) 3 (4) 5
(5) None of these

58. If '1' is subtracted form the third digit of each number and '1' is added to the first digit of each number, which of the following will be the sum of the second and third digits of the second lowest number?
(1) 13 (2) 9

(3) 8 (4) 6

(5) None of these

Directions (59-60): *Read the given information carefully and answer the given questions.*

There are 5 persons A, B, C, D and E. B is to the northeast of E. D is 2 km to the east of E, who is 6 km to the west of A. C is to the northwest of D and in the line of EB. D is 4 km the south of B.

59. What is the distance between D and A?

(1) 6 km (2) 4 km

(3) 3 km (4) 2 km

(5) None of these

60. In which direction is A with respect to B?

(1) Southeast (2) Southwest

(3) Northeast (4) Northwest

(5) None of these

Directions (61-63): *Study the following digit-letter-symbol sequence carefully and answer the questions given below:*

R * T J L 2 $ D = M # 8 C% B < K 1 & A W ? P E + Q @ 7 F 6

61. How many such numbers are there in the above sequence, each of which is immediately preceded by a consonant and immediately followed by a symbol?

(1) None (2) One

(3) Three (4) Four

(5) None of these

62. Which of the following is sixth to the left of eighteenth element from the left?

(1) % (2) C

(3) 1 (4) 8

(5) None of these

63. If the above sequence is written in reverse order then which of the following will be sixth to the right of sixteenth element from the right end?

(1) M (2) A

(3) B (4) ?

(5) None of these

64. If each of the odd position in the letter CAREFULLY is increased by 1 and each of the even position letter are decreased by 1 then which will be the new word?

(1) EZSDHTNKY (2) EZSDHTNKY

(3) DZSDGTMKZ (4) DYTFGTNKY

(5) None of these.

65. In a certain code, CHAMPION is written as NBIDMNHO. How is ELECTRON written in the code?

(1) FMDFMNQS (2) BDKDMNQS

(3) DFMFOPSU (4) DFMFMNQS

(5) None of these

Directions (66-70): *Study the following information carefully and answer the given questions.*

Five Movies-Go Goa, Chandni-Chawk to China, London Dreams, Chennai Express and Mumbai Metro are played in 5 halls-Golden, Diamond, platinum, Deluxe, and Galaxy in a PVR. These movies are rated by different stars-one, two, three, four and five. The show timing is also different for each movie, 9 am, 12 noon, 3 pm, 6 pm, and 9 pm.

- Chandni-Chawk to China is not played in Diamond or Galaxy hall.
- The show timing of Go Goa is not 6 pm or 9 pm while show timing of Chennai Express is 12 noon.
- Mumbai Metro is not one or four star movie but played in Diamond hall.
- London Dream and Chennai Express are neither played in Golden & Platinum hall nor two or four star movie. Five star rated movie is played at 9 pm
- Three star rated movie is played in Galaxy. Five star rated movie is played in Deluxe hall.
- Four star rated movie is played immediate after Mumbai Metro.

66. Movie 'Go Goa' is rated as?

(1) One star (2) Two star

(3) Three star (4) Four star

(5) Five star

67. Which of the following statement is true?

(1) Two star rated movie is played in Deluxe hall

(2) Mumbai Metro is played at 3 pm.

(3) Chennai Express is five star rated movie

(4) Chandni-Chawk to China is played in

Platinum hall
(5) None of the above

68. Which of the following matching is correct?
(1) London Dream-four star
(2) Go Goa-five star
(3) Mumbai Metro-6pm
(4) Chennai Express-Galaxy hall
(5) More than one of the above

69. What is the timing of the movie which is played in Deluxe hall?
(1) 9 am (2) 12 noon
(3) 3 pm (4) 6 pm
(5) 9 pm

70. Movie 'Mumbai Metro' is rated as?
(1) One star (2) Two star
(3) Three star (4) Four star
(5) Five star

Directions (71-72): *Study the following information carefully and answer the questions given below:*

Five family members V, W, X, Y and Z are sitting in a straight line facing north. Each of them somehow has a relation with V, who sits third to the right of his daughter. There are only two females in the family. X is an immediate neighbour of his mother. Y sits third to the right of Z, who sits at one end of the line. V sits with his wife. X is brother of W, who is niece of Z.

71. How is Z related to V?
(1) Father (2) Mother
(3) Brother (4) Can't be determined
(5) None of these

72. How is Y related to W?
(1) Mother (2) Father
(3) Brother (4) Can't be determined
(5) None of these

Directions (73-77): *Study the information carefully and answer the question given below.*

Eight persons- P, S, Q, R, U, B, J and C are sitting in a circle at equal distances. Three of them are facing opposite to center and other five are sitting facing the centre of the circle. Two persons are sitting between C and U and two are sitting between B and U. Q is sitting to the second left of J, who is facing the centre of the circle. S is facing the centre of the circle. S is sitting to the third right of B. R is not near to C. Q is sitting to the third left of R, who is second right of P, and among these three players one is facing opposite to the centre of the circle. U is not opposite to B and Q.

73. Which of the following sports persons is facing to the opposite of the centre?
(1) B (2) R
(3) U (4) Q
(5) None of these

74. Who is sitting third to the left of U?
(1) R (2) B
(3) S (4) C
(5) None of these

75. If all the people change their positions with the person sitting opposite to them then who is now sitting second to the left of R?
(1) U (2) P
(3) B (4) C
(5) None of these

76. Who is second right to J?
(1) B (2) C
(3) S or B (4) R or S
(5) C or R

77. How many people are sitting between C and R, when counting in anticlockwise direction from R?
(1) Three (2) None
(3) One (4) Two
(5) None of these

Directions (78-80): *Each of the questions below consists of a question and three statements numbered I, II and III given below it. You have to decide whether the data provided in the statements are sufficient to answer the question. Read all the three statements and Give answer:*

(1) If the data in Statement I and II are sufficient to answer the question while the data in Statement III is not required to answer the question
(2) If the data in Statement I and III are sufficient to answer the question, while the data in Statement II is not required to answer the question

(3) If the data in Statement II and III are sufficient to answer the question, while the data in Statement I is not required to answer the question

(4) If even the data in Statement I, II and III together are not sufficient to answer the question.

(5) If the data in all the Statement I, II and III together are necessary to answer the question.

78. Who among A, B, C, D and E is driving the four wheeler?

I. B and C are drunk.

II. D does not have the driving license.

III. D and C are sitting on the front row.

79. Who is the tallest or heaviest among A, B, C, D and E?

I. E is heavier than D and B. Neither D nor B is the shortest.

II. A is taller than B. Neither B nor C is the shortest.

III. C is shorter than B but lighter than B.

80. Which of the following persons is B married to amongst A, C, D and E who all belong to the same family?

I. No one among B, C or E is the oldest member of the family. D is the father of A.

II. C is the daughter of D. E is the youngest.

III. D has only two children and one of them is a mother. A is unmarried & is brother-in-law of B.

81. Windows 7 is an example of a(n)

(1) application software
(2) browser
(3) operating system
(4) shareware
(5) None of these

82. A(n) .... program provides access to Web resources.

(1) Web (2) ISP
(3) Browser (4) URL
(5) None of these

83. Which of the following is not a logic gate?

(1) AND (2) NOR
(3) NAND (4) NAT
(5) None of these

84. A modem could be attached to which port?

(1) Parallel port
(2) ASYNA port
(3) Keyboard connector
(4) Video port
(5) None of these

85. The binary system uses powers of

(1) 2 (2) 10
(3) 8 (4) 16
(5) None of these

86. Expand RDBMS.

(1) Relative Database Management System
(2) Rational Database Minimize System
(3) Relational Database Management System
(4) Relational Database Maximize System
(5) None of these

87. .... is a set of instructions.

(1) Hardware (2) Code
(3) Language (4) Program
(5) All of these

88. Which memory is nonvolatile and may be written only once?

(1) RAM (2) EE-ROM
(3) RAM (4) PROM
(5) None of these

89. Main storage is also called

(1) accumulator (2) control unit
(3) register unit (4) memory
(5) None of these

90. In which language is a source program written?

(1) English (2) Symbolic
(3) High-level (4) Machine
(5) None of these

Quantitative Aptitude

Directions (91-95): *Study the pie-charts carefully and answer the following question.*

Distribution of Laptops (HP and Asus) sold by six sellers

Total number of lap tops sold = 48,000

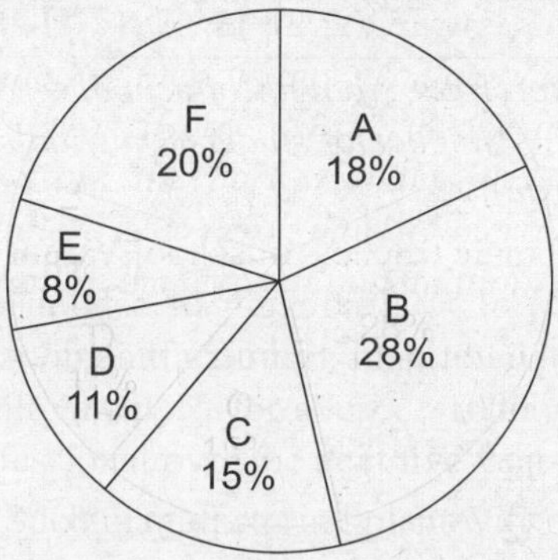

Number of Asus lap tops sold = 28,000

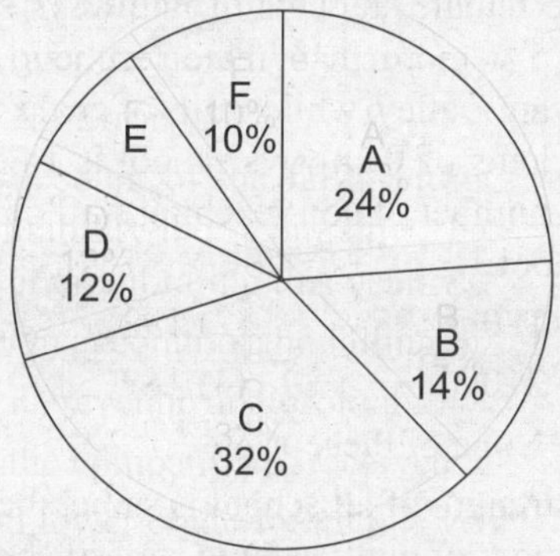

91. Number of HP Laptops sold by A and B together is approximately what percentage more or less than the number of Asus laptop sold by E and F together?

(1) 145% (2) 227%
(3) 127% (4) 245%
(5) 97%

92. Find the difference between the number of Asus laptop sold D and E together to the number of HP laptop sold by A, B and F together?

(1) 10,450 (2) 12,460
(3) 10,540 (4) 12,640
(5) 12,540

93. What is ratio of number of HP laptop sold by D and F together to HP laptop sold by B and E together?

(1) 139/109 (2) 109/139
(3) 113/127 (4) 127/113
(5) 121/147

94. Find the total profit earn by seller A if seller A earns Rs. 40 and Rs. 70 per laptop on HP and Asus respectively.

(1) Rs. 5,47,200 (2) Rs. 5,27,500
(3) Rs. 5,47,900 (4) Rs. 4,77,200
(5) Rs. 5,77,200

95. If seller E sells Asus laptop in loss at Rs. 30 each so at what price he should sell each HP laptop to gain Rs. 3,200 in total.

(1) Rs. 39 (2) Rs. 41
(3) Rs. 43 (4) Rs. 45
(5) None of these

96. A watch dealer sells watches at Rs. 800 per watch. However, he is forced to give two successive discounts of 10% and 15% respectively. However, he recovers the sales tax on the net sale price from the customer at 25% of the net price. Find the profit percentage if the C.P of watch is Rs. 600.

(1) 23.5% (2) 21.5%
(3) 25.5% (4) 27.5%
(5) 26.5%

97. The short and the long hands of a clock are 4 cm and 6 cm long respectively. What will be sum of distances travelled by their tips in 4 days? (Take $\pi = 3.14$)

(1) 954.56 cm (2) 3818.24 cm
(3) 2909.12 cm (4) 2703.56 cm
(5) None of these

98. A spherical cannon ball, 28 cm in diameter, is melted and cast into a right circular conical mould the base of which is 35 cm in diameter. Find the height of the cone correct up to two places of decimals.

(1) 8.96 cm (2) 35.84 cm
(3) 5.97 cm (4) 17.92 cm
(5) 30.92 cm

99. A train takes 3 seconds to cross a pole and 22

seconds to cross a 855 m long bridge. What is the time taken by the train (in seconds) to cross a 215 m long train coming at a speed of 90 km/hr from the opposite direction?

(1) 5 (2) 8
(3) 12 (4) 7
(5) 15

100. A 10 hectare field is reaped by 2 men, 3 women and 4 children together in 10 days. If working capabilities of a man, a woman and a child are in the ratio 5 : 4 : 2, then a 16 hectare field will be reaped by 6 men, 4 women and 7 children in.

(1) 5 days (2) 6 days
(3) 7 days (4) 8 days
(5) None of these

Directions (101-105): *In each of the following questions two equations are given. Solve the equations and give answer-*

(1) If $x < y$ (2) If $x \leq y$
(3) If $x > y$ (4) If $x \geq y$
(5) $x = y$ or relationship between x and y cannot be established

101. **I.** $35x^2 - 53x + 20 = 0$
II. $56y^2 - 97y + 42 = 0$

102. **I.** $18x^2 + 18x + 4 = 0$
II. $12y^2 + 29y + 14 = 0$

103. **I.** $8x^2 - 78x + 169 = 0$
II. $20y^2 - 117y + 169 = 0$

104. **I.** $6x^2 + 13x + 5 = 0$
II. $3y^2 + 11y + 10 = 0$

105. **I.** $6x + 7y = 52$
II. $14x + 4y = 35$

Directions (106-110): *Study the following table carefully and answer the questions that follow.*

The table shows the data related top six schools of India. Some values are missing which you need to find out and answer the questions accordingly.

Schools	Number of teachers	Ratio of male to female teachers	Ratio of teachers to students	Percentage of non-teaching staff
Vasant valley	480	15 : 17	- : -	15%
Woodstock	450	- : -	1 : 6	10%
DPS	–	3 : 2	3 : 20	–
Rishi Valley	510	8 : 7	3 : 10	–
Pathways	–	2 : 7	2 : 5	20%
DAV	–	- : -	2 : 7	15%

Note: Total strength of school = Number of teachers + Number of students + Number of non-teaching staff

106. If female teachers of school Vasant valley are 17% of total strength of school, then what is the ratio of teachers to students in that school?

(1) 32 : 55 (2) 5 : 11
(3) 32 : 53 (4) 23 : 53
(5) 5 : 13

107. The female students of Pathways school are 15 5% more than male teachers of school Vasant valley while ratio of male to female students of Pathways school is 14 : 13. Find the number of non-teaching staff of Pathways school.

(1) 180 (2) 192
(3) 210 (4) 189
(5) None of these

108. If strength of all school is same, then find the number of non-teaching staff of school DAV.

(1) 420 (2) 525
(3) 580 (4) 630
(5) None of these

109. If total strength and number of students of schools Woodstock and DPS are same, then teachers of DPS are what percent less than students of Woodstock?

(1) 80% (2) 85%
(3) 72% (4) 92%
(5) None of these

110. Find the difference in total strength of school Woodstock and that of Rishi valley.

(1) 980 (2) 840
(3) 780 (4) can't be determined
(5) None of these

111. Anil spends 25% of his monthly salary for his household expenditure and 12% on travelling. Out of the remaining, he spends 20% on clothes and saves the rest. If he saves Rs. 2520 every month, what is his monthly salary?

(1) Rs. 5000 (2) Rs. 15000
(3) Rs. 3000 (4) Rs. 10,00
(5) Rs. 8000

112. Raman and Nakul invested in a business. Raman invested Rs. 3000 and withdraw Rs. 1500 at the end of 8th month. Nakul invested Rs. 1000 initially and Rs. 3500 more at the end of 4th month but withdraw Rs. 1500 at the end of 7th month. At the year's end, they earned Rs. 1800. What should be Raman's share?

(1) 800 (2) 920
(3) 864 (4) 850
(5) 795

113. A can do a piece of work in 10 days, B can do the same work in 12 days and C in 15 days. They all started working together, but A leaves the work after 2 days and B leaves the work 3 days before the work is completed. For how many days the work lasted?

(1) 8 days (2) 10 days
(3) 7 days (4) 9 days
(5) 6 days

114. A shopkeeper sells shirts at the rate of Rs. 400 per shirt and allows a discount of 10% to all customers buying by full cash payment. Also, for all those customers who buy 10 shirts at a time, he counts 12 shirts. If a customer is willing to take both the discounts, what net effective discount can he avail?

(1) 37.5% (2) 12.5%
(3) 33.33% (4) 25%
(5) None of these

115. Subbu have a fan whose 5% of the selling price is equal to 6% of its cost price and 7% of the selling price exceeds 8% of its cost price by Rs 1. Find the profit.

(1) Rs 25 (2) Rs. 37.5
(3) Rs. 50 (4) Rs. 75
(5) Rs. 62.5

116. A sum of Rs. 1000 after 3 years at compound interest becomes a certain amount that is equal to the amount that is the result of a 3 years depreciation from Rs. 1728. Find the difference between the rates of CI and depreciation. (Given that CI is 10% p.a.)

(a) 21% (b) 12%
(c) 3% (d) 2%
(e) None of these

117. In a co-educational school there are 15 more girls than boys. If the number of girls is increased by 10% and the number of boys is also increased by 16%, there would be 9 more girls than the boys. What is the number of students in the school?

(1) 140 (2) 125
(3) 265 (4) 255
(5) 250

118. In Ramnagar colony, the ratio of school going children to non-school going children is 5 : 4. If in the next year, the number of non-school going children is increased by 20% making it 35,400, and the number of school going children remains same. Find the new ratio of school going children to non-school going children?

(1) 4 : 5 (2) 3 : 2
(3) 25 : 24 (4) Data inadequate
(5) None of these

119. There was one mess for 30 boarders in a certain hostel. If the number of boarders were increased by 10, the expenses of the mess would increase by Rs. 40 per month, while the average expenditure per head diminish by Rs. 2. Find the original monthly expenses.

(1) Rs. 390 (2) Rs. 360
(3) Rs. 410 (4) Rs. 480
(5) None of these

120. An empty container is filled with pure alcohol the alcohol is slowly to run out and when the container is one-fourth empty, it is replaced with water. Next, when the container is half empty it is again filled with water. Finally, when it is three fourth empty, it is again filled with water. What percentage of container is alcohol now?

(1) 8.25% (2) 11.75%

(3) 9.375% (4) 14.375%

(5) None of these

Directions (121-125): *Each question below is followed by two Statements (I) and (II). You have to determine whether the data given in the statements are sufficient for answering the question. You should use the data and your knowledge of Mathematics to choose between the possible answers.*

Give answer

(1) if the Statement (I) alone is sufficient to answer the question but the Statement (II) alone is not sufficient

(2) if the Statement (II) alone is sufficient to answer the question but the Statement (I) alone is not sufficient

(3) if both Statement (I) and (II) together are needed to answer the question

(4) if either the Statement (I) alone or Statement (II) alone is sufficient to answer the question

(5) if you cannot get the answer from the Statements (I) and (II) together but need even more data

121. In how many days 8 women can complete the work?

(I) 10 men & 12 Women can finish the work in 10/7 days.

(II) 5 Men and 6 women can finish the work in 20/7 days.

122. What is the radius of the circle?

(I) Length of a rectangle is 10% more than the breadth. Area of rectangle is 440 cm². Length of rectangle equals to circumference of circle.

(II) Circumference of circle is equal to side of square having area 484 cm².

123. Ram sold an item. Find the M.P of the item?

(I) Ram gave two successive discounts is 20% & 5% on marked price. But after that take 25% more on discounted price as tax. Ram can earn 40 more if he sell the item at MP.

(II) Ram gave two successive discount of MP *i.e.*, 15% & 20% whereas Ram kept M.P. 50% more than the C.P. of that item.

124. Find the amount invested by Jagriti?

(I) If Jagriti invested half of the amount in Yes Bank at 5% for 3 years and half the amount in Kotak Bank at 6% for 5 year, she got Rs. 4500 as Simple Interest.

(II) Jagriti will get 2420 more if she will invest in a bank at 10% p.a. for 3 year at compound interest rather than 10% p.a. for 2 year in same bank at compound interest.

125. What is the weight of Raju?

(I) There are four person Raju, Ramesh, Rajan, Rajguru. Average of weight of these four is 51.25. Average weight of Rajan and Rajguru is 47.5. Average weight of Ramesh & Rajguru is 57.5.

(II) In a class of 50 students having 30 kg as average weight If one students of weight 30 kg is replaced by Rajan then the average increases by 0.4.

Directions (126-130): *Study the following line graph and answer the questions that follow.*

The graph shows the percentage distribution of money spent by Avanish on Education, Household and Others in five different months. He spent only 60% of his monthly salary.

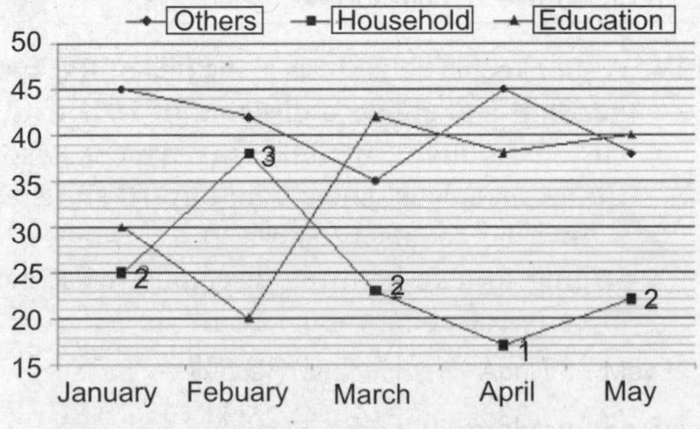

Note: Monthly income throughout the year remains constant. MONTHLY SALARY:- 50,000

126. In June, Avanish spent 25% less amount on others as compared to what he spent on others in May. Find the percentage contribution of money spent on others in June in monthly salary of June.

(1) 20.5% (2) 22.5%

(3) 17.1% (4) 23.2%
(5) None of these

127. Avanish invested 10% of the money spent on others in January in a business which gives him 10% interest per annum on amount invested. Find the interest earned by him in one year?
(1) Rs. 125.5 (2) Rs. 152
(3) Rs. 150 (4) Rs. 135
(5) None of these

128. What is the difference in amount saved and amount spent on education by Avanish in April?
(1) Rs. 12100 (2) Rs. 8600
(3) Rs. 7200 (4) Rs. 8500
(5) Rs. 7850

129. Find the total expenditure made in February except education?
(1) Rs. 24,000 (2) Rs. 24,400
(3) Rs. 22,400 (4) Rs. 20,400
(5) None of these

130. Find the ratio of money spent on Education in February to monthly salary in February?
(1) 3 : 22 (2) 4 : 27
(3) 5 : 29 (4) 8 : 35
(5) None of these

Directions (131-135): *What should come in place of question mark?*

131. 126 64 34 20 14 ?
(1) 12 (2) 10
(3) 8 (4) 6
(5) None of these

132. 4 6 14 44 ? 892
(1) 160 (2) 176
(3) 492 (4) 286
(5) None of these

133. 1011 13 21 69 ?
(1) 382 (2) 420
(3) 424 (4) 384
(5) None of these

134. 1534 20 ? 25 43 30
(1) 40 (2) 39
(3) 38 (4) 41
(5) None of these

135. 16 81 230 ? 472.5
(1) 105 (2) 108
(3) 148 (4) 156
(5) 178

Directions (136-140): *Study the following table carefully to answer the questions that follow*

Number of Gold coins (in hundred) produced in Five Different companies during Six Different month

Months	Companies				
	P	Q	R	S	T
Feb	96	56	54	103	92
March	78	134	63	125	117
April	84	156	58	95	119
May	114	149	103	154	143
June	102	133	78	149	138
July	167	147	87	127	127

136. What was the respective ratio between the number of Gold coins produced from company P in the month may and the number of Gold coins produced from company T in the month June?
(1) 38 : 41 (2) 23 : 21
(3) 19 : 21 (4) 19 : 23
(5) None of these

137. What was the total number of Gold coins produced from all the companies together in the month of March?
(1) 53500 (2) 51700
(3) 5.15 thousand (4) 51500
(5) None of these

138. In which company the number of the Gold coins continuously increased during the year February to July?
(1) Only R and T (2) Only Q
(3) Only P (4) Only Q and T
(5) None of these

139. In which Company was the number of

Gold coins produced out in the month May highest?

(1) Q (2) P
(3) T (4) S
(5) R

140. Number of Gold coins produced from company R in the month May was approximately what percentage of the number of Gold coins produced in the company T in the month March?

(1) 85 (2) 95
(3) 60 (4) 40
(5) 75

General/Financial Awareness

141. Dipika Pallikal is related to

(1) Golf (2) Badminton
(3) Squash (4) Swimming
(5) Table Tennis

142. The term "Deficit Financing" means the Government borrows money from the

(1) IMF (2) Local bodies
(3) RBI (4) Large corporate
(5) Public at large

143. Regional Rural Banks

(1) Have limited area of operation and access to refinance from NABARD.
(2) are required to lend only to weaker sections.
(3) are mandated to do only narrow banking.
(4) can only extend agricultural loans.
(5) have unrestricted area of operation.

144. Ngozi Okonjo-Iweala is holding which of the following positions at present?

(1) Chief of Asian Development Bank
(2) Director General of World Trade Organisation
(3) President of South Africa
(4) Chief of Morgan Stanley
(5) Chief of World Bank

145. What is the present reverse REPO rate in August 2023?

(1) 3.5% (2) 5.5%
(3) 4% (4) 4.5%
(5) 3.35%

146. General Assembly elections were held in which of the following South Indian states in May 2023?

(1) Andhra Pradesh (2) Kerala
(3) Tamil Nadu (4) Karnataka
(5) Telangana

147. What is the full form of the term FDI?

(1) Foreign Direct Investment
(2) Foreign Diverse Investment
(3) Fixed Deposit Investment
(4) Floating Deposit Investment
(5) Financial Derivatives in India

148. The erstwhile UTI Bank is presently known as

(1) ING Vysya Bank
(2) Yes Bank
(3) Indusind Bank (4) Axis Bank
(5) IDBI Bank

149. What percentage of an employee's wages is contributed to the Employees' Provident Fund (EPF) account?

(1) 8 (2) 10
(3) 12 (4) 14
(5) 15

150. Which of the following countries recently attained the status of world's fifth largest economy?

(1) Russia (2) Japan
(3) China (4) India
(5) Brazil

151. The *Kyoto Protocol* was adopted in 1997, but owing to a complex ratification process, it entered into force in

(1) 2005 (2) 2000
(3) 2010 (4) 2001
(5) 2002

152. Which of the following is NOT a Banking or Finance Company?

(1) Barclay (2) Lufthansa
(3) BNP Paribas (4) American Express
(5) HSBC

153. India and Russia were having some differences over which of the following nuclear power plants?
(1) Kaiga (2) Kudankulam
(3) Rawatbhata (4) Narora
(5) None of these

154. Excise duty is a tax levied on which of the following?
(1) Production of goods
(2) Purchase of goods
(3) Export of goods
(4) Sale of goods
(5) Movement of goods beyond municipal limits

155. Which ministry oversees the functioning of the Employees Provident Fund Organisation (EPFO)?
(1) Ministry of Finance
(2) Ministry of Commerce
(3) Ministry of Industry
(4) Ministry of Labour and Employment
(5) None of these

156. Which of the following is the unit of electrical current?
(1) Bar (2) Calorie
(3) Ampere (4) Decibel
(5) Angstrom

157. World Economic Forum meeting 2023 will be organised in
(1) New Delhi (2) Washington DC
(3) London (4) Davos
(5) Capetown

158. Which of the following awards is given to the coaches of sports persons?
(1) Kalidas Samman
(2) Dronacharya Award
(3) Arjuna Award
(4) Dada Saheb Phalke Award
(5) Saraswati Samman

159. Which of the following countries supply Uranium to India?
(1) Australia (2) Canada
(3) France (4) Kazakhstan
(5) All of the above

160. Which state saw the highest increase in MGNREGA job card deletions from 2021-22 to 2022-23?
(1) Jharkhand (2) Bihar
(3) West Bengal (4) Orissa
(5) Uttar Pradesh

161. Who among the following is a famous Sports person?
(1) Dhanush (2) Saina Nehwal
(3) Charles Correa (4) Ajit Singh
(5) Kim Jong-Un

162. Speed of a ship is expressed in
(1) Kilometre (2) Horsepower
(3) Ohm (4) Knot
(5) Coulomb

163. In which year did NongHyup Bank enter the Indian market?
(1) 2016 (2) 2014
(3) 2013 (4) 2002
(5) 1991

164. Who among the following has written the book Dr. Zhivago?
(1) Pearl S Buck (2) HG Wells
(3) Saul Bellow (4) Emile Zola
(5) Boris Pasternak

165. Yoshihiko Noda is the present Prime Minister of
(1) Myanmar (2) South Korea
(3) North Korea (4) Japan
(5) None of these

166. Major producer of mulberry silk in India is
(1) Jammu and Kashmir
(2) Jharkhand
(3) Karnataka
(4) Assam
(5) Himachal Pradesh

167. We come across the term 'PPP' in financial news nowadays. What does 'PPP' represent?
(1) Personal Per-capita Power

(2) Private Public Partnership
(3) Per-capita Potential for Purchases
(4) Present Purchasing Power
(5) Pure Purchase Parity

168. Many times we read the term 'ECB' in newspapers. What is the full form' of 'ECB'?
(1) Essential Commercial Banking
(2) European Credit Borrowing
(3) External Credit for Business
(4) External Commercial Borrowing
(5) None of These

169. What is meant by financial inclusion?
(1) Making available banking services at an affordable cost
(2) Opening savings accounts in rural areas without any deposit
(3) Opening any type of account without introduction
(4) Distributing money through rural branches
(5) Distributing wages through bank accounts

170. Which of these country is the largest producer of milk and milk products in the world?
(1) USA (2) China
(3) India (4) New Zealand
(5) None of These

171. Which of the following is the most important rabi crop of India?
(1) Rice (2) Millet
(3) Sugarcane (4) Groundnut
(5) Mustard

172. Who is the regulatory authority for insurance business in India?
(1) RBI (2) IRDP
(3) SEBI (4) NABARD
(5) IRDA

173. What is money laundering?
(1) Conversion of assets into cash
(2) Conversion of illegally obtained money into accountable money
(3) Conversion of cash into gold
(4) Conversion of gold into cash
(5) None of These

174. Golden revolution refers to the development of which of the following agricultural products?
(1) Oilseeds
(2) Pulses
(3) Horticultural products
(4) Cereals
(5) Fodder

175. When is Kargil Vijay Diwas celebrated in India?
(1) 26 June (2) 26 May
(3) 26 August (4) 26 April
(5) 26 July

176. Which country has officially applied to join the BRICS group of nations and expressed interest in becoming a shareholder member of the BRICS Bank?
(1) Sri Lanka (2) Bangladesh
(3) Canada (4) Iran
(5) Algeria

177. Bird flu is a disease which affects and spreads through?
(1) Cattle (2) Sheep
(3) Prawn (4) Silkworm
(5) Poultry

178. Which Indian state passed the Minimum Guaranteed Income Bill, setting an example for other states?
(1) Tripura (2) Bihar
(3) Uttar Pradesh (4) Tamil Nadu
(5) Rajasthan

179. How many official languages does the United Nations currently have?
(1) 2 (2) 4
(3) 6 (4) 8
(5) 5

180. The G-20 Summit will take place in
(1) Japan (2) India
(3) UK (4) USA
(5) Australia

181. In which policy, businesses are required to produce a valid BRC for availing export benefits?

(1) Fiscal Policy (2) Foreign Trade Policy
(3) Monetary Policy (4) Industrial Policy
(5) None of These

182. Which of the following currencies is used in Britain?
(1) Pound (2) Dollar
(3) Euro (4) France
(5) Pesso

183. Which of the following cups/trophies is associated with the game of Football?
(1) Grand Prix
(2) Rangaswami Cup
(3) Wimbledon Trophy
(4) FIFA Cup
(5) Ranji Trophy

184. The head office of the Bank of Maharashtra is located in which of the following cities?
(1) Kolkata (2) New Delhi
(3) Pune (4) Ahmedabad
(5) Mumbai

185. When was the India-Myanmar-Thailand Highway project first proposed?
(1) 2008 (2) 2006
(3) 2005 (4) 2002
(5) 2000

186. Which of the following terms is not used in the field of Economics?
(1) Balance of Trade
(2) Break Even Point
(3) Plasma
(4) Fiscal Deficit
(5) Capital Account Convertibility

187. "Carbon credit" is concerned with which one of these internationally sensitive issues?
(1) Deforestation
(2) Contract farming
(3) Rural infrastructure
(4) Diamond trading
(5) Protection of environment

188. Which of the following terms is used in the game of Cricket?
(1) Half Nelson
(2) Love
(3) Back Hand Drive
(4) Penalty Stroke
(5) Clean Bowled

189. Who achieved the highest medal count at the 25th Asian Athletics Championship 2023 in Bangkok, Thailand?
(1) India (2) Pakistan
(3) Japan (4) China
(5) None of these

190. What is the full form of the term ASBA?
(1) Allotment Supported by Blocked Amount
(2) Application Supported by Bank Amount
(3) Allotment Supported by Bank Account
(4) Application Supported by Blocked Amount
(5) Allotment and Social Banking Amount

Answers With Explanations

1. (1) According to the first sentence of the second paragraph, "The greatest concern of European specialists is the increasing number of young people who take their own lives."

2. (5) According to the first two sentences of the third paragraph, "Experts see the transformation of European society as the key to the recent increases in European suicides. The modernization of the workforce, the increasing social and geographical mobility and the consequent breakdown of old family structures and support networks all play a role."

3. (2) According to the third sentence of the third paragraph, "In a comparative study of suicide in 20 European countries over two decades, it was found that factors such as divorce, unemployment, the number of working women in a society, the number of children and the prevalence of religion, combined with the presence of violent crimes and alcohol abuse, are useful in predicting the rise and fall of suicide rates."

4. (2) According to the third sentence of the first paragraph, "While the traditionally high suicide rates in Austria, Hungary, Switzerland and Scandinavia have remained relatively stable, the low rates in Latin and Catholic countries have begun to grow dramatically in the last 20 years."

5. (1) According to the third last sentence of the first paragraph, "In parts of Hungary, which holds Europe's record for suicides with a rate of 41 a year per one lakh people, the rate among the elderly is 300."

6. (5) According to the third sentence of the last paragraph, "More and more people are beginning to consider the way they die as an equally personal choice."

7. (2)

8. (4) According to the second last sentence of the third paragraph, "As European Southern tier becomes more prosperous, families are becoming smaller, relationship less stable and suicides are increasing."

9. (2)
10. (1)
11. (4)
12. (4)
13. (3)
14. (1)
15. (2)
16. (4)

17. (3) Vivid and evocative are similar in meaning.

18. (3) Desultory and pertinent are opposite in meaning.

19. (3) Erudite and sagacious are similar in meaning.

20. (1) Awkward is an antonym of Debonair.

21. (3)
22. (5)
23. (1)
24. (4)
25. (4)
26. (5)
27. (4)
28. (1)
29. (5)
30. (5)
31. (5)
32. (2)
33. (3)
34. (4)
35. (1)
36. (3)

37. (4) Based on Subject-Verb agreement and its meaning, option (4) is the correct.

38. (1)
39. (2)
40. (4)

For questions (41-45):

Mobile Phone	Storage Space
F	1g b
B	500 mb
D	8 gb
E	32 gb
C	2 gb
G	256 mb
A	16 gb

41. (2)
42. (3)
43. (1)
44. (3)
45. (5)

46. (3)

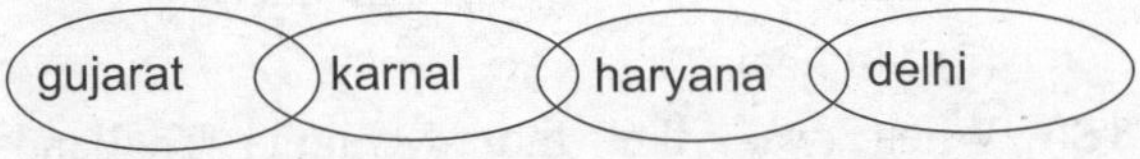

47. (4)

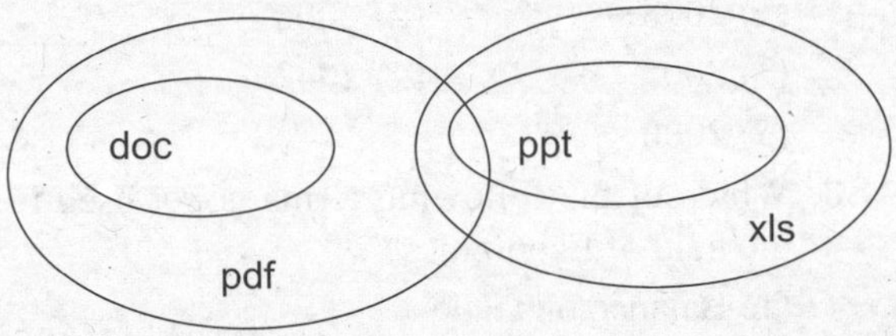

48. (3)

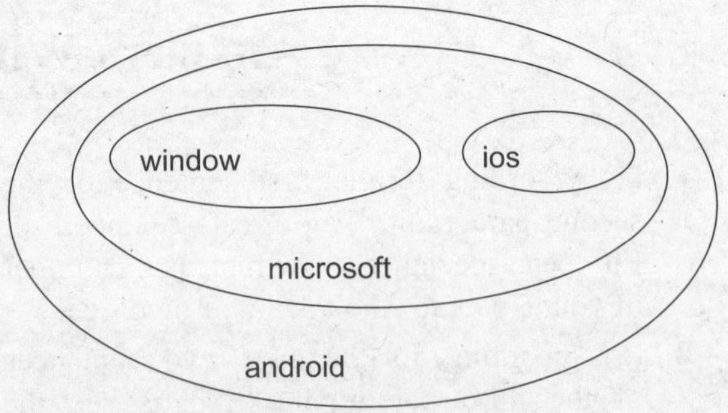

For questions (49-53):

Person	Mall	Colour

W	GIP	Violet
X	DLP	Green
Y	SRS	Blue
Z	GIP	Red
M	DLF	Purple
N	GIP	Black
O	SRS	White

49. (2)
50. (3)
51. (4)
52. (3)
53. (3)
54. (2)
55. (4)
56. (3)
57. (3)
58. (1)

For questions (59-60):

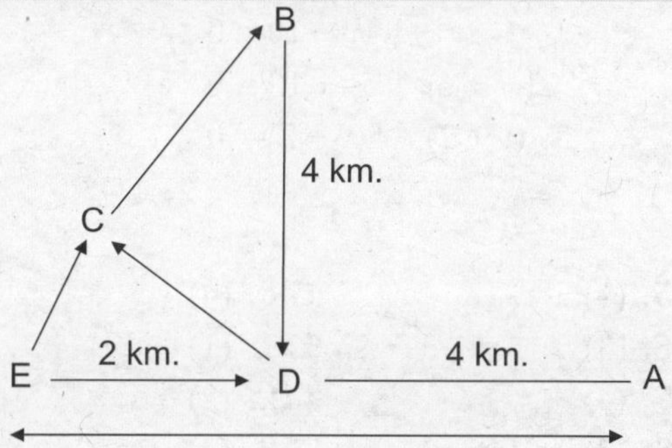

59. (2)
60. (1)
61. (5)
62. (4)
63. (4)
64. (1)
65. (3)

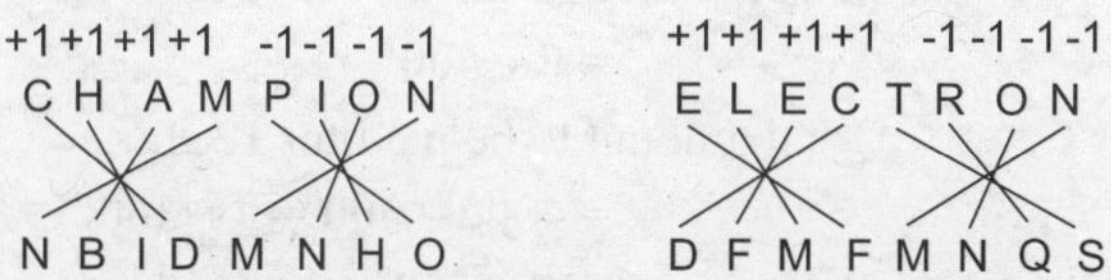

For questions (66-70):

Movie	Hall	Rating	Time
Go Goa	Golden/ Platinum	1 star	9 a.m
Chandni-Chowk to china	Golden/ Platinum	4 star	6 p.m
London Dreams	Deluxe	5 star	9 p.m
Chennai Express	Galaxy	3 star	12 noon
Mumbai Metro	Diamond	2 star	3 p.m

66. (1)
67. (2)
68. (4)
69. (5)
70. (2)

For questions (71-72):

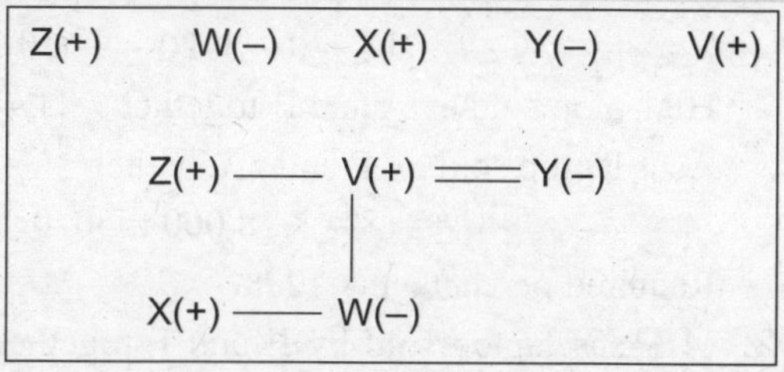

71. (3)
72. (1)

For questions (73-77):

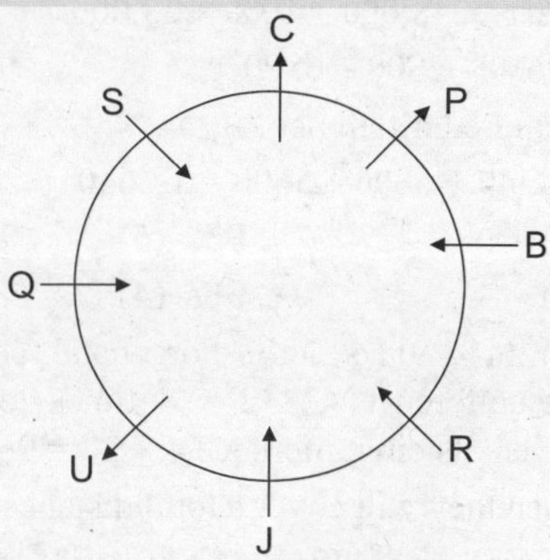

73. (3)
74. (2)
75. (1)
76. (1)
77. (4)
78. (4)
79. (2)
80. (5)

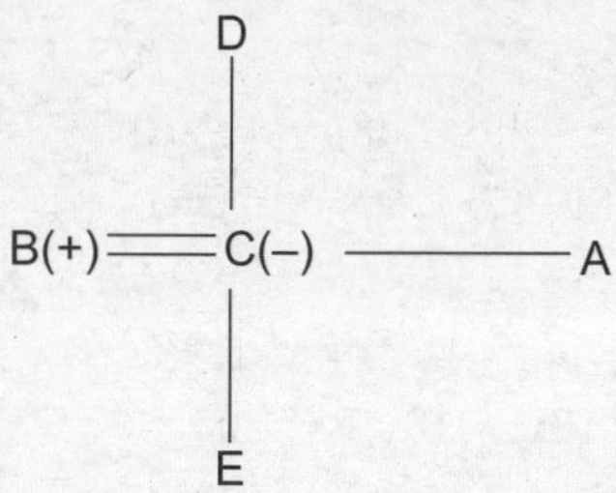

81. (3)
82. (3)
83. (4)
84. (1)
85. (1)
86. (3)

87. (3)

88. (4)

89. (4)

90. (3)

91. (3) HP laptop sold by A = 18% × 48,000 – 24% × 28,000

= 8640 – 6720 = 1920

HP laptop sold by B

= 28% × 48,000 – 14% × 28,000

= 13,440 – 3920 = 9,520

HP laptop sold by A and B together = 11,440

Asus laptop sold by E and F together

= 18% × 28,000 = 5040

Required percentage = 127%

92. (4) Asus laptop sold by E and F together = 20% × 28,000 = 5600

HP laptop sold by A and B together = 11,440

HP laptop sold by F

=20% × 48,000 – 10% × 28,000

=9600 – 2800 = 6800

Required difference

= 1440 + 6800 – 5600 = 12,640

93. (2)

94. (1)

95. (5)

96. (4)

97. (2) In 4 days, the short hand covers its circumference 4 × 2 = 8 times long hand covers its circumference 4 × 24 = 96 times.

Then they will cover a total distance of:

$(2 \times \pi \times 4)\ 8 + (2 \times \pi \times 6)\ 96 = 3818.24$ cm

98. (2)

99. (1)

100. (4)

101. (1) $35x^2 - 25x - 28x + 20 = 0$

$5x\,(7x - 5) - 4\,(7x - 5) = 0$

$x = 4/5,\ 5/7$

$56y^2 - 49y - 48y + 42 = 0$

$7y\,(8y - 7) - 6(8y - 7) = 0$

$y = 6/7,\ 7/8$

$x < y$

102. (4) I. $18x^2 + 18x + 4 = 0$

$3x(3x + 2) + 1(3x + 2) = 0$

$(3x + 1)\,(3x + 2) = 0$

$x = -1/3$ or $-2/3$

II. $12y^2 + 29y + 14 = 0$

$3y(4y + 7) + 2(4y + 7) = 0$

$y = -2/3$ or $-7/4$

$x \geq y$

103. (4) I. $8x^2 - 78x + 169 = 0$

$(2x - 13)\,(4x - 13) = 0$

$\therefore\ x = 13/2$ or $13/4$

II. $20y^2 - 117y + 169 = 0$

$(4y - 13)(5y - 13) = 0$

$\therefore\ y = 13/4$ or $13/5$

$\therefore\ x \geq y$

104. (4) I. $6x^2 + 13x + 5 = 0$

$6x^2 + 3x + 10x + 5 = 0$

$3x\,(2x + 1) + 5\,(2x + 1) = 0$

$\therefore\ x = -5/3, -1/2$

II. $3y^2 + 11y + 10 = 0$

$3y^2 + 11y + 10 = 0$

$3y^2 + 6y + 5y + 10 = 0$

$3y\,(y + 2) + 5(y + 2) = 0$

$y = -2, -5/3$

$x \geq y$

105. (1)

106. (3)

107. (4)

108. (2)

107. (2)

100. (4)

111. (1)

112. (2)

113. (3)

114. (4) Price of 12 shirts = 400 × 12 = Rs. 4800

Price of 10 shirts = 400 × 10 = Rs. 4000

Cash discount on 10 shirts = 10% of 4000

= Rs. 400

∴ Total amount to be paid for 12 shirts

= 4000 – 400 = Rs. 3600

Net discount availed = 25%

115. (3)

116. (2)

117. (3)

118. (3)

119. (2)

110. (3)

121. (5)

122. (4)

123. (1)

124. (4)

125. (3)

126. (3) Money spent = 60% × 50000 = 30,000

Money spent by Avanish on others in June

= 75% × 38% × 30000

= 8550

∴ % contribution = 17.1%

127. (4) Money invested by Avinash = 10% × 45% × 30,000

= Rs. 1350

Interest earned by him = 10% × 1350 = Rs. 135

128. (2) Amount saved in April = 40% × 50000 = Rs. 20,000

Amount spent on education

= 38% × 30,000 = Rs. 11,400

Required difference = Rs. 8600

129. (1)

130. (5)

131. (1) Difference between numbers are 62, 30, 14, 6, 2

132. (2)

133. (4)

134. (2) These are two series mix 15, 20 , 25, 20 .... and 34, 39, 43

135. (1)

136. (4)

137. (2)

138. (5)

139. (4)

140. (1)

141. (3)

142. (3)

143. (1)

144. (2) Ngozi Okonjo-Iweala is the Director General of the WTO, becoming the first woman and the first African to hold this position.

145. (5)

146. (4) Legislative *Assembly election* was held in *Karnataka* on 10 May 2023 to elect all 224 members of the *Karnataka* Legislative Assembly.

147. (1)

148. (4)

149. (3) The employee and the employer contribute to the EPF India scheme on a monthly basis in equal proportions of 12% of the basic salary and dearness allowance.

150. (4) *India* has overtaken the U.K. to become the world's fifth-largest economy and is now behind only the US, China, Japan and Germany.

151. (1)

152. (2)

153. (2)

154. (1)

155. (4) The Employees Provident Fund Organisation (EPFO) operates under the Ministry of Labour and Employment, Government of India.

156. (3)

157. (4)

158. (2)

159. (5) Currently, India imports uranium fuel from *Russia, Kazakhstan, Uzbekistan, France and Canada.*

160. (3) The number of MGNREGA job card deletions in West Bengal increased by over 5,000% from 1, 57, 309 in 2021-22 to 83, 36, 115 in 2022-23.

161. (2)

162. (4)

163. (1)

164. (5)

165. (4)

166. (3)

167. (2)

168. (4)

169. (1)

170. (3)

171. (5)

172. (5)

173. (2)

174. (3)

175. (5) Kargil Vijay Diwas is celebrated annually on 26th July to pay tribute to the bravery and valor of the Indian soldiers who fought and made the ultimate sacrifice during the Kargil War in 1999.

176. (5)

177. (5)

178. (5)

179. (3) The United Nations currently has six official languages: English, French, Spanish, Russian, Chinese, and Arabic.

180. (2)

181. (2)

182. (1)

183. (4)

184. (3)

185. (4)

186. (3)

187. (5)

188. (5)

189. (3)

190. (4)

IBPS Clerk Mains

Practice Set – 8

General English

Directions (1-8): *Read the following passage carefully and certain words in the passage are printed in bold letters to help you locate them easily while answering some of these questions.*

The Indian economy is currently passing through a phase of relatively slow growth. However, this should not cloud the fact that over the nine-year period beginning 2005-06, the average annual growth rate was 7.7 per cent. Against this background, the relevant question is whether India has the capability to grow at 8 to 9 per cent in a sustained way. In short, what is the potential rate of growth of India?

Normally, potential growth is measured using trends with some filters. In one sense, these are backward-looking measures, since they depend on historically observed data. In the case of measuring capacity utilisation in manufacturing, the maximum capacity is very often taken as the maximum output achieved in the recent period. Perhaps, in the case of determining the potential rate of growth of the economy also, one can take the maximum growth rate achieved in the recent past as the lowest estimate of the potential. However, this assumption will be valid only if there is reason to believe that the maximum growth rate achieved in the recent past was not a one-off event and that the growth rate achieved was robust and replicable.

India achieved a growth rate of 9.5 per cent in 2005-06, followed by 9.6 per cent and 9.3 per cent in the subsequent two years. After declining a bit in the wake of international financial crisis, the growth rate went back to 8.9 per cent in 2010-11. In many ways the growth rate achieved in the high phase period of 2005- 06 to 2007-08 was robust. The domestic savings rate during this period averaged 34.9 per cent of GDP. Similarly, the gross capital formation rate averaged 36.2 per cent. The current account deficit (CAD) remained low with an average of 1.2 per cent of GDP. Agricultural growth during this period averaged 5 per cent, and the annual manufacturing growth rate was 11 per cent. The capital flows were large but as the CAD remained low, the **accretion** to reserves amounted to $144 billion. Inflation during the period averaged 5.2 per cent. The combined fiscal deficit of the Centre and States was 5.2 per cent of GDP, well below the stipulated 6 per cent. Thus on many dimensions the growth rate was robust.

Unlike in the 1980s when the pick-up in growth was accompanied by deterioration in fiscal deficit and current account, the sharp increase in growth between 2005-06 and 2007-08 happened with the stability parameters at desired levels. Also, a booming external environment provided good support.

To assess whether the high growth phase can be replicated, we need to understand the factors that led to the slowdown since 2011-12. Complicating the analysis of this period is the revision of national income numbers with a new base. The two sets of numbers present a somewhat differing picture. According to the earlier series, the growth rate of the Indian economy fell below 5 per cent in 2012-13 and 2013-14. But the new series shows a decline below 5 per cent only in 2012-13. For 2013-14, the new series records a growth rate of 6.6 per cent, as against 4.7 per cent according to the earlier estimate. For 2014-15 and 2015-16, there is only one set of numbers, that is, according to the new series. For both the years the growth rate is above 7 per cent. These are good growth rates under any circumstance, let alone the current global situation. Anyway, we have come down from the growth rate of 9-plus per cent which we had seen earlier.

Three sets of reasons are attributed for the slowdown. First, the external environment had deteriorated sharply. The recovery from the crisis of 2008 was **tepid**. One country after another in the developed world came under pressure. Strangely, however, international commodity prices including crude oil prices remained high until a couple of years ago. All this had an adverse impact on developing countries, including India. However, it would be wrong to attribute the slowdown in India primarily to external factors. The domestic factors are the key. Second, there were severe supply bottlenecks. Agricultural production fell sharply in 2009-10 because of a severe drought. This triggered an inflation which lasted for several years thereafter. Coal output fell. Iron ore output fell, partly because of court decisions. The third set of reasons is basically non-economic which led collectively to a weakening of investment. A multitude of issues relating to scams and perceived delays in decision-making created an element of uncertainty in the minds of investors. New investments began to fall.

The rise in investment rate must be supported by a rise in the domestic saving rate. An increase in investment rate supported by a widening current account deficit is not sustainable and is fraught with serious consequences. Only a current account deficit in the region of 1 to 1.5 per cent is sustainable. Incremental capital output ratio is a catch-all variable which is influenced by a host of factors. Obviously, it depends on technology. It also depends upon the skill of the labour force which in turn depends on the quality of the education system. Another catch-all expression "ease of doing business" is also relevant (*i.e.*) bureaucratic hurdles which **impede** speedy execution of projects need to be removed. Thus improving the productivity of capital needs action on several fronts.

Making a prediction about the future is always hazardous. Many things can go wrong. The Indian economy in the recent past has shown that it has the **resilience** to grow at 8 to 9 per cent. Therefore achieving the required investment rate to support such a high growth is very much in the realm of possibility. However, we need to overcome the current phase of declining investment rate. Investment sentiment is influenced by non-economic factors as well. An environment of political and social **cohesion** is imperative. Equally, we can get the incremental capital- output ratio (ICOR) to a lower level. Raising the productivity of capital will require policy reforms including administrative reforms as well as firm-level improvements. The "potential" to grow at 8 to 9 per cent at least for a decade exists. We have to make it happen.

1. In context of the given passage, which of the following is/are the reason for economic slowdown of India?
(1) Jaunty recovery from the crisis of 2008
(2) Court's verdict to stop production of coal.
(3) Domestic barriers like draught, inflation etc.
(4) Various barriers introduced by the government.
(5) All of these

2. According to the given passage, what does 'ease of doing business imply?
(1) End of bureaucracy
(2) Eliminating nepotism
(3) Availability of funds
(4) Eliminating Red tapism
(5) Not clear from the passage

3. On what factors does incremental capital output ratio NOT depend?
(1) Technology
(2) Skilled labour
(3) Better education system
(4) Low fiscal deficit
(5) It depends on all the given options

4. On the basis of the given passage, which of the following options cannot be inferred?
(1) Corruption is one of the reasons for the economic slowdown of India
(2) There is a dissimilitude between the calculations based on new base and the previous one.
(3) The Indian economy experienced a great robust throughout the previous decade.
(4) Fiscal deficit below six percent is proviso.
(5) Nature also played an important role in slowing down Indian economy.

5. According to the given passage, which of the following option is the best reason which supports the author's conclusion that 'high growth is very much in the realm of possibility'?
(1) Flourishing service, agricultural and

manufacturing sectors of India.

(2) Policy reforms introduced by the current government.

(3) Increasing growth rate and investment rate

(4) India's potential to grow at a high rate

(5) None of these

6. On the basis of your reading, choose an appropriate title for the passage.

(1) The Indian economy: The phase of sluggish growth.

(2) India's potential.

(3) India's promising past results.

(4) Can India grow fast: An introspection

(5) Ease of doing business

Directions (7-8): *Choose the word/group of words which is **MOST SIMILAR** in meaning to the word/ group of words printed in bold as used in the passage.*

7. ACCRETION

(1) Adherence (2) Accumulation

(3) Approval (4) Devaluation

(5) Upsurge

8. IMPEDE

(1) Delay (2) Violate

(3) Defer (4) Taint

(5) Diagnose

Directions (9-15): *Read the following passage carefully and answer the questions given below it. Certain words have been printed in bold to help you to locate them while answering some of the questions.*

Brexit has **evoked** a **spate** of comments. These comments fall into broadly two categories. The first set of comments focusses on the short-term and medium- term impact of Brexit on the U.K., Europe and the rest of the world including India. The second goes into the reasons behind this decision of the British. Globalisation has been interpreted in many ways. In broad terms, globalisation denotes the free movement of goods, services, capital, funds, ideas, technology and people across countries. Many people think globalisation is a recent phenomenon. This is not true. This has been going on for centuries. What has made it unique in recent times is the speed of the movement. Great Britain and many other countries in Europe have reached the present level of economic development only because of this free movement. In both demographic and geographic terms, Britain is a small country. It is not the size of the domestic market that determined its growth. London could not have emerged as the financial centre of the world but for the free flow of capital.

The **gamut** of financial services offered by London is geared to meet world demand and not that of Britain alone. Even after the exit from the EU, Britain cannot remain as an isolated island. It has to be part of an international trade regime which allows for free trade. What then could have motivated a little more than 50 per cent of the population to come out of the EU? It has something to do with the nature of the relationship within the EU. The EU has evolved over the last seven decades. From a loose arrangement, it has become a tight bureaucratic organisation with its jurisdiction extending to multifarious activities. When the euro was created as a common currency, Britain opted out of it. The European Central Bank sets a common monetary policy stance for all member countries. This itself has been a source of irritation to many member countries. This came out prominently at the time of the Greek crisis. With the loss of one instrument of control — namely, the exchange rate variation — the entire burden of adjustment had to be through employment and output changes. As one commentator put it, the EU has moved up its aspiration from the idea of 'common' market to 'single' market. It is this transition which half of Britain has resented. The complex set of regulations **emanating** from Brussels has made at least a section of the British people feel that they have lost 'independence'. Some of the elite of Britain who voted to 'leave' feel this way. They think that control has moved to unelected bureaucrats in Brussels. What has induced the 'non-elite' to vote for Brexit was the EU's migration policy. The free movement of people has been the last straw that broke the camel's back. The low-paid jobs in the U.K. have been taken over by migrants predominantly from Eastern Europe. In an economy which has been growing slowly (even though the U.K. is a better performer than other European countries in recent years), this has come as a shock. The spirit of 'nationalism' still runs high. The poor in Britain feel that they have been cheated by the migrants. Absorbing migrants is not new for Britain. The Asian and African migrants constitute a significant proportion of the population. All this happened when the economy was strong and growing. But this is not the situation now, and the **resentment** is in one sense natural. However, looked at globally, the poor in the countries from which people migrate have benefited. The British have also gained to the extent that the free movement of people has enabled highly skilled professionals to find positions all over Europe. The 'leave' vote thus was motivated by two considerations: one, the degree of integration that the EU was trying to impose, and two, the migration policy which allowed a free movement of people across countries. Globalisation is not really the devil. If the EU arrangement had been restricted only to free movement of goods, services, capital and funds, it could not have led to any deep resentment. It is the attempt at greater economic integration that has been interpreted as a loss of sovereignty and resented. Globalisation, with its emphasis on efficiency (since goods and services will get produced at the least cost centres), can lead to greater inequality theoretically.

Within a country also, the more efficient including professionals gain disproportionately. This situation gets worse if economies are growing slowly. The U.S. has always prided itself on saying that the system they have is 'people's capitalism'. Inequalities do not matter much when economies are growing strongly and when new entrants to the labour force find employment easily. Countervailing measures are needed to take care of the adverse impact of globalisation. For this reason, we cannot throw the baby out with the bath water. The developed countries face a serious dilemma. They have reached a stage in their development when further growth will be slow. This will have implications for absorbing the labour that gets added to the market. Complicating the situation is technological development which is increasingly labour-saving. New technologies have a twofold impact. First, they reduce the demand for labour in general. Second, in particular they make unskilled and semi-skilled work redundant. They demand new skills for which retraining may be needed. Distribution of income has thus become an issue which needs to be dealt with directly. Brexit is not a blow against globalisation per se. Labour does not stand in the same category as capital, even though both are factors of production. Migration hurts when the economy is at a low ebb. Britain, along with other developed countries, faces a basic problem of coping with a growth potential which is far lower than the growth rate they had seen before 2008.

9. To what aspect this article is devoted by the author?

(1) Impact of Brexit on U.K and Europe.

(2) Impact of globalization.

(3) Motivation behind the vote against greater economic integration.

(4) The implications of Brexit on the migration in Britain.

(5) Countervailing measures that are needed to take care of the adverse impact of globalisation.

10. What has been the reason for the infuriation of the member countries of European Union?

(1) Technological development which is increasingly labour-saving.

(2) The increase in the EU's propensity towards single market.

(3) Britain's refusal to accept euro as its currency even after common monetary policy stance for all the members.

(4) The migration policy which allowed a free movement of people across countries.

(5) The increase of inequality in economically strong countries which has generated a new nationalism.

11. Which of the following is one of the reasons for major section of British people to vote against European Union?

(1) Low wages due to the abundance of labour force migrating from Asian countries to the Britain.

(2) Slow economic growth and incompetence of the new technologies because of which they are becoming more financially weak.

(3) The jurisdiction enjoyed by the unelected officials in Brussels.

(4) The spirit of nationalism among the some sections of British people.

(5) Discrimination of Britain by other member countries because of both demography and geography.

12. Which of the following statement is false regarding the impact of globalization?

(*i*) Globalization that stresses on productivity leads to inequality.

(*ii*) Globalization has been attributed as the primary reason for the loss of supremacy in British people by the author.

(*iii*) Globalization is a major factor which helped London in becoming a financial center of the World.

(1) Only (*ii*) (2) Both (*ii*) and (*iii*)
(3) Only (*iii*) (4) Both (*i*) and (*ii*)
(5) All of these.

13. What is the peril of migration?

(1) Complications in the technological development.

(2) Increase in the inequality in the economies growing at a faster rate like Britain.

(3) Redundant semi-skilled and skilled work in general.

(4) Disbursement of salary is becoming a major issue because of increased number of labour.

(5) None of these.

Directions (14-15): *Choose the word/group of words which is **MOST SIMILAR** in meaning to the word/ group of words printed in bold as used in the passage.*

14. EVOKED

(1) Aplomb (2) Subdue
(3) Extinguish (4) Elicit
(5) Obsolete

15. SPATE

(1) Meristematic (2) Deluge
(3) Paradox (4) Sparse
(5) Paucity

Directions (16-20): *In each of the following sentence there are three blank spaces. Below each sentence there are five options and each option consists of three words which can be filled up in the blanks in the sentence to make the sentence grammatically correct.*

16. Indian Cricket has seen many .... captains. But Dhoni was certainly a/an .... one in many ways. As skipper, he mainly focused on cultivating team spirit and creating .... for young players.

(1) exceptional, diminutive, chances.
(2) sturdy, serendipitous, chances
(3) stout, robust, opportunity
(4) Stalwart, extraordinary, opportunities.
(5) common, exceptional, prospects.

17. Pakistani's Defense Minister Khwaja Muhammad Asif, for all practical purposes, recently Israel with a .... nuclear attack, in response to a fake news report that the Israelis had said they would use nuclear .... against Pakistan if it sent ground troops to Syria.

(1) threatened, retaliatory, weapons
(2) Jeopardized, reciprocating, armor
(3) admonished, riposte, weapon
(4) rebuked, counter, armament
(5) rebuffed, retorted, weapons

18. The line seems to be a direct .... to the establishment of a caliphate. But those who know the context of Faiz the poet, the man and his work correctly interpret it as a communist vision of life, with the .... of the .... prevailing.

(1) Commendation, democracy, precariat
(2) Invocation, dictatorship, proletariat
(3) Intercession, autonomy, rabble
(4) Citation, anarchism, bourgeoisie
(5) Intervention, despot, common people

19. News and social media companies have a moral .... to ensure that they do not, directly or otherwise, deliberately .... the facts to their audiences and pass them off for news. If it is a post-truth world we ...., this becomes especially important.

(1) obligation, distort, desire
(2) commitment, tarnish, denounce

(3) responsibility, misrepresent, inhabit

(4) purport, besmirch ,stigmatize

(5) implication, enhance, reside

20. Activists in the country have long protested its .... society that essentially .... women from travelling, marrying or attending college without permission from a male relative, who is called their ....

(1) benevolent, forbid, steward

(2) Pre-Adamite, prevent, custodian

(3) pre-eminent, restrict, protector

(4) venerable, condemns, manciple.

(5) patriarchal, prohibits, guardian.

21. Five statements are given below, labelled a, b, c, d and e. Among these, four statements are in logical order and form a coherent paragraph. From the given options, choose the option that does not fit into the theme of the paragraph.

(1) This can be seen in the growing importance cities are receiving in the distinct "worlds" of government, business, think tanks, academia and civil society.

(2) After years of ambivalence, urbanization is increasingly being embraced, or at least acknowledged, in India.

(3) Each of these "worlds" is populated by experts in specific "fields" within the urban realm such as planning, environment, transport, housing, finance and health.

(4) sustainability is at the core of the "New Urban Agenda". A substantial portion is dedicated to various "transformative commitments for sustainable urban development"

(5) The multiple "fields" within these parallel "worlds" typically operate as silos and do not interact with the other "fields" and "worlds".

22. Five statements are given below, labelled a, b, c, d and e. Among these, four statements are in logical order and form a coherent paragraph. From the given options, choose the option that does not fit into the theme of the paragraph.

(1) It is often said that the urgent and the immediate are not the same as important.

(2) Therefore, one should not be surprised that the Indian corporate sector has kept its calls for lower interest rates and a competitive exchange rate on an auto-replay mode.

(3) Indeed, they are in conflict with one another.

(4) All the urgent and the immediate commentary on the decision by the newly constituted monetary policy committee (MPC) of the Reserve Bank of India (RBI) has already come out.

(5) RBI has released the minutes of the MPC meeting too. The bulk of it has been seen earlier in the press release that followed the meeting

23. Five statements are given below, labelled a, b, c, d and e. Among these, four statements are in logical order and form a coherent paragraph. From the given options, choose the option that does not fit into the theme of the paragraph.

(1) Notwithstanding the good monsoon this year after back-to-back drought years, most commentators agree that the rural economy and the agricultural sector may not be out of distress.

(2) Recent attempts by Rahul Gandhi to mobilize farmers during his Kisan Yatra might not revive the fortunes of the Congress party in Uttar Pradesh, but they did contribute to bringing the issues of farmers and agriculture to the political mainstream.

(3) It is also worth mentioning that most of them were seen as leaders of dominant farming communities or caste groups that benefited from rising profitability and price support.

(4) Given that almost half of the total workers in the country are still engaged in farming and the majority of households in rural areas are still dependent on agriculture, directly or indirectly, issues confronting

the farming community are naturally an important electoral plank.

(5) More so in an environment where rural areas, and the agricultural sector in particular, have been in some distress in recent years.

24. Five statements are given below, labelled a, b, c, d and e. Among these, four statements are in logical order and form a coherent paragraph. From the given options, choose the option that does not fit into the theme of the paragraph.

(1) Dyn is a part of the backbone of the Internet, since it is one of the companies that provides domain name services or DNS to Internet users, and translates simple English-based commands like "livemint.com" typed into a browser into the actual numeric addresses that the Internet's computers use to identify each website.

(2) Security firm Flashpoint has said that it believes that seemingly innocuous items such as video recorders, webcams, closed-circuit security cameras and the like were taken over by malware, and then, without their owners' knowledge, were used to help execute the massive cyber attack.

(3) This outage was astonishing in its ferocity, especially since it co-opted the much vaunted Internet of Things (IoT) into the attack.

(4) It claims that hundreds of thousands of such devices were co-opted into the attack by being infected with malware.

(5) This malware, called Mirai, was released by an anonymous hacker named Anna-senpai some weeks ago.

25. Five statements are given below, labelled a, b, c, d and e. Among these, four statements are in logical order and form a coherent paragraph. From the given options, choose the option that does not fit into the theme of the paragraph.

(1) The mathematician Richard K. Guy is arguably best known for discovering a glider. Assuming that's an intriguing-enough opening, let me explain. In 1970, the British mathematician John Conway invented a board game called, simply, "Life".

(2) Life happens on a grid of squares that stretch in every direction (imagine an infinite chessboard). Each square, or cell, is either alive or dead (or call it black or white, filled or empty).

(3) Now, this is not a game in the conventional sense: there's no way to "win", nor do you play against an opponent. In fact, Life doesn't even need a player as it proceeds. You just set up an initial state and then watch what happens.

(4) To start, you choose a certain number of cells to be live—at random, or in a pattern, whatever. Each cell now evolves according to a set of rules that considers its eight neighbours (left, right, above, below, and on the four corners).

(5) This is the endlessly fascinating question Conway's game raises, and this is why it was and remains today a much discussed favourite among mathematicians and computer scientists.

Directions (26-29): *In each of the following sentences four options are given. You are needed to identify the best way of writing the sentence in context of the correct usage of standard written English.*

26. The entire cast and crew of the film, enjoyed splashing in the pool, bathing in the ocean, and, particularly, to sun bathe on the shore.

(1) The entire cast and crew of the film, enjoyed splashing in the pool, bathing in the ocean, particularly to sun bathing on the shore.

(2) The entire cast and crew of the film, enjoyed splashing in the pool, to have a bath in the ocean, and, particularly, to sun bathe on the shore.

(3) The entire cast and crew of the film, enjoyed swimming in the pool to bathe in the ocean, and, particularly sun bathing on the shore.

(4) The entire cast and crew of the film, enjoyed swimming in the pool, bathing in the ocean, and, particularly, sun bathing on the shore.

(5) No error.

27. No officer had ought to be put into a situation where he was to choose between his love for his family and the responsibilities accompanying his duty.

(1) No officer would be put in a situation where he have to choose between his love for family and the responsibilities accompanying his duty.

(2) No officer had ought to be put into a situation in which he has to choose between his love for his family and the responsibilities accompanying his duty.

(3) No officer should be put into a situation where he has to choose between his love for his family and the responsibilities accompanying his duty.

(4) No officer ought to be put into a situation in which he has to choose between his love for this family and the responsibilities accompanying his duty.

(5) No error.

28. Being a realist, the detective could not accept the statement of the accused that UFOs had caused the disturbance.

(1) Being a realist that he was, the detective could not accept the statement of the accused that UFOs had caused the disturbance.

(2) Since he was a realist, the detective could not accept the statement of the accused that UFOs had caused the disturbance.

(3) Being that he was a realist, the detective could not accept the statement of the accused that UFOs had caused the disturbance.

(4) Realist that he was, the detective could not accept the statement of the accused that UFOs had caused the disturbance.

(5) No error

29. If we cooperate together by dividing up the booty, we shall be able to work together smoothly in the future.

(1) If we cooperate with one other by dividing up the booty, we will be able to work smoothly together in future.

(2) If we cooperate by dividing up the booty, we shall be able to work together smoothly in the future.

(3) If we cooperate by dividing up the booty together, we shall be able to work together smoothly in the future.

(4) If we cooperate with each other by dividing the booty, we shall be able to work together smoothly in the future.

(5) No error.

Directions (30–34): *Which of the words/phrases (1), (2), (3) and (4) given below should replace the words/ phrases given in bold in the following sentences to make it meaningful and grammatically correct. If the sentence is correct as it is and 'No correction is required', mark (5) as the answer.*

30. A very stout, ridged, hairy stem, the **petioled** leaves **compounded** of three broadly ovate, lobed and saw-edged divisions, downy on the underside, and the great **umbels**, which sometimes measure a foot across, all **bear out** the general impression of a Hercules of the fields.

(1) bracken, comprised, flower, bear out

(2) stemmed, composited, cluster, borne off

(3) axis, consist, species, bore

(4) rooted, embraced, flora, bear

(5) None of these

31. The judge **charged him** with a **penalty** rather than a prison sentence **yet** it was his first **misdemeanour**.

(1) indicted him, penance, as, mistake

(2) freed him, sanctions, because, fault

(3) vindicated him off, penalty, even though, wrongdoing

(4) let him off, fine, since, offence.

(5) None of these

32. Following the **footsteps** of many of his predecessors, he promptly **accorded** his election "capitulation" as a/an **infraction** on the divinely **granted** prerogatives of the Holy

See.

(1) pavement, adhered, dereliction, bequeath

(2) ideals, abjured, preservation, conferred

(3) example, repudiated, infringement, bestowed

(4) specimen, forbeared, contravention, entrusted

(5) None of these

33. "We **perceive** data science and data engineering **looming** as job roles this year. **In harmony with** the current trend, technical roles such as software developer and non-technical role such as digital marketing took top two spots as the most popular job **wholes**," Aspiring Minds Co-Founder and CEO Himanshu Aggarwal said.

(1) notice, receding, In step with, levels

(2) recognize, dawning, In compliance with, searches

(3) cloak, appearing, In accordance with, types

(4) see, emerging, In line with, categories

(5) None of these

34. The EU **inquired** to the crisis by implementing a series of financial **relief** mechanisms, such as the European Financial Stability Fund and the European Stability Mechanism, to **furnish** emergency loans to those countries most affected by **advancing** interest rates.

(1) reacted, sustain, divest, mounting

(2) responded, support, provide, skyrocketing

(3) rebutted, aid, deliver, plummeting, escalating

(4) excavated, support, disburse, spiraling

(5) None of these

Directions (35–36): *Sentences given in each question, when properly sequenced form a coherent paragraph. Each sentence is labeled with a letter. Choose the most logical order of sentences amongst the five choices given to construct a paragraph.*

35. A. The newspaper man, the flower seller, the milkman, the sweeper, they are all privy to the chatting and sharing of news that the elderly find comforting.

B. When we remove them from their homes, it is not only the family that they are being removed from, but all those other people that they see every day and whose joys and woes become their own.

C. In our system of living, the elderly at home have a circle of acquaintances, and friends.

D. The loneliness of the discarded elderly is manifold.

E. When we forcibly remove people from surroundings they have been part of for decades we put an un-mendable tear in the fabric of their lives.

(1) DECAB (2) ABDCE

(3) ECADB (4) DBAEC

(5) CBAED

36. A. Some of the worst cancers aren't detected by screening.

B. The only way to be sure is to look at the results of randomized trials comparing cancer deaths in screened and unscreened people.

C. So how can we be confident that getting a screening test regularly is a good idea?

D. Even when screening "works" in such trials, the size of the benefit observed is surprisingly low: Generally, regular screening reduces fatalities from various cancers between 15 percent and 25 percent.

E. They appear suddenly, between regular screenings, and are difficult to treat because they are so aggressive.

(1) DBAEC (2) AECBD

(3) ADBEC (4) ACBED

(5) ACBDE

Directions (37-40): *Read each of the following four sentences to find out whether there is any grammatical mistake/error in it. Choose the sentence with no grammatical error as the correct answer. If all of the given sentences are grammatically incorrect, mark (e) as an answer.*

37. (1) John Wanamaker, founder of the stores that bear his name, once confessed, I learnt 30 year ago that it is foolish to scold.

(2) Whether rich or poor, American or Indian, we all have the same emotions deep with us.

(3) This research indicate that we can no longer avoid significant warning during this century.

(4) Every modern society depends on the trust in the skills and ethics of a variety of institutions such as schools and colleges, hospital and markets.

(5) None of these

38. (1) Many of us have learnt not to make a public display of our emotions, particularly when they are negative.

(2) Though Indians have been increasingly taking up corner office in the international companies, Rahul is the first Indian to lead one of the top four accounting firms globally.

(3) Democracy was suspended not because it came under existential threat but because it has become an obstacle to political ambitions trotted out as the nation's solution.

(4) A virtual takeover of a bankrupt civil society by a coterie of individuals whom cornered tremendous power by being able to represent the state.

(5) None of these

39. (1) India has decided do away with the practice of put each imported food consignment through lab checks and switch to the international norm of random and risk based inspections.

(2) SP Sumit singh, along with Devesh Panday and DSP Hasan, headed separate terms that include cops from six police stations and investigators from the district police crime cell.

(3) Our emission standards are one-tenth that of global averages and far more stringent than even Europe.

(4) The university has received about 500 applicants for the course, out of them 50 will be shortlisted for the programme.

(5) None of these

40. (1) The Reserve bank of India lifted the ban upon imports of gold coins and medallions by banks and trading houses.

(2) President Pranab Mukherjee inaugurated Indian international trade fair 2016 in Pragati maiden in new Delhi.

(3) Three Indian, two women and one man were among the shortlisted 100 applicants whom were chosen for one-way trip to mars under one mission.

(4) Fasting not only deoxifies the system but also gives a person training in endurance, a spirit of acceptance and self control.

(5) None of these

Reasoning Ability & Computer Aptitude

Directions (41-44): *Study the following information carefully to answer the given questions.*

In a certain code language-

"work for earning money" is coded as "Go3 None5 Xor4 Farnin7"

"like six years passed" is coded as "Ti3 Qasse6 Zear5 Mik4"

"hence good amount received" is coded as "Seceive8 Ienc5 Hoo4 Bmoun6"

41. What is the code for "last earning was money"?

(1) Xa3 Mas4 Noney5 Farnin7

(2) None5 Xa3 Mas4 Darnin7

(3) None5 Mas4 Farnin7 Xa3

(4) Mas4 Lone5 Farnin7 Xa3

(5) None of these

42. If "money makes man perfect" is coded as "Nake5 Qerfec7 Na3 None5", then what is the code for "good people always perfect"?

(1) Qeople6 Hoo4 Blway6 Qerfec7

(2) None of these

(3) Hoo4 Qerfec7 Blway6 Qeopl6

(4) Qeople6 Hoo4 Qerfec7 Blway6

(5) Qerfec7 Blway6 Qeople5 Hoo5

43. What is the code for "hence always wrong hance"?

(1) Can't be determined
(2) Blway6 Iance5 Xron5 Ienc5
(3) Ianc5 Xron5 Blway5 Ienc5
(4) Ianc5 Xron5 Ienc4 Blways6
(5) Blway6 Ienc5 Ianc5 Xron5

44. "Farming" is coded as?
(1) None of these (2) Garmin7
(3) Gramin8 (4) Garing8
(5) Earnin7

Directions (45-50): *Read the given information carefully and answer the given questions.*

There are five units *i.e.* 1, 2, 3, 4 and 5. Each unit has a different height. Also each unit contains books and boxes. Unit 2 is above unit 1 and unit 3 is above unit 2 and so on. Every unit is belongs to different country *i.e.* Beijing, Paris, London, Sydney and Zurich. The total height of all five units is equal to 252″ ft.

**Total Height of Unit is equal to the total height of books plus total height of boxes in each unit.*

**Height of books is not equal to the height of boxes. Unless specified so.*

The books belongs to London is an even unit. The total height of unit 1 is 75″ ft. Sydney is not a unit 1. The total height of unit, which belongs to Sydney is 55″ ft. There is only one gap between London and Paris. The height of books and height of boxes in unit 3 are equal. The height of books in unit 2 is not less than 30″ ft. The books are in unit 4 is four more than books, which is in unit 3. The total height of London is not 37″ ft. The total height of unit, which contains 37″ ft is not taking a place, which is immediate above the unit, which contains 20″ ft more than the unit, which belongs to Sydney. The height of boxes in unit 2 is 23″ ft. Unit belongs to Zurich does not contain the equal height of books and boxes. The total height of unit 2 is a odd number and height is more than 50″ ft and less than 55″ ft. Unit 1 contains 23″ ft height of boxes more than unit 4 contains height of boxes and unit 5 contains 7″ ft height of books less than unit 1 contains.

45. What is the total height in unit 3?
(1) 37″ ft (2) None of these
(3) 32″ ft (4) 53″ ft
(5) 75″ ft

46. Unit 3 belongs to which country?
(1) Paris (2) Zurich
(3) Sydney (4) Beijing
(5) London

47. If 'Sydney' is related to 37″ ft in the same way as 'Beijing' is related to 53″ ft. Which of the following is 'Paris' related to, following the same pattern?
(1) 53″ ft (2) 37″ ft
(3) 75″ ft (4) None of these
(5) 32″ ft

48. Four of the following five are alike in a certain way and hence they form a group. Which one of the following does not belong to that group?
(1) Sydney (2) 32″ ft
(3) 75″ ft (4) Paris
(5) Beijing

49. What is the height of box in unit 4?
(1) 23′ ft (2) 17″ ft
(3) 27″ ft (4) 40″ ft
(5) 20″ ft

50. Which unit contains 30″ ft book?
(1) None of these (2) Unit 2
(3) Unit 3 (4) Unit 1
(5) Unit 5

Directions (51-55): *Read the given information carefully and answer the given questions.*

There are eight persons A, B, C, D, E, F, G and F are sitting around a circular table. All of them are facing the center, but not necessarily in the same order.

B sits third to the left of H. There are only one person sits between H and H's husband. G is the husband of A. D sits immediate left of B. C sits third right of A, but C is not immediate neighbor of H's husband. There are three person's sits between A and her husband. C is the spouse of F. B's spouse does not sits immediate right of A's husband.

51. Who sits second right of F?
(1) E (2) None of these
(3) D (4) G's wife

(5) B

52. How many person sits between E's wife and G's wife?

(1) None (2) Two
(3) One (4) Three
(5) Five

53. Four of the following five are alike in a certain way and hence they form a group. Which one of the following does not belong to that group?

(1) G (2) H
(3) B (4) E
(5) A

54. Who sits immediate left of H's husband?

(1) C's spouse (2) G
(3) None of these (4) H
(5) B's spouse

55. If C is related to B in the same way as E's wife is related to A's husband. Which of the following is 'G's wife' related to, following the same pattern?

(1) G (2) F
(3) D (4) H's husband
(5) None of these

Directions (56-59): *Each of the questions below consists of a question and three statements numbered I, II and III given below it. You have to decide whether the data provided in the statements are sufficient to answer the question.*

(1) If statement II and III are sufficient to answer the question, but statement I alone is not sufficient to answer the question.
(2) If all the statements I, II and III taken together are not sufficient to answer the questions.
(3) If statements I and II is sufficient to answer the question, but statement III is not sufficient to answer the question.
(4) If all the statements I, II and III taken together are sufficient to answer the questions.
(5) If statement I and III are sufficient to answer the question, but statement II alone is not sufficient to answer the question.

56. Who among A, B, C, D, E and F is the tallest?

I. Only two of them are taller than C.
II. D is shorter than F.
III. C is taller than A, but shorter than F and B.

57. How is M related to O?

I. J is the sister of K, who is the son of M. L is the brother of M.
II. L is the brother of M. M is the son of Q.
III. M is the son of R, who is the husband of Q. R is the brother of O.

58. Who amongst S, T, U, V, W and X is the tallest person?

I. X is taller than W but smaller than U. U is smaller than T.
II. U is taller than S and W but smaller than T. T is not the tallest person
III. V is taller than T and U. W is not the smallest person.

59. In which direction point D with respect to point M?

I. Point M is towards west of point E, who is the north-west of point P.
II. Point P is to the east of point S. Point M is the north of point S.
III. Point C is the west of point D. Point D is the west of point S.

60. "We have formulated a 10 point programme to curb molestation cases against woman and we are confident of restricting the eve-teasing cases with the help of our sincere cops"- Director General of Police of city 'X'.

Which of the following, if true, would weaken the statement?

(1) City 'X' is known among those cities where they are least crime records.
(2) City 'X' is the most populated city in the world.
(3) On several occasions women have complained against police cops and have charged them of indulging in eve-teasing.
(4) Literacy rate of city 'X' is the highest amongst all cities.
(5) Many NGOs are cooperating with the police forces in ensuring a peaceful life

in city 'X'.

Directions (61-65): *Read the given information carefully and answer the given questions.*

Two buses A and B starts their journey from same depot but not necessary in the same order. Bus A starts moving 6 km towards north direction to point P then take a right turn and move 18 km to reach point R, then take a left turn and move 12 km to reach point S. Point P, Q and R lies in a same line. Distance between P and Q is half of the distance between point Q and R. Bus B starts to move toward west 2 km more than point Q and R from depot and reach point W. than take a right turn and walk 18 km to reach point U. U, V and W lies in the same line as distance of V and W is double of the distance between U and V. from point U bus B take a right turn and reach point S. Point T lies between U and S in exact midway.

61. What is the total distance between U and S?

(1) 29 km (2) 32 km

(3) 36 km (4) 30 km

(5) 28 km

62. In which direction is point T with respect to point W?

(1) North (2) South

(3) North West (4) North East

(5) South West.

63. A boy want to go depot and starts walking toward north from Point W after reaching point V he suddenly realize that he is going to wrong direction. So what is the shortest route from point V to bus Depot?

(1) Back to point W then go to depot from there.

(2) From point V he should going to east direction 14 km than move toward south and reach depot.

(3) From point V going towards north to reach point U from there, he should reach point S than point R than P than depot.

(4) Both (1) and (2)

(5) Can't determine.

64. What is the distance between T and S?

(1) 14 km (2) 12 km

(3) 16 km (4) 18 km

(5) 6 km

65. Bus A is moving in which direction currently?

(1) West (2) North-east

(3) South (4) North

(5) East

66. A government survey released today shows that 80% of the people who fly are satisfied with the service they receive from the airlines in this country .Three interviewers stood outside a major airport and asked people leaving the terminal, "Do you have any complaints about the flight you just got off?" Only 20 percent responded "yes!"

Which of the following, if true, would most **undermine** the conclusion of the argument above?

(1) Sixty percent of the people coming out of the airline terminal were not people who had just gotten off a flight.

(2) One percent of the people approached by the interviewers refused to respond to their inquiries.

(3) The interviewers began their inquiry just after passengers were discharged from a flight that was 40 minutes late.

(4) The interviewers were able to speak to only 70 percent of the people leaving the terminal, but those people were selected at random.

(5) For six months following the day of the interviews, no official complaints were filled by any passenger with the Federal agency that regulated the airlines.

Directions (67-72): *Read the given information carefully and answer the given questions.*

There are seven persons in a family namely A, B, C, D, E, F and G. All of them related with each other in a order. Also each person has a different age. The information is given as-

A is older than B but younger than E. The third oldest person in the family is 38 year old. B is the sister of A. C is the father of A. The third youngest person of the family is 35 year old. G is the oldest person of the family. B is the niece of F. E is older than B. F is the husband of E. G and D are married couple. C's mother is 69 year old. C is younger than

F. Oldest person of the family is male member.

67. If total age of D and B is 75 year, then what is age of B?

(1) 40 year (2) 37 year
(3) 6 year (4) None of these
(5) 10 year

68. How is D related to A?

(1) Grandfather
(2) Mother
(3) Can't be determined
(4) Grandmother
(5) Father

69. Who among the following person is 35 year old?

(1) A (2) E
(3) F (4) C
(5) D

70. How many person are older than A?

(1) Six (2) Four
(3) None of these (4) Three
(5) Five

71. What is possible age of C?

(1) 52 year (2) 39 year
(3) 37 year (4) 29 year
(5) None of these

72. What is the possible age of oldest person of the family?

(1) 74 year (2) 68 year
(3) 62 year (4) 80 year
(5) Both (1) and (4)

73. **Statement:** The annual requirement of blood in our country is 6 million units whereas the generation is only 3.5 million units per annum at present.

Courses of action:

I. Blood donors should be attracted by telling them how the act of donating blood would improve their health.

II. Blood donors should be attracted by providing them monetary incentives.

III. More and more private blood banks should be encouraged.

(1) Either I or II follows
(2) I and II follow
(3) II and III follow
(4) All follow
(5) Only I follow

Directions (74-75): *Given below are pairs of events 'A' and 'B'. You have to read both the events 'A' and 'B' and decide their nature of relationship. You have to assume that the information given in 'A' and 'B' is true and you will not assume anything beyond the given information in deciding the answer. Mark answer*

(1) If 'A' is the effect and 'B' is its immediate and principal cause.
(2) If 'A' is the immediate and principal cause and 'B' is its effect.
(3) If 'A' is an effect but 'B' is not its immediate and principal cause.
(4) If 'B' is an effect but 'A' is not its immediate and principal cause.
(5) None of these

74. **Statement (A):** The government has decided to roll back the hike in the prices of cooking gas and kerosene.

Statement (B): Some ministers had resigned in protest against the hike in prices of cooking gas and other petroleum products.

75. **Statement (A):** A traveller found cockroaches in the crevices of his seat and also in the toilets of India's most prestigious train, the Rajdhani Express.

Statement (B): He drew the attention of catering manager, Western Railway, to the insects.

Directions (76-80): *Read the given information carefully and answer the given questions.*

There are eight persons namely A, B, C, D, E, F, G and H has born in the same month of different year i.e. 1969, 1972, 1978, 1981, 1989, 1997, 2000 and 2005. Their age are considered as on the same month of 2016.

G is born in even number year, but not born in the year, which does not divisible by 4. A is 36 year old now. B is 17 year older than F, who is 8 year younger than A. There are eight year gap between age of E and age of D. H is nine year younger than C, but not born in 2005. E was born earlier than G.

76. In which year does F born?
(1) 1969 (2) 1989
(3) 2005 (4) 1981
(5) 1978

77. What is the age of G in 2016?
(1) 11 year (2) 18 year
(3) 26 year (4) 16 year
(5) 35 year

78. Four of the following five are alike in a certain way and hence they form a group. Which one of the following does not belong to that group?
(1) 1969 (2) 1978
(3) 2005 (4) 1981
(5) 1997

79. By how many years B was born before E?
(1) 24 year (2) None of these
(3) 30 year (4) 19 year
(5) 25 year

80. How many years gap between C and D?
(1) 33 year (2) 16 year
(3) 36 year (4) None of these
(5) 27 year

81. In MODEMS
(1) several digital signals are multiplexed
(2) a digital signal changes some characteristic of a carrier wave
(3) digital signal is amplified
(4) All of these
(5) None of these

82. Which of the following can be used to control the movement of a cursor on a video screen?
(1) Mouse (2) OCR
(3) Card punch (4) Joystick
(5) None of these

83. Which method is used to connect a remote computer?
(1) Device (2) Dialup
(3) Diagnostic (4) Logic circuit
(5) None of these

84. What digits are representative at all binary numbers?
(1) 0 (2) 1
(3) Both (1) and (2) (4) 3
(5) None of these

85. ROM is an example of which of the following?
(1) volatile memory
(2) cache memory
(3) nonvolatile memory
(4) virtual memory
(5) None of these

86. Full form of LSI is:
(1) Low-scale Internet
(2) Large-Scale Internet
(3) Low-Scale Integration
(4) Large-Scale Integration
(5) Local-Scale Integration

87. TO correct error in a program:
(1) Debugging (2) Error moving
(3) Bugging (4) Delete
(5) Coding

88. Which memory is maximum in computer bits
(1) TB (2) GB
(3) MB (4) KB
(5) BIT

89. Writing set of instruction to run a software
(1) Coding (2) Buffering
(3) Decoding (4) Amplifying
(5) Debugging

90. How many bits are there in hexadecimal code:
(1) 16 (2) 0
(3) 2 (4) 4
(5) 32

Quantitative Aptitude

Directions (91-95): *What will come in the place of the question mark (?) in the following number series?*

91. 9 11 16 26 ? 69
(1) 40 (2) 41
(3) 42 (4) 43

(5) None of these

92. 3 4 10 33 136 ? 183

(1) 700 (2) 590
(3) 695 (4) 685
(5) None of these

93. 21 24 32 45 63 ?

(1) 85 (2) 86
(3) 84 (4) 82
(5) None of these

94. 6 3 3 6 24 ?

(1) 192 (2) 191
(3) 190 (4) 189
(5) None of these

95. 7 10 16 28 ? 100

(1) 49 (2) 53
(3) 50 (4) 51
(5) 52

96. 5% of one number (X) is 25% more than another number (Y). If the difference between the numbers is 96 then find the value of X?

(1) 90 (2) 100
(3) 92 (4) 96
(5) None of these

97. The ratio of A's age 3 years ago and B's age 5 years ago is 4 : 5. If A is 4 years younger than B then what is the present age of B?

(1) 16 (2) 14
(3) 11 (4) 15
(5) None of these

98. Two pipes A and B can fill a tank in 16 hrs and 12 hrs respectively. The capacity of the tank is 240 litres. Both the pipes are opened simultaneously and closed after 2 hrs. How much more water (In Liters) needed to fill the tank?

(1) 100 (2) 170
(3) 70 (4) 190
(5) None of these

99. A person cover 32 km downstream is 240 minutes and same person cover 48 km upstream in 1440 minutes. Then find the rate of current?

(1) 4 kmph (2) 5 kmph
(3) 3 kmph (4) 2 kmph
(5) None of these

100. The simple interest on a certain sum at 15% per annum for 5 year is Rs. 1500 more to the simple interest on the same at 12% per annum for the same period. Find the sum-

(1) Rs. 12000 (2) Rs. 12500
(3) Rs. 8000 (4) Rs. 10000
(5) None of these

101. The numerator of a fraction is decreased by 25% and the denominator is increased by 250%. If the resultant fraction is 6/5 what is the original fraction?

(1) 22/5 (2) 24/5
(3) 27/6 (4) 28/5
(5) 30/11

102. A dishonest vendor professes to sell fruits at the cost price but he uses a weight of 800 grams in lieu of 1 kg weight. Find his percentage gain.

(1) 22% (2) 24%
(3) 25% (4) 30%
(5) 20%

103. A is 2.5 times as good workman as B and A is able to finish the work in 50 days less than B. Find the time in which they can do it working together.

(1) $21\frac{18}{19}$ days (2) $23\frac{17}{21}$ days
(3) $22\frac{6}{7}$ days (4) $20\frac{3}{4}$ days
(5) $25\frac{1}{4}$ days–

104. The total of the ages of a class of 60 girls is 900 years. The average age of 20 girls is 12 years and that of the other 20 girls is 16 years. What is the average age of the remaining girls?

(1) 14 years (2) 15 years
(3) 16 years (4) 17 years
(5) none of these

105. Mr. Ankit invests 14% of his monthly income every month *i.e.* Rs. 1,750 in shares, 8% in Insurance policies and 7% in fixed deposits.

What is the total annual amount invested by him?

(1) Rs. 3275 (2) Rs. 3450
(3) Rs. 3625 (4) Rs. 3800
(5) none of these

Directions (106-110): *Given below is the table showing marks (out of 100) of 5 students A, B, C, D and E in class test on different days of a week.*

Set	A	B	C	D	E
Monday	74	65	36	59	84
Tuesday	69	68	70	51	72
Wednesday	49	82	75	64	59
Thursday	55	72	62	70	68
Friday	67	56	77	81	74

106. What is the difference between total score of B on Monday, Wednesday and Thursday together and the total score of E on Tuesday, Wednesday and Friday together?

(1) 12 (2) 14
(3) 10 (4) 20
(5) None of these

107. Marks of E on Monday is what percent more than marks of B on Thursday?

(1) 15% (2) 16.66%
(3) 20% (4) 25%
(5) None of these

108. What is the average marks scored by C on the given days?

(1) 60 (2) 62
(3) 52 (4) 64
(5) None of these

109. What is the ratio of total marks scored by C on Tuesday and Wednesday together to the total marks scored by D on the same days together ?

(1) 23 : 28 (2) 28 : 23
(3) 29 : 23 (4) 23 : 29
(5) None of these

110. Total marks scored by E on all days together are how much more than total marks scored by A on all days together?

(1) 43 (2) 45
(3) 55 (4) 65
(5) None of these

Directions (111-125): *What should come in place of question mark (?) in the following questions?*

111. 36% of 170 + ?% of 592 = 150

(1) 14.6 (2) 17.8
(3) 16.4 (4) 15
(5) None of these

112. $(12.11)^2 + (?)^2 = 732.2921$

(1) 20.2 (2) 24.2
(3) 23.1 (4) 19.2
(5) None of these

113. $288 \div ? \times 57 = 2052$

(1) 8 (2) 7
(3) 6 (4) 9
(5) None of these

114. $(1125 - 274 - 323) \div (875 - 654 - 155) = ?$

(1) 9 (2) 6
(3) 7 (4) 8
(5) None of these

115. $(42)^2 \div 6.3 \times 26 = ?$

(1) 7182 (2) 7269
(3) 7260 (4) 7240
(5) None of these

116. 115% of 4880 – 85% of 1640 = ?

(1) 4218 (2) 4368
(3) 4448 (4) 4628
(5) None of these

117. $3251 + 587 + 369 - ? = 3007$

(1) 1250 (2) 1300
(3) 1375 (4) 1400
(5) None of these

118. $\sqrt[3]{9261} \times \sqrt{62742241} = ? + 89$

(1) 166254 (2) 166259
(3) 166253 (4) 166252
(5) None of these

119. $18.6 \times 3 + 7.2 - 16.5 = ? + 21.7$

(1) 35.7 (2) 21.6
(3) 24.8 (4) 27.6
(5) None of these

120. $5.35 + 4.43 + 0.45 + 45.34 + 534 = ?$

(1) 597.27 (2) 589.57
(3) 596.87 (4) 596.67
(5) None of these

121. $\sqrt[3]{35937} \times 1331 = 121 \times ?$
(1) 443 (2) 673
(3) 363 (4) 303
(5) None of these

122. 0.5% of 674 of 0.8% of 225 = ?
(1) 7.066 (2) 9.12
(3) 6.066 (4) 5.17
(5) None of these

123. $\dfrac{854 \times 854 \times 854 - 276 \times 276\ 276}{854 \times 854 + 854 \times 276 + 276 \times 276} = ?$
(1) 1130 (2) 578
(3) 565 (4) 1156
(5) None of these

124. 56% of 225 + 20% of 150 = ? – 109
(1) 49 (2) 103
(3) 53 (4) 47
(5) None of these

125. 12% of 1885 = ? ÷ 6
(1) 1248.4 (2) 1292.2
(3) 1312.6 (4) 1357.2
(5) None of these

126. Rohit starts a business with Rs. 6,500 and after 8 months Shyam joins Rohit as his partner. After 4 years the profit is divided in the ratio of 13 : 12. What is Shyam's contribution in the capital?
(1) Rs. 7400 (2) Rs. 7200
(3) Rs. 7250 (4) Rs. 7630
(5) Rs. 7480

127. The speed of a boat in still water is 20 kmph and the rate of current is 4 kmph. The distance travelled by the boat downstream in 30 minutes is
(1) 8 km (2) 10 km
(3) 12 km (4) 14 km
(5) 16 km

128. Rs. 2,000 is invested at 10% p.a. on simple interest. If that interest is added to the principal after every 20 years, the amount will become Rs. 14,000 after
(1) 15 years (2) 33 years
(3) 16 years (4) 40 years
(5) None of these

129. Two trains 128 meters and 122 meters long are running towards each other on parallel lines at 48 kmph and 42 kmph respectively. In what time will they clear off each other from the moment they meet?
(1) 10 seconds (2) 12 seconds
(3) 18 seconds (4) 14 seconds
(5) 9 seconds

130. A boat running downstream covers 28 km in 7 hours, while for covering the same distance upstream it takes 14 hours. What is the speed of the boat in still water?
(1) 4 kmph (2) 3 kmph
(3) 4.2 kmph (4) 5 kmph
(5) 6 kmph

131. Ram sells a car to Mohan at a profit of 16% and Mohan sells it to Shyam at a profit of 25%. How much profit% Ram would have got if he had sold the car directly to Shyam at the price Shyam bought it?
(1) 41% (2) 42%
(3) 45% (4) 50%
(5) None of these

132. A sum on compound interest amounts to Rs. 2410 in 3 years and Rs. 2651 in 4 years. Find the sum.
(1) Rs. 1216 (2) Rs. 1500
(3) Rs. 1900 (4) Rs. 1600
(5) None of these

133. Ajay covers distance by car driving at 60 kmph and returns back to the starting point riding on a scooter at 45 kmph. What is his average speed?
(1) 50.12 km (2) 50.6 km
(3) 51.52 km (4) 51.42 km
(5) None of these

134. Two trains of length 120 m and 90 m respectively with the same speed pass a static pole in 8 seconds and 6 seconds respectively. In what time they will cross each other if they are moving in opposite directions?

(1) 14 seconds (2) 6 seconds
(3) 20 seconds (4) 7 seconds
(5) None of these

135. A train travelling at the speed of 50 kmph leaves from a station. Another train travelling at speed of 60 kmph leaves the same station after 7 hours in the same direction. They will meet after what distance?
(1) 1800 km (2) 2100 km
(3) 2400 km (4) 2700 km
(5) None of these

136. A alone would take 6 hours more to complete the job than if both A and B would work together. When B worked alone he took 1.5 hours more to complete the job and A and B worked together. How much time they will take if they work together?
(1) 3 hours (2) 4 hours
(3) 4.5 hours (4) 5 hours
(5) none of these

137. A dealer bought an item at 10% discount on its original price. He sold it at 35% more than the original price. What percentage profit did he get?
(1) 25% (2) 45%
(3) 22.5% (4) 50%
(5) 35%

138. The diameter of a circle is equal to the perimeter of a square whose area is 3136 sq cm. What is the circumference of the circle?
(1) 352 cm (2) 704 cm
(3) 39424 cm (4) Cannot be determined
(5) None of these

139. Cost of fencing a circular plot at the rate of Rs. 15 per m is Rs. 3300. What will be the cost of flooring the plot at the rate of Rs. 100 per square metre?
(1) Rs. 385000 (2) Rs. 220000
(3) Rs. 350000 (4) Cannot be determined
(5) None of these

140. Area of a rectangle is equal to the area of a circle whose radius is 14 cm. If the breadth of the rectangle is 22 cm, what is its length?
(1) 24 cm (2) 28 cm
(3) 26 cm (4) Cannot be determined
(5) None of these

General/Financial Awareness

141. 'May 1' is celebrated as the 'Labour Day'. This day is also celebrated as the formation day of which of the following States?
(1) Karnataka (2) Madhya Pradesh
(3) Telangana (4) Andhra Pradesh
(5) Gujarat

142. Which is the Capital of' Myanmar'?
(1) Naypyidaw
(2) Yangon
(3) Mandalay
(4) Other than those given as options
(5) Began

143. On the occasion of birthday of Dhyan Chand Indian celebrates National Sports Day on August 29 every year. Dhyan Chand was a famous
(1) cricket player (2) hockey player
(3) chess player (4) tennis player
(5) wrestling player

144. According to the India 'Tourism Statistics at Glance 2020' report released by the Ministry of Tourism, India's position in the world in terms of international tourists arrival is
(1) 52nd (2) 26th
(3) 19th (4) 14th
(5) Other than those given as options

145. Who amongst the following is the Minister of Home Affairs in Union Cabinet of India at present?
(1) Amit Shah (2) Nitin Gadkari
(3) Sushma Swaraj (4) Maneka Gandhi
(5) Rajnath Singh

146. For building up a data repository and fraud monitoring framework, Indian life following companies?

(1) CIBIL (2) CRIF High Mark
(3) Equifax (4) LexisNexis
(5) Experian

147. According to the Goldman Sachs report, by which year is India expected to surpass the United States to become the world's second-largest economy?

(1) 2035 (2) 2045
(3) 2050 (4) 2075
(5) 2080

148. Which of the following is NOT a type of Alternate Dispute Resolution (ADR)?

(1) Mediation (2) Conciliation
(3) Negotiation (4) Arbitration
(5) Litigation

149. Banks have to declare CAR in their balance sheet. What is the full form of CAR?

(1) Court Appointed Receiver
(2) Computer Assisted Retrieval
(3) Capital At Risk
(4) Computer Assisted Reporting
(5) Capital Adequacy Ratio

150. Who wrote the book 'The Monk Who Sold His Ferrari'?

(1) Spencer Johnson (2) Rhonda Byme
(3) Chetan Bhagat (4) Robin Sharma
(5) Rashmi

151. Which ministry is responsible for implementing the Nari Adalat initiative in India?

(1) Ministry of Women and Child Development
(2) Ministry of Law and Justice
(3) Ministry of Urban Development
(4) Ministry of External Affairs
(5) None of these

152. How often is the UN Global Survey on Digital and Sustainable Trade Facilitation conducted?

(1) Every year (2) Every 2 year
(3) Half yearly (4) Quarterly
(5) None of these

153. What is the new insurance cover provided under Pradhan Mantri Jan Aarogya Yojana in Gujarat?

(1) 1 lakh (2) 2 lakhs
(3) 5 lakhs (4) 8 lakhs
(5) 10 lakhs

154. The best indicator of economic development of any country is its

(1) Agriculture (2) Transport
(3) Gross production
(4) Per capita income
(5) None of these

155. Tagline 'Zindagi Ke Saath Bhi, Zindagi Ke Baad Bhi' is related to which insurance company?

(1) HDFC Life Insurance
(2) National Insurance Company
(3) Life Insurance Corporation of India
(4) United India Insurance Company Ltd
(5) None of these

156. UR Anantamurthy was a renowned

(1) Lok Sabha member
(2) Carnatic musician
(3) Cricket player
(4) Other than those given as options
(5) Kannada writer

157. The Govt. of India has launched a web portal named Khoyapaya.gov.in for which of the following?

(1) Distribution of food for the poor
(2) To track missing luggage in Railways
(3) For warning farmers about natural disasters
(4) Employment for the unemployed
(5) Information/Tracking related to or of missing children

158. Which country recently became a full member of the Shanghai Cooperation Organisation (SCO)?

(1) Iran (2) Russia
(3) China (4) India
(5) None of these

159. Which of the following is a credit information

company in India?

(1) CARE (2) ONICRA
(3) CIBIL (4) ICRA
(5) CISIL

160. A bank included in the second schedule or RBI is called as

(1) Commercial Bank
(2) Scheduled bank
(3) Cooperative bank
(4) National bank
(5) Regional Rural Bank

161. Which of the following cities will host the final match of 2016 World Cup Twenty-20 cricket match?

(1) Mumbai (2) Kolkata
(3) Ahmedabad (4) New Delhi
(5) Colombo

162. The 'World Wide Web' was invented by

(1) Robert Hooke
(2) Tommy Flowers
(3) Tim Burners-Lee
(4) Steve Jobs
(5) Gener Myron Amdahi

163. What is the interest rate for loans provided under the Swarnima Scheme?

(1) 10% (2) 3%
(3) 7.3% (4) 5%
(5) 7.5%

164. Insurance service provided by various banks is commonly known as

(1) Micro Finance (2) Portfolio Management
(3) Bancassurance (4) Investment Banking
(5) Merchant Banking

165. Where was India's first 'Police Drone Unit' launched?

(1) New Delhi (2) Lucknow
(3) Bangaluru (4) Chennai
(5) None of these

166. Which of the following is the largest State in terms of area?

(1) Maharashtra
(2) Uttar Pradesh
(3) Other than those given as options
(4) Madhya Pradesh
(5) Rajasthan

167. Who will serve as the regulatory body for all trading activities within India's carbon market?

(1) Ministry of Mines and Minerals
(2) National Thermal Power Corporation
(3) Power Corporation of India
(4) Central Electricity Regulatory Commission
(5) None of these

168. Who has been appointed as the Chief Financial Officer (CFO) of State Bank of India?

(1) Anita Bhardwaj (2) KR Kodavanti
(3) Amitabh Kant (4) KJ Rao
(5) None of these

169. What has New Zealand become the first country to ban?

(1) Plastic bottles (2) Plastic Cutlery
(3) Plastic bags (4) Alcohol
(5) Other than those given as options

170. Under Financial Inclusion plan, banks have been asked to issue Rupay cards. These cards come with EMV chip. What is the full form of EMV?

(1) Electronic Money Valet
(2) Empowered Money Valet
(3) Electronic Money Value
(4) Europay, Master Card and Visa
(5) Other than those given as options

171. Which of the following films won the maximum number of National Film Awards of India?

(1) Haider (2) Jogwa
(3) Godmother (4) Lagaan
(5) Bajirao Mastani

172. Who is the author of 'Midnight's Children'?

(1) V.D. Naipaul (2) Salman Rushdie
(3) Chetan Bhagat (4) Jeet Thayil
(5) Jhumpa Lahiri

173. Who, among the following, heads the Parliamentary Standing Committee on

Finance which deals with Goods and Service Tax (GST)?
(1) Yashwant Sinha
(2) Kapil Sibal
(3) Sushma Swaraj
(4) Montek Singh Ahluwalia
(5) Jaswant Singh

174. Who, at present, is the Vice President of India?
(1) M. Hamid Ansari
(2) M. Venkaiah Naidu
(3) Jagdeep Dhankhar
(4) Haribansh Narayana
(5) None of these

175. Who, among the following, did not win the Dhyanchand Award for 2022?
(1) S K Achanta
(2) Syed Ali
(3) Poornima Mahato
(4) Anil Mann
(5) Girraj Singh

176. Who, among the following, is the recipient of the Dronacharya Award 2022 in the field of Football?
(1) Mahavir Singh
(2) Narinder Singh Saini
(3) Bimal Prafulla Ghosh
(4) Raj Singh
(5) Sarpal Singh

177. In which state of India are the Sanchi Stupas located?
(1) Uttar Pradesh (2) Bihar
(3) Madhya Pradesh (4) Odisha
(5) Rajasthan

178. Which of the following films won the Best original song at the 95th Academy Awards?
(1) Hold my hand : Top Gun
(2) Naatu Naatu : RRR
(3) Lift me up : Black Panther
(4) Applause : Tell it like a woman
(5) None of these

179. Which term refers to the total value of all goods and services produced by all resident units during a certain period of time, minus depreciation?
(1) Gross Domestic Product
(2) Per Capita Product
(3) Gross National Product
(4) Net National Product
(5) Gross Capital formation

180. In the most common usage, CIS is associated with
(1) Citizen of Indian Source
(2) Centre for Internet Security
(3) Commonwealth of Independent States
(4) Computer and Information Science
(5) None of these

181. Who, at present, is the Chief of the Naval Staff of India?
(1) Madhvendra Singh
(2) Arun Prakash
(3) Suresh Mehta
(4) Nirmal Kumar Verma
(5) R Hari Kumar

182. The capital of Andaman & Nicobar Islands is
(1) Ross Island (2) Port Blair
(3) Car Nicobar (4) Viper Island
(5) Silvassa

183. What does 'UNCTAD' stand for?
(1) United Nations Conference on Trade and Development
(2) United Nations Convention on Troubled Darfur
(3) United National Commission on Tokyo Declaration
(4) United Nations Charter on Tariffs and Development
(5) United Nations Convention on Treatment of Dengue

184. Which day is celebrated as Independence Day in the United States?
(1) 3 July (2) 4 July
(3) 11 July (4) 15 July
(5) 21 July

185. With which sports is Mary Kom associated?
(1) Boxing (2) Wrestling

(3) Judo (4) Chess
(5) Weight lifting

186. Which country will host the 2024 Summer Olympic Games?
(1) Japan (2) Spain
(3) Brazil (4) France
(5) Canada

187. On which day is the United Nations Day celebrated?
(1) 2nd October (2) 14th August
(3) 16th September (4) 24th October
(5) 14 November

188. With which sports is Leander Paes associated?
(1) Soccer (2) Golf
(3) Tennis (4) Billiards
(5) Squash

189. Where is the headquarters of the International Civil Aviation Organization (ICAO) located?
(1) Sydney (2) Frankfurt
(3) Montreal (4) Paris
(5) New York

190. With which sports is Yelena Isinbayeva related?
(1) Long Jump (2) Gymnastics
(3) Tennis (4) Pole Vault
(5) Decathlon

Answers With Explanations

1. (3)
2. (4)
3. (4) According to the passage, the incremental capital output ratio depends on current account deficit (and not fiscal deficit).
4. (3)
5. (5)
6. (4)
7. (2) 'Accretion' and 'Accumulation' are most similar in meaning.
8. (1) 'Impede' and 'Delay' are most similar in meaning.
9. (3)
10. (2) From the passage, "European Central Bank sets a common monetary policy stance for all member countries".
11. (3) From the passage, "They think that control has moved to unelected bureaucrats in Brussels."
12. (1)
13. (5)
14. (4) 'Evoked' and 'elicit' are the most similar in meaning.
15. (2) 'Spate' and 'deluge' are the most similar in meaning.
16. (4)
17. (1)
18. (2)
19. (3)
20. (5)
21. (4)
22. (2)
23. (3)
24. (1)
25. (5)
26. (4)
27. (3)
28. (5)
29. (4)
30. (5)
31. (4)
32. (3)
33. (4)
34. (2)
35. (1)
36. (2)
37. (4)
38. (1)
39. (3)
40. (4)
41. (3)
42. (3)
43. (5)
44. (2)

For questions (45-50):

Unit	Total Height	Country	Height of books + height of Boxes
5	55″ ft	Sydney	28″ ft + 27″ ft
4	37″ ft	Paris	20″ ft + 17″ ft
3	32″ ft	Beijing	16″ ft + 16″ ft
2	53″ ft	London	30″ ft + 23″ ft
1	75″ ft	Zurich	35″ ft + 40″ ft

45. (3)
46. (4)
47. (5)
48. (4)
49. (2)
50. (2)

For questions (51-55):

51. (4) **54.** (1)
52. (2) **55.** (4)
53. (3) **56.** (2)
57. (5)

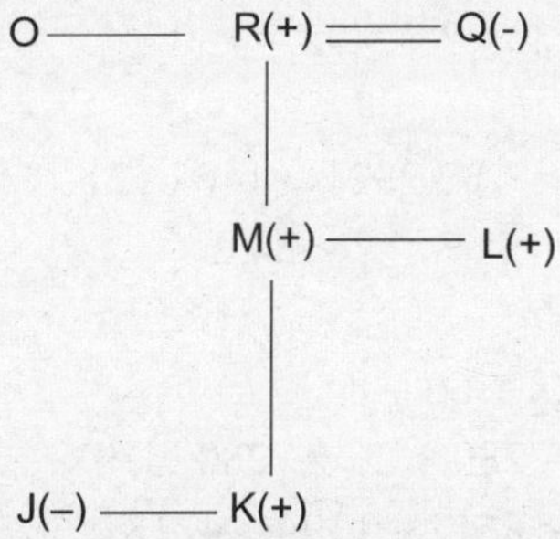

58. (5) V > T > U > X > W > S
59. (1)

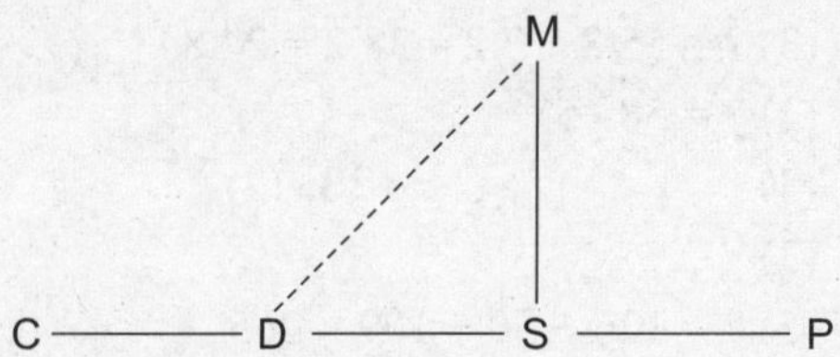

60. (3)
61. (2)

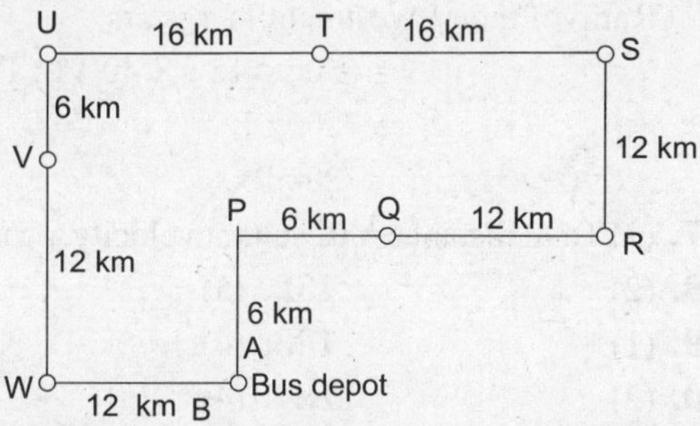

62. (4)

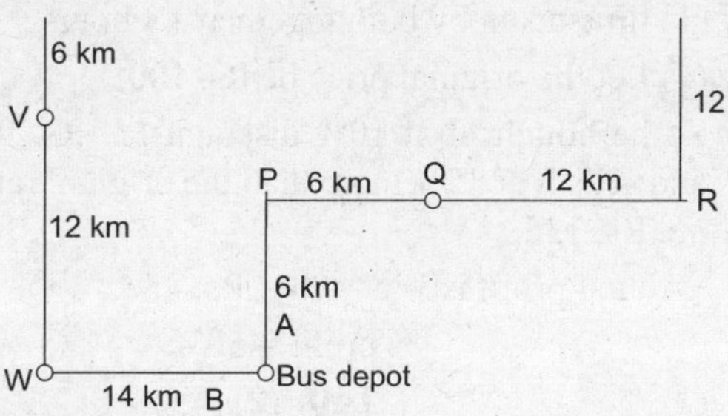

63. (4)

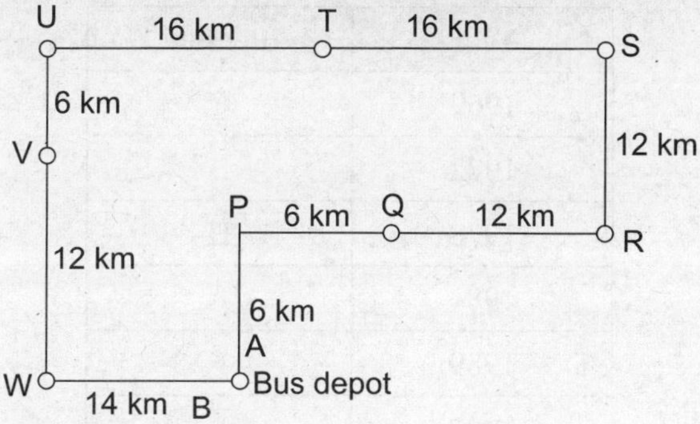

64. (3)

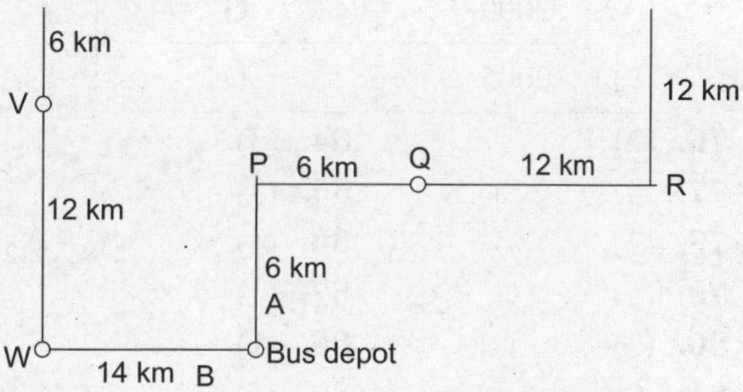

65. (4)

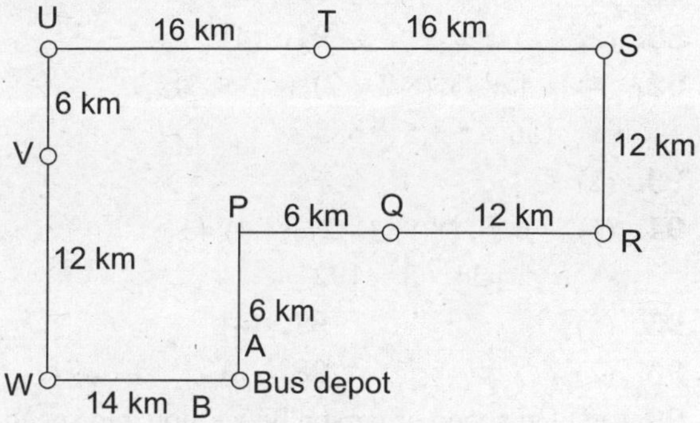

66. (1)

For questions (67-72):

69 38 35
G > D > F > C > E > A > B

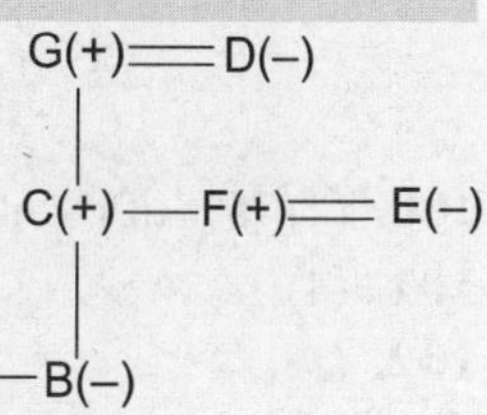

67. (3) **72.** (5)
68. (4) **73.** (5)
69. (2) **74.** (1)
70. (5) **75.** (2)
71. (3)

For questions (76-80):

Year	Person
1969	C
1972	B
1978	H
1981	A
1989	F
1997	E
2000	G
2005	D

76. (2)
77. (4)
78. (2)
79. (5)
80. (3)
81. (2)
82. (1)
83. (2)
84. (3)
85. (3)
86. (4)
87. (1)
88. (1)
89. (1)
90. (1)
91. (4)
92. (4) (× 1 + 1), (× 2 + 2), (× 3 + 3) .....

$136 \times 5 + 5 = 685$

93. (2)
94. (1) (× 0.5), (× 1), (× 2), (× 4), (× 8)

$24 \times 8 = 192$

95. (5)
96. (2)
97. (4)
98. (2)
99. (3) Let speed of person be x kmph and speed of current be y kmph.

$x + y = 8$

$x - y = 2$

$x = 5$ kmph, $y = 3$ kmph

100. (4) 75% of P – 60% of P = 1500 P = Rs. 10000
101. (4)
102. (3)
103. (2)
104. (4) $20\,(12) + 20\,(16) + 20x = 900$

$20x = 900 - 240 - 320$

$20x = 340$

$x = 17$ years

105. (5)
106. (2) Required difference

$= 65 + 82 + 72 - 72 + 59 + 74$

$= 219 - 205 = 14$

107. (2)
108. (4)
109. (3)
110. (1) Required difference = 357 – 314 = 43
111. (4) $61.2 + ? \times 5.92 = 150$

$? = 15$

112. (2) $?^2 = 732.2921 - 146.6521$

$? = 24.2$

113. (1)
114. (4) $528 \div 66 = 8$
115. (5) $? = 280 \times 26 = 7280$
116. (1) $? = 5612 - 1394 = 4218$
117. (5) $? = 4207 - 3007 = 1200$
118. (4) $? = 21 \times 7921 - 89 = 166252$
119. (3) $? = 55.8 + 7.2 - 38.2 = 24.8$
120. (2) $? = 589.57$
121. (3)
122. (3)
123. (2)
124. (5) $? = 126 + 30 + 109 = 265$
125. (4) $? = 226.2 \times 6 = 1357.2$
126. (2) Let shyam's Contribution be Rs. 'x'.
Ratio of their investment in 4 years

= 6500 4 12 : X 40 13 : 12

= 7800 : X

x = 7200 Rs.

127. (3) Total distance = Resultant velocity × Time
128. (2)
129. (1)
130. (2)
131. (3)
132. (5)
133. (4)
134. (4)
135. (2)
136. (1) time taken by both together = 3 hours
137. (4) Let the original price be Rs. 100.
So he bought it at 10% discount *i.e.* Rs. 90 and sells it at 35% more than the original rate *i.e.* Rs. 135.

Actual profit is 135 – 90 = Rs. 45

% profit = 50%

138. (2)
139. (1)
140. (2)
141. (5) In India, the first May Day was celebrated by The Labour Kisan Party of Hindustan in

Madras (now Chennai) in 1923. May 1 is also celebrated as 'Maharashtra Day' and 'Gujarat Day' to mark the statehood status of these two states in 1960.

142. (1) The capital of Myanmar is *Naypyidaw*. Yangon, also called Rangoon was the capital of the country from 1948 to 2006. Later it was changed.

143. (2) **145.** (1)

144. (3)

146. (5) *Life* insurance *companies* have selected Experian, a global data analytics *company,* to *build* a *data repository* and a *fraud monitoring framework.*

147. (4) The report predicts that India will overtake the US and become the world's second-largest economy by 2075.

148. (5) Litigation refers to the process of resolving disputes through the court system.

149. (5) *Capital Adequacy* Ratio : CAR

150. (4) The Monk Who Sold His Ferrari is a self-help book by Robin Sharma, a writer and motivational speaker.

151. (1)

152. (2)

153. (5) The insurance cover under Pradhan Mantri Jan Aarogya Yojana in Gujarat has been doubled from Rs. 5 lakhs to Rs. 10 lakhs.

154. (4) The best indicator of overall economic development of a nation is its per capita income.

155. (3)

156. (5) Udupi Rajagopalacharya Ananthamurthy was *an Indian contemporary writer and critic in the Kannada language.*

157. (5) The Khoya Paya portal is a citizen-based website to exchange information on missing and found children. It has been developed by the Ministry of Women and Child Development and the Department of Electronics and Information Technology.

158. (1) **159.** (3)

160. (2) Scheduled banks are those banks that are listed under Schedule II of the Reserve Bank of India Act, 1934.

161. (3) The final is scheduled to be played at the Narendra Modi Stadium, Ahmedabad on 19 November 2023.

162. (3) The World Wide Web was invented by the British physicist Tim Berners-Lee in 1989.

163. (4)

164. (3) Bancassurance means selling insurance product through banks.

165. (4)

166. (5) Rajasthan is the largest state in India in terms of area which covers 342,239 km 2 of land area.

167. (4) The Central Electricity Regulatory Commission (CERC) will act as the regulatory body responsible for overseeing all trading activities within the Indian carbon market, ensuring compliance and enforcing regulations.

168. (2) **169.** (3)

170. (4) EMV stands for Europay, Mastercard and Visa.

171. (5)

Movie and Year	No. of Awards won
Lagaan (2001)	8
Bajirao Mastani (2015)	7
Godmother (1998)	6
Jogwa (2008)	5
Haider (2014)	5

172. (2) Midnight's Children is a 1981 novel by Indian-British writer Salman Rushdie.

173. (1) *Yashwant Sinha* heads the parliamentary standing committee on finance which deals with Goods and Service Tax (GST).

174. (3) **176.** (3)

175. (1)

177. (3) Sanchi Stupa is a Buddhist complex, famous for its Great Stupa, on a hilltop at Sanchi Town in Raisen District of the State of Madhya Pradesh, India.

178. (2) **179.** (1)

180. (2) CIS is associated with *the Centre for Internet Security.* CIS is a nonprofit organization that provides the best cyber defence and security solutions.

181. (5)

182. (2)

183. (1)

184. (2)

185. (1)

186. (4)

187. (4) United Nations Day is an annual commemorative day, reflecting the official creation of the United Nations on 24 October 1945.

188. (3)

189. (3) The ICAO headquarters are located in the Quartier International of Montreal, Quebec, Canada.

190. (4)

IBPS Clerk Mains
Practice Set – 9

General English

Directions (1-10): *In the following passage there are blank each of which has been numbered. These numbers are printed below the passage and against each, five words are suggested, one of which fits the blank appropriately. Find out the appropriate word in each case.*

There was a man who had four sons. He **(1)** his sons to learn not to judge things too quickly. So he sent them each on a **(2)** in turn, to go and look at a pear tree that was a great distance away. The first son went in the winter, the second in the spring, the third in summer. and the youngest son in autumn. When they had all gone and come back, he **(3)** them together to **(4)** what they had seen. The first son said that the tree was ugly, bent, and twisted. The second son said, "No! It was covered with green buds and full of promise." The third son disagreed; he said it was laden with blossoms that **(5)** so sweet and looked so beautiful, it was the most graceful thing he had **(6)** seen. The last son disagreed all of them; he said it was ripe and drooping with fruit, full of life and with fulfilment. The man then **(7)** to his sons that they all were right, because they had each seen but only one **(8)** in the tree life. He told them that you **(9)** judge a tree, or a person, by only one season, and that the **(10)** of who they are and the pleasure, joy, and love that comes from that life can only be measured at the end, when all the seasons are over.

1. (1) created (2) wanted (3) placed (4) meant (5) teach

2. (1) quest (2) air plane (3) expedition (4) pilgrimage (5) requested

3. (1) followed (2) tied (3) called (4) said (5) bound

4. (1) all (2) predict (3) maintain (4) describe (5) talk

5. (1) was (2) fell (3) colour (4) smelled (5) cooked

6. (1) worriedly (2) mostly (3) ever (4) forever (5) forcefully

7. (1) tell (2) leaked (3) reprimanded (4) stood (5) explained

8. (1) flower (2) season (3) ground (4) more (5) leaf

9. (1) let (2) not (3) must (4) should (5) cannot

10. (1) essence (2) danger (3) tree (4) fear (5) journey

Directions (11-15): *Read the following passage carefully and answer the questions given below it.*

When Hurricane Harvey loomed off the coast of my home state of Texas, it seemed to fill the entire Gulf of Mexico. When it roared on land, it pummeled the towns of Rockport and Port Aransas, whose tawny beaches I've walked with my kids, pointing out the indigo sails of Portuguese man o' war jellyfish. Harvey's eye took direct aim at the University of Texas' Marine Science Institute, flattening not just the facility itself, but priceless samples awaiting analysis. After Harvey left Port Aransas, it spun back into the Gulf of Mexico over record sea temperatures as great as 4 degrees Fahrenheit above normal. Thermodynamic laws require that warmer air holds more water vapor. The heat armed the storm with a mighty arsenal of water vapor. Then Harvey returned to land, dumping a catastrophic amount of rain on Houston. My Facebook feed filled with pleas for rescue from the rising waters. Friends' houses flooded — houses that had always been on dry land before. A chemical plant blew up, twice. Toxic chemicals oozed from Superfund sites. Dozens died in the deluge, mostly by drowning. And all the while, alongside the heartbreak and horror, I kept thinking about a strange harbinger: jellyfish. Play Video Diaphanous in form yet menacing in sting, jellyfish have a powerful capacity to capture our imagination. They undulate in a primal rhythm, blinking open and closed like eyes that can peer into the soul of the sea. And what they are seeing are changes produced by us here on land. Because we burn fossil fuels, which release greenhouse gasses, not just the atmosphere but ocean waters are warming. At the same time, our ship traffic transports animals to new places, and sometimes these exotics find home-like conditions where in the past those conditions would have been unsuitable. That's what happened in the eastern Mediterranean, where a jellyfish from the tropical Indian Ocean has found warm, homey waters and now forms huge aggregations called blooms that stretch for tens of miles every summer. The fierce stings of these animals chase beach-goers out of the water. Their gooey bodies clog machinery at power plants, halting operations. Rampant coastal development provides new habitat for a jellyfish stage called a polyp that looks like a sea anemone. When it finds a hard surface like a dock or a jetty to grow on, a single polyp can proliferate into a dozen or even more medusae. And fields of polyps grow on those hard structures. That's likely what happened off the coast of Italy, where gas platforms are thought to be the home for a new invasion of jellyfish. In the twentieth century in the Adriatic Sea, moon jellies, pinkish with their characteristic four-leafed clover on top, were a rarity. Now they are ubiquitous. And as we wash pollution into our waters, we create low- oxygen environments. Some jellyfish, with their low metabolic rate due to their a-cellular jelly insides, can survive more easily there than fish, with their oxygen-guzzling muscled tissues. That is part of what happened in the Yellow Sea, where pollution is unchecked. It is the birthplace of a maroon jellyfish that reaches a weight of 500 pounds. Blooms of the creature were a once-a-generation event before 2000 — the kind of thing fishermen mentioned to their sons. But jellyzillas swept from China in the Tsushima Current, have plagued Japan's coast almost every year of the 21st century. In 2009, a fishing boat caught so many that their weight capsized the vessel. (Fortunately, the crewmembers were rescued.) And our lack of oversight of the fishing industry, which has removed more than 90% of the large fish from the seas, has depleted the predators of jellyfish as well as their competitors. Jellyfish are eaten by some fish, and jellyfish eat the same small zooplankton that fish do. The ecological vacuum left by unrestrained fishing can allow jellyfish to expand their influence in marine ecosystems. That's what happened off the coast of Namibia, once one of the world.

11. How is jellyfish able to survive in polluted water more than the other fishes?

(I) Jellyfish has oxygen guzzling muscled tissues.

(II) Due to low metabolic rate.

(III) Jellyfish eat small zooplankton to survive.

(1) Only (I)
(2) Only (II)
(3) Both (I) and (II)
(4) Both (II) and (III)
(5) All are correct

12. How Hurricane Harvey can be termed as devastating with reference to the passage?

(1) Many people died by drowning.
(2) Hurricane blew up the Chemical plants.
(3) Toxic chemicals got exuded from superfund sites.
(4) Hurricane flooded many houses
(5) All of the above

13. What is the author's main idea regarding the passage?

(1) How to ameliorate ecological imbalance.
(2) The author gave his opinion regarding jellyfish that what they know humans don't.
(3) Water pollution creating a low oxygen environment affecting aquatic life.
(4) Hurricane Harvey destroyed many lives.
(5) Endangered condition of Jellyfish

14. Which of the following statement (s) is/are true in context of the given passage?

(1) Maroon Jellyfish is found in Yellow sea where pollution is unchecked.

(2) Hurricane Harvey with strong winds battered the entire Gulf of Mexico.

(3) Jellyzillas sweeping from China have afflicted Japan's coast.

(4) Jellyfish survive more than other fishes in low oxygen environment

(5) All of the above

15. Which of the following statement regarding jellyfish is related to the country Namibia?

(1) The attenuation in the number of jellyfish is due to the low oxygen environment.

(2) The predators of Jellyfish are depleting because of uncontrolled fishing.

(3) Jellyfish can proliferate their population in the situation of ecological imbalance.

(4) Both (2) and (3)

(5) All are correct

Directions (16-21): *In each of the questions given below a sentence is given with one blank. Below each sentence FOUR words are given out of which two can fit the sentence. Five options are given with various combinations of these words. You have to choose the combination with the correct set of words which can fit in the given sentence.*

16. Would you like to have .... coffee?

A. much

B. more

C. some

D. many

(1) A-B (2) A-D

(3) B-C (4) C-D

(5) A-C

17. The Dysart Unified School District says they are investigating threats made .... the district and Dysart High School.

A. Towards

B. Against

C. For

D. After

(1) A-B (2) A-D

(3) B-C (4) C-D

(5) A-C

18. I was going .... to say hello when I realised that I couldn't remember his name.

A. beyond

B. Over

C. Through

D. Across

(1) A-B (2) A-D

(3) B-C (4) C-D

(5) B-D

19. In 1997 the sales tax was lowered to 4%, then in 2001 it was abolished ....

A. Together

B. Laterally

C. Completely

D. Altogether

(1) A-B (2) A-D

(3) B-C (4) C-D

(5) B-D

20. Children .... their parents' authority far more nowadays than they did in the past.

A. Dispute

B. Question

C. Confront

D. Challenge

(1) A-B (2) A-D

(3) B-C (4) C-D

(5) B-D

21. The United Nations has .... its authority to restore peace in the area.

A. Used

B. Blown

C. Exercised

D. refused

(1) A-C (2) A-D

(3) B-C (4) C-D

(5) B-D

Directions (22-30): *In each of the question given below a/an idiom/phrase is given in bold which is then followed by five options which then tries to decipher its meaning as used in the sentence. Choose the option which gives the meaning of the* *phrase most appropriately in context of the given sentence.*

22. She **comes across** really well on television.

(1) Discover (2) Express
(3) Behave (4) Offers
(5) Provide

23. The deal was completely open and **above board.**

(1) Mislead (2) Profitable
(3) Dupe (4) Respect
(5) Honest

24. For most businessmen, the central questions will **turn on** taxation.

(1) Matter (2) Consider
(3) Attack (4) Concern
(5) Unsettle

25. They sought a controlling interest rather than **a takeover**

(1) Spend (2) Partnership
(3) Endorse (4) Approve
(5) Buyout

26. I think he was just **putting on** an act to get sympathy

(1) Tolerate (2) Assume
(3) Perform (4) Deceive
(5) Effect

27. I can **put up with** the house being messy, but I hate it if it's not clean

(1) Ignore (2) Forget
(3) Delay (4) Remain
(5) Bear

28. He **gave in** to my suggestion after I had shown him the plans.

(1) Leave (2) Defeated
(3) Defy (4) Agree
(5) Resign

29. She **cut in** on a station wagon, forcing the driver to brake.

(1) Interrupt (2) Stop
(3) Collide (4) Too close
(5) Carve

30. Most patients find that the numbness from the injection **wears off** after about an hour.

(1) calm (2) Inflate
(3) Deepen (4) Fade
(5) Emerge

Directions (31-40): *In each of the questions given below a sentence is given which is then divided into five parts out of which last part is correct. There is an error in three part of the sentence and only one part is correct. You have to choose the part as your answer.*

31. After he had read (A)/the first two chapters (B)/to the novel, (C)/he had felt like (D)/ **reading the book in one sitting.** (E)

(1) After he had read
(2) the first two chapters
(3) to the novel
(4) he had felt like
(5) All are incorrect

32. Since most of the urban people (A)/have been lived (B)/at polluted areas (C)/they suffers from severe (D)/**diseases caused by pollution.** (E)

(1) Since most of the urban people
(2) have been lived
(3) at polluted areas
(4) they suffers from severe
(5) All are incorrect

33. Broadly speaking of a (A)/layman language disability (B)/could be (C)/classified in two groups (D)/**namely mental and physical.** (E)

(1) Broadly speaking of a
(2) layman language disability
(3) could be
(4) classified in two groups
(5) All are incorrect

34. Although there are some (A)/similarities at the qualification (B)/of both the candidate (C)/the differences among them (D)/**are considerably pronounced.** (E)

(1) Although there are some
(2) similarities at the qualification
(3) of both the candidate
(4) the differences among them
(5) All are incorrect

35. When the group of teenagers (A)/visits the

entertainment centre (B)/little did they knows (C)/that its outing (D)/**would lead them to a hospital.** (E)

(1) When the group of teenagers
(2) visits the entertainment centre
(3) little did they knows
(4) that its outing
(5) All are incorrect

36. If the present guidelines, (A)/the bank are required (B)/to obtaining a photograph (C)/from any persons (D)/**who wishes to open an account.** (E)

(1) If the present guidelines
(2) the bank are required
(3) the bank are required
(4) the bank are required
(5) All are incorrect

37. Although the clock struck twelve, (a)/we hear the big bang of (B)/the fire crackers and saw (C)/all the guests scream, (D)/**shouting and wishing each other with joy.** (E)

(1) Although the clock struck twelve
(2) we hear the big bang of
(3) the fire crackers and saw
(4) all the guests scream
(5) All are incorrect

38. The Rupali wanted (A)/to gets (B)/the clear picture about (C)/the incident so she spoke (D)/**to the victims.** (E)

(1) The Rupali wanted
(2) to gets
(3) the clear picture about
(4) the incident so she spoke
(5) All are incorrect

39. The centre has accepted (A)/the report of the judicial commission (B)/that indicted a former chief minister (C)/and six of his ministerial colleagues for corruption. (D)/**favouritism, nepotism and administrative impropriety.** (E)

(1) The centre has accepted
(2) the report of the judicial commission
(3) that indicted a former chief minister
(4) and six of his ministerial colleagues for corruption
(5) All are incorrect

40. Before invested, (A)/you should look at the (B)/overall business dynamics for the company (C)/along with its efficient management and (D)/**good corporate governance** (E)

(1) Before invested
(2) you should look at the
(3) overall business dynamics for the company
(4) along with its efficient management and
(5) All are incorrect

Quantitative Aptitude

Directions (41-45): *What approximate value should come in place of question mark (?) in the following questions?*

41. $(421.98 + 478.21) \div ? = 60.029$

(1) 6 (2) 8
(3) 9 (4) 12
(5) 15

42. $\sqrt{257} \times 19.17 + 8.15 \times 13.78 = ?$

(1) 406 (2) 450
(3) 432 (4) 416
(5) 392

43. $16.217 \times 23.88 + ? = 18.98 \times 32.12$

(1) 216 (2) 224
(3) 200 (4) 228
(5) 250

44. $27.897 \times 16.21 = ? \times 13.98 + 69.87$

(1) 15 (2) 22
(3) 27 (4) 32
(5) 39

45. $272.112 + 189.98 + 84.101 = ? \times 12.89 \times 6.11$

(1) 5 (2) 7
(3) 9 (4) 11
(5) 13

Directions (46-50): *What will come in the place of the question mark (?) in the following number series?*

46. 117.5, 117, 119, 111, 143, ?

(1) 9 (2) 12
(3) 15 (4) 18
(5) 21

47. 15, 12, 31, 148, ?

(1) 1039 (2) 1011
(3) 1012 (4) 1024
(5) 1027

48. 1, 13, 83, 419, 1679, ?

(1) 5029 (2) 5039
(3) 5019 (4) 5049
(5) 5059

49. 12, 25, 48, 99, 194, 393, ?

(1) 780 (2) 786
(3) 792 (4) 783
(5) 789

50. 3, 11, 31, 69, 131, ?

(1) 215 (2) 217
(3) 221 (4) 223
(5) 213

Directions (51-55): *Table given below shows number of tickets sold in six different theatres, number of tickets sold to children and remaining ticket sold to adults [male and female]. Study the data carefully and answer the following questions.*

Theatre	Ticket sold to children	Ticket sold to Adults (Male : Female)
C1	15	6 : 7
C2	10	3 : 4
C3	20	2 : 3
C4	14	6 : 5
C5	8	5 : 4
C6	12	9 : 8

Total 80 tickets are sold in each theatre.

51. Find the ratio of number of tickets sold to males by C3 and C6 theatre together to number of tickets sold to females by C3 and C5 theatre together.

(1) 14 : 19 (2) 15 : 17
(3) 20 : 23 (4) 16 : 19
(5) 14 : 17

52. Number of female who bought ticket from C2 and C4 theater together is what percent more than number of males who bought ticket from C5 theatre.

(1) 33.33% (2) 50%
(3) 66.66% (4) 75%
(5) 87.5%

53. If per ticket price for children, male and female is Rs. 150, Rs. 200 and Rs. 250 respectively. Then find the total revenue earn by C4 theater.

(1) 16600 (2) 15400
(3) 16800 (4) 15800
(5) 16400

54. Find the average number of male who bought tickets from C1, C2 and C3 theatre together.

(1) 30 (2) 28
(3) 32 (4) 34
(5) 36

55. Number of males who bought ticket from C4, C5 and C6 together is how much more than number of females who bought ticket from same theatres.

(1) 18 (2) 20
(3) 21 (4) 24
(5) 26

Directions (56-60): *In each of these questions, two equations (i) and (ii) are given. You have to solve both the equations and give answer*

(1) if $x > y$ (2) if $x \geq y$
(3) if $x < y$ (4) if $x \leq y$
(5) if $x = y$ or no relation can be established between x and y.

56. (*i*) $2x^2 - 5x + 3 = 0$
(*ii*) $3y^2 - 4y + 1 = 0$

57. (*i*) $x^2 - 17x + 72 = 0$
(*ii*) $y^2 - 27y + 180 = 0$

58. (*i*) $(x - 12)^2 = 0$
(*ii*) $y^2 - 21y + 108 = 0$

59. (*i*) $2x^2 + 7x + 5 = 0$

(ii) $3y^2+12y+9=0$

60. (i) $x^2+2x-35=0$

(ii) $y^2+15y+56=0$

Directions (61-65): *Bar graph given below shows the time taken by two trains in hr, on different days. Study the data carefully and answer the following questions:*

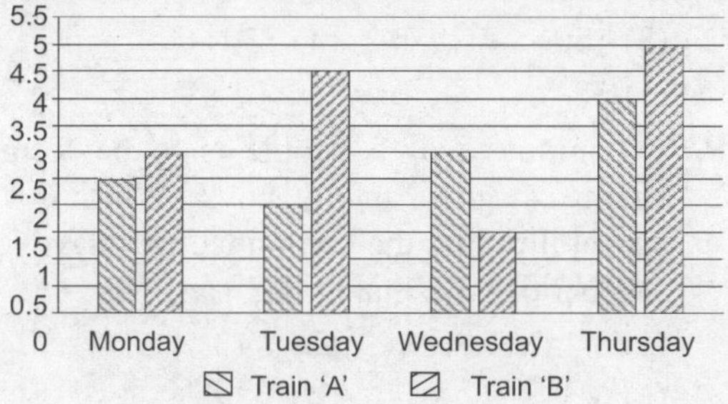

Both Train Cover 450 km distance on every day

61. Speed of train 'A' on Tuesday is what percent more than speed of train 'B' on Monday?

(1) 33.33% (2) 50%
(3) 66.66% (4) 75%
(5) 87.5%

62. Find the average speed of train 'B' on Tuesday and Train 'A' on Wednesday?

(1) 140 (2) 130
(3) 135 (4) 120
(5) 150

63. On Friday, speed of train 'A' increases by 60% and speed of train 'B' increases by 25% as compared to Thursday. Find the sum of the time taken by both trains separately to cover the same distance?

(1) 6.5 hr (2) 7.5 hr
(3) 6 hr (4) 7 hr
(5) 8 hr

64. Speed of train 'A' on Tuesday is how much less than speed of train 'B' on Wednesday?

(1) 50 km/hr (2) 60 km/hr
(3) 75 km/hr (4) 85 km/hr
(5) 100 km/hr

65. Find in how much time train 'A' can covert the given distance if speed of train 'A' increases by 60% on Tuesday?

(1) 3 hr (2) 2.5 hr
(3) 1.5 hr (4) 1.25 hr
(5) 1.75 hr

Directions (66-70): *The following questions are accompanied by two statements (A) and (B). You have to determine which statement(s) is/are sufficient/necessary to answer the questions*

(1) if the Statement 'A' alone is sufficient to answer the question but the Statement 'B' alone is not sufficient
(2) if the Statement 'B' alone is sufficient to answer the question but the Statement 'A' alone is not sufficient
(3) if both Statement 'A' and 'B' together are needed to answer the question
(4) if either the Statement 'A' alone or Statement 'B' alone is sufficient to answer the question
(5) if you cannot get the answer from both the Statements together

66. Is 'Z' a positive integer?

(A) $Z^7 > Z$
(B) $Z^8 > Z$

67. Find the value of $4^{1/a} + 4^{1/b}$?

(A) Sum of inverse of *a* and *b* is equals to 6/5
(B) Multiplication '*a*' and '*b*' is equals to 5

68. In how many days 14 men can complete a piece of work?

(A) If 18 women can complete the same piece of work in 24 days.
(B) If 28 children can complete the same piece of work in 56 days.

69. When one ball is drawn at random from an urn containing 25 balls, what is the chance that it is red?

(A) The urn contains 10 yellow and 8 green balls.
(B) The urn contains all colored balls.

70. Is '*w*' an integer?

(A) 3*w* is an odd number.
(B) 2*w* is an even number.

Directions (71-75): *Data regarding number of boys & girls in both the colleges is as follows:*

Average no. of Girls in St. Xavier College and Vijaya College is 210 & total number of boys in both the college is 810. Number of Girls is 2/3 of boys & number of Girls is 2/5 of number of Boys in St. Xavier college and in Vijaya College respectively.

71. Number of girls in Vijay college is what percent of the number of girls in St. Xavier College.

(1) 50% (2) 62.5%
(3) 75% (4) 66.66%
(5) 87.5%

72. Average number of girls in St. Xavier college and 'X' college is 320. If total number of students in 'X' college is 25% more than total number of students in St. Xavier college then find the number of boys in 'X' college.

(1) 450 (2) 400
(3) 375 (4) 350
(5) 300

73. Find the difference between the total number of students in Vijaya college to the total number of students in St. Xavier college.

(1) 15 (2) 20
(3) 25 (4) 30
(5) 35

74. Ratio between number of boys in Vijaya college to number of boys in 'Y' college is 9 : 13 and number of girls in 'Y' college is 20% less than that in Vijaya college. Find the total number of students in 'Y' college?

(1) 784 (2) 794
(3) 789 (4) 798
(5) 778

75. Number of boys in Vijaya college is what percent more than number of boys in St. Xavier college?

(1) 32.5% (2) 20%
(3) 50% (4) 37.5%
(5) 25%

76. 15 men can do a piece of work in 'X' days. 21 women can do a piece of work in 'X – 4' days. 35 men can do a piece of work in 'Y' days and 63 women can do a piece of work in 'Y – 4' days. Find the value of 'X'?

(1) 14 (2) 18
(3) 28 (4) 24
(5) 32

77. Cost price of article A is double then that of article B and shopkeeper mark up both the article 20% more than the cost price. If at the time of sale shopkeeper gave Rs. 9 discount and earn 17% profit on total. Find the cost price of article A?

(1) 100 (2) 200
(3) 150 (4) 250
(5) 50

78. A committee of 5 people is to be formed among 4 girls and 5 boys. What is the probability that the committee will have less number of boys than girls?

(1) 3/14 (2) 7/13
(3) 3/5 (4) 5/14
(5) None of these

79. A train running at 25 km/hr takes 18 seconds to pass a platform and it takes 12 seconds to pass a men walking at 5 km/hr in the opposite direction. Length of train in how much more than length of the platform (in m)

(1) 50 (2) 75
(3) 100 (4) 125
(5) 150

80. Satish and Bhavya entered into a partnership with Rs. 15000 and Rs. 18000 respectively. Abhishek joined them after '*x*' months and contributes Rs. 24000 and Bhavya left '*x*' month before the end of year. If they share profit at the end of the year. If they share profit in the ratio 10 : 9 : 12. Find the value of '*x*'.

(1) 4 month (2) 6 month
(3) 9 month (4) 3 month
(5) 8 month

81. Sakshi married 6 years ago. Today her age is 5/4 times her age at the time of her marriage and her son is 1/5 of her age. Find the ratio of Sakshi age to her son's age after 10 years?

(1) 3 : 1 (2) 5 : 2
(3) 5 : 3 (4) 3 : 2
(5) 4 : 1

82. Ravi invested Rs. 18000 in scheme 'A' which offers 15% p.a. at simple interest and Rs.

15000 in scheme 'B' which offers 18% p.a. at compound interest. Find the difference between the interest earn from these two schemes after two years?

(1) 468 (2) 396
(3) 456 (4) 486
(5) 482

83. An alloy of copper and aluminum has 40% copper. Another alloy of Copper and Zinc has Copper and Zinc in the ratio 2 : 7. These two alloys are mixed in ratio 5 : 3. Quantity of aluminum is what percent more/less than the quantity of copper in final alloy.

(1) 11.11% (2) 11.33%
(3) 12% (4) 13%
(5) 12.5%

84. Two boats, travelling at 5 Km/h and 10 Km/h respectively, head directly towards each other. They are now at a distance of 20 km from each other. How far apart are they (in Kms) one minute before they collide?

(1) 1/12 (2) 1/6
(3) 1/4 (4) 1/3
(5) None of these

85. If the volume and curved surface area of a cylinder 616 m^3 and 352 m^2 respectively, what is the total surface area of the cylinder (in m^2)?

(1) 429 (2) 419
(3) 435 (4) 421
(5) 417

86. In an alloy, zinc and copper are in the ratio 1 : 2. In the second alloy the same elements are in the ratio 2 : 3. In what ratio should these two alloys be mixed to form a new alloy in which the two elements are in ratio 5 : 8?

(1) 7 : 11 (2) 3 : 10
(3) 5 : 11 (4) 9 : 11
(5) None of these

87. 40 men, working 8 hours a day can do a piece of work in 15 days. Find the number of days in which second group of 60 men working 4 hrs a day can do twice the work. Assume that 3 men of the first group do as much work in 2 hour as 4 men of the second group do in 3 hrs.

(1) 60 days (2) 40 days
(3) 80 days (4) 70 days
(5) 75 days

88. A boat travel 75 km downstream and take same time as it travels 60 km in upstream. Speed of boat in downstream is what percent of the speed of boat in still water.

(1) 111.11% (2) 112.5%
(3) 113% (4) 140%
(5) 110%

89. A train crosses a pole in 24 sec. A second train of same length crosses a platform in 30 sec with a speed 20% more than the first train. Find out the ratio of length of train and length of platform.

(1) 2 : 1 (2) 3 : 1
(3) 2 : 3 (4) 3 : 2
(5) 1 : 2

90. A tank can be filled with water by two pipes A and B together in 36 minutes. If the pipe B was closed after 30 minutes, the tank is filled in 40 minutes. The pipe B can alone fill the tank in?

(1) 45 minutes (2) 60 minutes
(3) 75 minutes (4) 90 minutes
(5) 85 minutes

Reasoning Ability & Computer Aptitude

Directions (91-93): *Study the following information and answer the questions given below:*

There are seven given letters A, Y, E, R, S, P and L which are arranged from left to right with facing north direction. There are three letters between the S and E. There is only one letter between E and A. R is immediate left of S. Y is immediate left of E. P and L are adjacent to each other. L is not adjacent to R.

91. Who among the following is on extreme end?

(1) A, S (2) Y, S
(3) A, P (4) A, R
(5) E, S

92. Who among the following is immediate right

of P?

(1) R (2) L
(3) E (4) A
(5) Y

93. Which letter is adjacent to E?

(1) Y, P (2) Y, L
(3) A, S (4) S, L
(5) R, Y

Directions (94-96): *Study the following alphanumeric series carefully and answer the questions given below:*

7 A 6 P & R $ 4 Y Q% T @ 3 9 S I O 9 9 J L E U * K # 3

STEP I: The letters which are immediately preceded and immediately followed by a symbol are arranged in the end of the series in the alphabetical order. (They are arranged just after 3)

STEP II: The numbers which are immediately preceded by the letter and immediately followed by the Symbol are arranged between 9 and S in the increasing order.

STEP III: The numbers which are immediately followed by letter are interchanged its position with respect to the element just after it.

(STEP II is applied after STEP I and STEP III is applied after STEP II)

94. How many letters are arranged at the end of the series in the step-1?

(1) one (2) Three
(3) Four (4) Five
(5) More than five

95. Which among the following are the elements of the series which are second position from the left end and fifth position from the right end in step-III?

(1) 63 (2) 7#
(3) P# (4) AK
(5) 6#

96. How many symbols are immediately followed by numbers in step-III?

(1) one (2) Three
(3) Four (4) Five
(5) Two

Directions (97-99): *Study the following information carefully to answer the given question.*

There are Some boxes which are arranged one above another such that one box is placed at the bottom and another box is placed just above that box and all are arranged in the same order.

Only two boxes are there in between Orange box and box U and Orange box is above box U. There is only one box in between box P and box S. Box S is of Purple color and is placed above box R. There are three boxes in between Orange box and Green box. Green box is placed below U, which is not of blue colour. Only one box is placed in between box R and Orange box. More than four boxes are placed in between box P and Orange box. There are as same boxes placed between box S and the box which is of Orange colour as same as between the box which is of orange colour and the box which is of green colour. The box which is of green colour is placed at the bottom. Not more than two boxes are placed in between box V and box S. Box R is placed just above the box of blue colour. Box V is not an immediate neighbor of Box S.

97. How many boxes are there in the arrangement?

(1) Ten (2) Eleven
(3) Fourteen (4) Twelve
(5) None of these

98. How many boxes are there between box R and box U?

(1) Five (2) One
(3) Four (4) Two
(5) None of these

99. Which box is immediately above Orange box?

(1) S (2) R
(3) Purple box (4) V
(5) Green box

Directions (100-102): *Study the following alphanumeric series carefully and answer the questions given below:*

12AIFR 42WBOL 63EOCN 15TVMR 75GYTR

100. How many meaningful words can be formed from the letters of the words which are attached with the numbers in which at least one digit is even digit in the given alphanumeric series?

(1) one (2) two
(3) three (4) four
(5) More than four

101. The words are arranged according to the descending order of the numbers which are attached to them from left to right, then how many alphabets are between the letters of second letter from the left end and seventh letter from the right end?
(1) one (2) two
(3) three (4) four
(5) More than five

102. The letters which are attached with the numbers in which at least one is odd digit are arranged according to the ascending orders of their numbers from left to right and then all letters of the words together are arranged in the alphabetical order, then which of the following is the 9th letter from the right end?
(1) M (2) O
(3) N (4) R
(5) None of these

Directions (103-105): *Study the following information and answer the questions given below:*

There are AB axis in such a way that A is in north and B is in south direction. There is XY axis in such a way that X is in west direction and Y is in east direction. AB axis and XY axis intersect at a point Q in such a way that AQ is 15 m, QB is 17 m, QX is 12 m, QY is 24 m.

Mehul starts from point X and walks 20 m in south direction and then he turns his left and walks 32 m. Arun starts from point A and walks 20 m in east direction. Raju starts from point Y and walks 5 m in north direction and then he turns his left and walk 4 m and again he turns his left and walks 22 m.

103. Point B is in which direction with respect to Arun's current position?
(1) south (2) south-east
(3) south-west (4) west
(5) north-west

104. Point Y is in which direction with respect to Mehul's current position?
(1) north (2) east
(3) north-east (4) north-west
(5) south

105. What is distance between Raju's current position and Mehul's current position?
(1) 3 m (2) 5 m
(3) 13 m (4) 22 m
(5) 27 m

Directions (106-108): *Study the following information and answer the questions given below:*

106. Four friends are sitting around a circular table named M, N, O and P. Are they facing to the centre of table? If-

I. N is sitting second to the right of P. P is facing centre. O is sitting immediate right of N and P.

II. M is sitting immediate left of N. O is not sitting immediate left of M. O is sitting immediate right of P.

III. P is sitting immediate of M and O. N is sitting immediate left of M. O is sitting immediate left of P.

(1) If the data in statement I and II are sufficient to answer the question, while the data in statement III are not sufficient to answer the question.
(2) If the data in statement II and III are sufficient to answer the question, while the data in statement I is not sufficient to answer the question.
(3) If the data in statement I alone or in the statement II alone or in the statement III alone is sufficient to answer the question.
(4) If the data in all the statement I, II and III are necessary to answer the question.
(5) If the data in statement I and III are sufficient to answer the question, while the data in statement II is not sufficient to answer the question.

107. Six people A, B, C, D, E and F are living in six floor building each live in one of apartment of building. In building there are from I to VI floor. Ground floor is given number I, then II and so on. Who is living on Ground floor?

I. In which floor C and B are living there is only one floor between them. A is living in even number floor.

II. E is not living in even number floor. B is living in even number floor. B is not living in top floor.

III. D is living in odd number floor. In which floor D and A are living, there are two between them. E is living immediate next to C from down.

(1) If the data in statement I and II are sufficient to answer the question, while the data in statement III are not sufficient to answer the question.

(2) If the data in statement I and III are sufficient to answer the question, while the data in statement II is not sufficient to answer the question.

(3) If the data in statement II and III are sufficient to answer the question, while the data in statement I is not sufficient to answer the question.

(4) If the data in all the statement I, II and III are necessary to answer the question

(5) If the data in statement I alone or in the statement II alone or in the statement III alone is sufficient to answer the question.

108. Who is youngest among six family members G, H, I, J, K and L? (Each member is of different ages.)

I. G is the daughter-in-law of J, K is grandson of L, who is the father of H.

II. G is not youngest while L is the eldest.

III. H is the father of I, who is grandson of L. J is the wife of K's son and I's father

(1) If the data in statement I and II are sufficient to answer the question, while the data in statement III are not sufficient to answer the question.

(2) If the data in statement I alone or in the statement II alone or in the statement III alone is sufficient to answer the question.

(3) If the data in statement I and III are sufficient to answer the question, while the data in statement II is not sufficient to answer the question.

(4) If the data in statement II and III are sufficient to answer the question, while the data in statement I is not sufficient to answer the question.

(5) If the data in all the statement I, II and III are necessary to answer the question

Directions (109-111): *Study the following information and answer the questions given below:*

There is four triangles given in question on which we apply some operation individually on each triangle and then convert it into solution. We have to answer the questions from the triangle which comes after the operation applied on the given triangle.

For example-

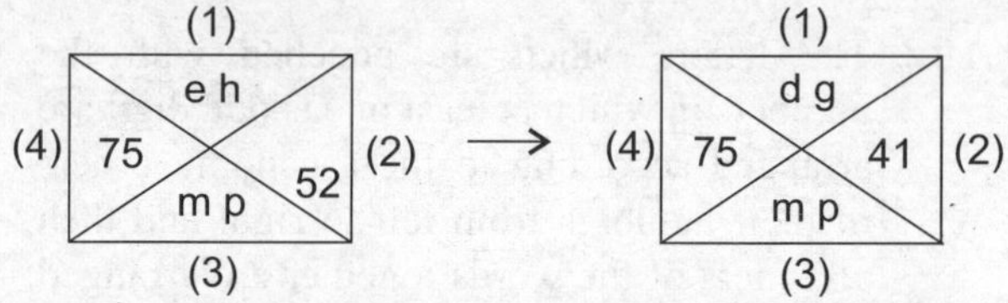

A. For triangle 1- if the total letter between given two letters in the triangle 1 is less than three then change each letter to previous letter according to English alphabetical series

B. For triangle 2- if the difference between given two digit is less than 5 then change the each digit to previous digit.

C. For triangle 3- if the total letters between given two letters is more than 5 then change the each letter to previous letter according to English alphabetical series.

D. For triangle 4- if the difference between given two digits is more than 2 then change each digits to previous digit.

Note: *If the above conditions are not applied then we write the digit and letter as it is in solution part.*

Based on the above example solve the given question.

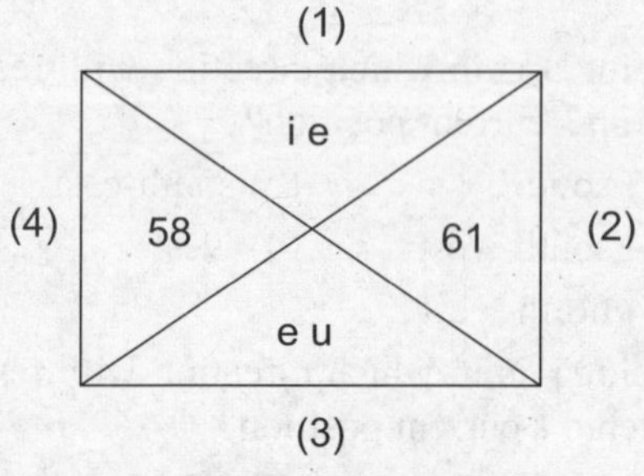

109. How many meaningful words are formed by letter combining from triangle 1 and triangle 3?

(1) None (2) Two
(3) Three (4) One
(5) Four

110. What is the sum of each digits which is obtained in triangle 2 and triangle 4?

(1) 17 (2) 18
(3) 19 (4) 20
(5) 16

111. Which of the following letter is obtained in triangle 3?

(1) *d*, *f* (2) *t*, *c*
(3) *d*, *t* (4) *d*, *v*
(5) *t*, *b*

Directions (112-114): *A word and number arrangement machine when given an input line of words and numbers rearranges them following a particular rule in each step. The following is an illustration of input and rearrangement.*

Input- acon 82 43 exam 16 acer loge 77 rope 22

Step I- care 82 acon 43 exam 16 loge 77 rope 22

Step II- cano 77 care 82 43 exam 16 loge rope 22

Step III- emax 43 cano 77 care 82 16 loge rope 22

Step IV- lego 22 emax 43 cano 77 care 82 16 rope

Step V- rpeo 16 lego 22 emax 43 cano 77 care 82

Input- 54 roll 39 back 87 25 cash seat 46 beat

112. In which of the following step 25 and seat are placed immediately?

(1) Step-III (2) Step-IV
(3) Step-III and Step-IV
(4) Step II
(5) None of these

113. How many elements are there between 54 and 39 in step-II?

(1) One (2) Two
(3) Three (4) Four
(5) None of these

114. Which elements are there between chsa and 54 in step-IV?

(1) 46, abck (2) eata, 46
(3) 87, 25 (4) rllo, seat
(5) None of these

Directions (115-117): *There are two rows given and to find out the resultant of a particular row we need to follow the following steps-*

Step 1: If an even number is followed by an odd (prime) number then the resultant will be the addition of both the numbers.

Step 2: If an odd number is followed by a perfect square then the resultant will be the difference of the square number and the odd number.

Step 3: If an odd number is followed by another odd number (but not a perfect square) then the resultant will be the addition of both the numbers.

Step 4: If an even number is followed by an odd (non-prime) number then the resultant will be the difference of the odd number and the even number.

Step 5: If an odd number is followed by an even number then the resultant comes by multiplying the numbers.

115. Find the sum of two rows

6	5	2
11	4	3

(1) 38 (2) 32
(3) 42 (4) 57
(5) None of the above

116. If the sum of the resultants of two rows is 44. Then find the value of X.

14	7	5
12	X	6

(1) 3 (2) 9
(3) 2 (4) 5
(5) None of the above

117. Find the difference between the resultant of first and second row.

7	4	8

11 9 13

(1) 2 (2) 3

(3) 8 (4) 9

(5) None of the above

Directions (118-120): *Study the following information carefully and answer the questions given below.*

There are five doctors of different types viz., Ophthalmologist, Orthopedic surgeon, Psychiatrist, General physician and Dentist in a hospital but not necessarily in same order. They attend their patients at different timing in a single day. The duration of their meeting with the patient is different. The total duration of the meeting with the patients by all doctors is of 11 hour. There is no gap between the meeting times of all doctors. The duration of meeting either full hour or half an hour but not in one third or one fourth.

The one who is orthopedic surgeon attends their patients from 12:30 to 3 pm. The dentist attends their patients immediate before or immediate after the Orthopedic surgeon. The meeting hour of Dentist with the patients is three hours. The duration of meeting with patients of General physician is more than duration of meeting of Psychiatrist with patients by 1 hour. General physician attends meeting just after the meeting of Psychiatrist. The general Physician does not attend patients at the last. The Ophthalmologist attends their patients before the Orthopedic surgeon but not immediate before. The duration of meeting of Ophthalmologist is of 1.5 hours. The timing of Psychiatrist meeting is after 6:00 am.

118. Who among the following attends patients from 3:00-6:00 pm?

(1) Ophthalmologist

(2) Psychiatrist

(3) General physician

(4) Dentist

(5) Orthopedic surgeon

119. Who among the following attends patients just after the Ophthalmologist?

(1) General physician

(2) Psychiatrist

(3) Orthopedic surgeon

(4) Dentist

(5) None of these

120. What is the duration (in hours) of the Psychiatrist's meeting with the patients?

(1) 2.5 hour (2) 3 hour

(3) 3.5 hour (4) 1.5 hour

(5) 2 hour

Directions (121-123): *Study the following information carefully and answer the questions given below:*

There are nine persons namely A, K, L, M, N, O, P, Q and R live on three different floors from one to three. Ground floor is number 1 and top floor is number third but not necessarily in the same order. There are three flats on each floor- flat-1, flat-2 and flat-3 from west to east such that flat-1 of third floor is exactly above flat-1 of second floor which is exactly above flat-1 of first floor and other flats are placed in the same way.

A lives in an even numbered flat. P lives just above M in a flat numbered 3. A does not live on the same floor on which P lives. O lives just above Q. Q does not live on the same floor on which M lives. N lives below M.L lives left to R.

121. Who lives in flat-3 of first floor?

(1) A (2) K

(3) P (4) N

(5) None of these

122. Who among the following lives immediate left to P?

(1) R (2) L

(3) O (4) Q

(5) None of these

123. How many persons live below M?

(1) Two (2) No one

(3) One (4) either (1) or (3)

(5) None of these

Directions (124-127): *In each of the questions below are given three statements followed by three conclusions number I, II and III. You have to take the given statements to be true even if they seem to be at variance from commonly known facts. Read the entire conclusion and then decide which of the given conclusions logically follows from the given statements disregarding commonly known facts.*

124. Statements: All pigs are Zebra. All Zebra are Rabbits. No Ant is are Pig.

Conclusions:

I. Some rabbit is Ant.

II. Some Zebra are Ant is a possibility.

III. Some Ant are Pig.

(1) Only I follows (2) Only II follows
(3) Only III follows (4) All follow
(5) None of these

125. Statements: Some bat are pen. Some pen are Shirt. No shirt is Coat.

Conclusions:

I. Some Coat is Pen.

II. Some Coat is shirt is a possibility.

III. All pen can be Coat

(1) None follows (2) only II follows
(3) only III follows (4) only I follows
(5) only either II or III follow

126. Statements: All Men are Rock. Some men are pearl. No Rock is Angel.

Conclusions:

I. Some men are not Angel.

II. All Pearl can be Angel is a possibility.

III. Some Angel can be Pearl is a possibility.

(1) only I and II follow
(2) only I and III follow
(3) only II and III follow
(4) All I, II and III follow
(5) None of these

127. Statements: Some Z are X Some X are not U Some V are U

Conclusions:

I. All U can be X

II. All V can never be Z

(1) Only I and II follow
(2) Only II follows
(3) Only I follows
(4) None follows
(5) None of these

Directions (128-130): *Study the following information carefully and answer the questions that follow:*

There are five cars – A, B, C, D, F – parked in a row facing north direction, but not necessarily in the same order. The distances between two adjacent bikes are successive multiples of three (*i.e.* if the distance between the 1st and the 2nd bike is 3 m, 1st and the 3rd bike is 6 m and between 1st and 4th bike is 9 m and soon.)

(*i.e.* suppose Car A is left end of the line at point R then the remaining people will stand at a distance as follows – 3 m, 6 m, 9 m .... from the end)

Car A is standing at the left end of the line. Two cars are standing between Car A and Car B. Car C stand second to the left of Car B. Car F is an immediate neighbor of Car C. Only one person stands between Car F and Car D. Car G which starts moving from point P which is 5 m in north from Car F. Car G moves 12 m in north-east direction till point Q. Point Q and Car D are in line vertically. Car D moves 4 m in the north direction and stops at point R. Car A moves in the direction to point R.

128. Car A at which of the following point after moving from its starting position?
(1) Point R
(2) Point P
(3) Between point P and Car F
(4) Can't be determined
(5) Point D

129. What is the shortest distance between Car D's new position and Car F's position?
(1) $\sqrt{41}$ m (2) $\sqrt{52}$ m
(3) 12 m (4) 21 m
(5) None of these

130. What is the distance between Car G's new position and Car D's old position?
(1) $\sqrt{41}$ m (2) $\sqrt{21}$ m
(3) $6\sqrt{3}+5$ m (4) $5\sqrt{3}$ m
(5) None of these

Directions (131-132): *In each question below is given a statement followed by two assumptions numbered I and II. An assumption is something supposed or taken for granted. You have to consider the statement and the following assumption and decide which of the assumption is implicit in the statement.*

Give answer
(1) If only assumption I is implicit
(2) If only assumption II is implicit
(3) If either I or II is implicit
(4) If neither I nor II is implicit
(5) If both I and II are implicit

131. Statement: Government should deploy army to rehabilitate the people displaced due to earthquake.

Assumptions

I. Army can be used for purposes other than waralso.

II. Only army can rehabilitate the displaced victims of earthquake.

132. Statement: A Government advertisement in public interest- "For a child's better mental health, admit him/her to a school only after five years of age."

Assumptions

I. A child cannot learn before he/she turns five.

II. Some school admit children who are below five years of age.

Directions (133-134): *In each question below, are given a statement followed by two courses of action numbered I and II. On the basis of the information given in the statement, you have to assume everything in the statement to be true, and then decide which of the suggested courses of action logically follow(s) for pursuing.*

Give answer:
(1) if only I follows.
(2) if only II follows.
(3) if either I or II follows.
(4) if neither I nor II follows.
(5) if both I and II follow.

133. Statement: A number of school children in the local schools have fallen ill after the consumption of their subsidized tiffin provided by the school authority.

Course of action

I. The tiffin facility of all schools should be discontinued with immediate effect.

II. The government should implement a system to certify the quality of tiffin provided by the school.

134. Statement: A huge rally will be organized by the people in the locality, on a religious occasion and the police was informed accordingly.

Course of action

I. Adequate police force should be deployed to over see the procession of the rally.

II. Vehicles on the road should be advised a diversion to avoid traffic congestion.

Directions (135-137): *Study the following information carefully and answer the questions given below:*

Eight persons namely J, K, L, M, N, O, P and Q are living in an eight-floor building with bottommost floor being the first floor while topmost floor being numbered as eighth floor. Only one person stays on one floor. All of them belong to the same family and there is only two married couple but they have different blood groups *i.e.* AB+, AB–, O–, B–, A–, A+, O+ and B+. Each of them participated and obtained different grade in a competitive exam viz. A, B, C, D, E, F, G and H but not necessarily in the same order. The grading is done in alphabetical order on the basis of their marks with top scorer obtaining A grade while the lowest scorer being given H grade.

L's maternal aunt does not live on eighth or first floor. The person who is the third lowest scorer lives on the fifth floor. K is the wife of Q and she has only one child. The person who scored sixth highest marks does not have B– blood group. The person whose blood group is AB– lives on an even-number floor. The person whose blood group is O– is an unmarried brother of Q. O is the sister-in-law of Q. L's grandmother has only one brother. The person whose blood group is AB+ lives on the top floor. The third highest scorer lives between K and L's grandmother. O obtained B grade and M's husband's brother-in-law scored the highest marks. M is the mother of Q. The person who obtained G grade has O– blood group and does not stay on the fifth floor. The person whose blood group is A+ lives on the seventh floor. N is the father of J, who is the uncle of L. K's father-in-law obtained E grade and lives on the sixth floor. The person who obtained D grade has A– blood group and lives on the third floor. The person who scored the lowest marks lives on first floor. Q's child and the one whose blood group is B+ live on an even-numbered floor. L's grandmother obtained F grade and L's uncle is the second lowest scorer. L does not have AB– blood group.

135. Who amongst the following has AB– blood group?
(1) N (2) Q
(3) J (4) M
(5) L

136. How is the person whose blood group is A– related to J?
(1) Brother-in-law (2) Brother
(3) Son (4) Sister-in-law
(5) Father

137. Who lives immediately above the one whose blood group is A–?
(1) Q
(2) O
(3) The one who scored the third highest marks
(4) The one who obtained F grade
(5) The one whose blood group is AB+.

138. Who amongst the following lives on an even numbered floor below the person whose blood group is O+?
(1) Q
(2) The one whose blood group is A–
(3) The one who obtained F grade
(4) The one who obtained C grade
(5) The one whose blood group is A+

139. **Statement:** A slump in home sales has pushed builders' inventory to "unsustainable levels" in the National Capital Region of Delhi, creating conditions for a real price correction that developers have so far avoided. Which of the following statements is inferred on the basis of the given statement?
(1) Demand for houses is quite low in most of the big cities.
(2) The high inventory level will hamper the ability of launching new projects by the builders.
(3) Builders in the market who have shown a good track record of delivering on time and on their promises, have been able to garner sales even in this slow market.
(4) Unless this unsold stock gets absorbed, it will be difficult for consumer confidence to come back in this market.
(5) High prices have pushed most of the on-sale apartments beyond the reach of average home buyers.

140. **Statement:** Next time, when you lose your baggage or meet with an accident while travelling by train, you need not run from pillar to post and wait for years before the cheque lands at your door.
Which of the following can be inferred from the given information? (An inference is something that is not directly stated but can be inferred from the given information.)
(1) There will be quick settlement of claims into the customer's account.
(2) All travellers' details will be linked with Aadhaar card.
(3) The loss will be covered by any insurance company through railways.
(4) There will be direct settlement of claim by the IRCTC.
(5) None of these

General/Financial Awareness

141. 'Cheque' and Demand Draft' come under the purview of which of the following Acts?
(1) Banking Regulation Act, 1949
(2) The Banking Companies Act–1949
(3) Chit Fund Act–1982
(4) Negotiable Instrument Act, 1881
(5) Other than the given options

142. Which of the following bank was acquired by HDFC Bank?
(1) ING Vysya Bank
(2) Catholic Syrian Bank
(3) Centurion Bank

(4) Karur Vysya Bank
(5) Lakshmi Vilas Bank

143. Which of the following is the first payment bank in India?
(1) Fino Pay Tech
(2) India Post Payments Bank
(3) Paytm Payment Bank
(4) Airtel Payment Bank
(5) None of these

144. The system of Cheque truncation was introduced in which of the following years?
(1) 2012 (2) 2010
(3) 2009 (4) 2008
(5) 2007

145. The Unified Payments Interface (UPI) launched by the National Payments Corporation of India (NPCI) would perform which of the following function(s)-
I. It would eliminate the need to exchange sensitive information about bank account numbers during a financial transaction.
II. It allows sharing of a bill among peers.
III. It allows individual to even request the money from its debtors.
(1) I and II only (2) II and III only
(3) I only (4) I, II and III
(5) III only

146. The book "The People's President: Dr. A.P.J Abdul Kalam" is authored by?
(1) Sourabh Duggal (2) S.M Khan
(3) Tarun Vijay (4) Vijay Kumar
(5) Khushwanth Singh

147. The Ministry of Shipping has issued a notification renaming Kandla Port Trust as .
(1) Subhash Chandra Bose Port Trust
(2) Jawahar Lal Port Trust
(3) Deendayal Port Trust
(4) Sardar Patel Port Trust
(5) Other than given options

148. PCA is a framework which is imposed by the Reserve Bank of India on banks with a higher percentage of Non Performing Assets. What does P stand for in 'PCA'?
(1) Public (2) Private
(3) Prompt (4) Partnership
(5) Parity

149. Who is the present Governor of Tamil Nadu?
(1) Banwarilal Purohit
(2) V. Shanmuganathan
(3) Keshari Nath Tripathi
(4) Ganga Prasad
(5) R N Ravi

150. In which of the following states is the Gorumara National Park located?
(1) Kerala (2) West Bengal
(3) Haryana (4) Madhya Pradesh
(5) None of these

151. The 15th BRICS Summit will be held in .... ?
(1) South Africa (2) Russia
(3) India (4) China
(5) Brazil

152. The Nobel Peace Prize was awarded to the International Campaign to Abolish Nuclear Weapons (ICAN) for drawing attention to the "catastrophic humanitarian consequences" of using nuclear weapons and for its efforts in a nuclear treaty. The headquarter of International Campaign to Abolish Nuclear Weapons (ICAN) is in ....
(1) Vienna, Austria
(2) Rome, Italy
(3) Geneva, Switzerland
(4) Melbourne, Australia
(5) Paris, France

153. Vijaywada is situated on the banks of which river?
(1) Godavari (2) Krishna
(3) Sutlej (4) Sabari
(5) Munneru

154. The National award-winning director and Film-maker was known for his dark satire "Jaane Bhi Do Yaaro?
(1) Rajan Rastogi (2) Kishore Kumar
(3) Kundan Shah (4) Suraj Singh
(5) None of these

155. The Rajiv Gandhi Orang National Park is located in ....

(1) West Bengal (2) Gujarat
(3) Maharashtra (4) Assam
(5) Kerala

156. What is the full form of BHIM?

(1) Bank Interface for Money
(2) Balance Interface for Mobile
(3) Bharat Interface for Mobile
(4) Bharat Interface for Money
(5) Bank Interbank for Money

157. Which state witnessed the largest decline in the number of poor, with 3.43 crore people escaping multidimensional poverty?

(1) West Bengal (2) Uttar Pradesh
(3) Rajasthan (4) Bihar
(5) Madhya Pradesh

158. Hidayatullah National Law University is in which state?

(1) Chhattisgarh (2) Madhya Pradesh
(3) Karnataka (4) West Bengal
(5) Manipur

159. 'PMSBY' is a social security scheme launched by the Government of India in 2015. Which of the following is the most appropriate explanation of the PMSBY?

(1) Life Insurance (2) Accident insurance
(3) Pension (4) Child care
(5) None of these

160. What is the purpose of cross-selling by Bank?

(1) To maintain SLR
(2) Liquidity in Market
(3) Fee Received (4) To maintain CRR
(5) To expand business

161. The Indian Museum is the largest and oldest museum in India which is located in ....

(1) Jaipur (2) Chennai
(3) Mumbai (4) New Delhi
(5) Kolkata

162. Bharatiya Reserve Bank Note Mudran Private Limited (BRBNMPL) was established by Reserve Bank of India (RBI) as its wholly owned subsidiary on 3rd February 1995. BRBNMPL manages 2 Presses one at Mysore and the other in:

(1) Bengaluru (2) Madurai
(3) Salboni (4) Kochi
(5) Durgapur

163. Reliance Stadium or Indian Petrochemicals Corporation Ltd Sports Complex Ground also known as the IPCL Ground is located in

(1) Mohali, Punjab
(2) Vadodara, Gujarat.
(3) Kochi, Kerala
(4) Indore, Madhya Pradesh
(5) Pune, Maharashtra

164. As per the Reserve Bank of India guidelines for licensing of Payments Banks and small finance bank, the promoter's minimum initial contribution to the paid-up equity capital of such banks shall at least be .... for the first five years from the commencement of its business.

(1) 25 percent (2) 30 percent
(3) 40 percent (4) 50 percent
(5) 15 percent

165. Which of the following committee recommended the establishment of Regional Rural Banks (RRBs) in each district in 1975?

(1) Mr. Gardgil Committee
(2) Mr. FF Nariman Committee
(3) M. Narisaman committee
(4) Bhagwati Committee
(5) C. Kamath Committee

166. SHG is a village-based financial intermediary committee usually composed of 10-20 local women or men. In 'SHG' G stands for:

(1) Generation (2) Gateway
(3) Group (4) Gross
(5) None of these

167. From which of the following states was Union Minister Prakash Javadekar elected to the upper house Rajya Sabha a Member of Parliament (Rajya Sabha) in 2014?

(1) Maharashtra (2) Madhya Pradesh
(3) Bihar (4) Chhattisgarh

(5) Uttar Pradesh

168. Tungabhadra Dam is in which state?
(1) Karnataka (2) Chhattisgarh
(3) West Bengal (4) Jharkhand
(5) Uttarakhand

169. Central Coalfields Limited (CCL) is a subsidiary of Coal India Limited (CIL). The headquarter of CCL is located at.
(1) Kolkata, West Bengal
(2) Chennai, Tamil Nadu
(3) Lucknow, Uttar Pradesh
(4) Raipur, Chhattisgarh
(5) Ranchi, Jharkhand

170. Under which of the following act was the 'Banking Codes and Standards Board of India' registered as a society?
(1) Banking Regulation Act, 1949
(2) Reserve Bank of India Act, 1934
(3) Banker's Books Evidence Act, 1891
(4) Societies Registration Act, 1860
(5) Negotiable Instrument Act, 1881

171. Every year 14th November is celebrated as ....
(1) World Tuberculosis Day
(2) World Diabetes Day
(3) World Cancer Day
(4) World Press Freedom Day
(5) World Habitat Day

172. The 'IDRBT' is established by the Reserve Bank of India (RBI) in 1996. It is a unique institution exclusively focused on:
(1) Rural Development
(2) Banking Technology
(3) Micro & Medium sector
(4) Science & Défense Technology
(5) Other than the given options

173. What is the capital of Venezuela?
(1) Caracas (2) Prague
(3) Lobamba (4) Tokyo
(5) None of these

174. Who among the following is the winner of the 2022 Nobel Prize for Literature?
(1) Alice Munro (2) Tomas Tranströmer
(3) Annie Ernaux (4) Mario Vargas Llosa
(5) None of these

175. Which of the following is the minimum capital requirement for Small and Payment Banks in India?
(1) 100 crores (2) 200 crores
(3) 300 crores (4) 500 crores
(5) 250 crores

176. Which of the following risks are associated with the calculation of Capital to Risk (weighted) Assets Ratio (CRAR)?
I. Operational Risk
II. Market Risk
III. Credit Risk
Select the correct option from the given option:
(1) Only I (2) Only I & II
(3) Only III (4) Only I & III
(5) All I, II & III

177. With which of the following sports is Pooja Kadian associated?
(1) Badminton (2) Chess
(3) Wrestling (4) Wushu
(5) Hockey

178. The Rural Infrastructure Development Fund (RIDF)wassetupbytheGovernmentin1995-96 for financing ongoing rural Infrastructure projects. The RIDF is maintained by the ....
(1) RBI (2) NABARD
(3) SIDBI (4) NPCI
(5) Regional Rural Banks

179. What does M in 'MUDRA' stand for?
(1) Micro (2) Money
(3) Management (4) Mobile
(5) Medium

180. Where is the headquarter of the Indian Council of Agricultural Research (ICAR)?
(1) Hyderabad (2) Kolkata
(3) New Delhi (4) Chennai
(5) Mumbai

181. India's first defense industrial park was set-up in which of the following states?

(1) Haryana (2) Punjab
(3) Jammu-Kashmir (4) Bihar
(5) Kerala

182. When is the World Day for International Justice observed?
(1) 17 August (2) 30 March
(3) 17 July (4) 23 September
(5) None of these

183. What does a negative WPI indicate?
(1) Deflationary pressure
(2) Inflationary pressure
(3) Balance pressure
(4) Indifferent pressure
(5) None of these

184. The Application Supported by Blocked Amount (ASBA) is related to which of the following sector?
(1) Insurance sector
(2) Export-Import
(3) Other than those given as options
(4) Capital market
(5) Commodity market

185. Coins upto .... paise are called as 'small coins.
(1) 50 (2) both 25 and 10
(3) 10 (4) 1
(5) 25

186. Where will the G20 Finance Ministers and Central Bank Governors meeting be held?
(1) Mumbai (2) New Delhi
(3) Chennai (4) Gandhi nagar
(5) Jaipur

187. How many entities voluntarily surrendered their NBFC licenses?
(1) 5 (2) 7
(3) 9 (4) 9
(5) 11

188. The first Olive Oil Refinery in Indian, has been set-up in which of the following states?
(1) Telangana (2) Madhya Pradesh
(3) Rajasthan (4) Gujarat
(5) Uttarakhand

189. Which country is the source of the Rafale Marine aircraft approved for procurement?
(1) Germany (2) Russia
(3) United Kingdom (4) Malaysia
(5) France

190. What percentage of increment will implementing partners receive in financial support under the SAMARTH scheme?
(1) 2% (2) 4%
(3) 5% (4) 6%
(5) 8%

Answers With Explanations

1. (2)
2. (1)
3. (3)
4. (4)
5. (4)
6. (3)
7. (5)
8. (2)
9. (5)
10. (1)
11. (3) Both the statements (I) and (II) are the reasons.
12. (5) All of the above reasons can make the hurricane.
13. (2)
14. (5) All of the above statements are related to the passage.
15. (4)
16. (3)
17. (1)
18. (5)
19. (4)
20. (5)
21. (1)
22. (3)
23. (5)
24. (4)
25. (5)
26. (4)
27. (5)
28. (4)
29. (4)
30. (4) 'Wears off' means lose effectiveness or intensity.
31. (1)
32. (1)
33. (4)
34. (1)
35. (5)
36. (5)

37. (3)

38. (4)

39. (4)

40. (2)

41. (5) $(422 + 478) \div ? \approx 60$

$? = 15$

42. (4) $? \approx \sqrt{256} \times 19 + 8 \times 14$

$? \approx 16 \times 19 + 8 \times 14 = 416$

43. (2) $16 \times 24 + ? \approx 19 \times 32$

$? = 608 - 384 = 224$

44. (3) $28 \times 16 \approx ? \times 14 + 70$

$448 \approx ? \times 14 + 70$

$? = 27$

45. (2) $272 + 190 + 84 \approx ? \times 13 \times 6$

$? \approx 7$

46. (3)

117.5 117 119 111 143 **15**

-0.5 $+2$ -8 $+32$ -128

-2^{-1} $+2^{+1}$ -2^{3} $+2^{5}$ -2^{7}

47. (5)

15 12 31 148 **1027**

×1–3 ×3–5 ×5–7 ×7–9

48. (2)

1 13 83 419 1679 **5039**

×7+6 ×6+5 ×5+4 ×4+3 ×3+2

49. (1)

12 25 48 99 194 393 **780**

×2+1 ×2–2 ×2+3 ×2–4 ×2+5 ×2–6

50. (4)

3 11 31 69 131 **223**

1^3+2 2^3+3 3^3+4 4^3+5 5^3+6 6^3+7

51. (2) Number of tickets sold to males by C3 and C6 theatre together = 24 + 36 = 60

Number of tickets sold to females by C3 and C5 theatre together = 36 + 32 = 68

Required ratio = 15 : 1

52. (4) Number of female who bought ticket from C2 and C4 theatre together = 40 + 30 = 70

Number of male who bought ticket from C5 theatre = 40

Required % = 75%

53. (3) Total revenue earns by C4 theatre = 2100 + 7200 + 7500 = 16800

54. (2) Number of male who bought ticket from C1, C2 and C3 together = 30 + 30 + 24 = 84

Required average = 28

55. (1) Number of males who bought ticket from C4, C5 and C6 together = 36 + 40 + 36 = 112

Number of females who bought ticket from C4, C5 and C6 together = 30 + 32 + 32 = 94

Required difference = 112 – 94 = 18

56. (2) (*i*) $2x^2 - 5x + 3 = 0$

$2x^2 - 2x - 3x + 3 = 0$

$2x(x - 1) - 3(x - 1) = 0$

$(x - 1)(2x - 3) = 0$

$x = 1, 3/2$

(*ii*) $3y^2 - 4y + 1 = 0$

$3y^2 - 3y - y + 1 = 0$

$3y(y - 1) - 1(y - 1) = 0$

$(3y - 1)(y - 1) = 0$

$x = 1/3, 1$

$x \geq y$

57. (3) (*i*) $x^2 - 17x + 72 = 0$

$x^2 - 9x - 8x + 72 = 0$

$x(x - 9) - 8(x - 9) = 0$

$(x - 8)(x - 9) = 0$

$x = 8, 9$

(*ii*) $y^2 - 27y + 180 = 0$

$y^2 - 12y - 15y + 180 = 0$

$y(y - 12) - 15(y - 12) = 0$

$(y - 15)(y - 12) = 0$

$y = 15, 12$

$y > x$

58. (2) (*i*) $(x - 12)^2 = 0$

$x - 12 = 0$

$x = 12$

(*ii*) $y^2 - 21y + 108 = 0$

$y^2 - 12y - 9y + 108 = 0$

$y(y - 12) - 9(y - 12) = 0$

$(y - 9)(y - 12) = 0$

$y = 9, 12$

$x \geq y$

59. (5) (*i*) $2x^2 + 7x + 5 = 0$

$2x^2 + 2x + 5x + 5 = 0$

$2x(x + 1) + 5(x + 1) = 0$

$(2x + 5)(x + 1) = 0$

$x = -5/2, -1$

(*ii*) $3y^2 + 12y + 9 = 0$

$3y^2 + 9y + 3y + 9 = 0$

$3y(y + 3) + 3(y + 3) = 0$

$(3y + 3)(y + 3) = 0$

$y = -1, -3$

No relation can be established.

60. (2) (*i*) $x^2 + 2x - 35 = 0$

$x^2 + 7x - 5x - 35 = 0$

$x(x + 7) - 5(x + 7) = 0$

$(x - 5)(x + 7) = 0$

$x = 5, -7$

(*ii*) $y^2 + 15y + 56 = 0$

$y^2 + 7y + 8y + 56 = 0$

$y(y + 7) + 6(y + 7) = 0$

$(y + 8)(y + 7) = 0$

$y = -8, -7$

$x \geq y$

61. (2) Speed of Train 'A' on Tuesday = 225 km/hr

Speed of train 'B' on Monday = 150 km/hr

Required % = 50%

62. (4) Speed of train 'B' on Tuesday = 100 km/hr

Speed of train 'A' on Wednesday = 150 km/hr

Average speed = 120 km/hr

63. (1) Speed of train 'A' on Friday = 180

Speed of train 'B' on Friday = 112.5

Required sum of time = 2.5 + 4 = 6.5 hr

64. (3) Speed of train 'A' on Tuesday = 225 km/h

Speed of train 'B' on Wednesday = 300 km/h

Required difference = 300 – 225 = 75 km/h

65. (4)
66. (1)
67. (3)
68. (5)
69. (5)
70. (3)

For questions (71-75)

	St. Xavier	Vijaya
Boys	360	450
Girls	240	180

71. (3) Required % = 75%

72. (4) Girls in 'X' college = 2 × 320 – 240 = 400

Total no. of students in 'X' colleges = 750

Number of boys in 'X' college = 750 – 400 = 350

73. (4) Required difference

= 450 + 180 – 360 – 240

= 630 – 600

= 30

74. (2)
75. (5)
76. (3)
77. (2)
78. (4)
79. (2)
80. (4)
81. (2)
82. (4)
83. (5)
84. (3)
85. (1)
86. (2)

87. (3) Let efficiency of men of first group be M_1 and second group be M_2

$3M_1 \times 2 = 4M_2 \times 3$

$M_1 = 2M_2$

$\text{Work} = 40\ M_1 \times 8 \times 15$

According to the question

$40M_1 \times 8 \times 15 \times 2 = 60M_2 \times 4 \times d$

$d = 80$ days

88. (1)
89. (1)
90. (4)

For questions (91-93):

A Y E L P R S

91. (1)
92. (1)
93. (2)
94. (2)
95. (2)
96. (5)

For questions (97-99):

Boxes	Colours
P	-----
-----	-----
S	Purple

-----	-----
R	-----
V	Blue
-----	Orange
-----	-----
-----	-----
U	----
-----	Green

97. (2)

98. (3)

99. (4)

100. (b) Five meaningful words: **Fair, Bowl, Blow, Cone, Once**

101. (2)

102. (3)

For questions (103-105):

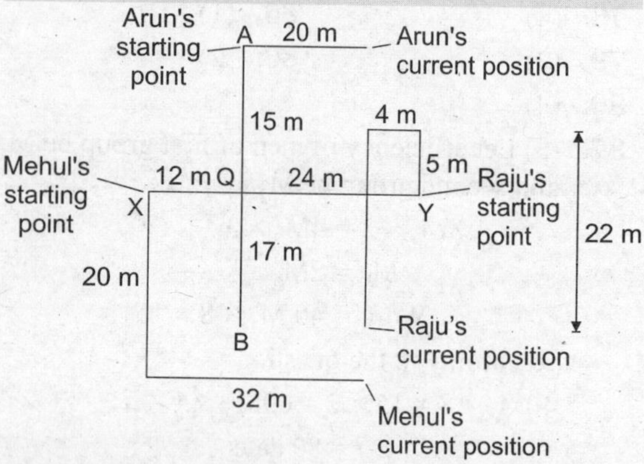

103. (3)

104. (3)

105. (1)

106. (3) **I.**

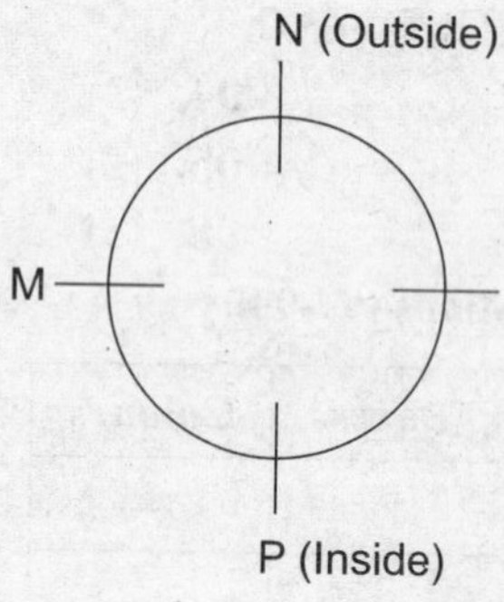

II.

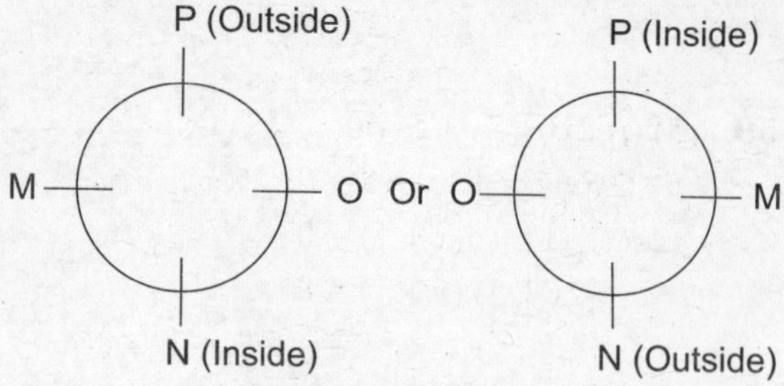

III.

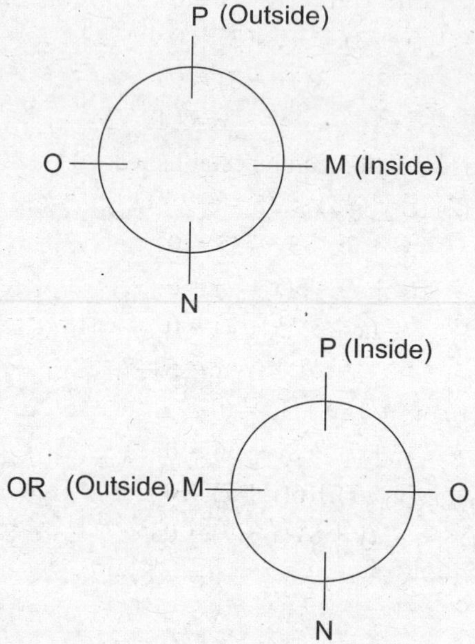

107. (3)

6. A
5. E
4. C
3. D
2. B
1. F

It is clear that F is living on the Ground floor

108. (4)

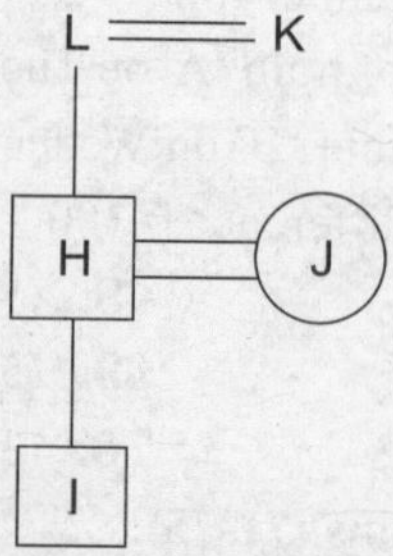

For questions (109-111):

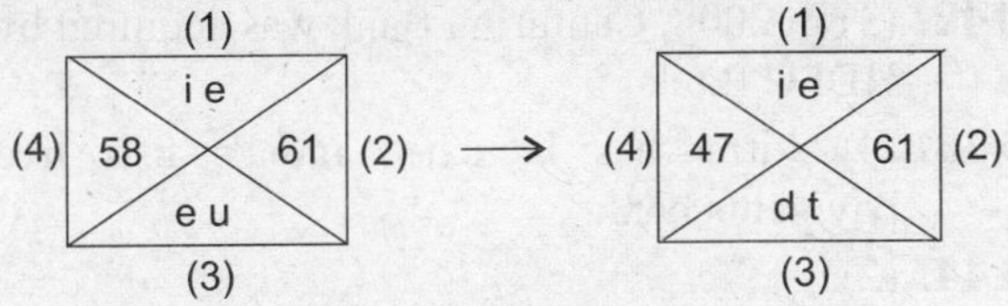

109. (3)
110. (2)
111. (3)

For questions (112-114):

- The word which comes first according to alphabetical series is arranged first and different arrangement is used in different step.
- Step 1 and 2- first and second letter are interchanged and third and fourth letter are interchanged Step 3 and 4- second and fourth letter are interchanged and rests are same.
- Step 5- First letter is unchanged, second letter is shifted to fourth place, third letter is shifted to second place, fourth letter is shifted to third place.
- Numbers start arranging as the highest number is arranged in 1st step then second highest number in second step and so on from left end after each word. And in the final step all the numbers are arranged in increasing order from left end.

Input- 54 roll 39 back 87 25 cash seat 46 beat

Step I- abkc 87 54 roll 39 25 cash seat 46 beat
Step II- eata 54 abkc 87 roll 39 25 cash seat 46
Step III- chsa 46 eata 54 abkc 87 roll 39 25seat
Step IV- rllo 39 chsa 46 eata 54 abkc 87 25seat
Step V- sate 25 rllo 39 chsa 46 eata 54 abkc87

112. (3)
113. (3)
114. (2)
115. (2)
116. (2)
117. (4)

For questions (118-120):

Doctors	Meeting hour
Ophthalmologist	7:00-8:30 am
Psychiatrist	8:30-10:00 am
General physician	10:00-12:30 am
Orthopedic surgeon	12:30-3:00 pm
Dentist	3:00-6:00 pm

118. (4)
119. (2)
120. (4)

For questions (121-123):

FLOOR	FLAT-1	FLAT-2	FLAT-3
THIRD	L	R	P
SECOND	O	K	M
FIRST	Q	A	N

or

FLOOR	FLAT-1	FLAT-2	FLAT-3
THIRD	L	R	P
SECOND	O	A	M
FIRST	Q	K	N

121. (4)
122. (1)
123. (3)
124. (2)

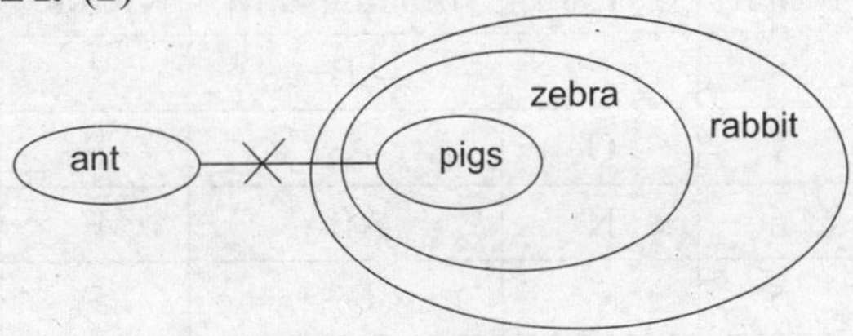

125. (1)

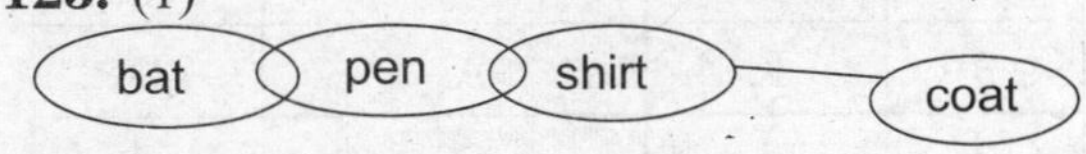

126. (2)

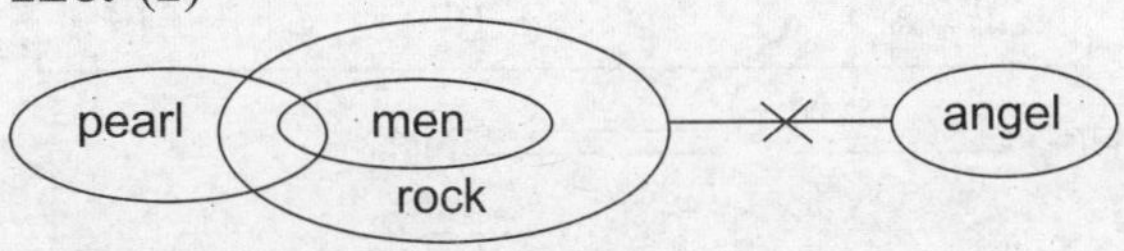

127. (3)

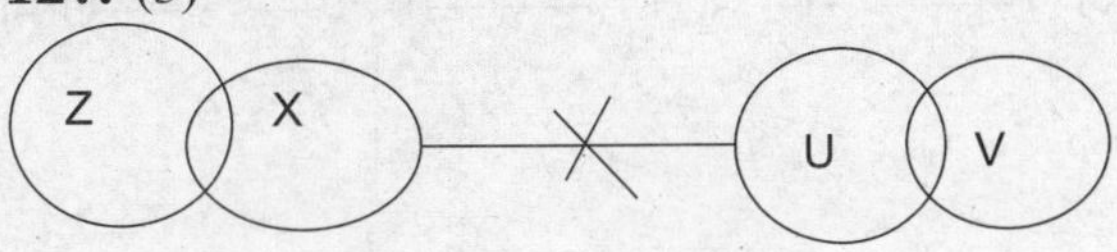

For questions (128-130):

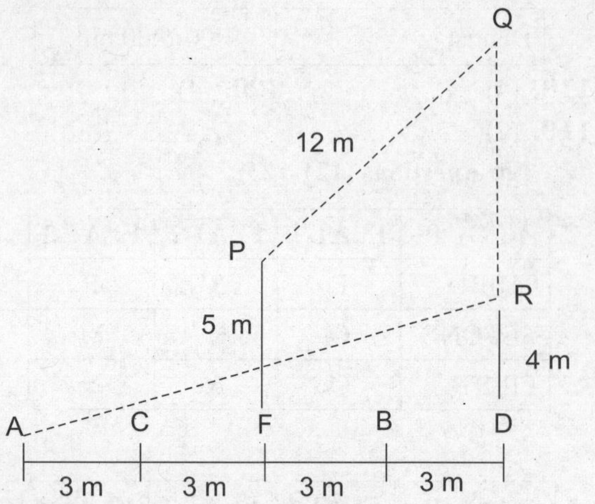

128. (4)

129. (2)

130. (3)

131. (1)

132. (2)

133. (2)

134. (5)

For questions (135-138):

Step 1.

Floor	Person	Blood group	Grade
8	P	AB+	A
7	O	A+	B
6	N	AB–	E
5	M	O+	F
4	L	B+	C
3	K	A–	D
2	J	O–	G
1	Q	B-	H

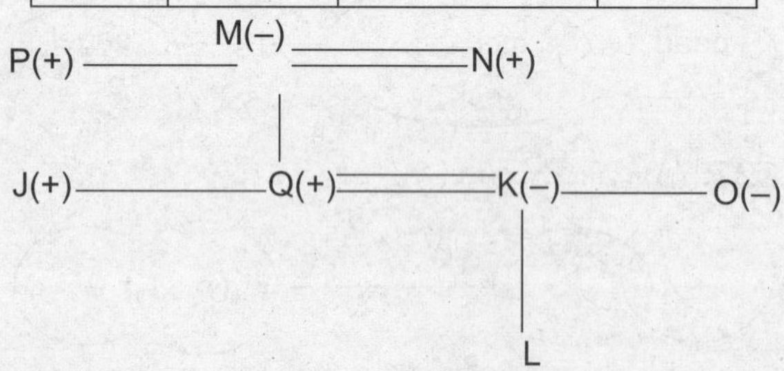

135. (1)

136. (4)

137. (3)

138. (4)

139. (5)

140. (1)

141. (4) Cheque and Demand Draft comes under Negotiable Instruments Act, 1881.

142. (3) In 2008, Centurion Bank was acquired by HDFC Bank.

143. (4) Airtel has launched India's first live payments bank.

144. (2)

145. (4) UPI is a flagship product of NPCI that will help India to move towards a cashless economy.

146. (2)

147. (3) The Ministry of Shipping has issued a notification renaming Kandla Port Trust as Deendayal Port Trust.

148. (3)

149. (5)

150. (2)

151. (1) The 15th edition of the annual BRICS (Brazil, Russia, India, China, South Africa) summit will be held in South Africa in August 2023.

152. (3) The headquarter of ICAN is in Geneva, Switzerland.

153. (2)

154. (3)

155. (4)

156. (4) BHIM-Bharat Interface for Money.

157. (2)

158. (1)

159. (2)

160. (5)

161. (5)

162. (3) The BRBNMPL manages 2 Presses one at Mysore in Karnataka and the other at Salboni in West Bengal.

163. (2)

164. (3)

165. (3)

166. (3)

167. (1)

168. (1)

169. (5)

170. (4) The Banking Codes and Standards Board of India was registered as a society under the Societies Registration Act, 1860, in February 2006.

171. (2) World Diabetes Day is the primary global awareness campaign focusing on diabetes mellitus and is held on November 14 each year. Children's Day is also celebrated on the birth anniversary of Jawaharlal Nehru.

172. (2)

173. (1)

174. (3)

175. (1)

176. (5) Capital Adequacy Ratio (CAR) is also

known as Capital to Risk (Weighted) Assets Ratio (CRAR), is the ratio of a bank's capital to its risk.

177. (4)

178. (1)

179. (1)

180. (3)

181. (5) The Indian government has approved setting up of India's first Defence Industrial Park at Ottappalam in Palakkad district of Kerala.

182. (3) The World Day for International Justice is observed on July 17 each year.

183. (1) A negative Wholesale Price Index (WPI) indicates deflationary pressure, meaning a general decrease in prices of goods and services.

184. (4) ASBA is an innovative investment process developed by SEBI to simplify the process of investing in Initial Public Offerings (IPOs).

185. (1) Coins in India are presently being issued in denominations of 50 paise, one rupee, two rupees, five rupees, ten rupees and twenty rupees.

186. (4)

187. (5) The RBI reported that 11 entities have voluntarily surrendered their NBFC licenses.

188. (3) The first Olive Oil Refinery in Indian, has been set-up in Lunkaransar, Rajasthan.

189. (5) The Rafale Marine aircraft will be procured from the French Government based on an Inter-Governmental Agreement (IGA).

190. (3) Implementing partners under the SAMARTH scheme will receive a 5% increment in financial support provided by the Ministry of Textiles.

IBPS Clerk Mains

Practice Set – 10

General English

Directions (1-8): *Read the following passage carefully and answer the questions given below them.*

With regard to employment, the term feminisation can be used to denote presence of women in a particular sector or industry where there is a disproportionate concentration of women; for instance, in the service industry, agriculture, or the garment industry. The Government of India in the Economic Survey (2017-2018) stated that the agricultural sector in India is undergoing feminisation. In the face of **shrinking** employment opportunities in agriculture, men diversified into the rural non-farm sector, and male out- migration emerged as a major livelihood strategy. Since women did not feature predominantly in either of these trends, most rural women are still engaged in agriculture, mostly as labourers and cultivators (with a disproportionate number of agricultural labourers being Dalit women).

One reason for the feminisation of agricultural labour is that capital prefers to employ women. Women are more willing to accept low-paid irregular work, are easy to hire and fire, are thought to be docile and hardworking, and certain jobs are typified as women's work. All these factors combined with gendered division of work are an important explanation for feminisation. Together, they keep production costs in check and enable capital accumulation. Against the backdrop of rural distress and agrarian crisis, rural men sought employment outside agriculture. Inside villages, they took to non-farm work as casual labourers in construction, brick kilns, mills, or worked as drivers, carpenters, teachers, and so on. An important point to note here is that such jobs, while more readily available and better remunerated than agricultural labour, are socially perceived as 'male work'. Many of these jobs are better paid, more esteemed, and involve **arduous** physical labour.

The participation of women in the rural, non-farm economy is few and far between, and depends on local socio-cultural value systems. In this context, women often remain in the villages, and therefore in agricultural work. At best, they are supplementary income earners; the concept of a 'breadwinner' is strongly associated with men. Social norms and a gendered division of labour. In line with patriarchal social roles, women are responsible for reproduction and care activities. With male out-migration, women have additionally taken on the role of providing for their households on a daily basis, since .... are irregular. This means that they now have to take care of their own farming and also work as agricultural wage labourers.

Within agriculture, there exists a gendered division of labour. Women undertake work such as weeding, threshing, and paddy transplantation—tasks that might not require physical strength. Patriarchy is so deeply rooted that even though women might do male tasks like ploughing and spade work in their own fields, they might not as wage labourers. A woman doing a 'man's job' would most likely invite **ridicule**.

1. As per Economic Survey (2017-18) what is/are the main reason(s) that agriculture in India is undergoing feminisation?

I. The challenges of agricultural employment in India.

II. Men ventured out to non-farm sectors and out- migrating for better prospects and stable livelihood.

(III) Women want to earn for themselves and build a career out of it.

(1) Only (I)
(2) Only (II)
(3) Only (I) and (III)
(4) Only (I) and (II)

(5) All (I), (II) and (III)

2. According to the passage, how do the local socio- cultural norms make rural women far less pliable than their male counterparts?

I. Since the "breadwinner" tag is only associated with the male population, women's income is considered as supplementary thus they mostly confine to villages and engage in agricultural activities.

II. The deeply rooted gender division society perceives women as a caregiver. With males out-migrating, women have taken the responsibility of aiding the family through their agricultural wages.

III. Even in farming, women only take those jobs that are not considered as "man's job" just to avoid getting ridiculed.

(1) Only (I) (2) Only (II)
(3) Only (III) (4) Only (I) and (III)
(5) All (I), (II) and (III)

3. Why capitalists prefer to employ women?

I. The conventional wisdom states that women are more likely to accept low paid irregular jobs and also, they are easy to hire and fire.

II. women are prejudiced to be docile and hardworking, and certain jobs are typified as women's work.

III. After nurturing the family, women want to earn extra income and capitalists use this in their favour.

(1) Only (I) (2) Only (II)
(3) Only (III) (4) Only (I) and (II)
(5) All (I), (II) and (III)

4. After going through the passage characterised author's tone.

(1) condescending (2) cynical
(3) laudatory (4) satirical
(5) acerbic

5. Which of the following words can fit grammatically and contextually into the blank given in the passage?

(1) remittances (2) supplementary
(3) invoice (4) evasions
(5) consideration

6. Which of the following words can REPLACE the word "**arduous**" given in the passage?

(1) fragile (2) onerous
(3) effortless (4) exciting
(5) None of these

7. Which of the following words can REPLACE the word "**ridicule**" given in the passage?

(1) applause (2) derision
(3) praise (4) approval
(5) None of these

8. Which of the following words is the OPPOSITE of "**shrinking**" as per passage?

(1) wither (2) shrivel
(3) expanding (4) condense
(5) None of these

Directions (9-13): *In the following paragraph few words are missing and for each of this word five options are given. Choose the correct option for the respective blank that is grammatically and contextually accurate.*

Water (9) .... is the lack of freshwater resources to satisfy water demand. It is (10) ....by partial or no satisfaction of expressed demand, economic competition for water quantity or quality, disputes between users, irreversible groundwater (11) ...., and negative effects on the environment. It affects every continent and was categorised in 2019 by the World Economic Forum as one of the largest global risks with respect to its (12) .... impact over the next decade.

One-third of the global population (2 billion people) live under situations of severe water scarcity at least one month of the year. Half a billion people in the world (13) .... by severe water scarcity all year round. Half of the world's largest cities have been facing water scarcity.

9. (1) drainage (2) clog
(3) scarcity (4) abundance
(5) surplus

10. (1) manifested (2) attested
(3) hidden (4) certify
(5) transparent

11. (1) augmentation (2) depletion
(3) expenditure (4) dwindle

(5) impoverishment

12. (1) latent (2) thinkable
(3) potential (4) probability
(5) reality

13. (1) Affected (2) effected
(3) aftermath (4) pompous
(5) grandiose

Directions (14-17): *Each question consists three sentences which may or may not have errors. Mark the correct sentence(s) as your answer. If there is no correct sentence then mark (5) that is "All sentences are incorrect".*

14. I. Before the exam she felt surely of excelling, but when the exam started, she realized that it is not going to be so easy.
II. I know that eventually he will succumb to me and confess that he has committed a crime
III. In his valedictory speech he said nothing worth listening to.
(1) Only (I) (2) Only (II)
(3) Only (III) (4) Only (I) and (II)
(5) All sentences are incorrect

15. I. Just before the match I asked him whom he thought was going to win.
II. My nephew, who is in Bangalore, is eager to travel to Delhi in this winter.
III. One of my uncles is seriously ill and is in the intensive care unit.
(1) Only (I) (2) Only (II)
(3) Only (III) (4) Only (II) and (III)
(5) All sentences are incorrect

16. I. The man was dressed simply but his eyes were beaming with knowledge.
II. when he used to walk along the road, a wild dog started chasing him.
III. A pair of trouser have been bought by me.
(1) Only (I) (2) Only (II)
(3) Only (III) (4) Only (I) and (III)
(5) All sentences are incorrect

17. I. The business tycoon returned back to the corridors of Indian cricket by bagging the franchise of the IPL.
II. Things will go the same as they were, unless you yourself look into it.
III. The thirsty dogs drank up all the water.
(1) Only (I) (2) Only (II)
(3) Only (III) (4) Only (I) and (III)
(5) All sentences are incorrect

Directions (18-25): *In each sentence some portion is in bold, which may or may not need improvement. Choose the correct replacement for that portion that makes the sentence grammatically and contextually correct. If the sentence is correct as it is, then mark "No improvement required".*

18. Prime Minister Narendra Modi expressed his gratitude to doctors, nurses and all **whom worked at** crossing the milestone of 100 crore covid doses.
(1) those who worked on
(2) those whom worked at
(3) those who worked upon
(4) whom working on
(5) No improvement required

19. The leader repeatedly said that his mission was not **by merely to achieve** hundred percent literacy.
(1) to more achieving
(2) merely to achieve
(3) for merely to achieve
(4) in order to achieve
(5) No improvement required

20. Stating that the lockdown had opened up new vistas such as conduct of online classes, the Madras High Court **impressed upon the need to continue** the virtual mode of education for the benefit of those in need of it.
(1) impressed by the need to continue
(2) impresses with the need to continue
(3) impressed along with need of continuing
(4) impresses from the need for continue
(5) No Improvement Required

21. **No sooner I saw** him than I ran away.
(1) As soon as I see
(2) No sooner did I see
(3) No sooner had I seen him
(4) No sooner had I seen him

(5) No improvement

22. Rohan met with an accident and immediately **admitted to the hospital.**

(1) admitted to hospital
(2) admitted to a hospital
(3) admitted into a hospital
(4) has admitted to a hospital
(5) No improvement required

23. Our journey to Manali was **far from being comfortable**, as the road was bumpy.

(1) far from comfortability
(2) far not comfortable
(3) far not comforting
(4) far and not being comfortable
(5) No improvement required

24. I **have been ringing the doorbell** five times but no one answered.

(1) Had been ringing the doorbell
(2) have rung the doorbell
(3) ringing the doorbell
(4) has rung the doorbell
(5) No improvement required

25. There **has been a sharp decline of** the profit of the company this year.

(1) have been a sharp decline of
(2) has a sharp decline in
(3) has been a sharp decline in
(4) have been a sharp decline
(5) No correction required

Directions (26-30): *In each question four words are given in bold, in which one of them might be misspelt or grammatically incorrect. Choose the incorrect word as your answer. If all the words are correct, mark (5) i.e. No correction required.*

26. What makes plastic so (A) **convenient** in our day-to-day lives it's (B) **cheap** also makes it (C) **ubiquoitous**, resulting in one of our planet's greatest environmental (D) **challenges.**

(1) A (2) B
(3) C (4) D
(5) No correction required

27. The country argues that deep and (A) **significent** cuts to fossil fuel use can (B) **affect** the development (C) **trajectory** of its and other (D) **developing** countries.

(1) A (2) B
(3) C (4) D
(5) No correction required

28. James was told to (A) **forfeit** all contact with (B) **convicted** felons if he did not want to (C) **violate** the terms of his (D) **payrole**.

(1) A (2) B
(3) C (4) D
(5) No correction required

29. While social media has mobilised help in a way our (A) **infrastructure** was unable to, and many could find the aid they needed in (B) **critical** times, what was once an escape from reality is now an (C) **overwelming** source of information and (D) **distressing** news.

(1) A (2) B
(3) C (4) D
(5) No correction required

30. Considering, however, the numbers of venomous and (A) **innocuous** snakes that occur in most (B) **tropical** countries, it might be supposed that (C) **mimicry** in this order of reptiles would be of commoner (D) **occurence** than appears to be the case.

(1) A (2) B
(3) C (4) D
(5) No correction required

Directions (31-35): *In the following questions words are given in bold, and correspondent to it three sentences are given using that word. Choose the sentence(s) where the correct usage of the word is done.*

31. Palpable

I. Because the bank was being robbed, the sense of fear among the patrons was palpable.

II. The hatred between the two sports teams was palpable and seemed to fill the entire stadium.

III. I was palpable to see my result of excelling in the exam with A grade.

(1) Only (I) (2) Only (II)
(3) Only (III) (4) Only (I) and (II)
(5) All (I), (II) and (III)

32. Coerce

I. The bully tried to coerce the small kids into giving him their lunch money.

II. According to the treasure map, the cave is located at the end of the coerce path that winds up the mountain

III. The bird carefully made a coerce nest out of twigs.

(1) Only (I) (2) Only (II)
(3) Only (III) (4) Only (I) and (II)
(5) All (I), (II) and (III)

33. Affiliate

I. The Global Hunger Report (GHR) has once again affiliate headlines in India for the country's poor ranking.

II. The India-China relationship is in a difficult place, with the past affiliate the present.

III. Jane is an atheist, and as such, she is not affiliated with any church in her community.

(1) Only (I) (2) Only (II)
(3) Only (III) (4) Only (II) and (III)
(5) All (I), (II) and (III)

34. Callow

I. I believed a lot of things in my callow youth that I do not believe now.

II. Amartya is a callow secretary who needs to take a few more computer classes.

III. He'd need to keep his senses sharp and try to put any such callow thoughts quite out of his mind.

(1) Only (I) (2) Only (II)
(3) Only (III) (4) Only (II) and (III)
(5) All (I), (II) and (III)

35. Wander

I. The bookworm loved to wander through the library and brush her fingers against the spines of the books.

II. "I wander what can have happened to the boy," he said; and he opened the door and looked out.

III. No wander, then, that he did not oftener stay to play on the common.

(1) Only (I) (2) Only (II)
(3) Only (III) (4) Only (II) and (III)
(5) All (I), (II) and (III)

Directions (36-40): *In the question below, the passage consists of five sentences. These are labelled as A, B, C, D and E. Find out the proper order for the five sentences and answer the questions based on that.*

(A) Globally, landslides lead to the expenditure of billions of bucks towards the rehabilitation of affected areas.

(B) Typically, pre-condition factors build up specific sub- surface conditions that build the sloping surface and cause landslides which endanger the livelihoods of folks living under these hills and mountains.

(C) Landslide, slope failure, slum is an uncontrollable downhill flow of rocks, earth, Junk or the mixture of the three.

(D) Because of these huge annual losses, most governments have instituted bodies to deal with landslides. As an example, the U.S. government created the National Landslides info Centre to gather and distribute all types of information associated with landslides.

(E) Thus, study of landslides is crucial considering the annual economic losses they create

36. Which of the following sentences is third after rearrangement?

(1) A (2) B
(3) C (4) D
(5) E

37. Which of the following sentences is first after rearrangement?

(1) A (2) B
(3) C (4) D
(5) E

38. Which of the following is fourth sentence after rearrangement?

(1) A (2) B

(3) C (4) D
(5) E

39. Which of the following is second sentence after rearrangement?
(1) A (2) B
(3) C (4) D
(5) E

40. Which of the following is fifth (last) sentence after rearrangement?
(1) A (2) B
(3) C (4) D
(5) E

Quantitative Aptitude

Directions (41-45): *What approximate value should come in the place of question (?) mark in following questions?*

41. $(0.99/7.98) \times 72.03 + (0.99/10.97) \times 120.95 - \sqrt{15.99} = \sqrt{?}$
(1) 144 (2) 324
(3) 576 (4) 196
(5) 256

42. $\sqrt{324.03} \times \sqrt{24.99} - 17.03 \times (2.09)^2 = \sqrt{?}$
(1) 144 (2) 784
(3) 400 (4) 484
(5) 576

43. $21.03 \times 5.99 + 8.99$ of 19.96% of $60.05 = ?$
(1) 234 (2) 222
(3) 232 (4) 242
(5) 228

44. $11.87 \times 13.08 - 55.03 \div 10.92 = ? + 99.98$
(1) 100 (2) 51
(3) 85 (4) 92
(5) 108

45. $53.08 + 77.98 - 33.11 + ? = 90.93$
(1) −1 (2) −15
(3) −7 (4) 11
(5) 17

46. A vessel contains mixture of milk and water in the ratio of 7 : 5 respectively. If 9 liters of mixture taken out and same quantity of water is added, then the ratio of milk to water in remaining mixture becomes 7 : 9, then find the initial quantity of milk in the mixture?
(1) 21 liters (2) 15 liters
(3) 20 liters (4) 7 liters
(5) 28 liters

47. Two pipes A & B can fill an empty tank in four hours and 'T' hours respectively. An outlet pipe C can empty the half of the same tank in four hours. If all three pipes open together in the tank, then they can fill the same tank in 4 hours 48 minutes. Find the value of 'T'?
(1) 8 (2) 12
(3) 4 (4) 2
(5) 1

48. An article marked up 30% above its cost price. Find the percentage of discount should offer on the article to make a profit of 4%?
(1) 10% (2) 5%
(3) 20% (4) 2%
(5) 9%

49. The breadth of a rectangle is 20 meters and area of a square is 125 meters^2 more than that of the rectangle. If the length of the rectangle is equal to side of square, then find the perimeter of rectangle?
(1) 90 m (2) 45 m
(3) 55 m (4) 80 m
(5) 75 m

50. Present age of father is four times of his son's present age and after three years age of father will be three times of his son's age. Find after how many years age of father will be 250% of his son's age?
(1) 6 (2) 5
(3) 4 (4) 9
(5) 10

51. A and B entered into a business by making investment of Rs. 12000 & Rs. X respectively. After six months A withdrew Rs. 2000 from his initial investment. If at the end of a year profit share of B is Rs. 3000 out of total profit of Rs. 5200, then find the value of X?
(1) 15000 (2) 30000

(3) 26000 (4) 50000
(5) 45000

52. Pallavi and Himanshi together can do a work in 120 days, while Himanshi and Ayush together can do the same work in 40 days. If Himanshi alone can do the same work in 180 days, then find in how many days Ayush, Himanshi and Pallavi together can do the same work?
(1) 18 days (2) 9 days
(3) 36 days (4) 6 days
(5) 60 days

53. The distance between two points A and B is 24 km. A boat travels from A to B and come back in six hours. If speed of stream is increases by 2 km/h, then boat takes six hours to travels from A to B in upstream. Find the speed of boat in still water?
(1) 6 km/h (2) 9 km/h
(3) 5 km/h (4) 7 km/h
(5) 10 km/h

54. A train travels 700 km with average speed of 70 km/h and after every 140 km train takes stoppage of 4 minutes. Find the time taken by the train to cover same distance without stoppage?
(1) 9 hr 4 min (2) 9 hr 48 min
(3) 9 hr 44 min (4) 10 hr 16 min
(5) 10 hr 44 min

55. The population of city P decreased by 20% every year and population of city Q decreased by 8% every year. If after two years population of city Q was 22088 more than that of city P and initially it was 20000 more than that of population of city P, then find the population of city Q initially?
(1) 30000 (2) 45000
(3) 42000 (4) 36000
(5) 54000

56. Deepak invested Rs. 4800 into two schemes A and B at same rate of interest. But Compound interest obtained from scheme A in 2 years is Rs. 50 more than the simple interest obtained from Schemes B for 4 years. If Deepak invested the total sum at simple interest for 8 years at same rate, then interest obtained becomes equal to the investment. Find the amount invested in scheme B?
(1) Rs. 2600 (2) Rs. 2000
(3) Rs. 1800 (4) Rs. 1600
(5) Rs. 2400

57. If we add 7 to the numerator of the fraction and increases denominator by 100% then both become equal. And when the numerator is increased by 300% and denominator is increased by 5 then it becomes twice of the original fraction. What will be the half of original fraction?
(1) 3/8 (2) 5/12
(3) 3/10 (4) 5/16
(5) 4/15

58. Running in opposite direction train B can cross train A in 10 seconds, while running in same direction train B can cross train A in 130/3 seconds. Train B can cross 300 meters long platform in 15 seconds and speed of train B is 144 km/hr. Find the length of train A?
(1) 250 m (2) 400 m
(3) 350 m (4) 300 m
(5) 450 m

59. A two–digit number decreased by 27 when its digits are reversed and difference between square of digit at unit place and square of the digit at tens place of the original number is same as difference between original number and the number obtained after reversing of digits. Find the original number?
(1) 52 (2) 74
(3) 85 (4) 63
(5) 96

60. There are three white and five black balls in a bag. In how many ways four balls should be selected such that there is at least one ball of each color?
(1) 55 (2) 90
(3) 45 (4) 65
(5) 130

Directions (61–65): *Paragraph given the information about certain number of masks sold by three companies (A, B & C). Read the data carefully and answer the questions.*

Company A: Total 100 mask sold and cost price of each mask is Rs. 20. 40% of total mask sold at profit of 20% and remaining at the profit of 10%.

Company B: Total 150 masks sold and cost price of each mask is Rs. 40. Company markup price of each mask 50% above its cost price and allow a discount of 10% on each mask.

Company C: Total money received by selling all the mask by company is Rs. 10800 and selling price of each mask is Rs. 100. Company gets a profit 25% on each mask.

61. Total masks sold by A and C together is what percent of total masks sold by B?
(1) 148.66% (2) 139.66%
(3) 135.66% (4) 138.66%
(5) 130.66%

62. Find the difference between total discount allowed by company B on each mask and cost price of each mask by company A?
(1) 18 (2) 12
(3) 11 (4) 14
(5) 15

63. Find the total cost price for the three companies together.
(1) Rs. 16440 (2) Rs. 16540
(3) Rs. 16640 (4) Rs. 16740
(5) Rs. 16840

64. Find the total amount received by all three companies by selling all the masks?
(1) Rs. 21280 (2) Rs. 21480
(3) Rs. 21680 (4) Rs. 21880
(5) Rs. 21180

65. If 40% of total masks of company A purchased by men and 30% of total masks of company B purchased by men, then find the difference between total masks purchased by women from company A and B?
(1) 42 marks (2) 48 marks
(3) 44 marks (4) 47 marks
(5) 45 marks

Directions (66-70): *Solve the given quadratic equations and mark the correct option based on your answer-*

66. I. $(2x - 7)^2 = 25$
II. $(4y - 1)^2 = 9$
(1) $x > y$ (2) $x \leq y$
(3) $x < y$ (4) $x \geq y$
(5) No relation can be established between x and y.

67. I. $(20/x^2) = 3 + (4/x)$
II. $(32/y^2) + 1 = (12/y)$
(1) $x > y$
(2) No relation can be established between x and y.
(3) $x \leq y$
(4) $\underline{x} < y$
(5) $x \geq y$

68. I. $x^2 + 8x + 15 = 0$
II. $2y^2 + 21y + 54 = 0$
(1) $x > y$
(2) $x \geq y$
(3) No relation can be established between x and y.
(4) $x \leq y$
(5) $x < y$

69. I. $(5/x) - (12/x^2) = (1/2)$
II. $2 + (20/y^2) = (13/y)$
(1) $x > y$ (2) $x \geq y$
(3) $x < y$ (4) $x \leq y$
(5) No relation can be established between x and y.

70. I. $3^{2x+4} = 9^{3x+4} \times 27^{(x+1)}$
II. $(y^2 + 18)/y = 9$
(1) $x > y$ (2) $x \geq y$
(3) $x < y$ (4) $x \leq y$
(5) No relation can be established between x and y.

Directions (71-75): *Table given below shows total number of vehicles (Public + Private) travels in five different years and number of public vehicles travels more than that of private vehicles in these five years. Read the data carefully and answer the questions.*

Years	Total number of vehicles (Public + Private) travels	Public vehicles travels more than that of private vehicles
2011	850	250
2012	1050	250
2013	1100	400
2014	800	200
2015	1200	400

71. Total private vehicles travel in 2013 is what percent more than total private vehicles travel in 2014?

(1) 66.66% (2) 22.33%
(3) 33.33% (4) 14.66%
(5) 16.66%

72. The ratio of males to females who travel in all vehicles in 2015 is 11 : 13 and number of males are 100 more than that of females who travel in private vehicles in 2015. Find the total females travel in public vehicles in 2015 (in each vehicle only one-person travel)?

(1) 440 (2) 540
(3) 250 (4) 400
(5) 500

73. Find the ratio of total private vehicles travel in 2011, 2012 & 2014 together to total number of public vehicles travel in 2013 & 2015 together?

(1) 15 : 11 (2) 11 : 31
(3) 15 : 13 (4) 20 : 17
(5) 20 : 31

74. 30% of total public vehicles travel in 2014 are three wheelers and rest are four wheelers, while 37.5% of total public vehicles travels in 2015 are three wheelers and rest are four wheelers. Find the difference between total four wheelers public vehicles travel in 2014 and 2015?

(1) 200 (2) 250
(3) 300 (4) 500
(5) 150

75. Find the sum of public vehicles travel in all the year?

(1) 3250 (2) 3200
(3) 3675 (4) 2300
(5) 1000

Directions (76-80): *Line graph shows monthly income and monthly saving of five different people (A, B, C, D & E) in year 2018. Read the data carefully and answer the questions.*

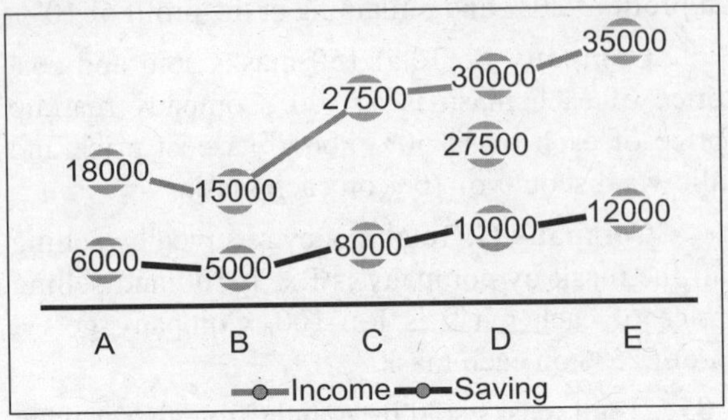

76. If expenditure of F is 25% more than that of A and the ratio of income to saving of F is 4 : 1, then find the saving of F?

(1) Rs. 15000 (2) Rs. 10000
(3) Rs. 5000 (4) Rs. 20000
(5) Rs. 9000

77. The expenditure of G is equal to difference between expenditure of B and D, while the saving of G is 50% of his income. If G spends 35% of his expenditure on food, 40% of his remaining expenditure on education and rest on house rent, then find the difference between G's saving and his expenditure on house rent?

(1) Rs. 1100 (2) Rs. 1200
(3) Rs. 1700 (4) Rs. 1300
(5) Rs. 1900

78. E spends 25% of his expenditure on travelling and remaining he spends on household and education. If amount spends on household is 650% of amount spends on education, then find the annual expenditure on education?

(1) Rs. 17600 (2) Rs. 37600
(3) Rs. 26600 (4) Rs. 27600
(5) Rs. 33600

79. Find the ratio of total expenditure of C for eight months to total expenditure of E for six months?

(1) 18 : 19 (2) 18 : 17

(3) 26 : 61 (4) 29 : 36
(5) 26 : 23

80. Monthly expenditure of B & E together is what percent (approx.) of total yearly expenditure of C?
(1) 4% (2) 14%
(3) 24% (4) 34%
(5) 44%

81. Ratio of present ages of two persons A and B is 3 : 2 and after four years ratio of their age (B : A) become 7 : 10. Then find the present age of B?
(1) 20 years (2) 18 years
(3) 24 years (4) 36 years
(5) 30 years

82. The difference between Circumference of circle A and diameter is 90 cm. If Radius of Circle B is 7 cm less than circle A then find area of Circle B?
(1) 556 cm^2 (2) 616 cm^2
(3) 588 cm^2 (4) 532 cm^2
(5) 630 cm^2

83. There are 40 children in a class in which boys are 4 more than the girls. Average weight of all the students is 42.5 kg and the average weight of all the girls is 48 kg then find the average weight of all the boys.
(1) 39.5 kg (2) 38 kg
(3) 40.5 kg (4) 36.75 kg
(5) 40.25 kg

Directions (84-88): *In each question two equations numbered (I) and (II) are given. Student should solve both the equations and mark appropriate answer.*
(1) If $x = y$ or no relation can be established
(2) If $x > y$
(3) If $x < y$
(4) If $x >= y$
(5) If $x <= y$

84. I. $8x^2 + 6x + 1 = 0$
II. $3y^2 + 7y + 2 = 0$

85. I. $x^2 = 196$
II. $y^2 - 26y + 169 = 0$

86. I. $9x^2 - 12x + 4 = 0$
II. $8y^2 - 9y + 1 = 0$

87. I. $x^2 - 15x + 56 = 0$
II. $y = \sqrt[3]{512}$

88. I. $3x^2 + 10x + 8 = 0$
II. $2y^2 + 3y + 1 = 0$

89. A man invested 15% of his monthly income in LIC and remaining gave to his mother. Mother spend 10% of it in household expenses and she had left with Rs. 30,600 then find the salary of man?
(1) Rs. 37,500 (2) Rs. 36,000
(3) Rs. 38,000 (4) Rs. 42,000
(5) Rs. 40,000

90. If 7 marks are awarded to right answer and 4 marks are penalty for wrong answer. Then Prabhat's score was 263. If he attempted 58 questions then find number of correctly attempted questions?
(1) 45 (2) 42
(3) 48 (4) 40
(5) 50

Reasoning Ability & Computer Aptitude

Directions (91-95): *Study the following information carefully and answer the questions given below.*

Fourteen persons sit in the two parallel rows such that each row contains seven persons. In Row 1- P, Q, R, S, T, U and V sit and face towards the south and in row2- A, B, C, D, E, F and G sit and face towards the north but not necessarily in the same order.

Two persons sit between V and R. R faces the one who sits at the extreme end. U faces F who sits third to the right of B. U doesn't sit adjacent to V. The number of persons sits between B and F is same as the persons sits between U and S. V faces one who sits third to the right of D. No one sits between T and P. G faces P and sits two places away from E. A sits to the left of C.

91. Who among the following persons sits third to the left of the one who faces R?
(1) B (2) E

(3) A (4) C
(5) F

92. Which among the following statement is not true?
(1) T sits at the extreme end.
(2) More than three persons sit between D and F
(3) B faces S
(4) G is not an immediate neighbor B
(5) All statements are true

93. How many persons sits between P and the one who faces A?
(1) One (2) Two
(3) Three (4) None
(5) More than three

94. Four of the following five are alike in a certain way and form a group. Who among the following person does not belong to the group?
(1) D (2) C
(3) R (4) T
(5) V

95. What is the position of A with respect to the one who faces T?
(1) Fifth to the left (2) Fourth to the right
(3) Immediate left (4) Second to the left
(5) None of these

Directions (96-98): *Study the following information carefully and answer the questions given below.*

Tim starts his walk from point G in the east direction, after walking 12 m he reaches at point H. From point H, he takes a left turn and walks 7 m to reach point F. From there he takes a right turn and walks 3 m to reach point K. Now, from point K he walks 5 m towards north and reaches at point C. Sam starts his walk from point D, after walking 4 m towards north he reaches at point B. From there he takes a right turn and walks 6 m to reach point E. Point E is 8 m towards north of point C.

96. In which direction is point K with respect to point B?
(1) South (2) South-east
(3) North east (4) North
(5) West

97. What is the shortest distance between Sam initial point and point C?
(1) $2\sqrt{13}$ m (2) $\sqrt{15}$ m
(3) 52 m (4) 50 m
(5) None of these

98. Four of the following five are alike in a certain way and form a group. Which among the following pair does not belong to the group?
(1) G-F (2) D-E
(3) G-C (4) F-E
(5) B-H

99. A family of three generation has seven members. J is nephew of Q. M is son-in-law of T. T has only two children. P is sister-in-law of S and has no siblings. T is the only brother of S. Gender of V and S is same. Q is unmarried member of the family. Find out how S is related to Q?
(1) Uncle (2) Mother
(3) Aunt (4) Sister
(5) Can't be determined

Directions (100-104): *Study the following information carefully and answer the questions given below.*

Six persons- A, B, C, D, E and F participated in the event on two different dates either 15 or 18 of three different months- March, April and May of the same year. The events are held in different cities- Indore, Agra, Bhopal, Dehradun, Delhi and Mumbai. All the information is not necessarily in the same order.

C participated on an odd numbered date in the month having odd number of days. Two persons participated between C and the person who participated in the event held in Mumbai. One event held between the event held in Dehradun and the event held in Mumbai. D participated in the event held in Dehradun but not in the month of March. Two persons participated between D and A who participated in the month having even number of days. E participated two persons before F. B doesn't participate in the event held in Delhi and Agra. The person who participated in the event held in Indore participated just before the person who participated in the event held in Agra. E doesn't participate in the event held in Indore.

100. Who among the following person participated in the event held in Delhi?

(1) A (2) F
(3) C (4) E
(5) None of these

101. How many persons participated between C and the one who participated on 18th April?

(1) One (2) Two
(3) Three (4) None
(5) More than three

102. Four of the following five are alike in a certain way and form a group. Who among the following person does not belong to the group?

(1) C (2) B
(3) E (4) D
(5) F

103. In which of the following cities does E participated in the event?

(1) Delhi (2) Bhopal
(3) Agra (4) Mumbai
(5) None of these

104. Which among the following statement (s) is/ are true?

(1) C participated in the month of May
(2) F participated after D
(3) More than two persons participated between E and D
(4) A participated in the event held in Indore
(5) All are true

Direction (105): *A word arrangement machine when given an input line of words rearranges them following a particular rule in each step. The following is an illustration of input and rearrangement.*

Input: Happy Doing Belt Active Crack First

Step I: Active Happy Doing Belt Crack First

Step II: Active Belt Happy Doing Crack First

Step III: Active Belt Crack Happy Doing First

Step IV: Active Belt Crack Doing Happy First

Step V: Active Belt Crack Doing First Happy

And step V is the last step of the arrangement.

As per the rule followed in the above steps, find out in each of the following questions the appropriate step for the given input:

Input: Visual Perk Ultimate Evaluate Famous Monk

105. Which among the following word is fourth to the left of sixth word from the left end in step III?

(1) Famous (2) Monk
(3) Evaluate (4) Perk
(5) None of these

Directions (106-110): *In each of the following questions, relationship between different elements is shown in the statements followed by three conclusions. Find the conclusion which is definitely true.*

106. Statements: $A \geq B = D > F; U = S \geq J \leq K = F$

Conclusions:

I. $K < B$
II. $F \geq S$
III. $F < U$

(1) Only I is true
(2) Only I and Either II or III are true
(3) Either II or III is true
(4) Both I and III are true
(5) All are true

107. Statements: $S \geq T \leq F < V; R \leq A < J \leq M; M = S > Z$

Conclusions:

I. $Z \leq T$
II. $R < S$
III. $M > T$

(1) Only I is true (2) Only II is true
(3) Only III is true (4) Both I and II are true
(5) All are true

108. Statements: $K \leq M = P; M \leq S > U; B \leq Q < P$

Conclusions:

I. $Q < S$
II. $B \leq K$
III. $P \leq U$

(1) Only I is true (2) Only II is true
(3) Only III is true (4) Both I and II are true
(5) All are true

109. Statements: $P \leq Q < S > R$; $U < T = R$; $Y \geq W > R$

Conclusions:

I. $S > Y$

II. $T < Y$

III. $U < S$

(1) Only I is true
(2) Only II is true
(3) Both II and III are true
(4) Both I and II are true
(5) All are true

110. Statements: $I \leq J < K = L$; $P < O \leq M \leq L$; $K < U \leq V$

Conclusions:

I. $M < V$

II. $J < O$

III. $P < K$

(1) Only I is true
(2) Only II is true
(3) Both II and III are true
(4) Both I and III are true
(5) All are true

Directions (111-115): *Study the given information carefully and answer the questions given below:*

Eleven persons work on different designations of a company. Their designations are: MD, CMD, CEO, COO, CTO, CFO, Sr. Manager, Manager, Team lead, Executive and trainee. The order of seniority is- MD is senior most designation and trainee is junior most designation.

Four persons are there between G and T who is junior to manager. D is senior to G but he is not MD and CEO. B is three designations junior to D. The number of designations between B and T is same as the number of persons senior to P. H is not senior to P but he is senior to team lead. More than four persons work between H and K. N is senior to K but junior to R. L is senior to V who is not just senior and just junior to B.

111. Who among the following works as Sr. Manager?
(1) H (2) R
(3) N (4) B
(5) None of these

112. How many persons work between L and G?
(1) Six (2) Two
(3) One (4) Four
(5) None of these

113. Who among the following is just junior to R?
(1) B (2) P
(3) V (4) N
(5) None of these

114. Which of the given combination is incorrect?
(1) MD-L (2) Team lead-N
(3) COO-H (4) Trainee-T
(5) CMD-K

115. If V and D interchanged their designations, then who among the following is four designations junior to V?
(1) N (2) R
(3) G (4) T
(5) None of these

Directions (116-120): *In each of the following questions, some statements are given followed by five conclusions. You have to take the given statements to be true even if they seem to be at variance with commonly known facts. Read all the conclusions and then decide which of the given conclusions logically follows from the given statements disregarding commonly known facts.*

116. Statements: Only coin is bank. Only a few currency is coin. Some note is currency. Some note is not press.

Conclusion:

(1) Some currency is not press
(2) Some currency is not coin
(3) All bank can be note
(4) No press is currency
(5) Some bank is currency

117. Statements: All line is music. Some singer is line. Only a few music is album. Only music is song.

Conclusion:

(1) Some song can be singer
(2) No album is line
(3) Some line is song
(4) Some part of music can never be album
(5) No singer is music

118. **Statements:** All shop is shirt. No shop is pant. Only a few pant is cotton. Only a few cloth is pant. Only cloth is silk.

Conclusion:
(1) All cotton being shirt is a possibility
(2) Some cloth is shop
(3) No shirt is pant
(4) Some cotton is not pant
(5) All silk can be shop

119. **Statements:** Some rays are alpha. All alpha are wave. Some color is wave. No band is alpha.

Conclusion:
(1) Some color is not band
(2) All rays are wave
(3) No color being alpha is a possibility
(4) All rays can be band
(5) Some color are rays

120. **Statements:** Some cat is dog. All dog are rat. Only rat is cow. No camel is rat.

Conclusion:
(1) All camel can be dog
(2) No camel is cat
(3) Some dog being cow is a possibility
(4) Some rat is not cat
(5) All cat can never be cow

Directions (121-125): *Read the following information carefully and answer the related questions:*

In a certain code language-

'Knowledge study under learning' is coded as '13 19 17 23'

'Area of knowledge' is coded as '13 29 11'

'Results of learning theory' is coded as '17 29 31 37'

'Theory under consideration' is coded as '19 31 41'

121. What is the code for 'theory'?
(1) 29 (2) 19
(3) 17 (4) 31
(5) None of these

122. What will be the code for 'results area'?
(1) 37 11 (2) 11 19
(3) 17 13 (4) 37 13
(5) None of these

123. The code '41' is used for which among the following words?
(1) Theory (2) Under
(3) Consideration (4) Learning
(5) None of these

124. Which among the following words are coded as '29 13'?
(1) Area study (2) Theory of
(3) Under knowledge
(4) Of knowledge
(5) None of these

125. What will be the possible code for 'known results'?
(1) 1317 (2) 3741
(3) 1537 (4) 2931
(5) 1113

Directions (126-130): *Read the given information carefully and answer the questions given below:*

Ten persons A to J sit around a circular table facing inside. The consecutive alphabetical named persons do not sit adjacent to each other. Ex- A doesn't sit adjacent to B, B doesn't adjacent to A and C.

F sits third to the right of A. One person sits between A and

G. B sits opposite to E. C and H are immediate neighbors. D sits second to the left of I. C neither sits opposite to I nor sits adjacent to A.C and J are not immediate neighbors.

126. How many persons sit between C and D?
(1) Four (2) Five
(3) Three (4) Two
(5) None of these

127. What is the position of B with respect to I?
(1) Third to the right
(2) Fourth to the left

(3) Immediate right
(4) Third to the left
(5) Seventh to the right

128. Who among the following sits opposite to G?
(1) C (2) F
(3) B (4) H
(5) I

129. Who among the following sits fourth to the right of H?
(1) A (2) G
(3) D (4) J
(5) None of these

130. Who among the following are immediate neighbors?
(1) G, J (2) F, H
(3) H, A (4) B, E
(5) C, F

131. If we have to move data from one place to another permanently then which shortcut will be used:
(1) copy paste (2) cut paste
(3) alt delete (4) alt shift
(5) none

132. Which is input in mentioned below
(1) Plotter (2) Scanner
(3) Mouse (4) None
(5) screen

133. Which is used to find any data on screen through cursor:
(1) Jockey (2) Mouse
(3) Scanner (4) Plotter
(5) None

134. Which is not Boolean in below mentioned:
(1) And (2) Plus
(3) Or (4) Not
(5) None

135. HTTP full form:
(1) Hyper tool text protocol
(2) Hyper text tool protocol
(3) Hyper text transfer protocol
(4) None
(5) both 1 and 2

136. Boot a system which is already on
(1) cold boot (2) warm boot
(3) hot boot (4) force boot
(5) none

137. Google is a
(1) browser (2) search engine
(3) software (4) none
(5) 1 and 2

138. Which is incorrect about RAM:
(1) Even in absence of power it stores data
(2) volatile
(3) is put on motherboard as memory circuit
(4) none
(5) both 1 & 2

139. Which is not binary from below mentioned:
(1) 0120211 (2) 010.110
(3) 101011 (4) 011111
(5) None

140. HTML full form:
(1) Heavy transfer mark up language
(2) hyper transfer make up language
(3) hyper text mark up language
(4) hyper text mock language

General/Financial Awareness

141. On which river is the Tehri Dam constructed?
(1) Son (2) Gandak
(3) Chambal (4) Bhagirathi
(5) Tapti

142. The currency of South Korea is
(1) Ringgit (2) Yuan
(3) Won (4) Peso
(5) Kyat

143. Under the restructured National Rural Livelihood Mission (NRLM), SCs and the STs will account for a minimum of 50% of financial assistance. Minorities will comprise
(1) 3% (2) 9%
(3) 15% (4) 21%
(5) 33%

144. The commencement year of the 17th Lok

Sabha is
(1) 2013 (2) 2014
(3) 2018 (4) 2019
(5) 2020

145. Which of the following financial institutions/ organizations aids the growth and development of micro, small and medium scale enterprises (MSME) in India?
(1) IRDA (2) SEBI
(3) NABARD (4) RBIt
(5) SIDBI

146. Indian player PV Sindhu is related to
(1) Badminton (2) Table Tennis
(3) Wrestling (4) Hockey
(5) None of these

147. Which of the following is the parliament of Bangladesh?
(1) Majlis (2) Shura
(3) Jatiya Sangsad (4) Jirga
(5) Sangosthi

148. From which country did India get INS Sindhurakshak submarine?
(1) France (2) Russia
(3) Sweden (4) Australia
(5) United States of America

149. Where is the headquarters of the Bank for International Settlements (BIS) located?
(1) Hong Kong (2) Vienna
(3) Mexico City (4) Basel
(5) Antwerp

150. 'MNREGA' stands for
(1) Mahatma Gandhi National Rural Employment Guarantee Act
(2) Modern New Rural Enterprise Growth Act
(3) Multi National Rural Empowerment Guarantee Act
(4) Modern New Rural Economic Growth Act
(5) Motilal Nehru Renewable Energy Guarantee Act

151. Which of the following areas come under Ayushman Bharat?
(1) Water (2) Roads
(3) Housing (4) Health
(5) Electricity

152. The Union Sports Ministry announced that Renjith Maheshwary would not be given Arjuna Award over the allegations of doping against him. With which sport is he associated?
(1) Marathon (2) Triple Jump
(3) Discuss Throw (4) Hurdle's Race
(5) Pole Vault

153. Who is the author of Bengali Romance novel 'Devdas'?
(1) Bimal Roy
(2) Sarat Chandra Chattopadhyay
(3) Sudhendu Ghosh
(4) Indra Sen
(5) Sumit Mitra

154. The capital of Mauritius is
(1) Port Louis (2) Camp Carol
(3) Britannia (4) Goodlands
(5) Union Park

155. Which of the following countries is not a member-state of ASEAN?
(1) Indonesia (2) Japan
(3) Malaysia (4) Philippines
(5) Singapore

156. Who, among the following is the Speaker of Lok Sabha?
(1) Om Birla
(2) Meira Kumar
(3) Haribansh Narayana
(4) Jagdeep Dhankhar
(5) Sushil Modi

157. Who, at present, is the Chairman of the NITI Aayog?
(1) Rajnath Singh
(2) Amit Shah
(3) Rajeev Kumar
(4) Narendra Modi
(5) Nirmala Sitharaman

158. Which of the following is not one of the Monitorable Targets of the 11th Five Year Plan (2007—12)?

(1) To increase the average GDP growth rate
(2) To increasing the literacy rate
(3) To increase energy efficiency
(4) To improve sex ratio
(5) To maximize the effect of global warming

159. What does the letter 'L' denote in the term LAF' as referred every now and then in relation to monetary policy of the RBI?
(1) Liquidity (2) Liability
(3) Leveraged (4) Longitudinal
(5) Linear

160. The European Union has adopted which of the following as a common currency?
(1) Dollar (2) Dinar
(3) Yen (4) Euro
(5) Peso

161. Government usually classifies its expenditure in term of planned and non-planned expenditure. Identify, which is the correct definition of Planned expenditure?
(1) It represents the expenditure of all the State Governments.
(2) It represents the total expenditure of the Central Government.
(3) It is the expenditure which is spent through centrally sponsored programmes and flagship schemes of Government.
(4) It represents the expenditure incurred on Defence.
(5) Other than those given as options.

162. Which of the following places in India does not have a Stock Exchange?
(1) Kolkata (2) Ahmedabad
(3) Mumbai (4) Delhi
(5) Udaipur

163. What is financial inclusion?
(1) To provide a permanent employment to the unemployed
(2) To provide a 100 days job to all those who are in need of a job
(3) To provide banking services to all those living in remote areas
(4) To ensure that all financial transactions amounting 5,000 and above are done through banks.
(5) To provide finances for all

164. Which of the following terms is used in banking and finance?
(1) Abiotic (2) Demand Deposit
(3) Fat scales (4) A diabetic
(5) Cathode

165. Which of the following is an economic term?
(1) Plaintiff (2) Bunker Blaster
(3) Deflation (4) Lampoon
(5) Zero Hour

166. What does the letter 'F' denote in the abbreviated name 'IIFCL'?
(1) Functional (2) Foreign
(3) Forwarded (4) Finance
(5) None of these

167. NAV is normally used in respect of schemes floated by ....
(1) Banks
(2) Mutual funds
(3) Insurance companies
(4) Merchant banker
(5) None of these

168. Money laundering refers to ....
(1) Conversion of assets into cash
(2) Conversion of money which is illegally obtained
(3) Conversion of cash into gold
(4) Conversion of gold into cash
(5) Money power

169. What is money laundering?
(1) Conversion of assets into cash
(2) Conversion of Money which is illegally obtained
(3) Conversion of cash into gold
(4) Conversion of gold into cash
(5) Conversion of gold into foreign currency

170. Expand the term ALM as used in Banking/ Finance sector.
(1) Asset Liability Management
(2) Asset Liability Maturity
(3) Asset Liability Mismatch

(4) Asset Liability Manpower
(5) Asset Liability Maintenance

171. Insurance cover for bank deposits in our country is provided by
(1) SBI (2) Government of India
(3) OG (4) LIC
(5) DICGC

172. The economy in which there is a mixture of public sector and private sector both, is called
(1) Closed economy (2) Mixed economy
(3) Open economy (4) Free trade economy
(5) Public economy

173. What does the letter 'P' denote in the term 'PAN' as used in financial transactions?
(1) Primary (2) Partial
(3) Permanent (4) Provisional
(5) Public

174. MCX is the index of which of the following stock exchanges of India?
(1) National Stock Exchange
(2) Bombay Stock Exchange
(3) Delhi Stock Exchange
(4) Kolkata Stock Exchange
(5) Multi Commodity Stock Exchange

175. The Central Board of Direct Taxes has made e-filing of income-tax returns mandatory for all assesses whose annual earnings exceed ....
(1) T 5 lakh during the fiscal
(2) T 10 lakh during the fiscal
(3) T 15 lakh during the fiscal
(4) T 20 lakh during the fiscal
(5) T 25 lakh during the fiscal

176. The process by which a life insurance policyholder can transfer all rights, title and interest under a policy contract to a third person is known as
(1) Assignment of the policy
(2) Hypothecation of the policy
(3) Reinvestment of the policy
(4) Negotiation of the policy
(5) Nomination of the policy

177. An Equity share is also commonly referred to as
(1) ordinary share
(2) debenture
(3) convertible share
(4) security receipt
(5) preferred stock

178. The abbreviation EMV stands for
(1) European Marginal Vat
(2) Expected Monetary Value
(3) Essential Monthly Voucher
(4) Europay, MasterCard and Visa
(5) None of these

179. Which of the following types of mutual funds is not marked with BROWN color?
(1) Diversified funds
(2) Income funds
(3) Sectoral funds (4) Index funds
(5) Large-cap funds

180. As per recent reports many countries are planning to introduce "Tobin Tax", the idea of which was given by a Nobel Prize winner economist James Tobin in 1978, Tobin Tax, if implemented will be levied on which of the following?
(1) On the interest income of corporates earned through major investments
(2) All cash transactions
(3) Services availed specifically by an elite group of people
(4) Foreign Exchange Transactions
(5) None of these

181. As per the findings of the World Bank, which of the following recent development in rural areas, has doubled the income of rural households, raised literacy rate by 10% and appreciated land prices by upto 80% ?
(1) Relief packages to the farmers
(2) Construction of all-weather roads
(3) Recharging of water bodies
(4) Rainwater harvesting
(5) None of these

182. What does SAPTA stand for:
(1) South Asian Preferential Trade Agreement
(2) South Asian Post Trade Agreement
(3) SAARC Preferential Trade Agreement
(4) SAARC Post Trade Agreement
(5) None of these

183. The present Foreign Trade policy of India will continue till-
(1) December 2012 (2) March 2013
(3) March 2014 (4) June 2013
(5) December 2014

184. Which of the following is a receipt listed in India and traded in rupees declaring ownership of shares of a foreign company?
(1) Indian Depository Receipt (IDR)
(2) European Depository Receipt (EDR)
(3) Global Depository Receipt (GDR)
(4) American Depository Receipt (ADR)
(5) Luxemburg Depository Receipt (LDR)

185. Exporters and importers in India are required to know 'FEMA' rules. What does the letter 'M' denote in the term '**FEMA**'?
(1) Money (2) Material
(3) Mega (4) Management
(5) Micro

186. Which of the following is a receipt listed in India and traded in rupees declaring ownership of shares of a foreign company?
(1) Indian Depository Receipt (IDR)
(2) European Depository Receipt (EDR)
(3) Global Depository Receipt (GDR)
(4) American Depository Receipt (ADR)
(5) Luxemburg Depository Receipt (LDR)

187. Which among the following Companies in India has a tie-up with the Japanese Financial Nomura for insurance market?
(1) ICICI Bank
(2) UCO Bank
(3) Kotak Finance
(4) Life Insurance Corporation of India
(5) None of the above

188. RuPay is an Indian domestic card scheme conceived and launched by
(1) National Payments Corporation of India (NPCI)
(2) Industrial Finance Corporation of India (IFCI)
(3) National Minorities Development & Finance Corporation (NDMC)
(4) National Handicapped Finance and Development Corporation (NHFDC)
(5) None of these

189. Which of the following is not insured by the DICGC (Deposit Insurance and Credit Guarantee Corporation)?
(1) All Indian commercial Banks
(2) Foreign Banks branches functioning in India
(3) Local Area Banks
(4) Cooperative Banks
(5) Primary cooperative societies

190. Which of the following was/ were not the subsidiary company of the General Insurance Corporation of India?
(1) National Insurance Company Limited
(2) Life Insurance Corporation
(3) New India Assurance Company Limited
(4) Oriental Insurance Company Limited
(5) United India Insurance Company Limited

Answers With Explanations

1. (4) **2.** (5)

3. (4) It is cleared from the second paragraph of the passage: "One reason for the feminisation of agricultural labour is that capital prefers to employ women. Women are more willing to accept low-paid irregular work, are easy to hire and fire, are thought to be docile and hardworking, and certain jobs are typified as women's work"

4. (5) **5.** (1)

6. (2)
7. (2)
8. (3)
9. (3)
10. (1)
11. (2)
12. (3) "potential" is the correct word as it means "possible".
13. (1)
14. (2)
15. (4)
16. (1)
17. (3)
18. (1) "who" should be used as it is in nominative case.
19. (2) "subject + be" infinitive (to + V1) is used.
20. (5)
21. (2) The correct form is "no sooner did I see".
22. (1) Because, when we are not talking about any then before all these nouns no article should be used.
23. (5)
24. (2) The correct structure is "S + has/have + v3".
25. (3)
26. (3)
27. (1)
28. (4) The correct spelling is "parole".
29. (3) The correct spelling is "overwhelming".
30. (4) The correct word is "occurrence".
31. (4)
32. (1)
33. (3)
34. (5)
35. (1)

For questions (36-40):

The correct sequence is "**CBEAD**"

36. (5)
37. (3)
38. (1)
39. (2)
40. (4)
41. (5)
42. (4)
43. (1) $21 \times 6 + 9$ of 20% of 60 = ?

$126 + 108 = ?$

$? = 234$

44. (2) $12 \times 13 - 55 \div 11 = ? + 100$

$? = 51$

45. (3)
46. (1)
47. (2)
48. (3)
49. (1) Let the length of rectangle and side of a square be 'l' m.

$l^2 = 125 + l \times 20$

$l^2 - 20l - 125 = 0$

$l = 25$ m

Perimeter of rectangle

$= 2 \times (l + b)$

$= 2 \times (25 + 20) = 90$ m

50. (1)
51. (1)
52. (3)
53. (2)
54. (3)
55. (2)
56. (4)
57. (3)
58. (3)
59. (4)
60. (4) **CASE I:**

Selection of 1 White and 3 black balls required number of ways = ${}^3C_1 \times {}^5C_3 = 30$

CASE II:

Selection of 3 White and 1 black balls

Required number of ways = ${}^3C_3 \times {}^5C_1 = 5$

CASE III:

Selection of 2 White and 2 black balls Req. number of ways

$= {}^3C_2 \times {}^5C_2 = 30$

Therefore, required number of ways

$= 30 + 5 + 30 = 65.$

For questions (61-65):

For company A

Total cost price of masks = 20×100 = Rs. 2000

Total selling price of masks

$=120\% \times 20 \times 40 + 110\% \times 20 \times 60 = 960 + 1320$ = Rs. 2280

For company B

Total cost price of masks = 150×40 = Rs. 6000

Total marked price of the mask

$=150 \times 40 \times 150\%$ = Rs. 9000

Total selling price of masks

$= 9000 \times 90\%$ = Rs. 8100

For company C

Let total masks be x units

Selling price = $100 \times x = 10800$

$x = 108$

Total cost price of masks = Rs. 80

61. (4) **62.** (4)

63. (3) Total cost price = 2000 + 6000 + 8640 = Rs. 16640

64. (5) Total selling price = 2280 + 8100 + 10800= Rs. 21180

65. (5)

66. (4) **I.** $(2x - 7)^2 = 25$

$\Rightarrow \quad 2x - 7 = \pm 5$

$\Rightarrow \quad x = 1, 6$

II. $(4y - 1)^2 = 9$

$\Rightarrow \quad 4y - 1 = \pm 3$

$y = 1, - ½$

$x \geq y$

67. (4) **I.** $3x^2 + 4x - 20 = 0$

$\Rightarrow \quad 3x^2 + 10x - 6x - 20 = 0$

$\Rightarrow \quad x(3x + 10) - 2(3x + 10) = 0$

$\Rightarrow \quad (x - 2)(3x + 10) = 0$

$\Rightarrow \quad x = 2, - 10/3$

II. $y^2 - 12y + 32 = 0$

$\Rightarrow \quad y^2 - 4y - 8y + 32 = 0$

$\Rightarrow \quad y(y - 4) - 8(y - 4) = 0$

$\Rightarrow \quad (y - 8)(y - 4) = 0$

$\Rightarrow \quad y = 8, 4$

$y > x$

68. (3) **I.** $x^2 + 8x + 15 = 0x^2 + 5x + 3x + 15 = 0$

$x(x + 5) + 3(x + 5) = 0$

$(x + 3)(x + 5)$

$x = - 3, - 5$

II. $2y^2 + 21y + 54 = 0$

$2y^2 + 12y + 9y + 54 = 0$

$2y(y + 6) + 9(y + 6) = 0$

$(2y + 9)(y + 6) = 0$

$y = - 9/2, - 6$

69. (2) Multiply by $2x^2$

$10x - 24 = x^2$

$\Rightarrow \quad x^2 - 10x + 24 = 0$

$\Rightarrow \quad x^2 - 6x - 4x + 24 = 0$

$\Rightarrow \quad x(x - 6) - 4(x - 6) = 0$

$\Rightarrow \quad (x - 4)(x - 6) = 0$

$\Rightarrow \quad x = 4, 6$

II. Multiply by y^2

$2y^2 + 20 = 13y$

$\Rightarrow \quad 2y^2 - 13y + 20 = 0$

$\Rightarrow \quad 2y^2 - 8y - 5y + 20 = 0$

$\Rightarrow \quad 2y(y - 4) - 5(y - 4) = 0$

$\Rightarrow \quad (2y - 5)(y - 4) = 0$

$\Rightarrow \quad y = 5/2, 4$

$x \geq y$

70. (3)

For questions (71-75):

In year 2011,

Let number of public vehicles and private vehicles are x and y.

$x - y = 250 \quad \text{... }(i)$

$x + y = 850 \quad \text{... }(ii)$

by equating (*i*) and (*ii*) $x = 550$ $y = 300$

Years	Public vehicle	Private vehicle
2011	550	300
2012	650	400
2013	750	350
2014	500	300
2015	800	400

71. (5) **74.** (5)

72. (5) **75.** (1)

73. (5)

For questions (76-80):

People	Income	Savings	Expenditure
A	18000	6000	12000
B	15000	5000	10000
C	27500	8000	19500
D	30000	10000	20000
E	35000	12000	23000

76. (3) **79.** (5)

77. (5) **80.** (4)

78. (5) **81.** (3)

82. (2) Let radius of circle A be r cm.

$2\pi r - 2r = 90$

$r = 21$ cm

Radius of circle B = 14 cm

Area of circle B = 616 cm^2

83. (2) Let the number of girls be x.

Then, boys $= x + 4$

$x + 4 + x = 40$ $x = 18$

Total weight of all students

$= 40 \times 42.5 = 1700$ kg

Total weight of girls $= 18 \times 48 = 864$ kg

Weight of all boys $= 1700 - 864 = 836$ kg

Average weight of all boys $= 836/22 = 38$ kg

84. (1) **87.** (5)

85. (1) **88.** (3)

86. (1)

89. (5) Let the salary of man be Rs. x

Amount given to mother $= 0.85\,x$

According to the question,

$0.85\,x \times 0.90 = 30{,}600$

$x =$ Rs. 40,000

90. (1) Let number of correct questions be x

Hence, incorrect question $= (58 - x)$

According to the question

$x \times 7 - (58 - x) \times 4 = 263$

$x = 45$

For questions (91-95):

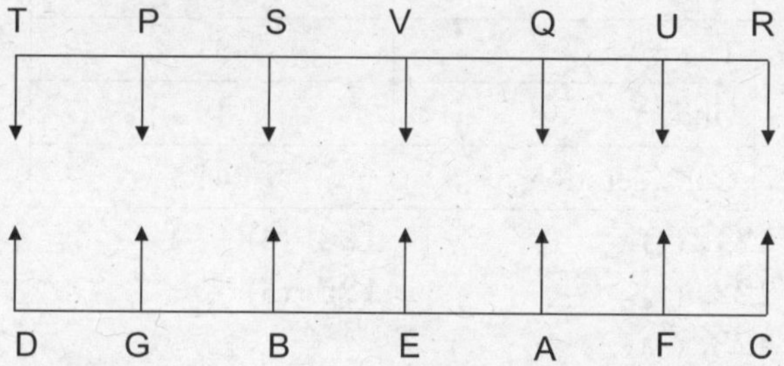

91. (2) **94.** (5)

92. (4) **95.** (2)

93. (2)

For questions (96-98):

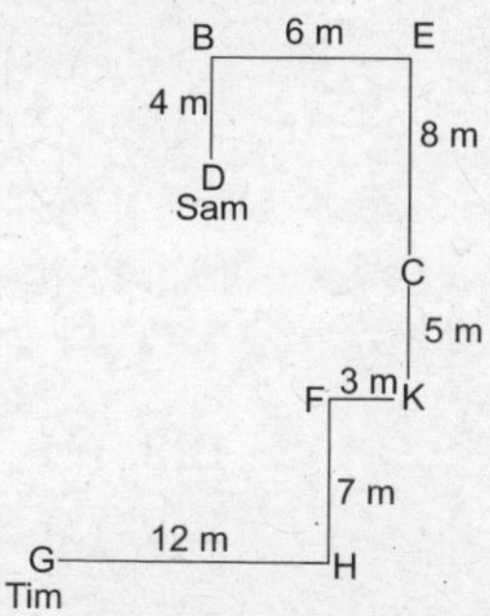

96. (2) **98.** (5)

97. (1)

99. (3) S is aunt of Q.

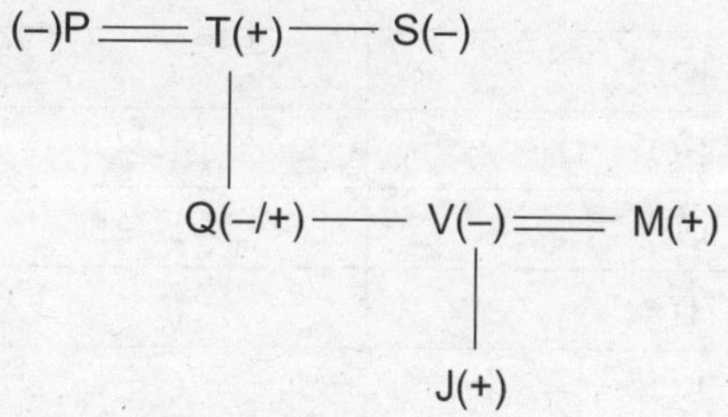

For questions (100-104):

Months	Persons	Cities
March 15	C	Indore
March 18	E	Agra
April 15	A	Delhi
April 18	F	Mumbai
May 15	B	Bhopal
May 18	D	Dehradun

100. (1) **103.** (3)

101. (2) **104.** (3)

102. (5) **105.** (1)

106. (2) **I.** $K < B$ (true)

II. $F \geq S$ (False)

III. $F < U$ (False)

107. (2) **I.** $Z \leq T$ (False)

II. $R < S$ (True)

III. $M > T$ (False)

108. (1) **I.** $Q < S$ (True)

II. $B \leq K$ (False)

III. $P \leq U$ (False)

109. (3) **I.** $S > Y$ (False)

II. $T < Y$ (True)

III. $U < S$ (True)

110. (4) **I.** $M < V$ (True)

II. $J < O$ (False)

III. $P < K$ (True)

For questions (111-115):

Designation	Persons
MD	L
CMD	V
CEO	P
COO	H
CTO	D
CFO	G
Sr. Manager	R
Manager	B
Team lead	N
Executive	K
Trainee	T

111. (2)
112. (4)
113. (1)
114. (5)
115. (1)
116. (2)

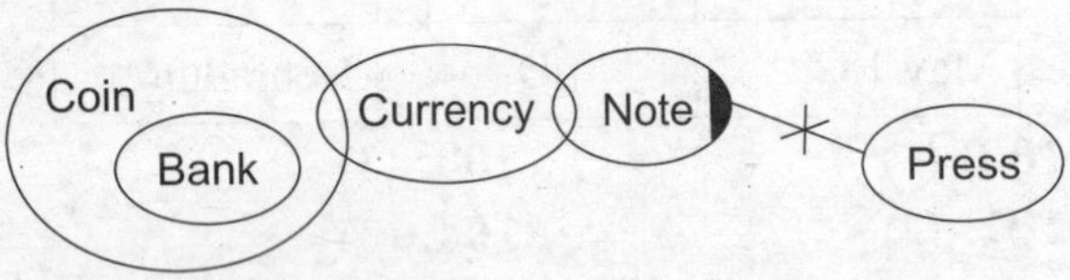

117. (4)

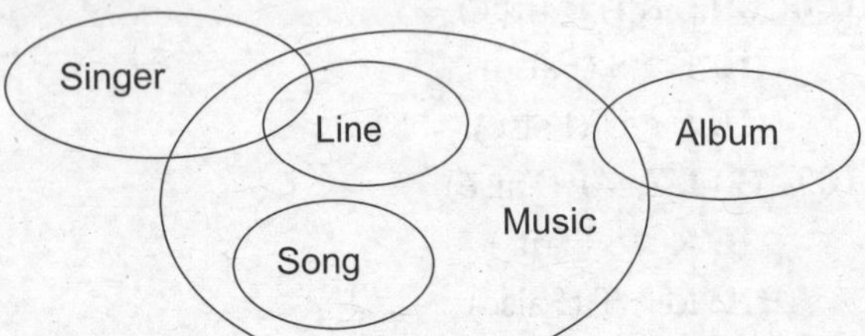

118. (1)

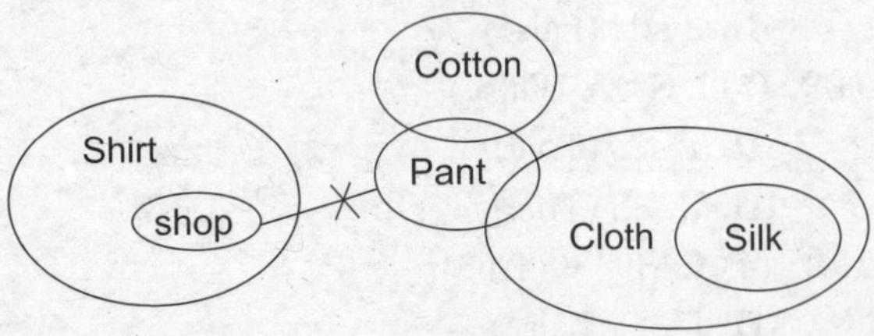

119. (3)

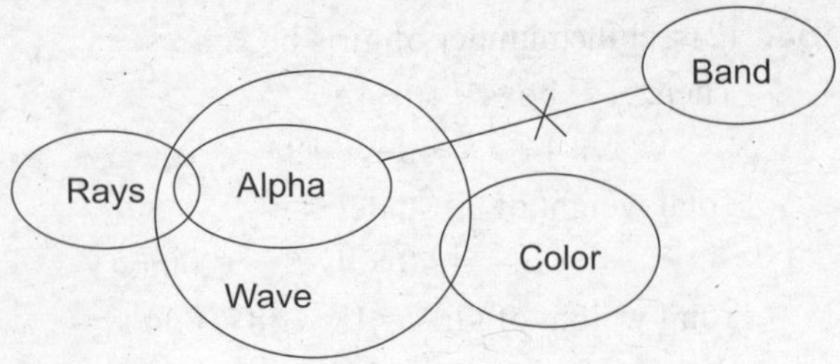

120. (5)

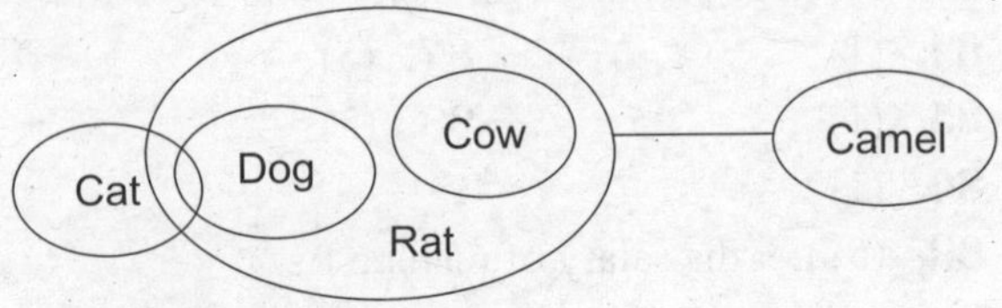

For questions (121-125):

Words	Codes
Knowledge	13
Study	23
Learning	17
Area	11
Of	29
Results	37
Theory	31
Under	19
Consideration	41

121. (4)
122. (1)
123. (3)
124. (4)
125. (3)

For questions (126-130):

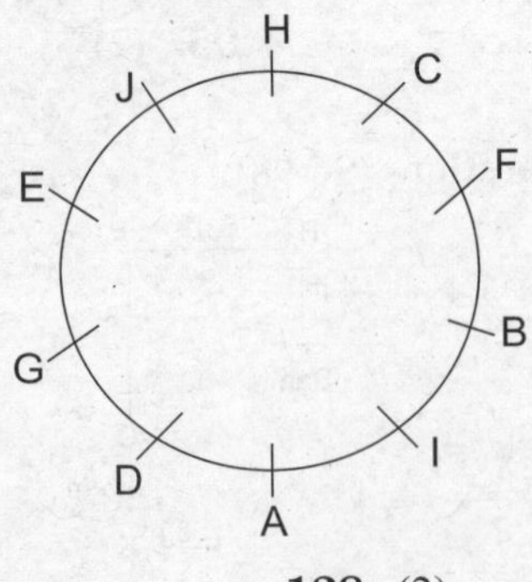

126. (1)
127. (3)
128. (2)
129. (3)

130. (5)
131. (2)
132. (2)
133. (2)
134. (2)
135. (3)
136. (2)
137. (2)
138. (1)
139. (1)
140. (3)
141. (4) Tehri Dam & Hydro Power Project (the multi-purpose river valley project) was constructed on River Bhagirathi.
142. (3)
143. (3)
144. (4)
145. (5) Small Industries Development Bank of India was set up in 1990 with the mission of empowering the Micro, Small, and Medium Enterprises (MSME) sector to contribute and balance regional financial institutions responsible for the promotion, financing, and development of the section.
146. (1)
147. (3)
148. (2) Sindhurakshak was constructed at the Admiralty Shipyard in Saint Petersburg, Russia. Construction of the submarine began in 1995. It was launched in June 1997 and delivered to India in December 1997.
149. (4) The BIS is based in Basel, Switzerland, with representative offices in Hong Kong and Mexico City.
150. (1)
151. (4)
152. (2)
153. (2) Devdas is a Bengali romance novel written by Sarat Chandra Chattopadhyay.
154. (1)
155. (2) ASEAN (Association of Southeast Asian Nations) is a political and economic union of 10 member states in Southeast Asia. These are: Brunei, Cambodia, Indonesia, Laos, Malaysia, Myanmar, the Philippines, Singapore, Thailand, and Vietnam.
156. (1)
157. (4) Prime Minister is the ex-officio chairman of NITI Aayog.
158. (5)
159. (1)
160. (4) The euro is the currency used by the Institutions of the European Union and is the official currency of the Eurozone, which consists of 17 of the 27 member states of the European Union.
161. (2)
162. (5)
163. (3)
164. (2)
165. (3)
166. (4)
167. (2)
168. (2)
169. (2)
170. (1)
171. (5)
172. (2) Mixed economy is an economic system in which both the public and private sector direct the economy, reflecting characteristics of both market economies and planned economies.
173. (2) Permanent Account Number (PAN)
174. (5)
175. (2)
176. (1)
177. (1)
178. (4)
179. (2)
180. (4)
181. (2)
182. (1)
183. (2)
184. (1) An IDR is a receipt, declaring ownership of shares of a foreign company. These receipts can be listed in India and traded in rupees.
185. (4)
186. (1)
187. (4)
188. (1)
189. (5)
190. (2)

IBPS Clerk Prelims, 2018

(Held on 8 December, 2018)

Based on Memory

Reasoning Ability

Directions (1-5): *Study the given information carefully and answer the given questions:*

Seven persons A, B, C, D, E, F and G are watching movies on different days of the week (starting on Monday and ending on Sunday) not necessarily in the same order. B is going to watch movie on Tuesday. F is going to watch movie on adjacent day of B. There are three days gap between the days on which F and A are going to watch movie. G is going to watch movie just after D. There are as many persons are watching movie between A and G, same as between D and C. C is watching movie before D but not just before.

1. Who among the following is going to watch movie on Wednesday?

(1) B (2) C
(3) F (4) E
(5) None of these

2. Who among the following person is going to watch movie just after A?

(1) C (2) D
(3) F (4) G
(5) None of these

3. If F and G interchange their days of watching movie, then on which day G is watching movie?

(1) Monday (2) Wednesday
(3) Friday (4) Saturday
(5) None of these

4. C is watching movie on which day?

(1) Friday (2) Saturday
(3) Wednesday (4) Thursday
(5) Tuesday

5. How many persons are watching movie between B and A?

(1) Two (2) Three
(3) One (4) Four
(5) None of these

Directions (6-8): *Study the following information carefully and answer the questions given below:*

There are six persons who all are of different height. A is taller than C and D but shorter than E. The one who is third shortest is 102 cm in height. B is taller than A. E is not the tallest. The one who is second tallest is 119 cm in height. Neither A nor C is the third shortest person among all. C is not the shortest among all. F is taller than D.

6. Who among the following is the second tallest?

(1) F (2) E
(3) A (4) C
(5) None of these

7. What will be the possible height of A?

(1) 120 cm (2) 100 cm
(3) 112 cm (4) 101 cm
(5) None of these

8. Who among the following is third shortest?

(1) A (2) C
(3) B (4) F
(5) None of these

Direction (9-13): *Study the following information carefully and answer the given questions.*

Twelve persons are sitting in two parallel rows at equal distance facing each other. Q, R, S, T, U and V are sitting in Row 1 facing south. B, C, D, E, F and G are sitting in Row 2 facing north (but not necessarily in the same order).

G sits third to the right of B and one of them sits at the end of the row. Q sits at the right end of the row. Three persons sit between Q and T. F sits to the immediate left of G. Two persons sit between F and C. C who faces R sits to the immediate right of E. S faces D. U sits to the immediate left of S.

9. Which of the following pair sits at the extreme ends of the Row 2?

(1) B and E (2) G and E
(3) B and C (4) G and C
(5) None of these

10. Who sits second to the left of the person facing V?

(1) B (2) D
(3) F (4) C
(5) G

11. What is the position of U with respect to R?

(1) Third to the left
(2) Second to the left
(3) Second to the right
(4) Third to the right
(5) None of these

12. Who is facing F?

(1) T (2) U
(3) Q (4) S
(5) None of these

13. If the positions of all persons sitting in Row 2 are arranged as per the English alphabetical order from left to right, then who among the following faces D?

(1) Q (2) R
(3) S (4) T
(5) None of these

Directions (14-16): *In each of the following questions some statements are given and these statements are followed by two conclusions numbered (I) and (II). You have to take the given statements to be true even if they seem to be at variance from commonly known facts. Read the conclusions and then decide which of the given conclusions logically follows from the given statements, disregarding commonly known facts.*

Give answer:

(1) If only (I) conclusion follows.
(2) If only (II) conclusion follows.
(3) If either (I) or (II) follows.
(4) If neither (I) nor (II) follows.
(5) If both (I) and (II) follow.

14. Statements: All DSLR are Lenses. Some Camera are DSLR.

Conclusions:

I. All camera is lenses.
II. Some lenses are camera.

15. Statements: All Label are Packets. All Mobiles are Cables.
Some Mobiles are packets.

Conclusions:

I. Some Label is mobile.
II. Some Cables are Label.

16. Statements: Some Book are Pen. Some Pens are Pencil.

Conclusions:

I. No Book is pencil.
II. All Pencils are Book.

Directions (17-21): *Study the following information to answer the given questions*

Eight students A, B, C, D, E, F, G and H are sitting around a square table in such a way four of them sit at four corners while four sit in the middle of each of the four sides. The one who sit at the corners face the centre and others facing outside.

A who faces the centre sits third to the left of F. E who faces the centre is not an immediate neighbour of F. Only one person sits between F and G. D sits second to right of B. B faces the centre. C is not an immediate neighbour of A.

17. Which one does not belong to that group out of five?

(1) B (2) C
(3) E (4) D
(5) A

18. Which will come in the place of?

BCE EHA AGD ?

(1) DFB (2) DGA
(3) DCG (4) DCF
(5) None of these

19. What is the position of G with respect to C?

(1) Third to the right
(2) Second to the left
(3) Second to the right
(4) Fourth to the right

(5) None of these

20. Who sits third to the left of B?

(1) H (2) A

(3) G (4) F

(5) None of these

21. Which is true from the given arrangement?

(1) G faces the centre

(2) B faces outside

(3) H faces inside

(4) A face the centre

(5) None of these

22. How many pairs of letter are there in the word 'DECLARING' (both backward and forward), each of which has as many letters between them as in the word as there are in the English alphabet?

(1) One (2) three

(3) Four (4) Five

(5) None of these

Directions (23-25): *Study the following information carefully and answer the questions given below:*

Point C is 15 m in the east of point F. Point A is 10 m west of point B which is 15 m north of point H. Point D is 15 west of point E. Point B is 15 m south of point C. Point E is 5 m east of point H. Point G is 15 m north of point A.

23. In which direction and at what distance is point G from point C?

(1) 10 m east (2) 5 m, east

(3) 10 m, west (4) 5 m, west

(5) None of these

24. Point D is in which direction with respect to point A?

(1) South (2) North

(3) North East (4) West

(5) None of these

25. Point F is in which direction with respect to point E?

(1) North East (2) South West

(3) South East (4) North West

(5) None of these

Directions (26-30): *Following questions are based on the five words given below, Study the following words and answer the following questions.*

TAP NOT MAT PQR STB

(The new words formed after performing the mentioned operations may not necessarily be a meaningful English word.)

26. If the given words are arranged in the order as they appear in a dictionary from right to left, which of the following will be second from the left end?

(1) MAT (2) NOT

(3) STB (4) TAP

(5) None of these

27. How many letters are there in the English alphabetical series between the third letter of the word which is second from the left end and the second letter of the word which is third from the right end?

(1) 20 (2) 19

(3) 18 (4) 17

(5) None of these

28. If in each of the word given, the second alphabet is replaced by its following alphabet and third alphabet is replaced by its preceding alphabet as per the English alphabetical order, then how many words thus formed will be without any vowels?

(1) None (2) One

(3) Two (4) Three

(5) Four

29. If the positions of the first and the third alphabet in each of the words given are interchanged, then how many meaningful word will be formed?

(1) Two (2) One

(3) Four (4) Three

(5) None

30. If in each of the given words, every consonant is changed to its previous letter and every vowel is changed to its next letter according to the English alphabetical series, then in how many words, thus formed, at least one vowels will appear?

(1) None (2) One

(3) Two (4) Three

(5) None of these

Directions (31-35): *Study the following information carefully and answer the questions given below:*

There are seven persons *i.e.* A, B, C, D, E, F and G. They all belongs to the different cities *i.e.* Kolkata, Mumbai, Chennai, Pune, Lucknow, Ahmadabad and Delhi but not necessarily in the same order. D belongs to Pune. Neither A nor F belongs to Kolkata. B belongs to Ahmedabad. C does not belong to Kolkata and Lucknow. G belongs to Mumbai. A does not belongs to Lucknow and Chennai.

31. Who among the following belongs to Kolkata?
(1) A (2) D
(3) F (4) G
(5) None of these

32. Which of the following statement is true?
(1) A belongs to Chennai
(2) G belongs to Delhi
(3) E belongs to Kolkata
(4) F belongs to Pune
(5) None of these

33. F belongs to which of the following City?
(1) Chennai (2) Mumbai
(3) Delhi (4) Lucknow
(5) None of these

34. Which of the following combination is true?
(1) A-Delhi (2) D-Pune
(3) E-Kolkata (4) All are correct
(5) All are incorrect

35. A belongs to which of the following city?
(1) Delhi (2) Mumbai
(3) Kolkata (4) Chennai
(5) None of these

Numerical Ability

Directions (36-40): *What will come in the place of question (?) mark in the following number series?*

36. 200, 193, 179, 158, ?, 95
(1) 135 (2) 133
(3) 132 (4) 130
(5) 128

37. 3, 43, 81, 115, 143, ?
(1) 163 (2) 172
(3) 166 (4) 160
(5) 168

38. 1, 6, 25, 76, 153, ?
(1) 152 (2) 154
(3) 153 (4) 155
(5) 156

39. 50, 54, 45, 61, 36, ?
(1) 66 (2) 72
(3) 75 (4) 80
(5) 84

40. 9, 45, 180, 540, ?, 1080
(1) 720 (2) 900
(3) 1080 (4) 1200
(5) 960

41. If the sum of upstream and downstream speed is 36 km/hr and the speed of the current is 3 km/hr. Then find time taken to cover 52.5 km in downward?
(1) 2 hr (2) 2.5 hr
(3) 3 hr (4) 3.5 hr
(5) 4 hr

42. A sum becomes 1.6 times of itself in five years at simple rate of interest. Find rate of interest per annum?
(1) 10% (2) 12.5%
(3) 15% (4) 12%
(5) 8.5%

Directions (43-52): *Calculate the exact value of the 'x' in the given following questions.*

43. $x^2 + (9^2 + 34) \div 5 = 39$
(1) 5 (2) 4
(3) 8 (4) 6
(5) 9

44. $6 \times 16 \times 5 \div 3 - x^2 = 96$
(1) 6 (2) 7
(3) 8 (4) 9
(5) 5

45. $\sqrt{124 + x + 169 = 18}$

(1) 27 (2) 28
(3) 29 (4) 30
(5) 31

46. $28^2 - x^3 = 7^3 + 225$
(1) 6 (2) 8
(3) 4 (4) 7
(5) 5

47. $298 - 13^2 - 2^3 = x \times 11$
(1) 51 (2) 41
(3) 21 (4) 11
(5) 31

48. $\sqrt[3]{729 + 3\frac{3}{5} \div x} = \sqrt{16 \times 9}$
(1) 1 (2) 1.4
(3) 1.2 (4) 1.6
(5) 2

49. $x\%$ of $300 + \sqrt{256} = 243 \div 3 + 7$
(1) 18 (2) 24
(3) 16 (4) 28
(5) 32

50. $x \times 3 \div 8 = \sqrt[3]{512} \times \sqrt{12^2}$
(1) 256 (2) 512
(3) 64 (4) 128
(5) 320

51. $136 \div 2^2 \times x = 17\%$ of $500 \div 10$
(1) 1 (2) 0.5
(3) 0.25 (4) 0.125
(5) 1.25

52. $1836 \div x \div 9 = 12$
(1) 9 (2) 11
(3) 13 (4) 15
(5) 17

53. Ratio of present ages of two persons A and B is 3 : 2 and after four years ratio of their age (B : A) become 7 : 10. Then find the present age of B?
(1) 20 years (2) 18 years
(3) 24 years (4) 36 years
(5) 30 years

54. The difference between Circumference of circle A and diameter is 90 cm . If Radius of Circle B is 7 cm less than circle A then find area of Circle B?
(1) 556 cm^2 (2) 616 cm^2
(3) 588 cm^2 (4) 532 cm^2
(5) 630 cm^2

55. There are 40 children in a class in which boys are 4 more than the girls. Average weight of all the students is 42.5 kg and the average weight of all the girls is 48 kg then find the average weight of all the boys.
(1) 39.5 kg (2) 38 kg
(3) 40.5 kg (4) 36.75 kg
(5) 40.25 kg

Directions (56-60): *In each question two equations numbered (I) and (II) are given. Student should solve both the equations and mark appropriate answer.*

(1) If $x = y$ or no relation can be established
(2) If $x > y$
(3) If $x < y$
(4) If $x >= y$
(5) If $x <= y$

56. I. $8x^2 + 6x + 1 = 0$
II. $3y^2 + 7y + 2 = 0$

57. I. $x^2 = 196$
II. $y^2 - 26y + 169 = 0$

58. I. $9x^2 - 12x + 4 = 0$
II. $8y^2 - 9y + 1 = 0$

59. I. $x^2 - 15x + 56 = 0$
II. $y = \sqrt[3]{512}$

60. I. $3x^2 + 10x + 8 = 0$
II. $2y^2 + 3y + 1 = 0$

61. A man invested 15% of his monthly income in LIC and remaining gave to his mother. Mother spend 10% of it in household expenses and she had left with Rs. 30,600 then find the salary of man?
(1) Rs. 37,500 (2) Rs. 36,000
(3) Rs. 38,000 (4) Rs. 42,000
(5) Rs. 40,000

62. If 7 marks are awarded to right answer and 4 marks are penalty for wrong answer. Then Prabhat's score was 263. If he attempted 58 questions then find number of correctly attempted questions?

(1) 45 (2) 42
(3) 48 (4) 40
(5) 50

63. In a city, 68% of population is literate in which ratio of male to female is 11 : 6. And ratio of illiterate male to female is 3 : 1. Find the ratio of literate female to illiterate female in that city.

(1) 3 : 2 (2) 2 : 1
(3) 3 : 1 (4) 4 : 1
(5) 5 : 2

64. Ratio of length to breadth of a rectangle is 4 : 3. If the area of that rectangle is 108 cm^2 and breadth of this rectangle is equal to the side of a square then find the area of that square.

(1) 49 cm^2 (2) 100 cm^2
(3) 64 cm^2 (4) 81 cm^2
(5) 121 cm^2

65. A is 1.5 times as efficient as that of B and C takes half time as compared to that of A. If A and B takes 12/5 days to complete half of the work then find the time taken by A and C together to complete the whole work?

(1) 7/3 days (2) 10/3 days
(3) 4/3 days (4) 5/3 days
(5) 8/3 days

Directions (66-70): *Given below table shows the number of cakes of five different types sold by a shopkeeper on four different days. Study the data and answer the questions that follow:*

Days/Type of Cake	A	B	C	D	E
Saturday	25	28	35	50	38
Sunday	35	65	48	42	47
Monday	38	60	40	24	29
Tuesday	46	54	55	44	30

66. What is the ratio of no. of cakes of type B sold by the shopkeeper on Saturday and Monday together to the no. of cakes of type E sold by him on the same days?

(1) 72 : 53 (2) 88 : 67
(3) 98 : 73 (4) 92 : 71
(5) 90 : 67

67. What is average no. of cakes of type C sold by shopkeeper on Saturday, Sunday and Tuesday?

(1) 38 (2) 40
(3) 42 (4) 44
(5) 46

68. The no. of cakes of type D and E sold together on Tuesday is what percent of the no. of cakes of type A and B sold together on Sunday?

(1) 72% (2) 75%
(3) 74% (4) 78%
(5) 80%

69. What is the difference between the total no. of cakes of all the given types sold by shopkeeper on Monday and the total no. of cakes of all the given types sold by shopkeeper on Tuesday?

(1) 38 (2) 44
(3) 42 (4) 40
(5) 45

70. If the no. of cakes of type F sold by the shopkeeper in given four days is 25% more than the no. of cakes sold of type D in all the given days, then find the no. of cakes sold of type F in all the given days.

(1) 164 (2) 160
(3) 180 (4) 200
(5) 240

English Language

Directions (71-76): *Read the following passage and answer the questions that follow it. Some words are highlighted to help you answer some of the questions.*

Conversations about the role of flexible working have shifted. It's no longer enough for companies to offer employees the option to either work from home or the office. Employees want to work from anywhere. Companies that want to attract and retain top talent, and ensure teams are highly productive, need to adapt their culture and technology to accommodate this shift in attitudes. And this is where the IT department can solidify its role as a valued contributor to the success of a company, by implementing technologies that enable secure and remote collaboration.

According to a recently commissioned Polycom survey, 24,000 respondents across 12 countries indicate that nearly two-thirds of today's global workforce take advantage of the anywhere working model. This is a significant shift since May of 2012 when only 14% of employees benefited from remote working. The survey results also provide insights into some of the concerns among companies in moving forward with the anywhere working model. Two significant concerns are a lack of trust and the perception that employees are not working as hard when they are not in the office. Also, among the 45-60-year-old age group, 59% worry that working anywhere will cause them to work longer hours. The fear of being always connected to work and overworking is a significant deterrent for this age group.

A good first step for companies to overcome the trust and perception concern is to ensure workers are measured by output and not by the hours they have worked, commonly referred to as 'presenteeism' Countries like Brazil lead the pack here with 80% of employees adopting the anywhere working model, and 64% respondents use video to communicate several times a day. When respondents were asked how their companies could improve trust and perceptions with the anywhere working model, the most popular recommendations were to: Equip workers with technology that is easy to use and which connects them to their colleagues; Ensure the same policies are applied to everyone in the business, regardless of seniority or their situation; and Provide guidelines on how to manage working from anywhere.

91% of those surveyed agreed that technology is a key factor in improving relationships and **fostering** better teamwork. This suggests that investing in the right technologies, in particular video collaboration, to get the most out of individuals and teams can help solve the lack of trust and perception concerns. And this is where the IT department can become a difference maker as they can implement technologies, such as video conferencing, to ensure colleagues can seamlessly collaborate wherever they are.

71. What is the shift in attitude of employees as discussed in the passage?

(I) They want to work in office.
(II) They want to work from home.
(III) They want to work from anywhere.

(1) Only (I) (2) Both (II) and (III)
(3) Only (III) (4) Only (II)
(5) None of (I), (II) and (III)

72. How could companies accommodate the recent shift in attitudes of employees as discussed in the passage?

(1) By offering work from home option to employees
(2) By enabling secure and remote collaboration
(3) By increasing the salaries of employees
(4) Options (1) and (2)
(5) None of the above

73. Which of the followings mention (s) the concern of the companies to accommodate the latest preference of employees for working styles?

(1) Lack of trust for employees;
(2) Perception that employees will not work hard anywhere apart from office;
(3) Working anywhere would make employees to work longer hours;
(4) Options (2) and (3)
(5) Options (1) and (2)

74. How could companies overcome their concerns for the latest preferences of employees for style of working?

(1) By not offering work from home model
(2) By measuring employees for the output, they generate and not by the hours they have worked
(3) By offering work from anywhere model
(4) By allowing only those who are interested to work from anywhere.
(5) None of the above

75. Which of the following opinions as expressed

in the survey about solving the trust and perception concerns of the companies in accommodating the latest preference of employees for style of work has received more than 91%?

(1) Investing in technology
(2) Providing guidelines on how to manage working from anywhere
(3) Ensuring the same policies are applied to everyone regardless of seniority
(4) Options (1) and (3)
(5) None of the above

76. Which of the following options has a meaning which is SIMILAR to the word '*fostering*'?

(1) asserting (2) focusing
(3) collaborating (4) encouraging
(5) admitting

Directions (77-81): *Rearrange the following five sentences (A), (B), (C), (D) and (E) in the proper sequence to form a meaningful paragraph and then answer the questions given below.*

(A) Crucially, this loss of sheen is reflected in the account books of the sport's controversial administrator, among the richest in the world.
(B) The total income that was distributed by BCCI among players is reduced because of lower income from media rights.
(C) Television viewership for the game has dropped 40% to a weekly 61 gross rating points (GRPs).
(D) A Board of Control for Cricket in India official said, however, that this was because India wasn't playing enough at home.
(E) Cricket seems to be losing its crowd-pulling power.

77. Which of the followings is the FOURTH sentence of the final sequence?

(1) A (2) D
(3) E (4) B
(5) C

78. Which of the followings is the FIRST sentence of the final sequence?

(1) E (2) C
(3) D (4) A
(5) B

79. Which of the followings is the SECOND sentence of the final sequence?

(1) E (2) A
(3) C (4) D
(5) B

80. Which of the followings is the THIRD sentence of the final sequence?

(1) E (2) A
(3) D (4) C
(5) B

81. Which of the followings is the FIFTH sentence of the final sequence?

(1) C (2) A
(3) E (4) D
(5) B

Directions (82-85): *In the following questions, a sentence is given consisting four highlighted words. Choose the option reflecting the word which is either misspelt or grammatically incorrect. If all the highlighted words are correct, choose option (5) i.e. "no error" as your answer choice.*

82. **Making** the **request** for a non-smoking room seemed **resonable** for everyone since the woman was **allergic** to smoke.

(1) Making (2) Request
(3) Resonable (4) Allergic
(5) No error

83. When we are **involved** in large-scale projects, we must make **judgements** on an **individual basis** about whether they are good or bad.

(1) involved (2) judgements
(3) individual (4) basis
(5) No error

84. Several **expriments** were tried, to **determine** positively **whether** or not she had any **perception** of sound.

(1) expriments (2) determine
(3) whether (4) perception
(5) No error

85. When the man gave the **terrific** persuasive speech at the **conference**, the observers **applaud** with gusto by **putting** their hands together.

(1) terrific (2) conference

(3) applaud (4) putting

(5) No error

Directions (86-90): *In the following questions two columns are given containing three sentences/ phrases each. In first column, sentences/phrases are A, B and C and in the second column the sentences/ phrases are D, E and F. A sentence/phrase from the first column may or may not connect with another sentence/phrase from the second column to make a grammatically and contextually correct sentence. Each question has five options which display the sequence(s) in which the sentences/phrases can be joined to form a grammatically and contextually correct sentence. Choose the correct combination of parts that make a meaningful sentence.*

86.

COLUMN I	COLUMN II
(A) There is emerging international recognition	(D) and create societies where all can live with hope and dignity
(B) It can serve as the driving force to restore hope	(E) our work makes us feel productive and empowered
(C) The earnest determination distilled in these words is the spirit we all need	(F) that women's participation is key to effective climate action

(1) C-F, A-D and A-E

(2) B-E

(3) A-F

(4) A-D and C-E

(5) A-F and B-E

87.

COLUMN I	COLUMN II
(A) Over time, there are changes that take place	(D) where they house an array of species
(B) In the case of primary succession,	(E) that ecological communities move from possessing very little species diversity
(C) In other cases, a pre-existing group of species is replaced by a new group of species,	(F) in the composition of species that constitute an ecological community.

(1) C-E, A-D and A-F

(2) B-D

(3) A-F

(4) B-E and C-D

(5) B-D

88.

Column I	Column II
(A) The increase in MSP for rabi crops comes	(D) The government said in a release
(B) There are notified crops	(E) Just ahead of the RBI monetary policy announcement
(C) For big companies, there are instances	(F) Of even the infrastructure getting damaged

(1) C-F (2) C-E and B-F

(3) A-E (4) C-F and A-E

(5) B-F, B-E and A-D

89.

Column I	Column II
(A) India will be the third largest aviation	(D) market globally a year sooner
(B) The biggest contribution in	(E) as the world's largest aviation
(C) Firstly, we are seeing an/a	(F) restrictive protectionist measures

(1) C-D, A-F and B-D

(2) B-F
(3) A-D
(4) C-E and B-D
(5) B-E

90.

COLUMN I	COLUMN II
(A) Researchers are only beginning to understand the power	(D) cannot be borne by science alone
(B) As our understanding grows, we will have the potential	(E) to edit out genes that cause fatal diseases
(C) The burden of gene editing	(F) would not be passed down the family tree

(1) A-D, B-E and B-D
(2) B-E and C-D
(3) A-F
(4) B-F and C-E
(5) C-E

Directions (91-95): *Given below are sentences consisting a blank in each. Identify the most suitable alternative among the five given that fits into the blank to make the sentence logical and meaningful.*

91. In .... to picking up milk from the grocery store, we also need to get some bread, because my cousin ate all of it this past week.
(1) further (2) addition
(3) computation (4) aftermath
(5) besides

92. He .... on things being done in the most efficient way and he usually does them that way himself.
(1) requesting (2) conserves
(3) urge (4) insists
(5) discourages

93. If the quality of your product meets with our customer's approval, we will place .... orders.
(1) interrupted (2) reduced
(3) regular (4) choice
(5) conditional

94. Tom seems to be unwilling to believe that Mary was the one who .... his credit cards.
(1) stole (2) run
(3) accept (4) delivery
(5) checking

95. The Circular will guide the regional investment .... and budgeting processes for FY 2020 Budget.
(1) programming (2) scheduled
(3) arrange (4) planned
(5) records

Direction (96-100): *The following questions consist of a sentence with a highlighted phrase which may or may not be grammatically or contextually correct. Choose the most suitable option that will replace the incorrect highlighted phrase to form a grammatically correct and meaningful sentence. If the given highlighted phrase is correct, choose option (5) i.e. "no replacement required" as your answer choice.*

96. India has suffered from terrorism. So has Pakistan. And **it turns out**, now the first world too is not immune.
(1) turning out to (2) it turns to
(3) it turned out to be
(4) it turning out
(5) No replacement required

97. The advocate declared in the court that his client **has prepared** to surrender.
(1) Was prepared to (2) Has been preparing for
(3) Was prepared at (4) Has prepared for
(5) No correction required

98. Any step that the Prime Minister takes to remove violence in the country **will be appreciate.**
(1) will appreciated (2) will have appreciated
(3) was appreciating (4) will be appreciated
(5) were appreciating

99. If this is freedom of speech, then it **must**

been curtailed immediately.

(1) have being curtailing

(2) must be curtailed

(3) must have been curtailed

(4) have been curtailed

(5) No correction required

100. When the police started asking questions, the suspect **clammed up.**

(1) camped down (2) clamped up

(3) clam out (4) clamed off

No Correction Required

Answers With Explanations

For questions (1-5):

Days	Persons
Mon	F
Tue	B
Wed	E
Thu	C
Fri	A
Sat	D
Sun	G

1. (4) **4.** (4)

2. (2) **5.** (1)

3. (1)

For questions (6-8):

B > E > A > F > C > D

6. (2)

7. (3)

8. (4)

For questions (9-13):

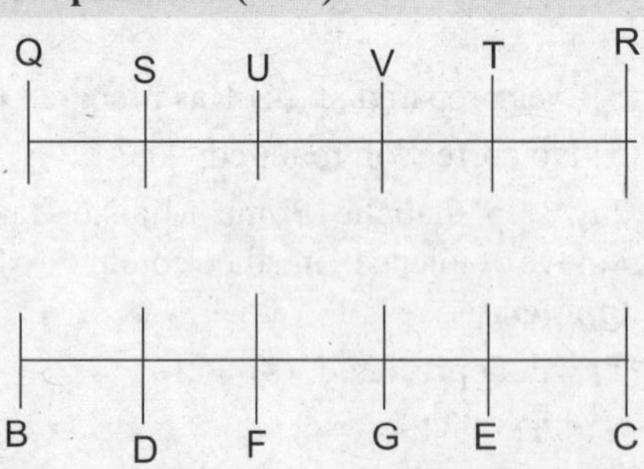

9. (3) **11.** (4)

10. (2) **12.** (2)

13. (5)

14. (2)

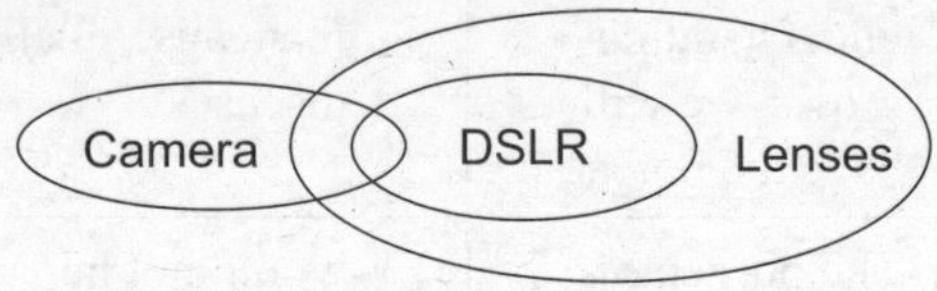

15. (4)

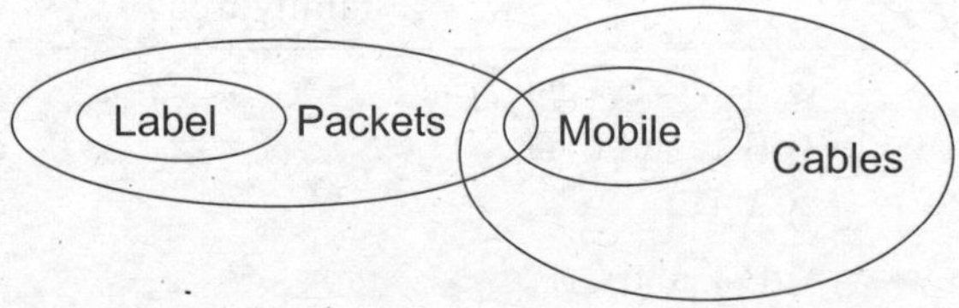

16. (4)

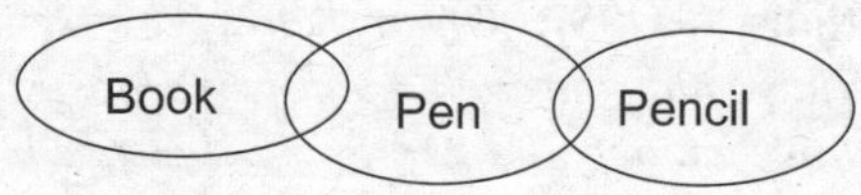

For questions (17-21):

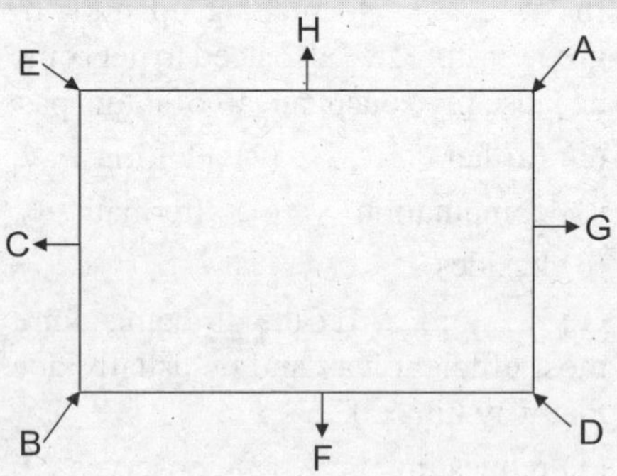

17. (2)

18. (1)

19. (4)

20. (1)

21. (4)

22. (4)

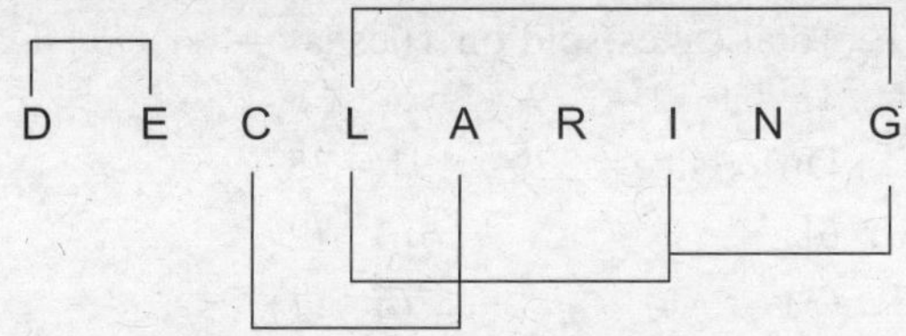

For questions (23-25):

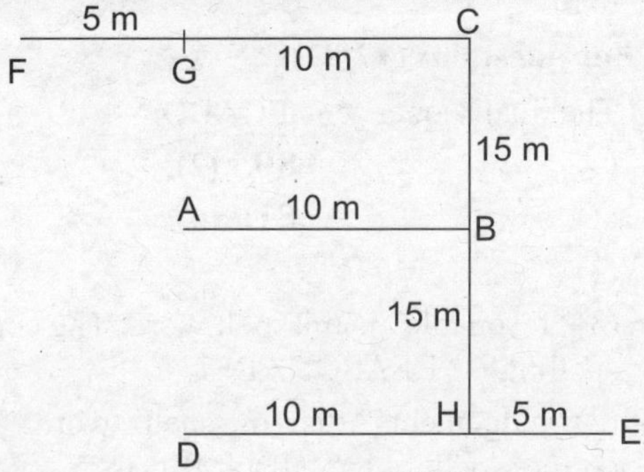

23. (3)

24. (1)

25. (4)

26. (3)

27. (3)

28. (4)

29. (4)

30. (4)

For questions (31-35):

Person	CITY
A	Delhi
B	Ahmedabad
C	Chennai
D	Pune
E	Kolkata
F	Lucknow
G	Mumbai

31. (5)

32. (3)

33. (4)

34. (4)

35. (1)

36. (4)

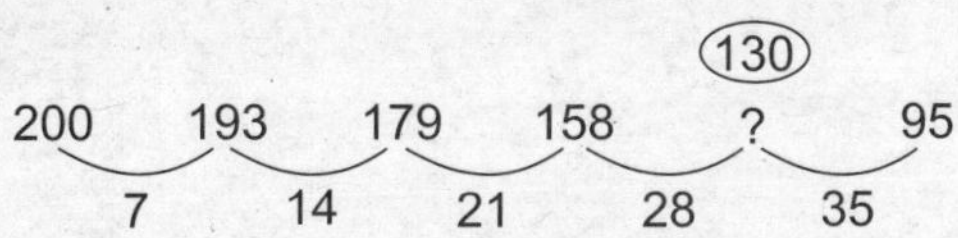

37. (1)

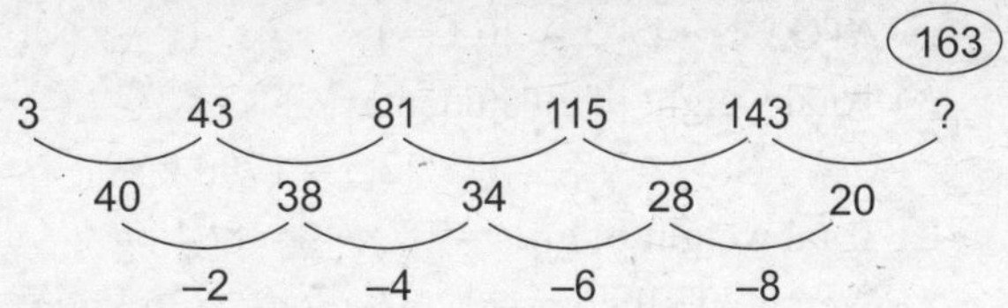

38. (2)

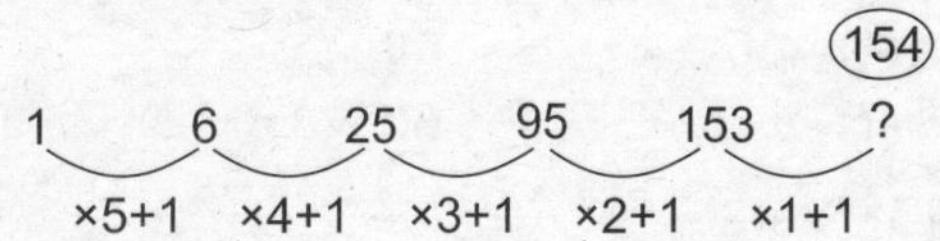

39. (2)

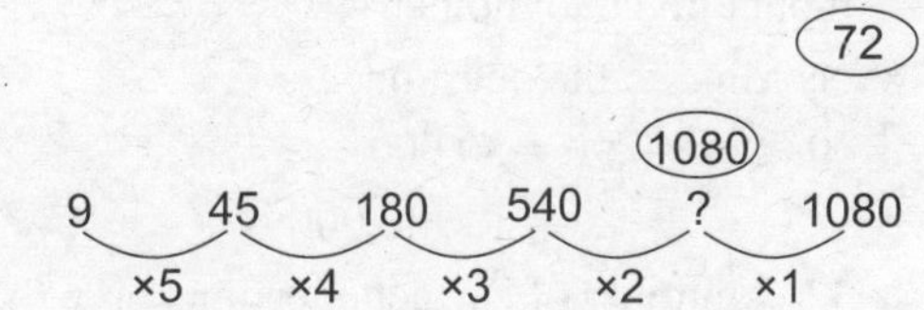

40. (3)

41. (2) Let the speed of boat in still water be x km/h.

$$x + 3 + x - 3 = 36$$

$$x = 18$$

Required time = 2.5 h

42. (4)

43. (2)

44. (3)

45. (5) $\sqrt{293} + x = 18$

Or, $293 + x = 324$

Or, $x = 324 - 293 = 31$

46. (1) $784 - x^2 = 343 + 225$

$$x^3 = 784 - 568 = 216$$

$$x = 6$$

47. (4) $298 - 169 - 8 = x \times 11$

$$121 = x \times 11$$

$$x = 11$$

48. (3)

49. (2)

50. (1)

51. (3)

52. (5)

53. (3)

54. (2) Let radius of circle A be r cm.

$$2\pi r - 2r = 90$$

$$r = 21 \text{ cm}$$

Radius of circle B = 14 cm Area of circle B = 616 cm^2

55. (2) Let the number of girls be x.

Then, boys = $x + 4$

ATQ $x + 4 + x = 40$ $x = 18$

Total weight of all students

$= 40 \times 42.5 = 1700$ kg

Total weight of girls $= 18 \times 48 = 864$ kg

Weight of all boys $= 1700 - 864 = 836$ kg

Average weight of all boys $= 836/22 = 38$ kg

56. (1)

57. (1)

58. (1)

59. (5)

60. (3)

61. (5) Let the salary of man be Rs. x

Amount given to mother $= 0.85\,x$

According to the question,

$0.85\,x \times 0.90 = 30{,}600$

$x =$ Rs. 40,000

62. (1) Let number of correct questions be x

Hence, incorrect question $= (58 - x)$

According to the question

$x \times 7 - (58 - x) \times 4 = 263$

$x = 45$

63. (3)

64. (4) Let the length and breadth of that rectangle be $4x$ and $3x$ cm respectively

$4x \times 3x = 108$

$x = 3$ cm

Breadth = 9 cm

Area of square = 81 cm^2

65. (5)

66. (2)

67. (5)

68. (3)

69. (1) Total cakes sold on Monday = 38 + 60 + 40 + 24 + 29 = 191

Total cakes sold on Tuesday = 46 + 54 + 55 + 44 + 30 = 229

Difference = 229 – 191 = 38

70. (4)

71. (3)

72. (2)

73. (5)

74. (2)

75. (1)

76. (4)

For questions (77-81):

The final sequence is ECABD.

77. (4)

78. (1)

79. (3)

80. (2)

81. (4)

82. (3) "resonable" is misspelt word. The correct spelling is "REASONABLE".

83. (2) "judgements" is misspelt word. The correct spelling is "JUDGMENTS".

84. (1) "expriments" is misspelt word. The correct spelling is "EXPERIMENTS".

85. (5)

86. (3)

87. (3

88. (4)

89. (3)

90. (2)

91. (2) "in addition to" is phrase.

92. (4)

93. (3)

94. (1)

95. (1)

96. (5)

97. (1) 'Has prepared to' should be replaced by 'was prepared to'.

98. (4) 'appreciate' should be replaced by 'appreciated'.

99. (2)

100. (5)

IBPS Clerk Mains, 2018

(Held on 20 January, 2019)

Based on Memory

General English

Directions (1-5): *Read the following passage and answer the questions as directed.*

Artificial intelligence (AI) is all the rage these days. A recent article noted that 'robots' — shorthand for AI in the tabloids — will be able to write a fiction bestseller within 50 years. I suppose that would be shocking to me as a novelist if most fiction bestsellers were not already being written by 'robots'. Or so one feels, keeping publishing and other vogues in mind: a bit of this, a bit of that, a dash of something else, and voila you have a bestseller! In that sense, perhaps the rise of AI will make us reconsider what we mean by human intelligence. This discussion has been neglected for far too long. Take my field: literature. The Chinese company, Cheers Publishing, lately offered a collection of poems written by a computer program. So, are poets, generally considered to be suicidal in any case, jumping off the cliffs in droves as a consequence? Well, this is a selection from one of the AI poems I found online: "The rain is blowing through the sea / A bird in the sky / A night of light and calm / Sunlight / Now in the sky / Cool heart / The savage north wind/ When I found a new world."

Yes, there are aspiring poets — and sometimes established ones — who write like this, connecting words centripetally or centrifugally to create an effect. I think they should have been pushed off literary cliffs a long time ago. Because this is not poetry; this is just the technique of assembling words like poetry. There is a difference between the intelligence required to write poetry and the skills required to write it. That poetic intelligence is lost without the required poetic skills, but the skills on their own do not **(A) suffice** either. The fact that lines like this, written by AI, can be considered poetry does not reflect on the intelligence of AI. It reflects on the intelligence of those readers, writers, critics, editors, publishers and academics who have not yet distinguished between gimmickry and mimicry on the one side and the actual freshness of a chiselled line on the other. But this is a small example. Surely, AI might also make **(B)** ...., including that of considering something like IQ to be a sufficient index of human mental capacity! Because if we think that AI can replace human intelligence, then we are simply not thinking hard enough.

(C) One of the major **(1) activity** here is that of considering **(2) intelligence** to be something **(3) different** from and raised above the **(4) failures** of living. This leads to the misconception that intelligence can be **(D)**.......... to something else — say, a robot — without becoming something else. Human intelligence cannot be passed on to something else: What is "passed on" is always a different kind of 'intelligence'. Even the arguments that AI — or, as in the past, robots — can enable human beings to lead a gloriously workless existence is based on a similar misconception. Because human intelligence is embedded in human existence, 'work' as human activity in the world is not something human beings can do without.

1. Which of the following words can replace the word given in **bold** in (A) without changing the meaning of the sentence?

(1) disperse (2) squander
(3) dissipate (4) serve
(5) spread

2. Out of the following options which option does support the statement **"There is a difference between the intelligence required to write poetry and the skills required to write it,"** made by the author in the paragraph?

(1) There are aspiring poets who write like

this, connecting words centripetally or centrifugally to create an effect, this is not poetry; this is just the technique of assembling words like poetry.

(2) that would be shocking to me as a novelist if most fiction bestsellers were not already being written by 'robots.'

(3) The lines written by AI considered as poetry does not reflect on the intelligence of AI.

(4) Both (2) and (3)

(5) None of the above

3. Which of the following phrases should fill the blank given in (B) to make it grammatically and contextually correct and meaningful?

(1) has always been a mistake to expect him to 'solve' problems without human effort

(2) us discover our basic lack of intelligence in other areas

(3) \often atheistic fans of AI who believe that it is 'The solution' are making the same mistake

(4) has had a crucial role in shaping cognitive capacity and brain evolution

(5) None of the Above

4. The sentence given in (C) has four words given in **bold**. Amongst given bolded words, which of the followings must replace each other to make the sentence contextually correct and meaningful.

(1) 2-4 (2) 2-3

(3) 1-4 (4) 3-4

(5) 1-3

5. Which of the following words given in the options should come at the place marked as 'D' in the above paragraph to make it grammatically and contextually meaningful and correct? Also, the word should fill the two sentences given below to make them contextually correct and meaningful?

I. They aim to prevent women from being .... to a secondary role.

II. United were .... to division two.

(1) forecasted (2) relegated

(3) researched (4) published

(5) vanished

Directions (6-10): *Read the following passage and answer the questions as directed.*

We expect individuals **(I)** to take charge of their lives, to assume responsibility for their decisions. But when individuals group together, a problem arises. Groups can't take charge of themselves, nor can every member simultaneously take charge of the entire group. Someone from the group is invariably asked to show the way, to become the primary agent, to lead. Yet, not everyone who occupies high office is a leader. A person who merely **(II)** or has management skills is not a leader. Moreover, not everyone who assumes the role of a leader is able to play it well. What qualities then make for a leader? Which **(A) virtues** are required to provide ethical leadership? I suppose there is little new **(III)**. But let me still give it a shot in the hope that it serves as a good reminder. And in the election year, why not focus on qualities necessary for political leadership?

If a person is chosen to lead the group, it is her responsibility to take care of the interest of each person of the entire group. This often **(B) ....** putting collective interest before her own interest or that of her preferred group. For this to happen, she must first be able to identify the common good, to have a grasp of what is acceptable to all, to have an inclusive vision. This requires an infinite capacity to listen to others, to learn from them, to have the intellectual ability to critically examine and evaluate what everyone wants and needs, and then put them all together. *Since this intellectual formulation can only be the first step, an estimate of the real quality of a decision is not known until it is implemented;* **...............(C) ....** . *This requires him to keep his ear to the ground, listen patiently to criticism to judge if his policies are working.* He must not be defensive when criticised, or evade uncomfortable questions, but face criticism head on and be able to sift the wheat from the chaff. It also necessitates that a leader show flexibility and an ability for course correction by admitting mistakes. He should know that one's stature is not diminished by accepting fallibility. A leader must be a good communicator, and that is greatly helped if he has a way with words. But all the rhetorical flourish is of no avail if the speech lacks sincerity and conviction. Finally, a good leader knows that nothing can be achieved without the collective expertise and wisdom of a support team.

It is equally tempting to pick those one has taken a fancy to, who are personally loyal. But such people often lack spine. **(D)** *Fearful people with poor ability can never offer good advice to their leader and could allow bad decisions to prevail that push the country down a ruinous path.* Besides, they are often among the first to backstab the leader once out of power. Thus, personal likes and dislikes too must be set aside.

6. Which of the following words can replace the word given in **bold** in (A) without changing the meaning of the sentence?

(1) gentry (2) Fortes
(3) rage (4) tantrum
(5) rampage

7. In the Question below three phrases are given which must be filled in the positions given in I, II and III in the passage. From the options given below, choose the correct order of phrases that should be filled in the positions given.

A. one can say on this matter
B. to be their own leaders
C. coordinates the actions of others

(1) ABC (2) CAB
(3) BCA (4) BAC
(5) ACB

8. Which of the following words should fill in the blank in (B) to make a contextually correct and meaningful sentence?

(1) arouse (2) entails
(3) sheers (4) garners
(5) evokes

9. Two sentences are given in italics on both sides of C. Which of the following statements can come in between the two sentences in place of C so as to maintain the continuity of the paragraph?

(1) this means that our leaders must owe supreme loyalty to nothing
(2) understand the purpose of the job, can speak their mind, and are able, without fear
(3) such persons can be identified only by one who possesses these qualities
(4) Its deficiencies begin to show up only when put into practice.
(5) None of the above

10. In the passage given, a sentence D is given in Italics. There may or may not be an error in one part of the sentence. Choose the part which has an error in it as your answer.

(1) Fearful people with poor ability can
(2) never offer good advice to their leader
(3) and could allow bad decisions to prevail
(4) that push the country down a ruinous path.
(5) no error

Directions (11-15): *Read the following passage and answer the questions as directed.*

Start-ups troubled by the so-called angel tax may soon receive some **(A)...** from the government. On Monday, the Centre set up a five-member working committee to look into revising the **(B)norms** of the angel tax imposed on start-ups. The tax, which was first introduced in 2012 to curb money-laundering through the **(i)** at bloated prices, has caused a lot of anguish among start-up investors in the country. Start- up owners have complained that income tax officials have asked many start-ups to cough up money when they try to attract capital into their entities by issuing new shares. For its part, the IT department fears that start-ups may be used as convenient tools to launder illegally acquired money, so a tax on investments beyond a certain threshold is **(ii). (C)** But while the **(1) unintended** of such an angel tax may be **(2) benefits**, the arbitrary nature of it means the cost of **(3) intent** consequences could be larger than the supposed **(4) justifiable**. In trying to curb money-laundering, Section 56(2) (viib) of the Indian Income Tax Act, 1961 gives income tax officials a free hand to harass even genuine start-ups looking to raise investments for their growth. Under the Act, the IT department is free to arbitrarily decide the fair value of a company's share and tax start-ups if the price at which their new shares are sold to investors is higher than the fair value of these shares. The broad-brush tax on all investments means an unnecessary cost is **(iii)** community simply because of the lack of better means at the government's disposal to tackle black money.

The committee set up by the government will, among other things, consider raising the threshold beyond which new investments into start-ups will be taxed. It is expected that start-ups with aggregate paid-up share capital and share premium of less than ₹ 25 crore, against the previous threshold of only ₹ 10 crore, will not be taxed while attracting new investment. This would definitely make life easier to a certain extent for angel investors and start-ups. But it will not address the real problem with the angel tax, which has to do with the unbridled power that it vests in the hands of the income tax authorities. Investors, foreign or domestic, may become wary of investing in new ideas when they are taxed while risking money on untested ventures. So the government should look to withdraw the angel tax and focus instead on building the capability to better identify and rein in illegal wealth. Otherwise it risks killing the nascent start-up ecosystem in the country.

11. Which of the following words should fill in the blank in (A) to make a contextually correct and meaningful sentence?

(1) collusion (2) commotion
(3) concession (4) digression
(5) fluctuation

12. Which of the following words can replace the word given in **bold** in (B) without changing the meaning of the sentence?

(1) Measures (2) Deviations
(3) Regulations (4) Standards
(5) Abbreviations

13. In the question below three phrases are given which must be filled in the positions given in i, ii and iii in the passage. From the options given below, choose the correct order of phrases that should be filled in the positions given.

A. necessary to deter such shady operations
B. sale of shares of private unlisted companies
C. imposed on the wider start-up

(1) ABC (2) CAB
(3) BCA (4) BAC
(5) ACB

14. The sentence given in C has four words given in **bold**. Amongst given bolded words, which of the followings must replace each other to make the sentence contextually correct and meaningful.

(1) 2-4 (2) 1-3
(3) 1-4 (4) 3-4
(5) Both (1) and (2)

15. As per the information given in the passage, out of the following options which option does **best explain the term "angel investor"**?

(1) Angel investors are those who don't look for the low risk investment that might yield a more reliable return, because those startups fail too.
(2) Angel investors are those who own shares in the business, not revenue, and not profits.
(3) An angel investor is an affluent individual who provides capital for a business start-up.
(4) Angel investors are often retired entrepreneurs or executives, who may be interested in angel investing for reasons that go beyond pure monetary return.
(5) None of the above

Directions (16-20): *In each of the following questions a grammatically correct and meaningful sentence is given with four words given in* **bold** *in each. Which of the following words should replace each other to form a meaningful and grammatically correct sentence. The meaning can be different from the one in question.*

16. The Central government is unable to provide the funds while Kerala has been stopped in its (A) **tracks** from seeking resources from (B) **abroad**, either from the Kerala (C) **diaspora** or from friendly (D) **overseas** governments.

(1) C-B (2) A-D
(3) B-D (4) A-B
(5) No Interchange Possible

17. Immediately the sympathies of the (A) **police**

and (B) **magistrates**, some sections of the media and (C) **public** opinion swing towards the (D)**perpetrator**, not the victim.

(1) A-C (2) A-B
(3) B-D (4) B-A
(5) No Interchange Possible

18. It is (A) **imperative** that there be course corrections; otherwise the (B) **exercise** runs the risk of fueling a (C) **parallel** movement against the state by those being (D) **victimised** now.

(1) A-D (2) A-C
(3) A-B (4) B-D
(5) No interchange is possible

19. The tsunami of 2004 and the (A) **threat** of piracy in the Indian Ocean provided India an (B) **opportunity** to test its new posture. Everybody was (C) **grateful**, but it made no difference to India's claim to (D) **permanent** membership.

(1) No interchange possible
(2) A-B
(3) B-C
(4) B-D
(5) A-D

20. The government has (A) **tampered** with institutions by appointing its own people to positions of (B) **authority**, and by using the (C) **Enforcement Directorate**, Income Tax authorities, the Central Bureau of Investigation and the (D) **police** as bulldozers to flatten out any site of opposition.

(1) A-C (2) B-D
(3) C-D and A-B (4) C-D
(5) A-D

Directions (21-25): *In each of the following questions a sentence is given with a word given in* **BOLD**. *Corresponding to each question three sentences are given with the use of the same word. From the options choose the sentences which give a DIFFERENT MEANING for the word used in the sentence above. The meaning used in the sentence(s) should be different from the one used in the main sentence.*

21. The leaders of our ruling **dispensation** seem to have no respect for the rule of law, nor for the rules that regulate speech in public spaces.

I. Because the soldier had saved his entire unit, the president gave him **dispensation** for his wartime crimes.
II. Scholarship is conveyed to a wider audience than under the old **dispensation**.
III. At the close of the Jubilee this **dispensation** was extended to all who had expired on the way to Rome.

(1) Only I (2) Only II
(3) Only III (4) Both I and II
(5) Both I and III

22. This is the latest instalment in the rather **sordid** story of institutional decay in India, overseen by the leaders of the Bharatiya Janata Party (BJP).

I. He remained, however, uncertain how to do so without immersing himself further in Lydia Larkin's **sordid** activities.
II. The overcrowded housing conditions were **sordid** and degrading.
III. Everyone knows of the bank's manager **sordid** plan to steal the money.

(1) Only III (2) Only II
(3) Both I and II (4) Only I
(5) Both II and III

23. Competitive federalism, in the context of interaction with foreign countries, **promoted** by Prime Minister Narendra Modi, has proved to be a double-edged sword.

I. In 1761 he was **promoted** to be member of council, under the presidency of Mr Vansittart, who had been introduced by Clive
II. The industry was actively **promoted** by a Frenchman named Jumel, in the service of Mehemet Ali, from 1820 onwards with great success.
III. He actively **promoted** the incorporation of the left bank of the Rhine with France.

(1) Only III (2) Both I and II
(3) Only I (4) Both II and III
(5) All of the above

24. When India's aspiration for permanent membership of the UN Security Council met with strong **resistance**, New Delhi hit upon the idea of forcing a vote in the General Assembly.

I. The president's healthcare plan drew a lot of **resistance** from his political rivals.

II. The employees' showed their **resistance** to the salary cuts by picketing outside the factory.

III. He also investigated electrical endosmosis and the electrical **resistance** of electrolytes.

(1) Only II (2) Both I and II
(3) Only II (4) Only III
(5) None of the above

25. The constitutional framework does not provide thick or **substantive** conceptions of how we shall think, and in what we shall believe.

I. Why should I take the herb when there is no **substantive** proof it will ease my pain

II. Not only do we hear of these varieties of practice, but also of the laying on of hands; together with prayer as a **substantive** rite unconnected with baptism.

III. They said no **substantive** objections to the agreement have been raised

(1) Only I (2) Only II
(3) Both II and III (4) All of the above
(5) None of the above

Directions (26-30): *In the questions given below a sentence is given with two blanks in each. Corresponding to each question two columns are given with three words in each column. Which combination of words from the two columns will perfectly fit into the blanks to make the sentence contextually correct and meaningful?*

26. Mutual political suspicion and a lack of .... of the complexities of the international situation have brought about a confrontation. The Chief Minister may have even made and tactical misjudgments.

Column I	Column II
A. Appreciation	D. Acceptable
B. Acknowledgement	E. Diplomatic
C. Plethora	F. Strategic

(1) C-E (2) A-F
(3) B-F and A-E (4) B-D
(5) C-D

27. The investigation also .... that another pilot flying as Staff On Duty entered the cockpit after pressing the cockpit buzzer several times. The pilot in command .... that he allowed the SOD inside the cockpit because the buzzer was distracting.

Column I	Column II
A. Divulged	D. Advanced
B. Rejected	E. Submitted
C. Communicated	F. Recommended

(1) C-D (2) B-E
(3) A-E (4) A-F
(5) B-E

28. A committee, chaired by Union Environment Minister Harsh Vardhan, has w i l d l i f e clearance to the Mumbai-Ahmedabad high speed train corridor that .... upon a flamingo sanctuary and the Sanjay Gandhi National Park, home to leopards, in Mumbai.

Column I	Column II
A. Alienated	D. Encroaches
B. Estranged	E. Repelled
C. Accorded	F. Admonish

(1) A-F (2) B-D and A-E
(3) C-F (4) C-D
(5) B-E

29. The CBI says there was no proper response to the earlier .... it sent to the Police Commissioner, and alleges that he could have destroyed evidence that was initially gathered by the Special Investigation Team that he had .... in the initial stage of the probe.

Column I	Column II
A. Declaration	D. Supervised
B. Summonses	E. Govern
C. Command	F. Administered

(1) A-D (2) C-E
(3) B-E (4) B-F and C-E
(5) B-F and B-D

30. Following Taylor, we can rightly wonder why political power should be exercised, implemented and .... without rules. Assertions of political power affect our interests and our projects.

Column I	Column II
A. fickle	D. sabotage
B. executed	E. adversely
C. finished	F. negatively

(1) A-E (2) C-D
(3) A-C and B-E (4) B-E
(5) C-F

Directions (31-35): *In the following questions, a grammatically correct and meaningful sentence is given which is divided into five parts, (A), (B), (C), (D) and (E). Part (E) is fixed and highlighted in* **BOLD**. *You have to arrange the other four parts to make a contextually and grammatically meaningful sentence (the meaning can be different from the one given in the question). If no such rearrangement is possible mark (5) as your answer i.e. 'No rearrangement is possible'.*

31. of formal and informal rules, assure (A)/ according to some norms that enable as well as (B) / institutions, as the embodiment (C)/ citizens that the government exercises power (D) /**regulate state capacity (E)**.
(1) ACBDE (2) CADBE
(3) DABCE (4) BACDE
(5) BDCAE

32. British rule, secularism was an article of faith across (A)/ the ideological spectrum, though only in a limited definition as (B) / the community-based template of political competition introduced under (C) / in the aftermath of Partition, seen as the outcome of (D) / **a seamless sense of national identity.** (E)
(1) BADAE (2) CBDAE
(3) ACBDE (4) DCABE
(5) CABDE

33. the exclusion was not based on gender or sex, but on religious (A) / by veteran lawyer K. Parasaran, sought a (B) / the Nair Service Society, represented (C) / review of the verdict on the ground that (D) / **faith in and character of the deity. (E)**
(1) DACBE (2) ABDCE
(3) CBDAE (4) BCDAE
(5) CBADE

34. represented by Solicitor General Tushar Mehta, (A) / while Mr. Venugopal said he did not (B) /on Mr. Bhushan, the government, (C) / want the court to impose any punishment (D) / **was of the opposite opinion. (E)**
(1) DABCE (2) BDCAE
(3) CDABE (4) ABCDE
(5) CDBAE

35. deposit-taking activities altogether, by making them an offence (A) /the principle is that the Bill would ban unregulated (B) / framework that only comes into effect (C) / ex-ante rather than the existing legislative-cum-regulatory (D) /**ex-post with considerable time lags. (E)**
(1) ADCBE (2) BACDE
(3) CDBAE (4) DABCE
(5) BADCE

Directions (36-40): *In the questions given below five words are given in which four of them have a similar meaning and one word is the antonym for the other four words. Choose the word, opposite in meaning to the other four, as your answer.*

36. (1) incommensurate (2) inordinate
(1) incommensurate (2) inordinate
(3) unsymmetrical (4) proportionate
(5) lopsided

37. (1) Dissipate (2) Lavish
(3) Splurge (4) Squander
(5) Retrieve

38. (1) fractious (2) affable
(3) grouchy (4) bad-tempered
(5) shrewish

39. (1) conciseness (2) eloquence
(3) rhetoric (4) magniloquence
(5) blarney

40. (1) eradicate (2) exterminate
(3) abolish (4) ratify
(5) quash

Reasoning Ability

Directions (41-44): *Study the following information to answer the given questions:*

Twelve persons are sitting around two circular table as one is inscribed in another one. All of them are facing towards the center.

A, B, C, D, E, F six persons are sitting around the inner circular table. P, Q, R, S, T, U six persons are sitting around the outer circular table.

Note: The persons of outer circular table are sitting exactly behind the persons sitting around the inner circular table.

B is sitting second to the right of E. R is an immediate neighbour of the one who is sitting behind B. Only one person sits between A and F (either from the left or from the right). A is not an immediate neighbour of B. P is sitting behind F. Only two persons sit between R and T (either from the left or from the right). U is an immediate neighbour of P. D is an immediate neighbour of A. T is not sitting behind D. Q is not an immediate neighbour of R.

41. Who among the following person is sitting third to the left of A?

(1) F (2) E
(3) D (4) B
(5) None of these

42. How many persons are sitting between S and P in the outer circle?

(1) One (2) More than three
(3) Three (4) None
(5) Two

43. Four of the following are alike in a certain way so form a group which of the following does not belong to the group?

(1) A, P (2) C, R
(3) E, T (4) B, U
(5) D, S

44. Who among the following person is sitting immediate right of S?

(1) P (2) T
(3) U (4) R
(5) Q

45. Six persons A, B, C, D, E and F lives on 6 different floors of a same building. Bottommost floor is first, the floor above it is second and so on till topmost floor which is sixth. A lives on odd numbered floor. C lives immediately below A. Two floors gap between floors of C and F. D lives immediately above F. B lives above E, who lives below F. How many persons live below E?

(1) None (2) One
(3) Two (4) Three
(5) Four

46. Seven letters are arranged in a linear arrangement to form a meaningful word. A is second to the left of I. L is to the left of N. Not more than two letters are placed between I and G. G is placed to the right of I. G is not neighbor of E and D. D and E are placed next to each other. Which letter is placed in exactly middle of the meaningful word so formed. If more than one word is formed mark your option as X?

(1) N (2) L
(3) X (4) E
(5) G

Directions (47-49): *Study the following information carefully to answer the given questions:*

A word and number arrangement machine when given an input line of words and numbers rearranges them following a particular rule. The following is an illustration of input and rearrangement.

INPUT—2538 5628 8516 7524 6325 2645

STEP I: 2358 2568 1568 2457 2356 2456

STEP II: 1568 2356 2358 2456 2457 2568

STEP III: 56 35 35 45 45 56

STEP IV: 11 8 8 9 9 11

Step IV is the last step of the rearrangement. As per the rules followed in the above steps, find out in each of the following questions the appropriate steps for the given input.

Input: 3846 9213 8273 7341 5218 3285 6925 4758

47. What will the addition of the numbers which is second, forth, sixth and eight from the left end in step IV?

(1) 32 (2) 23

(3) 38 (4) 40

(5) None of these

48. Which of the following would be the difference of the numbers which is 2nd from left end in step I and forth from right end in Step II?

(1) 1138 (2) 1287

(3) 1139 (4) 2125

(5) None of these

49. Which of the following element will be 3rd to the left of 7th from the left end in step III?

(1) 34 (2) 37

(3) 25 (4) 35

(5) None of these

Directions (50): *In the following question a statement is given followed by two more statements numbered as I and II. You have to read both the statement and decide which of them strength which of them strengthens or weakens the statement.*

50. The company A used to outsource its recruitment process for some years but this year the company has decided to conduct the recruitment process within the Organisation.

I. The employees who have been working in the Organisation are aware of that hard work is required to work in the company.

II. The company has decided to appoint three new persons in its senior level authority for the smooth recruitment process.

(1) Both I and II strengthens

(2) I strengthen while II weakens

(3) II strengthens while I is neutral

(4) Statement I and Statement II is neutral.

(5) Both I and II weakens.

Directions (51-54): *Study the following information carefully and answer the questions given below:*

Six boxes P, Q, R, S, T and U are placed in a stack one above other. Each contains different number of chocolates viz. 250, 190, 119, 175, 280 and 210.

Box P is placed immediately above box R. Three boxes placed between R and the box which contains 250 chocolates. Box which have 175 chocolates is just above the box which have 250 chocolates. One box placed between box T and the box which have 175 chocolates. U contains 210 chocolates. The box which contain 119 chocolates is placed below box U. Three boxes placed between box S and the box which have 119 chocolates. One box is placed between box Q and the box which have 190 chocolates.

51. Which box contains 210 chocolates?

(1) U (2) Q

(3) R (4) S

(5) P

52. Which box is placed at topmost position?

(1) U (2) Q

(3) R (4) S

(5) P

53. Box R and T together contains how many chocolates?

(1) 399 (2) 369

(3) 294 (4) 309

(5) 400

54. How many boxes are placed between box Q and the box which have 119 chocolates?

(1) one (2) two

(3) three (4) four

(5) none

Directions (55-57): *In each of the questions below are given some statements followed by some conclusions. You have to take the given statements to be true even if they seem to be at variance with commonly known facts. Read all the conclusions and then decide which of the given conclusions logically follows from the given statements, disregarding commonly known facts. Give answer.*

55. **Statements:** Some tube are bulb. All light are tube. All current are light.

Conclusions:

I. Some Current are bulb

II. Some light being bulb is a possibility.

III. Some tube are not current.

(1) Both I and III follows

(2) either I or II follows

(3) Only II follows (4) None follows

(5) None of these

56. Statements: Some file are copy. Some copy are eraser. No Pen is file.

Conclusions:

I. Some file are eraser

II. All pen can never be copy.

III. No file is eraser

(1) Only I follow (2) Only II follows

(3) Only III follows (4) Either I or III follows

(5) None of the above

57. Statements: Some file are copy. Some copy are eraser. No Pen is file.

Conclusions:

I. All copy can be pen.

II. Some copy can never be pen.

III. Some eraser being pen is a possibility.

(1) Only I follow (2) Only II follows

(3) Only III follows (4) Only II and III follows

(5) None of the above

Directions (58-64): *Study the following information carefully and answer the questions given below.*

Six persons J, K, L, M, N, O are born in six different years 1946, 1958, 1963, 1971, 1994, 2006. All of them like different colours Red, Black, Orange, Pink, White, Yellow.

Note: All the calculations of the ages are to be done on the basis of year 2019.

The sum of the ages of M and the one who likes Black colour is 86. The one who likes Pink colour was born in an even numbered year. M does not like red colour. The one who likes Pink colour is older than the one who likes Black colour. M does not like Pink colour. K is older than the one who like Pink colour. N likes Orange and was born in an odd numbered year. The sum of the ages of J and the one who likes Yellow colour is 81. O is younger than the one who likes orange colour. L does not like yellow colour.

58. Who among the following likes Red colour?

(1) J (2) O

(3) M (4) L

(5) None of these

59. How many persons born after O?

(1) Two (2) Four

(3) None (4) One

(5) Three

60. Which of the following statement is not correct regarding K?

(1) K is younger than M

(2) K likes Yellow

(3) K is elder to J

(4) The one who likes White is younger than K

(5) All are correct

61. In which of the following year J was born?

(1) 1994 (2) 1958

(3) 1971 (4) 2006

(5) 1946

62. Six persons L, M, N, O, P and Q sit in a linear row adjacent to each other facing north. Three persons sit between Q and P. N sits immediate left of Q. Two persons sit between N and M. How many persons sit to the left of M?

(1) one (2) two

(3) three (4) four

(5) None

63. Which of the following symbols should replace the sign (@) and (%) respectively in the given expression in order to make the expression $L \geq U$ and $R > J$ definitely true?

$L \geq K \geq P = N = J \ @ \ U \leq A \ \% \ R$

(1) $\leq, =$ (2) $\leq, \leq$

(3) $>, \leq$ (4) $=, <$

(5) $\geq, <$

64. Which of the following will be definitely true if the given expression $T \geq U \geq M = N < J = P < Q \leq R$ is definitely true?

(1) $T < J$ (2) $U > M$

(3) $R > N$ (4) $R \geq M$

(5) $T < P$

Directions (65-69): *Study the following information carefully and answer the questions given below.*

Twelve persons are born on three different dates 5, 12, 21 of four different months viz. March, May, September and November. Only one person is born on one date of a month. J was born on 5 of a month having 30 days. Only three persons were born between J and H. H does not born on an even date of a month. As many as persons born after H as born before A. Five persons born between A and D. Only two persons born between F and E. C born on an even date but immediately after K. Six person born between C and B. E born immediately before B. M born on an even date after L but before G.

65. How many persons born between C and F?

(1) Two (2) More than three
(3) Three (4) One
(5) None

66. Who among the following is born immediate before G?

(1) K (2) L
(3) J (4) M
(5) D

67. H born on which of the following day?

(1) 21 May (2) 12 March
(3) 5 September (4) 21 March
(5) 5 May

68. Which of the following statements is true?

(1) J and G both were born in same month
(2) F was born on odd date
(3) G was born on 5th
(4) B was born on 21st
(5) All are true.

69. In a certain code, numbers from (0-9) are coded as four alphabets i.e. '0389' is coded as 'AACD', '146' coded as 'ABA', then how is ' 257' coded?

(1) CBA (2) CDA
(3) BAC (4) AAD
(5) BCB

70. If all the letters of each given words are arranged in alphabetical order within the words, then in how many words third and fifth letter remains on the same position as earlier?

I. MBEKTYD
II. GPNAQUS
III. XCJRHO

(1) Only I (2) Only I and II
(3) All I, II and III (4) Only II
(5) None

Directions (71-72): *Study the following information carefully and answer the questions given below.*

The principal of St. Mary School organized extra classes for week students of X class and the concerned teachers are getting paid extra amount for the classes. But the average salary of teachers more or less remains the same.

71. Which of the following can be assumed from the given statement?

I. The students of class X of school Y will score more marks than students of St. Mary School.
II. Students of class X are not serious about exams.
III. Extra classes arranged by the principal for students of class X will help the students to score well in exams.

(1) Both I and II (2) Both II and III
(3) Only II (4) Only III
(5) None of these

72. What can be the reason behind the average of the salary remain same of teachers?

I. Student of class X attend the extra class two or three days in a week although the teachers provide the class regularly.
II. Teachers started taking more holidays after the commencement of the extra classes.
III. Teachers are already working overtime for checking and preparing homework for students on daily basis.

(1) Both I and II (2) Both II and III
(3) Only II (4) Only III
(5) None of these

Directions (73): *The tuda company is the third largest producer of steel with 1.5 lakh employees. The company is going to start a new unit by hiring 35% of its current employees. After its commencement the company will become the largest steel producer with 32.5 billion turnover.*

73. Which of the following can be inferred from the given statement?

I. The app. turnover of new unit of tuda company will be 1.5 million.

II. The company is required to hire 52000 employees.

III. With 52500 new employees of the new unit, the company will be able to reach the 32.5 million turnover.

IV. The turnover of the tuda company is now below 32.5 million.

(1) Both I and II (2) Both II and III
(3) Only IV (4) Only III
(5) Both III and IV

Directions (74-77): *Study the following information carefully and answer the questions given below.*

Ten persons are standing in a row facing north. All of them earn different amount viz. 3000, 4500, 5000, 7000, 8500, 10000. Three persons are standing between B and R. H is standing immediately ahead of B. L is standing adjacent to R. L is standing at extreme end. Six persons are standing between A and Y. Y is standing behind A. Only one person is standing between A and D. Q is standing ahead of G but behind Z. The following information is given for the amount earn by them—

S@P means S earn more than P. S#P means S earn less than P. S$P means S earn equal to P.

The amount earn by all of them is given below— A@Z$H@R$QG, YD#G, A#L#B

74. What will be the sum of the amount earn by Q, Z and L?
(1) 19000 (2) 18000
(3) 17000 (4) 20000
(5) 12000

75. How many persons are standing ahead of B?
(1) Two (2) More than three
(3) Three (4) One
(5) None

76. How many persons are standing between Q and R?
(1) Two (2) More than three
(3) Three (4) One
(5) None

77. How many persons earn less than G?
(1) Two (2) More than three
(3) Three (4) One
(5) None

Directions (78-80): *Study the following information carefully and answer the questions given below.*

A%B (7)- A is 12 m in north of B A$B (12)- A is 17 m in south of B A#B (32)- A is 37 m in east of B A&B (14)- A is 19 m in west of B

M%K (33), J#K (9), G%J (19), H&G (23), N$H (25)

78. K is in which direction with respect to G?
(1) North (2) West
(3) North-west (4) East
(5) South-west

79. If Z is the midpoint of the line formed between H and G, then what is the distance between H and Z?
(1) 12 m (2) 14 m
(3) 16 m (4) 17 m
(5) 30 m

80. If X is in west of J and lies on the line formed by H and N, then what is the distance between X and N?
(1) 10 m (2) 24 m
(3) 6 m (4) 16 m
(5) 14 m

Directions (81-85): *In each of the following below is given a group of letters followed by four combinations of digits/symbols numbered (a), (b), (c) and (d). You have to find out which of the combinations correctly represents the group of letters based on the following coding system and mark the number of that combination as the answer. If none of the four combinations correctly represents the group of letters, mark (e), i.e. 'None of these', as the answer-*

Note: More than one condition may apply.

Letter	Digit/Symbol
R	#
G	2
F	7
A	μ
P	%
Q	3
U	&
M	9

E	1
I	@
B	5
J	©
S	6
O	8
L	$

Conditions:

I. If first letter is vowel and last letter is consonant then both are coded with the code of the consonant.

II. If both the 2nd and the last letter is vowel, then their codes are to be interchanged.

III. If the second letter is a consonant and the 2nd last letter is a vowel, both are to be coded as the code for the vowel.

IV. If both 1st and fifth letter is consonant then both are coded as the code of third letter.

V. If only one condition is applied among the above given, then the code of first letter is interchanged with code of second letter and third letter code interchanged with 4th letter and so on after that applied condition.

81. AMGFIS

(1) 6@27@4 (2) 6@27@6
(3) 6@27#6 (4) 6@2@76
(5) None of these

82. PUGRLE

(1) 2122#& (2) 221#2&
(3) 212#&2 (4) 212#2&
(5) None of these

83. UAIMUI

(1) @&9@µ& (2) @&@9µ&
(3) @9&@µ& (4) @&99µ&
(5) None of these

84. MJGLBF

(1) ©2$227 (2) ©$2272
(3) ©$2227 (4) ©2$2$2
(5) None of these

85. GFPQMB

(1) %7%3%5 (2) 27%395
(3) 7%3%5% (4) %7%395
(5) None of these

86. **Statement:** The Union health ministry has made Aadhaar a compulsory document for tuberculosis patients to be able to avail treatment under the government's Revised National Tuberculosis Control Programme (RNTCP).

I. A person cannot take treatment of TB without Aadhar card.

II. Patients suffering from TB will be unable to get benefits under a central government scheme till they produce their Aadhaar card.

III. An individual eligible to receive the benefit under the scheme, is hereby, required to furnish proof of possession of Aadhaar number or undergo Aadhaar authentication.

IV. The World Health Organisation (WHO) recently said that tuberculosis epidemic in India was "larger" than what had been previously estimated.

Which of the following could be the inference of the given statement?

(1) Only II (2) Only I and III
(3) Only II and III (4) Only I
(5) None of these

87. **Statement:** The Captain Amarinder Singh-led government in Punjab has announced free education for girls in government schools and colleges from Nursery to PhD.

I. Good social welfare law. It is initially for girls as they are comparatively disadvantaged. Hopefully it will soon be followed by free education for everyone.

II. It is gender biased as if a poor or average person wants to educate his son for higher education he has to pay higher bills .If you are introducing a law / scheme / bills under no circumstance it should not favour any particular gender, if they are really concerned about education.

III. Do not differentiate a poor or average person on gender. A poor boy or man should also get free education as well.

Which of the following argument holds strong for the given statement?

(1) Only II (2) Only III
(3) Only II and III (4) Only I and II
(5) All of the above

Directions (88-90): *Study the given information carefully to answer the following questions:*

Six persons i.e. A, B, C, E, F and G who all are sitting around a circular table facing outside. They all are of different age. F is third youngest person. Only two persons sits between E and F. G sits second to the left of C, who is 20 years of age. The one who is second oldest person is of 24 years of age. G is elder than A and C but not the eldest. C sits on the immediate right of E. B is elder than A and G. A and G are not immediate neighbours. The one who is the youngest is less than 20 years of age. A is not younger than F.

88. What will be the possible age of A?
(1) 25 years (2) 20 years
(3) 27 years (4) 19 years
(5) 22 years

89. What is the position of G with respect to A?
(1) Third to the left (2) Second to the right
(3) second to the left
(4) Both (1) and (5)
(5) Third to the right

90. Who among the following is the youngest among all?
(1) A (2) E
(3) C (4) F
(5) None of these

Quantitative Aptitude

Directions (91-95): *In the given questions, two quantities are given, one as 'Quantity 1' and another as 'Quantity 2'. You have to determine relationship between two quantities and choose the appropriate option:*

91. A is twice as efficient as B. Both can complete a work together in 7.5 days.

Quantity 1: Time taken by B to complete the work alone.

Quantity 2: If C is 50% more efficient than A, then time taken by C to complete the work alone.

(1) Quantity 1 > Quantity 2
(2) Quantity 1 ≥ Quantity 2
(3) Quantity 2 > Quantity 1
(4) Quantity 2 ≥ Quantity 1
(5) Quantity 1 = Quantity 2 or Relation cannot be established

92. One of the roots of $2x^2 + bx - 5 = 0$ is 1.

Quantity 1: Value of the other root.

Quantity 2: 2.5

(1) Quantity 1 > Quantity 2
(2) Quantity 1 ≥ Quantity 2
(3) Quantity 2 > Quantity 1
(4) Quantity 2 ≥ Quantity 1
(5) Quantity 1 = Quantity 2 or Relation cannot be established

93. Two dices are rolled simultaneously.

Quantity 1: Probability that the sum of the numbers that appeared is a multiple of 5.

Quantity 2: 1/6

(1) Quantity 1 > Quantity 2
(2) Quantity 1 ≥ Quantity 2
(3) Quantity 2 > Quantity 1
(4) Quantity 2 ≥ Quantity 1
(5) Quantity 1 = Quantity 2 or Relation cannot be established

94. Sum of height and diameter of the cylinder is 28 meter.

Quantity 1: Curved surface area of the cylinder whose respective ratio of height to diameter is 3 : 4

Quantity 2: Curved surface area of the cylinder if height of cylinder is 10 m.

(1) Quantity 1 > Quantity 2
(2) Quantity 1 ≥ Quantity 2
(3) Quantity 2 > Quantity 1
(4) Quantity 2 ≥ Quantity 1
(5) Quantity 1 = Quantity 2 or Relation cannot be established

95. Product of digits of a two digits number 'N' is 21

Quantity 1: N

Quantity 2: 130–N

(1) Quantity 1 > Quantity 2
(2) Quantity 1 ≥ Quantity 2
(3) Quantity 2 > Quantity 1
(4) Quantity 2 ≥ Quantity 1
(5) Quantity 1 = Quantity 2 or Relation cannot be established

96. From container A containing 54 liter of mixture of milk and water in ratio of 8 : 1, 18 liter of the mixture is taken out and poured into container B in which ratio of milk to water is 3 : 1. If difference between total milk and total water in container B is 30 liter then find the quantity of initial mixture in container B.

(1) 30 Liter (2) 28 Liter
(3) 32 Liter (4) 36 Liter
(5) 40 Liter

97. In a match of 50 overs, team A's average runs for first thirty overs was 4.5 runs/over while for the remaining 20 overs the average was 5.5 runs/over. Team B chased the target and lost by 10 runs. Find the average runs per over scored by team B. (team B played all the 50 overs).

(1) 4.4 (2) 5.2
(3) 4.7 (4) 5.6
(5) 3.8

98. In a bag which contains 40 balls, there are 18 red balls and some green and blue balls. If two balls are picked up from the bag without replacement, then the probability of the first ball being red and second being green is 3/26. Find the number of blue balls in the bag.

(1) 16 (2) 12
(3) 10 (4) 14
(5) 8

99. A is 50% more efficient than B. They together start the work and 7/12th of work is left after 8 days. Find in what time B alone will complete the whole work.

(1) 36 days (2) 44 days
(3) 50 days (4) 40 days
(5) 48 days

Directions (100–105): *Given below table shows number of employees joined (at the beginning of the year) and left (at the end of the year) in three companies i.e. A, B and C in three years (2001, 2002 and 2003). Read the data carefully and answer the questions. (Some data are missing).*

Years	A		B		C	
	Joined	Left	Joined	Left	Joined	Left
2001	102		96	18	84	36
2002	78	24	72		108	
2003	112		144		124	28

100. In year 2000 total employee who joined A is 64 which is 32% of total employee working in A that year and total employee who left A in year 2000 and 2001 is 20 and 32 respectively. If employee left B in year 2002 is 16 and this company starts in 2001, then find total employee working in B at the end of 2002 is approximate what percent of total employee working in A at the end of 2002?

(1) 36% (2) 48%
(3) 52% (4) 44%
(5) 56%

101. The ratio of total employee who left B and C in the year 2002 is 7 : 9 and total employee working in B and C at the end of 2000 are 160 and 172 respectively. If total employee working at the end of 2003 in C is 406, then find total employee working in B at the end of 2002?

(1) 284 (2) 296
(3) 298 (4) 302
(5) 306

102. Total employee working in B at the end of 1999 is 220 and 28 employee left company in 2000, while 32 new employees joined the company. If respective ratio of employee left the company B in year 2002 and 2003 is 6 : 7 and total employee working in B at the end of 2003 is 466, then find total employee left B in 2002 and 2003 together?

(1) 52 (2) 48
(3) 42 (4) 36
(5) 32

103. The average of total employee left company A in the given three years is 21 and ratio of employee left in 2001 to in 2003 is 7 : 6. If company A start in 2001, then find total employee working in A at the end of 2002 is what percent more than total employee who joined company C in the year 2002?

(1) 20% (2) 15%
(3) 25% (4) 30%
(5) 22.5%

104. Total employee who left C in the year 2002 is 33.33% more than total employee who left A in same year and total employee who left B in 2002 is 62.5% of total employee who left C in same year. If all three companies start in 2001 and total 22 employee left A in 2001, then find the respective ratio of employee working in B, C and A at the end of 2002?

(1) 65 : 62 : 69 (2) 66 : 62 : 69
(3) 65 : 61 : 67 (4) 61 : 62 : 69
(5) 65 : 62 : 67

105. Each company start in 2001 and ratio of total employee left A in 2001 to that of B and C together in 2002 is 1 : 2. If total employee who left A in 2001 and that of B and C together in 2002 is 36 and total employee who left B in 2002 is 50% of employee who left C in same year, then find difference between total employee working in C at the end of 2003 and total employee working in A at the end of 2002?

(1) 92 (2) 82
(3) 72 (4) 96
(5) 86

Directions (106-111): *In each of these questions, two equations numbered I and II are given. You have to solve both the equation and give answer:*

(1) if $x < y$ (2) if $x \leq y$
(3) if $x > y$ (4) if $x \geq i$
(5) if $x = y$ or the relationship cannot be established

106. I. $2x^2 + 11x + 15 = 0$
II. $4y^2 + 13y + 9 = 0$

107. I. $x^2 - 36x + 324 = 0$
II. $y^2 - 35y + 216 = 0$

108. I. $x = (216)^{1/3}$
II. $y^2 = 6$

109. I. $2x^2 + 17x + 35 = 0$
II. $3y^2 + 17y + 24 = 0$

110. I. $x^2 + 72 = 108$
II. $y^3 + 581 = 365$

111. I. $8x^2 + 58x + 39 = 0$
II. $8y^2 - 14y - 15 = 0$

Directions (112-117): *Given pie chart shows percentage distribution of viewers of a TV channel in five different villages (A, B, C, D and E) and table shows number of viewers who subscribed the channel. Read the data carefully and answer the questions.*

Note: Total viewers = Total subscriber + Total unsubscribe

Total viewers = 3000

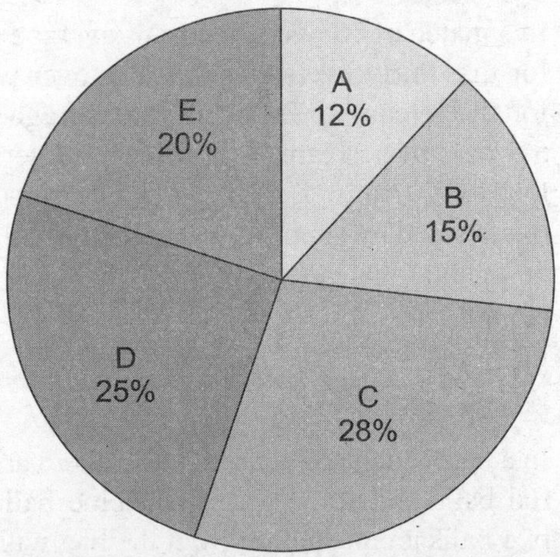

Villages	People who subscribed
A	220
B	250
C	440
D	350
E	180

112. Total unsubscribed viewers from B and E together is what percent more than total unsubscribed viewers from C?

(1) 50% (2) 55%
(3) 45% (4) 40%
(5) 42%

113. If total male unsubscribed viewers in D is 66.66% more than that of female unsubscribed viewers, then find ratio of total male unsubscribed viewers in D to total unsubscribed viewers in A and C together?

(1) 25 : 53 (2) 25 : 54
(3) 7 : 9 (4) 23 : 54
(5) 2 : 3

114. Find the central angle for total unsubscribed viewers in B and C and total subscribed viewers in E together with respect to total viewers?

(1) 133.6° (2) 136.6°
(3) 63.6° (4) 130.6°
(5) 93.6°

115. Out of total viewers in village C, 46.43% are female and 7/13th of total female are unsubscribed viewers, then find total unsubscribed male viewers from village C?

(1) 170 (2) 180
(3) 210 (4) 190
(5) 250

116. In another village F total subscribed viewers are 20% more than total unsubscribed viewers in village A and total subscribed viewers in village F are 3/7th of total viewers in that village. Find total unsubscribed viewers from village F is what percent less than total unsubscribed viewers from village C?

(1) 42% (2) 44%
(3) 48% (4) 46%
(5) 40%

117. If the above data given for the year 2017 and in 2018 total viewers increased by 40%, while percentage distribution of viewers of TV channel in five different villages remain same as in 2017. If number of subscribed viewers from village A, B, D and E in 2018 increased by 25%, 20%, 14% and 10% respectively and total subscribed viewer from all the five village in 2018 are 1400, then find total unsubscribed viewers from C in 2018?

(1) 942 (2) 952
(3) 948 (4) 956
(5) 964

Directions (118-122): *The following questions are accompanied by two statements A and B. You have to determine which statements(s) is/are sufficient/ necessary to answer the questions.*

(1) Statement A alone is sufficient to answer the question but statement B alone is not sufficient to answer the questions.
(2) Statement B alone is sufficient to answer the question but statement A alone is not sufficient to answer the question.
(3) Both the statements taken together are necessary to answer the questions, but neither of the statements alone is sufficient to answer the question.
(4) Either statement A or statement B by itself is sufficient to answer the question.
(5) Statements A and B taken together are not sufficient to answer the question

118. What is the value of rate of interest?

A. A sum of Rs. 8000 is invested at simple interest for 3 years in scheme A which offers a certain rate of interest. Amount obtained from scheme A is equal to the amount obtained when Rs. 9000 is invested in scheme B for 2 years at C.I.

B. Rate of interest for scheme B is same as rate of interest for scheme A.

119. 4 men and 18 women can do a piece of work in 2.5 days, then in how many days 12 woman can complete the same piece of work?

A. Ratio of efficiency of men to women is 3 : 2.

B. 6 men and 6 women can complete the same work in 4 days.

120. What will be speed of stream, if speed of boat in still water is 22.5 km/hr?

A. The time taken by boat to cover 120 km upstream is 4 hours more than time taken by boat to cover same distance in downstream.

B. Boat takes total 15 hours to cover 150 km in downstream and upstream.

121. What will be sum of two natural numbers X and Y?

A. X and Y both are multiple of 24, while X is 50% more than Y.

B. X/30 and Y/40 both are natural number.

122. There is $(2a + 16)$ students in a class with three streams, i.e. art, science and commerce. The ratio of students who take art to science is 4 : 1. Find total number of students in class.

A. Total students who take art is 8 more than total students who take commerce and probability of selecting one student who take science is 1/8.

B. Total commerce students in class are 25% less than total art students in the class.

Directions (123-128): *Given below bar graph (I) shows total students (Boys + girls) in thousands who have taken admissions in five different college and bar graph (II) shows percentage of girls taken admission in these five colleges. Read the data carefully and answer the questions.*

(I)

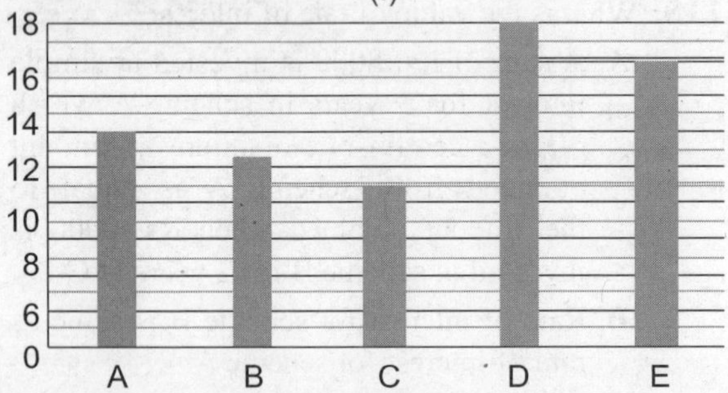

(II)

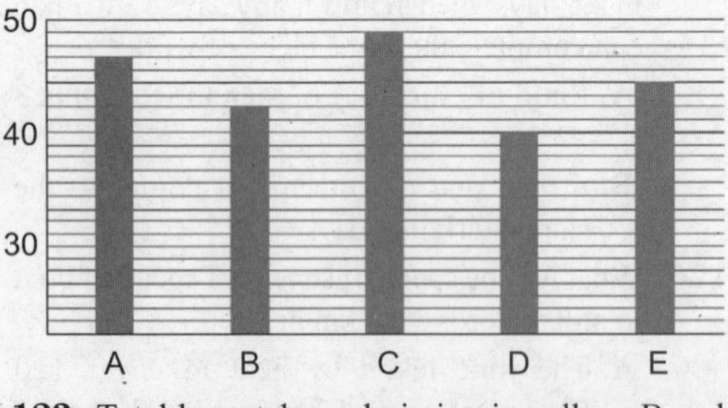

123. Total boys taken admission in college B and D together are what percent more than total boys taken admission in E?

(1) 92.5% (2) 97.5%
(3) 99.5% (4) 102.5%
(5) 84.5%

124. 75% and 80% of total girls taken admission in college A and C respectively appeared in exam and total students appeared in exam from A and C is 17910. If total boys appeared in exam from A is 6048, then find difference between boys who did not appeared in exam from college A and C?

(1) 438 (2) 428
(3) 418 (4) 408
(5) 448

125. Find the ratio of total boys taken admission in college A and B together to total girls taken admission in D and E together?

(1) 13 : 11 (2) 23 : 19
(3) 21 : 17 (4) 21 : 19
(5) None of these

126. If in college F total girls taken admission are 62.5% more than that of total girls taken admission in C and total boys taken admission in college E and F together is 20580, then find percentage of girls taken admission in college F?

(1) 33% (2) 43%
(3) 39% (4) 37%
(5) 45%

127. In each college there are only three streams (i.e. science, commerce and art) and in college B respective ratio of students taken admission in science, commerce and art is 2 : 1 : 4. If out of total girls taken admission in college B, 40% taken admission in science stream, 25% taken admission in commerce stream, then find difference between boys taken admission in art and science streams from college B?

(1) 3242 (2) 3464
(3) 3189 (4) 3345
(5) 2964

128. Find the average number of boys taken admission from all the five given colleges?

(1) 7992 (2) 7982
(3) 6848 (4) 7292
(5) None of these

129. There is a square field of area 'X' square

meters. A cylindrical ditch of radius 7 meters and depth 2 meters is dug, and the earth is taken out and spread over the remaining part of the square field, the height of square field which goes up by 0.77 meters. What is the value of 'X'?

(1) 548 m² (2) 524 m²
(3) 518 m² (4) 554 m²
(5) 504 m²

130. A man invested an amount at the rate of 10% p.a. on compound interest and after two years he again invested half of the initial amount. If man got Rs. 457. 2 Rs. as interest after three years, find the amount received by man after three years, if he invested same amount on simple interest at rate of 15% p.a.?

(1) Rs. 1740 (2) Rs. 1720
(3) Rs. 1760 (4) Rs. 1780
(5) None of these

131. A and B entered in a business by making investment of Rs. 4000 and Rs. 5500 respectively. After six months A and B withdrew Rs. 1000 and Rs. 1500 respectively and C joined them with capital of Rs. $4x$. If after one year and three months C received Rs. 2250 as profit share out of total profit of Rs. 12250, then find investment of C?

(1) Rs. 3600 (2) Rs. 3200
(3) Rs. 4400 (4) Rs. 3000
(5) Rs. 2800

132. Train A can cross a man in 8 sec and a 180 m long platform 'P' in 17 sec. If train A cross train B which is running in opposite direction at speed of 108 km/hr in 8 sec, then find time taken by train B to cross platform P?

(1) 16 sec (2) 11 sec
(3) 14 sec (4) 12 sec
(5) 15 sec

133. There are two shopkeepers, first shopkeeper calculates his profit percent on the selling price whereas the second shopkeeper calculates his profit percent on the cost price. If the selling price for both the shopkeeper is same and the difference between their profits is Rs. 175. Then, calculate the sum of the cost price for both the shopkeeper if the profit percent for the both shopkeeper is 25%?

(1) Rs. 5425 (2) Rs. 4875
(3) Rs. 4675 (4) Rs. 5275
(5) Rs. 5325

134. If 6 years are subtracted from the present age of Ayush and takes 25% of that then we get the present age of his only son. 4 years ago, his daughter's age is 7 years more than his son. Sum of daughter's present age and his wife's present age is 10 years more than Ayush's present age then find the present age of Ayush if average of present age of entire family is 30.25 yr?

(1) 45 year (2) 50 year
(3) 60 year (4) 40 year
(5) 36 year

135. 'X' is a bread seller who marked up price of each bread packet by 150% above and allow discounts of 40% and made a profit of Rs. 30 on each bread packet. If 'X' allows 37.5% discount on each packet, then find how much profit he gets on selling 80 bread packets?

(1) Rs. 2750 (2) Rs. 3200
(3) Rs. 2500 (4) Rs. 2700
(5) Rs. 2400

Directions (136-140): *Read the data carefully and answer the questions.*

A company is the producer of bottles and it used to sell bottles through distributor on a condition that on selling the stock of every 50 bottles, he will get Rs. 1000 as commission. The distributor is responsible to sell all those bottles to retailers. If he marks the bottles at the price which is 30% above the production cost (cost price) and allows a discount of Y%. He sells total of 'X' bottles which is 40 less than total received stock by him. Total production price of whole stock of bottles received by him to sell to retailers is Rs. 7.8 lakhs. The commission received by distributor is Rs. 7000 and he made a profit of Rs. 1.4 lakhs on selling the bottles.

136. What is value 'Y'?

(1) 9.69% (2) 7.69%
(3) 5.69% (4) 8.69%
(5) None of these

137. What will be ratio of Y : (X + 40)?

(1) 10 : 511 (2) 10 : 503
(3) 10 : 513 (4) 10 : 507
(5) 10 : 509

138. Instead of 'Y' employee allow 10% discount on one bottle, then percentage profit of distributor?

(1) 17% (2) 15%
(3) 12% (4) 10%
(5) 19%

139. If company added given commission in cost price and he give stock of (X + 450) bottles to another distributor who sold all stock, then find new cost price of one bottle?

(1) Rs. 2200 (2) Rs. 2020
(3) Rs. 2040 (4) Rs. 2060
(5) Rs. 2080

140. If distributor allowed two successive discounts of 5% and 12.5% on marked price, then find the profit made by distributor on selling of one bottle?

(1) Rs. 161.25 (2) Rs. 162.25
(3) Rs. 172.25 (4) Rs. 176.25
(5) Rs. 174.25

General Awareness

141. Who are the winners of this year's Ramon Magsaysay Award 2018 from India, regarded as the Asian version of the Nobel Prize?

(1) Bharat Vatwani and Sonam Wangchuk
(2) Kailash Satyarthi and Arvind Kejriwal
(3) Bhuwan Ribhu and Asmita Satyarthi
(4) Nadia Murad and Juan Manuel Santos
(5) None of the given option is true

142. Nearly .... crore jobs were created in the country in the 10-month period till June this year, as per a Central Statistics Office (CSO) report.

(1) 2.4 crore (2) 3.5 crore
(3) 6.9 crore (4) 1.2 crore
(5) 7.5 crore

143. Which organisation is a policy think tank of the Government of India, established with the aim to achieve Sustainable Development Goals and to enhance cooperative federalism by fostering the involvement of State Governments of India in the economic policy-making process using a bottom-up approach?

(1) RBI (2) IRDAI
(3) NITI Aayog (4) Planning Commission
(5) CBDT

144. The World Economic Outlook (WEO) is a survey conducted and published by:

(1) WTO (2) World Bank
(3) UNCTAD
(4) New Development Bank
(5) International Monetary Fund

145. Which country will chair the 2019 summit of the Association of Southeast Asian Nations (ASEAN)?

(1) Japan (2) Singapore
(3) China (4) Thailand
(5) Russia

146. Which Bank has bagged Hindi implementation award Rajbhasha Kirti Award for outstanding performance in implementing the Official Language Policy during 2017-18?

(1) Union Bank of India
(2) Indian Bank
(3) Punjab National Bank
(4) State Bank of India
(5) Bank of Baroda

147. Public Affairs Centre (PAC) engages in action research focusing on Sustainable Development Goals in the context of India. PAC situated in-?

(1) New Delhi (2) Bengaluru
(3) Mumbai (4) Kolkata
(5) Chennai

148. The Department of Industrial Policy and Promotion (DIPP), Ministry of Commerce and Industry, hosts a conference on Global Digital Content Market (GDCM) 2018 in which city?

(1) New Delhi (2) Bengaluru
(3) Mumbai (4) Kolkata
(5) Chennai

149. The Mahanadi is a major river in East Central India. It originates from which state?
(1) Jharkhand (2) West Bengal
(3) Odisha (4) Chhatisgarh
(5) Madhya Pradesh

150. Angelique Kerber is a/an .... professional tennis player and former world No. 1, and a three time Grand Slam champion.
(1) German (2) American
(3) France (4) Swiss
(5) Australian

151. Aaron James Finch is an Australian sports player. He play which sport?
(1) F1 Race (2) Football
(3) Badminton (4) Tennis
(5) Cricket

152. Indian Banks' Association, formed on 26 September 1946 as a representative body of management of banking in India operating in India – an association of Indian banks and financial institutions based in Mumbai. Who is present Chairman of IBA?
(1) Jatinder Bir Singh
(2) Dinabandhu Mohapatra
(3) Sunil Mehta
(4) Rajnish Kumar
(5) Chanda Kochhar

153. Who is the Chairman of HDFC Bank?
(1) Aditya Puri (2) Deepak Parekh
(3) Shikha Sharma (4) Amitabh Chaudhary
(5) Sandeep Bakhshi

154. Khelo India Youth Games, formerly Khelo India School Games, meaning Play India Youth Games, held annually in January or February, are the national level multidisciplinary grassroot games in India held for two categories, namely under- 17 years school students and under-21 college students. Khelo India Youth Games 2019 held in
(1) New Delhi (2) Lucknow
(3) Patna (4) Jaipur
(5) Pune

155. Recently, RBI has declared that how much percentage of demonetized money was back?
(1) 79.30% (2) 93.30%
(3) 88.30% (4) 99.30%
(5) 91.30%

156. What is the current reverse repo rate of RBI?
(1) 6.50% (2) 6.25%
(3) 6.75% (4) 4.00%
(5) 19.50%

157. Who is the committee head of the merger of the public sector banks?
(1) Raghuram Rajan (2) Bimal Jalan
(3) Arun Jaitley (4) YV Reddy
(5) Piyush Goyal

158. World's first thermal battery power plant is started in which state?
(1) Andhra Pradesh (2) Kerala
(3) Uttar Pradesh (4) Maharashtra
(5) Gujarat

159. The difference between exports and imports is called-?
(1) assets and liabilities
(2) balance of payment
(3) GDP (4) balance of trade
(5) depreciation

160. The 2018 ICC Women's World Twenty 20 was hosted in .... from 09th to 24th November 2018, during the 2018–19 international cricket season.
(1) Australia (2) West Indies
(3) South Africa (4) India
(5) New Zealand

161. Which of the following country to host the 11th BRICS Summit is scheduled for October 2019?
(1) India (2) China
(3) South Africa (4) Germany
(5) Brazil

162. What is the name of the book which was awarded the golden man Booker Prize 2018?
(1) The English Patient

(2) Everything Under
(3) The Long Take (4) Washington Black
(5) The Mars Room

163. What is the minimum paid-up equity capital for small finance banks?
(1) Rs. 10 crore (2) Rs. 500 crore
(3) Rs. 100 crore (4) Rs. 200 crore
(5) Rs. 1000 crore

164. Stan Lee, who passed away recently, was a comic writer with which of the following comic works was he as associated?
(1) Science fiction Comics
(2) Action/Adventur Comics
(3) Manga Comics
(4) Superhero Comics
(5) Marvel Comics

165. BOND-I is given by which institution?
(1) IMF (2) RBI
(3) ADB (4) World Bank
(5) SEBI

166. Eat right movement was launched by FSSAI selected whom as it's brand ambassador?
(1) MS Dhoni (2) Virat Kohli
(3) Rajkummar Rao (4) Amitabh Bachchan
(5) Nawazuddin Siddiqui

167. India has stated it aims to reduce the emissions intensity of its GDP by 33-35% by 2030 from 2005 levels and achieve .... of its cumulative electric power of around 350 GW installed capacity from non-fossil fuel-based energy resources, mainly renewable power.
(1) 20% (2) 40%
(3) 50% (4) 30%
(5) 10%

168. What is child sex ratio for 1000 males as per census 2011?
(1) 919 females (2) 921 females
(3) 927 females (4) 925 females
(5) 917 females

169. The Reserve Bank of India made a strong case for setting up a .... in India to address the twin balance sheet problem of the banking sector and the corporate sector.
(1) Public Credit Registration
(2) Public Credit Registry
(3) Public Credit Review
(4) Public Credit Reminder
(5) Public Commerce Registry

170. The .... is the second supersonic fighter developed by Hindustan Aeronautics Limited (HAL) after the HAL HF-24 Marut.
(1) Trishul (2) Prithavi
(3) Vikrant (4) Akash
(5) Tejas

171. Lok Adalat is one of the alternative dispute redressal mechanisms, it is a forum where disputes/cases pending in the court of law or at pre-litigation stage are settled/ compromised amicably. What is the minimum charge to file a case in a Lok Adalat?
(1) no court fee (2) Rs. 10
(3) Rs. 50 (4) Rs. 05
(5) Rs. 100

172. In 1970, an organized resistance to the destruction of forests spread throughout India and came to be known as-
(1) Save Silent Valley Movement
(2) Swadeshi Movement
(3) Namantar Andolan
(4) Chipko movement
(5) Narmada Bachao Andolan

173. Damdama lake is in which state?
(1) Punjab (2) Rajasthan
(3) Haryana (4) Uttar Pradesh
(5) Bihar

174. The United Nations' (UN) International Day Against Drug Abuse and Illicit Trafficking falls on
(1) 29th June (2) 21st June
(3) 12th June (4) 26th June
(5) 05th June

175. Which of the following ministry has Launched Mobile Application " Jan Dhan Darshak" as A Part of Financial Inclusion?
(1) Finance Ministry
(2) Ministry of Consumer Affairs, Food and Public Distribution

(3) Ministry of Human Resource Development
(4) Ministry of Parliamentary Affairs
(5) Ministry of Commerce and Industry

176. While India stands .... largest in number in terms of number of World Heritage properties in ASPAC (Asia and Pacific) region.
(1) fourth (2) third
(3) second (4) fifth
(5) first

177. Indian Air Force (IAF) for first time was participated in multinational air exercise .... 2018 (PB-18) in Australia hosted Royal Australian Air Force (RAAF).
(1) Desert Strike (2) Emerald Mercury
(3) Yudh Abyas (4) Nomadic Elephant
(5) Pitch Black

178. How much amount is available to one account holder of Pradhan Mantri Jan Dhan Yojana per household after six months of satisfactory conduct of the account?
(1) Rs. 5,000 (2) Rs. 10,000
(3) Rs. 2,000 (4) Rs. 15,000
(5) Rs. 20,000

179. Which of the following bank will allow its customers to make card-less cash withdrawals at over 100000 ATMs across India?
(1) Bank of Baroda (2) ICICI Bank
(3) AU Small Finance Bank
(4) State Bank of India
(5) Airtel Payments Bank

180. Cheques, Drafts, Pay Orders and Banker's Cheques are "valid for .... months from the date of instrument.
(1) 4 months (2) 1 months
(3) 6 months (4) 3 months
(5) 5 months

181. The four pillars of smart planning are vital to the success of Smart Cities and the Regional Smart City Initiative. Which of the following pillar is not them?
(1) MOBILITY (2) SUSTAINABILITY
(3) INFRASTRUCTURE
(4) CONNECTIVITY
(5) SECURITY

182. IRDAI has directed all third-party insurance companies to include vehicle insurance policies cover to vehicle owners-drivers of all vehicles (two-wheelers, three-wheelers, passenger vehicles and commercial vehicles) for an additional premium of-
(1) Rs. 500 (2) Rs. 750
(3) Rs. 10000 (4) Rs. 1000
(5) Rs. 5000

183. As per guidelines of the RBI, payments banks can accept demand deposits (savings and current) up to a maximum of .... per customer.
(1) Rs. 1,00,000 (2) Rs. 2,00,000
(3) Rs. 50,000 (4) Rs. 5,00,000
(5) Rs. 10,000

184. Public Sector Enterprises (PSEs) is comes under which ministry?
(1) Ministry of Heavy Industries and Public Enterprises
(2) Ministry of Environment, Forest and Climate Change
(3) Ministry of Personnel, Public Grievances and Pensions
(4) Ministry of Corporate Affairs
(5) Ministry of New and Renewable Energy

185. The 91st Academy Awards ceremony will honor the best films of 2018 and will take place at the Dolby Theatre in-
(1) Tokyo (2) Los Angeles
(3) Paris (4) Sydney
(5) London

186. The global Multidimensional Poverty Index (MPI) is an international measure of acute poverty covering over 100 developing countries. Global Multidimensional Poverty Index given by-
(1) UNESCO (2) UNCTAD
(3) UNDP (4) OECD
(5) UNEP

187. Under the Liberalised Remittance Scheme, Authorised Dealers may freely allow remittances by resident individuals up to USD .... per Financial Year for any permitted current or capital account transaction or a combination of both.

(1) USD 3,00,000 (2) USD 3,50,000
(3) USD 2,00,000 (4) USD 2,50,000
(5) USD 1,00,000

188. Digital wallet company Paytm has launched 'Paytm Money' app for mutual fund investments. The Paytm Money platform will be offering systematic investment plans (SIPs), starting at how much rupees per month?

(1) Rs. 300 (2) Rs. 400
(3) Rs. 200 (4) Rs. 500
(5) Rs. 100

189. Which of the following organisation has approved a $25-30 billion commitment plan for India for the 2019-22 period?

(1) United Nations (2) World Bank
(3) UNCTAD
(4) New Development Bank
(5) International Monetary Fund

190. Government has announced to fix MSP at a level of at least   per cent of the cost of production for kharif crops 2018-19 which redeems the promise made in the Union Budget for 2018-19.

(1) 50 per cent (2) 250 per cent
(3) 200 per cent (4) 100 per cent
(5) 150 per cent

Answers With Explanations

1. (4) 'Serve' is the most appropriate word to fill the blank.
2. (1)
3. (2)
4. (3)
5. (2)
6. (2)
7. (3) BCA will be the correct sequence.
8. (2)
9. (4)
10. (5)
11. (3)
12. (4) 'Standards' is the most appropriate word to fill the blank.
13. (4) BAC will be the correct option.
14. (5)
15. (3)
16. (3)
17. (2)
18. (5)
19. (5)
20. (4)
21. (5)
22. (2)
23. (3)
24. (4)
25. (5)
26. (3)
27. (3)
28. (4)
29. (5)
30. (4)
31. (2)
32. (4)
33. (3)
34. (2) The correct sequence is **BDCAE**.
35. (5) The correct sequence is **BADCE**.
36. (4)
37. (5)
38. (2)
39. (1)
40. (4)

For questions (41-44):

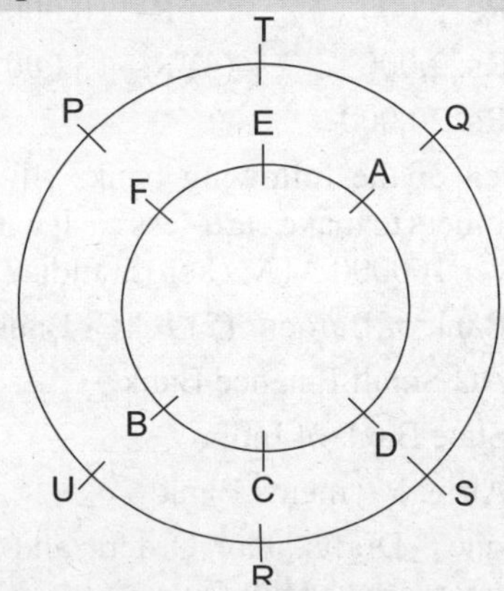

41. (4)
42. (5)
43. (1)
44. (5)
45. (1)

Floors	Persons
6.	D
5.	F
4.	B
3.	A
2.	C

1.	E

46. (3) ALIGNED, DEALING

For questions (47-49):

In the given Input-Output question the logic is—

For step I. All the digits of the given numbers are arranged in ascending order within the numbers.

For Step II. All the numbers obtained in step I are arranged in ascending order from the left end.

For Step III. First and last digits of the numbers are omitted.

For step IV. The digits of the numbers obtained in step III are added.

47. (3)
48. (3)
49. (4)
50. (3)

For questions (51-54):

Box	Chocolate
Q	175
S	250
T	190
U	210
P	280
R	119

51. (1)
52. (2)
53. (4)
54. (4)
55. (3)

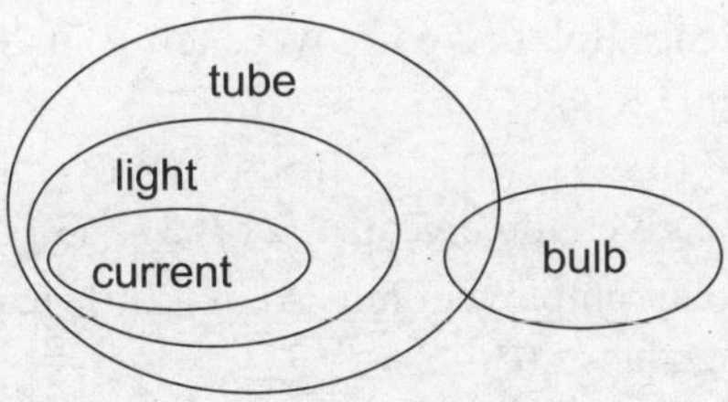

56. (4)

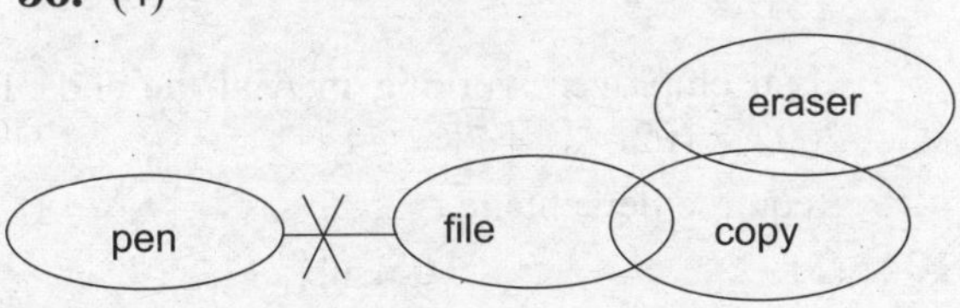

57. (4)

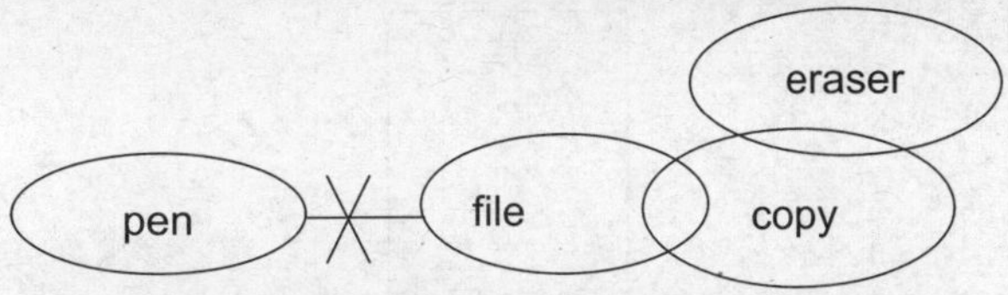

For questions (58-61):

Years	Ages	Persons	Colour
1946	73	M	White
1958	61	L	Red
1963	56	K	Yellow
1971	48	N	Orange
1994	25	J	Pink
2006	13	O	Black

58. (4)
59. (3)
60. (4)
61. (1)
62. (3)

N	Q	L/O	M	O/L	P

63. (4)
64. (3)

For questions (65-68):

Months↓/Date→	5th	12th	21st
March (31)	K	C	H
May (31)	D	F	L
September (30)	J	E	B
November (30)	A	M	G

65. (1)
66. (4)
67. (4)
68. (4)
69. (5)

0	1	2	3	4	5	6	7	8	9
A	A	B	A	B	C	A	B	C	D

70. (1)
71. (4)
72. (2)
73. (5)

For questions (74-77):

Persons
A
Z
D
H

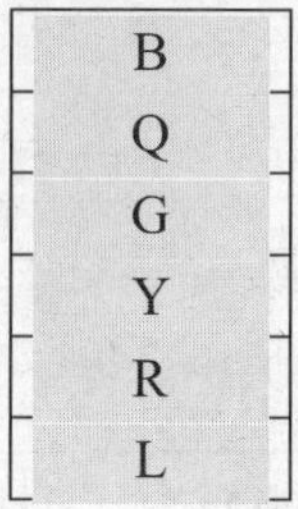

74. (2) **76.** (1)

75. (2) **77.** (1)

Solutions (78-80):

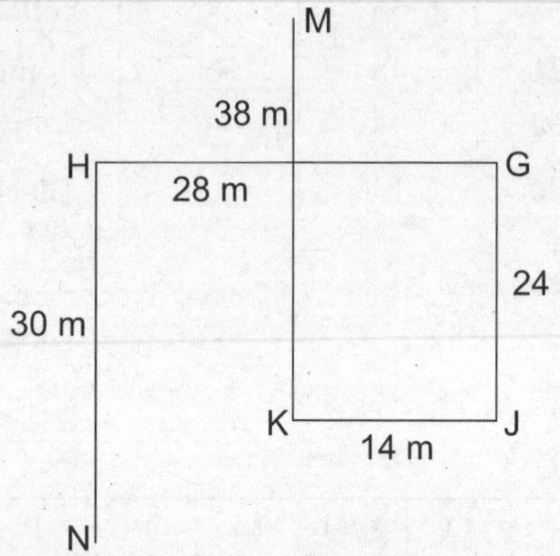

78. (5) **83.** (1)

79. (2) **84.** (5)

80. (3) **85.** (3)

81. (2) **86.** (3)

82. (4) **87.** (3)

For questions (88-90):

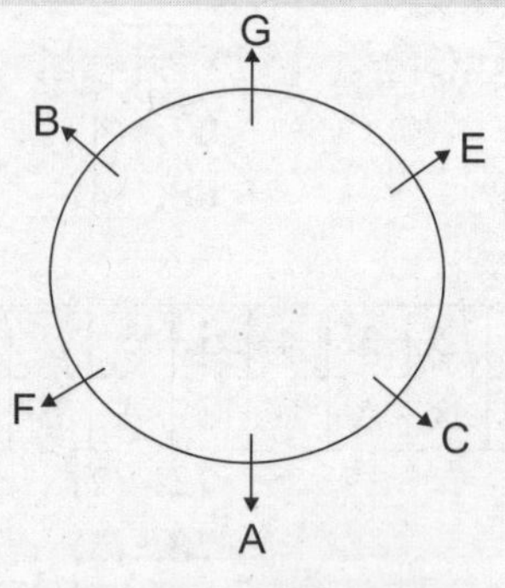

88. (5) **90.** (2)

89. (4)

91. (1) Efficiency ratio of A and B = 2 : 1

QUANTITY 1: Time taken by B = 45/2

QUANTITY 2: Efficiency of C = 3

$\therefore$ Time taken by C = 15/2 days

QUANTITY 1 > QUANTITY 2

92. (3) **94.** (1)

93. (1)

95. (5) There will be two numbers 73 and 37 whose product of digits is 21.

So if we take 73 then

Quantity 1 > Quantity 2

And if we take 37 then, Quantity 2 > Quantity 1

So no relation can be established.

96. (3) **99.** (5)

97. (3) **100.** (4)

98. (2)

101. (2) Let total employee who left B and C in the year 2002 be $7a$ and $9a$ respectively.

$172 + 84 - 36 + 108 - 9a + 124 - 28 = 406$

$9a = 424 - 406$

$9a = 18$

$a = 2$

Employee left B in 2002 = 14

Hence, total employee working in B at the end of 2002 = 160 + 96 − 18 + 72 − 14 = 296

102. (1) Total employee working in B at the end of 2000 = 220 − 28 + 32 = 224

Let total employee left B in 2002 and 2003 together be $6x$ and $7x$ respectively.

$224 + 96 - 18 + 72 - 6x + 144 - 7x = 466$

$13x = 518 - 466$

$13x = 52$

Hence, total 52 employees left B in 2002 and 2003 together.

103. (3) Total employee left A in the given three years = 21 × 3 = 63

Total employee left A in 2001 and 2003 together = 63 – 24 = 39

Total employee left A in 2001 = 39 × 7/13 = 21

Total employee working in A at the end of 2002 = 102 – 21 + 78 – 24 = 135

Required percentage = 25%

104. (5) **105.** (1)

106. (1) I. $2x^2 + 11x + 15 = 0$

$2x^2 + 6x + 5x + 15 = 0$

$$2x(x + 3) + 5(x + 3) = 0$$
$$(x + 3)(2x + 5) = 0$$
$$x = -3, -5/2$$
II. $4y^2 + 13y + 9 = 0$
$$4y^2 + 4y + 9y + 9 = 0$$
$$(y + 1)(4y + 9) = 0$$
$$y = -1, -9/4$$
$$y > x$$

107. (5) I. $x^2 - 36x + 324 = 0$
$$x^2 - 18x - 18x + 324 = 0$$
$$(x - 18)^2 = 0$$
$$x = 18, 18$$
II. $y^2 - 35y + 216 = 0$
$$y^2 - 27y - 8y + 216 = 0$$
$$(y - 27)(y - 8) = 0$$
$$y = 278$$
No relation

108. (3)
109. (1)

110. (4) I. $x^2 + 72 = 108$ $x^2 = 108 - 72 = 36$
$$x = \pm 6$$
II. $y^3 + 581 = 365$
$$y^3 = -216$$
$$y = -6$$
$$x \geq y$$

111. (2) I. $8x^2 + 58x + 39 = 0$
$$8x^2 + 52x + 6x + 39 = 0$$
$$4x(2x + 13) + 3(2x + 13) = 0$$
$$x = (-13)/2, (-3)/4$$
II. $8y^2 - 14y - 15 = 0$
$$8y^2 - 20y + 6y - 15 = 0$$
$$4y(2y - 5) + 3(2y - 5) = 0$$
$$y = 5/2, (-3)/4$$
$$y \geq x$$

112. (2)
113. (2)
114. (5)
115. (4)
116. (2)
117. (3)
118. (3)
119. (4)
120. (4)
121. (5)
122. (1)
123. (2)
124. (1)
125. (4)
126. (3)
127. (3)
128. (1)
129. (4)
130. (1)
131. (4)
132. (3)
133. (1)
134. (2)
135. (4)
136. (2)
137. (4)
138. (1)
139. (2)
140. (1)

141. (1) Two Indians Bharat Vatwani and Sonam Wangchuk are among the winners of this year's Ramon Magsaysay Award 2018, regarded as the Asian version of the Nobel Prize.

142. (4)
143. (3)
144. (5)

145. (4) Thailand chaired the first 2019 summit of the Association of Southeast Asian Nations.

146. (3)
147. (2)
148. (1)

149. (4) The river flows through the states of Chhattisgarh and Odisha.

150. (1)

151. (5) Aaron James Finch is an Australian international cricketer who captains the Australian cricket team in limited overs cricket.

152. (3) Punjab National Bank (PNB's) managing director and chief executive, Sunil Mehta was elected as new chairman of Indian Banks Association (IBA) for year 2018-19.

153. (2) Deepak Parekh is the Chairman of HDFC, India's leading housing finance company.

154. (5)
155. (4)
156. (2)
157. (3)
158. (1)
159. (4)
160. (2)

161. (5) Brazil to host the 11th BRICS Summit, scheduled for October 2019.

162. (1)

163. (3) The minimum paid-up equity capital for small finance banks shall be Rs. 100 crore.

164. (5)

165. (4) The World Bank launched bond-I.

166. (3)
167. (2)

168. (1) As per the Census, 2011 the child sex ratio (0-6 years) has shown a decline from 927 females per thousand males in 2001 to 919 females per thousand males in 2011.

169. (2)

170. (5)

171. (1) There is no court fee payable when a matter is filed in a Lok Adalat.

172. (4)

173. (3)

174. (4)

175. (1)

176. (3)

177. (5) Indian Air Force (IAF) for first time will participate in multinational air exercise Pitch Black – 18 (PB-18) in Australia hosted Royal Australian Air Force (RAAF).

178. (2)

179. (5)

180. (4)

181. (3)

182. (2)

183. (1)

184. (1)

185. (2)

186. (3)

187. (4)

188. (5)

189. (2)

190. (5)

IBPS Clerk Prelims, 2019

(Held on 7 December, 2019)

Based on Memory

Reasoning Ability

Directions (1-5): *Study the following information carefully and answer the questions given below:*

Eight persons A, B, C, D, E, F, G and H are going to watch movie in different months *i.e.* January, April. May, June, July, August, October and December but not necessarily in the same order.

F was going to watch movie in the month which has 30 days. There are three persons watching movie between F and C. H watches the movie just before A, who is watching the movie before B. B watches the movie just before C. H is watching the movie in the month which has maximum number of days but not in January. D is watching the movie in the month which has 30 days. G is watching the movie after D.

1. If E is related to F and H is related to C then, in the same way D is related to which of the following?

(1) H (2) F
(3) C (4) B
(5) A

2. Which of the following statement is true as per the given information?

(1) D is going to watch movie after F
(2) Two persons are watching movie between G and B
(3) B is watching the movie in January
(4) A is watching the movie in August
(5) None is true

3. The number of persons watching the movie between D and F is same as between B and?

(1) E (2) F
(3) H (4) A
(5) None of these

4. Four of the following five are alike in a certain way and hence they form a group. Which one of the following does not belong to that group?

(1) H (2) D
(3) C (4) B
(5) G

5. How many persons are watching the movie between B and D?

(1) Five (2) Three
(3) Four (4) Two
(5) None

Directions (6-10): *Study the following information carefully and answer the questions given below:*

A certain number of persons are sitting in a row facing in north direction. Four persons are sitting between P and Q. F sits second to the right of Q. One person sits between F and S. S sits at eighth position from one of the extreme ends. D sits third to the right of S. H sits fifth to the left of Q. Eight persons are sitting to the left of Q.

6. What is the maximum possible number of persons are sitting in a row?

(1) Twenty (2) Twenty-two
(3) Twenty-six (4) None of these
(5) Twenty-five

7. How many persons are sitting between P and S?

(1) Three (2) Five
(3) None (4) Two
(5) More than five

8. What is the position of D with respect to F?

(1) Fifth to the left
(2) Sixth to the right
(3) Second to the left
(4) Fifth to the right
(5) None of these

9. How many persons are sitting to the left of H?

(1) One (2) Three
(3) Two (4) Four
(5) None of these

10. If A is sitting exactly in between the P and D, then what is the position of A with respect to S?
(1) Third to the left
(2) None of these
(3) Third to the right
(4) Second to the left
(5) Second to the right

11. In the word 'CHLORINE', how many pairs of the letters have the same number of letters between them in the word as in alphabet?
(1) Four (2) Two
(3) One (4) Three
(5) More than four

Directions (12-15): *In each of the questions below are given some statements followed by some conclusions. You have to take the given statements to be true even if they seem to be at variance with commonly known facts. Read all the conclusions and then decide which of the given conclusions logically follows from the given statements disregarding commonly known facts.*

(1) If only conclusion I follows.
(2) If only conclusion II follows.
(3) If either conclusion I or II follows.
(4) If neither conclusion I nor II follows.
(5) If both conclusions I and II follow.

12. Statements: Only a few home is picnic. No picnic is mystery. All mystery is real.
Conclusions:
I. Some mystery are not picnic.
II. All home being picnic is a possibility.

13. Statements: Only a few strong is tough. Only a few tough is dark
Conclusions:
I. Some strong is not dark.
II. No tough is strong.

14. Statements: No network is dull. Only a few dull is fast. All fast is memory.
Conclusions:
I. Some memory are definitely not network.
II. Some dull are not network.

15. Statements: All tennis is football. All football is basketball. No basketball is cricket.
Conclusions:
I. No football is cricket.
II. All tennis is basketball.

Directions (16-20): *Study the following information carefully and answer the questions given below:*

Twelve persons are sitting in the two parallel rows containing six persons in each row in such a way that there is an equal distance between adjacent persons. In the first row, A, B, C, D, E and F are seated and all of them are facing north. In the second row, P, Q, R, S, T and U are seated and all of them are facing south. Therefore, in the given seating arrangement, each member seated in a row faces another member of the other row.

E sits 4th to the right of B. Q faces to E. The number of persons sit to the left of Q is same as sit to the right of S. F sits immediate to the left of D. A sits to the left of C and to the right of F. P faces the one who is an immediate neighbor of A. U is the only neighbor of Q. R sits to the right of T.

16. Four of the following five are alike in a certain way and hence they form a group. Which one of the following does not belong to that group?
(1) R (2) P
(3) U (4) C
(5) B

17. Who among the following faces to F?
(1) P (2) U
(3) S (4) R
(5) Either (1) or (3)

18. What is the position of F with respect to B?
(1) Immediate to the left
(2) 2nd to the left
(3) 3rd to the right
(4) 4th to the left
(5) Immediate to the right

19. Which of the following is true as per the given information?
(1) S sits to the immediate right of P
(2) U faces to A

(3) F sits at the extreme end
(4) Both (2) and (3) true
(5) All are true

20. Who among the following sits 3rd to the right T?
(1) U (2) None of these
(3) S (4) P
(5) R

Directions (21-25): *Study the following information carefully and answer the questions given below:*

Eight persons *i.e.* F, J, K, M, N, P, S and V are sitting around a square table. Four of them are sitting at the corners and remaining are sitting at the middle side of the table. The persons sitting at the corners faces away from the center and the persons sitting at the middle sides of the table faces towards the center. All the information is not necessarily in the same order.

F sits at the middle side of the table. N sits at the immediate left of V. Two persons sit between F and J. V sits at the immediate right of J. Three persons sit between S and N. M is an immediate neighbor of S. M is not an immediate neighbor of J. P faces inside.

21. How many persons are sitting between F and J when counting from the left of F?
(1) One (2) Two
(3) Three (4) Four
(5) More than four

22. Four of the following five are alike in a certain way and hence form a group, which of the following does not belong to the group?
(1) S (2) F
(3) J (4) K
(5) N

23. Which of the following statement is true?
(1) P sits second to the left of V
(2) N is an immediate neighbor of S
(3) Two persons sit between P and V
(4) M sits opposite to N
(5) J sits opposite to K.

24. Who among the following is sitting second to the left of M?
(1) P (2) V
(3) J (4) F
(5) None of these

25. Who among the following is sitting opposite to P?
(1) V (2) J
(3) F (4) M
(5) None of these

Directions (26-28): *Study the following information carefully and answer the questions given below:*

There are seven members in a family of three generation. A is mother of P. P is brother of G. K is married to G. S is aunt of M. K is child of L. S is sister of K.

26. If L is married to J, then how J is related to G?
(1) Grand daughter (2) Grand son
(3) Son-in-law (4) Daughter-in-law
(5) Can't be determined

27. If A is married to R, then how R is related to M?
(1) Grand father (2) Brother-in-law
(3) Uncle (4) None of these
(5) Can't be determined

28. How S is related to G?
(1) Sister (2) Sister-in-law
(3) Aunt (4) Mother-in-law
(5) None of these

29. If it is possible to make only one meaningful word with the 2nd, 5th, 8th and 9th letters of the word 'TRANSLATION' which would be the second letter of the word from the left? If more than one such word can be formed give 'Y' as the answer. If no such word can be formed, give 'Z' as your answer.
(1) Y (2) S
(3) T (4) Z
(5) R

Directions (30-33): *These questions are based on the following arrangement. Study the arrangement carefully to answer these questions.*

R Q D 8 H 9 L O P T E F M 6 I A 7 J 5 4 B

U 2 G

30. If all the numbers are remove from the series, then which of the following element is 10th from the left end?

(1) R (2) F
(3) M (4) B
(5) U

31. How many alphabets according to the English dictionary are between the elements which is 7th from the left end and 9th from the right end?

(1) Five (2) Three
(3) Seven (4) Ten
(5) Eight

32. Which of the following element is 3rd from the right of the element which is 11th from the left end?

(1) M (2) I
(3) A (4) 6
(5) R

33. How many such numbers are there in the above arrangement, each of which is immediately preceded by a consonant and also immediately followed by a consonant?

(1) Three (2) One
(3) Two (4) Four
(5) None of these

34. If in the number 485794362, 1 is added to each of the digit which is placed at even position and 1 is subtracted from each of the digit which is placed at odd position then how many digits are repeating in the number thus formed?

(1) Only 5 (2) Both 1 and 2
(3) Only 8 (4) Both 1 and 7
(5) None of these

35. Find the odd one out?

(1) BEH (2) JMP
(3) TWZ (4) CFI
(5) KOP

Numerical Ability

Directions (36-45): *Find the value of (?) in the following questions*

36. $\sqrt{124} + ? + 169 = 18$

(1) 34 (2) 31
(3) 33 (4) 35
(5) 32

37. $136 \div 2^2 \times ? = 17\%$ of $500 \div 10$

(1) 0.75 (2) 1.33
(3) 0.25 (4) 1.66
(5) 0.5

38. $115 \div 5 + 12 \times 6 = ? + 64 \div 4 - 35$

(1) 114 (2) 118
(3) 108 (4) 116
(5) 111

39. 41% of 600 − 250 = ? −77% of 900

(1) 693 (2) 675
(3) 684 (4) 679
(5) 689

40. $360/? = 73 + 3^3$

(1) 3.4 (2) 4.3
(3) 3.1 (4) 3.6
(5) 3.9

41. $\frac{1}{2} - \frac{3}{5} + 4\frac{2}{3} = ?\ \frac{5}{6}$

(1) $3\frac{11}{15}$ (2) $5\frac{11}{15}$
(3) $3\frac{11}{12}$ (4) $2\frac{11}{12}$
(5) $4\frac{11}{15}$

42. $65 \times 3 \div 13 + 67 - ?\ 2 = 81 \div 9 \times 2$

(1) 9 (2) 5
(3) 12 (4) 8
(5) 14

43. $(2744)^{1/3} + (18)^2 - 121 = ? - 69 \times 5$

(1) 658 (2) 568
(3) 666 (4) 656
(5) 562

44. $1111 \div 11 + 2002 \div 26 + 750 \div 25 = ?$

(1) 204 (2) 212
(3) 208 (4) 206
(5) 210

45. $\frac{5}{11} \times 121 + 1\frac{4}{9} \times 288 = 141 + ?$

(1) 333 (2) 327

(3) 335 (4) 330

(5) 329

Directions (46-50): *Given bar graph shows the number of residents residing in 4 societies in years 2008, 2018. Read the data carefully and answer the questions carefully.*

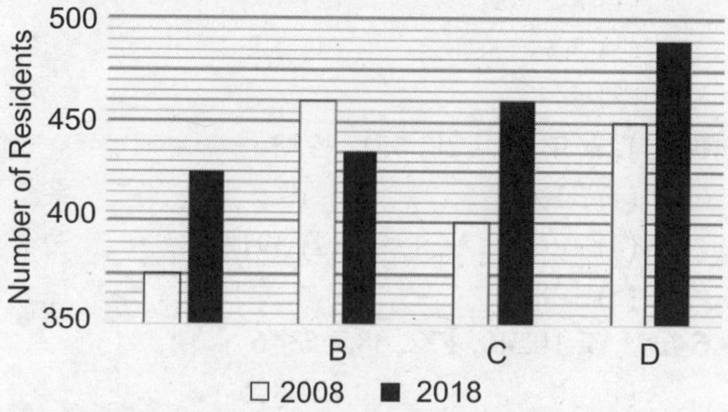

46. What is average of residents residing in society A in 2008, B in 2018, C in 2018 and D in 2008?

(1) 355 (2) 360

(3) 365 (4) 370

(5) 350

47. Residents residing in society B in 2008 are what percent more/less than average of residents residing in society D in 2008 and 2018?

(1) $5\frac{6}{11}\%$ (2) $3\frac{6}{11}\%$

(3) $6\frac{6}{11}\%$ (4) $7\frac{6}{11}\%$

(5) $4\frac{6}{11}\%$

48. Which society shows maximum percentage increase in no. of residents from year 2008 to 2018?

(1) Both A and C (2) Both A and D

(3) Both C and D (4) Both A and B

(5) None of these

49. What is ratio of all residents in all societies in 2008 to that of in 2018?

(1) 142 : 157 (2) 157 : 142

(3) 162 : 137 (4) 137 : 162

(5) 97 : 114

50. What is difference between number of residents residing in society A and B in 2018 together and that of in society C and D together in 2008?

(1) 30 (2) 24

(3) 20 (4) 28

(5) 26

51. A shopkeeper sells two pens, he sold 1 pen at profit and other pen at loss. SP of each of the two pens is Rs. 300 and profit percentage on 1 pen is equal to loss percentage on other. If overall loss of shopkeeper is 6.25%, then find difference between cost price of both pen.

(1) Rs. 350 (2) Rs. 100

(3) Rs. 240 (4) Rs. 160

(5) Rs. 300

52. A man received Rs. 3456 when he invested Rs. P at 12% p.a. at SI for 3 years. If he invested Rs. (P + 4400) at 15% p.a. at CI compounding annually for 2 years, then find the interest received by him.

(1) Rs. 4515 (2) Rs. 4960

(3) Rs. 4725 (4) Rs. 4185

(5) Rs. 4345

53. Time taken by a boat to cover 162 km each in downstream and in upstream is 14 hours and 24 minutes. If speed of stream is 6 km/hr., then find the time taken by boat to cover 240 km in upstream.

(1) $7\frac{1}{3}$ hours (2) $18\frac{2}{3}$ hours

(3) $9\frac{1}{3}$ hours (4) $16\frac{2}{3}$ hours

(5) $13\frac{1}{3}$ hours

54. C is 100% more efficient than B. A alone can complete a piece of work in 9 days and B and C together can complete the same work in 2^2 days. Find what portion of work will be completed, if A and B works together for 4 days.

(1) $\frac{13}{18}$ (2) $\frac{8}{9}$

(3) $\frac{5}{6}$ (4) $\frac{2}{3}$

(5) $\frac{17}{18}$

55. Ratio of age of P 2 years ago to age of R 2 years hence is 1 : 2 and Q's present age is 25% more than P's present age. If average of present age of P and R is 39 years, then find difference between P's age 5 years hence and R's present age.

(1) 12 years (2) 17 years

(3) 21 years (4) 15 years

(5) 14 years

Directions (56–60): *Solve the following quadratic equation and mark the answer as per instructions.*

56. **I.** $x^2 - 2x - 143 = 0$

II. $y^2 - 169 = 0$

(1) $x > y$ (2) $x < y$

(3) $x \leq y$ (4) $x \geq y$

(5) $x = y$ or no relation can be established

57. **I.** $x^2 - 7x - 18 = 0$

II. $y^2 - 19y + 90 = 0$

(1) $x \leq y$

(2) $x = y$ or no relation can be established

(3) $x > y$ (4) $x \geq y$

(5) $x < y$

58. **I.** $2x^2 + 5x + 3 = 0$

II. $y^2 + 4y - 12 = 0$

(1) $x \leq y$

(2) $x > y$

(3) $x = y$ or no relation can be established

(4) $x < y$ (5) $x \geq y$

59. **I.** $9x + 3y = 15$

II. $4x + 5y = 14$

(1) $x = y$ or no relation can be established

(2) $x > y$ (3) $x \leq y$

(4) $x < y$ (5) $x \geq y$

60. **I.** $2x^2 - x - 1 = 0$

II. $3y^2 - 5y + 2 = 0$

(1) $x \leq y$ (2) $x < y$

(3) $x = y$ or no relation can be established

(4) $x \geq y$ (5) $x > y$

Directions (61-65): *Find the wrong number in the following number series.*

61. 2, 3, 6, 15, 45, 156.5, 630

(1) 2 (2) 15

(3) 3 (4) 156.5

(5) 630

62. 36, 20, 12, 8, 6, 5.5, 4.5

(1) 8 (2) 36

(3) 5.5 (4) 4.5

(5) 6

63. 1, 3, 9, 31, 128, 651, 3913

(1) 31 (2) 3

(3) 1 (4) 3913

(5) 128

64. 2, 3, 10, 40, 172, 885, 5346

(1) 40 (2) 885

(3) 172 (4) 3

(5) 10

65. 5, 8, 16, 26, 50, 98, 194

(1) 5 (2) 194

(3) 8 (4) 16

(5) 98

66. A rectangular path of width 3 m is surrounding the garden whose length is 3 m more than its width. If cost of painting the path at rate of 0.5 Rs/m² is Rs. 273 then find the area of garden

(1) 1525 m² (2) 1804 m²

(3) 1776 m² (4) 1906 m²

(5) 1664 m²

67. In a class percentage of students who passed the exam is 60% and number of boys and girls who passed the exam is same. If boys who failed the exam are 200% more than girls who failed in exam then find the percentage of girls who failed out of total students

(1) 9% (2) 13%

(3) 10% (4) 12%

(5) 15%

68. A man invested Rs. X at 15% p.a. at SI for 4 years and Rs. (1.35 X) at 18% p.a. at SI for 3 years. If total interest received by man is Rs.

it would .... (81) for the more than 80 children present that day in a school in rural Uttar Pradesh (U.P.). This was somewhat similar to the one reported from U.P. a couple of months ago. In the earlier incident, a video showed plain chapatis being served with salt. The two videos made it to the national media; they also proved useful for the officers who .... (82) the mid-day meal scheme since they also depend on unauthorised video graphers to learn about the reality in schools. Each such revelation leads to the same (83) official statement: punish the guilty, locate the video-maker and deal with him/her. In the latest mid-meal story narrated above, authorities in U.P. have reportedly done the .... (84) needful, i.e. they have fired the apparent culprit who is a para-teacher.

79. (1) Balances (2) Stabilized
(3) Persistent (4) Stabilizing
(5) None of these.

80. (1) Stained (2) Retaliate
(3) Accusations (4) Blunder
(5) None of these.

81. (1) Suffice (2) Assent
(3) Patriotism (4) Benefit
(5) None of these.

82. (1) React (2) Negate
(3) Supervise (4) Unify
(5) None of these.

83. (1) Amalgamate (2) Reflexive
(3) Applicable (4) Unlikely
(5) None of these.

84. (1) Permit (2) Annihilate
(3) Customary (4) Stride
(5) None of these.

Directions (85-89): *Each question below has one blank, which is indicating that something has been omitted. Choose the most suitable option indicating the words that can be used to fill up the blank in the sentence to make it meaningfully complete.*

85. Maharashtra has been .... into a new party system over the past few years, with the BJP trying hard to replace the Congress as the dominant party in the State.
(*i*) Investigated (*ii*) Transitioning
(*iii*) Framing
(1) Only (*i*) (2) Only (*ii*)
(3) Both (*ii*) and (*iii*)
(4) Both (*i*) and (*ii*) (5) None of these

86. The theme song of Downton Abbey along with a panoramic shot of the imposing monarchic structure is enough to .... memories.
(*i*) Evoke (*ii*) Recall
(*iii*) Sent
(1) Only (*i*) (2) Only (*ii*)
(3) Both (*ii*) and (*iii*)
(4) Both (*i*) and (5) None of these

87. With tomato and onion prices continuing to soar, the Centre is considering a .... to increase cultivation of these staple vegetables in the north Indian region.
(*i*) Proposal (*ii*) Role
(*iii*) Novel
(1) Only (*i*) (2) Only (*ii*)
(3) Both (*ii*) and (*iii*)
(4) Both (*i*) and (*ii*) (5) None of these.

88. The Railways will speed up trains to reduce running time and maximise .... of infrastructure across its network.
(*i*) Collecting (*ii*) Effectiveness
(*iii*) Utilisation
(1) Only (*i*) (2) Only (*ii*)
(3) Both (*ii*) and (*iii*)
(4) Both (*i*) and (*ii*) (5) None of these

89. There could be more interest rate .... by the RBI as some of the members of the monetary policy committee have observed that growth is yet to bottom out
(*i*) Increment (*ii*) Cuts
(*iii*) Growths
(1) Only (*i*) (2) Only (*ii*)
(3) Both (*ii*) and (*iii*)
(4) Both (*i*) and (*ii*) (5) None of these

Directions (90-94): *In each of the questions given below four words are given in bold. These four words may or may not be in their correct position. The sentence is then followed by options with the correct combination of words that should replace each other in order to make the sentence* *grammatically and contextually correct. Find the correct combination of the words that replace each other. If the sentence is correct as it then select option (5) as your choice.*

90. Today, thermal **accounts** (A) capacity **generation** (B) for about two-thirds the **installed** (C) generation **capacity** (D) in the country.

(1) A-B (2) A-C
(3) B-D (4) C-D
(5) The sentence is correct

91. The IMF **followed** (A) the World Bank in **reducing** (B) its forecast for India's **economic** (C) growth in the current **financial** (D) year.

(1) A-B (2) A-C
(3) B-D (4) C-D
(5) The sentence is correct

92. In **pursuit** (A) of novel ways to draw **caught** (B) to the Big Prize, the **Academy** (C) seems to have been **attention** (D) on the wrong foot again.

(1) A-B (2) A-C
(3) B-D (4) C-B
(5) The sentence is correct

93. With **power** (A) growth, the **demand** (B) for **economic** (C) in India is only going to **increase** (D) further.

(1) A-B (2) A-C
(3) B-D (4) C-D
(5) The sentence is correct

94. The Air Quality Index of Delhi **worsened** (A) slightly and **expected** (B) in the "poor" category and is **stayed** (C) to further **deteriorate** (D) from the last week of the month.

(1) A-B (2) A-C
(3) B-C (4) C-D
(5) The sentence is correct

Directions (95-100): *The following questions consist of a sentence. Four of the words of the sentences are marked in bold, which may or may not be correctly spelled. Option corresponding to misspelt word is your answer. If there is no misspelled word in the sentence then choose (5), i.e., 'All are correct' as your answer.*

95. **Education**, for most of us, is a necessary public good central to the task of nation **building** and, like fresh air, is **neccessary** to make our **communities** come alive.

(1) Education (2) Building
(3) Neccessary (4) Communities
(5) All are correct

96. The Budget's **provisons** for collecting more in taxes from the **incomes** of the super-rich were aimed at **redistributing** wealth to bring about more **equitable** development.

(1) Provisons (2) Incomes
(3) Redistributing (4) Equitable
(5) All are correct

97. Ideas **rejected** more than two **decades** ago during the **liberalisaetion** phase are back in **circulation**.

(1) Rejected (2) Decades
(3) Liberalisaetion (4) Circulation
(5) All are correct

98. The proposal to **establish** a National Research Foundation, with an "**overarching** goal to enable a culture of research to **permeate** through our universities" needs to be **applauded** and widely supported.

(1) Establish (2) Overarching
(3) Permeate (4) Applauded
(5) All are correct

99. **Policymaking** has three **essenteal** ingredients: technical elements, **administrative** inputs and political goals and **packaging.**

(1) Policymaking (2) Essenteal
(3) Administrative (4) Packaging
(5) All are correct

100. The Central **Bureou** of Investigation has set up an Online Child Sexual **Abuse** and **Exploitation** Prevention/**Investigation** Unit.

(1) Bureou (2) Abuse
(3) Exploitation (4) Investigation
(5) All are correct

Answers With Explanations

For questions (1-5):

Month	Persons
January	E
April	D
May	G
June	F
July	H
August	A
October	B
December	C

1. (1)
2. (4)
3. (3)
4. (2)
5. (3)

For questions (6-10):

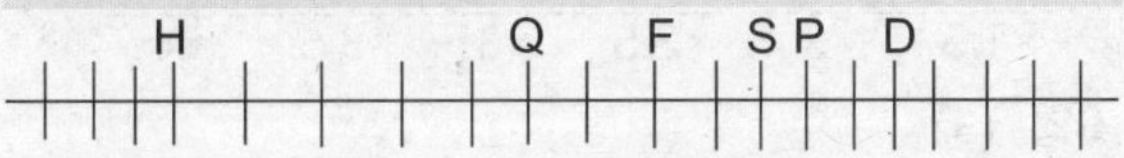

6. (1)
7. (3)
8. (4)
9. (2)
10. (5)
11. (3)

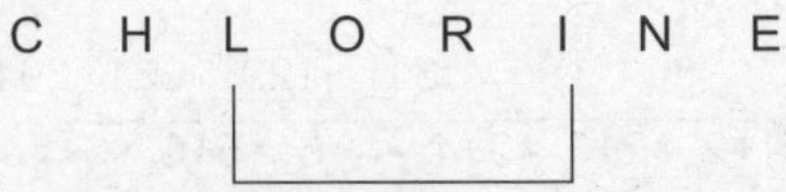

For questions (12-15):

12. (1)

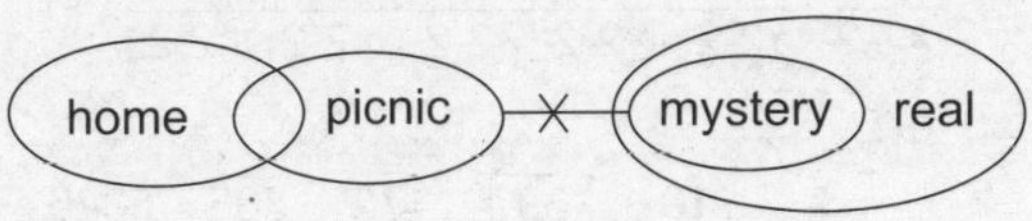

13. (4)

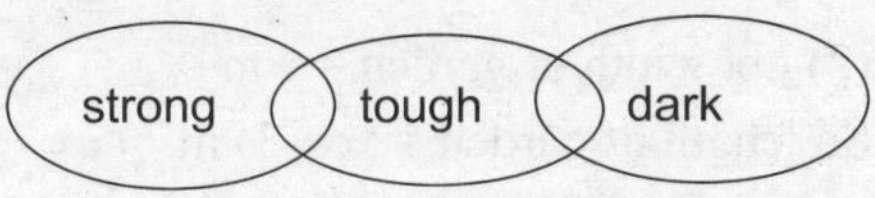

14. (5)

15. (5)

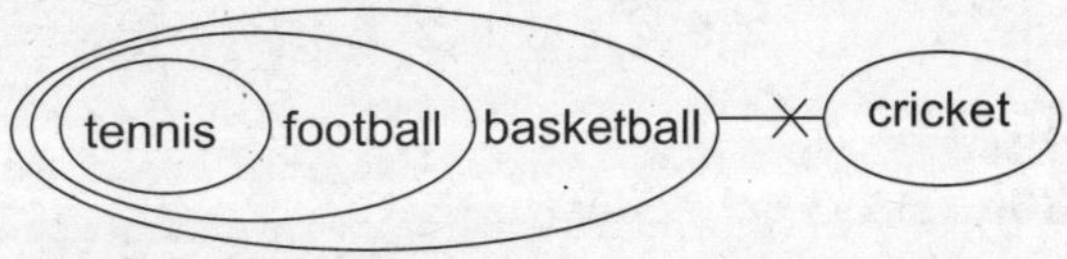

For questions (16-20):

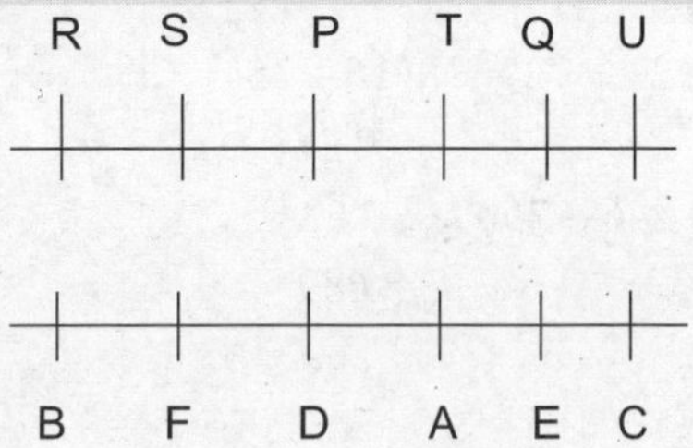

16. (2)
17. (3)
18. (5)
19. (1)
20. (5)

For questions (21-25):

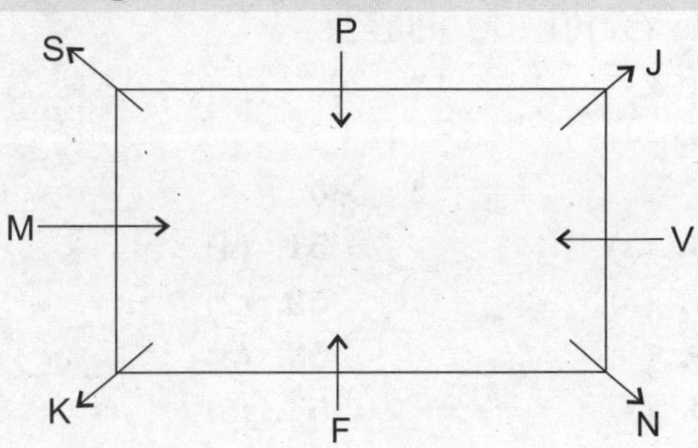

21. (4)
22. (2)
23. (5)
24. (1)
25. (3)

For questions (26-28):

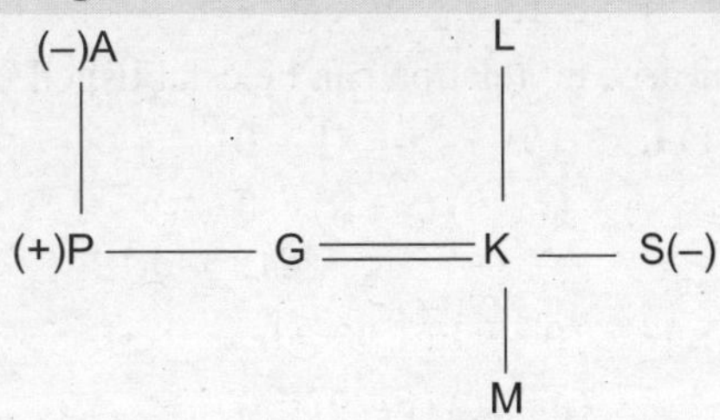

26. (5)
27. (1)
28. (2)
29. (3)

For questions (30-33):

30. (2)

31. (4)

32. (4)

33. (3)

34. (3)

4 8 5 7 9 4 3 6 2
3 9 4 8 8 5 2 7 1

35. (5)

36. (2) $293 + ? = 324$

$? = 31$

37. (3)

38. (1) $23 + 72 = ? + 16 - 35$

$? = 114$

39. (5) $246 - 250 = ? - 693$

$? = 689$

40. (4)

41. (1)

42. (4) $15 + 67 - ?^2 = 18$

$? = 8$

43. (5) $14 + 324 - 121 = ? - 345$

$? = 562$

44. (3) $101 + 77 + 30 = ?$

$? = 208$

45. (4) $55 + 416 = 141 + ?$

$? = 330$

46. (2)

47. (5)

48. (1)

49. (4)

50. (3)

51. (4)

52. (2)

53. (5)

54. (5)

55. (2)

56. (5) **I.** $x^2 - 13x + 11x - 143 = 0$

$(x - 13)(x + 11) = 0$ $x = -11, 13$

II. $y^2 = 169$

$y = \pm 13$

clearly, no relation can be established

57. (1) **I.** $x^2 - 9x + 2x - 18 = 0$

$(x - 9)(x + 2) = 0$

$x = -2, 9$

II. $y^2 - 10y - 9y + 90 = 0$

$(y - 10)(y - 9) = 0$

$y = 9, 10$

clearly, $x \leq y$

58. (3) **I.** $2x^2 + 3x + 2x + 3 = 0$

$(x + 1)(2x + 3) = 0$

$x = -1, -\frac{3}{2}$

II. $y^2 + 6y - 2y - 12 = 0$

$(y - 2)(y + 6) = 0$

$y = 2, -6$

clearly, no relation can be established

59. (4) (*ii*) × 9 – (*i*) × 4

On solving, $x = 1, y = 2$

clearly, $x < y$

60. (3) **I.** $2x^2 - 2x + x - 1 = 0$

$(2x + 1)(x - 1) = 0$

$x = -\frac{1}{2}, 1$

II. $3y^2 - 3y - 2y + 2 = 0$

$(3y - 2)(y - 1) = 0$

$y = \frac{2}{3}, 1$

clearly, no relation

61. (4)

2 3 6 15 45 [157.5] 630
×1.5 ×2 ×2.5 ×3 ×3.5 ×4

62. (3)

36 20 12 8 6 [5] 4.5
–16 –8 –4 –2 –1 –0.5
÷2 ÷2 ÷2 ÷2

63. (5)

1 3 9 31 [129] 651 3913
×1+2 ×2+3 ×3+4 ×4+5 ×5+6 ×6+7

64. (1)

5 8 [14] 26 50 98 194
×2-2 ×2-2 ×2-2 ×2-2 ×2-2 ×2-2

65. (4)

2 3 10 [39] 172 885 5346
$\times1+1^2$ $\times2+2^2$ $\times3+3^2$ $\times4+4^2$ $\times5+5^2$ $\times6+6^2$

66. (2) Let width of garden = x m

So length of garden = $(x + 3)$ m

According to the question

$(x + 6)(x + 9) - x(x + 3) = 273/0.5$

$x^2 + 15x + 54 - x^2 - 3x = 546$

$12x + 54 = 546$

$x = 41$

Area of garden $= 41 \times 44$

$= 1804\ m^2$

67. (3) Let total students be $100x$

Then passed students be $60x$

Passed boys and girls are $30x$ each.

Let failed girls $= y$

$y + 3y = 40x\ 4y = 40x$

$y = 10x$

Required percentage = 10%

68. (5)

70. (3)

69. (5)

71. (1) From first paragraph, 'The balance of an ecosystem depends on the presence of every type of animal. If one type of animal becomes too numerous or scarce, the entire balance of the ecosystem will change.'

72. (4) From second paragraph, 'Carnivores will feed on herbivores, omnivores, and other carnivores in an ecosystem. A natural community depends on the presence of carnivores to control the populations of other animals.'

73. (3) From last part of second paragraph, 'Carnivores depend on sufficient prey in the food chain to give them the food they need. If the herbivore population or the population of other carnivores declines in an ecosystem, carnivores may not survive.'

74. (5)

75. (2)

76. (2)

77. (3)

78. (1)

79. (2)

80. (4)

81. (1)

82. (3)

83. (2)

84. (3)

85. (2)

86. (4)

87. (1)

88. (3)

89. (2)

90. (1)

91. (5)

92. (3)

93. (2)

94. (3)

95. (3) Correct word is 'Necessary'.

96. (1) Correct word is 'Provisions'.

97. (3) Correct word is 'Liberalisation'.

98. (5) There is no spelling error.

99. (2) Correct word is 'essential'.

100. (1) Correct word is 'Bureau'.

IBPS Clerk Mains, 2019

(Held on 19 December, 2020)

Based on Memory

Reasoning Aptitude

Directions (1-5): *Study the following information carefully and answer the questions given below:*

Eight persons sit in a row such that some of them are facing in the north direction and some are facing in the south direction.

Note: No two adjacent persons are sitting according to the English alphabetical series for example, P is not an immediate neighbor of both O and Q, and so on.

C sits third from one of the extreme ends of the row. A sits third to the left of C. Only one person sits between A and B. Three persons sit between D and E. As many persons sit to the left of E as to the left of H. H faces north direction. Immediate neighbors of C face same direction. Persons sitting at the extreme end faces the same direction. G sits to the left of F. E faces opposite direction as A. Immediate neighbors of G faces the opposite direction. G does not face north direction.

1. How many persons sit between B and E?
(1) One (2) Two
(3) Three (4) Four
(5) More than four

2. Who among the following sits third to the right of H?
(1) F (2) E
(3) D (4) G
(5) A

3. Four of the following five are alike in a certain way and hence form a group which of the following does not belong to the group?
(1) FC (2) CH
(3) GA (4) DC
(5) HE

4. How many persons face south direction?
(1) Four (2) Two
(3) Three (4) One
(5) More than four

5. Which of the following statement is not true?
(1) H sits immediate left of E
(2) A sits between H and C
(3) D sits at an extreme end
(4) C sits immediate left of F.
(5) No one sits between A and G.

Directions (6-7): *In each of the questions below. Some statements are given followed by conclusions/ group of conclusions. You have to assume all the statements to be true even if they seem to be at variance from the commonly known facts and then decide which of the given conclusion given in the options logically follow from the information given in the statements:*

6. Statements: Only a few paint is color. No color is fabric. Only a few fabric is enamel.
(1) Some fabric is paint
(2) All paint can be fabric
(3) All enamel can be color
(4) Some paint is enamel
(5) All color can be paint

7. Statements: Only a few brush is nail. Only a few home is buyer. Some buyer is nail.
(1) Some buyer is not nail.
(2) Some nail is not home
(3) All brush is buyer
(4) Some brush is not nail.
(5) All home can be buyer.

Directions (8-10): *Digits in the number given in each of the following questions are to be coded based on the codes and the conditions given below:*

Elements	V	7	#	T	&	U	2	E	A

Codes	1	@	*n*	9	*h*	*	*f*	!	$

Conditions:

I. If first element is even number and last element is symbol then the codes for both of them is interchanged.

II. If any vowel is preceded by an odd number then their codes will be code of the odd number.

III. If the first element is odd number and last element is consonant then their codes will be the code of the first element.

IV. If any consonant is succeeded by symbol then their codes will be the code of the symbol.

Note: In each case either no or one or more than one condition is followed.

8. What is the code for 27AU#?

(1) n@$fn (2) n@@*f
(3) f@@*f (4) f@@*n
(5) n$@nf

9. What is the code for 7VU&A?

(1) @1*h$ (2) $1*h@
(3) $1*h$ (4) @1*h@
(5) None of these

10. What is the code for 7T&2V?

(1) @h9f@ (2) @hh@f
(3) @hhf@ (4) 1h9f@
(5) 1h9f1

Directions (11-13): *In each of the questions below. Some statements are given followed by conclusions/ group of conclusions. You have to assume all the statements to be true even if they seem to be at variance from the commonly known facts and then decide which of the given conclusion given in the options logically follow from the information given in the statements:*

11. Statements: Some nail is paint. Only a few paint is oil. All oil is dark.

(1) No dark is paint
(2) Some dark can be nail.
(3) Some paint can be dark.
(4) Some oil is nail.
(5) Some oil is not paint.

12. Statements: Only a few brush is wallet. All brush is money. Some money is enamel.

(1) Some enamel is wallet.
(2) Some money is not brush.
(3) All brush can be wallet.
(4) Some enamel is not money.
(5) All wallet can be brush.

13. Statements: No nail is pain. Nobody is pain. Only a few pain is arm.

(1) Some arm is body.
(2) Some body is nail.
(3) All nail can be arm.
(4) Some arm is not pain.
(5) All arm can be body.

14. Six persons A, B, C, D, E and F go to office on six different days of the week from Monday to Saturday. A go before Wednesday. Only two persons go between A and D. Three persons go between D and F. B goes after D. E goes before D but not immediately before D. In which of the following days C go to office?

(1) Monday (2) Tuesday
(3) Wednesday (4) Thursday
(5) None of these

Directions (15-19): *Study the following information carefully and answer the questions given below:*

Eight persons A, B, C, D, E, F, G and H sits around a circular table facing towards the center of the table. All of them go to eight different cities.

Only one person sits between F and the one who go to Pune. Three persons sit between the one who go to Pune and the one who go to Mumbai. D sits third to the left of the one who go to Pune. The one who is from Chennai sits second to the right of D. Three persons sit between the one who go to Chennai and the one who go to Bengaluru. H sits second to the right of G. H go to Delhi. G sits third to the left of A. The one who go to Chandigarh sits third to the left of G. B sits immediate right of the person who go to Jaipur. C does not go to Mumbai and Kolkata. E does not go to Chandigarh.

15. Who among the following go to Chandigarh?

(1) A (2) C
(3) D (4) B

(5) G

16. How many persons sit between A and G when counted from right of G?

(1) Two (2) Three
(3) Four (4) Five
(5) One

17. Who among the following sits second to the left of the one who is from Chennai?

(1) G (2) A
(3) D (4) B
(5) C

18. F go to which of the following city?

(1) Mumbai (2) Jaipur
(3) Bengaluru (4) Chennai
(5) Kolkata

19. Which of the following is true regarding B?

(1) B sits immediate left of D
(2) B go to Chennai
(3) B sits third right of A.
(4) C is immediate neighbor of B.
(5) B go to Bengaluru.

Direction (20): *Study the following information care-fully and answer the questions given below:*

There are six persons of different weights. Three persons are heavier than Rohan. Two person's weight is in between Sohan and Geeta. Rajesh is heavier than Rakesh but lighter than Ram. Neither Rakesh nor Geeta is lightest person. Weight of 2nd heaviest person is 66kg. Weight of all persons are in whole numbers.

20. What is the weight of Sohan?

(1) 67 kg (2) 65 kg
(3) 64 kg (4) 63 kg
(5) 62 kg

Directions (21-24): *Study the following information carefully and answer the questions given below:*

P@Q: It means that P is in East of Q
P#Q: It means that P is in West of Q
P$Q: It means that P is in North of Q
P%Q: It means that P is in South of Q
P(7)$Q means that P is 7m North of Q
P$@Q means that P is in North-east of Q

Paul and Raj are starting their journey from point V and U respectively and both reaches at point W as per the given information-

Paul- R(13)#V, S(8)%R, T(5)@S, X(4)%T, Y(10)#X, W(15)$Y

Raj- J(5)#U, K(11)$J, L(11)@K, M(4)$L, N(5)@M, W(10)%N

21. If point A(2)%R then, what is the direction and shortest distance of A with respect to U?

(1) A(15)$@U (2) A(16)@U
(3) A(16)$@U (4) A(15)@U
(5) None of these

22. Which of the following is true?

(1) M$@X (2) U%@N
(3) U#R (4) J%#V
(5) None is true

23. If B(5)@L and C(8)#W are true then, what is the shortest distance between B and C?

(1) 5 m (2) 10 m
(3) 15m (4) 20 m
(5) None of these

24. U is in which direction with respect to V?

(1) U$@V (2) U%@V
(3) U%#V (4) U#V
(5) None is true

Directions (25-29): *Study the following information carefully and answer the questions given below:*

Eleven persons buy things one after another. Only five persons buy things after P. Three persons buy things between P and Q. R buy things after S and before T. There are as many persons buy things before U as after V. More than three persons buy things between W and X who buy things just after P. Y buy things before Z and after R. No one buy things after T. Y buy things just after V. U buys after Q.

25. Who among the following buy things between X and Z?

(1) U and Y (2) U and V
(3) V and Y (4) P and Y
(5) None of these

26. Four of the following five are alike in certain way and hence form a group, find the one which does not belong to that group?

(1) QR (2) UX

(3) WU (4) XY
(5) PY

27. Which of the following statement is true?
(1) R buy things before U
(2) More than two persons buy things before S
(3) No one buy things before Q
(4) P buy things after Z
(5) None is true

28. How many persons buy things between Y and R?
(1) Three (2) Five
(3) Seven (4) Four
(5) None of these

29. Who among the following buy things just after U?
(1) Q (2) R
(3) S (4) T
(5) None of these

Directions (30-32): *Study the following information carefully and answer the questions given below:*

A meaningful eight letter word is going to formed. No two letters of this word are same. There are three letters between S and N. C is 2nd to the left of U which is to the left of T. D is either at extreme left or at extreme right. There are at least two letters are between D and O which is immediate left of U. T is at immediate right of N. I is not at extreme end.

30. What is the position of I with respect to C?
(1) 3rd to the right (2) 3rd to the left
(3) 2nd to the right (4) 2nd to the left
(5) None of these

31. Which of the following letter is 2nd from extreme left end?
(1) C (2) I
(3) O (4) U
(5) None of these

32. Which of the following is true regarding I?
(1) I is not an immediate neighbor of D
(2) Three letters are between I and C
(3) S is at immediate left of I
(4) T is not at extreme end
(5) None is true

Directions (33-37): *Study the following information carefully and answer the questions given below:*

Eight persons were born at different months in different years i.e. 1983, 1984, 1985, 1986. Two persons were born in each year. Ages are measured from 1st January 2020. Every person was born on 1st of every month.

There are 11 months gap between the births of L and K. Q and L were born in the month of 30 days. J is younger than N. P and L were born in same year. O was born just before K who is youngest, and both were born in the month which have 31 days. M is not less than 37 year. There are as many persons were born before Q as after L. There are 17 months difference between the age of M and J. There are 13 months difference between the ages of P and O. P was born before April. N was born on October.

33. What is the age of Q?
(1) 35 years 7 months
(2) 35 years 8 months
(3) 35 years 9 months
(4) 36 years 3 months
(5) None of these

34. Who among the following was born on September 1985?
(1) N (2) M
(3) O (4) Q
(5) None of these

35. Which of the following is true?
(1) N was born on June
(2) Q was born before the person who was born on September
(3) L was born before July
(4) Three persons were born between N and O
(5) None is true

36. Four of the following five are alike in certain way and hence form a group, find the one which does not belong to that group?
(1) M (2) N
(3) J (4) O
(5) K

37. In which of the following month youngest person was born?

(1) March (2) May
(3) June (4) August
(5) None of these

Directions (38-42): *Study the following information carefully and answer the questions given below:*

In a certain code language:

"group rate drive dare" is coded as "®£ $# ©¥ ©℗"

"nose final read less" is coded as "®¥ αμ %¥ Ω%"

"gear other mind most" is coded as "@¥ £& ®β Ω¥"

38. What is the code of "sure"?
(1) ©@ (2) &α
(3) %£ (4) ¥€
(5) None of these

39. What may be the code of "green grass"?
(1) Ω© £℘ (2) Ω$ ℘©
(3) ℘$ Ω© (4) £℘ Ω$
(5) None of these

40. If "epic" is coded as "□Ω" then, what is the code of "care"?
(1) #$ (2) *&
(3) @% (4) □℗
(5) None of these

41. Which of the following word may have code "&£"?
(1) Image (2) True
(3) This (4) Then
(5) None of these

42. Which of the following may have the code "□Ω %©"?
(1) Night Match (2) Great Walk
(3) Close Fight (4) Nice Draw
(5) None of these

Directions (43-47): *In the following questions, the symbols @, #, $, % and & are used with the following meaning as illustrated below-*

'P@Q' means 'P is neither smaller than nor equal to Q'

'P#Q' means 'P is neither greater than nor equal to Q'

'P$Q' means 'P is neither smaller than nor greater than Q'

'P%Q' means 'P is not greater than Q'

'P&Q' means 'P is not smaller than Q'

Now in each of the following questions assuming the given statements to be true, find which of the three conclusions I, II and III given below them is/are **definitely true** and give your answer accordingly.

43. Statement: N@V$W, W%K#L, L%R

Conclusions: **I.** L@N **II.** K#R **III.** V%R

(1) Only I (2) Both II and III
(3) Only I and II (4) Only II
(5) All I, II, III

44. Statement: J#K&L, L@M$O, O@N%G

Conclusions: **I.** G&M **II.** K@O **III.** M@G

(1) Either I or III (2) II and Either I or III
(3) Only I (4) I and Either II or III
(5) Both I and II

45. Statement: N#M&L; L#J&O; O&V

Conclusions: **I.** M@N **II.** J#V **III.** L%N

(1) Only I (2) Only II
(3) Both I and II (4) Both II and III
(5) None of these.

46. Statement: A@B&D; D%E#F; H@G&D

Conclusions: **I.** D#A **II.** F@D **III.** H%E

(1) Both I and II (2) Only II
(3) Both II and III (4) Only I
(5) All I, II, III

47. Statements: H#G; H#I&J; M#F%I

Conclusions: **I.** G%J **II.** F@H **III.** I@M

(1) Both I and II (2) Only I
(3) Only III (4) Both I and III
(5) Only II

Directions (48-50): *Each of the questions below consists of a question and two statements numbered as I and II given below it. You have to decide whether the data provided in the statements are sufficient to answer the question. Read all the two* *statements and give answer.*

48. Five persons live on a building of five floors. The ground floor is numbered as 1, floor just above is numbered as 2 and so on till the topmost floor which is numbered as 5. On which floor X lives?

I. A lives above 3rd floor. Two persons live between X and Y. X lives above A.

II. Two persons live between X and Y. X lives just above C. Y lives below X.

(1) Only I (2) Only II
(3) Either I or II (4) Neither I nor II
(5) Both I and II

49. What is the direction of L with respect to O?

I. A is 10 m north of L. M is 25 m north of L. B is 10 m south of O.

II. M is 5 m west of B. A is 15 m south of M. L is 10 m south of A.

(1) Either I or II (2) Only II
(3) Both I and II (4) Only I
(5) Neither I nor II

50. Five students P, Q, W, S and V have different heights. Who is the tallest person among them?

I. P is taller than Q, but he is not the tallest. Q is shorter than W.S is shorter than V.

II. Only three persons are shorter than P. Q is shorter than P and V. W is taller than S.

(1) Only II (2) Neither I nor II
(3) Only I (4) Either I or II
(5) Both I and II

Quantitative Aptitude

Directions (51–56): *Read the data carefully and answer the questions.*

There are 3 colleges A, B, C offering 3 courses mechanical engineering (ME), chemical engineering (CE) and electrical engineering (EE).

College A: Number of students in ME is 40 less than that of in EE and number of students in CE is 50% more than that of in ME.

College B: Number of students in EE is 20 less than that of in EE in college A. Number of students in CE is 340 which is 40 more than that of in CE in college A. Number of students in EE is 22^2% more than that of in ME.

College C: Number of students in ME is 40% less than that of in ME in college A. Number of students in CE is 40 less than that of in ME.

Total students in EE in all colleges together are 780.

51. How many students are in college C?

(1) 620 (2) 740
(3) 560 (4) 680
(5) 520

52. If 10% students of ME course from college A shifted to CE course in college C, then what is the difference between total number of students in CE in college C now and average of students in ME in all colleges now?

(1) 60 (2) 380
(3) 260 (4) 80
(5) 180

53. Number of students in EE in college B are what percent more/less than number of students in ME in college C?

(1) 75% (2) 87.33 %
(3) 83.33 % (4) 66.66%
(5) 50%

54. What is the ratio of total number of students in ME and CE together in college A to total number of students in CE and EE together in college B?

(1) 23 : 27 (2) 25 : 28
(3) 26 : 25 (4) 25 : 26
(5) 27 : 28

55. What is the difference between average of total number of students in EE in all colleges and average of total number of students in CE in all colleges?

(1) 30 (2) 60
(3) 40 (4) 20
(5) 50

56. Total students in college C are what percent of total students in college A? (approx.)

(1) 79% (2) 70%

(3) 100% (4) 73%
(5) 85%

57. A shopkeeper sets MRP of a product such that after giving 10% discount, he earns 12.5% profit. What will be his profit/loss percent if he allows a discount of 25%?
(1) 5% (2) 10.45%
(3) 8.33% (4) 6.25%
(5) 9.09%

58. A alone can fill a tank in 16 mins and B alone can fill the same tank in 'X' mins. C alone can empty the tank in 12 mins. A, B, and C together take min to fill the tank. What is the time taken by B alone to fill the tank?
(1) 12 min (2) 16 min
(3) 20 min (4) 24 min
(5) 18 min

59. A container contain 96 litre mixture of milk and water out of which 35% is water. 20 lit of mixture is taken out and 10 litre milk and 16 litre water are added in remaining mixture. Find the difference between quantity of milk and water in the final mixture after replacement.
(1) 15.4 lit (2) 16.8 lit
(3) 18.2 lit (4) 21.4 lit
(5) 19.8 lit

60. Train A having length 180 m crosses a platform thrice of its length in 36 sec. Train B having speed of 63 kmph crosses a standing man in 8 sec. find the time taken by both trains to cross each other when running in same direction.
(1) 100 sec (2) 120 sec
(3) 128 sec (4) 64 sec
(5) 92 sec

Directions (61-66): *Given table shows the total number of boys and girls in a class in 5 different years and percentage of boys and girls who participated in an event and percentage of total students who did not participate in event. Some data are missing which you have to calculate as per the information provided in question. Read the data carefully and answer the questions.*

Year	Total number of Boys and Girls in class	% of boys participated in event	% of girls participated in event	% of (boys + girls) not participated in event
2015	---	65	---	30
2016	360	---	25	15
2017	180	25	---	25
2018	300	---	80	10
2019	---	45	---	40

61. If there are 20% more students in 2019 as compared to previous year and number of girls who didn't participate in 2019 are 12, then what is the difference between no. of boys who participated in 2019 and total students who didn't participate in 2016?
(1) 68 (2) 54
(3) 72 (4) 44
(5) 84

62. Find ratio of no. of students who didn't participate in 2017 to no. of boys who participated in 2018 if all boys participated in 2018?
(1) 3 : 10 (2) 13 : 10
(3) None of these (4) 5 : 8
(5) 7 : 10

63. If average of total no. of students in 2015, 2016 and 2017 is 260 and 23 girls didn't participate in 2015, then find the difference between no. of boys and girls who participated in 2015?
(1) 6 (2) 36
(3) 42 (4) 14
(5) 26

64. Find average no. of students who didn't participate in 2016, 2017 and 2018.
(1) 39 (2) 44
(3) 41 (4) 46
(5) 43

65. If ratio of total boys to total girls in 2018 is 3 : 2, then boys who didn't participate in 2018 are what percent of total girls who participated in 2018?
(1) 16.66 % (2) 25%
(3) 6.25% (4) 5%
(5) 8.33%

66. If there are 200 boys in class in 2019 and number of girls who didn't participate in 2019 is 5 more than no. of students who didn't participate in 2017 then what is the ratio of no. of girls who participated in 2019 to total students who participated in 2018?

(1) 5 : 9 (2) Cannot be determined
(3) 20 : 27 (4) 5 : 8
(5) 5 : 6

Directions (67–68): *Read the information carefully and answer the questions.*

A and B started a business by investing Rs. 6000 and Rs. 12000 respectively. A left business after 'X' months and at same time C joined B with Rs. 7000. At the end of year, ratio of their profit share (A : B : C) is 18 : 48 : Z.

67. Find 'X'.

(1) 8 (2) 6
(3) 9 (4) 7
(5) 10

68. Find value of Z.

(1) 27 (2) 18
(3) 24 (4) 21
(5) 15

69. Present age of Father and mother is in ratio of 12 : 11 and after 12 years, this ratio becomes 15 : 14. Age of father is 22 years more than his son and age of mother is 20 years more than that of her daughter. Find sum of present age of son and daughter.

(1) 54 yrs (2) 48 yrs
(3) 52 yrs (4) 46 yrs
(5) 50 yrs

70. Difference between total CI and total SI on a certain sum at 20% per annum for 2 years is Rs. 420. What will be the simple interest earned on same sum at 25% per annum for 3 years?

(1) Rs. 5725 (2) Rs. 7875
(3) Rs. 6525 (4) Rs. 7000
(5) Rs. 7375

Directions (71-75): *What approximate value should come in place of question mark (?) in following questions? You are not expected to calculate the exact value.*

71. $40.05 \div 4.89 + ? = 72.93 - 18.95$

(1) 36 (2) 42
(3) 52 (4) 46
(5) 58

72. $9.87 \times 16.08 - 55.03 \div 10.92 = ? + 54.98$

(1) 100 (2) 115
(3) 85 (4) 92
(5) 108

73. $63.08 + 67.98 - 43.11 + ? = 89.93$

(1) 6 (2) 15
(3) 2 (4) 11
(5) 17

74. $79.87 + 23.06 = 12.98 \times 7.13 + ?$

(1) 2 (2) 21
(3) 7 (4) 17
(5) 12

75. $520.07 \div 13.02 - 3.89 \times 10.09 + 33.88 = ?$

(1) 39 (2) 34
(3) 29 (4) 25
(5) 45

76. A and B invested Rs. 6000 and Rs. 12000 respectively in a business. After 6 months, C joined them and B left after 9 months from the starting. If profit share of C at the end of one year is Rs. 18900 out of total profit which is Rs. 50400, then find amount invested by C?

(1) Rs. 18000 (2) Rs. 15000
(3) Rs. 17000 (4) Rs. 16000
(5) Rs. 14000

77. The area of a square is 1767 m^2 (approx.) and length of rectangle is one-third of side of that square. If breadth of rectangle is 4 m less than length of rectangle, then find difference between area of square and area of rectangle.

(1) 1609 m^2 (2) 1627 m^2
(3) 1664 m^2 (4) 1729 m^2
(5) 1709 m^2

78. A person sold an article for Rs. 802. If it is sold for Rs. 38 more, then selling price would be 20% more than cost price. What is the profit percent when article is sold at actual selling price?

(1) 18.75% (2) 16.67%
(3) 20% (4) 100/9%
(5) 102/7%

79. A boat takes 4 hrs to cover 'D' km in upstream and takes 3 hours to cover 'D-2' km in downstream. If speed of stream is 2 kmph, then find distance covered by boat in upstream in 3 hrs.

(1) 44 km (2) 48 km
(3) 42 km (4) 56 km
(5) 54 km

80. A dice is rolled twice what is the probability that the number in the second roll will be lesser than that in the first?

(1) 1/4 (2) 1/2
(3) 7/12 (4) 5/12
(5) 1/6

Directions (81–86): *Study the following data carefully and answer the following questions.*

The pie chart shows the percentage distribution of total girls in five different classes in March month of 2019 and table shows the percentage of boys more or less than the girls in respective class for the same month and year.

Percentage of Girls

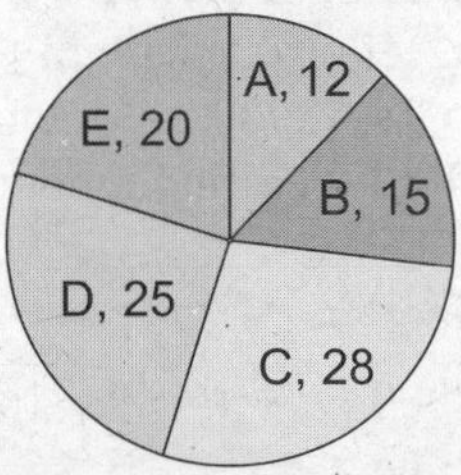

CLASS	% of boys more/less than girls
A	50% More
B	30% More
C	25% Less
D	24% More
E	25% More

81. What is the central angle for the percentage distribution of girls in class C?

(1) 100.8° (2) 100.0°
(3) 102.8° (4) 98.8°
(5) 90.8°

82. In April 2019, number of girls and boys in class C are increased by 14 2 7 % and 33 1 3 % respectively as compared to previous month. Total students in class C in April 2019 are what percent more or less than total students in class C in March 2019?

(1) 25.285% (2) 24.285%
(3) 28.571% (4) 30.285%
(5) 28.285%

83. What is the ratio of number of boys in class B to number of boys in class E?

(1) 33 : 50 (2) 39 : 49
(3) 44 : 47 (4) 37 : 40
(5) 39 : 50

84. What is the average of number of boys in class A, D and E if number of boys in class B are 195?

(1) 245.66 (2) 240.66
(3) 236.66 (4) 241.66
(5) 246.66

85. If the difference between boys and girls in class D are 216, then what is the sum of boys in class A and girls in class C?

(1) 1656 (2) 1545
(3) 1600 (4) 1664
(5) 1520

86. Total students in class B are what percent more/less than total students in class E?

(1) 27.88% (2) 27.55%
(3) 25.77% (4) 25.55%
(5) 23.33%

Directions (87-91): *Following are the questions based on two statements and answer the following based on the given statements.*

87. C alone can complete the work in 15 days. In what time C and A together can complete the whole work.

Statement I. A is 25% more efficient than B and B alone can complete the work in 20 days.

Statement II. Difference between the time

taken by A alone and B alone to complete the work is 22.5 days and time taken by C alone to finish the work is 10% more than the time taken by A and B together to complete the work.

(1) Statement I alone is sufficient to answer the question while statement II alone is not sufficient to answer the question.
(2) Statement II alone is sufficient to answer the question while statement I alone is not sufficient to answer the question.
(3) Both statements I and II together are required to answer the question.
(4) Either the statement I alone or Statement II alone is sufficient to answer the question.
(5) Question cannot be answered from any of the given statements or from both the statements.

88. Side of square is '*a*' cm. Find the value of '*a*'?

Statement I. Square is inscribed in a circle C1. Radius of circle C1 is 21 cm.

Statement II. Circle C2 is inscribed in the square. Radius of circle C2 is 28 cm.

(1) Statement I alone is sufficient to answer the question while statement II alone is not sufficient to answer the question
(2) Statement II alone is sufficient to answer the question while statement I alone is not sufficient to answer the question
(3) Both statements I and II together are required to answer the question.
(4) Either the statement I alone or Statement II alone is sufficient to answer the question
(5) Question cannot be answered from any of the given statements or from both the statements.

89. A boat covers 35 km in upstream and 35 km in downstream in total 4 hours. In what time it will cover 50 km upstream?

Statement I. Sum of upstream and downstream speed of the boat is 36 km/h

Statement II. Speed of water current is 20% of speed of boat in still water.

(1) Statement I alone is sufficient to answer the question while statement II alone is not sufficient to answer the question
(2) Statement II alone is sufficient to answer the question while statement I alone is not sufficient to answer the question
(3) Both statements I and II together are required to answer the question.
(4) Either the statement I alone or Statement II alone is sufficient to answer the question
(5) Question can not be answered from any of the given statements or from both the statements.

90. A train crosses a platform of twice of its length in 48 seconds. Find the speed of train?

Statement I. Train crosses a man walking at a speed of 4 m/s in the same direction as the direction of the train in 20 seconds

Statement II. After covering half of the platform, due to fault in the engine it covers remaining distance at a speed of which is 60% of its initial speed.

(1) Statement I alone is sufficient to answer the question while statement II alone is not sufficient to answer the question.
(2) Statement II alone is sufficient to answer the question while statement I alone is not sufficient to answer the question.
(3) Both statements I and II together are required to answer the question.
(4) Either the statement I alone or Statement II alone is sufficient to answer the question
(5) Question cannot be answered from any of the given statements or from both the statements.

91. Let x be total number of balls in a bag. Balls are of three different colors i.e. black, white and red. Calculate $(x - 1)$.

Statement I. Probability of getting a black ball is 1/6, a red ball is 1/6 and a white ball is $\frac{2}{3}$.

Statement II. If one white ball is lost, probability of not getting a white ball is 8/23 and initial number of white balls in bag is less than 27.

(1) Statement I alone is sufficient to answer the question but statement II alone is not sufficient to answer the question.

(2) Statement II alone is sufficient to answer the question but statement I alone is not sufficient to answer the question.

(3) Both the statements taken together are necessary to answer the questions, but neither of the statements alone is sufficient to answer the question.

(4) Either statement I or statement II by itself is sufficient to answer the question.

(5) Statements I and II taken together are not sufficient to answer the question.

Directions (92–97): *Line chart given below shows markup percent more than CP and discount percent given on MRP of seven different articles sold by a shopkeeper. Study the data carefully and answer the following questions.*

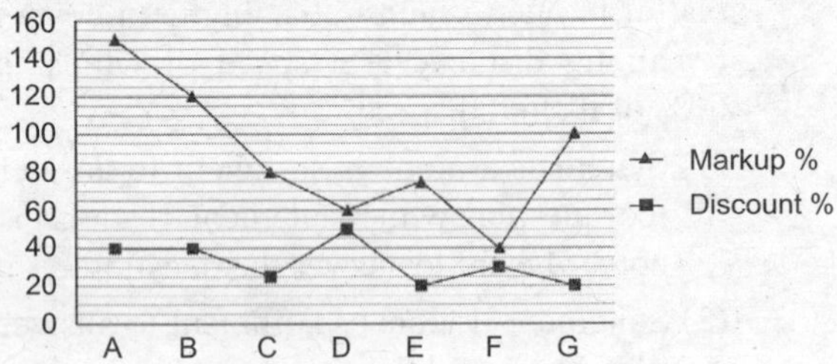

92. Cost price of article D is Rs. 320. If article D is sold at 20% profit rather than marking up and giving discount, then find the difference between the selling price obtained in both cases. (in Rs.)

(1) 120 (2) 128
(3) 90 (4) 144
(5) 165

93. If difference between selling price and cost price of article G is Rs. 150, then find the selling price of article G.

(1) Rs. 300 (2) Rs. 420
(3) Rs. 350 (4) Rs. 250
(5) Rs. 275

94. If selling price of article B is same as selling price of article E, then cost price of article B is what percent more than cost price of article E?

(1) 7.06% (2) 9.06%
(3) 5.06% (4) 4.06%
(5) 6.06%

95. What is the ratio of marked price to selling price of article C?

(1) 4 : 3 (2) 3 : 4
(3) 4 : 7 (4) 7 : 4
(5) 4 : 5

96. Total selling price of article A and article B together is what percent more than the marked price of article G ? (It is given that cost price of all articles are same)

(1) 48% (2) 42%
(3) 41% (4) 45%
(5) 47%

97. Cost price of article 'B' is Rs. 100 more than Cost price of article 'C' and marked price of article 'B' is Rs. 260 more than marked price of article 'C'. Find the difference between selling price of article B and article C?

(1) Rs. 128 (2) Rs. 124
(3) Rs. 136 (4) Rs. 180
(5) Rs. 156

98. Difference of speed of boat in downstream and upstream is 7 km/h and the time taken by the boat to travel 45 km in downstream is 80 minutes more than the time taken to travel 13 km in upstream. Due to cyclone, speed of current becomes twice and thus it can cover D km in upstream in time which is equal to new speed of current. Find D? (Note: speed of boat in still water is multiple of 5)

(1) 30 (2) 24
(3) 18 (4) 21
(5) 27

99. Ravi and Sneha got married 10 years ago and at that time ratio of their ages was 5 : 4. Ratio of present age of Ravi and Sneha is 7 : 6. After marriage they had seven children including a triplet and a twin. The ratio of present age of triplet, twin, sixth and the seventh child is 4 : 3 : 2 : 1. Find the largest possible value of the present total age of the family.

(1) 121 (2) 107
(3) 101 (4) 93

(5) None of the above

100. Shivam invested Rs. 3 lac in a scheme which is providing interest rate of '*r*'% per annum at CI and this scheme doubles the sum invested in 72 *r* years which is two times of rate of interest provided by the scheme. Find the total amount received by Shivam at the end of 48 years (in lac)?

(1) 45 (2) 50

(3) 64 (4) 32

(5) 48

General English

Directions (101-106): *Read the following passage and answer the following questions. Some words are highlighted to help you answer some of the questions.*

AI has several positive applications but the capability of AI systems to learn from experience and to perform autonomously for humans makes AI the most disruptive and self-transformative technology of the 21st century. If AI is not regulated properly, it is bound to have unmanageable implications. Imagine, for instance, the electricity supply suddenly stops while a robot is performing a surgery, and access to a doctor is lost? And what if a drone hits a human being? These questions have already confronted courts in the U.S. and Germany. All countries, including India, need to be legally prepared to face such kind of disruptive technology.

Predicting and analysing legal issues and their solutions, however, is not that simple. For instance, criminal law is going to face drastic challenges. What if an AI-based driverless car gets into an accident that causes harm to humans or damages property? Who should the courts hold liable for the same? In the U.S., there is a lot of discussion about regulation of AI. Germany is working on blemish present in it, like certain ethical rules for autonomous vehicles stipulating that human life should always have priority over property or animal life. China, Japan and Korea are following Germany in developing a law on self-driven cars. In India, NITI Aayog released a policy paper, 'National Strategy for Artificial Intelligence', in June 2018, which considered the importance of AI in different sectors. The Budget 2019 also proposed to launch a national programme on AI. While all these developments are taking place on the technological front, no comprehensive legislation to regulate this growing industry has been formulated in the country till date.

Apart from these aspects, strategists have also offered sober explorations of the future relationship between AI and nuclear weapons. Some of the most widely received **musings** on the issue, including a recent call for an AI- enabled "dead hand" to update America's aging nuclear command, control, and communications infrastructure, tend to obscure more than they ______ due to an insufficient understanding of the technologies involved. An appreciation for technical detail, however, is necessary to arrive at realistic assessments of any new technology, and particularly consequential where nuclear weapons are concerned. Some have warned that advances in AI could erode the fundamental logic of nuclear deterrence by enabling counter-force attacks against heretofore concealed and mobile nuclear forces. Such secure second- strike forces are considered the backbone of effective nuclear deterrence by assuring retaliation. Were they to become vulnerable to pre-emption, nuclear weapons would lose their deterrent value.

The exponential growth of sensors and data sources across all warfighting domains has analysts today facing an overabundance of information. Some strategists warn that the same AI-infused capabilities that allow for more prompt and precise strikes against time-critical conventional targets could also undermine deterrence stability and increase the risk of nuclear use. Specifically, AI-driven improvements to intelligence, surveillance, and reconnaissance would threaten the survivability of heretofore secure second-strike nuclear forces by providing technologically advanced nations with the ability to find, identify, track, and destroy their adversaries' mobile and concealed launch platforms. Transporter- erector launchers and ballistic missile submarines, traditionally used by nuclear powers to enhance the survivability of their deterrent forces, would be at greater risk. A country that acquired such an exquisite counter-force capability could not only hope to limit damage in case of a spiraling nuclear crisis but also negate its adversaries' nuclear deterrence "in one swift blow." Such an ability would undermine the nuclear deterrence calculus whereby the costs of imminent nuclear retaliation far outweigh any conceivable gains from aggression.

101. In accordance with the passage which of the following statement(s) negates the advancement of the AI technology?
(1) AI would diminish the whole idea of having a nuclear deterrence in the first place
(2) Absence of international monitoring authority for AI would lead to unbridled use
(3) Non-existence of jurisdictional responsibility of use of AI
(4) Both (1) and (3)
(5) None of these

102. Which of the following argument(s) can be rectified after reading the given passage?
(1) Machine intelligence is much different from human intelligence
(2) AI-improved counter-force capability would be considered as good enough to order a strike
(3) Use of AI in National security will make the conventional warfare strategies obsolete.
(4) AI is considered to be inanimate that holds the producer of the product liable for harm
(5) None of these.

103. Which of the following is similar to **'MUSINGS'** as used in the passage?
(1) contemplation (2) decimate
(3) nurture (4) tickle
(5) None of these.

104. 'No comprehensive legislation to regulate this growing industry has been formulated in the country till date' Why?
(1) dearth of technical whereabouts of the AI based mechanism in the concerned authorities
(2) dual use of AI i.e. both military and non-military.
(3) owing to political benefits of mass surveillance
(4) Both (2) and (3)
(5) None of these.

105. Select appropriate filler for the blank given in the passage.
(1) discard (2) flout
(3) embellish (4) illuminate
(e) None of these.

106. Which of the following suggestions regarding improvement of the AI have been suggested in the passage?
(1) Agreeing with the legal as well psychological aspects in different situations
(2) Ability to prioritize in life threatening situations
(3) prone to various manipulation that can alter decision making ability
(4) safeguard from hacking various malicious groups and organization
(5) None of these.

Directions (107-111): *In the following questions a sentence is provided which is divided in different parts. One of these parts is highlighted and is free from grammatical error. Remaining parts may or may not be grammatically or contextually correct. Choose the letter corresponding to the correct part as your answer.*

107. Noting Kathak exponent Manjari Chaturvedi **(A)**/is in for a shock when her **(B)/qawwali performance was stopped midway**/ by officials of the Uttar Pradesh government during **(C)**/a official cultural programme at a Lucknow **(D)**
(1) D (2) A
(3) B (4) C
(5) No Error

108. In a fortnight, about 30 peoples will **(A)**/join the National Cyber Forensic Lab to **(B)/assist security agencies in preventing,**/containing and investigate complex (C)/cybercrimes along the country**(D)**

(1) D (2) A
(3) B (4) C
(5) No Error

109. The fourth edition of 'The Death Penalty in India: Annual Statistics' **(A)**/published by Project 39A of NLU-Delhi said **(B)/the number of death sentences awarded**/ for murders involving sexual offences**(C)**/ in 2019 was at the highest in four years **(D)**

(1) D (2) A
(3) B (4) C
(5) No Error

110. The NGT have warned that local **(A)/ bodies will be liable to pay**/ a compensation of Rs. 1 millions per month **(B)**/for a population of above 1 million if there was **(C)**/continued failure to treated generated waste. **(D)**

(1) D (2) A
(3) B (4) C
(5) No Error

111. Under the NDPS Act, if there was prior **(A)**/ information about the recovery of narcotic drugs **(B)**/ or psychotropic substances to any person **(C)**/ the power of arrest such a person **(D)/ is not vested with the police officer.**

(1) D (2) A
(3) B (4) C
(5) No Error

Directions (112-117): *Read the following passage and answer the following questions. Some words are highlighted to help you answer some of the questions.*

The sweetest victory is the one that's most difficult. The one that requires you to reach down deep inside, to fight with everything you've got, to be willing to leave everything out there on the battlefield—without knowing, until that do-or-die moment, if your heroic effort will be enough. Society doesn't reward defeat, and you won't find many failures documented in history books. The exceptions are those failures that become stepping stones to later success. Such is the case with Thomas Edison, whose most memorable invention was the light bulb, which purportedly took him 1,000 tries before he developed a successful prototype. "How did it feel to fail 1,000 times?" a reporter asked. "I didn't fail 1,000 times," Edison responded. "The light bulb was an invention with 1,000 steps."

Unlike Edison, many of us avoid the prospect of failure. In fact, we're so focused on not failing that we don't aim for success, settling instead for a life of .... When we do make missteps, we **gloss** over them, selectively editing out the miscalculations or mistakes in our life's résumé. "Failure is not an option," NASA flight controller Jerry C. Bostick reportedly stated during the mission to bring the damaged Apollo 13 back to Earth, and that phrase has been etched into the collective memory ever since. To many in our success-driven society, failure isn't just considered a non-option—it's deemed a deficiency, says Kathryn Schulz, author of Being Wrong: Adventures in the Margin of Error. "Of all the things we are wrong about, this idea of error might well top the list," Schulz says. "It is our meta-mistake: We are wrong about what it means to be wrong. Far from being a sign of intellectual inferiority, the capacity to err is crucial to human cognition."

When we take a closer look at the great thinkers throughout history, a willingness to take on failure isn't a new or extraordinary thought at all. From the likes of Augustine, Darwin and Freud to the business mavericks and sports legends of today, failure is as powerful a tool as any in reaching great success. "Failure and defeat are life's greatest teachers [but] sadly, most people, and particularly conservative corporate cultures, don't want to go there," says Ralph Heath, managing partner of Synergy Leadership Group and author of Celebrating Failure: The Power of Taking Risks, Making Mistakes and Thinking Big. However, in today's post-recession economy, some employers are no longer shying away from failure—they're embracing it. According to a recent article in Business Week, many companies are deliberately seeking out those with track records reflecting both failure and success, believing that those who have been in the trenches, survived battle and come out on the other side have irreplaceable experience and perseverance.

When the rewards of success are great, embracing possible failure is key to taking on a variety of challenges, whether you're reinventing yourself by starting a new business or allowing yourself to trust another person to build a deeper relationship. "To achieve any worthy goal, you must take risks," says writer and speaker John C. Maxwell. "One of the biggest secrets to success is operating inside your strength zone but outside of your comfort zone," Heath says. Although you might fail incredibly, you might succeed incredibly—and that's why incredible risk and courage are requisite. Either way, you'll learn more than ever about your strengths, talents and resolve, and you'll strengthen your will for the next challenge. If this sounds like dangerous territory, it can be. But there are ways to ease into this fearless mindset.

112. As per the passage, what is common in all of the struggles which are later documented in the books?

(*i*) Efforts made throughout the struggles
(*ii*) Never give up attitude
(*iii*) Success at the end of their journey

(1) Only (*i*) (2) Only (*iii*)
(3) Both (*ii*) and (*iii*)
(4) Both (*iii*) and (*i*)
(5) All of these.

113. Which of the following statement(s) is/are not true in context of the given passage?

(1) High rewarding challenges require similar adaptability to varied failure possibility.
(2) As per Heath, risk taking ability is must to achieve any worthy goal
(3) Both (1) and (4)
(4) Human generally learn from the mistakes they make and the experience from those mistakes
(5) None of these.

114. Which of the following best describe the attitude of Thomas Edison as can be inferred from the second paragraph of the given passage?

(1) distressed (2) sedulous
(3) tense (4) indifferent
(5) None of these.

115. Which of the following statement(s) can be inferred from the given passage?

(1) History is filled with the stories of eminent person and their failures.
(2) Positive attitude is the key to tackle a problematic situation
(3) Recession have made the people to take failure positively
(4) Mangers have to stick their necks out a mile every day to get the job done
(5) None of these.

116. Select appropriate filler for the blank given in the passage.

(1) supremacy (2) abundant
(3) mediocrity (4) distinction
(5) None of these.

117. Which of the following is opposite in meaning to **'GLOSS'** as used in the passage?

(1) unveil (2) façade
(3) shimmer (4) conceal
(5) None of these.

Directions (118-120): *In the following questions, a paragraph is given which is provided with some blanks. These blanks have to be filled by one word from the options provided below. Choose the option which fills all the blanks without inducing any grammatical or contextual error.*

118. We are witnessing unprecedented .... in India. Such .... are the hallmark of a free, democratic society, whose logic demands that the voice of the people be heard by those in power and decisions be reached after proper discussion and consultation.

(1) fastenings (2) protests
(3) growth (4) debate
(5) None of these.

119. There could be more bad news on the ....front which saw a five-year high of 7.35% in December. The report from SBI said core .... could rise further on the back of telecom price increase and a larger increase could push headline .... closer to 8%.

(1) diplomatic (2) economic
(3) democratic (4) inflation
(5) None of these.

120. A bag containing a/an ...., placed near a ticket counter at the Mangaluru International Airport, triggered alarm on Monday morning. The bag was later removed and the .... defused through controlled explosion in an open area one kilometre away.

(1) ornament (2) confliction

(3) explosive (4) cash

(5) None of these.

Directions (121-125): *Read the following passage and answer the following questions. Some words are highlighted to help you answer some of the questions.*

Coffee first arrived in Europe from the Muslim world during the 17th century. It was amazing and it amazed, with an exoticness that charmed Europeans, its stimulating effect and the fact that it made a welcome change from traditional alcoholic beverages. Establishments serving coffee began to open, providing an environment for wonderful social, cultural and political exchange and, within a century, coffee had become part of everyday life.

It is not known exactly when coffee as a drink was discovered. However, we do know that the coffee plant originated in Ethiopia, where coffee beans were consumed either as a paste or as a drink, for their medicinal properties. The shrub was introduced to Yemen around the 14th century and it was then that the first coffee plantations were created. Muslim mystics and pilgrims appreciated coffee for its energising powers, so it travelled to Mecca. From that moment onwards, its success became unstoppable, bowling over Cairo, the Middle East and Constantinople, before arriving in Europe in the early 17th century. As expected, this new drink would come up against a few opponents. Religious clerics were suspicious and asked Pope Clement VIII to taste it. He allegedly declared that it would be a sin if only unbelievers were allowed to enjoy such a delicious drink. Like the pope, the privileged classes were charmed by coffee and quickly **embraced** its exoticism; 'turqueries' were particularly fashionable at that time. Intellectuals appreciated it for its ability to help one stay alert and to think clearly. Unlike chocolate, which remained a luxury for the privileged for a long time, coffee, which was less-expensive, was adopted by all levels of society and welcomed into homes during the 19th century. A morning cup of coffee gradually replaced traditional broths or soups and became established as a great classic.

The arrival of coffee was accompanied by a new trend as establishments serving coffee, just like the ones that existed in Constantinople and in Cairo, began to open all over Europe. They soon became meeting places, where people from a variety of backgrounds could get together, discuss and exchange ideas, without becoming intoxicated. In Paris, for example, Le Procope became a meeting place for artists and intellectuals - Montesquieu and Diderot were regular customers. The freedom of speech and the spirit of revolt which sometimes reigned in these establishments did not go unnoticed by the authorities. In London, cafés came to be considered dangerous and, in 1676, Charles II ordered their closure. However, as a result of public pressure, they reopened just a few days later.

What we call the coffee bean is actually more like a seed or pit it grows inside a thin-fleshed fruit not unlike a cherry, which ripens about nine months after the coffee plant flowers. In order to prepare the beans for roasting, they must first be removed from this outer casing using one of several techniques—a "washed," a "pulp natural," or a "natural" method—which may vary based on factors like regional climate, tradition, and the coffee's intended flavor profile. This can be a very tricky part of the life cycle of a coffee bean, as even the highest-quality crop can quickly be .... by mold, over-drying, inattentiveness, bad weather, or pest infestation.

121. Which of the following statement(s) is/are false in context of the given passage?

(1) Coffee leads to the rise of establishments which sometimes served as the origin of revolt.

(2) Coffee was first discovered in Ethiopia in middle eastern region of world.

(3) Both (*b*) and (*d*)

(4) Popularity of coffee around the world started from Europe.

(5) None of these.

122. Which of the following is similar in meaning to the word **'EMBRACED'** as used in the passage?

(1) repudiate (2) espouse

(3) obviate (4) renounce
(5) None of these.

123. Which of the following merits of the coffee have been mentioned in the passage?
(*i*) Energizing affects
(*ii*) Increased alertness
(*iii*) improved ability to think clearly
(1) Only (*i*) (2) Only (*ii*)
(3) Only (*iii*) (4) Both (*ii*) and (*iii*)
(5) All of the above

124. Select appropriate filler for the blank given in the passage.
(1) augmented (2) ruined
(3) exhausted (4) replenished
(5) None of these.

125. Which of the following statement(s) is/are in accordance with the passage?
(1) Use of coffee faced severed criticism from religious clerics
(2) widespread use of coffee helped chocolate in gaining popularity
(3) coffee fruit is grinded and roasted to obtain the coffee powder which is widely used
(4) Both (1) and (2)
(5) None of these.

Directions (126-130): *In the following questions five sentences which are in their jumbled form are given. Further these sentences have a highlighted part which may or may not form a contextually meaningful sentence. You have to swap the highlighted part with the other to make a contextually meaningful sentence and then rearrange those sentences to make a contextually meaningful paragraph. Later, answerer the follow up questions.*

A. Here, the example of Brazil, the only country where more than 100 million **most ambitious government health programme (*i*)**.
B. Achieving universal health coverage is a very complex task, **one interesting field of cooperation to explore in the strategic partnership is healthcare (*ii*)**.
C. It can also provide lessons for Ayushman Bharat, currently the world's largest and **inhabitants have a universal health system, is worth studying (*iii*)**.
D. As Brazilian President Jair Bolsonaro visits New Delhi this Republic Day, **especially for developing countries (*iv*)**.
E. Which in turn will Help in achieving universal coverage in India, a country with a population of 1.3 billion, **is a challenge of epic proportions (*v*)**.

126. Which of the following will be the second sentence after the rearrangement?
(1) C (2) A
(3) E (4) B
(5) D

127. Which of the following highlighted phrase should the phrase **'especially for developing countries'** interchanged with to make a contextually meaningful sentence?
(1) most ambitious government health programme
(2) one interesting field of cooperation to explore in the strategic partnership is healthcare
(3) inhabitants have a universal health system, is worth studying
(4) is a challenge of epic proportions
(5) No interchange required.

128. Select the correct pair of replacement from the options given below.
(1) (*i*)-(*ii*) (2) (*iii*)-(*iv*)
(3) (*ii*)-(*iii*) (4) (*i*)-(*iii*)
(5) None of these.

129. Which of the following will be the fifth sentence after the rearrangement?
(1) C (2) A
(3) E (4) B
(5) D

130. Which of the following will be the fourth sentence after the rearrangement?
(1) C (2) A
(3) E (4) B
(5) D

Directions (131-138): *In the following passage*

there are highlighted words, each of which has been numbered. These numbers are printed below the passage and against each, five options are given. In four options, one word is suggested in each option. Find out the appropriate word which can replace the highlighted word. If the highlighted word fits the passage, choose option '5' (No correction required) as the correct choice.

The Supreme Court allowed the government's **abrogation (131)** to take over the management of the **thriving (132)** real estate major Unitech Ltd. and appointed a new board of directors to steer the completion of pending projects and provide homes for over 12,000 investors in dire straits. A Bench of Justices D.Y. Chandrachud and M.R. Shah appointed former IAS officer Yudvir Singh Malik as the chairman and managing director of the new board while refusing to give a/an **vacant (133)** on the board to Unitech Group founder Ramesh Chandra at this stage.

"The idea of a professional board is to allow them to take control of the company and complete the pending projects in the interest of homebuyers," the court said. The board includes A.K. Mittal, ex-CMD of National Buildings Construction Corporation; Renu Sud Karnad, chairman of HDFC Credila Finance Service Pvt Ltd.; Jitu Virwani, CMD of Embassy Group; and Niranjan Hiranandani, managing director of Mumbai-based Hiranandani Group.

The court **subjugated (134)** the institution of any fresh cases against Unitech for two months. Old orders and enforcement of them also stand suspended for the period. Unitech promoters Sanjay Chandra and his brother Ajay Chandra are currently **granted (135)** in Tihar jail for allegedly **laying (136)** off homebuyers' money. The court said the probe into irregularities in the company would continue and said the work of a panel led by former Delhi High Court judge, Justice S.N. Dhingra, appointed to sell the company's assets and use the money in completion of pending projects, would continue to work till the new board comes up with a **resolution (137)** framework.

The court indicated that it would appoint a retired Supreme Court judge to monitor the preparation of resolution framework. The top court directed the present management of the company, forensic auditors, asset reconstruction companies, banks and financial institutions and state governments to **intend (138)** cooperation to the new board.

131. (1) inception (2) character
(3) adoption (4) proposal
(5) No correction required

132. (1) juvenile (2) embattled
(3) sprouting (4) endangered
(5) No correction required

133. (1) rite (2) abash
(3) berth (4) ramification
(5) No correction required

134. (1) barred (2) adjourned
(3) incurred (4) discord
(5) No correction required

135. (1) entitled (2) coveted
(3) lodged (4) melee
(5) No correction required

136. (1) taken (2) called
(3) pay (4) siphoning
(5) No correction required

137. (1) journal (2) intrinsic
(3) luscious (4) novice
(5) No correction required

138. (1) disseminate (2) extend
(3) squander (4) plummet
(5) No correction required

Directions (139-140): *Select the phrase/connector (STARTERS) from the given three options which can be used to form a single sentence from the two sentences given below, implying the same meaning as expressed in the statement sentences.*

139. China will step up efforts to contain the coronavirus outbreak ahead of the Lunar New Year holidays. 17 new cases of the virus have been confirmed and there is increasing possibility of spread of virus to other countries.

(*i*) In lieu of 17 new cases…
(*ii*) Owing to the 17 new cases….
(*iii*) Taking into consideration China's efforts to….

(1) Only (*i*) (2) Only (*ii*)
(3) Only (*iii*) (4) Both (*i*) and (*ii*)
(5) None of the above

140. Doubts were raised about the efficacy of the Right To Information Act in Haryana. Only 35% penalty has been recovered since the setting up of the Haryana State Information Commission in 2006.

(*i*) Citing the modus operandi of RTI ....
(*ii*) Stating the facts regarding cases under RTI ....
(*iii*) In what raises doubts about the efficacy ....

(1) Only (*i*) (2) Only (*ii*)
(3) Only (*iii*) (4) Both (*iii*) and (*i*)
(5) None of the above

General Awareness

141. The Mahanadi is a major river in East Central India. It originates from which state?
(1) Jharkhand (2) West Bengal
(3) Odisha (4) Chhatisgarh
(5) Madhya Pradesh

142. Angelique Kerber is a/an .... professional tennis player and former world No. 1, and a three time Grand Slam champion.
(1) German (2) American
(3) France (4) Swiss
(5) Australian

143. Aaron James Finch is an Australian sports player. He play which sport?
(1) F1 Race (2) Football
(3) Badminton (4) Tennis
(5) Cricket

144. Indian Banks' Association, formed on 26 September 1946 as a representative body of management of banking in India operating in India - an association of Indian banks and financial institutions based in Mumbai. Who is present Chairman of IBA?
(1) Jatinder Bir Singh
(2) Dinabandhu Mohapatra
(3) Sunil Mehta
(4) Rajnish Kumar
(5) Chanda Kochhar

145. Who is the Chairman of HDFC Bank?
(1) Aditya Puri (2) Deepak Parekh
(3) Shikha Sharma (4) Amitabh Chaudhary
(5) Sandeep Bakhshi

146. Khelo India Youth Games, formerly Khelo India School Games, meaning Play India Youth Games, held annually in January or February, are the national level multidisciplinary grassroot games in India held for two categories, namely under-17 years school students and under-21 college students. Khelo India Youth Games 2019 held in-
(1) New Delhi (2) Lucknow
(3) Patna (4) Jaipur
(5) Pune

147. Recently, RBI has declared that how much percentage of demonetized money was back?
(1) 79.30% (2) 93.30%
(3) 88.30% (4) 99.30%
(5) 91.30%

148. What is the current reverse repo rate of RBI?
(1) 6.50% (2) 6.25%
(3) 6.75% (4) 4.00%
(5) 19.50%

149. Who is the committee head of the merger of the public sector banks?
(1) Raghuram Rajan (2) Bimal Jalan
(3) Arun Jaitley (4) YV Reddy
(5) Piyush Goyal

150. World's first thermal battery power plant is started in which state?
(1) Andhra Pradesh (2) Kerala
(3) Uttar Pradesh (4) Maharashtra
(5) Gujarat

151. The difference between exports and imports is called-?
(1) assets and liabilities
(2) balance of payment

(3) GDP (4) balance of trade
(5) depreciation

152. The 2018 ICC Women's World Twenty20 was hosted in .... from 09th to 24th November 2018, during the 2018–19 international cricket season.
(1) Australia (2) West Indies
(3) South Africa (4) India
(5) New Zealand

153. Which of the following country to host the 11th BRICS Summit is scheduled for October 2019?
(1) India (2) China
(3) South Africa (4) Germany
(5) Brazil

154. What is the name of the book which was awarded the golden man Booker Prize 2018?
(1) The English Patient
(2) Everything Under
(3) The Long Take
(4) Washington Black
(5) The Mars Room

155. What is the minimum paid-up equity capital for small finance banks?
(1) Rs. 10 crore (2) Rs. 500 crore
(3) Rs. 100 crore (4) Rs. 200 crore
(5) Rs. 1000 crore

156. Stan Lee, who passed away recently, was a comic writer with which of the following comic works was he as associated?
(1) Science fiction Comics
(2) Action/Adventure Comics
(3) Manga Comics (4) Superhero Comics
(5) Marvel Comics

157. BOND-I is given by which institution?
(1) IMF (2) RBI
(3) ADB (4) World Bank
(5) SEBI

158. Eat right movement was launched by FSSAI selected whom as it's brand ambassador?
(1) MS Dhoni (2) Virat Kohli
(3) Rajkummar Rao (4) Amitabh Bachchan
(5) Nawazuddin Siddiqui

159. India has stated it aims to reduce the emissions intensity of its GDP by 33-35% by 2030 from 2005 levels and achieve .... of its cumulative electric power of around 350GW installed capacity from non-fossil fuel-based energy resources, mainly renewable power.
(1) 20% (2) 40%
(3) 50% (4) 30%
(5) 10%

160. What is child sex ratio for 1000 males as per census 2011?
(1) 919 females (2) 921 females
(3) 927 females (4) 925 females
(5) 917 females

161. The Reserve Bank of India made a strong case for setting up a .... in India to address the twin balance sheet problem of the banking sector and the corporate sector.
(1) Public Credit Registration
(2) Public Credit Registry
(3) Public Credit Review
(4) Public Credit Reminder
(5) Public Commerce Registry

162. The .... is the second supersonic fighter developed by Hindustan Aeronautics Limited (HAL) after the HAL HF-24 Marut.
(1) Trishul (2) Prithavi
(3) Vikrant (4) Akash
(5) Tejas

163. Lok Adalat is one of the alternative dispute redressal mechanisms, it is a forum where disputes/cases pending in the court of law or at pre-litigation stage are settled/ compromised amicably. What is the minimum charge to file a case in a Lok Adalat?
(1) no court fee (2) Rs. 10
(3) Rs. 50 (4) Rs. 05
(5) Rs. 100

164. In 1970, an organized resistance to the destruction of forests spread throughout India and came to be known as-
(1) Save Silent Valley Movement
(2) Swadeshi Movement
(3) Namantar Andolan

(4) Chipko movement
(5) Narmada Bachao Andolan

165. Damdama lake is in which state?
(1) Punjab (2) Rajasthan
(3) Haryana (4) Uttar Pradesh
(5) Bihar

166. The United Nations' (UN) International Day Against Drug Abuse and Illicit Trafficking falls on-
(1) 29th June (2) 21st June
(3) 12th June (4) 26th June
(5) 05th June

167. Which of the following ministry has Launched Mobile Application " Jan Dhan Darshak" as A Part of Financial Inclusion?
(1) Finance Ministry
(2) Ministry of Consumer Affairs, Food and Public Distribution
(3) Ministry of Human Resource Development
(4) Ministry of Parliamentary Affairs
(5) Ministry of Commerce and Industry

168. While India stands .... largest in number in terms of number of World Heritage properties in ASPAC (Asia and Pacific) region.
(1) fourth (2) third
(3) second (4) fifth
(5) first

169. Indian Air Force (IAF) for first time was participated in multinational air exercise .... 2018 (PB-18) in Australia hosted Royal Australian Air Force (RAAF).
(1) Desert Strike (2) Emerald Mercury
(3) Yudh Abyas (4) Nomadic Elephant
(5) Pitch Black

170. How much amount is available to one account holder of Pradhan Mantri Jan Dhan Yojana per household after six months of satisfactory conduct of the account?
(1) Rs. 5,000 (2) Rs. 10,000
(3) Rs. 2,000 (4) Rs. 15,000
(5) Rs. 20,000

171. Which of the following bank will allow its customers to make card-less cash withdrawals at over 100000 ATMs across India?
(1) Bank of Baroda
(2) ICICI Bank
(3) AU Small Finance Bank
(4) State Bank of India
(5) Airtel Payments Bank

172. Cheques, Drafts, Pay Orders and Banker's Cheques are "valid for .... months from the date of instrument.
(1) 4 months (2) 1 months
(3) 6 months (4) 3 months
(5) 5 months

173. The four pillars of smart planning are vital to the success of Smart Cities and the Regional Smart City Initiative. Which of the following pillar is not them?
(1) MOBILITY (2) SUSTAINABILITY
(3) INFRASTRUCTURE
(4) CONNECTIVITY
(5) SECURITY

174. IRDAI has directed all third-party insurance companies to include vehicle insurance policies cover to vehicle owners-drivers of all vehicles (two-wheelers, three-wheelers, passenger vehicles and commercial vehicles) for an additional premium of-
(1) Rs. 500 (2) Rs. 750
(3) Rs. 10000 (4) Rs. 1000
(5) Rs. 5000

175. As per guidelines of the RBI, payments banks can accept demand deposits (savings and current) up to a maximum of .... per customer.
(1) Rs. 1,00,000 (2) Rs. 2,00,000
(3) Rs. 50,000 (4) Rs. 5,00,000
(5) Rs. 10,000

176. Public Sector Enterprises (PSEs) is comes under which ministry?
(1) Ministry of Heavy Industries and Public Enterprises
(2) Ministry of Environment, Forest and Climate Change
(3) Ministry of Personnel, Public Grievances

and Pensions

(4) Ministry of Corporate Affairs

(5) Ministry of New and Renewable Energy

177. The 91st Academy Awards ceremony will honor the best films of 2018 and will take place at the Dolby Theatre in

(1) Tokyo (2) Los Angeles

(3) Paris (4) Sydney

(5) London

178. The global Multidimensional Poverty Index (MPI) is an international measure of acute poverty covering over 100 developing countries. Global Multidimensional Poverty Index given by

(1) UNESCO (2) UNCTAD

(3) UNDP (4) OECD

(5) UNEP

179. Under the Liberalised Remittance Scheme, Authorised Dealers may freely allow remittances by resident individuals up to USD .... per Financial Year for any permitted current or capital account transaction or a combination of both.

(1) USD 3,00,000 (2) USD 3,50,000

(3) USD 2,00,000 (4) USD 2,50,000

(5) USD 1,00,000

180. Digital wallet company Paytm has launched 'Paytm Money' app for mutual fund investments. The Paytm Money platform will be offering systematic investment plans (SIPs), starting at how much rupees per month?

(1) Rs. 300 (2) Rs. 400

(3) Rs. 200 (4) Rs. 500

(5) Rs. 100

181. Which of the following organisation has approved a $25-30 billion commitment plan for India for the 2019-22 period?

(1) United Nations (2) World Bank

(3) UNCTAD

(4) New Development Bank

(5) International Monetary Fund

182. Government has announced to fix MSP at a level of at least per cent of the cost of production for kharif crops 2018-19 which redeems the promise made in the Union Budget for 2018-19.

(1) 50 per cent (2) 250 per cent

(3) 200 per cent (4) 100 per cent

(5) 150 per cent

183. Who are the winners of this year's Ramon Magsaysay Award 2018 from India, regarded as the Asian version of the Nobel Prize?

(1) Bharat Vatwani and Sonam Wangchuk

(2) Kailash Satyarthi and Arvind Kejriwal

(3) Bhuwan Ribhu and Asmita Satyarthi

(4) Nadia Murad and Juan Manuel Santos

(5) None of the given option is true

184. Nearly .... crore jobs were created in the country in the 10-month period till June this year, as per a Central Statistics Office (CSO) report.

(1) 2.4 crore (2) 3.5 crore

(3) 6.9 crore (4) 1.2 crore

(5) 7.5 crore

185. Which organisation is a policy think tank of the Government of India, established with the aim to achieve Sustainable Development Goals and to enhance cooperative federalism by fostering the involvement of State Governments of India in the economic policy-making process using a bottom- up approach?

(1) RBI (2) IRDAI

(3) NITI Aayog (4) Planning Commission

(5) CBDT

186. The World Economic Outlook (WEO) is a survey conducted and published by-

(1) WTO (2) World Bank

(3) UNCTAD

(4) New Development Bank

(5) International Monetary Fund

187. Which country will chair the 2019 summit of the Association of Southeast Asian Nations (ASEAN)?

(1) Japan (2) Singapore

(3) China (4) Thailand

(5) Russia

188. Which Bank has bagged Hindi implementation award Rajbhasha Kirti Award for outstanding performance in implementing the Official Language Policy during 2017-18?

(1) Union Bank of India
(2) Indian Bank
(3) Punjab National Bank
(4) State Bank of India
(5) Bank of Baroda

189. Public Affairs Centre (PAC) engages in action research focusing on Sustainable Development Goals in the context of India. PAC situated in-?

(1) New Delhi (2) Bengaluru
(3) Mumbai (4) Kolkata
(5) Chennai

190. The Department of Industrial Policy and Promotion (DIPP), Ministry of Commerce and Industry, hosts a conference on Global Digital Content Market (GDCM) 2018 in which city?

(1) New Delhi (2) Bengaluru
(3) Mumbai (4) Kolkata
(5) Chennai

Answers With Explanations

For questions (1-5):

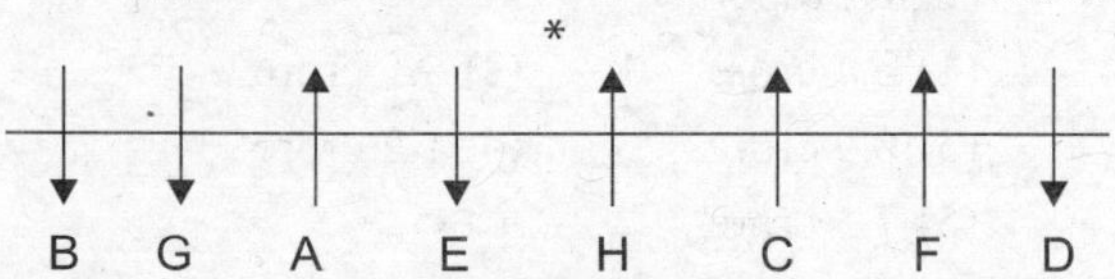

1. (2) **4.** (1)
2. (3) **5.** (2)
3. (4)
6. (5)

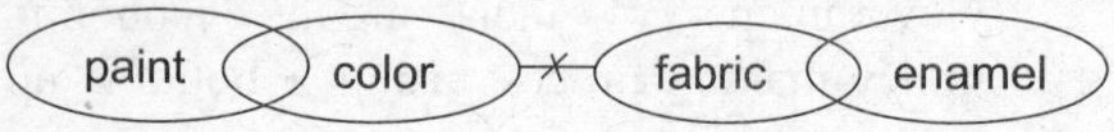

7. (4)

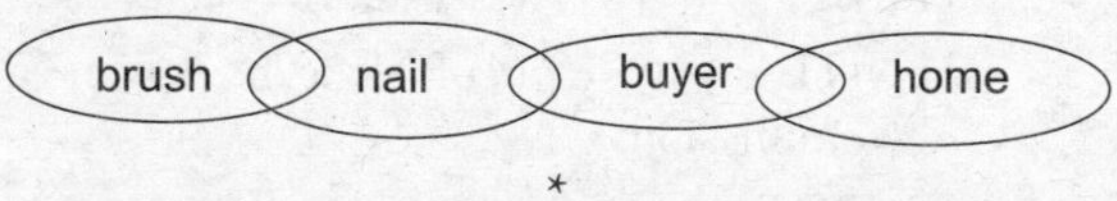

8. (2) Condition I and II is applied.
9. (1) No Condition is applied.
10. (3) Condition III and IV is applied.
11. (2)

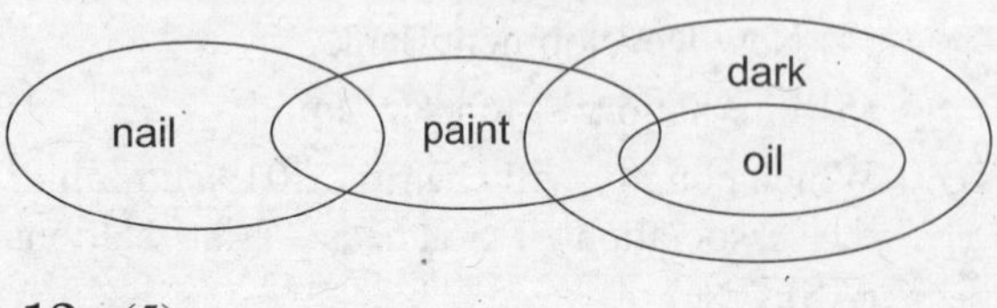

12. (5)

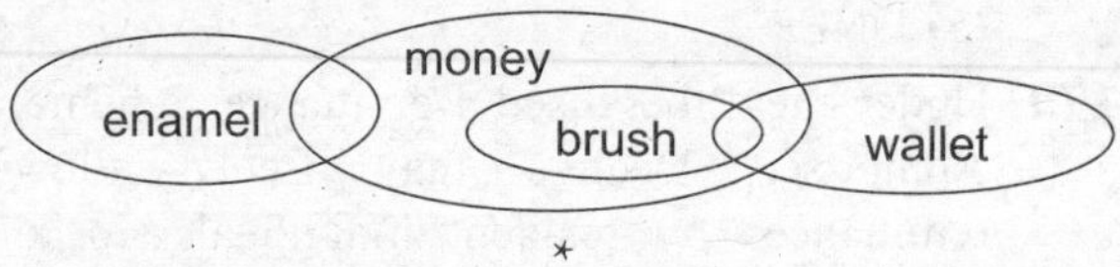

13. (3)

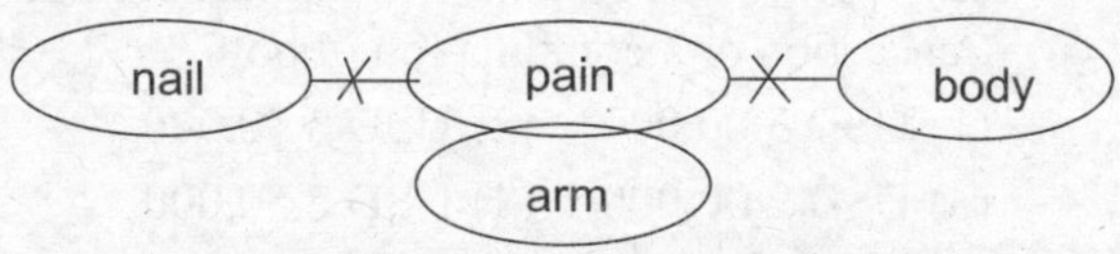

14. (4)

Days	Persons
Monday	F
Tuesday	A
Wednesday	E
Thursday	C
Friday	D
Saturday	B

For questions (15-19):

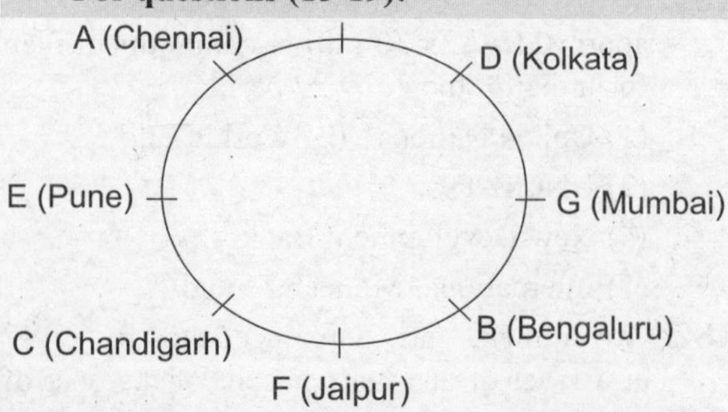

15. (2)

16. (1)

17. (3)

18. (2)

19. (5)

20. (5) All weights are in whole number so

Ram > Rajesh > Geeta > Rohan > Rakesh > Sohan

66 kg 65 kg 64 kg 63 kg 62 kg

21. (2)

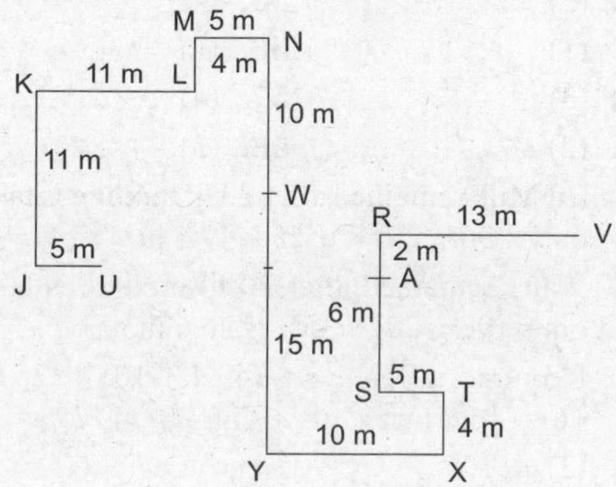

22. (4)

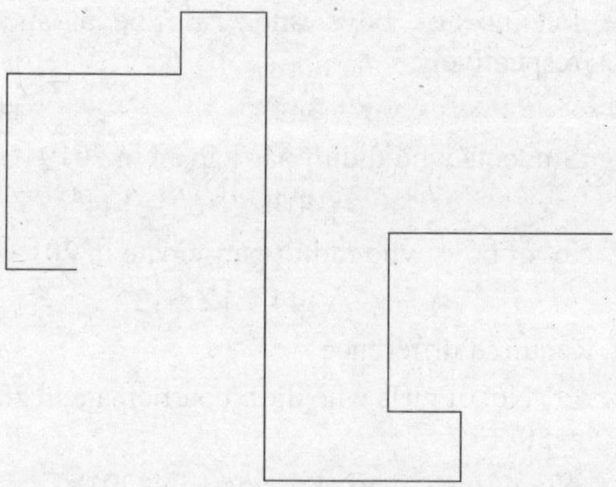

23. (2)

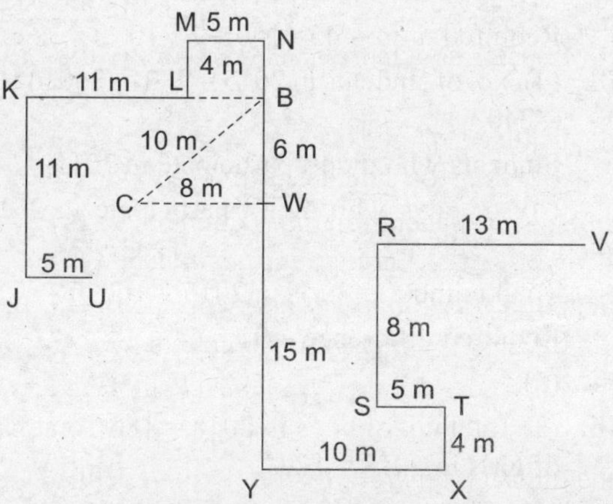

24. (3)

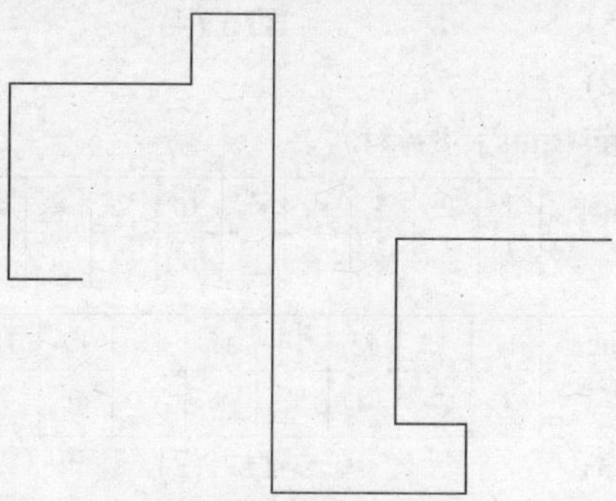

For questions (25-29):

W
Q
S
U
R
P
X
V
Y
Z
T

25. (3)

26. (4)

27. (5)

28. (1)

29. (2)

For questions (30-32):

Meaningful word is **DISCOUNT**

30. (4)

31. (2)

32. (5)

For questions (33-37):

Years	Months	Persons
1983	January	M
	October	N
1984	April	Q
	June	J
1985	February	P
	September	L
1986	March	O
	August	K

33. (3)

34. (5)

35. (2)

36. (3)

37. (4)

For questions (38-42):

difference	1	2	3	4	5	6	7	8	9	10
code	©	□	£	¥	β	α	Ω	μ	®	€

difference	11	12	13	14	15	16	17	18	19
code	@	℘	$	%	&	*	℗	∞	#

38. (3)

39. (2)

40. (4)

41. (2)

42. (3)

43. (4) **I.** L@N (false) **II.** K#R (true) **III.** V%R (false)

44. (2) **I.** G&M (false) **II.** K@O (true) **III.** M@G (false)

45. (1) **I.** M@N (true) **II.** J#V (false) **III.** L%N (false)

46. (1) **I.** D#A (true) **II.** F@D(true) **III.** H%E(false)

47. (3) **I.** G%J (false) **II.** F@H(false) **III.** I@M(true)

48. (1) From I we get following arrangement:

Floor	Persons
5	X
4	A
3	
2	Y
1	

49. (3)

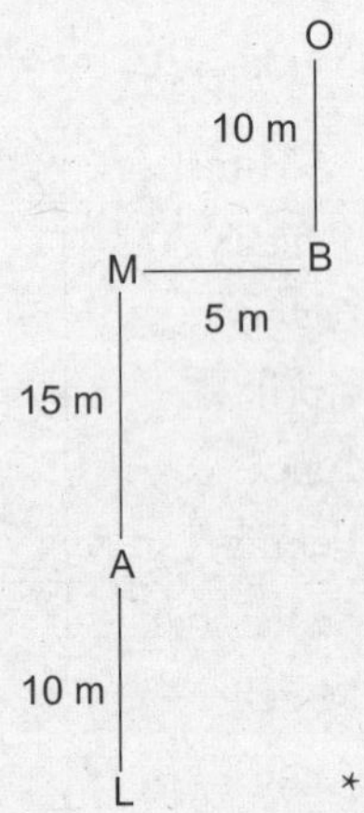

Thus, L is in south-west of O.

50. (2)

For questions (51–56):

College/Course	ME	CE	EE	Total
A	200	300	240	740
B	180	340	220	740
C	120	80	320	520

51. (5)

52. (1)

53. (3)

54. (2)

55. (4)

56. (2)

57. (4)

58. (3)

59. (*b*) Milk remained after 20 lit mixture is taken out = (96 – 20) × 65% = 49.4 lit

Water remained after 20 lit mixture is taken out = (96 – 20) × 35% = 26.6 lit

Required difference = (49.4 + 10) – (26.6 + 16) = 16.8 litre

60. (3)

61. (2) Total student in 2019 = 360

Let no. of boys and girls be x and y respectively.

$$x + y = 360 \quad ...(i)$$

Students who didn't participate in 2019

= 40% × 360 = 144

No. of boys who didn't participate in 2019

= 144 – 12 = 132

Required difference = 54

62. (1) No. of girls who didn't participate in 2018 = 30

No. of boys who participated in 2018

= 300 – (30/20) × 100 = 150

Required ratio = 45 : 150 = 3 : 10

63. (4) No. of students in 2015 = 780 – (360+180) = 240

Students who didn't participate in 2015 = 72

No. of boys who didn't participate in 2015 = 49

Total number of girls in 2015 = 100

Required difference = 91 – 77 = 14

64. (5)

65. (3) Total no. of boys in 2018 = 180 Total No. of girls in 2018 = 120

No. of students who didn't participate in 2018 = 30

No. of boys who didn't participate in 2018 = 30 – 24 = 6

66. (1) No. of boys who didn't participate in 2019 = 110

No. of girls who didn't participate in 2019 = 50

Total students in 2019 = 160 × 100 = 400

67. (3)
68. (4)
69. (5)
70. (2)

71. (2) $40 \div 5 + ? \approx 73 - 19$

$? = 46$

72. (1) $10 \times 16 - 55 \div 11 \approx ? + 55$

$? = 100$

73. (3) $63 + 68 - 43 + ? \approx 90$

$? = 2$

74. (5) $80 + 23 \approx 13 \times 7 + ?$

$? = 12$

75. (2) $520 \div 13 - 4 \times 10 + 34 \approx ?$

$? = 34$

76. (1) Let amount invested by C be Rs. X

Profit share ratio = A : B : C

= 6000 × 12 : 12000 × 9 : X × 6

= 12000 : 18000 : X

Hence $x = 18900$

77. (2) Side of square = 42 m (area of square ≈ 1764 m^2)

Length of rectangle = 14 m

Breadth of rectangle = 10 m

Required difference = 1767 – 140 = 1627 m^2

78. (5)
79. (3)
80. (4)
81. (1)
82. (3)

83. (5) Required ratio = 39 : 50

84. (5)

85. (1) Let girls in class D be $25x$

Then boys in D will be $31x$

$31x - 25x = 216$

$6x = 216$

$x = 36$

Boys in class A = $12x \times 150/100 = 18x$

Girls in class C = $28x$

Required sum = $18x + 28x = 46 \times 36 = 1656$

86. (5)
87. (4)
88. (4)
89. (4)
90. (1)
91. (2)
92. (2)
93. (4)
94. (5)
95. (1)
96. (3)
97. (5)
98. (4)
99. (2)
100. (5)
101. (4)
102. (3)
103. (1)
104. (5)
105. (4)
106. (2)

107. (4) 'Noting' is incorrect. So it should be 'noted'.

108. (3) 'Peoples' is incorrect because 'people' is plural. 'Investigate' is should be replaced by 'investigating' and 'along' should be replaced by 'around'. So, only part (B) is free from any error.

109. (5)

110. (4) 'Have' should be replaced by 'has' because 'NGT' is singular.

111. (3) 'Was' should be replaced by 'is' because the given sentence is in present tense.

112. (2)
113. (2)
114. (2)
115. (3)
116. (3)
117. (4)
118. (2)
119. (4)
120. (3)
121. (4)
122. (2)
123. (5)
124. (2)
125. (3)

For questions (126-130):

The final arrangement is DBACE.

126. (4)
127. (2)
128. (4)
129. (3)
130. (1)
131. (4)
132. (2)
133. (3)
134. (1)
135. (3)
136. (4)
137. (5)
138. (2)
139. (2)
140. (3)

141. (4) The river flows through the states of

Chhattisgarh and Odisha.

142. (1)

143. (5) Aaron James Finch is an Australian international cricketer who captains the Australian cricket team in limited overs cricket.

144. (3) Punjab National Bank (PNB's) managing director and chief executive, Sunil Mehta was elected as new chairman of Indian Banks Association (IBA) for year 2018-19.

145. (2) Deepak Parekh is the Chairman of HDFC, India's leading housing finance company.

146. (5) **150.** (1)

147. (4) **151.** (4)

148. (2) **152.** (2)

149. (3)

153. (5) Brazil to host the 11th BRICS Summit, scheduled for October 2019.

154. (1)

155. (3) The minimum paid-up equity capital for small finance banks shall be Rs. 100 crore.

156. (5)

157. (4) The World Bank launched bond-I.

158. (3) **159.** (2)

160. (1) As per the Census, 2011 the child sex ratio (0-6 years) has shown a decline from 927 females per thousand males in 2001 to 919 females per thousand males in 2011.

161. (2) **162.** (5)

163. (1) There is no court fee payable when a matter is filed in a Lok Adalat.

164. (4) **167.** (1)

165. (3) **168.** (3)

166. (4)

169. (5) Indian Air Force (IAF) for first time will participate in multinational air exercise Pitch Black – 18 (PB-18) in Australia hosted Royal Australian Air Force (RAAF).

170. (2) **177.** (2)

171. (5) **178.** (3)

172. (4) **179.** (4)

173. (3) **180.** (5)

174. (2) **181.** (2)

175. (1) **182.** (5)

176. (1)

183. (1) Two Indians Bharat Vatwani and Sonam Wangchuk are among the winners of this year's Ramon Magsaysay Award 2018, regarded as the Asian version of the Nobel Prize.

184. (4) **186.** (5)

185. (3)

187. (4) Thailand chaired the first 2019 summit of the Association of Southeast Asian Nations.

188. (3)

189. (2)

190. (1)

IBPS Clerk Prelims, 2020

(Held on 5 December, 2020)

Based on Memory

English Language

Directions (1-8): *Read the following passage and answer the following questions based on the given passage. Some of the words are highlighted which would help you to answer some of the questions given.*

A good night's sleep is utmost essential for overall good health. It is the time when the body rests, rejuvenates and recovers. An adult requires 7 to 8 hours of peaceful and quality sleep per day. Sleep deprivation can be defined as inability to complete the **sufficient** sleep-time required by the person.

Research has shown that even one night of sleep deprivation is equivalent to being intoxicated. Intentional sleep deprivation is mostly seen in young people and teenagers who prefer entertainment over sleep. Many workaholics also consider sleeping as a waste of precious time which is not true. Many a time because of work commitments such as working in night shifts or long hours may also interfere with quality sleep that an individual requires. Medical issues such as chronic illnesses, depression and sleep disorders such as obstructive sleep apnea can also be the reason for sleep deprivation.

You probably already have some understanding of the benefits of rest—and the costs of not getting it. Sleep allows us to consolidate and store memories, process emotional experiences, **replenish** glucose (the molecule that fuels the brain), and clear out beta-amyloid (the waste product that builds up in Alzheimer's patients and disrupts cognitive activity).

The most common sign and symptom of the fact that one is sleep deprived is fatigue, lethargy and feeling sleepy throughout the day. Other symptoms include mood disorders; sleep deprivation may lead to increasing irritability, desire to stay alone, rapid mood swings and more. Lack of sleep will also cause psychomotor instability meaning the person will find it difficult to focus and stand still at a place. Sleep deprivation will also cause issues with sight and hearing. An affected person may experience burning sensation in eyes, tingling and redness of eyes, light flashes and even hallucinations. He or she may also find it difficult to gauge distance at which a sound is originating. Other signs and symptoms of sleep deprivation include tingling sensations on the body, disorganization of thought and much more.

Negative effects of sleep deprivation are many. It affects both physical and mental health of a person negatively. The most common effect of sleep deprivation is drowsiness, tiredness, mood swings, irritability and reduced alertness. Although scientific knowledge of the physiological effects of sleep deprivation is relatively recent but researchers now believe that sleep deprivation can lead to disorders such as depression. Both short term sleep deprivation and chronic long term sleep deprivation can be very dangerous for the health as it has a direct impact on functioning of both heart and brain of an individual. Sleep loss also blunted activity in brain regions that normally **induce** social engagement. During sleep, regeneration of neurons happens in the cerebral cortex. Thus in a sleep deprived individual the brain fails to function optimally.

The simplest and easiest way to treat sleep deprivation is sleep more. Be it acute or chronic condition, a quality good night's sleep will help an individual (A) effectively. Fighting stress, eating a healthy and a balanced diet, avoiding alcohol are some other dos for a good night's sleep. Certain medications can also interfere with one's sleep thus consult your medical professional about the same. Exercising or indulging in an activity such as jogging, walk or swimming can also help one sleep better. Avoid usage of electronic gadgets before bedtime as they can interfere with one' sleep. Spending time in natural sunlight, Yoga, meditation and breathing exercises can also help one sleep better at night. Treating underlying medical cause if any will also help one sleep better and avoid sleep deprivation.

1. According to the passage, which among the following statements is true?

(1) Sleep allows us to enhance our ability of acquiring knowledge and process emotional experiences.
(2) An adult can function properly only with a quality sleep of 5-6 hours a day.
(3) Sleep deprivation can be cured only with a help of a medical professional.
(4) Both (1) and (2)
(5) All are true

2. What is/are the cause(s) of incompetency in a sleep deprived individual's brain?

(*i*) Clearing out of beta-amyloid that disrupts cognitive activity.
(*ii*) Sleep deprivation leads to drowsiness, tiredness and reduced alertness.
(*iii*) Reduction in the regrowth or repair of nervous tissues, cells or cell products in the cerebral cortex.

(1) Only (*i*) (2) Only (*iii*)
(3) Both (*i*) and (*iii*) (4) Both (*i*) and (*ii*)
(5) All (*i*) (*ii*) and (*iii*)

3. Choose the most suitable phrasal verb to fill the given blank (A) to make the sentence grammatically and contextually correct.

(1) drop back (2) break out
(3) come forward (4) bounce back
(5) fall out

4. Which among the followings is true according to the context of the passage?

(1) Fighting stress, eating a healthy and a balanced diet, avoiding alcohol cures depression
(2) Sleep deprivation means a state caused by inadequate quantity or quality of sleep.
(3) Sleep deprivation has negative effects on all the five senses of human body.
(4) Treating prolong and underlying medical cause can cause sleep deprivation.
(5) All are true

5. How can one safeguard oneself from sleep deprivation?

(*i*) Getting regular exercise during the day.
(*ii*) Refraining from using electronic devices right before bed
(*iii*) Limiting the consumption of alcohol

(1) Only (*i*) (2) Only (*iii*)
(3) Both (*i*) and (*iii*)
(4) Both (*i*) and (*ii*)
(5) All (*i*) (*ii*) and (*iii*)

Directions (6-7): *Choose the most suitable word that depicts the meaning of the highlighted word.*

6. SUFFICIENT

(1) Many (2) Adequate
(3) Restricted (4) Limited
(5) Wanting

7. INDUCE

(1) Hasten (2) Inspire
(3) Encourage (4) Advocate
(5) Evaluate

8. Which of the following word depicts the **opposite** meaning of the given word **REPLENISH**?

(1) Restore (2) Exhaust
(3) Recharge (4) Accelerate
(5) Modify

Directions (9-13): *In the following questions, a sentence is divided into four parts. Choose the part of the sentence which may contain a grammatical error in it. If all the parts of the sentence are grammatically correct and contextually meaningful, choose option (s) i.e. "no error" as your answer choice.*

9. Slicing a cake between pieces (A)/is a fun tradition that many (B)/newlyweds like to (C)/ incorporate into their ceremonies. (D)/ No Error (E)

(1) A (2) B
(3) C (4) D
(5) E

10. She had stayed up (A)/all night because (B)/ she had received (C)/bad news. (D)/No error.

(E)

(1) A (2) B

(3) C (4) D

(5) E

11. He as well as (A)/his friends (B)/were going (C)/ for picking. (D)/No Error (E)

(1) A (2) B

(3) C (4) D

(5) E

12. The coaching industry in India (A)/plays a pivotal role, (B)/as it contributes significant (C)/ revenue to the education sector. (D)/No Error (E)

(1) A (2) B

(3) C (4) D

(5) E

13. If I don't (A)/turn on my (B)/air conditioner, my (C)/house was hot. (D)/No error (E)

(1) A (2) B

(3) C (4) D

(5) E

Directions (14-17): *In the following question, sentences are given with a part in bold. The given phrase in the bold may or may not contain an error. The options following can replace the incorrect phrase. The correct phrase that is to be replaced will be your answer. If the sentences are correct then select 'No improvement required' as your answer.*

14. Everything is funny, as long as it is **happening too** somebody else.

(1) has been happening for

(2) is happening to

(3) was happening too

(4) could have happened to

(5) No improvement required

15. They recommend this book even though **they himself had** never read it.

(1) they themselves had

(2) they themself has

(3) it itself had (4) one oneself has

(5) No improvement required

16. This is the house **that Jack built it.**

(1) that Jack is building it

(2) Which Jack built it

(3) whom Jack built (4) that Jack built

(5) No improvement required

17. **In no way do I** agree with what you're saying.

(1) In no way I do (2) In no way I don't

(3) No way I don't (4) Do I in no way

(5) No improvement required

Directions (18-22): *In the following passage some words have been deleted. Fill in the blanks with the help of the alternatives given. Select the most appropriate option for each blank.*

According to some researchers, musical instruments came about .... **(18)** ...., depending on the available materials, and, in some cases, by the stimulus of the clamor of battle. The definition of a musical instrument is quite simple: it is an instrument that was created or .... **(19)** .... to make musical sounds. It is important to remember that the history of musical instruments dates back to the beginning of human culture. This tells us that man has always been drawn to music. The earliest musical instruments were used for rituals. For example, the trumpet-like ones were used to signal success in a hunt, or drum-like instruments were used in religious ceremonies.

Over time, cultures have developed the composition and performance of musical pieces for entertainment. Musical instruments have also .... **(20)** .... with the ever-changing applications. It appears that no one knows exactly where music came from. We are not talking here about who Elvis' singing predecessors were, not even about when the first musical instrument was invented. Researchers who have been interested in the physics of instruments believe that musical devices have always .... **(21)** .... pretty much on the materials that were available to each civilization. In other words, people worked with what they had. In time, traditional poetry was .... **(22)** .... alongside human noise-makers and got rhythms to them. Again, there is no exact data to back this up, so no one knows exactly when the first song was born. However, adding stories to melodies became a tradition that was carried on to our days and it does not seem like it will ever go out of fashion.

18. (1) deliberate (2) systematic (3) cautiously (4) randomly (5) anxiously

19. (1) concise (2) adapted (3) prohibited (4) distributed (5) immense

20. (1) subdued (2) evolved (3) Refine (4) Surge (5) diminished

21. (1) relatively (2) suspected (3) depended (4) aligned (5) sustained

22. (1) displayed (2) recited (3) elaborate (4) arranged (5) Remembered

Directions (23-26): *In each of the questions given below a sentence is given with three words in bold. Choose the option which gives the correct sequence of these words to make the sentence grammatically and contextually correct.*

23. The U.P. ordinance not only **conflict (A)** guaranteed fundamental rights but is also in **violates (B)** with **existing (C)** personal laws

(1) ABC (2) BAC (3) CAB (4) ACB (5) None of these

24. The **deficit (A)** changes in the sector brought in through the three laws have **aggravated (B)** the trust **abrupt (C)** of the government.

(1) ABC (2) CAB (3) BAC (4) CBA (5) None of these

25. The Chinese Communist Party initially **aftermath (A)** nationalism as a co-option **embraced (B)** in the **strategy (C)** of the Tiananmen Square massacre

(1) None of these (2) CAB (3) ABC (4) BCA (5) CBA

26. The Supreme Court has been asking States to **reservation (A)** quantifiable data to **justify (B)** their levels of **produce (C)**.

(1) None of these (2) CAB (3) ACB (4) BCA (5) CBA

Directions (27-30): *In the question given below, some sentences/phrases are given which have to be arranged in a proper sequence. Select the option which best defines the proper sequence and arranges the sentence in an appropriate way.*

27. A. Sidestepping debate
B. And discussion in Parliament
C. Discontent over the
D. Is a result of
E. New farm laws

(1) DEABC (2) EDABC (3) No rearrangement possible (4) AEBDC (5) CEDAB

28. A. Population-level vaccination plans
B. For COVID-19
C. Expecting from
D. The outcomes we are
E. It is crucial to define

(1) BCAED (2) CABED (3) EDCAB (4) DCABE (5) No rearrangement possible

29. A. WHO must
B. Work alongside
C. China in quickly
D. Origins of the virus
E. Uncovering the

(1) EBCDA (2) CAEBD (3) EBACD (4) ACDBE (5) ABCED

30. A. Public activity should
B. Be available
C. To the public
D. Only information
E. Bearing a nexus to

(1) DEABC (2) EDABC (3) No rearrangement possible (4) AEBDC (5) CEDAB

Numerical Ability

31. Train A running at a speed of 36 km/hr crosses train B in 20 seconds. Find the speed of train B (in km/hr), if the sum of the length of train A and B is 600 meters and both trains running in the opposite direction.

(1) 72 km/hr (2) 54 km/hr
(3) 48 km/hr (4) 108 km/hr
(5) 81 km/hr

32. A invests Rs. X in a business. After four months B joined him with Rs. 2X and A double his investment. If at the end of the year's total profit is Rs. 13950, then find the profit share of A?

(1) Rs. 7250 (2) Rs. 7750
(3) Rs. 8750 (4) Rs. 6750
(5) Rs. 7050

33. A man invested an amount in two schemes in the ratio of 2 : 3 at the rate of 20% p.a. and 10% p.a. on compound interest respectively. If the man gets a total interest of Rs. 1208 after two years from both the schemes, the find amount invested by man?

(1) Rs. 6000 (2) Rs. 4800
(3) Rs. 5000 (4) Rs. 4500
(5) Rs. 4000

34. The sum of the length of a rectangle and the side of a square is 72 meters. If the perimeter of the rectangle is 84 meters and the breadth of the rectangle is 18 meters, then find the measurement of the side of the square (in meters).

(1) 48 (2) 36
(3) 54 (4) 60
(5) 30

35. The ratio of time taken by A, B and C to complete work alone is 4 : 6 : 3 respectively. If all three together complete the work in 8 days, then find in how many days A alone complete three – fourth of the same work?

(1) 12 (2) 30
(3) 15 (4) 24
(5) 18

Directions (36–40): *In the following questions, there are two equations in x and y. You have to solve both the equations and give answer*

(1) if $x > y$ **(2)** if $x < y$
(3) if $x \geq y$ **(4)** if $x \leq y$
(5) if $x = y$ or there is no relation between x and y

36. **I.** $2x^2 - 3x + 1 = 0$
II. $2y^2 - 5y + 3 = 0$

37. **I.** $x^2 + 21x + 110 = 0$
II. $y^2 + 17y + 72 = 0$

38. **I.** $x^2 = 4$
II. $y^2 - 6y + 8 = 0$

39. **I.** $x^2 + 9x - 22 = 0$
II. $2y^2 - 7y + 6 = 0$

40. **I.** $6x^2 + 5x + 1 = 0$
II. $15y^2 + 11y + 2 = 0$

41. The population of a village is decreased by 10% in the first year and then increased by 20% in the second year. Find the population of the village at the end of the second year if two years ago it was 15,000?

(1) 16180 (2) 16200
(3) 16320 (4) 16360
(5) 16480

42. A shopkeeper marked up a shirt 50% above the cost price and allows successive discounts of 111/9% and 10% on it. If the difference between profit earned and discount given is Rs. 200 then find the marked price of the shirt?

(1) Rs. 2100 (2) Rs. 3000
(3) Rs. 2400 (4) Rs. 3600
(5) Rs. 3300

43. The downstream speed of a boat is 5 km/hr more than its upstream speed and the ratio of the speed of the boat in still water to the speed of the stream is 19 : 5. Find the total time taken by boat to travel 42 km downstream and 31.5 km upstream?

(1) 7½ hr (2) 8 hr
(3) 9 hr (4) 9½ hr
(5) 10 hr

44. A container contains a mixture of two liquids P and Q in the ratio 5 : 3. If 16 liter of the mixture is taken out and replaced with liquid Q, then the new ratio of liquid P to liquid Q becomes 1 : 1. Find the initial quantity of mixture in the container.

(1) 80 L (2) 60 L
(3) 70 L (4) 48 L
(5) 96 L

45. The ratio of the present age of A to B is 8 : 5 and the average of the present age of B and C is 35 years. If five years ago, the sum of ages of A and B is 55 years, then find the difference between the present age of A and C.

(1) 12 years (2) 5 years
(3) 9 years (4) 8 years
(5) 4 years

Directions (46 – 50): *The line graph given below shows the total number of posts (Photos + Videos) shared by six (A, B, C, D, E and F) people in December 2019. Read the data carefully and answer the questions.*

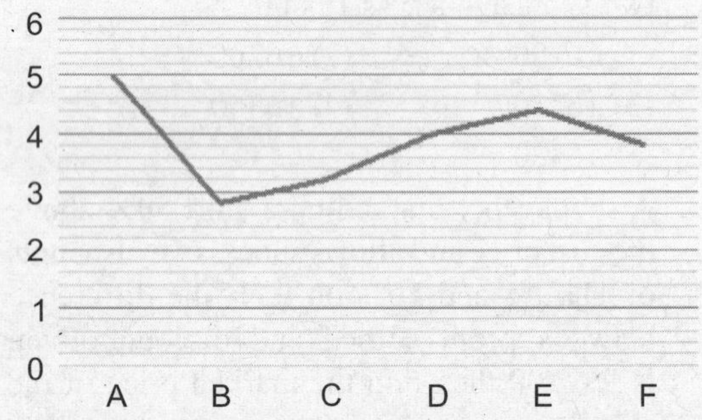

46. The total post shared by C is what percent less than the total post shared by D?

(1) 20% (2) 25%
(3) 15% (4) 10%
(5) 30%

47. In January 2020 total posts shared by B and F is 12 and 15 more than previous month respectively, then find the total number of the post shared by B and F in January 2020?

(1) 95 (2) 91
(3) 93 (4) 97
(5) 99

48. Find the average number of posts shared by A, C and F?

(1) 42 (2) 48
(3) 40 (4) 36
(5) 44

49. Total photos shared by E is four more than total videos shared by him, then find total videos shared by E?

(1) 24 (2) 20
(3) 28 (4) 22
(5) 30

50. If the ratio of total photos to total videos shared by B is 5 : 9, then find total photos shared by B?

(1) 10 (2) 18
(3) 12 (4) 14
(5) 16

Directions (51-65): *What will come in the place of question mark in following questions?*

51. $(? \div 5 \div 7) \times 14 + 112 = 420$

(1) 710 (2) 720
(3) 660 (4) 770
(5) 750

52. $(?)^{(4 \times 16 \div 32 + 1)} + 12^2 = 360$

(1) 4 (2) 6
(3) 8 (4) 2
(5) 3

53. 50% of $128 + (\sqrt{16})/2 \times 4 = ? + 10$

(1) 64 (2) 62
(3) 60 (4) 56
(5) 82

54. $\frac{\sqrt[3]{1331}}{11} + \sqrt{81} + ? = 27$

(1) 19 (2) 18
(3) 17 (4) 16
(5) 15

55. $(14)^2 + 179 + (5)^2 = (?)^2$

(1) 10 (2) 20
(3) 30 (4) 40
(5) 22

56. $28.5 \times 34 + 2320 \div 8 = (36)^2 - ?$

(1) 51 (2) 47

(3) 43 (4) 34
(5) 37

57. $47 \times 27 + 15600 \div 8 + 181 = ?$
(1) 3320 (2) 3420
(3) 3370 (4) 3400
(5) 3460

58. $112.5 \times 5 + 4560 \div 6 - 175 \times 7 = ?$
(1) 103.5 (2) 91.5
(3) 97.5 (4) 110.5
(5) 115.5

59. 80% of $? = \sqrt{250 \times 44 + 40\% \text{ of } 8500}$
(1) 80 (2) 120
(3) 150 (4) 180
(5) 240

60. $? \times 40 \div 24 \times 27 = \frac{594}{115} \times \frac{2300}{264}$
(1) 1 (2) 2
(3) 3 (4) 4
(5) 5

61. $? + 13 \times 50 = 420 + 45\%$ of $800 + 220$
(1) 300 (2) 350
(3) 400 (4) 450
(5) 250

62. 12% of $? + 12.5\%$ of $960 = 16 \times 12$
(1) 840 (2) 960
(3) 800 (4) 600
(5) 400

63. $15 \times ? + 20\%$ of $450 = 360$
(1) 12 (2) 20
(3) 24 (4) 16
(5) 18

64. 75% of $3/4 \times 8/9 \times 1800 = ? + 600$
(1) 300 (2) 400
(3) 250 (4) 480
(5) 540

65. $?\%$ of $900 + 500 = 4 \times 197$
(1) 28 (2) 25
(3) 36 (4) 40
(5) 32

Reasoning Ability

Directions (66-70): *Study the following information carefully and answer the question given below.*

Eight boxes are placed one above another. Only two boxes are placed between box U and T. Only one box is placed between box T and R. Only two boxes are placed between box R and V. Box V is placed below box R. Three boxes are placed between S and Q, both S and Q are placed above box T. Box W is placed below box V. Not more than one box is placed between box S and box P.

66. How many boxes are there between box T and box S?
(1) None (2) One
(3) Two (4) Three
(5) More than three

67. Which of the following box is placed immediately above box Q?
(1) W (2) U
(3) R (4) T
(5) None of these

68. Which of the following box is placed at the bottommost position?
(1) W (2) U
(3) R (4) T
(5) None of these

69. Which of the following box is placed immediately below box P?
(1) W (2) U
(3) R (4) T
(5) None of these

70. How many boxes are there between box W and box R?
(1) None (2) One
(3) Two (4) Three
(5) More than three

71. In the word **'BACKGROUND'** all consonants are written as their preceding letter and all vowels are written as their following letters. Then, how many letters repeated in the new arrangement?
(1) One (2) Two
(3) Four (4) Three

(5) More than four

Directions (72-76): *Study the following information carefully and answer the question given below-*

Six persons are arranged according to their weight in descending order from left to right. E is not the heaviest among all. A is heavier than F and C. F is heavier than B and D but not heavier than E. B and C are not the lightest among all. A is not just heavier than F. E is heavier than C, who is not the 3rd heaviest among all. Weight of the 2nd lightest person is 17 kg. Total weight of B and C is 44 kg. 2nd heaviest person is twice heavy to the one who is 2nd lightest. C is just lighter than F. Total weight of all the persons are 150 kg.

72. What may be the possible weight of F?

(1) 30 kg (2) 38 kg
(3) 24 kg (4) 25 kg
(5) None of these

73. The number of persons is heavier than F is same as the number of persons lighter than ....?

(1) A (2) C
(3) D (4) B
(5) None of these

74. If D is 10 kg lighter than B and F is 5 kg heavier than C then what is the weight of A?

(1) 23 kg (2) 43 kg
(3) 30 kg (4) 33 kg
(5) None of these

75. Four of the following five are alike in a certain way and so form a group. Find the one who does not belong to that group?

(1) E-C (2) F-A
(3) D-C (4) B-D
(5) F-B

76. Which of the following statement is true?

(1) Only one person is lighter to C
(2) D is the lightest among all
(3) A is lighter to D
(4) Weight of A is 50 kg
(5) None is true

Directions (77-80): *In these questions, relationship between different elements is shown in the statements. The statements are followed by conclusions.*

Give answer

(*a*) If only conclusion I is true
(*b*) If only conclusion II is true
(*c*) If either conclusion I or II is true
(*d*) If neither conclusion I nor II is true
(*e*) If both conclusions I and II are true

77. Statements: $F > R \geq T = E > W \leq Q$

Conclusions:

I. $E < F$ **II.** $Q \geq T$

78. Statements: $W = G \geq H \geq T = C \leq V \leq B$

Conclusions:

I. $T < G$ **II.** $C = G$

79. Statements: $K > I \geq G > F \leq T < R$

Conclusions:

I. $K > T$ **II.** $R > F$

80. Statements: $K < G \leq D < C > R \leq Y$

Conclusions:

I. $C > G$ **II.** $K < D$

81. In the Given number **'843576529'** How many such numerals will remain at the same position, when arranged in ascending order from left to right?

(1) More than Four (2) Four
(3) Two (4) Three
(5) One

Directions (82-86): *Study the following information carefully and answer the question given below-*

Eight persons A, B, C, D, E, F, G and H were born in the month of December of 4 different years *i.e.* 1956, 1957, 1958 and 1959 either on 14th or 23rd but not necessarily in the same order. E was born in the even numbered year but not the eldest among all. More than two persons were born between E and D. H was born just after D. There are as many persons born before H as same as born after B. G was born before F and after A and they all were born on the same date.

82. How many persons born before C?

(1) One (2) None
(3) Two (4) More than four
(5) Four

83. In which of the following year B was born?

(1) 1956
(2) 1959

(3) Either 1956 or 1959
(4) 1957
(5) 1958

84. How many persons were born between A and F?
(1) Three (2) Five
(3) Two (4) One
(5) None of these

85. Four of the following five are alike in a certain way and so form a group. Find the one who does not belong to that group?
(1) D (2) B
(3) E (4) C
(5) H

86. The number of persons born between G and H is same as between .... and ....?
(1) E, F (2) B, H
(3) C, B (4) D, G
(5) None of these

Directions (87-90): *In each question below are given some statements followed by two conclusions numbered I and II. You have to take the given statements to be true even if they seem to be at variance with commonly known facts and then decide which of the given conclusions logically follows from the given statements, disregarding commonly known facts. Give answer:*

87. Statements: Only a few Photo are Video. Only a few Frame are Video. All Frame are Camera.
Conclusions:
I. All Photo being Frame is a possibility.
II. Some Photo are not Camera.
(1) If both conclusions I and II follow.
(2) If only conclusion II follows.
(3) If only conclusion I follows.
(4) If neither conclusion I nor II follows.
(5) If either conclusion I or II follows.

88. Statements: Only a few City are Town. No Town is Village. All Village are Block.
Conclusions:
I. All City can be Village.
II. Some Block are not Town.
(1) If both conclusions I and II follow.
(2) If either conclusion I or II follows.
(3) If only conclusion I follows.
(4) If neither conclusion I nor II follows.
(5) If only conclusion II follows.

89. Statements: Some Bird are not Eagle. Some Eagle are Parrot.
Conclusions:
I. Some Parrot are Bird.
II. No Parrot is Bird.
(1) If only conclusion I follows.
(2) If either conclusion I or II follows.
(3) If both conclusions I and II follow.
(4) If neither conclusion I nor II follows.
(5) If only conclusion II follows.

90. Statements: Only Banana is Apple. Some Banana are Papaya.
Conclusions:
I. Some Apple being Papaya is a possibility.
II. All Banana can be Apple.
(1) If both conclusions I and II follow.
(2) If only conclusion I follows.
(3) If either conclusion I or II follows.
(4) If neither conclusion I nor II follows.
(5) If only conclusion II follows.

Direction (91-95): *Study the following information carefully and answer the questions given below:*

Eight persons D, E, F, G, M, O, P and S purchase some products one after another but not necessarily in the same order. At most two persons purchase before F. Only one-person purchase between D and F. P purchase just before S. One-person purchase between P and D. M purchase just before E. O purchase before G and after E.

91. How many persons purchase after D?
(1) None (2) Two
(3) More than three (4) One
(5) None of these

92. Who among the following purchase just after G?
(1) E (2) F
(3) O (4) P
(5) None of these

93. If all the persons are arranged in alphabetical order from top to bottom starting from D, then find how many persons remains at the same position (excluding D)?

(1) One (2) None
(3) Two (4) Four
(5) More than Four

94. Who among the following purchase exactly between D and F?

(1) E (2) O
(3) M (4) S
(5) None of these

95. How many persons purchase between E and P?

(1) Five (2) Four
(3) Three (4) None
(5) Two

96. How many pairs of letters are there in the word "**CHRISTMAS**" which has as many letters between them as we have in the English alphabetical series (from both forward and backward direction)?

(1) Three (2) One
(3) Two (4) None
(5) More than three

Direction (97-100): *Study the following arrangement carefully and answer the questions given below:*

3 9 1 8 1 2 5 8 6 3 6 4 2 5 2 8 5 2 6 4 5 1 4 9 4 7 3 2 7 2 5 9

97. How many 2'*s* is there in the above arrangement, each of which is immediately preceded by a digit which has a numerical value of more than 5?

(1) None (2) One
(3) Two (4) Three
(5) More than three

98. Which of the following number is seventh to the left of the twentieth from the left end of the above arrangement?

(1) 3 (2) 9
(3) 2 (4) 7
(5) 1

99. If all the even digits are removed from the above arrangements then, which of the following digit will be tenth from the right end of the arrangement?

(1) 9 (2) 5
(3) 1 (4) 3
(5) 7

100. How many such 1's is there in the above arrangement, each of which is immediately followed by a perfect square?

(1) None (2) One
(3) Two (4) Three
(5) More than three

Answers With Explanations

1. (1) From the 2nd paragraph, "Sleep allows us to consolidate and store memories, process emotional experiences, replenish glucose (the molecule that fuels the brain), and clear out beta- amyloid (the waste product that builds up in Alzheimer's patients and disrupts cognitive activity)."

2. (2) From the last sentence of the 3rd paragraph "During sleep, regeneration of neurons happens in the cerebral cortex. Thus, in a sleep deprived individual the brain fails to function optimally."

3. (4) **4.** (2)

5. (5)

6. (2) Sufficient means enough; adequate.

7. (3)

8. (2) Replenish means restore to a former level or condition.

9. (1) Replace 'between' by 'into'.

10. (1) The correct answer should be "She stayed up".

11. (3) 'were' must be replaced by 'was'.

12. (5)

13. (4) 'Was' must be replaced by 'is'.

14. (2) Replace "too" with "to"

15. (1) The correct phrase is "they themselves had".

16. (4)
17. (5)
18. (4)
19. (2)
20. (2)
21. (3)
22. (2)
23. (2)
24. (4)
25. (4)
26. (5)
27. (5)
28. (3)
29. (5)
30. (1)

31. (1) Let the speed of the train B be x km/h.
According to the question–
$20(36 + x) \times 5/18 = 600$
$3600 + 100x = 10800$
$100x = 7200$
$x = 72$ km/h

32. (2) Profit ratio of A : B = (X × 4 + 2X × 8) : (2X × 8)
= 20X : 16X = 5 : 4
Hence, profit of A = 13950 × 5/9 = Rs. 7750

33. (5)

34. (1) $2(l + 18) = 84$
$2l = 48$
$l = 24$ m
Hence, side of square = 72 – 24 = 48 m

35. (5) Ratio of efficiency of A, B and C = 3 : 2 : 4
Suppose that the total work
$=(3x + 2x + 4x) \times 8 = 72x$ unit
Required days = $72x \times 3/4 \times 1/3x = 18$ days

36. (4) **I.** $2x^2 - 2x - x + 1 = 0$
$2x(x - 1) - 1(x - 1) = 0$
$x = 1/2, 1$
II. $2y^2 - 2y - 3y + 3 = 0$
$2y(y - 1) - 3(y - 1) = 0$
$y = 3/2, 1$
$x \le y$

37. (2) **I.** $x^2 + 10x + 11x + 110 = 0$
$x(x + 10) + 11(x + 10) = 0$
$x = -10, -11$
II. $y^2 + 9y + 8y + 72 = 0$
$y(y + 9) + 8(y + 9)$
$y = -9, -8$
$x < y$

38. (4) **I.** $x = \pm 2$
II. $y^2 - 2y - 4y + 8 = 0$
$y(y - 2) - 4(y - 2) = 0$
$y = 2, 4$
$x \le y$

39. (5) **I.** $x^2 + 9x - 22 = 0$
$\Rightarrow x^2 + 11x - 2x - 22 = 0$
$\Rightarrow (x + 11)(x - 2) = 0$
$\Rightarrow x = -11, 2$
II. $2y^2 - 7y + 6 = 0$
$\Rightarrow 2y^2 - 4y - 3y + 6 = 0$
$\Rightarrow 2y(y - 2) - 3(y - 2) = 0$
$\Rightarrow (y - 2)(2y - 3) = 0$
$\Rightarrow y = 2, 3/2$
No relation

40. (5) **I.** $6x^2 + 5x + 1 = 0$
$6x^2 + 3x + 2x + 1 = 0$
$3x(2x + 1) + 1(2x + 1) = 0$
$x = -1/2$ or $-1/3$
II. $15y^2 + 11y + 2 = 0$
$15y^2 + 6y + 5y + 2 = 0$
$3y(5y + 2) + 1(5y + 2) = 0$
$\therefore y = -2/5$ or $-1/3$
$\therefore$ no relation can be established

41. (2) Required population = 15000 × 0.9 × 1.2 = 16200

42. (2) Let the CP of shirt be Rs. $100x$
Then MP = Rs. $150x$
SP = $150x \times 8/9 \times 9/10$ = Rs. $120x$
Profit = Rs. $20x$
Discount given = Rs. $30x$ ATQ,
$10x = 200$
$\Rightarrow x = 20$
MP = Rs. 3000

43. (2) Let the speed of boat in still water be x km/h and that of stream be y km/h.
According to the question
$(x + y) - (x - y) = 5$
$\Rightarrow y = 2.5$ km/hr
$x = 2.5 \times 19/5 = 9.5$ km/h

Required time = 8h

44. (1) Let initial quantity of liquid P and Q in container be $5x$ and $3x$ respectively.

Hence,

$5x - 10 = 4x$

$x = 10$

Initial quantity of mixture

$= (5 + 3) \times 10 = 80$ liter

45. (2) Let the present age of B be $5x$ years.

Present age of A = $5x \times 8/5 = 8x$ years

Present age of C = $35 \times 2 - 5x = (70 - 5x)$ years

According to the question,

$(8x - 5) + (5x - 5) = 55$

$x = 5$

Required difference = $(70 - 5x) - 8x = 5$ years

46. (1) Required percentage = (40 − 32)/100 = 20%

47. (3) Required sum = (28 + 12) + (38 + 15) = 93

48. (1) Required average = (50 + 32 + 38)/3 = 40

49. (2) Let total videos shared by E be x.

Total photos shared by E = $(x + 4)$

According to the question–

$x + x + 4 = 44$ $2x = 40$

$x = 20$

50. (1)

51. (4) $(? \div 5 \div 7) \times 14 = 308$

$? = 22 \times 35$

$? = 770$

52. (2) $?^3 + 144 = 360$

$?^3 = 216$

$? = 6$

53. (2) **54.** (3)

55. (2) $196 + 179 + 25 = (?)^2$

$(?)^2 = 400$

$? = 20$

56. (5) $28.5 \times 34 + 2320 \div 8 = (36)^2 - ?$

$969 + 290 = 1296 - ?$

$1259 = 1296 - ?$

$? = 1296 - 1259 = 37$

57. (4) $? = 47 \times 27 + 15600 \div 8 + 181$

$= 1269 + 1950 + 181$

$= 3400$

58. (3) $? = 112.5 \times 5 + 4560 \div 6 - 175 \times 7$

$= 562.5 + 760 - 1225$

$= 1322.5 - 1225$

$= 97.5$

59. (3) **60.** (1)

61. (2) $? + 13 \times 50 = 420 + 45/100 \times 800 + 220$

$\Rightarrow$ $? + 650 = 420 + 360 + 220$

$\Rightarrow$ $? = 1000 - 650 = 350$

62. (4) **64.** (1)

63. (5) **65.** (5)

For questions (66-70):

Boxes
S
P
U
R
Q
T
V
W

66. (5) **69.** (2)

67. (3) **70.** (4)

68. (1)

71. (1)

B A C K G R O U N D

A B B J F Q P V M C

For questions (72-76):

A > E > F > C > B > D

34 27 17

72. (1) **75.** (4)

73. (2) **76.** (2)

74. (4)

77. (1) **I.** E < F (True) **II.** Q ≥ T (False)

78. (3) **I.** T < G (False) **II.** C = G (False)

79. (2) **I.** K > T (False) **II.** R > F (True)

80. (5) **I.** C > G (True) **II.** K < D (True)

81. (4)

8 4 3 [5] 7 [6] 5 2 [9]

2 3 4 [5] 5 [6] 7 8 [9]

For questions (82-86):

Years	Month	Date	Persons
1956	December	14	D
		23	H
1957		14	C
		23	A
1958		14	E
		23	G
1959		14	B
		23	F

82. (3)

83. (2)

84. (1)

85. (5)

86. (3)

87. (3)

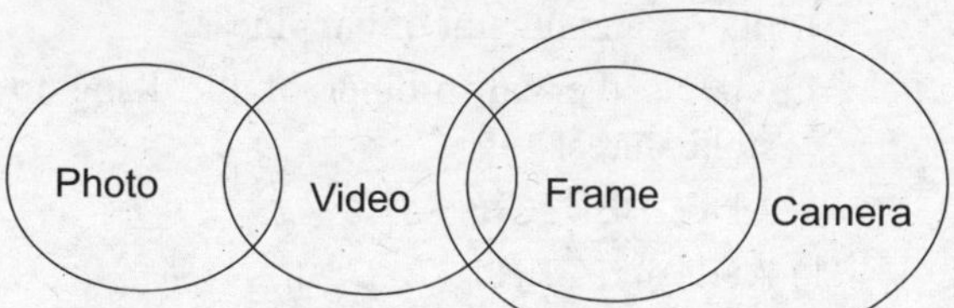

88. (5)

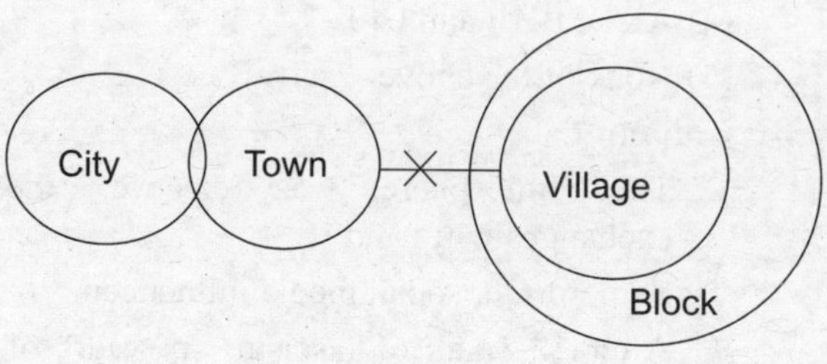

89. (2)

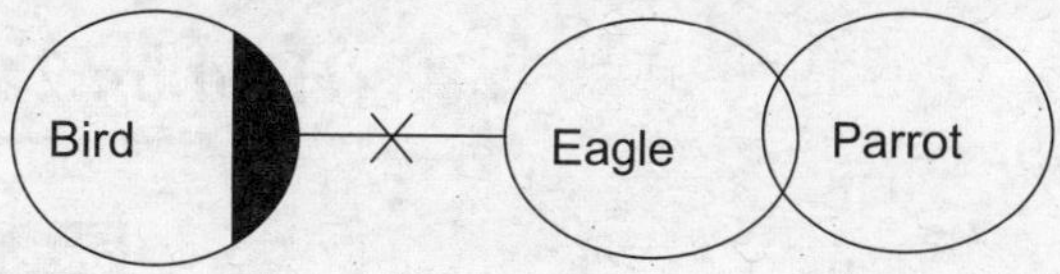

90. (4)

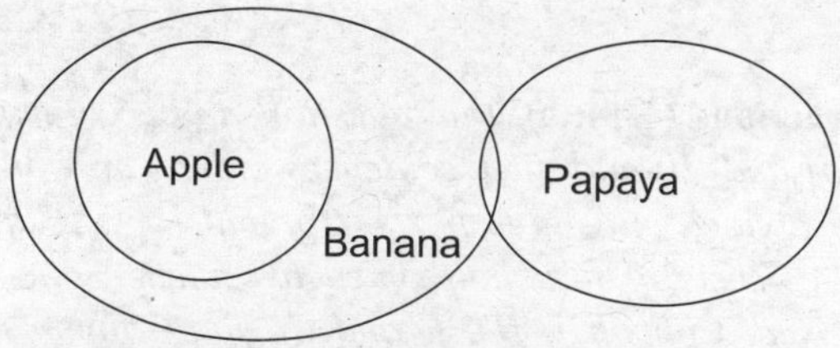

For questions (91-95):

Persons
M
E
F
O
D
G
P
S

91. (5)

92. (4)

93. (4)

94. (2)

95. (2)

96. (3)

97. (2)

98. (3)

99. (2)

100. (2)

IBPS Clerk Mains, 2020

(Held on 24 January, 2021)

Based on Memory

General English

Directions (1-5): *In this question, three columns (I, II and III) and three sentences are given, which are divided into three parts. Column I (A, B and C) consists of first half of each sentence and it is fixed. Column II (D, E and F) and Column III (G, H and I) consist of the remaining half of each sentence. Match column I with column II and III, so that the sentences formed are both meaningful and grammatically correct. Choose the correct option as your answer.*

1. Column I

A. On 19 October 2017, the astronomer Robert Weryk

B. With her laptop in front of her

C. Mr. Zuckerman's extreme environmentalist anti-immigration sentiments

Column II

D. spotted an extraordinary splinter of rock, just a few hundred metres across,

E. is motivated by the presumption that the place we live is special

F. she's listening intently to a giant pair of headphones

Column III

G. Applying the technology in native town of California

H. held upside down so that the strap hangs below her chin

I. tumbling through our inner solar system

(1) ADI, BFH and CEG

(2) AID, BHF and CGE

(3) AIB, BHD and CGF

(4) ADI and BFH

(5) None of the above

2. Column I

A. Speculation might well be the creative engine of science

B. Democracy is a form of government based upon the fundamental assumption

C. The accused have been charged with conspiring with a senior royal

Column II

D. but it's only when flights of imagination are followed up by intellectually

E. of equality of all individuals and of their equal rights to life

F. against the monarch, while seeking foreign assistance

Column III

G. honest, rigorous critique that we have a chance of learning more about our world

H. liberty and pursuit of happiness

I. who is the half-brother of the King to stoke unrest

ADG, BEH, CIF

(1) AGD and BEH

(2) ADH, BEG and CFI

(3) ADG, BEH and CIF

(4) AGD, BHE and CFI

(5) None of the above

3. Column I

A. The atmosphere was electric, the exchanges witty and

B. Someformer social media influencers

C. After 12 years of fascism, six years of war, and the concentrated

Column II

D. highlight the dangers of curating a self-image with little purchase in reality

E. genocidal killing of the Holocaust

F. and thus the debates were well attended

by professors and students alike

Column III

G. the arguments well thought out and well-honed,

H. have turned against their platforms and chosen to

I. investment to market is extremely risky. AGF and BHD

(1) AFG, BEH and CFI

(2) AFI, BHE, and CIF

(3) AGF and BHD

(4) AFG and CDH

(5) None of the above

4. Column I

A. The actress took her second vaccine shot

B. Detailed reports from the north Germany suggest that

C. Renaissance philosophy started in the mid-14th century

Column II

D. for Covid exactly a month after her first dose

E. in one city alone, some 100,000 people bought confiscated

F. and saw the flowering of humanism, the rejection of scholasticism

Column III

G. and shared the update with fans on Instagram on Tuesday

H. goods from various auctions during the Nazi regime

I. and the renewal of interest in the ancients

(1) ADG, BEH and CFI

(2) AGD, BHE and CIF

(3) ADH, BEI and CFG

(4) AFH, BDI and CGE

(5) None of the above

5. Column I

A. Nihilism, over the course of time, has been given

B. Some people are lucky enough to look back at

C. The leader of the opposition vehemently criticized and slammed

Column II

D. many meanings and has been interpreted in

E. as benefitted from the work-from- home and remote education boom

F. the list of hospitals was provided by the government

Column III

G. many differentways by philosophers through-out history

H. most of them being state-run hospitals

I. vaccines, especially in the rural area

(1) AEG and CFI (2) BEI

(3) AGF, BEH and CFI

(4) ADG

(5) None of the above

Directions (6-11): *Read the passage carefully and answer the questions that follow. A word is given in bold to help you locate it while answering on of them.*

I don't think it's too soon to say that the COVID-19 global pandemic will likely be one of the defining events of 2020, and that it will have implications that last well into the decade. The situation is rapidly changing. The amount of people deemed safe to gather in a single place has dwindled from thousands, to hundreds, to ten. Restaurants, bars, movie theaters, and gyms in many major cities are shutting down. Meanwhile many office workers are facing new challenges of working remotely full time.

Essentially, people are coming to terms with the realities of our interconnected world and how difficult it is to temporarily separate those connections to others. To say that we are living in unprecedented times feels like an understatement. We received responses from many on how people are approaching this period of isolation and uncertainty in huge overnight changes to their shopping behaviors. From bulk- buying to online shopping, people are changing what they're buying, when, and how.

As more cities are going under lockdowns, nonessential businesses are being ordered to close, and customers are generally avoiding public places.

Limiting shopping for all but necessary essentials is becoming a new normal. Brands are having to adapt and be flexible to meet changing needs. As people have embraced social distancing as a way to slow the spread of the pandemic, there has naturally been a **drop-off** in brick-and-mortar shopping. That would seem to mean there would likely be an increase in online shopping as people turn to e-commerce to purchase the items they might have otherwise purchased in person.

No doubt, online retail has played a huge role in keeping the U.S. economy from suffering even greater damage during the pandemic. **Stay-at-home orders and consumer** .... Online retail still doesn't completely satisfy most consumers, though. A study reported 90% of surveyed shoppers stated high shipping fees and home delivery lasting more than two days would deter an online purchase.

Amazon (the nation's second largest retailer behind only Walmart) cracked the code with its Prime service, offering free shipping and two-day (or faster) turnaround. Not surprisingly, Amazon saw tremendous sales growth in 2020. Other national retailers, including Walmart and Target, have poured resources into strengthening their online shipping services.

For example, customers shop for items online, then pick up their merchandise either in the store or, even more conveniently, curbside in their cars.

However, the market shift in retail is posing tremendous challenges to small retailers: challenges that COVID-19 exacerbated. Surely, engaging in e-commerce is more than simply setting up a website and waiting for orders.

6. Which of the following word/phrase can replace the highlighted phrase in the passage?
Drop off
(1) Rachet down (2) Distend
(3) Taper off (4) Both 1 and 3
(5) All 1, 2 and 3

7. Which of the following assumptions strengthen the given argument in the passage?
Surely, engaging in e-commerce is more than simply setting up a website and waiting for orders.
A. E-commerce business involves a huge costs related to software, sales tax accounting and SEO.
B. The investors are augment their profits without adhering to tax liabilities.
C. Consumer behavior and loyalty is much dependent on their safety during the pandemic and immediate access to the retail products.
(1) Only A (2) Only B
(3) Both A and C (4) Both B and C
(5) All of these

8. Which of the following statements best describes the main idea of the passage?
A. Understanding the COVID-19 Effect on Online Shopping behavior
B. Understanding the impact of pandemic on online retail industry
C. How has pandemic led to revival of brick and mortar shopping
(1) Only A (2) Only B
(3) Both B and C (4) Only C
(5) Both A and B

9. Which of the following can best describe the tone of the passage?
(1) Commiserating (2) Grandiose
(3) Derisive (4) Dogmatic
(5) Incendiary

10. What does the author mean when he mentions:
"To say that we are living in unprecedented times feels like an understatement."
(1) The author means that the overnight changes that this pandemic has caused people to incorporate in them is though unwelcomed, but people are pushing hard to adapt themselves to it. Such situation have never been experienced before but the way people have adapted to it, we can say that the intensity of the challenge seems less now.
(2) The overnight changes, isolation, separation from interconnected world, people are much affected and they are finding it hard to adapt to the new normal.

(3) The intensity of the pandemic currently is quite low and people are able to adapt to it easily, seeming that such an experience is not anything new for them.

(4) Both 1 and 2

(5) Both 2 and 3

11. Which of the following statements should precede the emboldened line in the passage?

For example, customers shop for items online, then pick up their merchandise either in the store or, even more conveniently, curbside in their cars.

(1) As online momentum builds, online return volumes will inevitably rise – putting intense pressure on profit margins.

(2) For many businesses striving to remain relevant and survive the disruption, their transition will likely mean a challenging readjustment as business models are aligned with the 'new normal'.

(3) Omni-channel marketing — which combines the strengths of online and in-person retail — offers opportunities for brick-and-mortar retailers to serve customers in this new environment of increased comfort with web shopping.

(4) As the European retail industry undergoes a period of transformation, businesses need to adopt a more detailed and data-driven approach to profitability.

(5) Before using the product, consumers should check that product they received is what they actually ordered by comparing its description at the point of purchase with the product packaging information, and that there is no visible damage.

Directions (12-17): *Read the given passage carefully and answer the questions that follow. Certain word (s) are printed in bold to help you locate them while answering some of these.*

Genghis Khan got his dying wish: despite attempts by archaeologists and scientists to find the Mongolian ruler's final resting place, the location remains a secret 800 years after his death. The search for his tomb, though, has inspired an **innovative** project that could help protect polar bears.

"I randomly tuned into the radio one night and heard an expert talking about the use of synthetic **aperture** radar [SAR] to look for Genghis Khan's tomb," says a researcher involved in the project. "They were using SAR to penetrate layers of forest canopy in upper Mongolia, looking for the ruins of a burial structure."

Talking to engineers, the researcher learnt that SAR is used by the military to detect enemy camps, tanks and vehicles hidden beneath **camouflage** and is being studied as a potential tool for finding avalanche survivors. He and his team had been looking for a technology to detect polar bear dens. "It was very **serendipitous** that I heard that broadcast," he says. Successful pilot tests using SAR to find simulated polar bear dens took place in Alaska's Prudhoe Bay in 2014 and 2015. The project was resurrected with trials in March 2021 on a snowy mountain plateau in Utah's Manti-La Sal national forest. A SAR device was fitted to a Cessna O- 2A Skymaster that flew 3,000 ft (900 metres) over researchers and students digging dens a metre under the snow. With a lack of polar bears in Utah, students crawled inside to act as targets, or laid out simulated bears made from cardboard and tinfoil.

Building dens is a critical period for polar bears. For months, **vulnerable** cubs rely on their mother's milk and the safety of the den to survive. As polar bears are driven further inland by <u>receding sea ice</u>, denning areas and oil and gas activity increasingly overlap. Disturbances can push fearful mothers to abandon their dens. The chances of survival for ....

With fewer than 26,000 polar bears thought to be left globally and an estimated decline of 40% in some populations, such as the southern Beaufort Sea, every den and bear counts.

SAR detects objects by sending pulses of radio waves; sensors pick up the echo or "bounce" to map an area. The aim is to find the right frequency, a sweet spot, which can penetrate snow but still detect a bear. Getting reliable data on denning sites is vital. "The <u>Arctic</u> national wildlife refuge is the perfect example," says a researcher. "Industry wants to go in and pump oil. If we have a tool that definitively says exactly where polar bear dens are, that means keeping people away from those places.

If we want bears, we need baby bears, so we've got to protect those dens."

12. Which of the following assumptions are supported by the passage?

I. Synthetic Aperture Radar can penetrate denser surfaces for the most effective remote sensing among extant remote sensors.

II. Global Warming is directly related to the endangerment of polar bears.

III. Researchers need approximate data on denning sites to better protect them.

(1) Only I (2) Only II
(3) Both I and II (4) Both II and III
(5) All I, II, and III

13. Given below is a possible inference that can be drawn from the facts stated in the passage. You have to examine the inference in the context of the passage and decide upon its degree of truth or falsity.

"Synthetic Aperture Radar is an amplitude-based remote sensing that tries to find the right amplitude of the echoes reflecting off surfaces and targets."

(1) Definitely true (2) True
(3) False (4) Definitely false
(5) Cannot be determined

14. Which of the following themes is being discussed in the passage?

(1) Climate change and its impact on arctic fauna.
(2) Scientific Research as a way forward to combat climate change and species extinction.
(3) Remote sensing as a way of combating the extinction of endangered species.
(4) The role of sound wave frequency in developing modern remote sensing AI.
(5) None of the above

15. Which of the following options correctly describe the tone of the passage?

(1) Caustic (2) Informative
(3) Assertive (4) Deprecatory
(5) Condescending

16. Which of the following can effectively fill the blank in the fifth paragraph of the passage?

(1) the weak and undeveloped cubs prematurely out on the snow and ice, are drastically reduced.
(2) the strong and well developed cubs prematurely out on the snow and ice, are drastically reduced.
(3) the weak and hyperdeveloped cubs out on the snow and ice, are drastically increased.
(4) Both 1 and 3
(5) None of the above.

17. Which of the following words as used in the passage can be replaced by the word "Fortuitous"?

(1) Innovative (2) Aperture
(3) Camouflage (4) Serendipitous
(5) Vulnerable

Directions (18-20): *Four statements are given below at A, B, C and D. There may be some errors in the given statements. Mark the incorrect statement as the answer. If all the statements are incorrect, mark E i.e. All are incorrect as the answer.*

18. (1) A 400-year old lake on Hawaii island was evaporated due to lava from the weeks-long eruption of the Kilauea volcano, which paved over tide pools and coral gardens, leading to death of a number of sea creatures.

(2) On Hawaii island, lava from the weeks-long eruption of the Kilauea volcano has paved over tide pools and coral gardens, boiled a 400-year-old lake until it evaporated and killed a number of sea creatures.

(3) The evaporation of a 400-year old lake on Hawaii island resulted due to the spread of lava from the weeks- long eruption of the Kilauea volcano, which paved over tide pools and coral gardens and a number of sea creatures.

(4) Death of a number of sea creatures resulted from a 400-year old lake on Hawaii island evaporating due to lava from the weeks-long eruption of the Kilauea volcano, which paved over tide

pools and coral gardens.

(5) All are incorrect

19. (1) The National Award-winning actor, Naseeruddin Shah, has acted in more than 100 films till date and knows the industry like the back of his hand.

(2) Luckily, the television series have also done a lot of permanent damage by propagating completely outdated and miscredited situations by showing the woman to always be at his husband's beck and call.

(3) I see hope from those filmmakers because they are making movies without the pressure of a producer sitting on their heads and without having to worry about the budget.

(4) Shah feels that most kids born into the industry believe that the industry owes them something by accommodating them.

(5) All are incorrect

20. (1) From the gorgeous scenery and rich history to the culture and the personalities of the people who live here, the unique aspects of Scotland are so appealing that it should surely be our next travel destination.

(2) The Scottish Highlands are just as beautiful as you've imagined and they let you see the Scotland of your imagination.

(3) Not all of Scotland is lush green – the coastline is lined with beautiful white sandy beaches where you can dig your toes in the sand and listen to the roaring waves crashing onto the land.

(4) The best way to feel the rhythm of traditional Scottish music is by attend a Scottish dance event for which you can dance in couples or small groups.

(5) All are incorrect

Directions (21-23): *Out of the five statements given below, only one is grammatically correct. Choose the correct statement as your answer.*

21. (1) Tape worms are those organisms which can breed in your intestine, which means they can also share the nutrition and fats of your food.

(2) People who practice KEN diet aren't allowed to eat or drink anything for a span of 10 days, and they even have to get a pipe inserted through their nose for the supply of basic nutrients.

(3) Fascinating architecture - whether modern or historic - always attracts tourism because it's indicative of the kind of beauty only humans and not so machines can together create.

(4) Push-ups are one of the exercise which strengthen your arms and upper body but give you a great physique.

(5) However the movie didn't gain as much attention in India, Zubaan was the first Bollywood film to open the 20th edition of the Busan International Film Festival.

22. (1) 2018 so far has been the year of movies and shows that struck a chord with the audience, not just for their story lines, but also for some amazing performances by certain actors.

(2) The subject of the film demanded the actors to portray a myriad range of human emotion, especially vulnerability in the farce of emotional loss.

(3) Adele's mother was a brilliant guitar player and a young Adele had begun developing an interest in music from her mother's age.

(4) While studying in one of the most renowned schools of performing arts, Adele wanted to make her career in Artists and Repertoire, which entails overlooking the artistic development of recording artists and songwriters.

(5) Not only is she a critically acclaimed singer, she's an incredible human being who's bold, powerful, and believes in taking charge of her own life.

23. (1) Not to far from the realms of the Thar desert, its shape-shifting sand dunes, mighty forts and palaces, the Kalbeliya dancers and scorching heat, there lies a city with lush green forests, pleasant weather and plenty of flora or fauna.

(2) Achalgarh fort was build by Maharana Kumbha, the ruler of Mewar, who built a total of 32 forts in Rajasthan during his reign.

(3) Krem Puri Cave is an incredibly complex maze of hundred of short passages and long stretches of corridors which are interconnected in a big network.

(4) The Shyok River meets the Nubra or Siachan River to form the beautiful Nubra valley separates the Ladakh and Karakoram mountain ranges.

(5) The Bhimbekta caves were discovered quite recently in 1957 and were declared a UNESCO World Heritage Site only in 2003.

Direction (24): *In the following question, three statements have been given, and a word has been highlighted in each of them which may be the synonym or antonym of the word given in bold. Identify the statement(s) in which the word fits contextually to convey a logical meaning.*

24. Hurdle

I. By going around the world in his wheelchair, Rick Hansen showed the world that an **impediment** shouldn't stop you from achieving your goals.

II. Bored, restless, fearful, she retreated to the back of the cave, searching it again for any sort of door or anything that might **aid** her escape.

III. If you're in the middle of a blistering guitar solo on an electric, you can **fudge** the details a little bit in a way that would never fly on an acoustic.

(1) Only I (2) Only II
(3) Both II and III (4) Both I and II
(5) All I, II and III

Direction (25-28): *In the following question, three statements have been given, and a word has been highlighted in each of them which may be the synonym or antonym of the word given in bold. Identify the statement(s) in which the word fits contextually to convey a logical meaning.*

25. Convert

I. Before going on the trip, he **changed** the currency to ensure no hassle during the vacation.

II. The **apostate** firmly believed in his decision to leave the order following the discovery of its criminal activities.

III. The **translate** was quickly edging into an agitated argument.

(1) Both I and II (2) Both I and III
(3) Both II and III (4) Only I
(5) Only II

26. Remedial

I. The **therapeutic** sessions helped her a lot in coming to terms with the trauma of being orphaned at the age of five.

II. Despite being discharged from the hospital, he was advised to remain on **palliative** care.

III. The audience was quickly becoming **restorative** and demanded that the artist begin the performance immediately.

(1) Both I and III (2) Both I and II
(3) Only III (4) Both II and III
(5) None of the above

27. Abscond

I. For a minute there, the policemen thought that the thief was going to **bolt** and run away from custody.

II. Today's seizure was by far the biggest **seizure** of cannabis by the police force of the state.

III. Ayush **escaped** after slaying his brother, but he couldn't avoid the lingering sense of guilt.

(1) Only I (2) Only II
(3) Only III (4) Both I and III
(5) All I, II and III

28. Adamant

I. The king **resolved** to avenge his father's death by conquering the southern province by fair means or foul.

II. Due to pandemic, students are not able to take proper examinations and their grades in many cases might not be **satisfactory**.

III. Passengers in large numbers were seen

proceeding towards the railway stations to catch the train.

(1) Only I (2) Only II
(3) Only III (4) Both I and II
(5) All I, II and III

Directions (29-34): *In the following question, six statements have been given. All the given sentences, when rearranged, form a coherent paragraph. Arrange the parts to form coherent and grammatically correct passage and answer the questions that follow.*

A. The happiness first infected the zeitgeist with the publication of Laurie Garrett's The Coming Plague (1994) and Richard Preston's Hot Zone (1995).

B. But there's something in these scenarios not logical as there is nothing new in the intimate contact between animals and people because our hominid ancestors lived on wildlife before we ever evolved into Homo sapiens.

C. the fear about pandemic is confirmed by historical memory (1)/ history like black confetti (2)/ because over the time, plagues have killed a (3)/ lot of people, and deadly diseases litter (4)

D. According to the evolutionary epidemiologists, the most dangerous infectious diseases are **almost always not animal diseases fresh broken into the human species**, but diseases adapted to humanity over time: smallpox, malaria, tuberculosis, leprosy, typhus, yellow fever, polio.

E. One of the early records is that of the Antonine Plague in the year 165 CE, killed the Marcus Aurelius and millions of his subjects while the Black Death of 1348-50, spread by human fleas and from human lung to human lung, killed tens of millions.

F. Great Australian virologist Frank Macfarlane Burnet, argued (1)/ the plagues were a result from (2) human intrusion into the natural world (3)/ Studying these events, many health experts, including the (4)

29. Out of the given sentences, which of the following is incoherent to the theme of the passage?

(1) D (2) B
(3) C (4) F
(5) A

30. What should be the correct sequence of statement labelled C?

(1) 1324 (2) 1342
(3) 2134 (4) 3124
(5) No changes required

31. What should be the correct sequence of statement labelled F?

(1) 1243 (2) 3214
(3) 2413 (4) 4123
(5) No changes required

32. Which of the following will be the second statement after rearrangement?

(1) E (2) B
(3) C (4) D
(5) F

33. Which of the following will be the last statement after rearrangement?

(1) A (2) B
(3) E (4) D
(5) F

34. In statement D, a part of the sentence is highlighted. Below the sentence, alternatives to the emboldened part are given as (A), (B), (C) and (D), which may help improve the sentence. Choose the correct alternative out of the given five options. In case the given sentence is correct, the answer will be option (E), i.e., 'No correction required'.

(1) almost always not animal diseases freshly broken into the human species
(2) almost always not animal diseases refresh broken into the human species
(3) almost always not animal diseases fresh broken into the human specimen
(4) almost always not animalish diseases fresh broken into the human species
(5) No correction required.

35. Convert

I. Before going on the trip, he **changed** the

currency to ensure no hassle during the vacation.

II. The **apostate** firmly believed in his decision to leave the order following the discovery of its criminal activities.

III. The **translate** was quickly edging into an agitated argument.

(1) Both I and II (2) Both I and III
(3) Both II and III (4) Only I
(5) Only II

36. Remedial

I. The **therapeutic** sessions helped her a lot in coming to terms with the trauma of being orphaned at the age of five.

II. Despite being discharged from the hospital, he was advised to remain on **palliative** care.

III. The audience was quickly becoming **restorative** and demanded that the artist begin the performance immediately.

(1) Both I and III (2) Both I and II
(3) Only III (4) Both II and III
(5) None of the above

Directions (37-38): *The following question carries a statement with two blanks. From the given options, choose the option that would fit in both the blanks to make the sentence grammatically correct and meaningful.*

37. The "................." election of four new hereditary peers to the House of Lords has shown how a "few dozen ...." have more sway than thousands of voters and campaigners say.

A. mad, ill-bred
B. sensible, countess
C. asinine, commoner
D. ludicrous, aristocrat
E. grandee, quotidian

38. In the short panel discussion at the end of the conference an .... voice asked whether digital architecture is really ...., in a social and political sense.

(1) afraid, stringent (2) shrieky, profound
(3) intrepid, radical (4) cowardly, draconian
(5) plucky, lament

Directions (39-40): *A sentence with two blanks is given, followed by five options. The correct answer must fill both the blanks, to make the sentence meaningfully and grammatically correct.*

39. While conducting the research into the rationale behind the country's propagandising, the scholars .... that the country's .... elite's anxiety to present themselves as a homogeneous group was, ironically, a byproduct of their nation's Mediterranean geography.

(1) Determined (2) Lettered
(3) Grave (4) Read
(5) None of the above

40. Despite inflicting .... on the 'Other' for generations, the white people of specific ethnic and religious backgrounds are .... up about soon becoming the electoral minority in the regions they currently dominate because of immigration, both legal and illegal, and differing fertility rates among the relevant groups.

(1) Damage (2) Bruises
(3) Wound (4) Triggered
(5) None of the above

Quantitative Aptitude

Directions (41-46): *Study the following pie charts and answer the given questions.*

The pie chart given below shows the total number of employees (male and female) working in 5 companies – A, B, C, D and E .

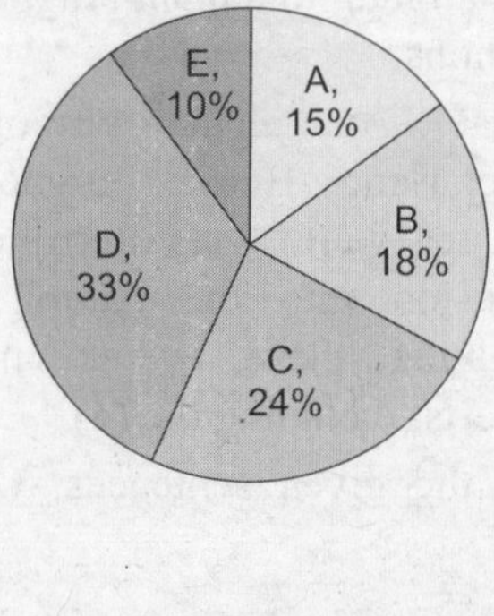

The below pie chart shows the number of male employees working in 5 companies – A, B, C, D and E.

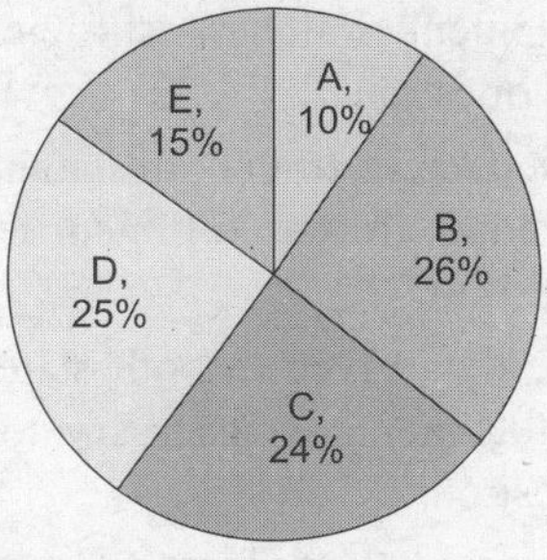

Note:

I. The difference of the total number of employees (male and female) working in companies A and B is 21.

II. The number of male employees working in company A is 800/21% of the total number of employees working in company A.

41. What is the central angle of total number of male employees working in company A?

(1) 36° (2) 45°
(3) 54° (4) 60°
(5) 75°

42. What is the average number of female employees working in the given 5 companies?

(1) 50 (2) 48
(3) 54 (4) 70
(5) None of these

43. What is the ratio of number of female employees working in companies C and E?

(1) 36 : 5 (2) 18 : 5
(3) 8 : 1 (4) 6 : 1
(5) None of these

44. Number of female employees working in company B is what percent less than the number of male employees working in company D?

(1) 63% (2) 72%
(3) 22% (4) 78%
(5) None of these

45. Find the difference of number of female employees working in the companies A and D.

(1) 86 (2) 206
(3) 65 (4) 66
(5) None of these

46. Only 12.5% of female employees and 18.75% of male employees working in the company C are post graduate, find the total number of post graduate employees working in the company C.

(1) 18 (2) 24
(3) 27 (4) 30
(5) None of these

47. There are total 80 students in a class. The number of boys who were not present in the class is 4 less than the number of girls who were not present. The number of girls who were present was two-third more than girls who were not present. 40 boys were present in the class. Find the total number of girls in the class.

(1) 28 (2) 40
(3) 32 (4) 30
(5) 48

48. There are two villages X and Y. Number of females in village X and female in village Y is equal. Number of male in village Y is 25% less than the number of males in village X. If the number of females in village Y reduced by 50% and the number of males in village Y becomes 50% more than that of village X then total population of village Y will remain same. Find the ratio of total population of village X and village Y.

(1) 7 : 6 (2) 5 : 6
(3) 10 : 9 (4) 12 : 7
(5) None of these

49. A container has 160 litres of pure milk and X litres of milk was drawn and replaced with same quantity of water. Now milk becomes three times of water. If 20 litres of mixture was taken out and replaced with same quantity of water, find the quantity of water in final mixture.

(1) 64 litres (2) 72 litres
(3) 40 litres (4) 55 litres
(5) 50 litres

50. An article is marked up by X% and sold on 0.5 X% of discount and earns profit of 8%. Find the value of X if the value of X is more than 20 .

(1) 80 (2) 70
(3) 60 (4) 90
(5) 84

51. A invests Rs. 9780 in a scheme A at R% rate of simple interest for 3 years. He reinvests the interest amount in scheme B at 20% rate of interest on compound interest for 2 years. He received Rs. 6337.44 after 2 years. Find the value of R.

(1) 24 (2) 20
(3) 15 (4) 30
(5) 28

52. 60 men can complete a piece of work on time. 40 men can complete the same work in 12 more days. Find in how many days can 18 men complete 3/5th of the work.

(1) 50 days (2) 48 days
(3) 60 days (4) 72 days
(5) None of these

Directions (53-56): *Each question below is followed by two statements I and II. You have to determine whether the data given in the statement is sufficient for answering the question. You should use the data and your knowledge of Mathematics to choose the best possible answer.*

53. There is a series of three consecutive odd numbers and another series of three consecutive even numbers. Find the difference between sums of both series.

Statement I: Middle value of odd number series is 7 more than the middle value of even number series.

Statement II: Sum of smallest number of odd number series and largest number of even number series is 57.

(1) The data in statement I alone is sufficient to answer the question, while the data in statement II alone is not sufficient to answer the question
(2) The data in statement II alone is sufficient to answer the question, while the data in statement I alone is not sufficient to answer the question
(3) The data either in statement I alone or in statement II alone is sufficient to answer the question
(4) The data given in both statements I and II together are not sufficient to answer the question
(5) The data given in both statements I and II together are necessary to answer the question.

54. In a class, 52% students fail in English and 42% students fail in Mathematics. Find the percentage of students who passed in both exams.

Statement I: 48% students passed in English.

Statement II: 25% students passed in only Mathematics.

(1) The data in statement I alone is sufficient to answer the question, while the data in statement II alone is not sufficient to answer the question
(2) The data in statement II alone is sufficient to answer the question, while the data in statement I alone is not sufficient to answer the question
(3) The data either in statement I alone or in statement II alone is sufficient to answer the question
(4) The data given in both statements I and II together are not sufficient to answer the question
(5) The data given in both statements I and II together are necessary to answer the question.

55. There is a path around a square field. Find the area of the square field.

Statement I: Width of path around the square field is 2 m.

Statement II: Total area of the path is 136 m^2.

(1) The data in statement I alone is sufficient to answer the question, while the data in statement II alone is not sufficient to answer the question.
(2) The data in statement II alone is sufficient

to answer the question, while the data in statement I alone is not sufficient to answer the question.

(3) The data either in statement I alone or in statement II alone is sufficient to answer the question.

(4) The data given in both statements I and II together are not sufficient to answer the question.

(5) The data given in both statements I and II together are necessary to answer the question.

56. The ratio of monthly incomes of Ananya to Shaila is 5 : 6 and the ratio of their monthly savings is 2 : 3. What is the monthly expenditure of Shaila?

Statement I: The ratio of monthly income and monthly savings of Ananya is 5 : 2 respectively.

Statement II: The monthly expenditure of Ananya and Shaila is equal.

(1) The data in statement I alone is sufficient to answer the question, while the data in statement II alone is not sufficient to answer the question

(2) The data in statement II alone is sufficient to answer the question, while the data in statement I alone is not sufficient to answer the question

(3) The data either in statement I alone or in statement II alone is sufficient to answer the question

(4) The data given in both statements I and II together are not sufficient to answer the question

(5) The data given in both statements I and II together are necessary to answer the question.

57. $x^2 - \frac{23x^2}{\sqrt{46x^2 + 54x^2}} + k = 0$. If one root of this quadratic equation is 3/2, find the value of other root value.

(1) 3/5 (2) 4/5

(3) 4/7 (4) 2/3

(5) None of these

Directions (58-59): *Study the following information carefully and answer the question given below. Some equations and conditions are given.*

Equations	Conditions
a. $10x^2 - x - 3 = 0$	**d.** 50 times of largest root value is divisible by 6.
b. $4y^2 + 8y - 5 = 0$	**e.** Product of both root value is between –1 and –2.
c. $2z^2 + 9z - 35 = 0$	**f.** Sum of both root value will be positive value.

58. In the following the combination of equation and condition are satisfying each other?

(1) b-d (2) c-e

(3) a-d (4) b-f

(5) None of these

59. In the following the combination of equation and condition are satisfying each other?

(1) b-f (2) b-e

(3) c-d (4) a-e

(5) None of these

Directions (60-64): *What approximate value will come in place of the question mark (?) in the following question? (You are not expected to calculate the exact value)*

60. $\frac{1214.23 + 2312.03 - 825.98}{5.97} \times 2 = ? + 99.80$

(1) 750 (2) 720

(3) 800 (4) 840

(5) 850

61. $(15.99)^2 + (11.01)^2 - (9.98)^2 = ? + 124.001$

(1) 157 (2) 146

(3) 172 (4) 153

(5) 168

62. 74.9% of 719.99 – $?^2$ – 40% of 250.01 = $\sqrt{1370}$

(1) 25 (2) 20

(3) 32 (4) 16

(5) 12

63. $\frac{40.12 \times 14.99}{12.001} + 24.01 - 5.001 \times 31.899 = ?$

(1) –86 (2) –71
(3) 77 (4) 82
(5) –93

64. 59.98% of 640.09 – $?^3$ = 84.02% of 250 – 168.9

(1) 15 (2) 10
(3) 7 (4) 5
(5) 12

65. The ratio of the age of Anmol 5 years ago to the age of Prashant after 4 years is 4 : 5. Anmol is 5 years older than Prashant. Anmol is 4 years younger than Keshav. The age of Keshav is how much percentage more than that of Prashant?

(1) 45.5% (2) 52%
(3) 56.25% (4) 52.45%
(5) 60%

66. A shopkeeper mixed X litres sanitizer of one variety cost Rs. 240 per litres and (X – 12) litres sanitizer of other variety cost Rs. 280 per litres and after selling the mixture at Rs. 309 per litres, he got a profit of 20%. Find the value of X.

(1) 60 (2) 42
(3) 54 (4) 48
(5) None of these

67. P and Q started a business with the capital of Rs. 24000 and Rs. 32500. After x months R also joined them with the capital of Rs. 40000 while after $(x + 4)$ months, Q withdrawn all his investment and the ratio of the profit share of P to R after one year is 4 : 5. After how many months did Q withdraw the amount?

(1) 6 months (2) 8 months
(3) 5 months (4) 7 months
(5) None of these

68. Two bottles were purchased at the same price. One was sold at 25% profit and second was sold at a price which was Rs. 2160 less than the price at which first was sold. If the overall profit earned by selling both the bottles was 10%. What was the Cost price of one bottle?

(1) Rs. 5400 (2) Rs. 7200
(3) Rs. 9000 (4) Rs. 8400
(5) Rs. 7500

69. A container contains 765 litres mixture of milk and water in the ratio of 10 : 7 respectively. If 20% mixture was taken out and 2X litre milk and (3X – 32) litre water is added in the remaining mixture, then the ratio of the milk to water in the final mixture becomes 6 : 5. What is the difference between the quantity of milk and water in the final mixture?

(1) 80 litres (2) 60 litres
(3) 75 litres (4) 120 litres
(5) 90 litres

Directions (70-73): *Study the following information carefully and answer the questions that follow.*

Four people (P, Q, R, S) have certain amount of money in their wallets. The currency notes in the wallet of the four people were in only 3 denominations. (D-I, D-II, D-III)

The table given below shows the total amount that the four people have and the amount of the three different denominations for the four people.

The amount with S is missing from the table.

Person	Amount (in Rs.)	Denomination (D-I (in Rs.)	Denomination D-II (in Rs.)	Denomination d-III (in Rs.)
P	1120	50	20	10
Q	3250	100	20	5
R	5400	200	50	20
S	–	20	10	5

It is also known that each of the 4 people had the same number of currency notes for each of the denominations i.e. For person P: Number of notes of denomination D-I = Number of notes of denomination D-II = Number of notes of denomination D-III. This holds true for all the 4 people.

70. T has currency notes of three denominations - Rs. 500, Rs. 20 and Rs. 10 . If T has total amount of Rs. 3710 in his wallet, then the number of currency notes of each denomination that T has is how much less than the number of currency notes that P has?

All the above given conditions apply to T as well.

(1) 10 (2) 8
(3) 6 (4) 7
(5) 9

71. The amount with S in his wallet is less than Rs. 1000 and the number of notes of each denomination with S lies between 20 and 30 and is a prime number. Find the total number of currency notes with S.

(1) 66 (2) 72
(3) 69 (4) 75
(5) 87

72. What is the difference between the number of currency notes of each denomination of P and Q?

(1) 12 (2) 15
(3) 8 (4) 10
(5) None of these

73. Another person A has Rs. 25 more in his wallet than the average of the amount with Q and R together. A has minimum two notes of Rs. 2000 and notes of denomination of Rs. 200 and Rs. 50. What is the possible number of notes of Rs. 50 denomination that A could have? All the above given conditions apply to A as well.

(1) 5 (2) 3
(3) 4 (4) 2
(5) 6

Directions (74-75): *Study the following information carefully and answer the questions that follow.*

Car A: Car travels a certain distance in 6 hours and distance travelled by car A is 16.66% less than that travelled by car B.

Car B: Car travels a certain distance in 7 hour and 12 minutes with the speed of 50 km/h.

Car C: Car travels 400 km distance with twice the speed of car B.

74. If the speed of car A is decreased by 2 km/h and speed of car B is increased by 10%, find the difference between the distances travelled by both the cars in 4 hours.

(1) 32 km (2) 40 km
(3) 28 km (4) 35 km
(5) None of these

75. Car D travelled 40% more distance than that by car A in 10 hours, find the speed of car D.

(1) 50 km/h (2) 42 km/h
(3) 48 km/h (4) 54 km/h
(5) None of these

76. Train A whose length is 345 m can cross a pole in 23 seconds. If the speed of train A is increased by 50% the time taken by train A to cross the platform is 24 seconds. What is the ratio of the length of train A to the length of the platform?

(1) 10 : 7 (2) 23 : 13
(3) 15 : 9 (4) 24 : 17
(5) None of these

77. The ratio of the speed of boat to speed of the stream is 7 : 2. The taken by boat to cover 450 km distance upstream is 20 hours more than that to cover the same distance downstream. What is the difference between the upstream and downstream speed of the boat?

(1) 15 km/h (2) 12 km/h
(3) 6 km/h (4) 8 km/h
(5) None of these

78. Sanjana and Ritika has equal amount. Sanjana invested one-third of her amount at the rate of 12% p.a. on simple interest and the remaining amount at the rate of R% p.a. on simple interest while Ritika invested the amount at the rate of 10% p.a. on compound interest. If the interest received by both of them at the end of two years is equal, find the value of R.

(1) 11.25 (2) 10.25
(3) 9.75 (4) 8.5
(5) None of these

79. Manan can complete a piece of work in 24 days while Komal can complete it in 40 days. They work together for 8 days and the rest work is completed by Akshay in 7 days. If they get Rs. 2400 for the whole work, find the share of Manan, Komal and Akshay respectively.

(1) Rs. 600, Rs. 700, Rs. 1100
(2) Rs. 800, Rs. 600, Rs. 1000

(3) Rs. 600, Rs. 540, Rs. 1260
(4) Rs. 750, Rs. 450, Rs. 1200
(5) None of these

Directions (80-85): *Study the following information carefully and answer the questions that follow.*

There are three different Guns A, B and C. Different numbers of bullets are fired from each Gun. A few of them hit the target while others missed.

Gun A: 70% of the total number of fired bullets missed the target.

Gun B: Total 900 bullets were fired and 33.33% hit the target.

Gun C: 450 bullets hit the target. The number of bullets that hit the target by Gun A is 20% less than that by Gun B . The number of bullets that missed the target by Gun C is 6.25% less than the number of bullets fired by Gun A. Time gap between the firing of two bullets is 5 seconds, 3 seconds and 7 seconds for Gun A, Gun B and Gun C respectively.

80. If Gun C fired continuously from 12:30 pm to 12:34 pm and not any time before that, then how many bullets were left to be fired by Gun C after this period of shooting?
(1) 1165 (2) 1164
(3) 1156 (4) 1157
(5) 1158

81. Find the average of the number of bullets that hit the target by all three Guns together.
(1) 290 (2) 360
(3) 250 (4) 330
(5) None of these

82. If all the Guns started firing at 12.00 pm, how many total bullets would be left to be fired by the 3 guns after 30 minutes? (It is known that none of the guns fired any time before 12:00 pm).
(1) 1683 (2) 1720
(3) 1672 (4) 1540
(5) None of these

83. Number of bullets fired by Gun A in 10 minutes is approximately how much percentage more than the number of bullets fired by Gun B in 4 minutes?
(1) 30% (2) 45%
(3) 49% (4) 64%
(5) 60%

84. The number of bullets that hit the target by Gun D is equal to the number of bullets that hit the target by Gun B and the total number of bullets fired by Gun D is equal to the average of the number of total bullets fired by Gun A and C. What is the number of bullets that missed the target by Gun D?
(1) 800 (2) 500
(3) 600 (4) 700
(5) None of these

85. What is the ratio of the number of bullets fired by gun C that missed the target to the number of bullets fired by Gun A?
(1) 8 : 5 (2) 14 : 9
(3) 12 : 7 (4) 14 : 11
(5) 15 : 16

86. A certain sum is invested on simple interest at the rate of R% and becomes Rs. 8120 in three years and Rs. 9800 in 5 years. If the same sum is invested at the rate of (R + 5)% on compound interest, find the interest received after 2 years.
(1) Rs. 2550 (2) Rs. 2644
(3) Rs. 2655 (4) Rs. 2464
(5) None of these

87. Ashok and Dharma started a business with the capital of Rs. (X + 600) and Rs. (X – 400) respectively. After 6 months they made additional investment of Rs. 1200 and Rs. 3000 respectively. At the end of the year, profit share of Ashok out of total profit of Rs. 10480 is Rs. 5280. Find the value of X.
(1) 4800 (2) 5400
(3) 5200 (4) 6400
(5) 6000

88. A bag contains total 20 balls in which x are yellow balls, $(x + 4)$ are green balls and y are red balls. If the probability of picking 1 red ball is 1/5, find the number of green balls in the bag.
(1) 8 (2) 12
(3) 10 (4) 6

(5) 15

89. The ratio of the volume of two cylinder C_1 and C_2 is 5 : 16 respectively and the height of the two cylinders C_1 and C_2 is 5 : 4 respectively. If the radius of cylinder C_1 is 7 cm and the total surface area of cylinder C_1 is 748 cm^2, find the total surface area of cylinder C_2.

(1) 1936 cm^2 (2) 1744 cm^2
(3) 1824 cm^2 (4) 2024 cm^2
(5) None of these

90. The ratio of the two numbers P and Q is 5 : 7, when 22 is added in the P and 35 is added in Q, the ratio becomes 7 : 10. 48% of Q is what percentage of 60% of P?

(1) 108% (2) 80%
(3) 112% (4) 120%
(5) 90%

Reasoning Ability

Directions (91-95): *Study the following information carefully and answer the question based on it.*

Nine people A, B, C, D, E, F, G, H, and I have meetings on different dates viz. 5th, 11th, and 14th of different months viz. September, November, and December. They own different number of shops viz. 1, 2, 3, 4, 5 and 6 and different number of apartments which is double the number of shops. Not more than two people own the same number of apartments.

Two persons have meetings between A and B, A being first to attend the meeting among themselves. B owns 4 apartments. D and F both joined the meeting in the same month having 30 days, D's meeting is scheduled before F. E, who owns the least number of shops, attends meeting immediately before G, who attends the meeting in a month having more than 30 days. A and E owns the same number of apartments. More than two persons have meeting between B and E. Number of shops I owns is 4 less than H, who own an odd number of shops. H does not attend the meeting immediately after or before B or E. C has not attended the meeting before H. C's meeting is not scheduled adjacent to E or H's. D owns an odd prime number of shops but not more than 4. Number of apartments F owns is double of the same that D owns. Difference between the numbers of C and G is 1, C owns smaller number of shops owned than G. G owns an even number of shops but not prime.

91. The sum of apartments owned by C, H, and I is ....

(1) 16 (2) 22
(3) 18 (4) 20
(5) 12

92. How many people have meetings between B and G?

(1) 3 (2) 4
(3) 1 (4) 0
(5) 2

93. The difference between the number of apartments owned by F and H?

(1) 1 (2) 0
(3) 3 (4) 2
(5) 4

94. Who among them have meeting on 11th November?

(1) F (2) D
(3) B (4) I
(5) E

95. If A is related to D, B is related to I, then C is related to

(1) G (2) H
(3) E (4) F
(5) None of the above

Directions (96): *Study the following information and answer the given questions.*

96. If a meaningful word can be formed using 3rd letter of SECURITY, 2nd and 5th letter of PURITY, 6th letter of ENSURE and 1st letter of AMPULE, what is the second letter of the newly formed word? If more than one word can be formed, mark your answer as X. If no such word can be formed, mark your answer as Z.

(1) C (2) A
(3) E (4) X
(5) Z

Directions (97-98): *Study the following information and answer the given question.*

A @ B means A is the daughter of B

A and B means A is the father of B, A $ B means A is the brother of B

A # B means A is the husband of B

97. P #Q@KLMQO

How is P related to K?

(1) Son-in-law (2) Son
(3) Daughter (4) Brother
(5) None of the above

98. L#K, L$B, K&P

How many people are female in the family?

(1) 3 (2) 2
(3) 1 (4) 0
(5) Cannot be determined

Directions (99-104): *Study the following information and answer the given questions.*

Certain number of people sit around a circular table and face outside the center of the table. Two people sit between I and T. Two people sit between H and X. One people sits between O and A. I sits second to the left of Y. The number of people sit between T and A is same as the number of people sit between T and N. A sits second to the left of I. N sits third to the left of H. U sits second to the right of X and sits to the immediate left of O.

99. How many people are seated around the table?

(1) 20 (2) 22
(3) 26 (4) 21
(5) 27

100. In which position is I with respect to O?

(1) 4th to the left (2) 3rd to the right
(3) 6th to the left (4) 7th to the right
(5) None of the above

101. How many people are seated between X and T when counted clockwise from T?

(1) 9 (2) 11
(3) 8 (4) 10
(5) 7

102. N is seated .... to the .... of U?

(1) 11th, right (2) 3rd, right
(3) 5th, left (4) 8th, right
(5) 7th, left

103. If A and T interchange their positions, then A is .... to the left of O?

(1) 7th (2) 5th
(3) 2nd (4) 8th
(5) 9th

104. How many people are seated between Y and H, when counted anti-clockwise from H?

(1) 9 (2) 7
(3) 8 (4) 11
(5) None of the above

Directions (105-109): *Study the following information and answer the given questions.*

A number arrangement machine when given an input line of numbers rearranges them following a particular rule. The following is an illustration of input and rearrangement.

Input: [2|3] [4|5] [7|5] [4|5] [3|1] [4|3]

Step I: [6|8] [11|10] [7|4]

Step II: [48] [88] [110] [70] [28]

Step III: [48] [110] [42]

Step IV: [70] [68]

Step V: [02]

Step IV is the last step of the rearrangement. As per the rules followed in the above steps, find out in each of the following questions the appropriate steps for the given input.

Input: [3|2] [5|4] [5|7] [3|7] [2|3] [3|4]

105. Which of the following is in the final step?

(1) 31 (2) 13
(3) 07 (4) 22
(5) 35

106. What is the sum of the numbers in step IV?

(1) 189 (2) 209
(3) 312 (4) 267
(5) None of the above

107. What is the 3rd number from the left of step

II?

(1) 35 (2) 48
(3) 112 (4) 48
(5) 70

108. What is the difference between the largest and the smallest numbers in step I?

(1) 5 (2) 6
(3) 7 (4) 2
(5) 3

109. Which of the following is the factors of the smallest number in step IV?

(1) 3 (2) 4
(3) 5 (4) 7
(5) 9

Direction (110): *Below in each question are given two statements I and II. These statements may be either independent causes or may be effects of independent causes or a common cause. One of these statements may be the effect of the other statement. Read both the statements and decide which of the following answer choice correctly depicts the relationship between these two statements.*

110. Statement I: The state is facing huge water crisis along with air pollution.

Statement II: Natural sources of water and use of private vehicles are increased.

(1) I is the cause and II is the effect.
(2) I is the effect and II is the cause.
(3) Both I and IIare effect of independent causes.
(4) Both I and II are effect of common causes.
(5) None of the above

Directions (111): *A statement is given followed by three courses of action numbered I, II, and III. The candidate is required to grasp the statement, analyze the problem or policy it mentions and then decide which of the courses of action logically follow(s).*

111. Statement: An accountant of a company has found that a huge amount of money is missing from the shelf.

Courses of action:

I. He should inform the police about the same and ask them to strictly enquire about the suspects.

II. He should inform his manager and other authorities as soon as possible.

III. He should not inform anyone and keep silence about the incident as he might get dragged in this case.

(1) Only I follows.
(2) Only II follows.
(3) Both I and II follow
(4) Both II and III follow
(5) Only III follows

Directions (112): *A statement is given followed by three courses of action numbered I, II, and III. The candidate is required to grasp the statement, analyze the problem or policy it mentions and then decide which of the courses of action logically follow(s).*

112. Statement:

Priya has broken his brother's laptop by mistake and scared of getting scolded.

Courses of action:

I. She should throw the broken laptop out of the window silently so that no one gets to know who has broken it.

II. She should leave the house and run away as her brother will scold her bad.

(1) Only I follows.
(2) Only II follows.
(3) Both I and II follow
(4) Neither I and II follow
(5) None of the above

113. How many such pairs of letters are there in the word CROCODILE each of which has as many letters between them as in the English alphabet in both forward and backward directions?

(1) 3 (2) 5
(3) 7 (4) 2
(5) 0

Directions (114-118): *Study the following information and answer the given questions.*

Six people A, B, C, D, E, and F have joined the company XYZ in the years 2001 to 2006 but not necessarily in the same order. They have laptops of different companies, viz. Acer, HP, Lenovo of different colours, viz. Black, Silver and Blue. Not more than two people have laptop of the same brands. Not more than three people have laptops of the same colour.

Note: One person may be senior or junior to another person in terms of their joining date to the company. .

A is the only person to use a Blue laptop but the brand he use is also used by D. C is the first person to join the company. Only one person has joined after B. A has joined the company in a year which is not divisible by 2. Only one person has joined the company between E and F, who has Acer laptop. E is senior to F. People who use Acer laptops use Black coloured laptops. Only two people joined the company between the ones who use Acer and Lenovo laptops, the one having Acer laptop is senior to the other person. D is not the juniormost person. People having Lenovo laptops use Silver coloured laptops.

114. Who among the following uses Lenovo laptop?

(1) C (2) D
(3) A (4) B
(5) None of the above

115. The Blue laptop is of which brand?

(1) Lenovo (2) HP
(3) Acer (4) Either Lenovo or HP
(5) Either HP or Acer

116. Who joined the company in the year 2004?

(1) C (2) D
(3) E (4) B
(5) None of the above

117. How many people uses Black laptop?

(1) 2 (2) 1
(3) 3 (4) Either 1 or 2
(5) None of the above

118. How many people join the company between A and F?

(1) 2 (2) 1
(3) 3 (4) 4
(5) 5

119. Statement: A seventeen-year-old girl has registered in a social media platform where only people above eighteen years old are allowed. She has put wrong information while filling the form and system of verification is not available in that platform yet.

Assumptions:

I. Anybody can register themselves in the platform with wrong information as no system is available to verify.

II. Opening an account with fake identity proof is not a criminal offense.

(1) Only I follows (2) Only II follows
(3) Either I or II follows
(4) Both I and II follow
(5) None of the above

120. Statement: Taxation on private vehicles will increase the price of them and make people more reluctant to buy their own vehicles which will in turn reduce air pollution in the country as more people will start using public transports that are limited in number.

Assumptions:

I. Taxation can solve any problems in the country by putting restrictions on people's choices.

II. This was the only way to reduce air pollution in the nation.

(1) Only I follows
(2) Only II follows
(3) Either I or II follows
(4) Both I and II follow
(5) None of the above

121. Which of the following is false according to the given statement?

S@I, R&Q, P$Q, Q#L, R#S

(1) P is brother of Q.
(2) L is the daughter-in-law of R.
(3) I is the mother of S.
(4) R is son-in-law of I.
(5) L is the sister-in-law of P.

Directions (122-126): *Study the following information carefully and answer the given questions.*

Twelve people i.e., A, B, C, D, E, F, G, H, I,

J, K, and L sitting in three rows i.e. Row 1, Row 2 and Row 3 and all are facing to the north. Row 1 is to north of Row 2 and Row 2 is to the north of Row 3. They are sitting in the manner that three people sit in Row 1, six people sit in Row 2 and three people sit in Row 3. People of Row 1 sit opposite to the people of Row 2 who are sitting on the left most side and the other three people of Row 2 sit opposite to people of Row 3. They are sitting with equidistance to each other.

A sits second from one of the extreme ends of the row 2. I sits to the south of J. Two people sit between D and G who sits opposite to F. K sits to the immediate right of the one who sits opposite to A. D sits to the immediate left of A . One person sits between C and the one who sits opposite to F. E sits either to the south east or to the south west of C. L sits opposite to the one who sits adjacent to E. B sits to the north west of L but not adjacent to F. E doesn't sit at the end of any row.

122. Who sits opposite to H?

(1) D (2) A
(3) L (4) C
(5) None of these

123. How many people sit between A and the one who sits opposite to F?

A. Two B. One
C. Three D. More than three
E. None

124. How many people sit to the left of the one who sits opposite to E?

(1) One (2) Five
(3) Three (4) Four
(5) Two

125. What is the direction of A with respect to the one who sits opposite to C?

(1) South (2) North east
(3) North (4) South east
(5) None of these

126. If in the middle row all the people arranged from left to right in the English alphabetical order then the position of which amongst the following remains unchanged?

(1) Two (2) Three
(3) None (4) One
(5) None of these

Direction (127-131): *Each of the questions below consists of a question and three statements numbered I, II and III. You have to decide whether the data provided in the statements are sufficient to answer the question. Read all the three statements and give answer accordingly.*

127. Six friends P, Q, R, S, T and U are standing in a row. All of them are facing towards North. Who is standing between R and T?

Statement I: P is standing second from the left end. R is standing third to the left of Q who is near to T.

Statement II: Q isn't the immediate neighbor of U who doesn't sit any extreme ends of the row.

Statement III: T isn't the immediate neighbor of P.

(1) If the data in statement I and statement II is sufficient to answer the question.
(2) If the data in statement I and statement III is sufficient to answer the question.
(3) If the data in statement II and statement III is sufficient to answer the question.
(4) If the data in all the statements I, II and III together is sufficient to answer the question.
(5) If the data in all the statements I, II and III together isn't sufficient to answer the question.

128. Six professionals Doctor, Artist, Dancer, Painter, Singer and Teacher are travelling to Hyderabad in a week starting from Monday to Sunday, only one person travels on one day. On one day of the week no person is travelled. On which day of the week no one is travelled?

Statement I: Dancer travelled on one of the days after Wednesday but not on Sunday. Only one person has travelled between Dancer and Doctor but Doctor doesn't travel on last day of the week. Two persons travelled between Doctor and Teacher.

Statement II: Sunday is not the day when no one is travelled and painter is not travelled on Sunday. Doctor travelled before Teacher.

Two persons travelled between Painter and Holiday.

Statement III: Artist travelled before holiday. There is three-day gap between holiday and the day on which Singer travelled.

(1) If the data in statement I alone is sufficient to answer the question, while the data in statement II alone or in statement III alone is not sufficient to answer the question.

(2) If the data in Statement II alone is sufficient to answer the question, while the data in statement I alone or in statement III is not sufficient to answer the question.

(3) If the data in Statement III alone is sufficient to answer the question, while the data in statement I alone or in statement II is not sufficient to answer the question.

(4) If the data in all the statements I, II and III together isn't sufficient to answer the question.

(5) If the data in all the statements I, II and III together is sufficient to answer the question.

129. There are five pens Q, R, S, T and U are placed on the table according to their height with five being the tallest and 1 being the smallest position. All the pens are placed in a vertical line from smallest to tallest pen. What is the position of pen S?

Statement I: T is the tallest among the all. R is just placed behind Q but not on even numbered position.

Statement II: T doesn't place at even numbered position.

Statement III: U doesn't place at even numbered position and T is placed after U.

(1) If the data in statement I alone is sufficient to answer the question, while the data in statement II alone or in statement III alone is not sufficient to answer the question.

(2) If the data in Statement II alone is sufficient to answer the question, while the data in statement I alone or in statement III is not sufficient to answer the question.

(3) If the data in Statement III alone is sufficient to answer the question, while the data in statement I alone or in statement II is not sufficient to answer the question.

(4) If the data in all the statements I, II and III together isn't sufficient to answer the question.

(5) If the data in all the statements I, II and III together is sufficient to answer the question.

130. Six persons namely B, N, S, P, O and M who likes different activities – Dancing, Fighting, Singing, Karate, Painting and Mixing but not necessarily in the same order. S likes Dancing and M likes neither Fighting nor Singing. Who among the following likes Karate?

Statement I: B likes Painting and N doesn't like Fighting.

Statement II: O likes Singing and P doesn't like Painting.

Statement III: N likes neither Painting nor Singing.

(1) If the data in statement I alone is sufficient to answer the question, while the data in statement II alone or in statement III alone is not sufficient to answer the question.

(2) If the data in Statement II alone is sufficient to answer the question, while the data in statement I alone or in statement III is not sufficient to answer the question.

(3) If the data in Statement III alone is sufficient to answer the question, while the data in statement I alone or in statement II is not sufficient to answer the question.

(4) If the data in all the statements I, II and III together isn't sufficient to answer the question.

(5) If the data in all the statements I, II and III together is sufficient to answer the question.

131. How many people are there in the row if there are more than five people between B and Z?

Statement I: O is at third from the left end and D is sixteenth from the right end of the row.

Statement II: Z is sitting seventh to the right of B.

Statement III: There is twenty-two people between D and O which includes B and Z.

(1) If the data in statement I alone is sufficient to answer the question, while the data in statement II alone or in statement III alone is not sufficient to answer the question.

(2) If the data in Statement II alone is sufficient to answer the question, while the data in statement I alone or in statement III is not sufficient to answer the question.

(3) If the data in Statement III alone is sufficient to answer the question, while the data in statement I alone or in statement II is not sufficient to answer the question.

(4) If the data in all the statements I, II and III together isn't sufficient to answer the question.

(5) If the data in all the statements I, II and III together is sufficient to answer the question.

132. Choose the word which is different from the rest.

(1) BLUE – EULB

(2) RAINBOW – WOBNIAR

(3) PUPIL – LIPUP (4) CLOUD – DUOLC

(5) KDAHU – UHADK

133. Statement: Should government impose capital punishment in robbery cases?

Arguments:

I. Yes, it will reduce robbery cases in the country.

II. Yes, capital punishment is the only way to stop any kind of crime in the country.

(1) Only I is strong (2) Only II is strong

(3) Either I or II is strong

(4) Both I and II are strong

(5) None of the above

134. Statement: Should government ban tobacco production in the country?

Arguments:

I. Yes, this will reduce smoking habits of people.

II. No, this will increase unemployment rate in the country.

(1) Only II is strong (2) Only I is strong

(3) Either I or II is strong

(4) Both I and II are strong

(5) None of the above

Directions (135-139): *Study the following information carefully and answer the given questions.*

Eight persons A, B, C, D, P, Q, R and S are sitting in straight line and facing north but not necessarily in the same order. They all work in a company and have different designations i.e., CEO, Director, Branch Manager, Senior Manager, Manager, Assistant Manager, Clerk and Attendant but not necessarily in the same order. CEO is the senior-most post and Attendant is the junior-most.

E sits fourth to the right of the one who is Branch Manager. Only two persons sit between the one who is Branch Manager and D. Only two persons sit between the one who is Director and G who is not Clerk. C does not sit at the extreme ends of the row. The one who is junior-most does not sit at the extreme end of the row. A is not Manager. The one who is just senior than C is an immediate neighbor of D. Only one person sits between H and the one who is Manager. Number of persons sit to the right of the one who is CEO is same as the number of persons sit between A and D. The one who is Director does not sit at extreme end of the row. The one who is Clerk does not sit to the left of the one who is Manager. C who is an immediate neighbor of the one who is Branch Manager sits third to the left of A. The one who is senior Manager is not an immediate neighbor of the one who is Director. F sits third to the left of the one who is Clerk. E is not senior Manager.

135. Who amongst the following is the Senior Manager?

(1) H (2) A

(3) G (4) F

(5) C

136. How many people sit between F and the one who is CEO?
(1) Two (2) One
(3) Three (4) None
(5) Four

137. What is the designation of D?
(1) Senior Manager (2) Manager
(3) Director (4) Clerk
(5) None of these

138. How many people sit to the left of the one who is Manager?
(1) Three (2) Two
(3) One (4) None
(5) Four

139. What is the position of the one who is Attendant with respect to the one who is Branch Manager?
(1) Second to the left (2) Immediate right
(3) Third to the right (4) Immediate left
(5) None of these

140. SURROUNDINGS is coded as RUSDNUORSGNI, ENVIRONMENT is coded as NEIVNORTNEM, then how is PROTECTION coded as?
(1) ORPCERSSNI (2) TNOITRPCED
(3) ORPCETNOIT (4) ORPCETSBHI
(5) None of the above

General Awareness

141. What amount has been proposed for further recapitalization of public sector banks?
(1) Rs. 20,000 crores
(2) Rs. 30,000 crores
(3) Rs. 40,000 crores
(4) Rs. 50,000 crores
(5) Rs. 80,000 crores

142. Who monitors the Priority Sector Lending (PSL) in commercial banks?
(1) Reserve Bank of India (RBI)
(2) Small Industries Development Bank of India (SIDBI)
(3) National Bank for Agriculture and Rural Development (NABARD)
(4) Government of India (GOI)
(5) Securities and Exchange Board of India (SEBI)

143. The world's longest sandstone cave "Krem Puri" has been discovered in which state of India?
(1) Andhra Pradesh (2) Meghalaya
(3) Tripura (4) Maharashtra
(5) Odisha

144. How many Ombudsman office are there in India?
(1) 21 (2) 22
(3) 23 (4) 24
(5) 25

145. Who among the following is the co-founder and CEO of Twitter?
(1) Bill Gates (2) Narayan Murthy
(3) Jack Dorsey (4) Tim Berners-Lee
(5) None of the above

146. RBI was nationalised in the year ....
(1) 1934 (2) 1935
(3) 1949 (4) 1950
(5) 1951

147. India's first wetland conservation center 'Centre for Wetland Conservation and Management (CWCM)' has been be set up in which city of India?
(1) Kolkata (2) Kochi
(3) Chennai (4) Mumbai
(5) Bhubaneswar

148. What is the validity period of 'Electoral bonds'?
(1) 10 days (2) 30 days
(3) 20 days (4) 12 days
(5) 15 days

149. Mutual Funds are regulated in the country by
(1) IRDAI
(2) Association of Mutual Funds of India (AMFI)
(3) NABARD

(4) Securities and Exchange Board of India
(5) Reserve Bank of India

150. Renowned personality Ustad Ghulam Mustafa Khan passed away recently, he was a veteran ....
(1) Flute Maestro (2) Tabla Maestro
(3) Sitar Maestro (4) Classical Musician
(5) Piano Maestro

151. Which company has ranked first most-valued IT services brand globally, according to a report by Brand Finance?
(1) Accenture (2) IBM
(3) Tata Consultancy Services (TCS)
(4) Infosys
(5) Wipro

152. Which of the following Asian countries has Nikkei as its stock market index?
(1) China (2) Singapore
(3) Japan (4) South Korea
(5) Hong Kong

153. The 'ICC Men's T20I Cricketer of the Decade' has been awarded to?
(1) Virat Kohli (2) Kane Williamson
(3) Steve Smith (4) Rashid Khan
(5) None of these

154. What is percentage of government holding in NABARD?
(1) 99.6% (2) 0.4%
(3) 100% (4) 75%
(5) 56%

155. The headquarters of the 'United Nations World Tourism Organization' is situated in:
(1) Madrid, Spain
(2) Gland, Switzerland
(3) Washington DC, USA
(4) Paris, France
(5) Frankfurt, Germany

156. West Bengal legislative assembly consists of how many seats?
(1) 292 (2) 294
(3) 296 (4) 298
(5) 299

157. Which of the following country has been elected as President of the International Solar Alliance?
(1) USA (2) Russia
(3) India (4) Japan
(5) None of these

158. Recently, Hawker Culture of which country has been inscribed on the UNESCO's Representative List of the Intangible Cultural Heritage of Humanity?
(1) Indonesia (2) China
(3) Vietnam (4) Singapore
(5) None of these

159. The Chairman of the National Disaster Management Authority (NDMA) is ....
(1) National Security Advisor
(2) Prime Minister of India
(3) Chief of DRDO
(4) Home Minister of India
(5) None of these

160. Which payment gateway company has decided to close its operation in India?
(1) MobiKwik (2) Razor pay
(3) PayPal (4) Lazypay
(5) None of the above

161. The Foxconn of toy world to set up India's first toy cluster in
(1) Madhya Pradesh (2) Karnataka
(3) Kerala (4) Rajasthan
(5) Haryana

162. Maradona scored 'hand of god' goal against which country?
(1) Germany (2) France
(3) Portugal (4) Spain
(5) England

163. Which of the following became the first company to launch an Electric tractor in India?
(1) Sonalika Group
(2) Tractor and Farm Equipment (TAFE) Ltd.
(3) Mahindra and Mahindra
(4) Swaraj Tractors

(5) Escorts Agri Machinery

164. FASTag works on which of the following technologies?

(1) Phone Early Warning System (PEWS)

(2) Radio Frequency Identification (RFID) technology

(3) Accelerometer

(4) Near Field Technology

(5) GPS Technology

165. What is the name given to India's first indigenous 9 mm machine pistol jointly developed by the Defence Research and Development Organisation (DRDO) and the Indian Army?

(1) Glock 17 (2) SIG Sauer P226

(3) ASMI (4) Beretta 92FS

(5) Agram 2000

166. Which of the following is not related to 'bank to bank' transfer mechanism?

(1) NEFT (2) RTGS

(3) Cheque (4) Depository Receipt

(5) IMPS

167. Which of the following Musical Instruments is played by Ustad Shahid Parvez Khan?

(1) Santoor (2) Sitar

(3) Veena (4) Flute

(5) Tabla

168. The Light House Projects inaugurated by the prime minister will be undertaken in six cities. Which of the following is not one among them?

(1) Dhanbad in Jharkhand

(2) Rajkot in Gujarat

(3) Agartala in Tripura

(4) Indore in Madhya Pradesh

(5) Lucknow in Uttar Pradesh

169. ICICI Bank has launched its Representative office in which nation?

(1) France (2) USA

(3) Nepal (4) Indonesia

(5) Myanmar

170. Which Indian women wrestler has won silver medal at the individual Wrestling World Cup in the women's 57 kg category which took place in Belgrade, Serbia?

(1) Sakshi Malik (2) Vinesh Phogat

(3) Alka Tomar (4) Kavita Devi

(5) Anshu Malik

171. Adivasi Mela 2021 was organised in

(1) Bhubaneswar (2) Cuttack

(3) Balasore (4) Sambalpur

(5) Rourkela

172. The Tapovan Vishnugad power plant is owned by which corporation?

(1) ONGC (2) BPCL

(3) NTPC (4) GAIL

(5) CIL

173. According to the 'India Energy Outlook 2021', India will become .... largest energy consumer by 2030, surpassing European Union?

(1) 1st (2) 2nd

(3) 3rd (4) 4th

(5) 5th

174. What is the name of the umbrella program for the Roads and Highways sector in India?

(1) Setu Bharatam (2) Bharatmala Pariyojana

(3) Smart City Mission

(4) Accessible India Project

(5) Digital India Mission

175. Which organization is responsible for setting up the world's largest zoo in Gujarat's Jamnagar district?

(1) NTPC

(2) Reliance Industries Limited (RIL)

(3) Adani Groups

(4) Larsen and Toubro

(5) Tata Motors

176. What is the maturity period of the Senior Citizen Saving Scheme?

(1) 4 years (2) 5 years

(3) 6 years (4) 7 years

(5) 8 years

177. Kishor Biyani is the CEO of which company on which SEBI has imposed a penalty?

(1) Hindalco Industries

(2) Reliance Pvt Ltd
(3) Adani Groups
(4) Future Retail Ltd
(5) None of the above

178. Which company is known for cleaning up of Non-performing Asset (NPA)?
(1) Negotiable Instrument Company
(2) Asset Reconstruction Company
(3) Department of Economic and Policy Research
(4) Asset Arrangement Company
(5) None of the above

179. World's largest renewable energy park has been inaugurated in ....
(1) Madhya Pradesh (2) Gujarat
(3) Rajasthan (4) Maharashtra
(5) Punjab

180. Who is the author of the book titled as "Struggle is my life"?
(1) Nelson Mandela
(2) Jawaharlal Nehru
(3) Mahatma Gandhi
(4) Barack Obama
(5) Morissana Kouyate

181. Finance Minister of India has announced reduction in residency limit for Indian citizens to set up one-person companies (OPC) from 182 days to ....
(1) 110 days (2) 120 days
(3) 130 days (4) 140 days
(5) 150 days

182. India has recently released a commemorative postage stamp to mark the .... anniversary of the United Nations Organisations.
(1) 73rd (2) 74th
(3) 75th (4) 76th
(5) 77th

183. Flight Lieutenant Bhawna Kant is the first female fighter pilot to participate in the Republic Day Parade 2021. She hails from which State?
(1) Uttar Pradesh (2) Madhya Pradesh
(3) Jharkhand (4) Bihar
(5) Odisha

184. Which nation is planning to set up the first nuclear reactor on the moon by the end of 2026?
(1) Russia (2) USA
(3) UK (4) China
(5) France

185. Rajesh Sharma has replaced which of the following person as the CEO of Ayushman Bharat scheme?
(1) Amitabh Kant (2) Indu Bhushan
(3) Randeep Guleria (4) Rajeev Khosla
(5) Harsh Vardhan

186. Which of the following is the 1st international movie of Irfan Khan's?
(1) The Namesake
(2) New York
(3) The Amazing Spider-Man
(4) Jurassic World
(5) The Warrior

187. The minimum loan size eligible for debt recovery under the Securitisation and Reconstruction of Financial Assets and Enforcement of Security Interest (SARFAESI) Act, 2002 is proposed to be reduced from the existing level of Rs. 50 lakhs to ....
(1) Rs. 5 lakhs (2) Rs. 10 lakhs
(3) Rs. 15 lakhs (4) Rs. 20 lakhs
(5) Rs. 25 lakhs

188. According to India Energy Outlook 2021, published by the International Energy Agency (IEA) by which year India will overtake the European Union as the world's third-largest energy consumer?
(1) 2025 (2) 2027
(3) 2028 (4) 2030
(5) 2032

189. Which of the following national park is not located in Madhya Pradesh?
(1) Van Vihar National Park
(2) Kanha National Park
(3) Ranthambore National Park

(4) Bhandavgarh National Park
(5) None of the above

190. The National Pollution Control Day is observed every year on which date?
(1) 1st December (2) 2nd December
(3) 3rd December (4) 4th December
(5) 5th December

Answers With Explanations

1. (4)
2. (3)
3. (3)
4. (1)
5. (4)
6. (4)
7. (3)
8. (5)
9. (2)
10. (1)
11. (3)
12. (3)
13. (4)
14. (3)
15. (2)
16. (1)
17. (4)
18. (3)
19. (2)
20. (4)
21. (2)

41. (1) The difference of the total no. of employees working in companies A and B = 21

Total no. of employees working in all the given 5 companies = [21/(18 – 15)] × 100 = 700

No. of employees working in the company A = (15/100) × 700 = 105

Hence, no. of male employees working in the company A = 800/21% of 105 = 40

Total no. of male employees working in all the given 5 companies = (40/10) × 100 = 400

The central angle of total no. of male employees working in company A = (10/100) × 360° = 36°

22. (1)
23. (5)
24. (4)
25. (1) Convert:
26. (2)
27. (4)
28. (1)
29. (5)
30. (2)
31. (4)
32. (1)
33. (4)
34. (1) 'Fresh' should be replaced by 'freshly'.
35. (1)
36. (2)
37. (3)
38. (3)
39. (1)
40. (3)

42. (5) Required average = (700 – 400)/5 = 60

43. (1) The ratio of no. of female employees working in companies C and E

= (24/100) × 700 – (24/100) × 400 : (10/100) × 700 – (15/100) × 400

= (168 – 96) : (70 – 60) = 72 : 10 = 36 : 5

44. (4) The no. of female employees working in company B = 18/100 × 700 – 26/100 × 400 = 126 – 104 = 22

The no. of male employees working in company D =25/100 × 400 = 100

Hence, the required percentage =(100 – 22)/100 = 78%

45. (4) The no. of female employees working in company A = (15/100) × 700 – (10/100) × 400

= 105 – 40 = 65

The no. of female employees working in company D = (33/100) × 700 – (25/100) × 400

= 231 – 100 = 131

Hence, the required difference = 131 – 65 = 66

46. (3) The no. of post graduate male employees working in company C = 18.75% of 24/100 × 400 = 3/16 × 96 = 18

The no. of post graduate female employees working in company C = 12.5% of (24/100) × 700 – (24/100) × 400 = (1/8) × 72 = 9

Hence, the total no. of post graduate employees working in the company C = 18 + 9 = 27

47. (3) Let the no. of girls who were not present in the class be $3x$.

The no. of boys who were not present in the

class = $3x - 4$

The no. of girls who were present = $3x \times 5/3$ = $5x$

The no. of boys who were present = 40

According to the question,

$$3x + 3x - 4 + 5x + 40 = 80$$

$$\Rightarrow \quad 11x = 44$$

$$\Rightarrow \quad x = 4$$

The total no. of girls in the class = $8 \times 4 = 32$

48. (3) Let the number of females in village X be a.

The number of females in village Y = a

The number of males in village X = b. The number of males in village Y = $0.75b$

According to the data provided in the question, we get:

$$a \times 0.50 + b \times 1.50 = 0.75b + a$$

$$\Rightarrow \quad 0.50a + 1.5b = 0.75b + a$$

$$\Rightarrow \quad 0.50a = 0.75b$$

$$\Rightarrow \quad 2a = 3b$$

$$\Rightarrow \quad a = 1.5b \quad ...(1)$$

Total population in village X = $a + b$ = $1.5b + b = 2.5b$ (From equation 1) Total population in village Y = $a + 0.75b = 1.5b + 0.75b = 2.25b$

Required ratio = $2.5b : 2.25b = 10 : 9$

49. (4) According to the data provided in the question, we get:

$$(160 - x) = 3x$$

$$\Rightarrow \quad 160 = 4x$$

$$\Rightarrow \quad x = 40$$

The quantity of milk in the container

= 160 – 40 = 120 litres

The quantity of water in the container

= 40 litres

Ratio of the milk to water in the container

= 120 : 40 = 3 : 1

The quantity of milk that is taken out

$\frac{3}{4} \times 20$ = 15 litres

The quantity of water that is taken out

= $1/4 \times 20$ = 5 litres

Quantity of the water in the final mixture

= 40 – 5 + 20 = 55 litres

50. (1)

51. (3)

52. (2) Let 60 men can complete the work be x days.

According to the question,

$$60 \times x = 40 \times (x + 12)$$

$$\Rightarrow \quad 60x = 40x + 480$$

$$\Rightarrow \quad 20x = 480$$

$$\Rightarrow \quad x = 24$$

Let 18 men can complete the work in y days.

According to the data provided in the question, we get:

$$\frac{60 \times 24}{1} = \frac{18 \times y}{\frac{3}{5}}$$

$$\Rightarrow \quad 60 \times 24 = 30y$$

$$\Rightarrow \quad y = 48$$

53. (1) Let the odd numbers = $a, a + 2, a + 4$

Sum of odd numbers = $a + a + 2 + a + 4 = 3a + 6$

The even numbers = $b, b + 2, b + 4$

Sum of even numbers = $b + b + 2 + b + 4 = 3b + 6$

Statement I:

$$a + 2 - (b + 2) = 7$$

$$\Rightarrow \quad a - b = 7$$

Required difference = $3a + 6 - (3b + 6) = 3a - 3b$

$$= 3(a - b) = 3 \times 7 = 21$$

Statement I alone is sufficient to answer the question.

Statement II:

$$a + b + 4 = 57$$

$$\Rightarrow \quad a + b = 53$$

Statement II alone is not sufficient to answer the question.

54. (2) Students passed in English = 100 – 52 = 48%

Students passed in Mathematics = 100 – 42 = 58%

Statement I:

Students passed in English = 100 – 52 = 48%

Statement I alone is not sufficient to answer the question.

Statement II:

Students passed in both English and Mathematics = 58 – 25 = 33%

Statement II alone is sufficient to answer the question.

55. (5) Let the side of the square be a m.

Statement I:

Width of path around the square field = 2 m

Statement I alone is not sufficient to answer the question.

Statement II:

Total area of the path = 136 m^2

Statement I alone is not sufficient to answer the question.

Both statement I and statement II: $(a + 4)^2 - a^2 = 136$

$\Rightarrow \quad a^2 + 16 + 2a - a^2 = 136$

$\Rightarrow \quad 2a = 120$

$\Rightarrow \quad a = 60$ m

Area of the square field = $60^2 = 3600$ m^2

Both statement I and statement II together are necessary to answer the question.

56. (4) Let the monthly income of Ananya be Rs. $5x$.

Monthly income of Shaila = Rs. $6x$

Monthly saving of Ananya = Rs. $2y$

Monthly saving of Shaila = Rs. $3y$

Statement I:

$$\frac{5x}{2y} = \frac{5}{2}$$

$\Rightarrow \quad x = y$

Statement I alone is not sufficient to answer the question.

Statement II:

$$5x - 2y = 6x - 3y$$

$\Rightarrow \quad x = y$

Statement I alone is not sufficient to answer the question.

Both statement I and II:

In both the statements, same equation came.

Both Statements I and II together are not sufficient to answer the question.

57. (2)

58. (3)

59. (2)

60. (3)

61. (4)

62. (2)

63. (1)

64. (3)

65. (3)

66. (3)

67. (2)

68. (2) Let the CP of each bottle be Rs. x.

CP of both the bottles = Rs. $2x$

SP of both the bottles = $2x \times 110\%$ = Rs. $2.2x$

SP of the first bottle = 125% of x = Rs. $1.25x$

SP of the second bottle = Rs. $(1.25x - 2160)$

According to the question

$$1.25x + 1.25x - 2160 = 2.2x$$

$\Rightarrow \quad 2.5x - 2.2x = 2160$

$\Rightarrow \quad x = 7200$

CP of the each bottle = Rs. 7200

69. (1) The quantity of water in the mixture

$$= \frac{765}{17} \times 10 = 450 \text{ litres}$$

The quantity of milk in the mixture

$$= \frac{765}{17} \times 7 = 315 \text{ litres}$$

The quantity of the mixture that is taken out

$$= 765 \times 0.20 = 153 \text{ litres}$$

According to the question-

$$\frac{450 - 153 \times \frac{10}{17} + 2X}{315 - 153 \times \frac{7}{17} + 3X - 32} = \frac{6}{5}$$

$$\frac{450 - 90 + 2X}{315 - 63 + 3X - 32} = \frac{6}{5}$$

$\Rightarrow 5(360 + 2X) = 6(220 + 3X)$

$\Rightarrow 1800 + 10X = 1320 + 18X$

$\Rightarrow \quad 8X = 480$

$\Rightarrow \quad X = 60$

Quantity of milk in the final mixture = 450 – 90 + 120 = 480 litres

Quantity of water in the final mixture = 315 – 63 + 148 = 400 litres

Required difference = 480 – 400 = 80 litres

70. (4)

71. (3)

72. (1)

73. (2)

74. (3)

75. (2)

76. (2)

77. (4) Let the speed of the boat be $7x$ km/h.

Then, the speed of the stream = $2x$ km/h

According to the question-

$$\frac{450}{7x-2x}-\frac{450}{7x+2x}=20$$

$$\Rightarrow \quad \frac{90}{x}-\frac{50}{x}=20$$

$$\Rightarrow \quad 40=20x$$

$$\Rightarrow \quad x=2$$

Speed of the boat in still water = 7 × 2 = 14 km/h

Speed of the stream = 2 × 2 = 4 km/h

Speed of the boat in upstream = 14 – 4 = 10 km/h

Speed of the boat in downstream = 14 + 4 = 18 km/h

Required difference = 18 – 10 = 8 km/h

78. (3)

79. (4) Let the total work be 120 units. (LCM of 24 and 40)

Amount of the work done by Manan in one day = 120/24 = 5 units

Amount of the work done by Komal in one day = 120/40 = 3 units

Amount of the work done by Manan and Komal together in 8 days = 8 × 8 = 64 units

Remaining amount of the work = 120 – 64 = 56 units

Time taken by Akshay to done 56 units of work = 7 days

Amount of the work done by Komal in one day = 56/7 = 8 units

Ratio of the efficiencies of Manan, Komal and Akshay = 5 : 3 : 8

$$\text{Share of Manan} = \frac{5}{16}\times 2400 = \text{Rs. } 750$$

$$\text{Share of Komal} = \frac{3}{16}\times 2400 = \text{Rs. } 450$$

$$\text{Share of Akshay} = \frac{8}{16}\times 2400 = \text{Rs. } 1200$$

80. (1)

81. (4)

82. (5)

83. (3)

84. (4)

85. (5)

86. (4) Simple interest earned in 2 years

= 9800 – 8120 = Rs. 1680

Simple interest earned in 3 years

= 1680/2 × 3 = Rs. 2520

Sum = 8120 – 2520 = Rs. 5600

According to the question-

2520 = 5600 × R% × 3

$\Rightarrow$ R = 15

Rate of interest for CI

= 15 + 5 = 20%

$$\text{CI} = 5600\left(1+\frac{20}{100}\right)^2 - 5600$$

= 8064 – 5600 = Rs. 2464

87. (2)

88. (3)

89. (1)

90. (3)

For questions (91-95)

Months	Dates	Persons	Number of Shops	Number of Apartments
September	5th	A	1	2
(30 days)	11th	D	3	6
	14th	F	6	12
November	5th	B	2	4
(30 days)	11th	I	1	2
	14th	H	5	10
December	5th	C	3	6
(31 days)	11th	E	1	2
	14th	G	4	8

91. (3)

92. (2)

93. (4)

94. (4)

95. (3)

96. (1) 3rd letter of SECURITY, 2nd and 5th letter of PURITY, 6th letter of ENSURE and 1st letter of AMPULE are C, U, T, E, A. The newly formed word is ACUTE.

97. (1)

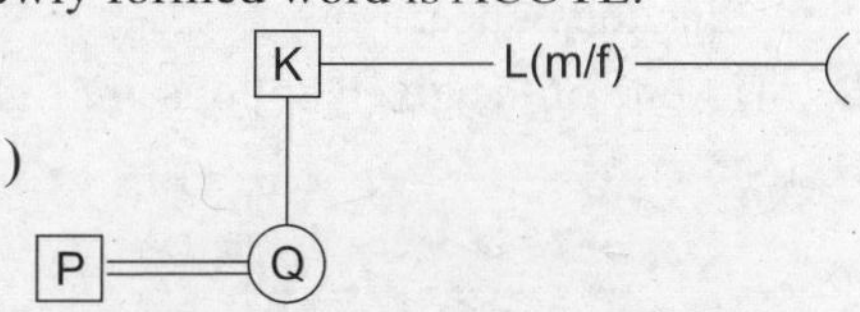

98. (5)

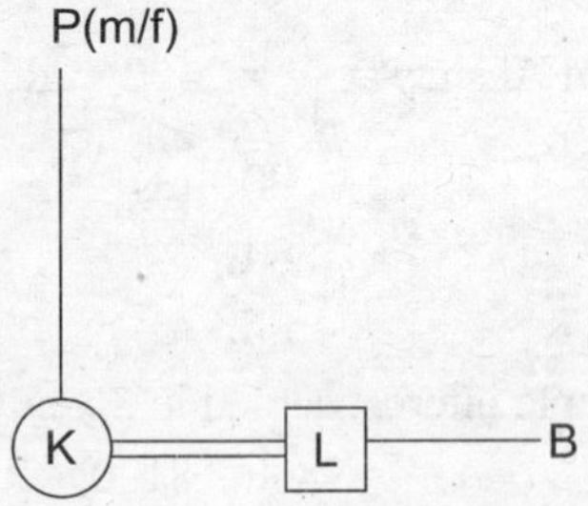

For questions (99-104)

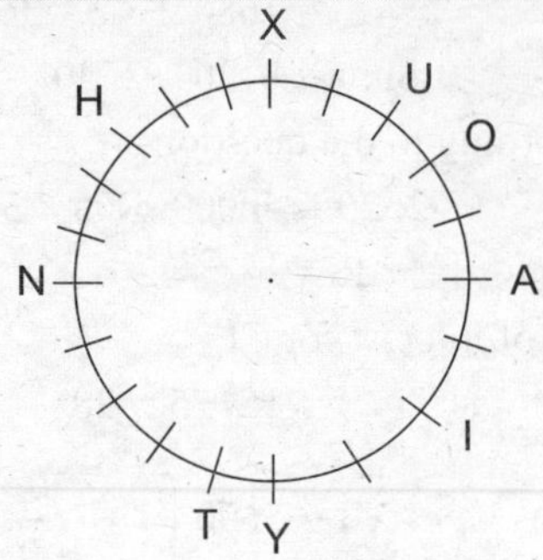

99. (4)
100. (1)
101. (4)
102. (4)
103. (1)
104. (3)

For questions (105-109):

Input:	3 2	5 4	5 7	3 7	2 3	3 4
Step I:	8 6		8 14		5 7	
Step II:	48	48	112	70	35	
Step III:	00	112	35			
Step IV:	112	77				
Step V:	35					

105. (5)
106. (1)
107. (3)
108. (2)
109. (4)

110. (2) Increase in use of natural sources of water and private vehicles causes water crisis and air pollution.

111. (3) He should inform his seniors before calling the police.

112. (4) None of the given options are right to do.

113. (5)

C	R	O	C	O	D	I	L	E
3	18	15	3	15	4	9	12	5

For questions (1114-118):

Years	People	Laptops	Colours
2001	C	Acer	Black
2002	D	HP	Black
2003	A	Lenovo	Silver
2004	E	Lenovo	Silver
2005	B	HP	Blue
2006	F	Acer	Black

114. (3)
115. (2)
116. (3)
117. (3)
118. (1)
119. (1)
120. (5)

121. (3)

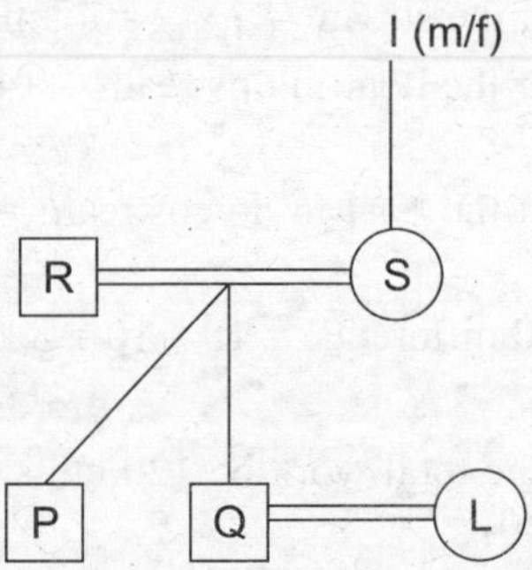

For questions (122-126):

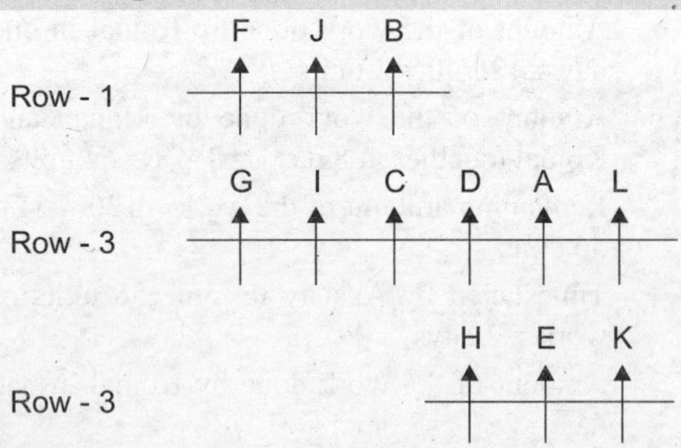

122. (1)
123. (3)
124. (4)
125. (4)
126. (4)
127. (1)
128. (5)
129. (4)
130. (4)
131. (5)
132. (5)
133. (5)
134. (1)

For questions (135-139):

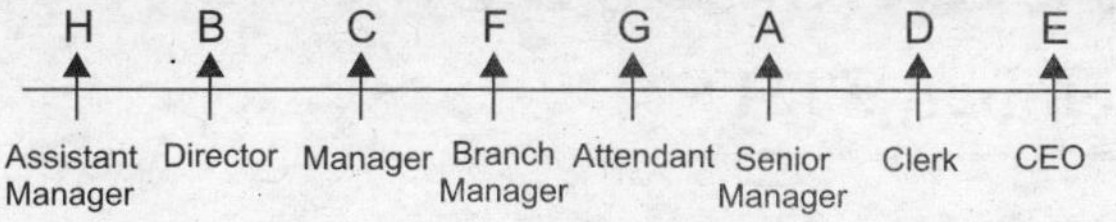

135. (2)
136. (3)
137. (4)
138. (2)
139. (2)
140. (3)
141. (1)
142. (1)
143. (2)
144. (2)
145. (3)

146. (3) The Reserve Bank of India (RBI) commenced its operations on 1 April 1935 during the British Rule in accordance with the provisions of the Reserve Bank of India Act, 1934. The original share capital was divided into shares of 100 each fully paid, which were initially owned entirely by private shareholders. Following India's independence on 15 August 1947, the RBI was nationalized on 1 January 1949.

147. (3) Coinciding with the World Wetland Day, India got its first specialised institution - Centre for Wetland Conservation and Management (CWCM) - in Chennai.

148. (5) Electoral bonds can be purchased for any value in multiples of Rs. 1,000, Rs. 10,000, Rs. 10 lakh, and Rs. 1 crore from any of the specified branches of the State Bank of India. The life of the bond will be for 15 days.

149. (4) Mutual Funds are regulated in the country by Securities and Exchange Board of India

150. (4)
151. (1)

152. (3) Nikkei is the stock market index of Japan.

153. (4) The award of 'ICC Men's T20I Cricketer of the Decade' has been awarded to Rashid Khan. The ICC Awards of the Decade recognize the best players across Cricket over the past ten years.

154. (3)
155. (1)
156. (2)
157. (3)
158. (4)
159. (2)
160. (3)
161. (2)
162. (5)
163. (1)
164. (2)
165. (3)
166. (4)
167. (2)
168. (1)
169. (3)
170. (5)
171. (1)
172. (3)
173. (3)
174. (2)
175. (2)
176. (2)
177. (4)
178. (5)
179. (2)
180. (1)
181. (2)
182. (3)
183. (4)
184. (2)
185. (2)
186. (5)
187. (4)
188. (4)
189. (3)
190. (2)

IBPS Clerk Prelims, 2021

(Held on 12 December, 2021)

Based on Memory

English Language

Directions : *Read the given passage carefully and answer the questions that follow:*

The grave water situation in Cape Town in South Africa is a wake-up call to everybody across the globe –from policy makers to the common man. A similar crisis is looming large in other cities in the world as people continue to be **cautious** in their use of water.

The situation is so worrisome that 12 world leaders –11 heads of state and a special adviser of a high-level panel on water –wrote an open letter to global leaders a week ago warning that the world is facing a water crisis and issued a New Agenda for Water Action. Observing that we need to make "every drop count", they called for a new approach: rethinking how we understand, value and manage water as a precious resource, and catalysing change and building partnerships to achieve the water-related goals of the 2030 Agenda for Sustainable Development.

The panel mentioned the need to put in place policies that will allow for at least a doubling of water infrastructure investment in the next five years. It called for governments, communities, the private sector, and researchers to **collaborate**.

In India, a growing population, lack of adequate planning, crumbling infrastructure, indiscriminate drilling of borewells, large-scale consumption of water, and a false sense of entitlement in using water carelessly are causing water shortages. Unless **(*A*) *minimise*** measures are taken to **(*B*) *drastic*** water usage, the day may not be far off when authorities will be **(*C*) *forced*** to **(*D*) *ration*** water supply in cities like Bengaluru, which has been ranked second in the list of 11 global cities which might face the imminent threat of running out of drinking water. Already, water is being supplied on alternate days in certain cities, and for a limited duration in some places.

1. The panel discussed the importance of implementing policies that will produce results in how many years?

(1) Five years (2) Four years
(3) Eleven years (4) Two years
(5) Three years

2. Who wrote an open letter to global leaders?

(1) 12 world leaders
(2) 11 heads of state
(3) a special adviser of a high-level panel on water
(4) both A and B
(5) All the above

3. Which of the following is/are the methods of new approach to conserve water?

(1) achieve the water-related goals of the 2025 Agenda
(2) value and manage water as a precious resource
(3) build partnerships with developed countries
(4) understand the methods of crumbling infrastructure
(5) All the above

4. What are the causes of water shortages in India?

(1) a growing population
(2) crumbling infrastructure
(3) indiscriminate drilling of bore-wells,
(4) a false sense of entitlement in using water carelessly
(5) All the above

5. Which city ranked second in the list of 11 global cities which might soon face the shortage of drinking water?

(1) Hyderabad (2) Bengaluru

(3) Delhi (4) Mumbai
(5) Chennai

6. What is the **SYNONYM** of the word 'collaborate' used in the given passage?

(1) Cooperate (2) Disagree
(3) Refuse (4) Condemn
(5) None of these

7. In the given sentence, the highlighted word might be used inappropriately. Choose the most suitable word that fits in the given sentence:

A similar crisis is looming large in other cities in the world as people continue to be **cautious** in their use of water.

(1) watchful (2) attentive
(3) careful (4) reckless
(5) None of these

8. Rearrange the highlighted words to make the sentence meaningful:

Unless ***(A) minimise*** *measures are taken to* ***(B)drastic*** *water usage, the day may not be far off when authorities will be* ***(C) forced*** *to* ***(D) ration*** *water supply in cities like Bengaluru.*

(1) Only A-B (2) Only B-C
(3) Only B-D (4) Both C-D and A-B
(5) No Improvement

Directions (9-13): *Rearrange the given six statements A, B, C, D, E, and F and answer the questions that follow.*

A. A primitive bacterium was engulfed by our oldest ancestor – a solo, free-floating cell.

B. Today, trillions of these bacterial descendants live within our bodies, churning out ATP, the molecular energy source that sustains our cells.

C. The two fused to form a mutually beneficial relationship that has lasted more than a billion years, with the latter providing a safe, comfortable home and the former becoming a powerhouse, fuelling the processes necessary to maintain life.

D. Despite being inextricably integrated into the machinery of the human body, mitochondria also carry remnants of their bacterial past, such as their own set of DNA.

E. Long before the earliest animals swam through the water-covered surface of Earth's ancient past, one of the most important encounters in the history of life took place.

F. That's the best hypothesis to date for how the cellular components, or organelles, known as mitochondria came to be.

9. Which of the following is THIRD sentence of the rearranged paragraph?

(1) F (2) D
(3) E (4) A
(5) C

10. Which of the following is FIFTH sentence of the rearranged paragraph?

(1) B (2) F
(3) E (4) A
(5) C

11. Which of the following is FIRST sentence of the rearranged paragraph?

(1) A (2) D
(3) F (4) E
(5) C

12. Which of the following is LAST sentence of the rearranged paragraph?

(1) E (2) D
(3) A (4) B
(5) F

13. What is the correct sequence of the given sentences?

(1) AECFBD (2) CAEFBD
(3) FCEABD (4) EACFBD
(5) DCEFBA

Directions (14-18): *A Sentence is given with four words highlighted in bold which may or may not be in their proper place, you have to interchange them in order to make sentences contextually and meaningfully correct.*

14. Amid criticism that it did not enforce steps to **banned (a)** the spread of COVID-19 during the **vigour (b)** campaign for Assembly elections in four States and one Union Territory with sufficient **protracted (c)**, the Election Commission of India has now **curb (d)** victory processions after the results are declared on May 2.

(1) a-d, b-c (2) a-b
(3) c-d (4) a-c, b-d
(5) None of the above

15. Covering an entire State in as few phases as possible will help localize the **potential (a)** for violence, prevent the spread of tension due to the fatigue **(b)** of the campaign, besides reducing the **virulence (c)** of forces **deployed (d)** throughout the campaign, up to the day of counting.

(1) a-d (2) b-c
(3) c-d (4) b-a
(5) None of the above

16. The Central government has **opened (a)** the responsibility of vaccinating people in the 18-44 age groups to the States, and **transferred (b)** up vaccine **providing (c)** to market forces, at a time when discussions around the world are about an intellectual property (IP) waiver for COVID-19 vaccines and **pricing (d)** free vaccines.

(1) a-c, b-d (2) b-c, a-d
(3) a-b, c-d (4) d-a
(5) None of the above

17. The important objective in the policy is to **achieve (a)** vaccination but the way in which the new policy is **designed (b)** we may not **accelerate (c)** that, precisely because it **fragments (d)** the market.

(1) b-d (2) b-c
(3) c-d (4) a-c
(5) None of the above

18. The International Monetary Fund is likely to **estimates (A)** its global economic growth **lower (B)** due to the new omicron **turmoil (C)** of the coronavirus, this is yet another sign of the **variant (D)** unleashed by the ever changing pandemic.

(1) A-B and C-D (2) A-D and B-C
(3) C-D (4) A- B
(5) No exchange required

Directions (19-24): *In each of the following questions, a sentence has been divided into five parts out of which one part is erroneous. You are required to choose the option which is grammatically or contextually incorrect.*

19. The Madhya Police arrested **(a)**/four people, including **(b)**/a professional Kabaddi player, **(c)**/for their alleged **(d)**/involving in arms trafficking.**(e)**

(1) a (2) b
(3) c (4) d
(5) e

20. Describing Lord Buddha as the inspiration **(a)**/for India's Constitution even today, **(b)**/ Prime Minister Narendra Modi said Buddha **(c)**/reside in the soul of humanity **(d)**/and connects different cultures and countries. **(e)**

(1) a (2) b
(3) c (4) d
(5) e

21. The National Highways Authority of India (NHAI) said **(a)**/that an expert committee **(b)**/will constituted to probe the reasons **(c)**/for the collapse of a segment of an **(d)**/ under-construction flyover in Maharashtra's Nagpur. **(e)**

(1) a (2) b
(3) c (4) d
(5) e

22. The Commission for Air Quality Management (CAQM) is strictly **(a)**/complying with dust mitigation **(b)**/measures at Construction and Demolition (C&D) **(c)**/cites in the National Capital Region (NCR), **(d)**/said the Government of India on Wednesday. **(e)**

(1) a (2) b
(3) c (4) d
(5) e

23. Addressing the nation, **(a)**/Prime Minister Narendra Modi said **(b)**/India's vaccination programme **(c)**/were science-born, **(d)**/ science- driven and science-based. **(e)**

(1) a (2) b

(3) c (4) D
(5) e

24. The External Affairs Minister unveiled a **(a)**/ plaque at Ra'anana in northern Israel **(b)**/in the memory of Indian soldiers **(c)**/who laid off their lives **(d)**/in the Battle of Tabsor during World War I. **(e)**

(1) a (2) b
(3) c (4) d
(5) e

Directions (25-30): *Each question below has one blank, which is indicating that something has been omitted. Choose the most suitable option indicating the words that can be used to fill up the blank in the sentence to make it meaningfully complete.*

25. On December 30, Prime Minister Narendra modi launched a hash tag (#IndiaSupportsCAA) on Twitter .... the whole country with his government and those who support the CAA. If India supports the CAA, are those protesting tens of thousands out on the streets not Indian?

(1) Criticizing (2) Enormous
(3) Conflating (4) Comparing
(5) None of the above.

26. To act as a .... force against an expansive China, the US, Japan, Australia and India formed the Quad.

(1) Contrast (2) Countervailing
(3) Liquidity (4) Murky
(5) None of the above.

27. Marico's biggest achievement isn't the profits or turnover or popularity. It's breaking new ground despite competing .... with multinationals.

(1) Bib and tucker (2) Neck and neck
(3) Nip and tuck (4) Both (2) and (3)
(5) None of the above

28. My commitment to the sport will never change .... of the outcome towards the award, but getting it will greatly benefit the sport,

(1) Despite (2) Therefore
(3) Irrespective (4) Determined
(5) None of the above

29. Both the Congress and BJP claim .... that they do not differentiate between caste Hindus and the Dalits. The fact is they both do.

(1) Vociferously (2) Angrily
(3) Arguments (4) Neatly
(5) None of the above

30. Once the disrespectful worker was gone, the office was no longer filled with scornful ....

(1) adherence (2) sanctions
(3) derision (4) assistance
(5) None of these

Numerical Ability

Directions (31-44): *What value should come in the place of (?) in the following questions?*

31. $(50\%\text{ of }?)/3 = \sqrt{1600 \times 5}$

(1) 700 (2) 1200
(3) 900 (4) 1000
(5) 800

32. $\sqrt[3]{1331} + 5 \times ? = 16^2 + 15 \times 8 - 215$

(1) 30 (2) 50
(3) 70 (4) 60
(5) 40

33. $\sqrt{(125 + 20 \times 5)} + \sqrt{?} = 15\%\text{ of }240$

(1) 361 (2) 256
(3) 441 (4) 529
(5) 324

34. $25\%\text{ of }480 + 5/8 \times 120 + ? = 25^2$

(1) 510 (2) 350
(3) 270 (4) 320
(5) 430

35. $8^? + 20 \times 15 = 312 + 375 + 5^3$

(1) 2 (2) 3
(3) 1 (4) 4
(5) 5

36. $40\%\text{ of }2500 - ? = 36\%\text{ of }500 + 420$

(1) 750 (2) 100
(3) 550 (4) 400
(5) 250

37. 480 × 0.5 + ? = 20 × 360/15 + 175
(1) 415 (2) 210
(3) 360 (4) 545
(5) 470

38. 75% of ? + 840/7 = (205 + 95) × 2
(1) 360 (2) 480
(3) 640 (4) 560
(5) 400

39. $65/4 \times 120/13 - ?^2 = 25^3/5^3$
(1) 10 (2) 5
(3) 15 (4) 25
(5) 20

40. $15^2 \times 4 - 345 = ? + 210 + 155$
(1) 170 (2) 140
(3) 110 (4) 190
(5) 150

41. 216 + ? × 7 = 15 × 10 + 16 × 5
(1) 5 (2) 9
(3) 7 (4) 4
(5) 2

42. $64^5 \times 10^2/32^5 = 5^2 \times ?$
(1) 128 (2) 144
(3) 102 (4) 154
(5) 126

43. 440 + 275 + ? = 3500/5 + 250
(1) 215 (2) 345
(3) 235 (4) 405
(5) 385

44. 24% of 550 + 105/5 = ? – 147
(1) 700 (2) 300
(3) 500 (4) 600
(5) 400

Directions (45-49): *What value should come in the place of (?) in the following number series?*

45. 72, 73, 78, 87, ?, 117
(1) 112 (2) 107
(3) 95 (4) 100
(5) 93

46. 48, 52, 61, 86, 135, ?
(1) 256 (2) 235
(3) 184 (4) 216
(5) 279

47. 51, ?, 70, 92, 129, 186
(1) 57 (2) 55
(3) 58 (4) 59
(5) 54

48. 32, 16, 16, 32, ?, 1024
(1) 48 (2) 80
(3) 128 (4) 96
(5) 160

49. 250, 50, 200, 40, 160, ?
(1) 15 (2) 32
(3) 20 (4) 25
(5) 10

Directions (50-54): *Read the following information carefully and answer the questions.*

The given table shows the number of pens, pencils and erasers distributed to three different classes *i.e.* I, II and III.

	Class I	Class II	Class III
Pen	56	75	84
Pencil	60	55	85
Eraser	44	66	70

50. The number of pens and erasers distributed in class III is how much more/less than the number of pencils distributed in class I and II together?
(1) 30 more (2) 18 less
(3) 39 more (4) 25 less
(5) None of these

51. If the number of pens distributed in class IV is 25% more than that of class I and the ratio of the number of pens to the total number of items distributed in class IV is 1 : 4, then find the number of pencils and erasers distributed in class IV?
(1) 210 (2) 140
(3) 350 (4) 280
(5) None of these

52. Find the ratio of the number of pencils distributed in all three classes together to the number of pens, pencils and erasers distributed in class I?

(1) 8 : 9 (2) 7 : 6
(3) 3 : 2 (4) 5 : 4
(5) None of these

53. The number of pencils distributed in classes II and III is what percentage more than the number of pens and erasers distributed in class I?

(1) 25% (2) 40%
(3) 75% (4) 10%
(5) None of these

54. If the number of pencils and papers distributed in class II is 32 more than the average number of erasers distributed in classes II and III together, then find the ratio of the number of pens and papers distributed in class II?

(1) 5 : 6 (2) 9 : 7
(3) 4 : 3 (4) 1 : 2
(5) None of these

Directions (55-57): *Read the following information carefully and answer the questions.*

There are a certain number of people in three different villages *i.e.* A, B and C. Ratio of the number of people in villages A and C is 5 : 4 and the number of people in village B is 40% less than that of village A. Ratio of the number of males in village A to the number of females in village B is 5 : 2. The number of females in villages A and B is 30 more and 15 less than that of village C respectively. The average number of females in all three villages is 50.

55. Find the difference between the number of males in villages A and B together and the total number of people in village C?

(1) 20 (2) 35
(3) 50 (4) 15
(5) None of these

56. If the total number of people in village D is 4/3rd of the total number of people in village A and the number of males in village D is 50 more than that of females, then find the number of males in village D?

(1) 125 (2) 75
(3) 145 (4) 95
(5) None of these

57. Find the ratio of the number of males in village C to the average number of males and females in village B?

(1) 3 : 8 (2) 4 : 7
(3) 5 : 3 (4) 2 : 1
(5) None of these

58. The breadth of a rectangle is 4/5th of its length and the perimeter of the rectangle is 108 cm, then find the area of the rectangle?

(1) 540 cm^2 (2) 810 cm^2
(3) 630 cm^2 (4) 720 cm^2
(5) None of these

59. A and B together complete $66\frac{2}{3}\%$ of the work in 20 days and the efficiency of A is 50% more than that of B. If A, B and C together complete the work in 10 days, then how many days B and C together complete the whole work?

(1) 12.5 days (2) 7.5 days
(3) 10.5 days (4) 17.5 days
(5) None of these

60. A shopkeeper sold an article at a loss of 25%. If he sold the same article for Rs. 378 more, then he would earn a profit of 20%. Find the cost price of the article?

(1) Rs. 560 (2) Rs. 720
(3) Rs. 600 (4) Rs. 840
(5) None of these

61. 5 years ago, the ratio of the age of Palani and Baba is 7 : 5. If Ramar is 17 years elder than Baba and the average age of Palani, Baba and Ramar is 39 years, then find the age of Baba 2 years hence?

(1) 28 years (2) 54 years
(3) 32 years (4) 44 years
(5) None of these

62. Murali invested Rs. 5500 in simple interest at the rate of R% per annum for 5 years. After 5 years, the total amount received by Murali is 20% more than its investment, then find the value of R?

(1) 16 (2) 24
(3) 18 (4) 20
(5) None of these

63. A and B started a business with the investment of Rs. x and Rs. $(x + 4000)$ respectively and the investment time of A and B is 24 and 16 months respectively. If the profit share of B is Rs. 1440 out of the total profit of the business is Rs. 2400, then find the value (in Rs.) of x?

(1) 3200 (2) 7200
(3) 4000 (4) 5200
(5) None of these

64. A vessel contains 90 liters of milk and the rest is water which is 1/4th of the mixture of the vessel. If 36 liters of mixture is taken out and added x liters of water, then the ratio of milk and water becomes 7 : 4. Then find the value of x?

(1) 20 (2) 10
(3) 9 (4) 15
(5) None of these

65. Ratio of the speed of the boat in still water and stream is 7 : 2. If the boat covers 432 km downstream in 6 hours, then find the time taken by boat to cover 280 km upstream?

(1) 4 hours (2) 5 hours
(3) 7 hours (4) 8 hours
(5) None of these

Reasoning Ability

Directions (66-70): *Study the following information carefully and answer the below questions.*

Seven persons- A, B, C, D, E, F, and G are working in the bank with different positions. The designations are in decreasing order such as Chairman and Managing Director (CMD), Executive Director (ED), General Manager (GM), Deputy General Manager (DGM), Assistant General Manager (AGM), PO and Clerk but not necessarily in the same order.

Three persons are working between F and D who is senior to F. The number of persons senior to D is the same as the number of persons junior to C. Only one person works between D and E. A neither works as ED nor PO. G is senior to B but not senior to D.

66. Who among the following person works as PO?

(1) The one who works immediately senior to C
(2) The one who works immediately junior to G
(3) D
(4) A
(5) F

67. Who among the following persons are senior to A?

I. F II. B
III. D IV. G

(1) Only I and IV (2) Only I and III
(3) Only III and IV (4) Only II and III
(5) Only I and II

68. How many persons work senior to E?

(1) Three (2) Four
(3) Five (4) Two
(5) One

69. What is the designation of F?

(1) CMD (2) AGM
(3) DGM (4) PO
(5) Clerk

70. Four of the five among the following are similar in such a way to form a group, which one of the following doesn't belong to the group?

(1) DC (2) DE
(3) GA (4) EF
(5) FC

Directions (71-74): *Study the following information carefully and answer the questions given below.*

N G U 5 K S 6 7 Q E 8 R A 1 T 3 Y O Z 2 M 4 J 9

71. How many numbers are there between the elements which are sixth from the left end and fourth from the right end?

(1) Five (2) Seven
(3) Six (4) Four
(5) Three

72. How many even numbers are immediately preceded by consonants in the given series?

(1) Two (2) Three
(3) One (4) None
(5) Four

73. Which of the following element is sixth to the left of the element which is tenth from the right end?
(1) K (2) 5
(3) 7 (4) E
(5) Q

74. What is the position of "3" with respect to "M"
(1) Fourth to the left (2) Third to the left
(3) Fifth to the left (4) Second to the left
(5) Sixth to the left

75. How many pairs of letters are there in the word "SIDEWAY" each of which has as many letters between them as in the English alphabetical series (Both forward and backward direction)?
(1) One (2) Two
(3) Four (4) More than four
(5) Three

Directions (76-80): *Study the following information carefully and answer the below questions.*

Seven boxes- L, M, N, O, P, Q, and R are kept one above another on seven different shelves but not necessarily in the same order. The lowermost shelf is numbered as one and the topmost shelf is numbered as seven. Box Q is kept three boxes above box R. Only one box is kept between R and P. Box P is not kept adjacent to box Q. The number of boxes kept between Q and P is the same as the number of boxes kept between O and M. Box N is kept above box L which is kept above box M. Box O is not kept adjacent to Box N.

76. Which of the following box is kept on the sixth shelf?
(1) Box O (2) Box Q
(3) Box L (4) Box R
(5) Box M

77. How many boxes are kept between N and P?
(1) Three (2) Two
(3) One (4) Four
(5) None

78. Box M is kept on shelf.
(1) Fifth (2) Fourth
(3) Third (4) Second
(5) First

79. Four of the five among the following are similar in such a way to form a group, which one of the following doesn't belong to the group?
(1) OQ (2) RP
(3) NL (4) RM
(5) MP

80. If all the boxes are arranged in alphabetical order from the top, then how many boxes are remaining unchanged in their position?
(1) Four (2) Three
(3) Two (4) None
(5) One

Directions (81-83): *Study the following information carefully and answer the below questions.*

Point L is 14 m east of point M. Point P is 4 m east of Point S which is 6 m north of Point Q. Point U is 9 m south of Point X. Point M is 9 m north of point P. Point X is 10 m west of Point Z. Point Q is 8 m west of point U.

81. What is the distance between points L and Z?
(1) 7 m (2) 4 m
(3) 5 m (4) 6 m
(5) 3 m

82. What is the direction of M with respect to U?
(1) East (2) North-West
(3) North-East (4) South
(5) South-west

83. Four of the following are alike in a certain way and hence form a group. Which of the following ones does not belong to the group?
(1) SM (2) US
(3) PL (4) QZ
(5) UZ

84. If "ACROSS" is coded as "CETQUU", in the same way, "CLIENT" is coded as "ENKGPV", then what is the code for "DEFINE"?
(1) GFHKPG (2) BGHKPG
(3) EGHLPG (4) FGHKPG

(5) FGHLQG

85. If in the number "256374815", the odd digits are increased by 2, and the even digits are decreased by 1, then which of the following digits are repeated more than two times?

(1) Only 9 (2) Only 5
(3) Both 3 and 5 (4) Both 3 and 7
(5) Only 7

Directions (86-90): *Study the following information carefully and answer the below questions.*

A certain number of persons are sitting in the linear row and facing north. S sits sixth from one of the ends. G sits fourth to the left of S. Only two persons are sitting between S and L. G and L are not immediate neighbours. Eight persons are sitting between M and G. U sits second to the left of M. Only three persons are sitting between U and K. More than two persons sitting between M and K. The number of persons sitting to the left of K is the same as the number of persons sitting to the right of X who sits to the right of L. More than three persons sitting between S and X.

86. Who among the following person sits to the right of S?

(1) U (2) M
(3) L (4) K
(5) G

87. Who among the following person sitting between M and L?

I. G II. S
III. X IV. K

(1) Only I and II (2) Only III and IV
(3) Only I and III (4) Only II and IV
(5) All I, II, III and IV

88. How many persons are sitting in the linear row?

(1) 24 (2) 25
(3) 23 (4) 22
(5) 21

89. How many persons sitting between M and S?

(1) 13 (2) 09
(3) 10 (4) 11
(5) 12

90. What is the position of U from the left end?

(1) Seventh (2) Sixth
(3) Fourth (4) Fifth
(5) Third

Directions (91-95): *Study the following information carefully and answer the questions given below.*

Ten persons are sitting in the two parallel rows and facing each other. In Row 1 A, B, C, D, and E are sitting and facing south. In row 2 H, I, J, K and L are sitting and facing north but not necessarily in the same order. I sits third to the right of L. B sits opposite to L. A sits second to the left of B. The number of persons sitting between B and A is the same as the number of persons sitting between L and K. C and I sitting opposite to each other. Neither D nor E sits adjacent to C. E sits to the left of B. J and E does not sit opposite to each other.

91. Who among the following person sits second to the right of H?

(1) K
(2) The one who sits immediate right of J
(3) The one who sits immediate left of L
(4) I
(5) None of the above

92. Who among the following person sits between B and C?

(1) E (2) A
(3) D (4) Both (1) and (2)
(5) Both (2) and (3)

93. Who among the following pair does not sit opposite to each other?

(1) DJ (2) BH
(3) CI (4) AK
(5) None of the above

94. Who among the following person sits opposite to K?

(1) The one who sits immediate right of B
(2) J
(3) The one who sits third to the left of D
(4) The one who sits immediate left of A
(5) E

95. Four of the following five are alike in a certain way and hence form a group. Who among the following person does not belong to the group?

(1) The one who sits immediate left of L

(2) The one who sits immediate right of K

(3) The one who sits opposite to I

(4) The one who sits second to the right of E

(5) L

Directions (96-98): *In each of the following questions, the relationship between different elements is shown in the statements followed by two conclusions. Find the conclusion which is definitely true.*

96. Statements:

$S \leq D < I = M \leq P = H > O$

Conclusions:

I. $H > D$ II. $P \geq S$

(1) If only conclusion I is true

(2) If only conclusion II is true

(3) If either conclusion I or II is true

(4) If neither conclusion I nor II is true

(5) If both conclusions I and II are true

97. Statements:

$X \leq G < N < Y = P > H > Q$

Conclusions:

I. $P > X$ II. $N < Q$

(1) If only conclusion I is true.

(2) If only conclusion II is true.

(3) If either conclusion I or II is true.

(4) If neither conclusion I nor II is true.

(5) If both conclusions I and II are true.

98. Statements:

$G > Q \geq B = S \geq N = T \geq Z$

Conclusions:

I. $Q > Z$ II. $Z = Q$

(1) If only conclusion I is true.

(2) If only conclusion II is true.

(3) If either conclusion I or II is true.

(4) If neither conclusion I nor II is true.

(5) If both conclusions I and II are true.

Directions (99-100): *Study the following statements and then decide which of the given conclusions logically follows from the given statements disregarding commonly known facts.*

99. Statement

Only a few Arrow is Cross.

No Cross is Rhombus.

All Rhombus is Minus.

Conclusion

I. Some Minus can be Cross

II. No Arrow is Rhombus

(1) If Only conclusion I follows.

(2) If Only conclusion II follows.

(3) If either conclusion I or II follows.

(4) If Neither conclusion I nor II follows.

(5) If both conclusions I and II follow.

100. Statement

Only a few Cylinder is Cube.

All Cylinder is Heart.

No Cube is Oval.

Conclusion

I. Some Cylinder is not an Oval

II. All Cube can be Heart

(1) If Only conclusion I follows.

(2) If Only conclusion II follows.

(3) If either conclusion I or II follows.

(4) If Neither conclusion I nor II follows.

(5) If both conclusions I and II follow.

Answers With Explanations

1. (1) It is mentioned in the given passage that "The panel mentioned the need to put in place policies that will allow for at least a doubling of water infrastructure investment in the next five years."
2. (5)
3. (2) It is mentioned in the given passage that "Observing that we need to make "every drop count", they called for a new approach: rethinking how we understand, value and manage water as a precious resource, and catalysing change and building partnerships to achieve the water-related goals of the 2030 Agenda for Sustainable Development."
4. (5) It is mentioned in the given passage that "In India, a growing population, lack of adequate planning, crumbling infrastructure, indiscriminate drilling of bore-wells, large-scale consumption of water, and a false sense of entitlement in using water carelessly are causing water shortages".
5. (2) It is mentioned in the given passage that "the day may not be far off when authorities will be forced to ration water supply in cities like Bengaluru, which has been ranked second in the list of 11 global cities which might face the imminent threat of running out of drinking water."
6. (4) The word 'reckless' which means 'careless' fits correctly in the sentence.
7. (1)
8. (5)
9. (1)
10. (4)
11. (1)
12. (2)
13. (4) The correct sequence of the given sentences is EACFBD.
14. (1)
15. (2)
16. (3)
17. (4)
18. (1)
19. (5) "Involving" should be replaced by the noun "involvement".
20. (4) "Reside" should be replaced by "resides" because Budhha is a singular noun.
21. (3) "Will" should be replaced by "will be".
22. (4)
23. (4) "Were" must be replaced by "was".
24. (4) "Laid off" should be replaced by "laid down".
25. (3)
26. (2)
27. (3)
28. (3)
29. (1)
30. (3)
31. (2) $(50\% \text{ of } ?)/3 = \sqrt{1600 \times 5}$ $(50 \times ?/100)$

$$= 40 \times 5 \times 3$$
$$?/2 = 600$$
$$? = 1200$$

32. (1) $\sqrt{1331} + 5 \times ? = 162 + 15 \times 8 - 215$

$$11 + 5 \times ? = 256 + 120 - 215$$
$$5 \times ? = 150$$
$$? = 30$$

33. (3) $\sqrt{(125 + 20 \times 5)} + \sqrt{?} = 15\% \text{ of } 240$

$$\sqrt{225} + \sqrt{?} = 36$$
$$\sqrt{?} = 21$$
$$? = 441$$

34. (5) $25\% \text{ of } 480 + 5/8 \times 120 + ? = 25^2$

$$120 + 75 + ? = 625$$
$$? = 430$$

35. (2) $8^? + 20 \times 15 = 312 + 375 + 5^3$

$$8^? = 312 + 375 + 125 - 300$$
$$8^? = 512$$
$$8^? = 8^3$$
$$? = 3$$

36. (4) $40\% \text{ of } 2500 - ? = 36\% \text{ of } 500 + 420$

$$1000 - ? = 180 + 420$$
$$? = 400$$

37. (1) $480 \times 0.5 + ? = 20 \times 360/15 + 175$

$$240 + ? = 480 + 175$$
$$? = 655 - 240 = 415$$

38. (3) $75\% \text{ of } ? + 840/7 = (205 + 95) \times 2$

$$3 \times ?/4 + 120 = 300 \times 2$$
$$3 \times ?/4 = 480$$
$$? = 640$$

39. (2) $65/4 \times 120/13 - ?^2 = 25^3/5^3$

$150 - ?^2 = (25/5)^3$
$150 - 125 = ?^2$
$?^2 = 25$
$? = 5$

40. (4) $15^2 \times 4 - 345 = ? + 210 + 155$
$900 - 345 = ? + 365$
$? = 190$

41. (5) $216 + ? \times 7 = 15 \times 10 + 16 \times 5$
$216 + ? \times 7 = 150 + 80$
$? \times 7 = 14$
$? = 2$

42. (1) $64^5 \times 10^2/32^5 = 5^2 \times ?$
$(64/32)^5 \times 10^2 = 5^2 \times ?$
$2^5 \times 10^2/5^2 = ?$
$? = 128$

43. (2) $440 + 275 + ? = 3500/5 + 250$
$440 + 275 + ? = 700 + 250$
$? = 235$

44. (2) 24% of $550 + 105/5 = ? - 147$
$132 + 21 + 147 = ?$
$? = 300$

45. (4) $72 + 1 = 73$
$73 + 5 = 78$
$78 + 9 = 87$
$87 + 13 = 100$
$100 + 17 = 117$

46. (1) $48 + 2^2 = 52$
$52 + 3^2 = 61$
$61 + 5^2 = 86$
$86 + 7^2 = 135$
$135 + 11^2 = \mathbf{256}$

47. (3)

48. (3) $32 \times 0.5 = 16$
$16 \times 1 = 16$
$16 \times 2 = 32$
$32 \times 4 = 128$
$128 \times 8 = 1024$

49. (2) $250/5 = 50$
$50 \times 4 = 200$
$200/5 = 40$
$40 \times 4 = 160$
$160/5 = \mathbf{32}$

50. (3) Required answer = 84 + 70 – (60 + 55)
= 39 more

51. (1) The number of pens distributed in class IV
$= 56 \times 125/100 = 70$

The number of pens, pencils and erasers distributed in class IV = $70 \times 4/1 = 280$

The number of pencils and erasers distributed in class IV = 280 – 70 = 210

52. (4) The number of pencils distributed in all three class = 60 + 55 + 85 = 200

The number of pens, pencils and erasers distributed in class I = 56 + 60 + 44 = 160

Ratio = 200 : 160 = 5 : 4

53. (2) The number of pencils distributed in classes II and III = 55 + 85 = 140

The number of pens and erasers distributed in class I = 56 + 44 = 100

Percentage = (140 – 100)/100*100 = 40%

54. (5) The average number of erasers distributed in classes II and III = (66 + 70)/2 = 68

The number of pencils and papers distributed in class II = 68 + 32 = 100

The number of papers distributed in class II = 100 – 55 = 45

Ratio = 75 : 45 = 5 : 3

For questions (55-57):

Village	Total	Males	Females
A	150	75	75
B	90	60	30
C	120	75	45

55. (4) Required difference = 75 + 60 – 120 = 15

56. (1) The total number of people in village D
$= 150 \times 4/3 = 200$

. The number of males in village D
= (200 + 50) /2 = 125

57. (3) The average number of males and females in village B = 90/2 = 45

Required ratio = 75 : 45 = 5 : 3

58. (4) Suppose the length of the rectangle = $5x$ cm

Hence, the breadth of the rectangle = $5x \times 4/5$

$= 4x$

According to the question

$2 \times (5x + 4x) = 108$

$x = 54/9 = 6$

The length of the rectangle = $5 \times 6 = 30$ cm

The breadth of the rectangle = $4 \times 6 = 24$ cm

Area of the rectangle = $30 \times 24 = 720$ cm^2

59. (1) A and B together complete the work = $20 \times 3/2 = 30$ days

Ratio of the efficiency of A and B = 3 : 2 $1/2x + 1/3x = 1/30$

$3 + 2 = x/5$

$x = 25$

A alone complete the work = $2 \times 25 = 50$ days

B alone complete the work = $3 \times 25 = 75$ days

C alone complete the work = y days

$A + B + C = 1/10$

$1/50 + 1/75 + 1/y = 1/10$

$1/y = 1/15y = 15$

Required days = $1/75 + 1/15 = (1 + 5)/75 = 2/25$ or 12.5 days

60. (4) Let the CP of an article be x.

Article sold at 25% loss = $x \times 75/100 = 3x/4$

According to the question

$3x/4 + 378 = x \times 120/100$

$3x/4 + 378 = 6x/5$

$x = 840$

61. (3)

62. (2)

63. (1) Share of A and B = 960 : 1440 = 2 : 3

$x \times 24/[(x + 4000) \times 16] = 2/3$

$9x/4 = x + 4000$

$5x = 16000$

$x = 3200$

64. (4) Milk in vessel = 90 liters

Water in vessel = $90 \times 1/3 = 30$ liters

$(90 - 36 \times 3/4)/(30 - 36 \times 1/4 + x)$

$= 7/4$ $63/(21 + x) = 7/4$

$36 = 21 + x$

$x = 15$

65. (3) Speed of the boat = $7x$

Speed of the stream = $2x$

Downstream speed of the boat

$= 432/6 = 72$ km/hr

Speed of the boat = $72 \times 7x/(7x + 2x) = 56$ km/hr

Speed of the stream = $72 - 56 = 16$ km/hr

Upstream speed of the boat = $56 - 16 = 40$ km/hr

Required time = $280/40 = 7$ hours

For questions (66-70):

Designation	Person
CMD	D
ED	G
GM	E
DGM	A
AGM	F
PO	B
Clerk	C

66. (1)

67. (3)

68. (4)

69. (2)

70. (1)

71. (3) Given series

N G U 5 K **S 6** 7 Q E 8 R A 1 T 3 Y O **Z 2** **M** 4 J 9

72. (2) Given series

N G U 5 K S 6 7 Q E 8 R A 1 T 3 Y O Z 2 M 4 J 9

Required order → Consonants-Even number

73. (5) Given series

N G U 5 K S 6 7 **Q** E 8 R A 1 T 3 Y O Z 2 M 4 J 9

74. (3) Given series

N G U 5 K S 6 7 Q E 8 R A 1 T **3** Y O Z 2 **M** 4 J 9

75. (4) Given series

N G U 5 K **S6** 7 Q E 8 R A 1 T 3 Y O Z **2M** 4 J 9

For questions (76-80):

Shelves	Boxes
7	O
6	Q

5	N
4	L
3	R
2	M
1	P

76. (2)
77. (1)
78. (4)
79. (2)
80. (5)

For questions (81-83):

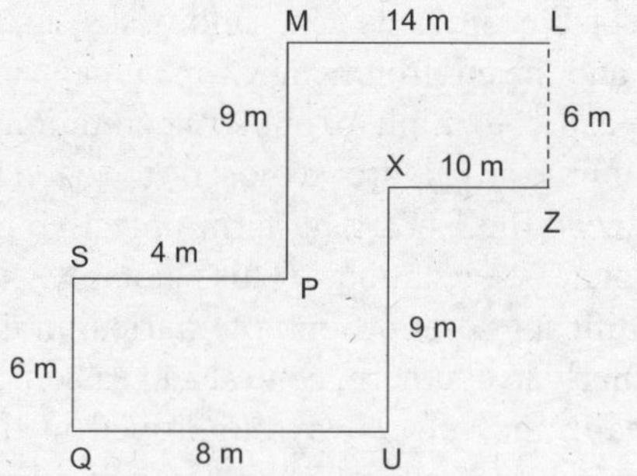

81. (4)
82. (2)
83. (2)
84. (4) ACROSS → Alphabet + 2→ A + 2 = C in the same way,
D → F, E → G, F → H, I → K, N → P, E → G
85. (5) 256374815 175593737

For questions (86-90):

Final Arrangement

86. (3)
87. (1)
88. (2)
89. (5)
90. (4)

For questions (91-95):

Final Arrangement

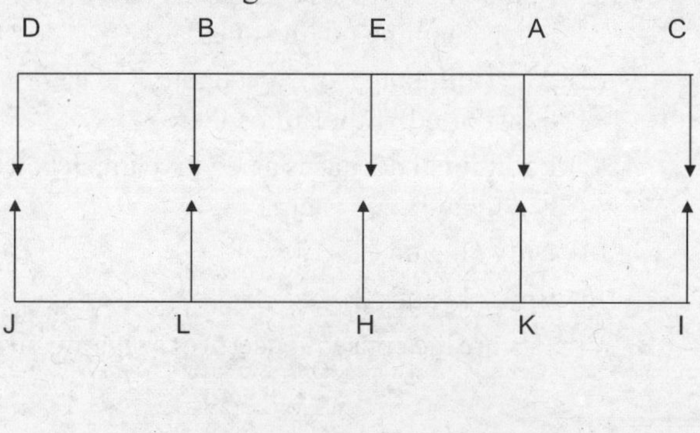

91. (4)
92. (4)
93. (2)
94. (3)
95. (5)
96. (1) I. H > D (D < I = M ≤ P = H) True
II. P ≥ S (S ≤ D < I = M ≤ P) False
Only conclusion I is true
97. (1) I. P > X (X ≤ G < N < Y = P) → True
II. N < Q (N < Y = P > H > Q)→ False
Only conclusion I is true.
98. (3) I. Q > Z (Q ≥ B = S ≥ N = T ≥ Z) → False
II. Z = Q (Q ≥ B = S ≥ N = T ≥ Z) → False
Either conclusion I or II is true.
99. (1)

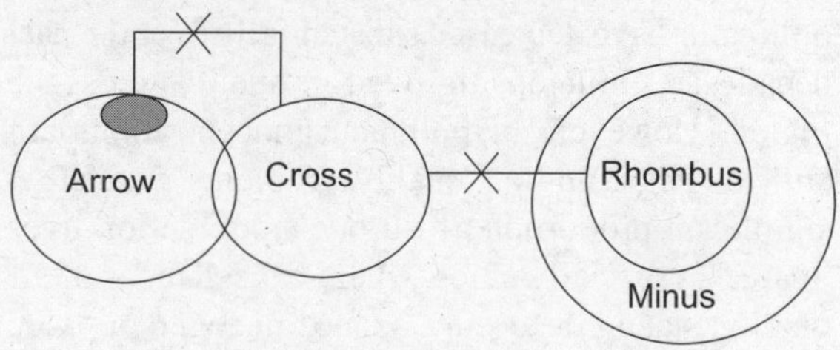

Only conclusion I follows.

100. (5)

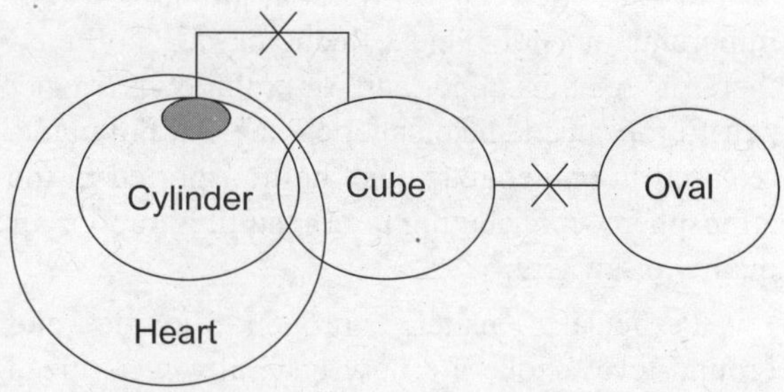

Both conclusions I and II follow.

IBPS Clerk Mains, 2021

(Held on 25 January, 2022)

Based on Memory

General English

Directions (1-7): *Read the following passage and answer the questions given below. Some words are highlighted to help you answer some of the questions.*

Air pollution harms human health and the environment. In Europe, emissions of many air pollutants have decreased substantially over the past decades, resulting in improved air quality across the region. However, air pollutant concentrations are still too high, and air quality problems **persist**. A significant proportion of Europe's population lives in areas, especially cities, where exceedances of air quality standards occur: ozone, nitrogen dioxide and particulate matter (PM) pollution pose serious health risks. Several countries have exceeded one or more of their 2010 emission limits for four important air pollutants. Reducing air pollution therefore remains important. Air pollution is a local, pan-European and hemispheric issue. Air pollutants released in one country may be transported in the atmosphere, contributing to or resulting in poor air quality elsewhere.

Particulate matter, nitrogen dioxide and ground-level ozone are now generally recognized as the three pollutants that most significantly affect human health. Long-term and peak exposures to these pollutants range in severity of impact, from impairing the respiratory system to premature death. Around 90 % of city dwellers in Europe are exposed to pollutants at concentrations higher than the air quality levels deemed harmful to health. Air pollution is causing damage to human health and ecosystems. Large parts of the population do not live in a healthy environment, according to current standards. To get on a sustainable path, Europe will have to be ambitious and go beyond current legislation. Acidification was substantially reduced between 1990 and 2010 in Europe's sensitive ecosystem areas that were subjected to acid deposition of excess sulfur and nitrogen compounds. The EU's long-term objective is to achieve levels of air quality that do not result in unacceptable impacts on, and risks to, human health and the environment. Crop damage is caused by exposure to high ozone concentrations. Most agricultural crops are exposed to ozone levels that exceed the EU's long-term objective intended to protect vegetation. This notably includes a significant proportion of agricultural areas, particularly in southern, central and eastern Europe. Air quality has not always improved in line with the general decrease of **anthropogenic emissions** of air pollutants. There is not always a clear linear relationship between decreasing emissions and the concentrations of air pollutants observed in the air. Targeted efforts to reduce emissions are therefore still required to further protect human health and the environment in Europe. The European Environment Agency (EEA) is the European Union's air pollution data center; it supports the implementation of EU legislation linked to air emissions and air quality. The EEA also contributes to the evaluation of EU air pollution policies and to the development of long-term strategies to improve air quality in Europe.

1. What, according to the author, is/are driving and adding to poor air quality in various parts of the world?

(1) Pollutants that are exposed to higher levels than the quality standards.

(2) Air pollutants of a country that are transported in the atmosphere.

(3) Pollution that causes a negative impact on health and ecosystems.

(4) Only (1) and (3)

(5) Both (1) and (2)

2. What is/are the consequence(s) of a significant

reduction in air pollutants over the last few decades?

(1) The level of suffering caused by air pollution has decreased.

(2) There has been a significant improvement in the quality of the air.

(3) Pollution levels in the air are becoming unacceptably high.

(4) Several countries have exceeded their limits for emissions.

(5) All of these

3. Which of the following factors contribute to the deterioration of the respiratory system and early mortality?

(1) transportation of air pollutants in the air.

(2) maximum exposures to ground-level ozone.

(3) long-term exposures to nitrogen dioxide.

(4) Only (1) and (2)

(5) Only (2) and (3)

4. Which of the following statements is/are correct based on the information provided regarding the European Environment Agency (EEA)?

(*i*) It is the air pollution data center of the European Union.

(*ii*) It helps in the review of the air pollution policies of the UN.

(*iii*) It contributes to European air quality improvement plans.

(1) Only (*iii*) (2) Only (*ii*) and (*iii*)

(3) Only (*ii*) (4) Only (*i*) and (*iii*)

(5) All of these

5. Why is it necessary to make targeted efforts to minimize emissions?

(1) to better safeguard human health in the interest of a sustainable society.

(2) to strengthen environmental and natural vegetation preservation.

(3) to cut down on the number of pollutants accumulated in the acid.

(4) Both (1) and (2)

(5) None of these

6. Which of the following statements most accurately describes the phrase **"anthropogenic emissions"** as used in the passage?

(1) a type of emission that ensures the long-term viability of nature.

(2) an emission that brings humans and the environment closer together.

(3) human-caused emissions that are less detrimental to the environment.

(4) human-caused emissions of greenhouse gases and pollutants.

(5) emissions that have a serious impact on species and wildlife.

7. Choose the most appropriate synonym of the word **'PERSIST'**, as highlighted in the given passage.

(1) forswear (2) renounce

(3) persevere (4) abandon

(5) evacuate

Directions (8-14): *Read the following passage and answer the questions given below. Some words are highlighted to help you answer some of the questions.*

Whether you're the reader who rips through a new book each week or the one still **slogging through** that bestseller your friend recommended months ago, psychologists say your time is being well spent. And if it's been a while since your last date with a good book, the experts have a few reasons that might convince you to give it another go. One of the benefits of reading is simply that it provides enjoyment and pleasure. It can provide an escape from boredom or stress. Plus, reading has been shown to help us better understand and interact with other people, keep our brains sharp, expand our world views and grow as individuals. Stories allow us to feel connected with others and part of something bigger than ourselves. Reading can give us a sense of belongingness that we all instinctively want as human beings.

It's more likely to get lost in a book if you're reading a high-quality text, but "quality" in this case is subjective and something that gets determined by you. For some, it's a quick-moving plot that's **critical**, while for others engaging characters or a poetic writing style is most important if you want to get lost in the storyline. And some people are just more interested in one type of story versus another. Stories about other people teach us to be the types of people we want to be. Reading makes us think and feel in new and different ways. You give up some of your own habits and thoughts, and you take on your own idea of being a different person in circumstances that you might otherwise never had been in. Researchers at a University showed in an experiment that reading actually satisfies that need for human connection because it can mimic what we feel during real social interactions.

Back in 2009, Oatley and his colleagues found that after reading one of two different versions of the same story - one an original piece of fiction and the other a retelling of the same story written in a non-fiction style - participants who read fiction changed in their personality traits more than those who read the non- fiction version of the story and reported feeling higher levels of emotions. Throughout life, reading activities aid to rejuvenate navigational learning skills and contextual memory. Objectively, Oatley and his colleagues haven't measured whether these changes might be labeled as "good" or "positive," but he says to think about it in terms of personal growth akin to how we want kids to grow and develop in their own ways. It is very important in the social world to understand others, to understand ourselves, and not just get stuck.

8. What is/are the advantage(s) of reading that the author describes in the passage?

(1) It can be a fun way to pass the time when you're bored.

(2) It brings pleasure and enjoyment.

(3) It maintains our minds sharp and broadens our horizons.

(4) Only (1) and (3)

(5) All of these

9. What did university researchers demonstrate in an experiment?

(1) Reading satisfies our want for interaction with people.

(2) Reading helps us feel the same way we do in real-life social situations.

(3) After reading fiction, the majority of people's personality features alter.

(4) Only (1) and (2)

(5) Only (2) and (3)

10. What, in the opinion of the author, is subjective and determined by the reader?

(1) Presence of mind while reading

(2) Quality while reading a book

(3) Engaging characters in a book

(4) A poetic writing style in a book

(5) All of these

11. Which of the following statements is/are correct based on the information provided in the given passage?

(*i*) Other people's stories teach us how to be the people we aspire to be.

(*ii*) Reading encourages us to think and behave in new and different ways.

(*iii*) If you wish to get immersed in the story, you'll need a poetic writing style.

(1) Only (*iii*) (2) Only (*ii*) and (*iii*)

(3) Only (*ii*) (4) Only (*i*) and (*iii*)

(5) All of these

12. Choose the most appropriate antonym of the word **"CRITICAL"**, as highlighted in the given passage?

(1) crucial (2) decisive

(3) exigent (4) pivotal

(5) trivial

13. Which of the following idioms best illustrates the phrase **"slogging through"** as used in the passage?

(1) let it all hang out

(2) hammer away at

(3) be of the opinion that

(4) push the boat out

(5) let one's hair down

14. Choose the most appropriate synonym of the word **'REJUVENATE'**, as highlighted in the given passage.

(1) impair (2) impede

(3) uplift (4) shrink

(5) blunt

Directions (15-21): *In the following paragraph, a*

few words have been omitted, each of which has been numbered. Select the most appropriate word from the given options to fill in the given blanks correctly in terms of contextual meaning and grammatical accuracy.

To ensure that visually impaired litigants are able to effectively pursue and .... (15) .... their legal rights, the Delhi High Court has asked the government to provide them with the court documents in Braille script. Moreover, the right to justice includes the right to receive documents, which legally .... (16) .... the parties to a communication mode and language that they can easily .... (17) .... The court's direction came while hearing an anticipatory bail plea filed by a visually impaired man. It is mandated to make available all necessary facilities and equipment to .... (18) .... the recording of testimonies, arguments or opinions given by persons with disabilities in their preferred language and means of communication," the court said while .... (19) .... the government to make arrangements to provide the documents in Braille. Taking note of the submission, the Judge said, "The parties are entitled to be well versed with the proceedings of the litigation they .... (20) .... and the documents which materially affect their legal rights. Section 12 of the Rights of Persons with Disabilities Act, 2016 creates a .... (21) .... on the state for providing access to justice to differently-abled persons".

15. (1) cushion (2) protect
(3) insulate (4) fortify
(5) All of these

16. (1) averts (2) prevents
(3) entitles (4) obviates
(5) hampers

17. (1) preclude (2) restrain
(3) obturate (4) decipher
(5) All of these

18. (1) expedite (2) trammel
(3) encumber (4) constrain
(5) forestall

19. (1) promising (2) occupying
(3) engaging (4) dictating
(5) All of these

20. (1) tenant (2) sheath
(3) pursue (4) desert
(5) strand

21. (1) directive (2) injunction
(3) mandate (4) ordinance
(5) All of these

Directions (22-23): *Rearrange the following statements in the proper sequence to form a meaningful paragraph and then answer the questions given below.*

(A) This is due to Russia's war on Ukraine, which have impacted the region when it was already experiencing fragile growth and rising commodity prices.

(B) However, the impact was indirect, rather than direct, given the relatively low proportion of exports and imports that go to and come from Russia and Ukraine.

(C) India is projected to grow at a slower rate over the current fiscal year, the World Bank said in its bi- annual South Asia Economic Focus.

(D) Given these challenges, governments need to carefully plan monetary and fiscal policies to counter external shocks and protect the vulnerable.

(E) The impact of the war has seen faster inflation, deteriorating current account balances and growing fiscal deficits.

22. Which of the following will be the correct sequence of the given statements to form a coherent paragraph?
(1) ACEDB (2) CDBEA
(3) EABCD (4) CAEBD
(5) DBEAC

23. Which one of the following statements contains an error?
(1) C (2) E
(3) A (4) D
(5) B

Direction (24-28): *In each of the questions given below, a statement with a highlighted phrase is given. The highlighted phrase may or may not have been used correctly in the given statements. Choose the appropriate phrase/phrases from the given options which could replace the highlighted* *one to make the statements grammatically and contextually correct. If the highlighted phrase is correct and needs no replacement then choose option "e" as your response.*

24. The Constitution states that the official language used for communication shall be the language **that have been in use since** the adoption of the Constitution.

(*i*) that has been in using since
(*ii*) that had been in use since
(*iii*) that has been in use since
(1) Only (*iii*) (2) Only (*i*) and (*iii*)
(3) Only (*ii*) (4) Only (*i*) and (*ii*)
(5) No correction required

25. Official figures show **retail inflation has increased significant** just four days after the RBI stated it would emphasize inflation over growth.

(*i*) retail inflation has increased significantly
(*ii*) retail inflation have been increasing rapidly
(*iii*) inflation in the retail sector has risen sharply
(1) Only (*i*) and (*iii*) (2) Only (*iii*)
(3) Only (*i*) and (*ii*) (4) Only (*ii*)
(5) No correction required

26. The recent corona virus pandemic **has taught us all a lot about what** a large-scale, global public health problem looks like.

(*i*) has thought us a lot about all what
(*ii*) has taught a lot us all about which
(*iii*) have taught all us a lot about what
(1) Only (*iii*) (2) Only (*i*) and (*iii*)
(3) Only (*ii*) (4) Only (*i*) and (*ii*)
(5) No correction required

27. Given the long list of diplomats from across the world, one may presume that India **was actively involved in resolving** the European crisis.

(*i*) was actively involving in resolving
(*ii*) was active involved into resolving
(*iii*) was actively involve for resolving
(1) Only (*i*) and (*iii*) (2) Only (*iii*)
(3) Only (*i*) and (*ii*) (4) Only (*ii*)
(5) No correction required

28. Despite the border crisis, India's commerce with China has achieved new highs, **and it continues to be a largest beneficiary** of Asian Infrastructure and Investment Bank financing.

(*i*) it continue to be the largest beneficiary
(*ii*) it continues to be the largest beneficiary
(*iii*) it continue to be the largest beneficial
(1) Only (*iii*) (2) Only (*i*) and (*iii*)
(3) Only (*ii*) (4) Only (*i*) and (*ii*)
(5) No correction required

Directions (29-31): *In the following questions, two columns are given containing three sentences/phrases each. In the first column, sentences/phrases are A, B and C and in the second column, the sentences/phrases are D, E and F. A sentence/phrase from the first column may or may not connect with another sentence/phrase from the second column. Each question has five options, four of which display the sequence(s) in which the sentences/phrases can be joined to form a grammatically and contextually correct sentence. Choose the appropriate option. If none of the given options forms a correct sentence after combination, mark (e), i.e. "None of these" as your answer.*

29. COLUMN I

(A) It shall not apply to the transport of any live elephant through
(B) The Delhi government will issue new COVID-19 guidelines
(C) Such person has obtained prior permission from the government

COLUMN II

(D) not to encourage the sale and purchase of captive elephants.
(E) hold a final round of meeting on its report on the legislation.
(F) for schools in view of the slight rise in viral cases in the city.

(1) Only A-E and B-D
(2) Only B-F
(3) Only A-F and B-E
(4) Only C-E
(5) None of these

30. COLUMN I

(A) Chief Minister warned that the government will not spare anyone found indulging in riots

(B) It reminded the Governor of the need to discharge constitutional duties constructively

(C) It was done while pointing to the cordiality and productive relationship enjoyed by them

COLUMN II

(D) and the official protocols and courtesies extended to the constitutional head of the State.

(E) a phenomenon associated with a warming of the Central Pacific and drying up of the rains.

(F) current indication has suggested normal rainfall in the northern parts of peninsular India.

(1) Only A-E and B-D
(2) Only C-E
(3) Only A-F and B-E
(4) Only B-F
(5) None of these

31. COLUMN I

(A) Nefarious attempts were being constantly made to undermine

(B) The authority has decided to launch an investigation and audit

(C) The Prime Minister made the announcement while paying homage

COLUMN II

(D) provide students foundational education in language and specialized education.

(E) on getting complaints about a school increasing fees according to its wishes.

(F) they have been established by the city government in partnership with them.

(1) Only A-D and B-F
(2) Only C-F
(3) Only A-E and B-D
(4) Only B-E
(5) None of these

Directions (32-36): *In each of the questions given below, two sentences with a blank in each are given. The given blanks must be filled with the same word. Select a word or words from the choices below that can be used to fill in both of the given blanks.*

32. (A) There needs to be a basic rethink on the .... of the inflation-targeting framework itself.

(B) Fortunately, the medicine had the .... to reduce the amount of pain John was feeling.

(*i*) neglect (*ii*) efficacy
(*iii*) sinking

(1) Only (*ii*) (2) Only (*i*) and (*iii*)
(3) All of these (4) Only (*i*) and (*ii*)
(5) Only (*iii*)

33. (A) The .... way to control inflation for India is for us to create jobs and output.

(B) The scholar's .... goal was to get his research published in a medical journal.

(*i*) reckless (*ii*) ultimate
(*iii*) eventual

(1) Only (*iii*) (2) Only (*i*) and (*ii*)
(3) All of these (4) Only (*ii*) and (*iii*)
(5) Only (*ii*)

34. (A) Nowadays, people's .... of inflation is far higher than what the CPI number indicates.

(B) Your .... of the world around you is dictated primarily by your five senses.

(*i*) pomposity
(*ii*) affectation
(*iii*) perception

(1) Only (*ii*) (2) All of these
(3) Only (*i*) and (*iii*) (4) Only (*i*) and (*ii*)
(5) Only (*iii*)

35. (A) Our country is being .... by religious divisions that have reached a new and dangerous level.

(B) Bullies have .... the victims by making fun of them and encouraging others to do so as well.

(*i*) mortified (*ii*) humiliated
(*iii*) appeased

(1) Only (*ii*) (2) Only (*i*) and (*iii*)
(3) All of these (4) Only (*i*) and (*ii*)
(5) Only (*iii*)

36. (A) A fundamental freedom is .... when the freedom of conscience is harmed.

(B) Our ability to make rational decisions is sometimes .... by our emotions.

(*i*) impaired (*ii*) blunted
(*iii*) vitiated

(1) Only (*ii*) (2) All of these
(3) Only (*i*) and (*iii*) (4) Only (*i*) and (*ii*)
(5) Only (*iii*)

37. Five grammatically correct and contextually meaningful sentences are given in this question. A paragraph can be formed by rearranging four of these sentences. You must select the sentence that is incoherent and does not fit in with the rest of the sentences.

(1) The second system permits the social insurance fund to cover private healthcare spending.
(2) Universal health care has become a well-accepted objective of public policy around the world.
(3) In the first approach, health care is provided as a free public service, just like a public library.
(4) This rapid expansion in transportation is one of India's most massive changes since liberation.
(5) The basic idea of universal health care is that no one should be deprived of quality health care.

Directions (38-40): *In each of the following questions, three statements are given. For each question, three starters are also given which can be used to integrate all three statements into a meaningful and coherent composition. Select a starter or starters from the following options that can be used to combine the given statements in a grammatically accurate and contextually meaningful manner.*

38. (A) training future leaders of India's public transportation system,

(B) Indian Railways officers will need to work together

(C) because they will be serving in the organization for decades

(*i*) however (*ii*) apart from
(*iii*) anyhow

(1) Only (*ii*) (2) Only (*i*) and (*iii*)
(3) All of these (4) Only (*i*) and (*ii*)
(5) Only (*iii*)

39. (A) merging services to adapt training for newly hired officers,

(B) early and mid-career training programs are also required

(C) since the focus should be on increasing the ability to manage

(*i*) in addition to (*ii*) nevertheless
(*iii*) besides

(1) Only (*ii*) (2) Only (*i*) and (*iii*)
(3) Only (*iii*) (4) Only (*i*) and (*ii*)
(5) All of these

40. (A) in a system based on social insurance, public service is crucial because,

(B) in the absence of public health institutions, patients are at risk of racing to

(C) expensive hospitals every other day, wasting resources and increasing costs

(*i*) due to (*ii*) even
(*iii*) instead

(1) Only (*iii*) (2) Only (*i*) and (*iii*)
(3) All of these (4) Only (*i*) and (*ii*)
(5) Only (*ii*)

Reasoning Ability

Directions (41-45): *Study the following information carefully and answer the given questions.*

There are three rows i.e., row 1, row 2 and row 3 such that row 2 is in the north of row 3 and row 1 is in the north of row 2. Six persons sit in each row. All of them face the north direction. The persons sit in row 1 are exactly opposite to persons sit in row 2 and vice versa and the persons sit in row 2 are exactly opposite to persons sit in row 3 and vice versa. The persons are from A to R as per the English alphabetical series. All the information is not necessarily in the same order.

Q sits third to the left of G. Q sits at the extreme end. A sits to the north of Q. Two persons sit between A and the one who sits immediate left of H. The one who sits to the north of H is the only neighbor of B. N sits second to the left of E. E sits neither adjacent to G nor at the extreme end. One person sits between B and C. C doesn't sit adjacent to N. The number of persons sits between A and H is same as between L and D who sits south of R. R sits at the extreme end. P sits second to the left of J in the same row as C. F sits just next to J. O sits to the south east of K. G and I are not immediate neighbours.

41. How many persons sit between Q and the one who sits immediate right of O?

(1) One (2) Two
(3) Three (4) None
(5) More than three

42. Which among the following statement(s) is/are true?

I. A and H sit in the same row
II. H sits to the north west of G
III. K sits at the extreme end

(1) Both I and II (2) Both II and III
(3) Only I (4) Both I and III
(5) Only III

43. Four of the following five are alike in a certain way and thus form a group. Which of the following one does not belong to the group?

(1) N-Q (2) I-L
(3) C-N (4) E-D
(5) H-M

44. Who among the following sits third to the left of the person who sits at extreme end in row1?

(1) J (2) C
(3) K (4) E
(5) M

45. If all the persons sit in row 3 are arranged in the alphabetical order from left to right, then the position of how many persons remains unchanged?

(1) One (2) Two
(3) Three (4) None
(5) More than three

Directions (46-49): *Study the following information carefully to answer the given questions. In a certain code language:*

"More migrated towards pound" is written as '6EN 7DQ 9SU 10DN'

"Hold the laugh store" is written as '6DI 5EU 7ET 7HM'

"Wait recorded from changes" is written as '10DS 6MG 6TX 9SD'

46. In the given coding language, which of the following will be the code for "Puzzled"?

(1) 6EN (2) 4UY
(3) 8RD (4) 9DQ
(5) None of these

47. In the given coding language, which of the following will be the code for "Stronger"?

(1) 10DR (2) 6DN
(3) 7RK (4) 10RU
(5) None of these

48. Which of the following words could be coded as "7KC 8TN"?

(1) Death Magnet (2) Black Magic
(3) Black Magnet (4) Track Progress
(5) Blue Moon

49. Which of the following will be the code for 'Mental'?

(1) 5ON (2) 7LM
(3) 8LN (4) 5QL
(5) None of these

50. With restaurants affected due to the COVID-19 crisis, a restaurant in Pune has come up with a unique scheme to attract customers with 'Win a Bullet bike' contest for those who finish a massive Bullet Thali within an hour. Bullet Thali is a massive non-veg thali which consists of around 12 types of dishes made with 4 kgs of mutton and fried fish. The owner is happy that the response has been great and people are visiting to try the thali and participating in this unique contest. As per owner, the hotel sells around 65 Thali daily.

Which of the following can be inferred from the above statement?

(I) Bullet bike has a huge craze and demand among people in Pune.

(II) Promotion is only source to make restaurant popular and gain income.

(III) Non-vegetarians are more in count as compared to Vegetarians in Pune.

(1) Only II (2) Only I and III
(3) Only I (4) Only III
(5) Only II and III

Directions (51-55): *Study the given information and answer the related questions:*

Nine persons K, L, M, N, O, P, Q, R and T visit Balaji temple in three months i.e., May, August and November on 5th, 7th and 20th of the same year. They go by different vehicles. All the information is not necessarily in the same order as given.

R goes by airplane on even date. Four persons visit between R and the one goes by bus. P visits two person before the one who goes by bus. The number of persons visit after P is two more than the number of persons visit before L. T goes by train just after the one goes by car and both of them visits in different months. Three persons visit between T and M. M and the one who goes by chopper do not visit in the same month. The person who goes by taxi visits before K who visits before the one who goes by Chopper and they all three visits on the same date. N goes by Bike. O does not go by chopper and bike but visits after the one who goes by boat. One of them goes by Jeep.

51. Which among the following combination is correct?

(1) Q- chopper (2) O-bus
(3) K-Jeep (4) M-boat
(5) All are correct

52. How many persons visits between Q and the one who goes by bike?

(1) None (2) One
(3) Two (4) Three
(5) More than three

53. Who among the following visits on 20th August?

(1) T (2) L
(3) P (4) R
(5) None of these

54. .... goes by bus on .... ?

(1) O, 5th August (2) K, 5th August
(3) O, 5th May (4) Q, 20th May
(5) P, 20th November

55. If N is related to airplane, P is related to chopper, in the same way, ... is related to car?

(1) K (2) O
(3) T (4) M
(5) None of these

Directions (56-60): *A number arrangement machine when given an input line of numbers rearranges them following a particular rule in each step. The following is an illustration of input and rearrangement.*

Input: 2375 9824 1673 8253 4213 5184

Step I: 2357 2489 1367 2358 1234 1458

Step II: 7532 9842 7631 8532 4321 8541

Step III: 4321 7532 7631 8532 8541 9842

Step IV: 32 53 63 53 54 84

Step V: 1 2 3 2 1 4

Step V is the last step of the input. As per the rules followed in the above step, find out the appropriate step for the given output.

Input: 3472 6721 9733 7123 5361 8417

56. In which of the following step the elements "9733 7321 6531" found in the same order?

(1) Step I (2) Step IV
(3) Step III (4) Step II
(5) no such step

57. What is difference between the fourth element from the left in step IV and fourth element from the right in step V?

(1) 31 (2) 63
(3) 42 (4) 61
(5) None of these

58. How many steps will be required to complete the rearrangement?

(1) V (2) IV

(3) II (4) More than VI

(5) VI

59. Which of the following element would be at the third from the right of the element which is sixth from the right end in step II?

(1) 9733 (2) 6531

(3) 7123 (4) 8417

(5) None of these

60. Which element is exactly between the third element from left end and second element from right end in step III?

(1) 7321 (2) 7621

(3) 8741 (4) 6531

(5) Can't be determined

Directions (61-62): *Dismissing four petitions challenging the collection of fine in cars when the drivers were found without a mask, the Delhi high court said it is mandatory to wear a mask in a private car even when the driver is alone in the car, as a vehicle is considered a public place. The high court said a mask acts as Suraksha Kavach, which would prevent the spread of the deadly virus.*

61. Which of the following diminish the verdict issued by Delhi High Court?

(1) There will be penalty if anyone will break the rules to wear mask.

(2) Delhi government has decided to distribute masks at public places.

(3) Mask is not compulsory for police personnel if they are driving alone.

(4) Delhi Transport department has also made compulsory to wear masks in DTC buses and DMRC.

(5) Both (2) and (4)

62. Which of the following can be hypothesized from the above statement?

(I) People will follow the rules to wear mask even they are alone in car.

(II) Awareness among people will be spread as court has termed "Suraksha Kavach" to mask.

(III) Less car will be seen on the roads of Delhi after verdict of High Court.

(1) Only III (2) Only I and II

(3) Only II and III (4) Only II

(5) All I, II and III

Direction (63-65): *Study the given information and answer the following questions:*

Four persons Rohan, Vikas, Deepak and Yash are married to four girls named Pragya, Surbhi, Poonam, Anjana. They all have four kids (one each) named Tina, Anu, Monty, Puja. All the information is not necessarily in the same order as given.

Puja is not the child of Rohan and Vikas. Surbhi is not married to Vikas and Deepak. Yash is not the father of Puja nor married to Surbhi and Poonam. Anjana is not the mother of Puja and Tina. The mother of Anu is not married to Vikas. Poonam is neither the mother of Monty nor the wife of Deepak. Monty is not the child of Yash.

63. Who among the following is the child of Pragya?

(1) Tina (2) Monty

(3) Puja (4) Anu

(5) Can't be determined

64. Which among the following combination is correct?

(1) Poonam- Rohan (2) Anjana- Deepak

(3) Surbhi- Vikas (4) Pragya- Puja

(5) Poonam- Anu

65. Which among the following statement is/are true?

(1) Surbhi is the mother of Anu

(2) Rohan is the husband of Surbhi

(3) Poonam is the wife of Rohan

(4) Puja is not the child of Pragya

(5) Vikas is the husband of Anjana

Directions (66-69): *Each of the questions below consists of a question and two statements numbered I, and II given below it. You have to decide whether the data provided in the statements are sufficient to answer the question. Read all the statements and answer the following questions.*

(1) If the data in statement I alone is sufficient to answer

(2) If the data in statement II alone is

sufficient to answer

(3) If the data either in statement I alone or in statement II alone is sufficient to answer

(4) If the data given in both statements, I and II together are not sufficient to answer

(5) If the data in both the statements I and II together are necessary to answer

66. Seven persons are attending the seminar on seven consecutive days starting from Monday. Who among the following attends the class on Saturday?

Statement I: Three persons attend class between A and E. G attends class just before the one who attends class two persons after C. F attends class before D.

Statement II: More than one person attend class before A. G attends class two persons after F. F attends class after Wednesday. The number of persons attends class before A is one more than after G.

67. Eight persons-A, B, C, D, E, F, G and H go to market one after the other but not necessarily in the same order. Who among the following goes first to the market?

Statement I: Two persons go between G and C. A goes just after C who goes three persons before F. The number of persons goes after H is same as before G. H does not go before F.

Statement II: More than two persons go between C and H. G goes before E who doesn't go last to the market. Neither A nor D goes to the market last.

68. Eight persons sit around a circular table and face outwards. Who among the following sits second to the left of W?

Statement I: R sits opposite to the one who sits immediate right of S. Two persons sit between W and the one who sits immediate left of P.

Statement II: V sits adjacent to S. T sits second to the left of S. R is an immediate neighbor of T but not S. P is an immediate neighbor of both W and S.

69. A family of three generation have six members. How many male members are there in the family? **Statement I:** S is nephew of T. Q is sister-in-law of T and vice versa. N is grandparent of only child of O. S is not married.

Statement II: T is unmarried. O is the only son of N and is married. M is parent of T.

Directions (70-74): *Study the following information carefully to answer the given questions.*

Seven friends Hema, Vikas, Piya, Neema, Kiran, Shiv and Arya are going to visit famous places of India named as Hawa mehal, Golden temple, Taj mahal, Red fort, Robbers cave, Qutub minar and Lotus temple. Each of them goes on different days of the same week starting from Sunday. All the information is not necessarily in the same order.

Vikas goes to either Taj mahal or Golden temple but not on Monday. The number of persons who goes between Arya and Vikas is same as the number of persons who goes between Arya and kiran. Only one person goes between Hema and Neema. Arya doesn't go to Hawa mahal and Qutub minar. Shiv goes to Golden temple. Piya goes just after Arya but not on the last day of the week. The one who goes on Wednesday goes to Red fort. More than three persons goes before Piya. Vikas goes before Piya who doesn't goes to Robbers cave and Hawa mehal. Neema goes after Vikas. Kiran goes to Lotus temple.

70. Who among the following goes on Thursday?

(1) The one who goes to Lotus temple

(2) Arya

(3) Neema

(4) Shiv

(5) The one who goes just after Hema

71. How many persons go between Shiv and Piya?

(1) One (2) Two

(3) Three (4) Four

(5) Five

72. Who among the following goes to robbers cave?

(1) Neema (2) Shiv

(3) None of these (4) Arya

(5) Hema

73. Four of the following five are alike in a

certain way and hence form a group. Which is the one that does not belong to the group?

(1) Shiv-Hawa mahal

(2) Hema-Taj mahal

(3) Neema-Red Fort

(4) Piya-Lotus Temple

(5) Arya-Qutub Minar

74. Which of the following statement is not true?

(1) Shiv goes on Sunday

(2) Neema goes to Red Fort

(3) Only two persons goes between Vikas and Piya

(4) Piya goes on Friday

(5) Kiran goes On Monday

Directions (75-78): *Study the following information and answer the related questions:*

A#B means A is the father of B

A%B means A is the child of B A&B means A is the brother of B, A@B means A is the sister of B , A*B means A is the wife of B

75. If the expression **'R#B%H%C&L'** is true, then what is the relation of C with respect R?

(1) Sister (2) Father-in-law

(3) Uncle (4) Mother

(5) None of these

76. Who among the following is the father of S according to the expression **'S@K&T%V*N&G'**?

(1) N (2) G

(3) S (4) T

(5) Can't be determined

77. According to the expression **'U*K, E%K, E&J, J*F#H'**, find, how many children K has?

(1) Three (2) One

(3) Can't be determined

(4) Two

(5) None of these

78. In the expression, **'A#W@Z&K*C, K%D'**, find the number of females in the family?

(1) Five (2) Four

(3) Three (4) Two

(5) None of these

Directions (79-80): *With an increased variability of monsoons and rapidly depleting groundwater tables, large parts of India are reeling under water stress and drought like situation. Here, one intervention that has been tried out in various States, and perhaps needs to be taken up on a bigger scale, is the construction of farm ponds, it can be cost-effective structures that transform rural livelihoods. They can help enhance water control, contribute to agriculture intensification and boost farm incomes.*

79. Which of the following can diminish the importance farm ponds?

(1) Farm Ponds is cost effective and it transform rural livelihoods.

(2) It will help to enhance water control, agricultural reforms and can boost farmers' incomes.

(3) It can used as intermediate storage which may leads to evaporation loss.

(4) Both (*a*) and (*b*)

(5) Both (*b*) and (*c*)

80. Which of the following statement(s) is/are false in context of the given statement?

(1) The problem of lower water table has captivated the entire country.

(2) Farm ponds can help in the process of water control.

(3) Construction of farm ponds hamper the agricultural modification and rural subsistence.

(4) Farm ponds can be a viable investment option

(5) None of these.

Directions (81-84): *Study the following alphanumeric series carefully and answer the questions given below:*

U 3 7 @ # 4 5 T & ! F U 9 M 6 3 © G 5 Ω 3 A Z 5 2 € 8 β L P 3

STEP I: The numbers which are immediately preceded by a letter are arranged to the immediate right of the element which is third from the right end (in the series) in ascending order.

STEP II: The symbol which is immediately followed by a letter is interchanged its position with respect to the element just before it.

STEP III: The letters which are immediately preceded by a symbol are dropped from the series. (STEP II is applied after STEP I and STEP III is applied after STEP II)

81. How many numbers are arranged at the end of the series in the step-I?
(1) One (2) Three
(3) Four (4) Five
(5) More than five

82. How many numbers are immediately followed by symbols in step-II?
(1) One (2) Two
(3) Four (4) Five
(5) None of these

83. Which of the following letter is 6th to the right of 3rd symbol from the left end in step III?
(1) L (2) U
(3) T (4) M
(5) None of these

84. What is sum of numbers which are 6th from the right end in step I and 5th from the left end in step III? 3 + 3 = 6
(1) 11 (2) 12
(3) 6 (4) 13
(5) None of these

85. Owner of Restaurant A has decided to decrease the price of Full Thali to attract the customers while the Owner of Restaurant B will keep the price unchanged. Both the owner has same motive to increase the customer base and increase their income.
Which of the following can be hypothesized from the above statement?
(I) All the Customer of Restaurant B will move to Restaurant A to avail the benefit of price slashed.
(II) Some of the customer will think quality of Restaurant A is not as good as Restaurant B.
(III) Infrastructure and kitchen of Restaurant B is more modern and spacious.
(1) Only I and II (2) Only III
(3) Only II and III (4) Only I and III
(5) None of them

Directions (86-90): *Study the following information carefully and answer the given questions.*

Eight Cricketers- A, B, C, D, E, F, G and H sit around a circular table facing the center in a dinner party but not necessarily in the same order. Each one of them is from a different country. F sits second to right of the cricketer who is from South Africa. B is not from West Indies. Only one person sits between C and the cricketer who is from Sri Lanka. H sits third to left of the cricketer who is from New Zealand. The cricketer who is from Australia sits second to left of the cricketer who is from Zimbabwe. The cricketer who is from India is an immediate neighbor of the cricketer who is from South Africa. Two cricketers sit between the cricketer who is from India and B. C and E are immediate neighbors of each other. Neither C nor E is an immediate neighbor of B and the cricketer who is from South Africa. The cricketer who is from England sits second to right of D. D is neither the cricketer of South Africa nor India. G and the cricketer who is from West Indies are immediate neighbors of each other.

86. Who among the following sits second to the right of the cricketer who is from West Indies?
(1) B (2) H
(3) The cricketer who is from India
(4) E
(5) None of these

87. Who among the following cricketer is from Zimbabwe?
(1) C (2) F
(3) B (4) G
(5) None of these

88. Who among the following sits opposite to E?
(1) A (2) H
(3) G (4) B
(5) None of these

89. Which of the following statement is true about A?
(1) A is from Australia
(2) G is an immediate neighbor of A
(3) A sits opposite to the one who sits second

to the left of D

(4) H does not sit immediate right of A

(5) None is true

90. F is from which country?

(1) India (2) England

(3) South Africa (4) West Indies

(5) None of these

Quantitative Aptitude

Directions (91-93): *A set of 2 equations is given below. Read the information carefully and answer the question based on it.*

1. $x^2 - px + q = 0$ … … Equation (I)

2. $x^2 - (p - 2) + (q - 4) = 0$ ….. Equation (II)

Equation (I) has 'm' and 3 as its roots while equation (II) has 'm' and 1 as its roots.

91. Find the value of 'm'.

(1) 3 (2) 2

(3) 4 (4) 6

(5) 5

92. Find the value of '$2p + q$'.

(1) 12 (2) 8

(3) 17 (4) 16

(5) 10

93. Another equation (III) $a^2 - 7a + 10 = 0$ is given. Which of the following is/are correct about it?

A. Roots of equation (III) are less than that of equation (II).

B. Equation (III) has one root equal to value of 'm'.

C. Equation (III) has roots greater than $(q - p)$.

(1) Only A and C (2) Only A and B

(3) Only B and C (4) None of the above

(5) All of the above

94. There are two trains A and B. Train A starts from point X at 8 AM towards point Y. Another train B starts at 9 AM from point Y towards point X. If they meet at 11 AM and speed of A is 24 kmph, while that of B is 36 kmph. Find distance between X and Y?

(1) 144 km (2) 156 km

(3) 160 km (4) 136 km

(5) None of these

95. Average age of A, B and C is 20 years and average age of B and C was 12 years when A was born. If B is 21 years old, then find the age of C 6 years hence?

(1) 27 years (2) 21 years

(3) 33 years (4) 39 years

(5) 18 years

96. A boat covers a certain distance in upstream in 6 hours 2 minutes and comes back to starting point with current in 2 hours 56 minutes. If boat's upstream speed is 15.05 kmph, then find the distance (approximately) travelled by boat in downstream in 7 hours?

(1) 240 km (2) 180 km

(3) 210 km (4) 150 km

(5) 105 km

97. An article is marked up by P% above the cost price. If shopkeeper offers discount of 25% and still earns a profit of 35%. For earning a profit of 71%, how much discount should be offered by shopkeeper?

(1) 12.5% (2) 10%

(3) 7.5% (4) 5%

(5) None of these

98. A two-digit number decreases by 18 when it's both digits are written in reverse order. If unit digit of original number is equal to the unit digit of 22^6. Find the product of both digits of the number?

(1) 24 (2) 35

(3) 15 (4) 30

(5) 48

Directions (99-103): *In a class, there are total 50 students in class and each student study at least one of three subjects – Mathematics, Science and Hindi. No student studies both Science and Mathematics but not Hindi. Four students study all of these subjects. Sum of number of students who study only Hindi and only Mathematics is 11. 40% of number of students who study only Science is equal to the* *number of students who study only Hindi. Number of students who study both Hindi and Science but not Mathematics is equal to thrice the number of students who study all these subjects. Number of students who study both Hindi and Mathematics but not Science is 33.33% less than number of students who study both Hindi and Science but not Mathematics.*

99. What is the number of students who study both Hindi and Science?

(1) 16 (2) 18
(3) 12 (4) 15
(5) 14

100. What is the number of students who study exactly two subjects?

(1) 24 (2) 26
(3) 20 (4) 28
(5) 22

101. Find the number of students who study only Science is what percentage more or less than that who study both Hindi and Science but not Mathematics?

(1) 20% (2) 33.33%
(3) 16.66% (4) 25%
(5) 40%

102. Number of students who do not study Mathematics is how much more or less that that who do not study Hindi?

(1) 3 (2) 10
(3) 11 (4) 17
(5) 13

103. What is the ratio of number of students who study Hindi to the number of students who do not study Hindi and Mathematics?

(1) 1 : 2 (2) 3 : 2
(3) 4 : 3 (4) 2 : 1
(5) 3 : 1

Directions (104-107): *There are two villages A and B. Ratio of population of village A and that of village B is 3 : 2. Ratio of male population to female population in village A is X : Y and that in village B is Y : X. Difference between the number of males in village A and that of female in village B is 880.*

104. Find the number of females in village B?

(1) 2640 (2) 880
(3) 1320 (4) 1760
(5) Can't be determined

105. Find the number of males in village A?

(1) 880 (2) 1760
(3) 2640 (4) 2520
(5) Can't be determined

106. Number of females in village B is how much percent more/less than that of village A?

(1) 33.33% (2) 66.66%
(3) 40% (4) None of these
(5) Can't be determined

107. If female population in village A is 120 more than male population in same village, then find the total population of village B?

(1) 3600 (2) 5400
(3) 4500 (4) 2700
(5) Can't be determined

Directions (108-110): *A set of 2 number series is given below. Both series follow a similar pattern. Answer the questions based on it using information given below:*

I. 5, 6, 13, 40, 161, 806

II. 2, p, q, r, s

108. Find the value of s.

(1) 22 (2) 82
(3) 89 (4) 84
(5) 77

109. If nth term of series II is 2677, then find the value of 'n'.

(1) 11 (2) 13
(3) 9 (4) 7
(5) 8

110. Find the value of $(r - pq)$.

(1) –3 (2) 5
(3) 0 (4) –1
(5) 1

Directions (111-115): *Read the given data carefully and answer the question based on it.*

There are 3 vessels named – A, B and C. All contain mixture of milk, water and juice. Vessel B contains mixture of volume 150 liters. Ratio of quantity of juice and water in vessel B is 3 : 2 while that of milk and water is 1 : 2. Water in vessel B is

66.67% more than juice in vessel C. Juice in vessel A is 80% of total juice in vessel B and C taken together. Water in vessel C is 20% less than juice in vessel B. In vessel A, ratio of water and juice is 5 : 6. Ratio between milk and water in vessel C is 5 : 4. Milk in vessel A is 2% less than total milk in vessels B and C together.

111. Find the ratio between total milk in vessel A and B together and water in vessel B and C together.
(1) 123 : 110 (2) 87 : 74
(3) 117 : 101 (4) 134 : 115
(5) None of these

112. If 36 liters' mixture from vessel A is taken out, then find the difference between quantity of juice in vessel A and that in vessel B.
(1) 5 liters (2) 12 liters
(3) 3 liters (4) 1 liters
(5) 7 liters

113. Find the sum of amount of quantity in vessel B and that in vessel A together.
(1) 315 liters (2) 402 liters
(3) 417 liters (4) 354 liters
(5) 378 liters

114. From vessel B, 9 liters of mixture is taken out, in next step, 18 liters mixture is again taken out from same vessel. In final step, 27 liters mixtures is taken out from same vessel, then find the difference between amount of milk and juice remained finally in this vessel.
(1) 16 liters (2) 32 liters
(3) 24 liters (4) 28 liters
(5) 36 liters

115. If from vessel A, vessel B and vessel C 20%, 40% and 55% quantity taken out and put into another vessel X, then find the difference between quantity of water and juice in the mixture.
(1) 4.2 liters (2) 5.4 liters
(3) 3.7 liters (4) 4.7 liters
(5) 6.3 liters

116. Average weight of 5 students in a class increases by 4 kg when weight of teacher is also included. If sum of average weight of 5 students and weight of teacher is 104 kg. Find the weight of teacher?
(1) 48 kg (2) 54 kg
(3) 64 kg (4) 72 kg
(5) 42 kg

117. X men can finish a work in Y days. 0.9 X women can finish 1/3rd of the same work in (Y-8) days. If 0.8 X women can complete 1/3rd of the work in 36 days. Find 0.5 X men can finish 1/4th of the same work in how many days?
(1) 10 days (2) 80 days
(3) 40 days (4) 20 days
(5) 60 days

118. A man spends 25% of his monthly salary on Rent and 32% on Groceries. He invests remaining salary in the ratio of 11 : 5 in Mutual Funds and Fixed Deposits. If difference between his yearly mutual funds and fixed deposit amount is Rs. 77400, then find the amount he spends each month on Groceries.
(1) Rs. 12800 (2) Rs. 9600
(3) Rs. 6400 (4) Rs. 7200
(5) Rs. 11200

119. A bag has balls of three colors. It has 8 red balls, x green balls and y blue balls. If probability of picking one green ball and that of picking one blue ball out of bag is equal, then find the number of blue balls. Probability of picking one red ball is 0.5.
(1) 2 (2) 4
(3) 5 (4) 6
(5) 3

120. A man invests Rs. X in a scheme at 12% rate of interest for 8 years. After 8 years, he reinvests the amount received at same rate of interest for same time duration. If interest received from reinvestment is Rs. 5730.4 more than Rs. X. Find the value of X.
(1) 6500 (2) 5400
(3) 7800 (4) 5900
(5) None of these

121. A person took a loan of Rs. 1500 from an investor at 20% per annum on compound interest for 2 years. But he paid only 80% of amount after 2 years. And investor put some penalty on remaining amount. He paid Rs. 520 including penalty amount after some time. Find the value of penalty amount.

(1) Rs. 104 (2) Rs. 76
(3) Rs. 58 (4) Rs. 92
(5) Rs. 88

122. Pipe A can fill half of the tank in 6 hours 2 min. Pipe B can fill the same tank completely in 18 hours 5 min while pipe C can empty the fully filled tank in 9 hours. If all the pipes are opened simultaneously then in how much time (approx.) 80% of tank will be filled.

(1) 29 hours (2) 24 hours
(3) 35 hours (4) 33 hours
(5) 27 hours

123. A and B invest in a business in the ratio of 2 : 3. After X months, B left the business while C joins the business with twice of investment as compared to that of B. C invests for 2 months more than B. After a year, C received 5/9th share of total profit. Find the time period for which B invested the amount?

(1) 4 months (2) 6 months
(3) 8 months (4) 5 months
(5) 7 months

124. A, B and C invest in a business. A invests twice as compared to B and C invests 90% more than A's investment. If all invest for same duration and earned a total profit of Rs. 2109, then find the approximate profit share of A?

(1) Rs. 300 (2) Rs. 1140
(3) Rs. 880 (4) Rs. 620
(5) Rs. 710

125. Cost price of an article is Rs. X and its marked price is 400% more than cost price. To gain a profit of 100%, what percent of discount should be offered on this particular article?

(1) 60% (2) 40%
(3) 50% (4) 75%
(5) 100%

Directions (126-130): *In the given questions, two quantities are given, one as Quantity I and another as Quantity II. You have to determine relationship between two quantities and choose the appropriate option*

(1) Quantity I > Quantity II
(2) Quantity I < Quantity II
(3) Quantity I ≤ Quantity II
(4) Quantity I ≤ Quantity II
(5) Quantity I = Quantity II or No relation

126. **Quantity I:** $(2x - 1) = 3$

Quantity II: $y^{-2} = \sqrt{625}$

127. A's age '*x*' years ago is equal to B's age after '*x*' years. Present age of C is twice of the present age of B and C's age '*x*' years ago is equal to A's age after 2*x* years.

Quantity I: 6 years

Quantity II: Difference between present age of A and C.

128. A person offers same discount percent on two articles X and Y. He marks up articles by 40% and 15% respectively above the cost price and selling price of article X and Y are Rs. 280 and Rs. 276 respectively.

Quantity I: Cost price of article Y.

Quantity II: marked price of article X.

129. Ratio of area of a circle and area of rectangle is 11 : 15. Breadth of rectangle is twice of the radius of circle. Sum of length and breadth of rectangle is 58 cm.

Quantity I: 600 cm^2

Quantity II: Area of rectangle (in cm^2)

130. 1: $2^3x^+y = \sqrt{32}$

2: $2(^3x+^5y)^{/2} = \sqrt{3}$

Quantity I: $(x + y)$

Quantity II: 2

Direction (131-136): *Table given below shows total people (male + female) live in five (P, Q, R, S, and T) different societies in the year 2020 and it also shows ratio of male to female in these five societies in year 2020. Read the data carefully and answer the questions.*

Note: Neither any people left nor any people came to live in 2020.

Societies	Total people (male + female)	Ratio of male to female Male : Female
P	160	5 : 3
Q	220	15 : 7
R	240	11 : 13
S	200	3 : 2
T	210	11 : 10

131. Find the average number of females in societies Q, R and T?

(1) 120 (2) 140
(3) 100 (4) 80
(5) 90

132. In the year 2021, 20% male from R left the society and no new people come in society R. If the ratio of male to female in 2021 in society R is 4 : 5, then find the number of females who left the society R in 2021?

(1) 10 (2) 16
(3) 24 (4) 20
(5) 30

133. There is another society X in which number of people are 20% more than the number of people in society P. In society X there are some houses. In society X there are ten houses in which four people live in each house, ten house in which six people live in each house, five house in which eight people live in each house and in remaining house there is two people live in each house. Find total number of houses in society X?

(1) 51 (2) 67
(3) 82 (4) 98
(5) 47

134. Total number of females in society S is what percent more or less than total number of females in society T?

(1) 15% (2) 20%
(3) 25% (4) 10%
(5) 7.5%

135. The ratio of number of people in society T to that of in society N is 21 : 24 and number of males in society N is 66^2 % of number of females in society N. Find the number of males in society N?

(1) 84 (2) 36
(3) 54 (4) 96
(5) 72

136. Total number of males in 2021 in society P is equal to the average number of males in 2020 in societies Q and R and number of females in 2021 in society P is 10 less than the number of males in 2021 in that society. Find the number of people in 2021 in society P?

(1) 220 (2) 240
(3) 250 (4) 260
(5) 270

Directions (137-140): *What approximate value should come in place of question mark (?) in the following questions?*

137. $44.04 \div 3.97 \times 7.49 \div 2.54 + 3 = \sqrt{?}$

(1) 6 (2) 36
(3) 24 (4) 1296
(5) 216

138. $\sqrt{37.54}$ % of 400.08 + 75.07% of 59.92 = ?

(1) 7 (2) 14
(3) 49 (4) 98
(5) 196

139. $(9.01)^3 + (7.94)^3 + 5.12 \times 17.95 = ?^3$

(1) 11 (2) 15
(3) 13 (4) 10
(5) 14

140. 62.01% of ? + $(24.04)^2 = (30.99)^2 - \sqrt{169.01}$

(1) 660 (2) 600
(3) 640 (4) 720
(5) 780

General Awareness

141. RBI was nationalised in the year ....

(1) 1934 (2) 1935
(3) 1949 (4) 1950
(5) 1951

142. India's first wetland conservation center 'Centre for Wetland Conservation and Management (CWCM)' has been be set up in which city of India?

(1) Kolkata (2) Kochi
(3) Chennai (4) Mumbai
(5) Bhubaneswar

143. What is the validity period of 'Electoral bonds'?

(1) 10 days (2) 30 days
(3) 20 days (4) 12 days
(5) 15 days

144. Mutual Funds are regulated in the country by

(1) IRDAI
(2) Association of Mutual Funds of India (AMFI)
(3) NABARD
(4) Securities and Exchange Board of India
(5) Reserve Bank of India

145. Renowned personality Ustad Ghulam Mustafa Khan passed away recently, he was a veteran ....

(1) Flute Maestro (2) Tabla Maestro
(3) Sitar Maestro (4) Classical Musician
(5) Piano Maestro

146. Which company has ranked first most-valued IT services brand globally, according to a report by Brand Finance?

(1) Accenture (2) IBM
(3) Tata Consultancy Services (TCS)
(4) Infosys (5) Wipro

147. Which of the following Asian countries has Nikkei as its stock market index?

(1) China (2) Singapore
(3) Japan (4) South Korea
(5) Hong Kong

148. The 'ICC Men's T20I Cricketer of the Decade' has been awarded to?

(1) Virat Kohli (2) Kane Williamson
(3) Steve Smith (4) Rashid Khan
(5) None of these

149. What is percentage of government holding in NABARD?

(1) 99.6% (2) 0.4%
(3) 100% (4) 75%
(5) 56%

150. The headquarters of the 'United Nations World Tourism Organization is situated in:

(1) Madrid, Spain (2) Gland, Switzerland
(3) Washington DC, USA
(4) Paris, France
(5) Frankfurt, Germany

151. West Bengal legislative assembly consists of how many seats?

(1) 292 (2) 294
(3) 296 (4) 298
(5) 299

152. Which of the following country has been elected as President of the International Solar Alliance?

(1) USA (2) Russia
(3) India (4) Japan
(5) None of these

153. Recently, Hawker Culture of which country has been inscribed on the UNESCO's Representative List of the Intangible Cultural Heritage of Humanity?

(1) Indonesia (2) China
(3) Vietnam (4) Singapore
(5) None of these

154. The Chairman of the National Disaster Management Authority (NDMA) is .

(1) National Security Advisor
(2) Prime Minister of India
(3) Chief of DRDO
(4) Home Minister of India
(5) None of these

155. Which payment gateway company has decided to close its operation in India?

(1) MobiKwik (2) Razor pay
(3) PayPal (4) Lazypay
(5) None of the above

156. The Foxconn of toy world to set up India's first toy cluster in

(1) Madhya Pradesh (2) Karnataka
(3) Kerala (4) Rajasthan

(5) Haryana

157. Maradona scored 'hand of god' goal against which country?
(1) Germany (2) France
(3) Portugal (4) Spain
(5) England

158. Which of the following became the first company to launch an Electric tractor in India?
(1) Sonalika Group
(2) Tractor and Farm Equipment (TAFE) Ltd.
(3) Mahindra and Mahindra
(4) Swaraj Tractors
(5) Escorts Agri Machinery

159. FASTag works on which of the following technologies?
(1) Phone Early Warning System (PEWS)
(2) Radio Frequency Identification (RFID) technology
(3) Accelerometer (4) Near Field Technology
(5) GPS Technology

160. What is the name given to India's first indigenous 9 mm machine pistol jointly developed by the Defence Research and Development Organisation (DRDO) and the Indian Army?
(1) Glock 17 (2) SIG Sauer P226
(3) ASMI (4) Beretta 92FS
(5) Agram 2000

161. Which of the following is not related to 'bank to bank' transfer mechanism?
(1) NEFT (2) RTGS
(3) Cheque (4) Depository Receipt
(5) IMPS

162. Which of the following Musical Instruments is played by Ustad Shahid Parvez Khan?
(1) Santoor (2) Sitar
(3) Veena (4) Flute
(5) Tabla

163. The Light House Projects inaugurated by the prime minister will be undertaken in six cities. Which of the following is not one among them?
(1) Dhanbad in Jharkhand
(2) Rajkot in Gujarat
(3) Agartala in Tripura
(4) Indore in Madhya Pradesh
(5) Lucknow in Uttar Pradesh

164. ICICI Bank has launched its Representative office in which nation?
(1) France (2) USA
(3) Nepal (4) Indonesia
(5) Myanmar

165. Which Indian women wrestler has won silver medal at the individual Wrestling World Cup in the women's 57 kg category which took place in Belgrade, Serbia?
(1) Sakshi Malik (2) Vinesh Phogat
(3) Alka Tomar (4) Kavita Devi
(5) Anshu Malik

166. Adivasi Mela 2021 was organised in ....
(1) Bhubaneswar (2) Cuttack
(3) Balasore (4) Sambalpur
(5) Rourkela

167. The Tapovan Vishnugad power plant is owned by which corporation?
(1) ONGC (2) BPCL
(3) NTPC (4) GAIL
(5) CIL

168. According to the 'India Energy Outlook 2021', India will become largest energy consumer by 2030, surpassing European Union?
(1) 1st (2) 2nd
(3) 3rd (4) 4th
(5) 5th

169. What is the name of the umbrella program for the Roads and Highways sector in India?
(1) Setu Bharatam (2) Bharatmala Pariyojana
(3) Smart City Mission
(4) Accessible India Project
(5) Digital India Mission

170. Which organization is responsible for setting

up the world's largest zoo in Gujarat's Jamnagar district?

(1) NTPC
(2) Reliance Industries Limited (RIL)
(3) Adani Groups (4) Larsen and Toubro
(5) Tata Motors

171. What is the maturity period of the Senior Citizen Saving Scheme?
(1) 4 years (2) 5 years
(3) 6 years (4) 7 years
(5) 8 years

172. Kishor Biyani is the CEO of which company on which SEBI has imposed a penalty?
(1) Hindalco Industries
(2) Reliance Pvt Ltd
(3) Adani Groups (4) Future Retail Ltd
(5) None of the above

173. Which company is known for cleaning up of Non-performing Asset (NPA)?
(1) Negotiable Instrument Company
(2) Asset Reconstruction Company
(3) Department of Economic and Policy Research
(4) Asset Arrangement Company
(5) None of the above

174. World's largest renewable energy park has been inaugurated in
(1) Madhya Pradesh (2) Gujarat
(3) Rajasthan (4) Maharashtra
(5) Punjab

175. Who is the author of the book titled as "Struggle is my life"?
(1) Nelson Mandela (2) Jawaharlal Nehru
(3) Mahatma Gandhi (4) Barack Obama
(5) Morissana Kouyate

176. Finance Minister of India has announced reduction in residency limit for Indian citizens to set up one-person companies (OPC) from 182 days to ....
(1) 110 days (2) 120 days
(3) 130 days (4) 140 days
(5) 150 days

177. India has recently released a commemorative postage stamp to mark the .... anniversary of the United Nations Organisations.
(1) 73rd (2) 74th
(3) 75th (4) 76th
(5) 77th

178. Flight Lieutenant Bhawna Kant is the first female fighter pilot to participate in the Republic Day Parade 2021. She hails from which State?
(1) Uttar Pradesh (2) Madhya Pradesh
(3) Jharkhand (4) Bihar
(5) Odisha

179. Which nation is planning to set up the first nuclear reactor on the moon by the end of 2026?
(1) Russia (2) USA
(3) UK (4) China
(5) France

180. Rajesh Sharma has replaced which of the following person as the CEO of Ayushman Bharat scheme?
(1) Amitabh Kant (2) Indu Bhushan
(3) Randeep Guleria (4) Rajeev Khosla
(5) Harsh Vardhan

181. Which of the following is the 1st international movie of Irfan Khan's?
(1) The Namesake (2) New York
(3) The Amazing Spider-Man
(4) Jurassic World
(5) The Warrior

182. The minimum loan size eligible for debt recovery under the Securitisation and Reconstruction of Financial Assets and Enforcement of Security Interest (SARFAESI) Act, 2002 is proposed to be reduced from the existing level of Rs. 50 lakhs to ....
(1) Rs. 5 lakhs (2) Rs. 10 lakhs
(3) Rs. 15 lakhs (4) Rs. 20 lakhs
(5) Rs. 25 lakhs

183. According to India Energy Outlook 2021, published by the International Energy Agency (IEA) by which year India will overtake the

European Union as the world's third-largest energy consumer?

(1) 2025 (2) 2027
(3) 2028 (4) 2030
(5) 2032

184. Which of the following national park is not located in Madhya Pradesh?

(1) Van Vihar National Park
(2) Kanha National Park
(3) Ranthambore National Park
(4) Bhandavgarh National Park
(5) None of the above

185. The National Pollution Control Day is observed every year on which date?

(1) 1st December (2) 2nd December
(3) 3rd December (4) 4th December
(5) 5th December

186. What amount has been proposed for further recapitalization of public sector banks?

(1) Rs. 20,000 crores
(2) Rs. 30,000 crores
(3) Rs. 40,000 crores
(4) Rs. 50,000 crores
(5) Rs. 80,000 crores

187. Who monitors the Priority Sector Lending (PSL) in commercial banks?

(1) Reserve Bank of India (RBI)
(2) Small Industries Development Bank of India (SIDBI)
(3) National Bank for Agriculture and Rural Development (NABARD)
(4) Government of India (GOI)
(5) Securities and Exchange Board of India (SEBI)

188. The world's longest sandstone cave "Krem Puri" has been discovered in which state of India?

(1) Andhra Pradesh (2) Meghalaya
(3) Tripura (4) Maharashtra
(5) Odisha

189. How many Ombudsman office are there in India?

(1) 21 (2) 22
(3) 23 (4) 24
(5) 25

190. Who among the following is the co-founder and CEO of Twitter?

(1) Bill Gates (2) Narayan Murthy
(3) Jack Dorsey (4) Tim Berners-Lee
(5) None of the above

Answers With Explanations

1. (2) According to the last line of the first paragraph "Air pollutants released in one country may be transported in the atmosphere, contributing to or resulting in poor air quality elsewhere."

2. (2) According to the starting line of the first paragraph "Air pollution harms human health and the environment. In Europe, emissions of many air pollutants have decreased substantially over the past decades, resulting in improved air quality across the region."

3. (5) According to the starting lines of the second paragraph, "Particulate matter, nitrogen dioxide and ground-level ozone are now generally recognized as the three pollutants that most significantly affect human health. Long-term and peak exposures to these pollutants range in severity of impact, from impairing the respiratory system to premature death."

4. (4) According to the last line of the third paragraph, "The European Environment Agency (EEA) is the European Union's air pollution data center, and it assists in the execution of EU regulations concerning air emissions and quality. The EEA also assists in the evaluation of EU air pollution legislation as well as the formulation of long-term initiatives to improve Europe's air quality." So, only (*i*) and (*iii*) statements are correct based on the information provided.

5. (4) According to the sixth line of the last paragraph "Targeted efforts to reduce emissions are therefore still required to further protect human health and the environment in Europe."

6. (4)

7. (3) "Persist" means continue to exist; be prolonged. So, the meaning of 'persevere' is same.

8. (5) According to the fourth line of the first paragraph, "One of the benefits of reading is simply that it provides enjoyment and pleasure. It can provide an escape from boredom or stress. Plus, reading has been shown to help us better understand and interact with other people, keep our brains sharp, expand our world views and grow as individuals."

9. (4) According to the last line of the second paragraph, "Researchers at a University showed in an experiment that reading actually satisfies that need for human connection because it can mimic what we feel during real social interactions."

10. (2) According to the starting line of the second paragraph, "It's more likely to get lost in a book if you're reading a high-quality text, but "quality" in this case is subjective and something that gets determined by you."

11. (5)
12. (5)
13. (2)
14. (3)
15. (5)
16. (3)
17. (4)
18. (1)
19. (4)
20. (3)
21. (5)
22. (4)

23. (3) "Have" must be replaced with "has".

24. (1) Since 'language' is a singular noun, so, 'have' must be replaced by 'has' along with the 1st form of the verb "use".

25. (1)
26. (5)
27. (5)
28. (3)
29. (2)
30. (5)

31. (4) The correct sentence: "The authority has decided to launch an investigation and audit on getting complaints about a school increasing fees according to its wishes."

32. (1)
33. (4)
34. (5)
35. (4)
36. (2)
37. (4)
38. (1)
39. (2)
40. (5)

For questions (41-45):

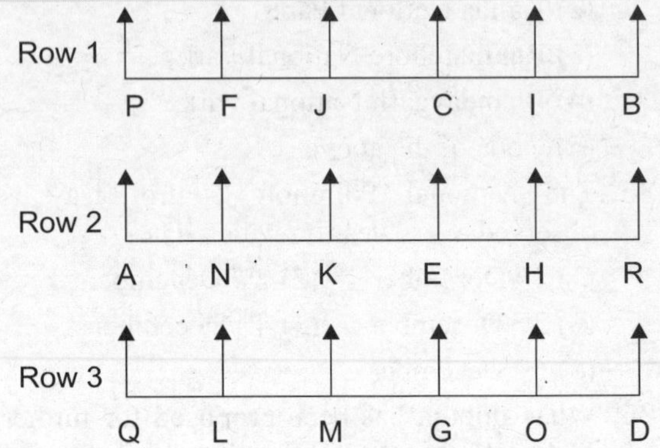

41. (5)
42. (3)
43. (4)
44. (1)
45. (1)

For questions (46-49):

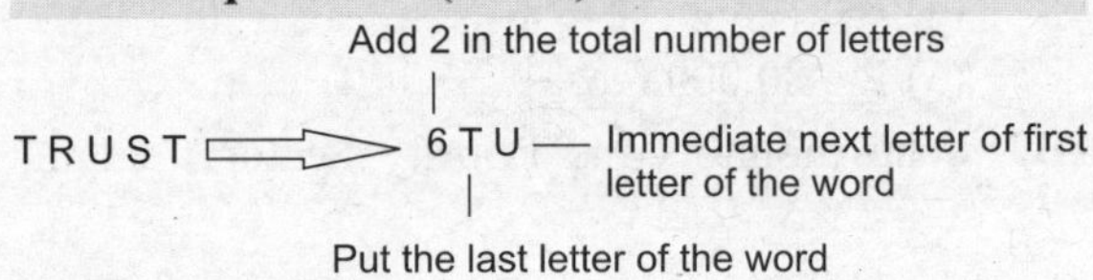

46. (4)
47. (5)
48. (3)
49. (3)
50. (3)

For questions (51-55):

Month	Date	Person	Vehicle
May	5	N	Bike
	7	Π	Taxi
	20	M	Boat
August	5	O	Bus
	7	K	Jeep
	20	L	Car
November	5	T	Train
	7	Q	Chopper
	20	R	Airplane

51. (5)
52. (5)
53. (2)
54. (1)
55. (2)

For questions (56-60):

Step I: All Digits are arranged in increasing order within the number

Step II: All Digits are arranged in decreasing order within the number

Step III: Number are arranged in increasing order

Step IV: Eliminate first and last digit of the number

Step V: Difference between the digits with in the number

Input: 3472 6721 9733 7123 5361 8417

Step I: 2347 1267 3379 1237 1356 1478

Step II: 7432 7621 9733 7321 6531 8741

Step III: 6531 7321 7432 7621, 8741 9733

Step IV: 53 32 43 62 74 73

Step V: 2 1 1 4 3 4

56. (4)
57. (4)
58. (1)
59. (5)
60. (2)
61. (3)
62. (2)

For questions (63-65):

Male	Female	Kids
Deepak	Pragya	Puja
Yash	Anjana	Anu
Rohan	Surbhi	Monty
Vikas	Poonam	Tina

63. (3)
64. (4)
65. (2)
66. (2)

Days	Persons
Monday	
Tuesday	
Wednesday	A
Thursday	F
Friday	
Saturday	G
Sunday	

67. (1)

Persons
G
C
A
F
H

68. (2) S sits second to the left of W.

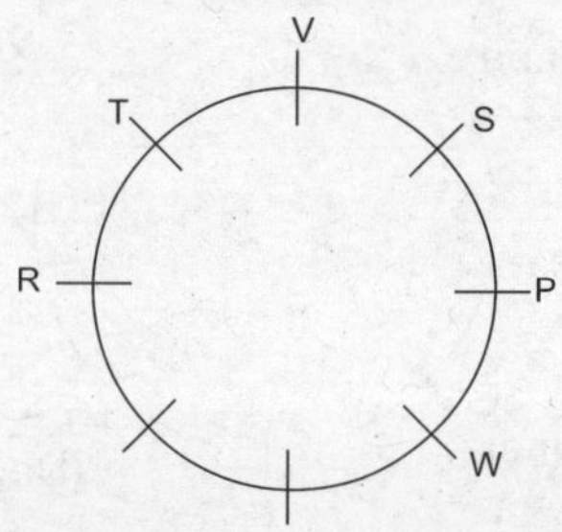

69. (5)

For questions (70-74):

Days	Persons	Places
Sunday	Shiv	Golden temple
Monday	Hema	Hawa mehal
Tuesday	Vikas	Taj mahal
Wednesday	Neema	Red fort
Thursday	Arya	Robbers cave
Friday	Piya	Qutub minar
Saturday	Kiran	Lotus temple

70. (2)
71. (4)
72. (4)
73. (3)
74. (5)
75. (2) C is the father-in-law of R.
76. (1) N is the father of S.
77. (4) K has two children, E and J.
78. (3) Three females are there in the family- D, K, W

79. (3) **80.** (3)

For questions (81-84):

U 3 7 @ # 4 5 T & ! F U 9 M 6 3 © G 5 Ω 3 A Z 5 2 € 8 β L P 3

STEP I - U 7 @ # 4 5 T & ! F U M 3 © G Ω 3 A Z 2 € 8 β L 3 3 5 5 6 9 P

STEP II - U 7 @ # 4 5 T ! & F U M © 3 G Ω 3 A Z 2 € β 8 L 3 3 5 5 6 9 P

STEP III - U 7 @ # 4 5 T ! & U M © 3 G Ω 3 A Z 2 € β 8 L 3 3 5 5 6 9 P

81. (5) **84.** (3)
82. (2) **85.** (3)
83. (1)

For questions (86-90):

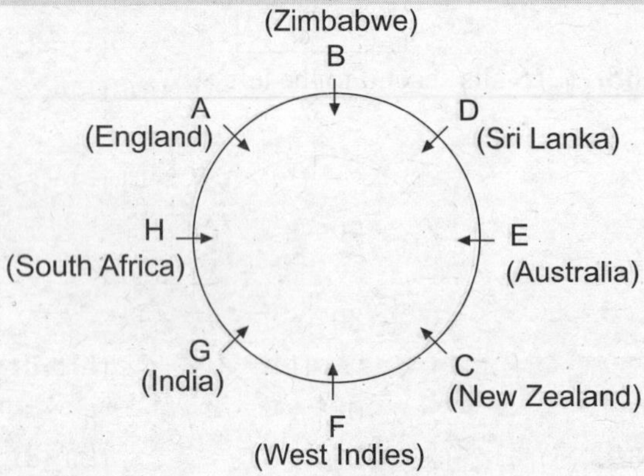

86. (4) **89.** (3)
87. (3) **90.** (4)
88. (2)

Solutions (91-93): From equation (I)

$m + 3 = p$ and $3m = q$

From equation (II)

$m + 1 = p - 2$ and $m = q - 4$

From equations (I) and (II),

$3(q - 4) = q$

$3q - 12 = q$

$q = 6$

Hence, $M = 6/3 = 2$

$p = 2 + 1 + 2 = 5$

91. (2) **93.** (3)
92. (4)
94. (1) Required distance = 24 × 3 + 36 × 2 = 144 km

95. (3) Let present age of A, B and C be a, b and c years respectively.

According to the question,

$a + b + c = 60$

$a + c = 39$

$$\frac{(21 - a) + (c - a)}{2} = 12$$

$21 - a + c - a = 24$

$21 + c - 2a = 24$

$c - 2a = 3$

$39 - a - 2a = 3$

$$a = \frac{36}{3} = 12$$

$c = 27$

So, required age = 27 + 6 = 33 years

96. (3) Distance covered by boat in upstream = 6 × 15 = 90

Downstream speed of boat =90/3 = 30 kmph

So, required distance = 30 × 7 = 210 km

97. (4) **98.** (1)

For questions (99-103):

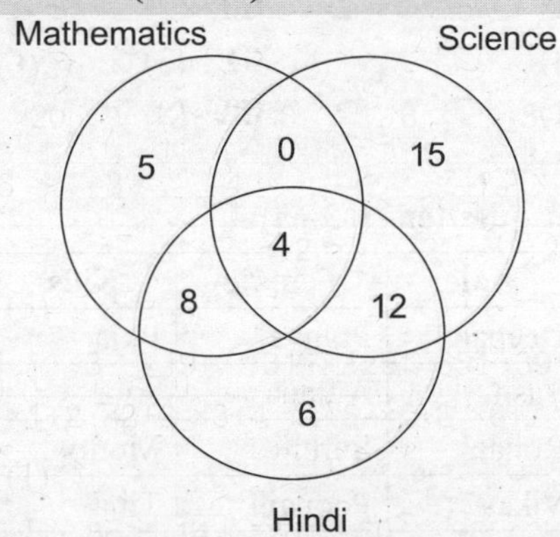

99. (1) **104.** (4)
100. (3) **105.** (3)
101. (4) **106.** (5)
102. (5) **107.** (1)
103. (4)

For questions (108-110):

The pattern of the series I: 5 × 1 + 1 = 6

6 × 2 + 1 = 13

13 × 3 + 1 = 40

40 × 4 + 1 = 161

161 × 5 + 1 = 806

Hence, series II will be:

$p = 2 \times 1 + 1 = 3$

$q = 3 \times 2 + 1 = 7$

$r = 7 \times 3 + 1 = 22$

$s = 22 \times 4 + 1 = 89$

108. (3) **110.** (5)

109. (4)

For questions (111-115):

Vessel	Quantity of Milk	Quantity of water	Quantity of Juice	Total
A	98	70	84	252
B	25	50	75	150
C	75	60	30	165
Total	198	180	189	567

111. (1) Required ratio = (98 + 25) : (50 + 60)

= 123 : 110

112. (3) **125.** (1)
113. (2) **126.** (5)
114. (2) **127.** (5)
115. (3) **128.** (2)
116. (3) **129.** (2)
117. (4) **130.** (2)
118. (1) **131.** (3)
119. (2) **132.** (4)
120. (1) **133.** (1)
121. (5) **134.** (2)
122. (1) **135.** (4)
123. (3) **136.** (3)
124. (4) **137.** (4)

138. (2) $\sqrt{37.5\% \times 400} + 75\% \times 60 = ?$

$? = \sqrt{150 + 45}$

$? = \sqrt{196}$

$? = 14$

139. (1) $729 + 512 + 5 \times 18 = ?^3$

$1241 + 90 = ?^3$

$1331 = ?^3$

$? = 11$

140. (2)

141. (3) The Reserve Bank of India (RBI) commenced its operations on 1 April 1935 during the British Rule in accordance with the provisions of the Reserve Bank of India Act, 1934. The original share capital was divided into shares of 100 each fully paid, which were initially owned entirely by private shareholders. Following India's independence on 15 August 1947, the RBI was nationalized on 1 January 1949.

142. (3) Coinciding with the World Wetland Day, India got its first specialised institution - Centre for Wetland Conservation and Management (CWCM) – in Chennai.

143. (5) Electoral bonds can be purchased for any value in multiples of Rs. 1,000, Rs. 10,000, Rs. 10 lakh, and Rs. 1 crore from any of the specified branches of the State Bank of India. The life of the bond will be for **15 days**.

144. (4) Mutual Funds are regulated in the country by Securities and Exchange Board of India

145. (4) **146.** (1)

147. (3) Nikkei is the stock market index of Japan.

148. (4) The award of 'ICC Men's T20I Cricketer of the Decade' has been awarded to Rashid Khan. The ICC Awards of the Decade recognize the best players across Cricket over the past ten years.

149. (3) **167.** (3) **185.** (2)
150. (1) **168.** (3) **186.** (1)
151. (2) **169.** (2) **187.** (1)
152. (3) **170.** (2) **188.** (2)
153. (4) **171.** (2) **189.** (2)
154. (2) **172.** (4) **190.** (3)
155. (3) **173.** (5)
156. (2) **174.** (2)
157. (5) **175.** (1)
158. (1) **176.** (2)
159. (2) **177.** (3)
160. (3) **178.** (4)
161. (4) **179.** (2)
162. (2) **180.** (2)
163. (1) **181.** (5)
164. (3) **182.** (4)
165. (5) **183.** (4)
166. (1) **184.** (3)

IBPS Clerk Prelims, 2022

(Held on 3 September, 2022)

Based on Memory

English Language

Directions (1-8): *Read the given passage and answer the following questions based on that.*

Home is where the heart is, or so goes the adage. But the human heart did not always crave a still hearth. In fact, before the emergence of agrarian societies, the early humans journeyed along the roads taken by their prey — hunter-gatherer societies were mobile and the road was their life. But with the rise of agrarianism, humans learnt to put down their roots and a life of journeys became something to be frowned upon. Yet, vestiges of the wandering spirit persist. In the year, 2000, Herman and Candelaria Zapp set out in a car from Buenos Aires to travel the world. The Zapps' home is the road — literally and proverbially. They have had four children in different countries, and in an era of strict visa regimes and rising **insularity**, managed to treat borders as what they truly are — arbitrary and artificial lines on a map. The world was a different place when the Zapps set out — there were no smartphones, the internet was in its **infancy**, a site of knowledge and hope rather than disinformation and division, the twin towers towered over New York, and Russia was a diminutive shell stripped of its Soviet grandeur. It is tempting to imagine that the Zapps .... Kishore Kumar's immortal song, "Musafir hoon yaaron, na ghar hai na thikana", as they covered great distances across a changing world.

The Zapps, interestingly, are not an anomaly. Latest estimates show that over one million Americans live permanently in recreational vehicles with no permanent address. Many are retired, but many others work part of the year, just long enough to keep them going for a few months or so. It is easy to romanticize the lifestyle and the idea of freedom that it brings. But in most countries, people without a stationary home are subjected to intense legal scrutiny. Law enforcement institutions are even prejudiced against specific communities. For example, in the United States of America, there are legislations that make it illegal to sit on the sidewalk, to camp or sleep anywhere in a downtown area or to hang around in a public place without an apparent purpose. The intent seems to encourage sanitization of space of some kinds of human presences. These laws are not unique to the US. Anti-vagrancy laws have existed for hundreds of years — think of the persecution of gypsies across Europe. In the old United Kingdom, vagrants could be put in jail, sold as slaves, or sometimes even killed for no other reason than wandering. Colonial India, too, had witnessed the purge of nomadic communities, most notably under the guise of the campaign against thuggees.

1. According to the passage, what changes has human society seen from the pre-agrarian era to the present?

(1) Modern humans have diverged their dependency from agriculture, unlike their primitive ancestor whose livelihood was solely based on that

(2) From being a hunter-gatherer nomad society, it evolved into a settled agrarian society

(3) The immense technological advancement in recent years makes it possible to envisage services that were seen as utopian in pre- agrarian era

(4) All of these

(5) None of these

2. What was NOT the global situation when the Zapps embarked on their journey?

(1) The world was witnessing the inception of the internet

(2) The twin towers were standing tall in New York

(3) Post dissolution of Soviet Union, Russia was still in its timid state.
(4) The world was going through an acute economic crisis due to surge in oil prices.
(5) None of these

3. How do the itinerant Americans sustain their lives?
(1) Few of them are retired and thus continued their rest of the lives by travelling on their recreational vehicles
(2) Some of them are engaged in work for a few months of a year and use the rest for travelling
(3) Prominent travel companies and independent organisations sponsor those people who actively travel
(4) Only (1) and (2)
(5) Only (2) and (3)

4. How are the countries treating the new age wanderer?
(1) They are subject to legal scrutiny in many countries because of their lack of possession of land.
(2) Many countries assess their livelihood and put their earnings on the tax slab.
(3) Many law enforcement agencies are biased towards these travellers
(4) Only (1) and (3)
(5) All of these

5. Which of the following is FALSE according to the data given in the passage?
(1) Thuggees are predominantly nomadic people of colonial India
(2) Germany has a prohibition law for sitting on the sidewalks.
(3) UK has criminalized wandering, to the extent of giving out death sentences.
(4) The Zapps couple had started off from Buenos Aires in the year 2000.
(5) None of these

6. Which of the following words can fit into the blank given in the passage?
(1) hummed (2) iterated
(3) cherished (4) longed
(5) enunciated

7. Which word from among the following words most closely represents the antonym of the highlighted word "infancy" keeping in consideration its intended meaning in the passage?
(1) service (2) apprehension
(3) perseverance (4) maturity
(5) intelligence

8. Choose the word from among the following which is most similar in meaning to the highlighted word "insularity" in accordance with its meaning in the given text.
(1) irritation (2) inflexibility
(3) disbelief (4) freedom
(5) awareness

Directions (9-14): *In the following passage there are blanks, each of which has been numbered. These numbers are printed below the passage and against each, five options are given. Find out the appropriate word which fits the blank appropriately.*

Filmmaking research is a form of practice research that .... (9) into production practices, techniques, modes and genres used in cinema, television and online. The outputs are films that may include .... (10), documentary and hybrid forms. Filmmaking research pushes at the boundaries of traditional filmmaking and traditional research methods by adopting distinct (11) to professional and critical practices. This is in contrast to typical industry research where commercial pressures dominate. There have been .... (12) success stories that demonstrate this potential.

Filmmaking research is a developing area and films produced within the academy are growing in number. In both the UK and Australia, this research has tended to .... (13) in one of two disciplines, creative arts (fine art, experimental, video art) or media, communication and film studies (fiction film, documentary). This has made it fragmented, sometimes difficult to identify and subject to different forms of support and .... (14). Researchers come from a range of backgrounds, many moving from industry into academia seeking to reframe their work within

Higher Education.

9. (1) probes (2) enquires
(3) inquests (4) surveys
(5) investigate

10. (1) friction (2) segregation
(3) accede (4) fiction
(5) purport

11. (1) regulations (2) adversaries
(3) approaches (4) assistances
(5) intervals

12. (1) expressed (2) threatening
(3) overlooked (4) mocking
(5) spectacular

13. (1) reside (2) accommodate
(3) occupy (4) fuller
(5) lament

14. (1) ample (2) wither
(3) engagement (4) enrollments
(5) alliance

Directions (15): *A word has been given below, and following it are provided three sentences which use the word. Mark the correct option from the options given below which indicates the sentence or combination of sentences with correct usage of the word.*

15. pore

(*i*) After I was given the manuscript for my first title role in the play, I began to **pore** over the script for hours.

(*ii*) It is **pore** that people show identification before being allowed to board a commercial aircraft.

(*iii*) Before I sign the contract, I decided it would be best for me to **pore** through it so that the job would run smoothly.

(1) Both (*i*) and (*ii*) (2) Both (*i*) and (*iii*)
(3) Only (*ii*) (4) Both (*ii*) and (*iii*)
(5) All of these

Directions (16-20): *Given below are five sentences, each of which has been jumbled up in an order which makes the text incoherent. Mark the option which gives the meaningful rearrangement of the parts of the sentence as the answer.*

16. The property, they (A)/had to undergo a (B)/ in order to purchase (C)/lengthy application process (D).

(1) BDAC (2) DACB
(3) ADBC (4) CABD
(5) No rearrangement require

17. Constituted the battlefields (A)/of World War Two, encompassing (B)/much of the globe (C)/ many conflicts and fronts (D).

(1) DABC (2) BACD
(3) ADCB (4) BDCA
(5) No rearrangement required

18. We received a package (A)/not notice the mail (B)/yesterday but did (C)/until early this morning (D).

(1) DCBA (2) BDAC
(3) ACBD (4) CADB
(5) No rearrangement required

19. The venomous black widow (A)/are often killed (B)/because they resemble (C)/ perfectly harmless spiders (D).

(1) BCDA (2) DBCA
(3) ADCB (4) CABD
(5) No rearrangement required

20. Look for new jobs (A)/were rigid and uncompromising, (B)/leaving the workers to (C)/many of the company's rules (D).

(1) CDBA (2) ACBD
(3) DBCA (4) CABD
(5) No rearrangement required

Directions (21-25): *Given below are five sentences, with four words highlighted in each sentence. One of these words may be the misspelt form of a word, making the sentence contextually incoherent. Mark the option which depicts the corresponding letter to the incorrectly spelled word, or mark option (e) if there is none.*

21. Pat didn't mean to loose (A) her mother's favourite (B) bracelet but hasn't been able to locate (C) it since she wore (D) it last week.

(1) A (2) B
(3) C (4) D
(5) No spelling errors

22. The unweary (A) gamblers lost all their (B) money when they carelessly (C) put all their chips on the wrong (D) tile.

(1) A (2) B
(3) C (4) D
(5) No spelling errors

23. Taking a position as curator (A) at the museum (B), the woman hoped to spread (C) her love for sports memorablia (D) to others.
(1) A (2) B
(3) C (4) D
(5) No spelling errors

24. As my father's only surviving (A) sister, my aunt took great (B) care of my aging (C) grandparents until they both passed away recently (D).
(1) A (2) B
(3) C (4) D
(5) No spelling errors

25. Because of technical (A) difficulties (B), the sound of the music floctuated (C) during the concert (D).
(1) A (2) B
(3) C (4) D
(5) No spelling errors

Directions (26-30): *Which of the phrase/ word from the options (a), (b), (c) and (d) given below each sentence should replace the phrase printed in bold letters to make the sentence grammatically correct? If the sentence is correct as it is, mark (5) i.e., "No replacement required" as the answer.*

26. Jeff was given a medal of honor **in recognition by** the twenty-five years he spent fighting for his country.
(1) of recognition by
(2) in recognition of
(3) by recognition of
(4) in recognition at
(5) No correction required

27. INS Vikrant is a unique reflection of India **becoming self-reliance.**
(1) becomes self-reliant
(2) became self-reliant
(3) become self-reliance
(4) becoming self-reliant
(5) No replacement required

28. There **have been a steady** spike in cases of cybercrime in the last five years.
(1) has been a stead (2) has been a steady
(3) has been a steadily
(4) has a steady
(5) No replacement required

29. It is vital that every Indian **takes a pledge to eliminate** discrimination and enable equity.
(1) take a pledge to eliminate
(2) took a pledge to eliminate
(3) takes a pledges to eliminate
(4) take a pledge to elimination
(5) No replacement required

30. He was worried that the anger **would erupt and led** to a law-and-order situation.
(1) would erupts and lead
(2) would erupt and lead
(3) would erupted and led
(4) would erupt and leads
(5) No replacement required

Numerical Ability

Directions (31-35): *What will come in the place of question (?) mark in following number series?*

31. 50, 75, 175, 400, 800, ?
(1) 1435 (2) 1425
(3) 1415 (4) 1405
(5) 1375

32. 8, 18, 38, 78, ?, 318
(1) 178 (2) 168
(3) 154 (4) 148
(5) 158

33. 41, ?, 53, 64, 77, 94
(1) 48 (2) 46
(3) 43 (4) 49
(5) 41

34. 215, ?, 89, 47, 19, 5
(1) 136 (2) 139
(3) 143 (4) 145
(5) 141

35. 1, 9, 36, 100, 225, ?

(1) 441 (2) 443

(3) 447 (4) 431

(5) 451

Directions (36-40): *Line graph given below shows total number of boats and ships manufactured by four different companies in 2020 and it also show total number of ships manufactured by these four companies. Read the line graph carefully and answer the questions.*

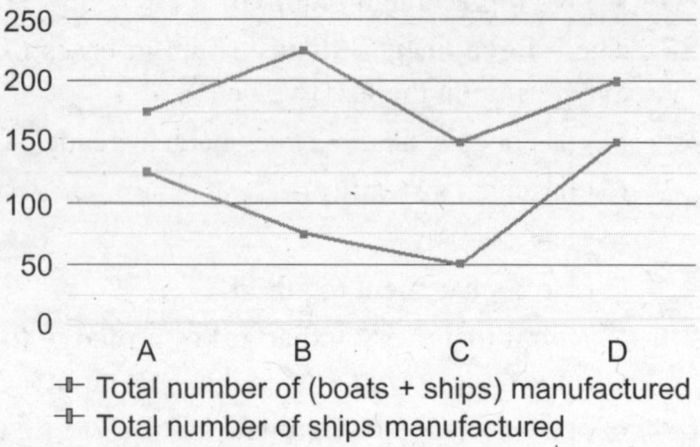

36. If two-third of total boats manufactured by B are used by general people and rest used by fishermen, then find total boats used by fishermen are what percent of total ships manufactured by A?

(1) 30% (2) 33.33%

(3) 40% (4) 37.5%

(5) 50%

37. If total number of boats and ships manufactured by A in 2021 is 40% more than that of in year 2020 and total number of ships manufactured by A in 2021 is equal to that of in 2020, then find the total number of boats manufactured by A in 2021?

(1) 115 (2) 105

(3) 75 (4) 85

(5) 120

38. Find the ratio of total boats manufactured by C and D together to total ships manufactured by B and C together?

(1) 6 : 7 (2) 6 : 5

(3) 5 : 4 (4) 3 : 4

(5) 3 : 5

39. If manufacturing cost of each boat for company D is Rs. 4600, then find the total cost (in Rs.) of all boats manufactured by D?

(1) 240000 (2) 236000

(3) 233000 (4) 220000

(5) 230000

40. Total boats and ships manufactured by A and B together is what percent more than total boats manufactured by A and D together?

(1) 300% (2) 175%

(3) 250% (4) 400%

(5) 350%

41. Six years ago, sum of age of Amit and Den is 20 years. Mohit is six years younger than Amit and the average of present age of Mohit and Den is 13 years. Find the present age of Den?

(1) 16 years (2) Can't determined

(3) 20 years (4) 14 years

(5) 24 years

42. The perimeter of semicircle is 36 cm and the radius of the semicircle is equal to the breath of a rectangle. If area of rectangle is 147 cm^2, then find the length of rectangle?

(1) 10.5 cm (2) 28 cm

(3) 14 cm (4) 21 cm

(5) 35 cm

43. Sum of six consecutive odd numbers is 150 more than average of these six numbers. Find the sum of highest and lowest number?

(1) 60 (2) 50

(3) 70 (4) 45

(5) 55

44. P and Q started a business by investing Rs. X and Rs. (X + 100) respectively. After three months, P withdrew 40% of his initial investment. If at the end of year, P got Rs. 210 as profit share out of total profit of Rs. 530, then find the value of (in Rs.) X?

(1) 1750 (2) 1250

(3) 2500 (4) 1500

(5) 2000

45. A man invested Rs. P on simple interest at 18% p.a. for three years and received Rs. (0.5P+100) as interest. If man invested Rs. (P + 3500) on compound interest at 10% p.a. for two years, then find amount gets by man?

(1) Rs. 7240 (2) Rs. 7260
(3) Rs. 7280 (4) Rs. 7460
(5) Rs. 7040

46. Pipe A can fill a tank in 4 hours and pipe B can fill the same tank in 6 hours. If A, B and pipe C can together fill the same tank in 3 hours, then find time taken by pipe C to empty the tank?

(1) 24 hours (2) 12 hours
(3) 16 hours (4) 8 hours
(5) 18 hours

47. The ratio of marked price to selling price of an article is 5 : 3 and shopkeeper gets a profit of 40%. If shopkeeper sells the article at its marked price, then the difference between cost price and marked price of article is Rs. 400. Find the cost price of the article?

(1) Rs. 540 (2) Rs. 480
(3) Rs. 600 (4) Rs. 300
(5) Rs. 360

48. A vessel contains mixture of milk and water in the ratio of 7 : 3. If 50 liter of milk is added into the mixture, then the quantity of milk becomes 80% of the resulting mixture. Find the initial quantity of milk in the mixture?

(1) 112 liters (2) 105 liters
(3) 84 liters (4) 70 liters
(5) 56 liters

49. Ram alone can complete a work in 40 days. If Ram and Shayam together take 37.5% less time than Ram to complete the same work, then find in how many days Shayam alone can complete the work?

(1) 56.66 days (2) 58 days
(3) 50 days (4) 66.66 days
(5) 33.33 days

50. Arun spent 60% of his monthly salary on accommodation, 15% of remaining salary on entertainment and remaining salary he saved. If the difference of amount spent on accommodation and his saving is Rs. 3510, then find his monthly salary?

(1) Rs. 12,500 (2) Rs. 13,500
(3) Rs. 12,800 (4) Rs. 14,000
(5) Rs. 15,000

51. The length of train A is half of the length of train B and the ratio of speed of train A to B is 4 : 3. If train A and B can cross 100 meters long platform in 5 sec. and 10 sec. respectively, then find the length (in meters) of train B?

(1) 200 (2) 180
(3) 140 (4) 240
(5) 120

52. The ratio of speed of boat in downstream to that of in upstream is 4 : 1 and total time taken by boat to cover a certain distance in downstream and upstream together is 10 hours. Find the time taken by boat to cover the same distance in still water?

(1) 3 hours and 24 minutes
(2) 3 hours and 12 minutes
(3) 3 hours and 10 minutes
(4) 3 hours and 15 minutes
(5) 3 hours and 20 minutes

Directions (53-65): *What will come in the place of question (?) mark in following questions?*

53. 64% of 2500 + 75% of 1600 = ? × 112

(1) 28 (2) 21
(3) 24 (4) 32
(5) 25

54. 55% of 1400 + $?^2$ +282= $(12)^3$

(1) 28 (2) 24
(3) 26 (4) 36
(5) 16

55. $\frac{7.5\% \text{ of } 7200}{?} + 450 = 15\% \text{ of } 3200$

(1) 15 (2) 24
(3) 20 (4) 18
(5) 12

56. $?^2 + 224 - 96 = 85\%$ of 280 + 34

(1) 18 (2) 12
(3) 16 (4) 14
(5) 8

57. $\sqrt{1521} + (21)^2 - 18 \times 5 = 5 \times ?$

(1) 80 (2) 78

(3) 64 (4) 70
(5) 96

58. $? \times 7 + 337 = (5)^3 + 436$
(1) 36 (2) 44
(3) 48 (4) 45
(5) 32

59. $? \div 6 + (12)^2 - \sqrt{2304} = (14)^2$
(1) 1100 (2) 400
(3) 600 (4) 900
(5) 1500

60. $(? \times 48) \div 54 + 8^2 = 96$
(1) 45 (2) 36
(3) 72 (4) 54
(5) None of these

61. $2\frac{1}{3} + 5\frac{2}{3} - 3\frac{3}{4} = ? - 8\frac{3}{4}$
(1) 14 (2) 13
(3) 12 (4) 15
(5) 16

62. $\frac{2^5 \times 3^6}{9^2 \times 4^2} + 7 = (?)^2$
(1) 4 (2) 5
(3) 7 (4) 6
(5) 3

63. $9097 \div 11 \div 10 = ? + 15.7$
(1) 87 (2) 77
(3) 67 (4) 57
(5) 47

64. $15 \times 12 - 10 \times 11 = -15 \times 17 + ?$
(1) 330 (2) 345
(3) 335 (4) 325
(5) 365

65. $35 \times 5 + 19 \times 7 + ? = (20)^2$
(1) 95 (2) 103
(3) 97 (4) 92
(5) 90

Reasoning Ability

66. Find the odd one out?
(1) DGJE (2) KNQL
(3) UXZU (4) CFID
(5) MPSN

Directions (67-70): *Study the following information carefully and answer the questions given below:*

A certain number of persons sit in a row and all of them face towards the north. Q sits second to the right of M. Two persons sit between J and Q. W sits second to the right of J and sits third from the extreme right end. Five persons sit between W and S. The number of persons sits to the left of S is same as the number of persons sits to the right of W. K is the only neighbour of P. K sits to the right of J.

67. How many persons sit in the row?
(1) 13 (2) 11
(3) 10 (4) 15
(5) 17

68. What is the position of Q with respect to W?
(1) Fourth to the left
(2) Fifth to the right
(3) Second to the right
(4) Fifth to the left (5) Third to the left

69. Which among the following statement(s) is/are true?
I. P sits at the extreme right end
II. More than three persons sit to the left of Q
III. M sits adjacent to S
(1) Both I and II (2) Both II and III
(3) Only I (4) Both I and III
(5) Only III

70. Four of the following five are alike in a certain way and thus form a group. Who among the following does not belong to the group?
(1) M (2) W
(3) P (4) Q
(5) K

Directions (71-73): *In these questions, relationship between different elements is shown in the statements. The statements are followed by two conclusions. Give answer.*

(1) If only conclusion I is true

(2) If only conclusion II is true
(3) If either conclusion I or II is true
(4) If neither conclusion I nor II is true
(5) If both conclusions I and II are true

71. **Statements:** $Q \geq W > Y = E \leq U < P > S \leq T$
Conclusions
I: $Y < P$ **II:** $W > S$

72. **Statements:** $M \leq B > H = A \geq D < L = C$
Conclusions:
I: $H > L$ **II:** $A \leq C$

73. **Statements:** $K > M \leq Z < E \geq V = X < C$
Conclusions:
I: $E \geq C$ **II:** $V < M$

Directions (74-78): *Study the following information carefully and answer the questions given below:*

Eight persons A, B, C, D, E, F, G and H sit around a square table such that four persons sit at corner and the remaining four sit at the middle of the sides of the table but not necessarily in the same order. The persons sit at the corner face towards the center of the table and the persons sit at the middle of the side face away from the center of the table.

E sits second to the right of B. Two persons sit between B and H. F sits to the immediate right of H. The number of persons sits between H and D is same as the number of persons sits between D and G. D sits at the corner of the table. A sits adjacent to D.

74. Who among the following sits third to the left of C?
(1) A (2) B
(3) D (4) E
(5) H

75. How many persons sit between E and H when counts to the left of H?
(1) Two (2) Three
(3) One (4) None
(5) More than three

76. What is the position of C with respect to G?
(1) Second to the right
(2) Second to the left
(3) Immediate left
(4) Third to the right
(5) None of these

77. Which among the following statement(s) is/are not true?
(1) A sits to the immediate left of H
(2) Three persons sit between D and C
(3) E sits opposite to A
(4) B sits at the corner of the table
(5) All are true

78. Four of the following five are alike in a certain way and thus form a group. Who among the following does not belong to the group?
(1) E (2) F
(3) D (4) A
(5) B

Directions (79-82): *Study the following number series carefully and answer the questions given below:*

9 8 4 6 3 7 2 9 4 1 5 2 5 9 1 4 3 6 9 1 8 2 9 4 5 7 6 1

79. How many prime numbers are in the above series each of which is immediately preceded by an even number and immediately followed by odd number?
(1) Three (2) Five
(3) Four (4) Six
(5) More than six

80. What is the sum of the odd numbers which are immediately followed by the number which is multiple of 3?
(1) 11 (2) 15
(3) 17 (4) 13
(5) 19

81. Which among the following number is 9th to the left of the number which is 7th from the right end?
(1) 2 (2) 1
(3) 9 (4) 5
(5) 8

82. How many even numbers are between the numbers which are 9th from the right end and 3rd from the left end?
(1) Six (2) Five
(3) Four (4) Three
(5) Two

83. If we form a four-letter meaningful word with 1st, 5th, 6th and 8th letter from the left end of the word "**CRITERIA**" (Using each letter once), then what would be the third letter of that meaningful word? If no meaningful word is formed, then mark the answer as X. If more than one meaningful word is formed then mark the answer as Z.

(1) C (2) R
(3) A (4) Z
(5) X

Directions (84-88): *Study the following information carefully and answer the questions given below:*

Seven persons have different designations *i.e.* Vice Chancellor (VC), Director (DR), Director of nursing (DN), Head of Department (HOD), Principal, Professor and Assistant professor in a company. The order of seniority is the same as given above *i.e.* Vice Chancellor (VC) is the senior-most designation and Assistant professor is the junior-most designation.

At most two persons are senior to R. Two designations gap between R and V who is not a professor. One designation gap between P and T and both of them are senior to V. There are as many persons junior to P as senior to U. S is junior to Q.

84. How many persons are senior to Q?

(1) Three (2) One
(3) Four (4) Two
(5) None

85. Who among the following is designated as Principal?

(1) P (2) Q
(3) T (4) V
(5) S

86. The number of persons designated between R and U is same as the number of persons designated before ....

(1) S (2) V
(3) Q (4) T
(5) None of these

87. Who among the following is three post junior to the one who is just senior to R?

(1) Q
(2) Director (DR)
(3) S
(4) Director of nursing (DN)
(5) Both Q and Director of nursing (DN)

88. If all the persons are arranged according to the alphabetical order from top to bottom then how many persons remain unchanged except (P)?

(1) One (2) Two
(3) None (4) Three
(5) None of these

Directions (89-91): *In each of the questions below, some statements are given followed by some conclusions. You have to take the given statements to be true even if they seem to be at variance with commonly known facts. Read all the conclusions and then decide which of the given conclusions logically follow from the given statements, disregarding commonly known facts. Give answer*

(1) If only conclusion I follows.
(2) If only conclusion II follows.
(3) If either conclusion I or II follows.
(4) If neither conclusion I nor II follows.
(5) If both conclusions I and II follow.

89. Statements: Some juice are mango. Only a few mango are orange.

Conclusions:

I. Some Juice are not mango

II. All Orange being mango is a possibility

90. Statements: No Bell is Clock. All Bell is Ring.

Conclusions:

I. Some Clock is Ring

II. No Ring is Clock

91. Statements: Only Car is Train. Some Ship are Car

Conclusions:

I. Some Ship are not Train

II. All Car being Ship is a possibility

Directions (92-96): *Study the following information carefully and answer the questions given below:*

Seven persons H, J, K, L, M, N and O buy a product on different day one after another but not necessarily in the same order.

One person buys product between H and O.

Two persons buy product between O and N. N buys product neither just before nor just after H. K buys product just before J and after O. L buys product two days before M.

92. How many persons buy product between L and K?
(1) More than four (2) Three
(3) None (4) Two
(5) One

93. The number of persons buy product between J and N is same as the number of persons buy product before ....
(1) L (2) M
(3) O (4) H
(5) None of these

94. Which of the following statement is true?
I. More than two persons buy product after K
II. O buys product just after M
III. Only one person buys product before H
(1) Both I and III are true
(2) Both II and III are true
(3) Only I is true (4) Only II is true
(5) None is true

95. How many persons buy product after N?
(1) One (2) Two
(3) More than four (4) Four
(5) None of these

96. Four of the following five are alike in a certain way and hence form a group. Which of the following does not belong to that group?
(1) M-L (2) L-H
(3) O-M (4) J-N
(5) K-O

Directions (97-99): *Study the following information carefully and answer the questions given below:*

L has two daughters. C is the unmarried sister-in-law of H. K is the father of G. K is the only sibling of C. P is the spouse of L. W is the maternal uncle of H. L is the maternal grandmother of M who is sibling of G. S is the sister-in-law of K. G is the only grandson of J who is not female.

97. How many married couple are live in the family?
(1) Four (2) One
(3) Three (4) Two
(5) None of these

98. How is L related to K?
(1) Sister (2) Niece
(3) Mother-in-law (4) Sister-in-law
(5) Mother

99. Who is the sister-in-law of H?
(1) C (2) M
(3) L (4) Either C or M
(5) None of these

100. In the word '**PAGINATE**', how many pairs of the letters have the same number of letters between them (both forward and backward direction) in the word as in the alphabetical series?
(1) Four (2) Two
(3) One (4) Three
(5) More than four

Answers With Explanations

1. (2) From the first paragraph of the given passage, the option (2) is true.

2. (4)

3. (4) The first few lines of the second paragraph of the passage can be used to deduce the answer.

4. (4) From the second paragraph, the options (1) and (3) are correct. So, option (4) is the right answer.

5. (2) Sentence (2) is false.

6. (1) The appropriate word is "hummed".

7. (4)

8. (2)

9. (2)

10. (4)

11. (3)

12. (5)

13. (1)

14. (3)

15. (2)

16. (4)

17. (1)

18. (3)

19. (2)

20. (3)

21. (1) The correct spelling will be "lose".

22. (1) The correct spelling will be "unwary".

23. (4) The correct spelling will be "memorabilia".

24. (5) All the highlighted words are spelt correctly.

25. (3) The correct spelling will be "fluctuated".

26. (2)

27. (4) The given sentence is in present continuous tense hence 'become' should be in gerund form.

28. (2)

29. (5) The highlighted phrase is correct hence no improvement required.

30. (2)

31. (2) $50 + 5^2 = 75$

$75 + 10^2 = 175$

$175 + 15^2 = 400$

$400 + 20^2 = 800$

$? = 800 + 25^2 = \mathbf{1425}$

32. (5) $8 + 10 = 18$

$18 + 20 = 38$

$38 + 40 = 78$

$? = 78 + 80 = 158$

$158 + 160 = 318$

33. (2) $? = 41 + 5 = 46$

$46 + 7 = 53$

$53 + 11 = 64$

$64 + 13 = 77$

$77 + 17 = 94$

34. (4) $? = 215 - (14 \times 5) = 145$

$145 - (14 \times 4) = 89$

$89 - (14 \times 3) = 47$

$47 - (14 \times 2) = 19$

$19 - (14 \times 1) = 5$

35. (1) $-1 + 2^3 = 9$

$9 + 3^3 = 36$

$36 + 4^3 = 100$

$100 + 5^3 = 225$

$? = 225 + 6^3 = \mathbf{441}$

For questions (36-40):

Companies	Total number of boats manufactured	Total number of ships manufactured
A	(175 – 125) = 50	125
B	(225 – 75) = 150	75
C	(150 – 50) = 100	50
D	(200 – 150) = 50	150

36. (3) Total boats used by fishermen

$= 150 \times 1/3 = 50$

Required percentage $= 50 \times (1/125) \times 100 = 40\%$

37. (5) Total number of boats and ships manufactured by A in 2021 $= 175 \times (140/100) = 245$

Total number of boats manufactured by A in 2021 $= 245 - 125 = 120$

38. (2) Required ratio $= (100 + 50)/(75 + 50) = 6 : 5$

39. (5) Total cost of all boats manufactured by

D = 50 × 4600 = 230000 Rs.

40. (1) Total boats and ships manufactured by A and B = (175 + 225) = 400 Total boats manufactured by A and D = (50 + 50) = 100

Required percentage

={(400 – 100)/100} × 100 = 300%

41. (2) Let the present age of Amit, Den and Mohit be 'a', 'd' and 'm' respectively

According to the question-

$a + d = 20 + 2 \times 6 = 32$ ...(*i*)

$a - m = 6$ ...(*ii*)

And, $m + d = 26$ ...(*iii*)

From (*i*), (*ii*), (*iii*) we get

$32 - a + a - 6 = 26$

$26 = 26$

We cannot determine the age of Den

42. **(4)** $\pi r + 2r = 36$

$\frac{22}{7} \times r + 2r = 36$

$r = 7$ cm

Length of rectangle = 147/7 = 21 cm

43. **(1)** Let six consecutive odd numbers = $x, x + 2, x + 4, x + 6, x + 8, x + 10$ According to the question-

$6x + 30 - (x + 5) = 150$

$5x + 25 = 150$

$x = 25$

Required sum = 25 + 35 = 60

44. (4) **45.** (2)

46. (2) Total capacity of tank = LCM of 4, 6 and 3 = 12 unit

Efficiency of pipe A = 12/4 = 3 units/hour

Efficiency of pipe B = 12/6 = 2 units/hour

Efficiency of pipe (A + B + C)

= 12/4 = 4 units/hour

So, efficiency of pipe C = 4 – (3 + 2)

=–1 unit/hour (pipe C is an outlet pipe)

Required time = 12 hours

47. (4) **48.** (4)

49. (4) Time taken by Ram and Shayam together = 40 × 5/8 = 25 days

Total work = 200 unit (LCM of 40 and 25)

Efficiency of Shayam = (200/25) – (200/40)

= 3 units/day

Required days = 200/3 days

50. (2) **57.** (2)

51. (1) **58.** (5)

52. (2) **59.** (3)

53. (5) **60.** (2)

54. (3) **61.** (2)

55. (4) **62.** (2)

56. (2) **63.** (3)

64. **(4)** 180 – 110 = – 255 + ?

? = 70 + 255

? = 325

65. **(4)** 175 + 133 + ? = 400

? = 92

66. (3)

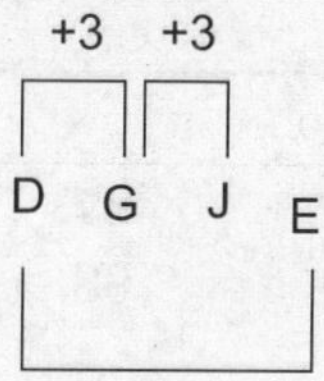

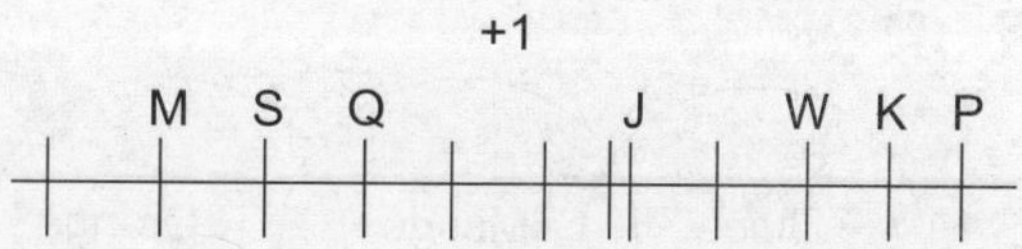

For questions (67-70):

67. (2) **69.** (4)

68. (4) **70.** (3)

For questions (71-73):

71. (1) **72.** (3)

73. (4)

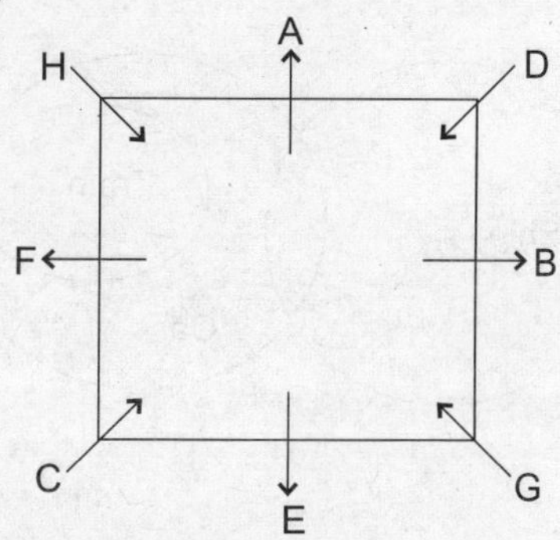

For questions (74-78):

74. (1)

75. (5)
76. (2)
77. (4)
78. (3)

For questions (79-82):

79. (3)
80. (2)
81. (4)
82. (1)
83. (4)

For questions (84-88):

Designations	Person
Vice Chancellor (VC)	P
Director (DR)	R
Director of nursing (DN)	T
Head of Department (HOD)	Q
Principal	V
Professor	S
Assistant professor	U

84. (1)
85. (4)
86. (2)
87. (1)
88. (3)
89. (2)

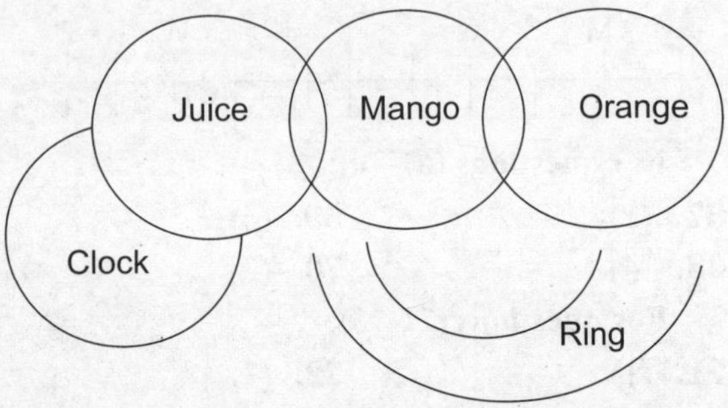

90. (3)

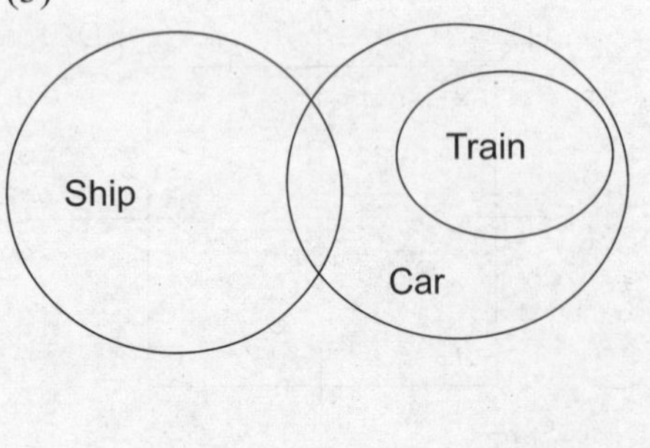

91. (1)

For questions (92-96):

Persons
L
H
M
O
K
J
N

92. (2)
93. (1)
94. (2)
95. (5)
96. (1)

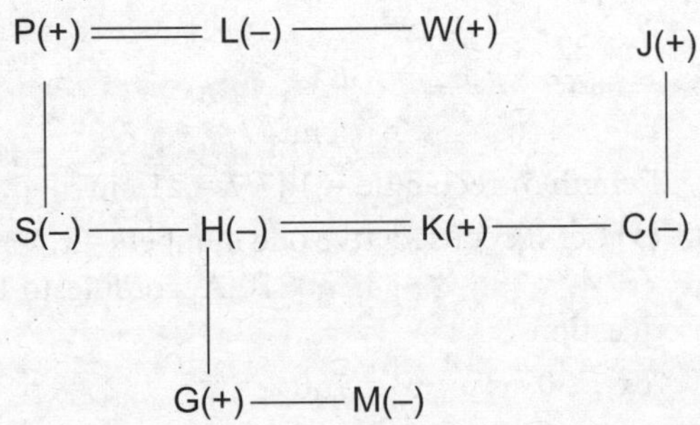

For questions (97-99):

97. (4)
98. (3)
99. (1)

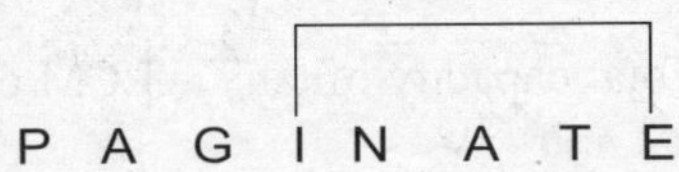

100. (3)

IBPS Clerk Mains, 2022

(Held on 8 January, 2022)

Based on Memory

General Awareness

1. In June 2022, who launched new portal NIRYAT (National Import-Export Record for Yearly Analysis of Trade)?
(1) Amit Shah (2) Ram Nath Kovind
(3) Narendra Modi (4) Piyush Goyal
(5) None of the above

2. Which Schedule of the Constitution provides for Anti-Defection Law?
(1) 10th (2) 7th
(3) 3rd (4) 1st
(5) None of the above

3. How many diseases are covered under National Vector Borne Disease Control Programme?
(1) 4 (2) 5
(3) 6 (4) 7
(5) None of the above

4. What is MFLOPS?
(1) It is used to measure the state of the CPU.
(2) It is used to measure the speed of CPU.
(3) It is a memory unit.
(4) It is used to measure memory access time.
(5) None of the above

5. In July 2022, Scientists working with the Large Hadron Collider (LHC) have discovered subatomic particles never seen before.
(1) 2 (2) 3
(3) 4 (4) 5
(5) None of the above

6. .... is a short-term unsecured promissory note issued by reputed business organisations at a price lower than its face value and redeemable at par.
(1) Treasury bill (2) Commercial paper
(3) Certificate of deposit
(4) Promissory note
(5) None of the above

7. Consider the following statements:
A. According to the Constitution of India, a person shall be disqualified from being a member of a legislative assembly if s/he holds any office of profit under the Union or state government.
B. According to the Representation of People Act, 1951, a person is disqualified from being a member of a legislative assembly if s/he has failed to lodge an account of his/her election expenses within the time.
Which of the statements given above is/are correct?
(1) A Only (2) B Only
(3) Both A and B (4) Neither A nor B
(5) None of the above

8. Which of the following department is mainly responsible for policy issues relating to Public Sector Banks (PSBs)?
(1) Financial Intelligence Unit-India (FIU-IND)
(2) Targeted Public Distribution System (TPDS)
(3) Centralised Public Grievance Redressal and Monitoring System (CPGRAMS)
(4) The Department of Financial Services (DFS)
(5) None of the above

9. RBI (RBI) on August 9, 2021, under the Deendayal Antyodaya Yojana-National Rural Livelihoods Mission (DAY-NRLM) has extended mortgage-free loans to self-help groups of ten lakhs has been increased from ....
(1) twelve lakh (2) sixteen lakh

(3) fourteen lakh (4) twenty lakh
(5) None of the above

10. Consider the following statements regarding Cryptocurrencies.

A. It is a digital currency in which encryption techniques are used to regulate the generation of units of currency and verify the transfer of funds, operating independently of a central bank.

B. Supreme Court had allowed banks and financial institutions to reinstate services related to cryptocurrencies by setting aside the RBI's 2018 circular that had prohibited them based on the ground of "proportionality".

Which of the statements given above is/are correct?
(1) A only (2) B only
(3) Both A and B (4) Neither A nor B
(5) None of the above

11. When is the International Day of Democracy observed?
(1) 13 September (2) 14 September
(3) 15 September (4) 16 September
(5) None of the above

12. Insurance Regulatory and Development Authority of India (IRDAI) recently announced that no need to submit separately in order to have new annuity products of National Pension Scheme (NPS).
(1) Digital Life Certificate
(2) Proposal Form
(3) Health Certificate
(4) Police Verification Certificate
(5) Salary Slip

13. Which regulatory body in India has unveiled a rupee settlement system for international trade in July 2022?
(1) Securities and Exchange Board of India (SEBI)
(2) Competition Commission of India (CCI)
(3) Insurance Regulatory and Development Authority
(4) Reserve Bank of India (RBI)
(5) None of the above/More than one of the above.

14. On July 19, Four entities of the eight that commenced testing of their products in the second cohort under the ....'s regulatory sandbox structure themed "Cross Border Payments" have completed the "Test Phase",
(1) Securities Exchange Board of India
(2) Insurance Regulatory and Development Authority
(3) Reserve Bank of India
(4) Banks Board Bureau
(5) None of these

15. The RBI has made the code mandatory for all participants undertaking transactions in the markets regulated by the RBI.
(1) Visual Entity Identifier
(2) Legal Entity Identifier
(3) Legit Entity Identifier
(4) Stock Entity Identifier
(5) Transaction Entity Identifier

16. As per a statement by Finance Minister Nirmala Sitharaman, SBI will invest how much per cent equity in Yes Bank with other investors also being invited?
(1) 30 (2) 49
(3) 51 (4) 60
(5) 75

17. The Competition Commission of India (CCI) approves acquisition of stake in IDFC Asset Management Company Limited and IDFC AMC Trustee Company Limited by ...., ChrysCapital and GIC.
(1) Bajaj Finserv Ltd
(2) L & T Finance Holdings Ltd
(3) Equitas Holdings Ltd
(4) Bandhan Financial Holdings Ltd
(5) Muthoot Finance Ltd

18. Which of the following is the electronic trading platform for natural rubber?
(1) eRube (2) eNam
(3) mRubber (4) eRubber
(5) mRube

19. In the Aarogya Sanjeevani policy provided by the insurers, what is the minimum amount sum insured (in rupees) provided under the policy?

(1) 5000 (2) 50,000
(3) 1,50,000 (4) 5,00,000
(5) None of the above

20. Which of the following is also known as the bad bank of India?

(1) NCLT (2) NARCL
(3) NCLAT (4) NARLC
(5) SARFAESI

21. "The Reserve Bank has released the eligibility criteria for entities to be categorized as 'Specified User' of Credit Information Companies (CICs)." Choose the incorrect option(s) regarding the aforesaid statement? (January, 2021)

(1) The criteria set out the requirements for the entities to become eligible as Specified User of CIC under the Credit Information Companies (Amendment) Regulations, 2021.
(2) The company should have a net worth of not less than ₹ 5 crores as per the latest audited balance sheet and should meet the requirement on a continuing basis.
(3) A 'specified user' should be a company incorporated in India or a statutory corporation established in the country.
(4) The company shall have at least three years of experience in running the business or activity of processing information.
(5) The criteria set out the requirements for the entities to become eligible as Specified User of CIC under clause (j) of Regulation 3 of the Credit Information Companies (Amendment) Regulations, 2021.

22. Which of the following is not a small savings scheme?

(1) PPF (2) NSC
(3) Post Office Time Deposit Scheme
(4) Senior Citizen Savings Scheme
(5) All of the above are small savings schemes

23. Recently in July 2022, Maryna Viazovska has won the Fields Medal 2022. The award is related to which field?

(1) Physics (2) Mathematics
(3) Biology (4) Statistics
(5) Chemistry

24. As per RBI data, what is the amount remitted by Indians in Q1FY23 under the Liberalised Remittance Scheme (LRS)?

(1) USD 3.65 billion
(2) USD 8.76 billion
(3) USD 5.87 billion
(4) USD 7.62 billion
(5) USD 6.04 billion

25. Which of the following has recently been accorded with the status of a 'Maharatna' Central Public Sector Enterprise, giving it greater operational and financial autonomy?

(1) Cochin Shipyard Ltd
(2) RailTel Corporation of India
(3) BrahMos Aerospace
(4) REC Ltd
(5) National Dairy Development Board

26. As per the Union Budget, 2022-2023, "Alternate Minimum Tax" paid by "Cooperative societies" are brought down to how much % from previous 18.5%?

(1) 15% (2) 14%
(3) 16% (4) 12%
(5) 16.5%

27. Who has tendered his resignation from the post of Indian Olympic Association (IOA) President?

(1) Venkataramani Sumantran
(2) Shrikant Madhav Vaidya
(3) Narinder Batra
(4) Shri Gurdeep Singh
(5) None of the above

28. Which country has recently become India's top trading partner in 2021-22?

(1) Japan
(2) United States of America

(3) China (4) Germany
(5) France

29. Which of the following company has been given the 'Maharatna' company status by the union government in September 2022?
(1) REC Limited (2) Coal India Limited
(3) Indian Oil Corporation Limited
(4) NTPC Ltd.
(5) None of the above

30. Reserve Bank Governor Shaktikanta Das on October 6 launched a new 'SupTech' initiative ...., which is the bank's Advanced Supervisory Monitoring System and is expected to make the supervisory processes more robust.
(1) UNNAT (2) LAKSHYA
(3) VIGIL (4) CHASE
(5) DAKSH

31. Which of the following theme has been selected by the Reserve Bank of India (RBI) for Financial Literacy Week in February 2022?
(1) "Go Digital, Go Secure"
(2) "Economy in Digital Era"
(3) "Go Digital, Go Cashless"
(4) "Creating Digital Economy"
(5) "Digital is the Future"

32. As per the United Nations-Habitat's World Cities Report 2022, India's urban population is estimated to stand at .... in 2035.
(1) 775 Million (2) 675 Million
(3) 575 Million (4) 475 Million
(5) 375 Million

33. The Department of Fisheries aims to bring 'Blue Revolution' through sustainable development of the fisheries sector with an investment of Rs. 20,050 crore for a period of five years, starting .... in all states/ union territories.
(1) 2020-21 to 2025-26
(2) 2021-22 to 2024-25
(3) 2021-22 to 2025-26
(4) 2020-21 to 2024-25
(5) 2021-22 to 2023-24

34. Often seen in the news, Chabahar Port is located in
(1) Persian Gulf (2) Gulf of Oman
(3) Gulf of Mannar (4) Gulfs of Turkey
(5) None of the above

35. Which of the following is the oldest grandslam tournament in tennis?
(1) US Open (2) French Open
(3) Wimbledon (4) Australian Open
(5) Indian Open

36. In June 2022, which portal of the Ministry of Commerce was launched by Narendra Modi to access all the information necessary related to India's foreign trade?
(1) NIRYAT (2) HARBINGER
(3) EXPERT (4) AYUSH
(5) None of these

37. Organization related to "Read Data Book" or "Red List" is
(1) U.T.E.S. (2) I.U.C.N.
(3) I.B.W.C. (4) W.W.F.
(5) W.T.O

38. What is the rank of India in the UNDP's Human Development Index 2021, released in September 2022?
(1) 132nd (2) 71st
(3) 165th (4) 121st
(5) 134th

39. Who is the Secretary General of NATO?
(1) Antonio Guterres
(2) Jens Stoltenberg
(3) Admiral Rob Bauer
(4) Stuart Peach (5) Gladwyn Jebb

40. According to the latest update, India's government and the .... are in talks to introduce a risk-sharing mechanism to compensate banks giving loans for electric vehicle purchases, as the country seeks to decarbonize the transport sector.
(1) New Development Bank
(2) International Renewable Energy Agency
(3) Asian Development Bank
(4) World Bank

(5) International Finance Corporation

41. 'SVANidhi se Samriddhi' program has been launched by the Ministry of Housing and Urban Affairs in additional 126 cities across 14 States/ UTs. The cabinet approved the extension of the scheme "Prime Minister Street Vendor's AtmaNirbhar Nidhi (PM SVANidhi)" to which date?

(1) March 2022 (2) December 2024
(3) June 2023 (4) June 2024
(5) March 2024

42. Which of the following has set up a committee to develop a comprehensive framework on the right to repair?

(1) Department of Chemicals and Petrochemicals
(2) Department of Telecommunications
(3) Department of Defence Production
(4) Department of Consumer Affairs
(5) Department of Food and Public Distribution

43. When was the National Payments Corporation of India (NPCI) incorporated?

(1) 2008 (2) 2014
(3) 2015 (4) 2012
(5) 2006

44. Recently in July 2022, Shinzo Abe passed away at the age of 67 after being shot while giving a campaign speech. He was the former Prime Minister of ....

(1) United Kingdom
(2) Japan
(3) Russia
(4) Israel
(5) South Korea

45. The GST council is headed by the:

(1) SEBI chairman (2) Prime minister
(3) RBI governor (4) Union finance minister
(5) None of the above

46. The gross GST revenue collected in the month of August 2022 stood at Rs. .... crore.

(1) 1,43,612 (2) 1,52,678
(3) 1,87,560 (4) 2,98,560
(5) 1,35,827

47. Government has extended the line for levy of GST compensation cess by nearly 4 years till which date?

(1) 2026 (2) 2030
(3) 2050 (4) 2024
(5) 2023

48. International Tiger day is celebrated by WWF every year, Where is the headquarters of WWF is located?

(1) United Arab Emirates
(2) Switzerland
(3) USA (4) Philippines
(5) California

49. Which state has topped the 'State Ranking Index for National Food Security Act' 2022?

(1) Gujarat (2) Punjab
(3) Odisha (4) Kerala
(5) Chhattisgarh

50. Which of the following countries are a part of G-7 Grouping?

(1) France, USA, Germany, Spain
(2) Canada, France, Germany, Italy
(3) United Kingdom, Austria, Germany, Italy
(4) USA, France, Japan, China
(5) None of the above

General English

Directions (51-57): *Read the passage and answer the questions that follow. Some words may be highlighted for you. Pay careful attention.*

Elon Musk's SpaceX has been testing the Starlink satellite broadband service which boasts of a speed boost of around 300 mbps and latency reduction to around 20 ms. Musk **confirmed** the speed boost in **response** to a tweet by a user who received the Starlink broadband kit in the United States and shared a screenshot of the service **offering** them broadband speeds of 130 mbps. "Speed will double to ~ 300 Mb/s and latency will drop to ~ 20 ms later this year," he said. During the beta testing phase, Starlink offered users a broadband speed between 50 mbps and 150 mbps with the latency expected between 20 ms and 40 ms, depending on location. In this phase, the Starlink kit included a phased-arrayed satellite dish, a tripod and a Wi-Fi router. SpaceX says that the Starlink satellite broadband service will cover most of the Earth by the end of the year which means that the service could also be expanded in India although there is no confirmed roadmap for the same. SpaceX has already submitted its recommendations to the Telecom Regulatory Authority of India (TRAI) last year for introducing satellite broadband in India.

"Most of Earth by end of the year, all by next year, then it's about densifying coverage. Important to note that cellular will always have the advantage in dense urban areas. Satellites are best for low to medium population density areas," tweeted Musk.

51. How is Starlink satellite supposed to reach India?
(1) By connections
(2) By flight
(3) By covering most parts of the earth
(4) By occupying its land
(5) None of the above

52. During the beta testing period, what speed range does the broadband service provide?
(1) Speed between 20 mbps to 40 mbps.
(2) Speed of around 300 mbps
(3) Speed between 50 mbps to 150 mbps.
(4) Speed of 20 mbps
(5) None of the above

53. Give another word for the underlined word in the given line - "SpaceX has already submitted its recommendations to the Telecom Regulatory Authority of India (TRAI) last year for introducing satellite broadband in India."
(1) Reject (2) Counsel
(3) Refuse (4) Decline
(5) None of the above

54. During the beta testing, what does a Starlink kit provide its users?
(1) Expensive services
(2) Phased-arrayed satellite dish, a tripod and a Wi-Fi router
(3) Free service
(4) Free data
(5) None of the above

55. Find a word which has the opposite meaning for the underlined word in the given line – "Musk confirmed the speed boost in response to a tweet by a user who received the Starlink broadband kit in the United States and shared a screenshot of the service **offering** them broadband speeds of 130 mbps."
(1) Provide (2) Recommend
(3) Withdrawing (4) Propose
(5) None of the above

56. Give the correct antonym for the word **"confirmed"**.
(1) Contradicted (2) Established
(3) Firm (4) Settled
(5) None of the above

57. Give the synonym for the word **"response"**.
(1) Dissatisfy (2) Deny
(3) Leave (4) Reply
(5) None of the above

Directions (58-63): *Read the passage carefully and answer the following questions given below.*

It's no secret that Mount Everest, the jewel in Nepal's Himalayan crown, is the world's premier mountain. It's one of those facts embedded in childhood, like knowing that Neil Armstrong was the first person to walk on the moon or that blue whales are the largest animals ever to have lived. You may be surprised to hear, then, that other peaks could conceivably be considered Earth's tallest; it just depends how you measure them.

So, judging by different **parameters** — including tallest by altitude, tallest from base to top and tallest based on being the farthest point from Earth's center — what is the tallest mountain in the world?

"In order to have comparability in measurements, it is necessary to have a consistent baseline," Martin Price, a professor and founding director of the Centre for Mountain Studies at the University of Highlands and Islands in Scotland.

"Historically, and even now, elevation is usually given as height above mean sea level," said Price. "However, this has to be with reference to a standard mean sea level, which has to be defined. Sea levels are different in different parts of the world, and they're changing due to climate change."

As a result, "**elevation** is now measured in relation to the mathematically defined geoid of the Earth," he said. The geoid is, according to the National Oceanic and Atmospheric Administration "a model of global mean sea level that is used to measure precise surface elevations." This average is used to ascertain the height of mountains, a process that sometimes requires an aero plane to fly "back and forth over a mountain in a series of parallel lines to measure how much gravity pulls down on its peak," according to GIM International. These measurements, in conjunction with GPS readings, provide incredibly accurate elevation readings.

"In order to have comparability in measurements, it is necessary to have a consistent baseline," Martin Price, a professor and founding director of the Centre for Mountain Studies at the University of Highlands and Islands in Scotland.

So, all mountains are measured from sea level, predominantly for convenience and consistency, but what if measurements were simply taken from base to peak? Would Everest still top the charts? The answer is a mountainous "no." That honor would go to Mauna Kea, an inactive volcano in Hawaii. Should we, therefore, regard Mauna Kea as the tallest mountain on Earth? **"It all depends on the perspective you take,"** Price said. "If there were no oceans on our planet, there would be no debate! You could draw comparisons to the highest mountains on other bodies in our solar system, which have no oceans."

58. What does the author tries to infer in the said line: "It all depends on the perspective you take."

(1) It depends on your skills.

(2) It depends on how you take measurements.

(3) It depends on your framework and definition

(4) Both 1 and 2

(5) All of these

59. The given sentence is divided into (A), (B), (C), (D) and (E). Find the error if there is any. If there is no error, mark option (E) as "No error".

"In order to have comparability in (A) measurements, it is necessary to have (B) a consistent baseline," Martin Price, a professor and founding director (C) of the Centre for Mountain Studies at the University of Highlands and Islands in Scotland (D). No error (E).

(1) "In order to have comparability in

(2) measurements, it is necessary to have

(3) a consistent baseline," Martin Price, a professor and founding director

(4) of the Centre for Mountain Studies at the University of Highlands and Islands in Scotland

(5) No error

60. Choose the correct synonym for the word **'parameters'**.

(1) Criterion. (2) Guideline

(3) Constant. (4) Specification.

(5) All of these.

61. Give the antonym for 'Elevation'

(1) Surge (2) Disdain

(3) Demotion (4) Both (2) and (3)

(5) All of these.

62. What is 'geoid' according to the National Oceanic and Atmospheric Administration?

(1) A model of sea level that is used to measure precise surface elevations.

(2) A model of global mean sea level that is used to measure precise sea elevations.

(3) A model of global mean sea level that is used to measure precise surface elevations.

(4) A model of global mean surface level that is used to measure precise sea and surface elevations.

(5) None of these.

63. What is necessary in order to have comparability in measurements?

(1) Consistent temperature.

(2) Consistent baseline.

(3) Varied measurements.

(4) Consistent GPS readings

(5) None of these.

Directions (64-67): *In the following question, two columns are given containing three phrases each. The phrases are labelled A, B and C in the first column and P, Q and R in the second column. A phrase from the first column may or may not connect with a phrase in the second column to make it grammatically and contextually meaningful sentence. Identify the correct option given below that gives the correct sequence(s) in which one or more sentence can be formed. If one of the options make it possible for a meaningful sentence to be formed, indicate 'None of these' as your answer.*

64.

Column 1	Column 2
(A) Showing more emotions at work could be the secret to better staff morale in this hybrid world of work, with almost nine in 10 (87%) agreeing.	(P) LinkedIn also launched a new feature, 'funny reaction' for its members.
(B) Seven in 10 (70%) professionals believe there was a stigma around sharing feelings at work.	(Q) That doing so makes them more productive and boosts feelings of belonging, said a study released by LinkedIn on Tuesday.
(C) To accommodate professionals changing need for expressing emotions.	(R) Due to this, over a quarter of professionals are still worried about wearing their hearts on their sleeves.

(1) A-R, B-P, C-Q (2) A-Q, B-P

(3) A-Q, B-R, C-P (4) B-R, C-Q

(5) None of these

65.

Column 1	Column 2
(A) The trigger for the reforms in China were the twin projections of power by the US,	(P) to wage a modern war that could proscribe foreign powers from intervening in the region.
(B) The Chinese Communist Party leadership recognised that it lacked the technological prowess	(Q) namely the Gulf War of 1990 and the Taiwan Strait Crisis of 1995.
(C) In the wake of the Kargil War in 1999, India also started seriously thinking of reforming and modernizing	(R) its defence forces and command and control structures.

(1) A-Q, B-R, C-P (2) A-R, B-P, C-Q

(3) A-R, C-Q (4) A-Q, B-P, C-R

(5) None of these

66.

Column 1	Column 2
(A) 'Hermit' is the latest sophisticated spyware in the news, and it is believed to have	(P) the kernel information, model, manufacturer, OS, security patch, phone number, etc.
(B) Once installed on a device, it can record audio on the device,	(Q) carry out unauthorised calls, and carry out many unauthorised activities.
(C) It can also take pictures on the device, steal device information such as details about applications,	(R) targeted iPhones and Android devices in Italy and Kazakhstan.

(1) A-Q, C-R (2) A-P, B-Q, C-R

(3) A-R, B-Q, C-P (4) A-Q, B-R, C-P

(5) None of these

67.

Column 1	Column 2
(A) Under the anti-defection law, a member of a legislature can be disqualified	(P) were found in a truck on the road that stretches all the way to the U.S.- Mexico border.
(B) On Friday, a three-judge Bench of the top court had rejected a petition	(Q) if he or she has voluntarily given up membership of their political party.
(C) The police received an update on the situation from a worker of a building	(R) expressed the party's solidarity with the family members of former Lok Sabha member.

(1) B-P (2) C-Q
(3) B-R (4) A-Q
(5) None of these

Directions (68-72): *Seven sentences are given, in which the last sentence is fixed; also one sentence is going to be filled with the appropriate word. Arrange the sentences to form a meaningful paragraph. Out of the seven sentences, there is one sentence that does not fit into the theme of the passage thus formed. Read the sentences carefully and answer the questions that follow.*

A. India began its own Green Revolution program of plant breeding, irrigation development, and financing of agrochemicals.
B. A rapid expansion of small landowners did occur, but the peasantry as a whole did not acquire land.
C. The result of the White Revolution was that the rural population could be separated into three groups: prosperous farmers, small landowners, and village laborers.
D. In their place, though, emerged a new group of commercial farmers, and many previously large landowning families, such as the Pahlavi family, managed to renovate themselves into these commercial farmers.
E. Only roughly half of the rural population received any land, and many of the people who did receive land did not receive enough to themselves.
F. Land reform, which was the focus of the White Revolution, did what it was intended to do, weaken the nobles and landlords.
G. The first group was the only group to really benefit from the land reforms, and this group consisted of former village headmen, bailiffs, and some former landlords.

68. Find the sentence which doesn't fit into the context.
(1) C (2) D
(3) E (4) A
(5) B

69. Find the appropriate word to fill in the blank.
Only roughly half of the rural population received any land, and many of the people who did receive land did not receive enough to .... themselves.
(1) Torment (2) Sustain
(3) Plague (4) Agonize
(5) Excruciate

70. Which of the following should be the **FIFTH** sentence after rearrangement?
(1) F (2) A
(3) C (4) E
(5) B

71. Which of the following should be the **FOURTH** sentence after rearrangement?
(1) E (2) D
(3) C (4) A
(5) B

72. Which of the following should be the **SECOND** sentence after rearrangement?
(1) A (2) F
(3) C (4) B
(5) D

Directions (73-77): *In the question below, there are two statements. Each statement consists of two blanks. You have to choose the option which provides the correct set of words that fit both the blanks in both the statements appropriately and in the same order making them meaningful and grammatically correct.*

73. A major fire gutted a leading textile showroom in Surat, with fire and rescue services .... struggling to .... the blaze in an operation extending for over 10 hours.

Lake Superior and Abrahm fire .... reached the spot to .... the blaze. Officials brought the fire under control with the help of three fire engines.

(1) People, desiccate

(2) Personal, dehydrate

(3) Personnel, douse

(4) Security, dry

(5) Private, start

74. Abhishek was lauded for .... handling India's trade talks with RCEP, the China-led body that India didn't .... join.

Aamir Khan and Alaya F .... play unwilling dad and persistent daughter, though Tony Kakkar's film .... runs out of gas.

(1) Nimbly, immediately

(2) Deftly, Eventually

(3) gracefully, instantly

(4) Doubtfully, Lastly

(5) Unskillfully, Finally

75. Maintaining the status quo on tax rates also sends a strong signal to the .... that the government is committed to a long-term stable and predictable tax policy, despite the current fiscal ....

With institutional clients to worry about, the pros duly cut positions across the board while retail ...., who are free from such ...., charged on.

(1) Exporters, Allowance

(2) Importers, Allowance

(3) Investors, Constraints

(4) Financers, Liberty

(5) Importers, Freedom

76. The real advantage of this lens is that each area blends .... into the other, and even better, building an .... set that binds the lens and other parts of the telescope.

To determine your bridal style, first consider your wedding theme, as your overall hairstyle should mesh easily and .... with your vision giving rise to an .... appearance that takes the surrounding along with your desire.

(1) Brokenly, included

(2) Seamlessly, inclusive

(3) Abruptly, excluded

(4) Smooth, excluded

(5) Suddenly, exclusive

77. His eyes seemed to have .... all the fire of the world, and his tone was ...., his features being calm.

After his blood was .... we concluded that stimulants and strychnine may be given, but they should be avoided until it is certain the bleeding has been properly ...., as they tend to increase it.

(1) Get, constricted

(2) Collected, controlled

(3) withdrawn, owned

(4) Taken, owned

(5) Withdrawn, vague

Directions (78-80): *Which of the phrases given in the options should replace the word/phrase that is underlined in the sentence to make it grammatically correct? If the sentence is correct as it is and no correction is required, select 'No correction required' as the answer.*

78. Academies have been male bastions with the significant **inclusion** of women scientists, irrespective of their contributions and work.

(1) embracing (2) exclusion

(3) banishment (4) adoption

(5) assimilation

79. Resource management ought to give sufficient importance to the regeneration and

desolation of these material resources as well as the subtle resource that resides within us.

(1) reinvention (2) extinction
(3) reanimation (4) revitalization
(5) annihilation

80. The anti-dumping statute gives American firms an internationally recognised tool to seek relief from the **harmful** impacts of unfair import prices.

(1) encouraging (2) adverse
(3) adversely (4) favourable
(5) prosperous

Directions (81-86): *In the question below, a sentence is given. From the options, choose the one that conveys the same meaning as the given statement. If all of them convey the same meaning, mark E as your response.*

81. Corporate organizations have usually well-defined processes, which makes it a lot more difficult to get things done or influence the big picture.

A. Communication between the employees and the founders or management is open and transparent.

B. Many people are involved in the decisions and the decision process is often quite long and as logical as possible.

C. This fast-paced, dynamic environment can be extremely exciting and provides many opportunities to learn!

D. The work can differ from day to day and your roles and tasks can change entirely from one week to the next.

E. All are correct.

(1) A (2) B
(3) C (4) D
(5) E

82. Marketing is the activity, set of institutions, and processes for creating, communicating, delivering, and exchanging offerings that have value for customers.

A. It aims at promoting goods and services, pricing them, and making them available to customers.

B. It involves a substantial investment, interestingly, sales are the business process that generates revenue for the business.

C. The exchange of commodities for money; the action of selling something.

D. The main focus is to increase sales and maximize revenue.

E. All are correct.

(1) A (2) B
(3) C (4) D
(5) E

83. With physical learning, mentors and teachers have to be present in the classroom on location and only a limited number of students could benefit from this.

A. This tech-oriented approach to learning has helped students save a lot of time and their testimonials are living proof of this.

B. The biggest advantage is that you can literally learn from anywhere you like.

C. The commute up and down will take away a huge part of your time and not to mention the risks associated with travel and the energy you end up draining in the process.

D. Students can virtually be present inside the classrooms of some of the best teachers in the industry.

E. All are correct.

(1) A (2) B
(3) C (4) D
(5) E

84. Fellowship is focused on the development of a student by offering them study in a specific field.

A. It is offered to students or trainees interested in exploring and gaining more work experience in a particular industry.

B. It is mainly for undergraduate students in their final year, however, fresh graduates can also apply for it after they complete their studies.

C. For an internship program, companies display what they have on their websites or through other media and candidates have to apply.

D. It supports a range of different activities for purposes of research, graduates studies, developing community- based organizations, providing opportunities for exploring a field of work, and offering training.

E. All are correct.

(1) A (2) B
(3) C (4) D
(5) E

85. It is being constantly evolved for the inclusion of better-proven techniques for curing ailments and it also includes forms of treatment from alternative medicine fields once they are clinically tested and proven.

A. In this form of medication, the body of an ill person is exposed to similar kinds of other diseases, this helps them boost their immune system and fight against the disease.

B. In this form of medication, the body of an ill person is exposed to similar kinds of other diseases as it aims at curing the entire body.

C. It is also known as Modern Medicine and is based on proofs and successful clinical trials of medications.

D. A system of alternative medicine, which was developed by German physician Samuel Hahnemann, Homeopathy translates into 'similar suffering'.

E. All are correct.

(1) A (2) B
(3) C (4) D
(5) E

86. At a hospital, you see doctors with a variety of backgrounds who work together to deal with your medical concerns.

A. They typically cover the primary care needs of populations in local communities, in contrast to larger hospitals.

B. You may not always get the specialized care you need during your stay, but you can learn about the next steps in your care plan.

C. It may have extended hours and be open during evenings, weekends, and holidays.

D. A general clinic may not have the technology to help if you have a condition that requires specialized knowledge.

E. All are correct.

(1) A (2) B
(3) C (4) D
(5) E

Directions (87-90): *In the sentence, certain words are in bold and numbered from A to E, which are the possible pairs to be interchanged. Choose the pair(s) of words which need to be interchanged to make the sentence grammatically correct and meaningful.*

87. The company uses AI software **(A) installed** in the cameras to **(B) generating** video footage of traffic, **(C) analyse** data that helps local **(D) authorities** to plan traffic **(E) management.**

(1) A-C (2) B-D and A-E
(3) B-C (4) A-D
(5) C-E

88. The project has far-reaching **(A) notably** across cancer research, perhaps most **(B) consequences** in helping clinicians design treatment **(C) regimens** for individual cancer patients—bringing us closer to making what's called **(D) precision** medicine a **(E) reality**.

(1) A-B (2) C-D
(3) A-D (4) D-E
(5) None of these

89. Despite this **(A) unidentified** and the efforts of thousands of scientists working to **(B) ward** off dangerous new **(C) outbreaks**, the coronavirus behind COVID-19 was **(D) network** when it launched into an **(E) unprepared** world at the end of 2019.

(1) B-C (2) D-E
(3) A-D (4) A-C
(5) None of these

90. It is true that salmon and other fish have been **(A) banished** from rivers and **(B) depredations** in which they once **(C)**

abounded, but this was not **(D) owing** to the great **(E) creeks** of fishermen, as has generally been supposed.

(1) A-B (2) B-E
(3) C-D (4) D-E
(5) None of these

Reasoning Ability

Directions (91-94): *Read the given information and answer the following questions:*

Seven persons attends the interview in a week starting from Monday and ends on Sunday and they like different items T-shirt, Shoes, Top, Jeans, Bag, TV and Refrigerator, but not necessarily in the same order. Three persons attend the interview between R and the one who likes Refrigerator. Only two persons attend the interview after the one who likes Jeans. R attends the interview before the one who likes Refrigerator. Only one person attends the interview between N and the one who likes Top. The one who likes T-shirt attends the interview immediately before the one who likes Top. W does not like Top. The one who likes Bag attends the interview immediately before R. As many persons attend the interview before W as after N. G attends the interview immediately after the one who likes TV. N and G does not attend the interview consecutively. K attends the interview immediately after L. W does not like Shoes. P is one of the persons.

91. Four of the following five are like in a certain way based on the above arrangement. Find which of the following one does not belong to the group?

(1) G-Jeans (2) R-Shoes
(3) N-Top (4) W-T-shirt
(5) L-TV

92. Who among the following person attends the class immediately after K?

(1) G
(2) The one who bought refrigerator
(3) The one who bought bag
(4) P
(5) W

93. If P is related to Bag, R is related to Top, in the same way K is related to which of the following item?

(1) Refrigerator (2) Shoes
(3) Jean (4) TV
(5) Tops

94. How many persons attend the class after the one who bought shoes?

(1) No one (2) 1
(3) 2 (4) 3
(5) None of the above

Directions (95-98): *Read the given information and answer the following questions:*

In a hexagon arrangement, at each corner a triangle is placed which is denoted by two letters and two numbers. Below are given some of the conditions:

A. If the number is perfect square, then only the number is reduced by 1.
B. If there is at least one vowel then change it to the succeeding alphabet.
C. If both digits are odd then increase those digits by 2.
D. If any one of the consonants is greater than M in alphabetical order then change it to the previous alphabet.

Note: If no condition is applied then there will be no change. Apply the above given conditions to find the output. More than one condition is applicable.

For example,

	Input	Output
Triangle 1	4, 9	3, 8
Triangle 2	*u*, *p*	*v*, *o*
Triangle 3	2, 3	2, 3
Triangle 4	*e*, *r*	*f*, *q*
Triangle 5	*j*, *k*	*j*, *k*
Triangle 6	3, 3	5, 5

As per the rules followed in the above steps, find the steps required to rearrange the given input and answer the questions based on it.

Input

	Input
Triangle 1	r, p
Triangle 2	e, s
Triangle 3	5, 5
Triangle 4	t, x
Triangle 5	d, g
Triangle 6	2, 3

95. How many letters are there between the first letter of the output of triangle 1 and second letter of output of triangle 5?

(1) 11 (2) 8
(3) 10 (4) 7
(5) None of the above

96. What is the output of triangle 4?

(1) *u, y* (2) *t, x*
(3) *s, x* (4) *s, w*
(5) *t, r*

97. What is the sum of first number of output of triangle 3 and the second number of output of triangle 6?

(1) 10 (2) 9
(3) 8 (4) 7
(5) 6

98. What is the sum of the product of numbers of output of triangle 3 and product of numbers of output of triangle 6?

(1) 31 (2) 55
(3) 49 (4) 61
(5) None of the above

99. In the given word "AUTHORISE" replace the consonants with the succeeding letter as per the English alphabet series and vowel with their preceding letter as per the English alphabet series. Then arrange the letters in reverse alphabetical order from right to left. Which of the following letter is third from the left end after arrangement?

(1) D (2) H
(3) I (4) N
(5) S

Directions (100-102): *In the questions below are given three statements followed by conclusions given in the options. You have to take the given statements to be true even if they seem to be variance with commonly known facts. Read all the conclusions and then decide which of the given conclusions definitely follow from the given statements disregarding commonly known facts.*

100. Statement:

Some apples are mango.
No mango is papaya.
Only a few papayas are kiwi.

Conclusion:

I. Some papayas are not kiwi
II. All mangoes are kiwi is a possibility
III. Some apples are not kiwi

(1) Only III follows
(2) Both I and II follows
(3) Both I and III follows
(4) Either I or II and III follows
(5) All I, II, III follows

101. Statement:

Some fruits are jam
Only a few jams are butter.
All butter is gee

Conclusion:

I. All gee can be jam
II. Some butters are not jam
III. All butter are fruit is a possibility

(1) Only II (2) Both I and II
(3) Both I and III
(4) Either I or II and III
(5) All I, II, III

102. Statement:

Only a few cars are van.
All van is jeep
No jeep is bus

Conclusion:

I. Some buses are car.
II. No bus is car.
III. All jeep are car is a possibility.

(1) Only III follows
(2) Both I and II follows

(3) Both I and III follows

(4) Either I or II and III follows

(5) All I, II, III follows

Directions (103-106): *In each of the questions below consists of a question and two statements numbered I and II given below it. You have to decide whether the data provided in the statements are sufficient to answer the question. Read both the statements and Give answer.*

103. There are six family members G, K, S, T, R and V in a family. How is V related to R?

Statement I: G is the father of V. K is the grandson of S. T is the wife of R.

Statement II: K is the son of T. T is the daughter of S. V is the sibling of S.

(1) If the data in statement I alone are sufficient to answer the question, while the data in statement II alone are not sufficient to answer the question

(2) If the data in statement II alone are sufficient to answer the question, while the data in statement I alone are not sufficient to answer the question

(3) If the data either in statement, I alone or in statement II alone are sufficient to answer the question

(4) If the data given in both statements I and II together are not sufficient to answer the question

(5) If the data in both statements I and II together are necessary to answer the question

104. Seven persons P, Q, R, S, T, U and V attend the seminar in a week starting from Monday and ending on Sunday. In which of the following day does S attend the seminar?

Statement I: P attend the seminar after three persons. Two persons have attended the seminar in between P and T. U attends the seminar just after T. Q attend the seminar on Saturday.

Statement II: R attend the seminar just after P. Only one person attends the seminar between R and V. V and Q attend the seminar in an adjacent day.

(1) If the data in statement I alone are sufficient to answer the question, while the data in statement II alone are not sufficient to answer the question

(2) If the data in statement II alone are sufficient to answer the question, while the data in statement I alone are not sufficient to answer the question

(3) If the data either in statement I alone or in statement II alone are sufficient to answer the question

(4) If the data given in both statements I and II together are not sufficient to answer the question

(5) If the data in both statements I and II together are necessary to answer the question

105. Six persons K, L, M, N, O and P are sitting in a circular table facing inside the table. Who among the following sits to the immediate left of K?

Statement I: O sits second to the left of N. M sits third to the right of N. Only one person sits between M and L.

Statement II: P sits second to the right of N. Two persons sit between P and L. M sits to the immediate left of O.

(1) If the data in statement I alone are sufficient to answer the question, while the data in statement II alone are not sufficient to answer the question

(2) If the data in statement II alone are sufficient to answer the question, while the data in statement I alone are not sufficient to answer the question

(3) If the data either in statement, I alone or in statement II alone are sufficient to answer the question

(4) If the data given in both statements I and II together are not sufficient to answer the question

(5) If the data in both statements I and II together are necessary to answer the question

106. Six friends A, B, C, D, E and F are of different weights. Whose weight is the lightest?

Statement I: A is heavier than C. C is heavier

than both E and F.

Statement II: B is heavier than D who is heavier than E. E is not the lightest person.

(1) If the data in statement I alone are sufficient to answer the question, while the data in statement II alone are not sufficient to answer the question

(2) If the data in statement II alone are sufficient to answer the question, while the data in statement I alone are not sufficient to answer the question

(3) If the data either in statement, I alone or in statement II alone are sufficient to answer the question

(4) If the data given in both statements I and II together are not sufficient to answer the question

(5) If the data in both statements I and II together are necessary to answer the question

Directions (107-108): *Study the following information carefully and answer the questions given below.*

X + Y – X is the brother of Y

X % Y – X is the mother of Y

X ! Y – X is the father of Y

X * Y – X is the sister of Y

X # Y – X is the daughter of Y

X @ Y – X is the son of Y

X ~ Y – X is elder than Y

$ – in-law

© - grand

Example:

If X %$ Y → X is the mother-in-law of Y, X * $ Y → X is sister-in-law of Y

If X ©% Y → X is Grand Mother of Y, X © # Y → X is Granddaughter of Y

M # P © % J; N + $ R; O + $ B ! $ S % J # R; P * O ~ B; N @ $ B; B ~ P

107. If the age of O is 49 and age of P is 46 then what may be the age of B?

(1) 48 (2) 45
(3) 50 (4) 46
(5) 44

108. Which of the following pair is incorrect relation?

(1) M * $ S (2) R + $ N
(3) R @ B (4) M * B
(5) J # S

Directions (109-111): *In the following questions, the symbols @, +, ©, $ and # are used with the following meaning:*

'A @ B' means 'A is neither greater than nor equal to B'.

'A + B' means 'A is not smaller than B'.

'A © B' means 'A is not greater than B'.

'A $ B' means 'A is neither smaller than nor greater than B'.

'A # B' means 'A is neither smaller than nor equal to B'.

109. Statements: 3 $ 9 + 7 © 8 # 6; 7 @ 6 + 5; 6 + 4 © 2

Conclusions:

I. 9 # 5

II. 2 @ 8

III. 7 @ 3

(1) Only conclusions I and III follow

(2) Only conclusion II follows

(3) Only conclusions II and III follow

(4) Only conclusion I follows

(5) None follow

110. Statements: G © U + N $ K; R # P @ N + M; P + Q # D

Conclusions:

I. U # Q

II. R # U

III. D @ R

(1) Only conclusions I and III follow

(2) Only conclusion II follows

(3) Only conclusions II and III follow

(4) Only conclusion I follows

(5) None follow

111. Statements: P # R © T + C; I $ G @ T; P + H

Conclusions:

I. T # I

II. T @ H
III. P @ T
(1) Only conclusion I and III follow
(2) Only conclusion II follows
(3) Only conclusion II and III follow
(4) Only conclusion I follows
(5) None follow

Directions (112-115): *Read the given information and answer the following questions:*

In the given matrix rows are numbered from top to bottom i.e., I, II, III and IV and columns are numbered left to right i.e., I, II, III and IV. Some of the places is filled with respective colors in the matrix, and some are missing. To find the respective color of the missing places on the matrix fill it in a way such that no same color is repeated in a row nor in a column.

There are four colors i.e., red, green, blue, and yellow and a specific numerical value is assigned to each place in the matrix which is the value associated with each colour and the value assigned to these colors is, 2, 3, 4 and 5 respectively.

Now resultant of rows and columns are written in specific manner. For each row, write associated numerical value from left to right in that row and for a column write respective numerical value from bottom to top.

Blue			
		Green	
	Red		
Yellow		Red	

112. In which of the following pair blue and green are consecutive?
(1) Row I, Row III (2) Row II, Row III
(3) Row II, Row IV (4) Row I, Row II
(5) None of these

113. Which of the following resultant is divisible by 4?
(1) Row II (2) Row III
(3) Row IV (4) Column I
(5) Column II

114. What is the difference of resultant of row IV and column IV?
(1) 2000 (2) 2032
(3) 1754 (4) 1881
(5) 1672

115. If the resultant of a row is even, then add 222 to get the new resultant and if the resultant of column is odd then subtract 111 to get the new resultant. After rearrangement which of the following is true?
I. Resultant of row I is less than the resultant of column III
II. A difference of resultant of row II and column I is odd
III. Sum of the digits of resultant of row IV is even
(1) Only I and II (2) Only II and III
(3) Only III (4) Only II
(5) All of the above

Directions (116-120): *Read the given information and answer the following questions:*

21 persons work in bank at different post. The posts are in decreasing order i.e., Chairman, GM, Manager, AM, PO and Clerk. It is known that in any post the number of persons posted were one more than the number of persons posted in the immediate senior post. For example: If 4 person works as a PO then 5 persons work as a clerk. E works as a manager and is just senior to Z. C and G work at same post and were senior to E. F, Q and R work at same post and were junior to Z. A is just junior to W but just senior to R. P, T and Y work at same post but not with A. V is junior to Z but senior to J. K and O work at same post but does not work as a clerk. S does not work along with U and P. D is senior to M and junior to S. U and B work at same place.

116. O work at which post?
(1) GM (2) Manager
(3) AM (4) PO
(5) Clerk

117. Which of the following is at same post with C?
(1) E (2) W
(3) Z (4) A
(5) G

118. How many persons were at same post with Y

(excluding Y)?

(1) 2 (2) 3
(3) 4 (4) 5
(5) 1

119. Who among the following works as manager?

(1) Z (2) D
(3) E (4) More than one option
(5) None of these

120. How many persons are junior to S?

(1) 6 (2) 11
(3) 15 (4) 18
(5) 20

Directions (121-124): *Read the given information and answer the following questions:*

Eight persons A to H live in a four Storey building. The ground floor is numbered 1. Each floor consists of two flats i.e., Flat P and Flat Q. Flat P is to the west of Flat Q. Only one person lives in each flat. Each of them like different games i.e., cricket, chess, tennis, volleyball, skating, basketball, football and hockey, not necessarily in the same order. Floor 2 of flat P is just above the floor 1 of flat P and so on.

C lives on second floor and lives just below the person who likes chess. One floor is between the person who likes skating and football and both of them live in flat P. The person who likes Tennis and A lives on same floor but different flat. One floor is between the person who likes cricket and A. Number of floors above D is same as number of floors below G, who lives below D in different flat. The person who likes basketball lives in west of E. No person lives in west of the person who likes chess and C. The person who likes volleyball lives two floors above B. F does not like skating. The person who likes cricket lives on an odd number floor. B lives just below H.

121. How many floors are between A and E?

(1) None (2) One
(3) Two (4) Can't be determined
(5) None of the above

122. Which of the following statement is true?

(1) E likes hockey. (2) B lives on 3rd floor.
(3) D lives just above H.
(4) C lives on 1st floor.
(5) None of these

123. H likes which game?

(1) Volleyball (2) Chess
(3) Hockey (4) Skating
(5) Tennis

124. Who likes football?

(1) The one who lives just above A
(2) The one who lives just below B
(3) C (4) D
(5) G

Directions (125-126): *Read the given information and answer the following questions:*

In a company XYZ, during the training program few organizations are organized in a day for different departments i.e., HR, IT and Admin. Two HR, Two IT and one Admin orientation session with each session being of 1 hour. Also, for the new joinee a two-hour departmental training is organized on this day. These sessions are organized from 10 am to 7 pm. Two breaks are there between these sessions, 1 pm to 2 pm lunch and 5 pm to 6 pm tea.

None of the same department orientation are consecutive including breaks (for example: If HR orientation is at 12 pm slot then the other HR orientation can't be at 2 pm nor 11 pm slot). None of the HR orientation is after tea. Xena, who was the invigilator of these orientation session, left the departmental training session at 4 : 30 pm due to some personal reason for few minutes. First slot is not of HR. Last slot is of IT orientation. Admin session is just before one of the breaks.

125. Which sessions are between the two breaks?

(1) HR and Admin
(2) Admin and Departmental training
(3) IT and HR
(4) IT and Departmental training
(5) HR and Departmental training

126. How many sessions are there between the two IT sessions excluding breaks?

(1) 3 (2) 4
(3) 5 (4) 6
(5) 2

Directions (127-130): *Read the given information and answer the following questions:*

Nine persons Arnold, Barry, Charlie, Dove, Erwin, Frank, Gerald, Henry and John was born in different years on the same date in the month of June. Calculation is done from the base year of 2022. No person is younger than 5 years nor older than 75 years. Note: If it's given age of "A" is equal to the last two digit of the birth year of B then it can be the last digits or the reverse of last two digits.

Arnold was born in the year 1985. Age difference between Erwin and Frank is 12 years. Barry's age is equal to the last two digits of birth year of Arnold. Charlie's age is equal to the last two digits of birth year of Barry.

Dove's age is equal to the last two digits of birth year of Charlie. Erwin's age is equal to the last two digits of birth year of Dove. Gerald's age is sum of the digits of birth year of Frank. John is 6 years younger than Gerald. Henry is 9 years younger than Gerald.

127. Find the odd one out.
(1) Gerald (2) Frank
(3) Henry (4) Erwin
(5) Arnold

128. Who is the eldest person among them?
(1) Arnold (2) Barry
(3) Charlie (4) Dove
(5) Erwin

129. Erwin was born in which year?
(1) 1962 (2) 1960
(3) 1953 (4) 1967
(5) 1979

130. What is the difference of age between youngest and 3rd eldest?
(1) 31 (2) 26
(3) 24 (4) 38
(5) 22

Directions (131-134): *Study the following information carefully and answer the questions given below:*

A number and word arrangement machine when given an input line of numbers and words rearranges them following a particular rule in each step. The following is an illustration of input and rearrangement

Input:	**2193**	**4638**	**1825**	**2437**	**4769**	**5225**
Step I:	1825	2193	2437	4638	4769	5225
Step II:	1258	1239	2347	3468	4679	2255
Step III:	313	312	511	714	1016	410
Step IV:	9	6	5	28	6	0
Step V:	28	9	6	6	5	0

Step V is the last step.

As per the rules followed in the above steps, find the steps required to rearrange the given input and answer the questions based on it.

Input: 6482 5113 9438 2799 6619 4431

131. What is the sum of the digits of last three numbers in step V?
(1) 26 (2) 28
(3) 14 (4) 18
(5) None of these

132. What is the addition of the largest number and the smallest number in step IV?
(1) 82 (2) 88
(3) 102 (4) 84
(5) 40

133. What is the product of second digit of the second number from the left end and third digit of the third number from the right end in step III?
(1) 40 (2) 35
(3) 32 (4) 72
(5) 30

134. What is the difference between second largest number in step I and second smallest number in step II?
(1) 4376 (2) 5375
(3) 3755 (4) 7355
(5) 5275

Directions (135-136): *Study the following information carefully and answer the below questions:*

Statement: "Sudden decline in GST tax collection pulled down overall rise in gross direct tax mobilization in the first half of the current year, ruling out any pickup in growth in the first quarter of the year, indicating that the government will find it difficult to meet its tax target for this year."

Inferences:

I. GST tax collection rise only in the first quarter of the current year.

II. Industrial production and development slowed down in the first half of the year.

III. The government has achieved the target of corporate as well as GST tax collection in comparison to previous year.

IV. Poor tax collection in the GST tax collection pulled down the economy of our country.

V. The government is likely to face difficulties in achieving the target of collection of GST tax due to slowdown in production and the government has forecast a growth in GST tax.

135. Which of the inferences numbered (I), (II), (III), (IV), and (V) can be concluded from the fact/information given in the statement?

(1) Only II (2) Only II and V

(3) Only III and IV (4) Only IV

(5) Only III

136. **Statement:** Computers can finish the task with the help of coding languages which are comprehensible for human beings but the computer needs the compiler software to read those commands.

What are the conclusions that will be derived from the above passage?

(1) Computers can work by themselves to complete a task. (2) Humans need to train the computers to do a certain task by using the specific commands.

(3) Both options (IV) and (V) follow.

(4) Computer systems use certain conversion methods to read the codes.

(5) Computers cannot do the tasks without the help of the compiler software.

Directions (137-138): *Read the following paragraph carefully and answer the question that follows:*

137. **Statement:** Players like Amazon and Flipkart as well as industry watchers noted that the need for social distancing and prioritizing safety during the pandemic led to millions of people turning to e-commerce platforms this past year, not only in metros but also in tier III regions and beyond.

Inferences:

I. The pandemic brought about a "structural shift" in shopping behavior with more and more customers and businesses relying on e-commerce.

II. The Indian e-commerce market has been one of the biggest beneficiaries of the pandemic.

III. The new normal of working and learning from home also fueled demand for consumer electronic products.

(1) Only III follows (2) Only I and III follow

(3) Only II follows

(4) Only I and either II or III follows

(5) Only I and II follow

138. In the question, the statement is given followed by some inferences. You must consider the statement to be true even if it seems to be at variance from commonly known facts. You must decide which of the given inference, if any, is a strong argument.

Statement: Aishwarya likes to write from a very young age especially, she likes to write poetries. She also maintains a journal for her poetries which she plans to publish as an anthology.

What are the facts that can be inferred from the above passage?

(1) Aishwarya always likes to write poetry

(2) Aishwarya has written many poems

(3) Aishwarya has good poetic skills

(4) Aishwarya is planning to publish an anthology

(5) Aishwarya had an inborn talent to write poetry

139. Read the given statement and with that information answer the following question carefully:

After GST and demonetization, rising interest rates are set to hurt SMEs. Interest rates for loans against property (LAP) extended to small and medium-sized enterprises (SMEs) are set to rise in the coming months of 2018. 'Rising interest rates, in addition to the muted operating environment for small businesses in India, will lead to an increase in delinquencies on LAP extended to SMEs'. The introduction of the goods and services tax (GST) in July 2017 and the government's demonetization policy have placed stress on the SME sector, which rising interest rates will exacerbate.

Which of the following can be logically inferred from the statement above?

(1) In addition to rising delinquencies over the last few years would force lenders to be more cautious while underwriting loans. This would limit refinancing options, adversely affecting existing borrowers.

(2) But losses will be limited because these loans are secured and have relatively low loan-to-value ratios.

(3) Rising interest rates will limit refinancing options and increase repayment amounts, increasing risks for asset backed securities (ABS) backed by LAP to SMEs.

(4) The ABS (asset backed securities) backed by LAP extended to SMEs have non-amortizing cash reserves, substantial excess spread and the possibility to extend the life of the loans and hence the life of the transactions.

(5) None can be inferred

140. Read the passage given below carefully and answer the given question:

Statement: An oil painting by the late Chinese French artist Zao Wou Ki became the most expensive oil painting ever sold at auction by an Asian artist. The painting fetched $65 million in the auction at Sotheby's Hong Kong.

Which of the following does not support the statement?

I. The oil painting by the late Chinese-French artist became the most expensive oil painting ever sold at auction.

II. The auction at Sotheby's Hong Kong on the painting fetched $65 million which is the highest till date for any artist.

III. Zao Wou-Ki was an Asian artist to ever sell the most expensive oil painting.

(1) Only I (2) Only II

(3) Only I and II (4) Only II and III

(5) All of the above

Quantitative Aptitude

Directions (141-145): *Answer the questions based on the information given below.*

The pie chart given below shows the percentage distribution of students present in different sections of 5th class of a school on Monday.

The percentage distribution of students present

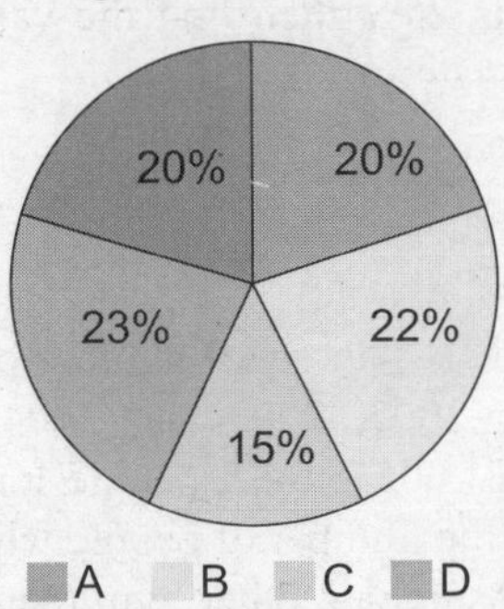

Note:

I. Difference between the number of students present in section 'A' and section 'B' is 4.

II. In each of the sections 'B', 'C', 'D', and 'E', the total number of students (Present + Absent) is less than 51.

III. No section has full attendance.

141. If absent students in section 'A' is 40% more than the present students and the ratio of absent students (Boys + Girls) is 5 : 3, then find the absent girl students in section 'A' is what percentage of the total present students in section 'C'?

(1) 40% (2) 50%

(3) 60% (4) 70%

(5) 80%

142. If 10 students who were present in section 'A', shifted to section 'C', then what is the sum of the maximum and minimum possible total (present + absent) students in section 'C'?

(1) 40 (2) 41
(3) 50 (4) 90
(5) 91

143. What is the difference between the maximum possible value of absent students in section 'B' and 3rd minimum possible value of absent students in section 'E'?

(1) 2 (2) 3
(3) 4 (4) 5
(5) 6

144. If the value of absent students in section 'C' is greater than 7 and the total number of students (present + absent) in section 'C' is a 'square' number, then what is the difference between the absent students in section 'C' and total present students in section 'A' and section 'E' together?

(1) 61 (2) 62
(3) 63 (4) 64
(5) 65

145. If it is given that the sum of maximum and minimum possible values of absent students in section 'D' is 4, then what is the maximum total number of students (Present + absent) in section 'D'?

(1) 46 (2) 47
(3) 48 (4) 49
(5) 50

146. A question is followed by 2 statements. Study the following statements carefully and state whether they are sufficient to answer the question.

A student appears in an examination where his marks in biology is 20 marks more than what he got in Physics. Find his marks in biology?

Statement I: Average marks of Physics and Chemistry is 71.5. The ratio of marks of Practical and Theory in Physics is 6 : 5 and in chemistry, it is 15 : 7.

Statement II: Ratio of marks obtained in the theory exam of physics and chemistry is 1 : 2. The ratio of marks of Physics and Chemistry is 5 : 8.

(1) Statement I alone is sufficient
(2) Statement II alone is sufficient
(3) Neither of the statement is sufficient
(4) Both I and II together is sufficient
(5) Either I or II is sufficient

147. A train can cross a car which is running with speed 40 km/h in same direction as that of train in 18 seconds while the train can cross a platform of length half of the length of train in 13.5 seconds, then what is the length of the platform?

(1) 150 m (2) 100 m
(3) 120 m (4) 80 m
(5) None of these

Directions (148-152): *Answer the questions based on the information given below.*

The line graph given below shows the total number of members (Males + Females) in four fitness gyms for the year 2001 and 2005.

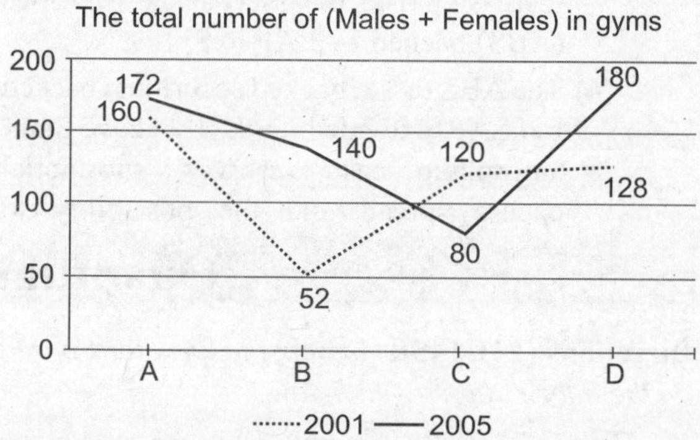

148. If in gym 'B', the percentage increase of the gym members from 2001 to 2003 is x%, from 2003 to 2004 is 20% and from 2004 to 2005 is 25% then find the value of 'x' ? (approximately)

(1) 75.5% (2) 76.5%
(3) 77.5% (4) 79.5%
(5) 80.5%

149. If in gym 'B', an equal number of members joined in 2002, 2003 and 2004 and from 2001 and 2005 only 5 people left the gym, then find the number of people who joined in 2002. (Assume no other gym member left or joined in any given year other than the given data)

(1) 31 (2) 32
(3) 33 (4) 34
(5) 35

150. If the total number of male gym members in gym 'C' and gym 'A' together in 2001 is 100 and in 2001, the total number of male members in gym 'A' was 75% of the total gym members in gym 'B' in 2001, then find the total number of female gym members in gym 'C' in 2001 is what percent of the total number of gym members in gym 'C' in 2005?

(1) 71.25% (2) 72.50%
(3) 73.75% (4) 74.25%
(5) 75.75%

151. If in 2005, the ratio of the number of female to male gym members in gym 'C' is 9 : 7 respectively and only in the year 2004 few members left the gym in which the number of females was 15%, then how many female members were there initially in gym 'C' in 2001?

(1) 51 (2) 52
(3) 53 (4) 54
(5) 55

152. In 2002, in gym D, the percentage increase of total members from the previous year is 25% in which males are 37.5% of the new gym members who joined and the new male members are 20% more than the number of male members present in the previous year. In 2004, 20 female members joined the gym. Find the ratio of the number of female members initially in 2001 and the number of female members in 2005. (Assume no other member joined or left in any year other than the given data)

(1) 59 : 79 (2) 61 : 79
(3) 67 : 79 (4) 71 : 79
(5) 73 : 79

Directions (153-156): *Answer the questions based on the information given below.*

There are four companies A, B, C, and D. Data given below shows the number of products sold and unsold by these shopkeepers.

The total number of products manufactured by 'A' is 120, and the ratio of sold and unsold products of company 'B' is 3 : 1. The total number of products manufactured by company 'B' and 'D' is 260, and the difference between the number of unsold and sold products by 'C' is 90. The total number of products manufactured by 'C' is 150 which is 12 less than that of products sold by 'D'. The difference between the products unsold by 'B' and 'D' is 2. The number of products sold by 'A' is x% as that of 'B'.

Note: The number of products sold by each company is more than that of products unsold.

153. If the total number of products sold by all companies together is 432, then find the number of unsold products by company 'D' is how much percent more or less that of 'A'?

(1) 25% (2) 30%
(3) 40% (4) 50%
(5) 60%

154. If the number of products sold by company 'A' is 140% more than the products unsold by company 'C', then find the value of 'x'?

(1) 120% (2) 125%
(3) 133.33% (4) 150%
(5) 166.66%

155. If the number of products unsold by 'A' is 30, and the number of products manufactured by 'E' is thrice that of company 'D', then find the number of unsold products of company 'E', if the sold products of company 'E' is $2x$.

(1) 60 (2) 80
(3) 100 (4) 120
(5) 240

156. If the difference between the number of products sold by 'C' and the total products manufactured by 'D' is 'Y' and the total number of products manufactured by 'B' is 'Z', then 'Y' is how much percent more or less than that of 'Z'?

(1) 20% (2) 25%
(3) 33.33% (4) 37.5%
(5) 50%

157. Consider the following number series and answer the question based on this.

18, 10, 12, 27, x, p $z + 4 = x - 27$

Find the value of p?

(1) 899 (2) 900

(3) 901 (4) 902

(5) 903

158. Which of the following is true about the value of z?

(1) z is an even number.

(2) z is a prime number.

(3) z is a perfect square number.

(4) z is greater than 90.

(5) Sum of digits of z is more than 20.

159. **Series I :** 14, x, 37, 53, 72

Series II : 48, x, 26, 53, 213, 1705

Series III : 8, 15, x, 35, 48, 63

The value of x is 24.

In which of the following series 'x' is not satisfied properly?

(1) Only I (2) Only II

(3) Only III (4) Only I and II

(5) Only II and III

Directions (160-164): *Answer the questions based on the information given below.*

The table given below shows the data of the total funds of 4 different companies and funds denoted by each company to 3 different NGOs.

Company	Total fund (Rs.)	% donated to NGO 'A'	% donated to NGO 'B'	% donated to NGO 'C'
W	Rs. 12000	32%	---	24%
X	---	64%	16%	Rs. 1905
Y	---	33%	---	27%
Z	Rs. 13500	---	52%	---

Note: (1) Sum of the percentage distribution in each company is 100.

(2) Ratio between the total funds of company 'W' to company 'Y' is 4 : 5 respectively.

(3) Some of the values are missing.

160. If the fund donated to NGO 'B' by company 'W' was distributed to an orphan child and elder person in 9 : 7 respectively, then find the difference between the fund donated to the elder person of NGO 'B' and the total fund of company 'X'?

(1) Rs. 7115 (2) Rs. 7215

(3) Rs. 7315 (4) Rs. 7415

(5) Rs. 7515

161. If the total fund of company 'X' is part of their 'actual plan' and it is only 40% of their actual fund then the total fund donated to NGO 'A' and NGO 'B' by company 'X' is what percent of their actual fund?

(1) 30% (2) 31%

(3) 32% (4) 33%

(5) 34%

162. If 20% of the fund donated to NGO 'B' by the company 'Y' was utilized in 'women's development and the rest was for 'rural development' then find the ratio between the fund utilized in women's development by NGO 'B' and fund donated by company 'Z' to NGO 'B'?

(1) 20 : 101 (2) 20 : 103

(3) 20 : 107 (4) 20 : 111

(5) 20 : 117

163. If the fund donated by company Z in NGO 'A' and NGO 'C' was in the ratio of 4 : 5, then find the fund donated to NGO 'C' was what percent of the total fund of company 'Z'?

(1) 13.33% (2) 16.66%

(3) 26.66% (4) 33.33%

(5) 42.22%

164. If another company 'V' has a fund that was 30% more than that of company 'Y' and company 'V' donated 30%, 25%, and 45% to NGO 'A', NGO 'B', and NGO 'C' respectively then find the sum of the fund donated to NGO 'C' by company 'V' and fund donated to NGO 'A' by company 'X'?

(1) Rs. 11871 (2) Rs. 12871

(3) Rs. 13871 (4) Rs. 14871

(5) Rs. 15871

Directions (165-169): *In this question two equations numbered I and II are given. You have to solve both the equations and find out the correct option.*

165. I. $x^2 - 17x + 72 = 0$

II. $y^2 - 17y + 70 = 0$

(1) $x > y$ (2) $x < y$

(3) $x \geq y$ (4) $x \leq y$

(5) $x = y$ or no relationship could be established

166. I. $x^2 - 56x + 343 = 0$

II. $2y^2 + 23y + 60 = 0$

(1) $x > y$ (2) $y \leq x$

(3) $y \geq x$ (4) $x < y$

(5) Either $x = y$ or Relation between x and y cannot be established.

167. I. $x^2 - 5x + 6 = 0$

II. $y^2 - 9y + 20 = 0$

(1) $x > y$ (2) $x < y$

(3) $x \geq y$ (4) $x \leq y$

(5) $x = y$ or relationship between x and y cannot be established

168. I. $x^2 - 2x - 35 = 0$

II. $y^2 + y - 42 = 0$

(1) $x > y$ (2) $y \leq x$

(3) $y \geq x$ (4) $x < y$

(5) Either $x = y$ or Relationship between x and y cannot be established.

169. I. $2x^2 - 13x + 21 = 0$

II. $3y^2 - 16y + 21 = 0$

(1) $x > y$ (2) $y \leq x$

(3) $y \geq x$ (4) $x < y$

(5) Either $x = y$ or Relationship between x and y cannot be established.

170. What approximate value should come in the place of question mark (?) in the following question?

$79.99 \times 24.14 \times 6.97 \div 27.98 = ?2 + 38.99$

(1) 31 (2) 29

(3) 19 (4) 23

(5) 21

171. What approximate value should come in the place of the question mark '?' in the following question?

17.77% of 399.99 + 42.14% of 249.99 = ? – 15.99% of 199.98

(1) 219 (2) 209

(3) 229 (4) 199

(5) 239

172. What approximate value will come in the place of the question mark '?' in the following question?

$(6.95 \times 7.988) - (12.004 \times \sqrt{9.012}) = ? - 10.895$

(1) 40 (2) 45

(3) 31 (4) 25

(5) 37

173. What approximate value should come in the place of question mark (?) in the following question?

$(45.875 - 34.75) \times (23.89 - 15.99) = ? + (34.87 - 17.98)$

(1) 80 (2) 65

(3) 71 (4) 75

(5) 78

Directions (174-175): *The question consists of two statements numbered "I" and "II" given below it. You have to decide whether the data provided in the statements are sufficient to answer the question or not and choose the correct option accordingly.*

174. An alloy contains zinc and copper in the ratio of 12 : 11 respectively. Find the original quantity of copper in the alloy?

Statement I: If 20% of the alloy is replaced with the same quantity of copper then the ratio of the zinc to copper becomes 48 : 67.

Statement II: If 125 kg of copper is added to the alloy, then the ratio of zinc to copper becomes 3 : 4.

(1) The data in statement I alone is sufficient to answer, while the data in statement II alone is not sufficient to answer the question.

(2) The data in statement II alone is sufficient to answer, while the data in statement I alone is not sufficient to answer the question.

(3) The data either in statement I alone or in statement II alone are sufficient to answer the question.

(4) The data given in both statements I and II together are not sufficient to answer the question.

(5) The data in both statements I and II together are necessary to answer the

question.

175. The ratio of the cost prices of articles 'A', 'B' and 'C' is 8 : 5 : 3. The percentage by which article 'A', article 'B' and article 'C' are marked up is 80%, 60%, and 40% respectively. Find the cost price of article 'C' ?

Statement (I): The ratio of the selling prices of article 'A', article 'B', and article 'C' is 10 : 7 : 13.

Statement (II): Total profit earned on the three articles is Rs. 120 less than the total discount given on the three articles together.

(1) The data in statement I alone is sufficient to answer, while the data in statement II alone is not sufficient to answer the question.
(2) The data in statement II alone is sufficient to answer, while the data in statement I alone is not sufficient to answer the question.
(3) The data either in statement I alone or in statement II alone are sufficient to answer the question.
(4) The data given in both statements I and II together are not sufficient to answer the question.
(5) The data in both statements I and II together are necessary to answer the question.

176. Given question contains a statement followed by two statements are numbered as Quantity I and Quantity II. On solving these statements, we get quantities I and II respectively. Solve both quantities and choose the correct option.

If $a^5 = 32$ and $b^6 = 64$

Quantity I: Value of b.

Quantity II: Value of a.

(1) Quantity I > Quantity II
(2) Quantity II > Quantity I
(3) Quantity II ≥ Quantity I
(4) Quantity I ≥ Quantity II
(5) Cannot be determined

177. A receives 1/15th of the total profit and the remaining is divided between B and C in the ratio of 3 : 4. If the difference between the profit shares of C and A is Rs. 2800. What is B's share?

(1) Rs. 2000 (2) Rs. 2200
(3) Rs. 2300 (4) Rs. 2400
(5) None of these

178. Narender can do 4/5th of work in 20 days. The efficiency of Ajay is 25% more than that of Narender. Both Narender and Ajay started working together and left the work after five days. Neha completed the remaining work in 11 days. The efficiency of Neha is how much percent more/less than that of Narender?

(1) 25% less (2) 20% less
(3) 20% more (4) 25% more
(5) None of these

179. A bag contains 8 red and 5 blue balls. Two balls are drawn randomly. Find the probability that one ball is red and other is blue.

(1) 20/39 (2) 10/29
(3) 25/39 (4) 1/13
(5) None of the above

180. Difference between compound interest and simple interest on Rs. 7200 for 2 years at x% per annum is Rs. 200. Find the value of x.

(1) 15% (2) 15.1%
(3) 16.2 % (4) 18%
(5) None of the above

181. The total time taken by the boat to go 'x' km upstream and then return back to a certain distance is 6 hours. The ratio of the speed boat in still water to the speed of the stream is 8 : 1, respectively. If the upstream distance covered is 50 km more than the downstream distance covered and the boat can cover $(3x + 60)$ km in still water in 12 hours, then find the value of 'x'?

(1) 120 km (2) 128 km
(3) 140 km (4) 150 km
(5) 158 km

182. A person can cover a distance between A and B at a speed of 45 km/hr. On the return journey, he covers 180 km with 30 km/hr, and after that, he takes a different route on the return journey which increases his total distance by 15 km. If the speed of the car on the extended route is 60 km/hr. If it takes 90 min more while returning then find the distance between A and B.

(1) 310 km (2) 315 km
(3) 320 km (4) 325 km
(5) 330 km

183. The age of the mother 4 years ago was 6 times the age of her son at that time. The age of the mother after 6 years will be 8/3 times the age of the son at the time. Find the difference between the mother's age after 2 years and the present age of the son.

(1) 2 : 3 (2) 3 : 2
(3) 4 : 1 (4) 5 : 2
(5) 6 : 5

184. The volume of a cylinder is 13552 cube cm and the diameter of the cylinder is equal to the side of a square whose perimeter is 112 cm. Find the curved surface area of the cylinder.

(1) 1345 sq. cm (2) 1540 sq. cm
(3) 1856 sq. cm (4) 1936 sq. cm
(5) 2090 sq. cm

185. There are 6 consecutive odd numbers. If the product of the 1st and the 2nd number is 483, then find the average of all the numbers.

(1) 22 (2) 24
(3) 26 (4) 27
(5) 28

186. The ratio of the number of boys to the number of girls is 8 : 5 and the average age of the whole class is 'x' and the average age of girls is '$x - 2$' then find the average age of boys in the class.

(1) $x - 1.25$ (2) $x + 1.25$
(3) $x + 2$ (4) $x - 2$
(5) $x + 2.5$

187. Profit earned on an article when it is sold for Rs. 672 is 25% more than the loss when it is sold for Rs. 470.4. If a person marked up the article by 50% on purchasing price and sold it after allowing two successive discounts of 20%. Find the selling price of the article.

(1) Rs. 534.4 (2) Rs. 536.5
(3) Rs. 537.6 (4) Rs. 538.7
(5) Rs. 539.8

188. Profit earned on selling a table for Rs. 'X + 1600' is 50% more than the loss incurred on selling the table for Rs. 'X + 100'. Had the table been sold for Rs. 'X', there would have been a loss of 43.75%. What is the cost price of the table?

(1) Rs. 1500 (2) Rs. 1600
(3) Rs. 1800 (4) Rs. 2000
(5) Rs. 2400

189. The question consists of two statements numbered "I" and "II" given below it. You have to decide whether the data provided in the statements are sufficient to answer the question or not and choose the correct option accordingly.

Find the time of the journey of Kush to reach school on time from his home given that the distance between his home and school is 280 km.

Statement I: If Kush travels with a speed of $(x + 3)$ km/hr, he reaches the school from home on time.

Statement II: If Kush travels with a speed of $(x - 3)$ km/hr, he will be late by six hours.

(1) The data in statement I alone is sufficient to answer, while the data in statement II alone is not sufficient to answer the question.
(2) The data in statement II alone is sufficient to answer, while the data in statement I alone is not sufficient to answer the question.
(3) The data either in statement I alone or in statement II alone are sufficient to answer the question.
(4) The data given in both statements I and II together are not sufficient to answer the question.
(5) The data in both statements I and II together are necessary to answer the question.

190. Yash spends 25% of his monthly salary on EMI. From the remaining, he spends 30% on the rent, 10% on food, 45% on groceries, and 15% on video blogging. If the difference between the amount spend on EMI and food is Rs. 945 then find the monthly salary of Yash.

(1) Rs. 5200 (2) Rs. 5300 (3) Rs. 5400 (4) Rs. 5500 (5) Rs. 5600

Answers With Explanations

1. (3)
2. (1)
3. (3)
4. (2)
5. (2)
6. (2)
7. (3)
8. (4)
9. (4)
10. (3)
11. (3)
12. (2)
13. (4)
14. (3)
15. (2)
16. (2)
17. (4)
18. (5)
19. (2)
20. (2)
21. (2)
22. (5)
23. (2)
24. (5)
25. (4)
26. (1)
27. (3)
28. (2)
29. (1)
30. (5)
31. (1)
32. (2)
33. (4)
34. (2)
35. (3)
36. (1)
37. (2)
38. (1)
39. (2)
40. (4)
41. (2)
42. (4)
43. (1)
44. (2)
45. (4)
46. (1)
47. (1)
48. (2)
49. (3)
50. (2)
51. (3)
52. (3)
53. (2)
54. (2)
55. (3)
56. (1)
57. (4)
58. (5)
59. (5)
60. (5)
61. (4)
62. (3)
63. (2)
64. (3)
65. (4)
66. (3)
67. (4)
68. (4)
69. (2)
70. (3)
71. (1)
72. (5)
73. (3)
74. (2)
75. (3)
76. (2)
77. (2)
78. (2)
79. (4)
80. (2)
81. (2)
82. (1)
83. (3)
84. (4)
85. (3)
86. (2)
87. (3)
88. (1)
89. (3)
90. (2)
91. (4)
92. (5)
93. (4)
94. (5)
95. (5)
96. (4)
97. (1)
98. (2)
99. (3)
100. (2)
101. (1)
102. (4)
103. (4)
104. (5)
105. (2)
106. (5)
107. (1)
108. (4)
109. (5)
110. (1)
111. (4)
112. (4)
113. (4)
114. (4)
115. (3)
116. (3)
117. (5)
118. (4)
119. (4)
120. (5)
121. (2)
122. (3)
123. (5)
124. (1)
125. (5)
126. (2)
127. (1)
128. (4)
129. (4)
130. (4)
131. (4)
132. (2)
133. (3)
134. (5)
135. (2)
136. (3)
137. (5)
138. (3)
139. (1)
140. (3)
141. (4)
142. (5)
143. (2)
144. (1)
145. (4)
146. (4)
147. (2)
148. (4)
149. (1)
150. (3)
151. (1)
152. (1)
153. (3)
154. (1)
155. (2)
156. (2)
157. (3)
158. (3)
159. (2)
160. (2)
161. (3)
162. (5)
163. (3)
164. (4)
165. (5)
166. (1)
167. (2)
168. (5)
169. (2)
170. (5)
171. (2)
172. (3)
173. (3)
174. (2)
175. (4)
176. (3)
177. (4)
178. (4)
179. (1)
180. (3)
181. (3)
182. (2)
183. (3)
184. (4)
185. (3)
186. (2)
187. (3)
188. (2)
189. (5)
190. (3)